# FINANCIAL MARKETS
# AND THE ECONOMY

FIFTH EDITION

# FINANCIAL MARKETS AND THE ECONOMY

**Charles N. Henning**
*University of Washington*

**William Pigott**
*University of Washington*

**Robert Haney Scott**
*University of California, Chico*

PRENTICE HALL, Englewood Cliffs, New Jersey 07632

Library of Congress Cataloging-in-Publication Data

Henning, Charles N.
    Financial markets and the economy / Charles N. Henning, William
Pigott, Robert Haney Scott. -- 5th ed.
        p.    cm.
    Includes bibliographies and index.
    ISBN 0-13-316894-8
    1. Finance--United States.  2. Financial institutions--United
States.  3. Money market--United States.  4. Capital market--United
States.   I. Pigott, William.            II. Scott, Robert Haney.
III. Title.
HG181.H37  1988
332'.0973--dc19                                    87-24413
                                                   CIP

Editorial/production supervision and
  interior design: *Nancy Savio-Marcello*
Cover design: *Photo Plus Art*
Manufacturing buyer: *Ed O'Dougherty*

 © 1988, 1984, 1981, 1978, 1975 by Prentice-Hall, Inc.
A Division of Simon & Schuster
Englewood Cliffs, New Jersey 07632

Printed in the United States of America

10  9  8  7  6  5  4  3  2

ISBN 0-13-316894-8  01

PRENTICE-HALL INTERNATIONAL (UK) LIMITED, *London*
PRENTICE-HALL OF AUSTRALIA PTY. LIMITED, *Sydney*
PRENTICE-HALL CANADA INC., *Toronto*
PRENTICE-HALL HISPANOAMERICANA, S.A., *Mexico*
PRENTICE-HALL OF INDIA PRIVATE LIMITED, *New Delhi*
PRENTICE-HALL OF JAPAN, INC., *Tokyo*
SIMON & SCHUSTER ASIA PTE. LTD., *Singapore*
EDITORA PRENTICE-HALL DO BRASIL, LTDA., *Rio de Janeiro*

# CONTENTS

# FOREWORD

This appears to be the volume that teachers of money and banking and financial institutions have been waiting for.

It has long been recognized that the student is short-changed when his or her first, and frequently only, course in macrofinance concentrates on money and banking to the exclusion of the other financial institutions and the operation of the financial marketplace. Up to now, however, it has been difficult for the teacher to find a volume that integrates financial institutions and markets and that also indicates the relevance of these institutions and markets to the economy in general.

*Financial Markets and the Economy* does the job. It explains money and banking in simple terms, it gives a good picture of the other financial institutions, and it shows the workings of the money and capital markets in terms the student can not only understand but can also examine with interest.

The topics covered in this volume are the topics covered in the financial press and in the financially related committees in the halls of Congress and the various state legislatures.

A student will leave this text with a good dose of theory but will also understand why financial institutions are modifying their functions today, why the Federal Reserve is under pressure to refine its goals, and why the tax-exempt bond is being threatened with extinction.

Frequently, text writers get so wrapped up in their own studies that they lose perspective as to what a student should really be required to retain. This volume is not subject to that criticism. Rather, it shows thorough research of both the academic as well as the institutional literature of finance and places topics in good perspective without emphasis to extreme on pet topics of the authors.

Professors Henning, Pigott, and Scott have found the prime void in the availability of textbooks on finance. They appear to have filled this void to a degree that will merit appreciation not only from professors but also from the full gamut of students—ranging from the newest to those reviewing for perspective in preparation for Ph.D. orals.

PAUL S. NADLER
*Professor of Finance*
*Graduate School of Business Administration*
*Rutgers University*

# PREFACE
# TO THE FIFTH EDITION

Our aim in this book is to cover the *financial* part of macroeconomics: saving, investment, and the financial institutions and financial markets through which saving flows to provide funds to ultimate borrowers for investment (and, to a limited extent, to consumers for consumer borrowing). Interest rates are determined in the credit markets by the interaction of the supply of saving (including that part of saving arising from the creation of new money) and the demand for borrowing.

The pace of change in financial instruments, financial institutions, and financial markets has not slowed since publication of our earlier editions. If anything, it has speeded up in the 1980s. Creation of money by commercial banks, always a limited but important part of the supply of saving, is still a part, but money can now be created by any depository institution that holds checkable deposits. Thus the uniqueness of commercial banks, a basis for discussing them at length in books on money and banking, is being undermined. In fact, the concept of financial institutions as a unique group is also being undermined, as institutions that are not basically financial in nature—such as Sears, Roebuck—engage in financial activities through subsidiaries that deal in securities, provide savings and loan facilities, engage in mortgage banking, and provide insurance. Instead of a financial institutions sector, we now have a financial *services* industry.

The heart of the book is still the determination of interest rates through the generation of saving, the flow of saving through financial institutions and markets, and the demand for borrowing. We discuss both the asset choice theories of Keynes (in a two-asset model) and of Tobin (in a multi-asset model) and the flow theory of

Robertson (loanable funds theory). In a loanable funds theory, demand for borrowing is the fundamental basis for interest (although of course supply of funds is the other blade of Marshall's scissors), and borrowing for investment purposes is based on the *productivity* of investment. Thus this theory differs from the Keynesian theory in which the supply of and the demand for *money* determine the interest rate.

Changes in the financial markets resulting from the inflation of the 1970s and the legislation of the early 1980s (especially the Depository Institutions Deregulation and Monetary Control Act of 1980, the Economic Recovery Tax Act [ERTA] of 1981, and the Depository Institutions Act of 1982 [the Garn-St Germain bill]) are covered in some detail. The Tax Reform Act of 1986 and the Competitive Equality Banking Act of 1987 are also discussed at relevant points.

Economic goals such as high employment, a relatively stable price level, and economic growth are regularly discussed in economic reports; but equally important are such goals as the encouragement of business enterprise, adequate defense, and prevention of pollution of the environment. We trace the impact of financial measures designed to achieve these goals on inflation, business activity, and the role of the government in the financial markets. The change in monetary policy in the autumn of 1979 and the subsequent changes in techniques of controlling money are discussed in detail. Finally, we consider some of the issues in fiscal policy and management of the national debt.

Gunter Dufey, Professor of International Business and Finance, University of Michigan, was most helpful in reviewing and suggesting minor changes in the sections on Eurodollars in Chapters 1 and 9 for the fourth edition.

Our aim in writing the first edition of this book was to provide a text integrating the analysis of financial institutions, services, and markets and showing their relationship to the economy and to attainment of such goals as high employment, moderation of inflation, more rapid economic growth, and deregulation, where appropriate, to permit financial markets to provide better service to savers, lenders, and borrowers. This aim remains the same, but significant legislation, technological changes, and new theories required changes reflecting the economic situation of the 1980s.

CHARLES N. HENNING
WILLIAM PIGOTT
ROBERT HANEY SCOTT
*Seattle, Washington*

# PREFACE
# TO THE FIRST EDITION

This book presents an overview of our financial system and the role it plays in the economy. It is designed for use in courses in financial institutions and markets. The only prerequisite for students is a course in the principles of economics. The book may also be used in courses in money and banking, especially by instructors who wish to stress the manner in which financial institutions and markets play a role in the transmission of macrofinancial policy actions to various sectors of the economy and to GNP. The book is of moderate length and is especially suited to one-quarter courses, or to one-semester courses especially if additional readings are assigned.

We hope that the book fills a void that we believe exists because purely descriptive texts give insufficient attention to financial markets, the intermediary process, and the role and the determination of interest rates. Moreover, such texts do not give students a sense of the importance of the financial system for the economy. Traditional money and banking texts usually focus on banks only as creators of money. They often ignore other functions of banks and the other financial institutions, both of which are important in the process of financial intermediation.

The book can be used in conjunction with a book of readings or with readings selected by instructors. To aid in selection, an extensive and up-to-date bibliography, with annotations indicating the significance of various readings, follows each chapter. Many readings are available on request from the Federal Reserve System and sometimes from other sources, in classroom quantities.

The book is policy oriented because of the significant impact that macrofinancial policies have on financial markets. A discussion of goals and monetary theory is provided as a review for some students. Since schools of business administration and departments of economics are requiring fewer specific prerequisites for courses beyond the introductory level, instructors cannot assume a uniformity of background among their students.

International aspects of finance could have been treated by themselves in one or more chapters, but we chose to discuss such aspects where appropriate. Chapters 8, 9, and 10 include discussion of the influence exercised by foreign demand for and supply of loanable funds, the Eurodollar market, and the Eurobond market, and matters relating to the international balance of payments are included in the chapters dealing with policy.

An effort has been made to include recent important developments such as progress toward an electronic funds transfer system, the Hunt Commission report, and the Administration's proposals for financial reform. In the area of international finance, attention is given to recent developments in foreign exchange markets and to measures to reform the world monetary system. Similar effort has been made to discuss controversial areas in theory and policy such as the term structure of interest rates, the high employment budget, and the appropriate guides to Federal Reserve policy.

At the same time, we must recognize that change is a hallmark of the financial system. Institutions and markets are in a continual state of flux; monetary and credit conditions change over time; the policy questions of today may not be those of tomorrow. We urge the reader, therefore, to view this textbook only as an introduction to the study of financial markets and the economy, and to keep abreast of financial developments by perusing current issues of financial publications such as those listed in the Selected References at the end of each chapter. Such a practice will not only keep the reader "up to date," but will provide the excitement and flavor of the financial world that a textbook can only suggest.

The authors wish to acknowledge many helpful comments made by three reviewers—Professor Paul Nadler, Rutgers University; Dr. Paul Horvitz, Director of Research, Federal Deposit Insurance Corporation; and Professor George H. Hempel, Washington University, St. Louis. These reviewers are, of course, not responsible for any errors or omissions. Several colleagues in the faculty of the Graduate School of Business Administration, University of Washington, also helped by reading and commenting on certain chapters: Peter Frost, Alan Hess, and Charles W. Haley. Finally, the careful typing of several drafts of the manuscript by Joanne Beaurain merits the authors' appreciation.

CHARLES N. HENNING
WILLIAM PIGOTT
ROBERT HANEY SCOTT
*Seattle, Washington*

# INTRODUCTION TO OUR FINANCIAL SYSTEM: AN OVERVIEW OF MARKETS AND INSTITUTIONS

In a modern economy, income is partly spent for consumption and partly saved. Money saving is channeled into investment via a variety of financial institutions and markets that provide borrowers with funds needed *now*, and at the same time provide lenders with a variety of financial assets. An efficient financial system assures the flow of such loanable funds into their most desired uses.

The process of the flow of saving into investment is complex in a modern economy. Many types of financial institutions and markets act as intermediaries between borrowers and lenders. Financial markets establish the interest rates at which present funds are exchanged for future funds. The right to have funds in the future is indicated by financial assets or claims, held by lenders.

Changes in financial markets and institutions affect both the total level of economic activity and the allocation of funds to various sectors of the economy. Chapters 1 and 2 introduce the analysis of the financial system: Chapter 1 presents an overview of the institutions and markets and a brief introductory discussion of the determination of interest rates. Chapter 2 includes more detailed discussion of relations between saving and investment and an introduction to flow of funds accounting, an organized framework for data on flows of funds among financial institutions and financial markets.

## FINANCIAL MARKETS AND INSTITUTIONS

A highly developed financial system is a hallmark of a modern exchange economy. The markets and institutions that comprise this system facilitate the efficient production of goods and services, thereby contributing to the society's well-being and to a rising standard of living. The financial system channels the nation's saving into its highest and best uses. It does this by bringing together those who have funds to lend and those who wish to borrow to finance their expenditures.

Activity in financial markets involves the exchange of one financial asset for another. In most exchanges, lenders exchange money for other financial assets that provide a future return. In effect, they buy a *claim* against someone's money holdings at a future date—they buy an IOU. These IOUs, or "securities," provide returns in the form of interest or dividends. In some cases the lender may hold a security until it matures, that is, until the borrower repays the loan on the specified date. In other cases, the lender may sell the security to someone else before it matures. Thus, although the borrower continues to use loaned funds, the lender is now a different person. We say that lenders "supply loanable funds" to the market whereas borrowers "demand loanable funds."

When individuals buy and sell outstanding or newly issued claims, they are "adjusting their portfolios," *portfolios* meaning the groups of financial assets they hold. Individuals dispose of some assets and acquire others because they wish to obtain a higher return, change the marketability of the assets they hold, or change the riskiness of the assets they hold.

Besides exchanging financial assets to adjust portfolios, individuals may wish, for example, to reduce holdings of financial assets to consume more or to invest in real assets. For example, one may sell a bond to pay for a vacation, or to acquire funds to invest in a house or a business. Thus, financial markets allow individuals to adjust their holdings of assets to suit their preferences.

## INTEREST RATES AND SECURITIES PRICES

Economists use "market demand and supply" as the analytical frame of reference when they "explain" the price and quantity of goods and services. The same analytical technique is useful when looking at financial markets. The theory of financial markets is developed more extensively in later chapters, but a simple demand and supply analysis is useful until then.

The first thing to observe is that, while we express the price or cost of, say, oranges as 30 cents per pound, we usually express the "price" or cost of borrowed funds in terms of an interest *rate* or an interest *yield*. If money is obtained by selling a bond, those who buy the bond pay, say, $1,000 now in return for $1,000 a year from now if the maturity of the bond is one year. If they also receive $60 in interest a year from now, the interest rate is 6 percent per annum. The sum of $60 can be viewed as the rental cost of the use of $1,000 for a year. The 6 percent rate is termed the *coupon rate.*

On the other hand, instead of referring to the supply and demand for *funds,* we can refer to the supply of, and demand for, *securities.* In the preceding example, the price of the *security* that called for payment of $1,060 one year from today was $1,000. Thus, transactions in financial markets may be looked at in two ways: (1) lending and borrowing of loanable funds or (2) purchasing and selling securities.

In Figure 1–1(a) solid lines show supply and demand curves for loanable funds. The supply curve for funds is upward sloping. The rate of interest is on the vertical axis and the quantity of loanable funds is measured on the horizontal axis. The supply curve shows that at higher interest rates lenders will supply more funds in the market. The demand curve for funds is downward sloping. This indicates that those who wish to borrow funds will borrow larger amounts at lower interest rates. The interaction of market forces of demand and supply will determine the interest rate and the amount of loanable funds being exchanged in the market.

In Figure 1–1(b), the price of securities (*not* the interest rate) is measured on the vertical axis, and the volume of securities is measured on the horizontal axis. Here, the supply curve represents borrowing by those who offer securities for sale in the market. At higher prices more will be offered for sale; that is, more funds will be borrowed. Thus, the curve showing the supply of securities at various prices contains the *same information* as the curve in Figure 1–1(a) that showed the demand for funds at various interest rates.

**FIGURE 1–1**
**Interest Rates and Securities Prices**

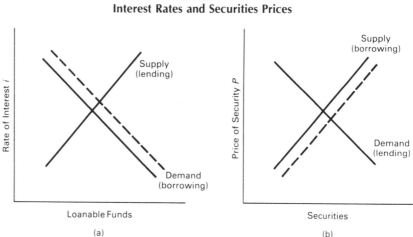

Loanable Funds

(a)

Securities

(b)

Similarly, the demand curve for securities in Figure 1–1(b) slopes down to show that lenders will buy more of them at a lower price. This demand curve for securities contains the same information as the supply curve for loanable funds in Figure 1–1(a).

An increase in demand for funds can be shown by a rightward shift in the demand curve in Figure 1–1(a) as illustrated by the dashed line. Such a shift might arise from a federal budget deficit; that is, when the government spends more than it receives in taxes, it borrows funds in the market to make up the difference. The new intersection of the demand and supply curves indicates a higher rate of interest and a larger volume of funds exchanged in the market.

This *same phenomenon* can be shown in Figure 1–1(b) as an increase in the supply of securities depicted by the dashed supply curve. The government offers more bonds in the market, and, given the demand for securities, their price must fall. Similar analysis can be applied to the curves when there is an increase in the supply of funds rather than an increase in demand for funds. In this case, the supply curve in Figure 1–1(a) would shift rightward and the demand curve for securities in Figure 1–1(b) would also shift rightward.

Let us again consider the bond having a 6 percent coupon interest rate, on which, if the bond matures at the end of one year, the holder will receive $1,060. This can be expressed in the formula

$$P + Pi = R$$

in which $P$ is the face value of the bond, $i$ is the coupon interest rate, and $R$ is the return to be received, including both face value and interest. We use $R$ as the *amount* to be received.

Those who buy bonds obtain a *market yield* (interest rate) that is usually different from the coupon rate. This yield varies inversely with the market price of the securities. By factoring out $P$ and dividing both sides by $1 + i$, the formula may be rewritten as

$$P = \frac{R}{1 + i}$$

If interest rates change, the yield on the 6 percent coupon bond will rise or fall with the rates on comparable securities. The price will also vary, but *inversely* with the yield. The values in the preceding formula are

$$\$1,000 = \frac{\$1,060}{1.06}$$

If interest rates on comparable securities rise to 10 percent, the dollar return to be obtained remains the same, but the yield must be 10 percent if the investor is to do as well as on similar securities. Hence the price at which the bond sells—its *present value*—becomes

$$P = \frac{\$1,060}{1.10} = \$963.63$$

Thus a 6 percent coupon bond would sell at $963.63 if the market interest rate (for example, the rate on comparable newly issued bonds) were 10 percent. This rate is often termed a *discount* rate, since the $1,060 to be received one year in the future is being discounted to obtain its present value. Securities prices vary inversely with interest rates. There are three interrelated variables: the return to be obtained, the discount rate, and the present value or price. If any two of these are known, the third can be determined from the formula[1]

$$P = \frac{R}{1 + i}$$

Interest rate formulas are developed further in subsequent chapters. It is more important to note here that interest rates are market prices that influence the behavior of borrowers and lenders, as shown in Figure 1–1. Through interest rates, financial markets allocate resources to saving or to consumption and allocate saving to investment in goods that produce more goods and/or services later.

## FUNCTIONS OF FINANCIAL MARKETS

Financial markets perform an *economic* function. They facilitate the transfer of real economic resources from lenders to borrowers. Lenders have earned money incomes and wish to save part of their earnings for future use. They can earn interest on their savings by lending their purchasing power to someone who wishes to obtain command over real resources (by purchasing labor services, plant and equipment, land, and so on). Thus, initially real resources flow to borrowers and away from lenders. Lenders reduce their present consumption but expect to have higher income (and higher consumption) in the future when the loan matures. When borrowers use the borrowed funds productively—by investing in new machines, for example—they will produce a larger income, thereby raising their own real standard of living and that of others in the economy.

By facilitating transfers of real resources, financial markets serve the nation's economy and its citizens. Under a free enterprise pricing system, profit-seeking entre-

---

[1] The formula for bond prices is of course more complicated because of the number of periods (years or semiannual periods) involved and because of the compounding of interest.

preneurs provide people with commodities that they are willing and able to pay for. As consumer desires change over time, it is necessary that factors of production flow readily into the hands of producers who respond to those changing desires. Because financial markets permit shifts of real resources far more efficiently than do the barter agreements that would be necessary in their absence, such markets are highly productive; in a modern highly developed economy, they are essential.

Financial markets also perform a *financial* function. They provide borrowers with funds (purchasing power) that they want or need to have *now* to carry out their plans. Also, they provide lenders with earning assets so that a lender's wealth may be held in a productive form without the necessity of direct ownership of real assets. There is, of course, no sharp dichotomy between *economic* and *financial* functions of financial markets. In general, when real resources are affected we refer to economic functions. But many financial transfers have only slight effects upon real resource allocation, and in these cases we refer to *financial* functions.

## THE DIVERSITY OF FINANCIAL MARKETS

When we speak of "the financial market," we treat funds or securities exchanged as if they were homogeneous—as if there were only one type of fund or one security. This is, of course, an oversimplification; there are, in fact, dozens of financial markets in which a wide variety of securities are exchanged, and the term "loanable funds" covers the funds supplied for many different types of loans. Among the more important differences are differences in purposes of loans, in time period or maturities of loans, in credit risks involved, and in collateral required. Some loans to consumers are made for housing or other durables; business loans finance the purchase of inventory or plant and equipment; loans to governmental units supplement their tax receipts. In the case of most borrowers, there are various degrees of risk of default that lenders are willing to assume only if the promised interest rate is high enough to compensate for the additional exposure. Some loan transactions require borrowers to pledge specific assets that can be sold to protect lenders. There are mortgage markets, markets for corporate bonds, government securities, tax-exempt bonds, foreign securities, and many others. The markets in which these securities are traded reflect differences in purposes, maturities, and risks.

Loan markets also differ geographically. Local loans may be made by banks, retail firms, and finance companies. Mortgage markets are mostly local or regional, with mortgage money for local construction supplied by local savings institutions. In larger localities there are often regional securities exchanges. The securities of large well-known corporations are traded nationally or even internationally. U.S. government securities are bought and sold by individuals and firms located around the world. National and international exchanges of funds occur in telephone and telegraphic markets, with principal connections in headquarters in such major markets as New York, London, Frankfurt, Tokyo, and Zurich. These centers handle orders from nearly everywhere on earth.

Although financial markets are distinct and diverse, they are closely interconnected. Transfer costs—costs involved in effecting an exchange of securities between market participants—are quite low in comparison with those attached to exchange of real commodities. Although new issues of securities and the processing of new loan applications may have significant transfer costs, the trading of outstanding paper certificates or notes is usually not expensive; therefore, connections between various financial markets may be maintained without great cost per dollar of lending.

Security price and yield information flows rapidly and freely throughout financial markets. Also, borrowers and lenders are nearly always involved in several markets at the same time. A bank diversifies its portfolio of loans and investments among many types of financial instruments. Many financial managers easily switch from one market to another. A private citizen often "lends" to more than one financial institution at a time. He or she may own an insurance policy, a savings account, a demand deposit in a commercial bank, some government bonds, and other financial assets. Borrowers also typically use a variety of sources of funds. Financial markets are interconnected because borrowers and lenders have many options and alternatives in both sources and uses of funds.

In an efficient market, funds flow freely and rapidly among various sources and uses. Insofar as financial instruments are substitutable for each other, changes in supply and demand in one sector of a market have a rapid spillover effect into adjacent markets. Rapidity and strength of such spillover effects depend, of course, upon the degree of substitutability—the greater the degree of substitutability, the stronger and more immediate the transmission of effects. When markets are closely linked, interest rates in the linked markets move up and down together as supply and demand conditions change.

## THE CLASSIFICATION OF FINANCIAL MARKETS

To analyze the numerous financial markets in an economy, it is useful to divide them into categories. In doing so, however, we recognize that any attempt to classify markets is arbitrary; the lines drawn are not clear-cut in practice.

### Primary and Secondary Markets

First, there are markets for new issues of securities and markets for existing claims. The markets for new issues of securities are *primary* markets. Here, consumers, managers of business firms, and government units issue new securities to raise funds to finance their expenditures. These securities may be purchased directly by financial institutions or other lenders who have funds to invest. However, most new issues of private long-term securities and of state and local (but not federal) obligations are initially purchased by investment bankers or underwriters. After the underwriter has purchased the securities they are resold in the market and any profit to the underwriter will be determined by the spread between the initial purchase price and the resale price.

Markets for existing claims (financial assets) are known as *secondary* markets. Since the original issuers are not obligated to redeem securities until maturity, these markets allow investors to exchange securities for money before they mature. Thus, active secondary markets enhance the value of financial assets. The ease and convenience with which such assets can be sold prior to maturity without a significant loss is a measure of their "liquidity"—a concept we will examine in greater detail in subsequent chapters.

### Markets for Loans and Markets for Securities

A second way of classifying financial markets is to divide them into markets for loans and markets for securities. A loan is usually negotiated directly between the borrower and the lender; they deal face to face. In contrast, securities markets are impersonal or open markets; buyers and sellers of securities are usually unknown to each other and usually trade through brokers or dealers. Most consumer credit to finance the purchase of durables and of housing takes the form of loans. Business firms also obtain loans, principally from commercial banks, especially for short-term needs. Most large business firms rely on both loans and the sale of securities to obtain needed funds.

Some loans, having been made by one institution, may be sold to another institution in a secondary market; this is especially true for mortgage loans. On the other hand, some securities issues are negotiated directly by borrowers with lenders, as in the so-called *private placement* of bonds issued by a business firm and sold to an insurance company. Therefore, whether or not borrowers and lenders are known to each other does not always provide a sufficient criterion for distinguishing between a loan market and a securities market.

Securities markets may be subdivided into other categories. For example, there are markets for debt instruments, such as bonds, and there are markets for equities, such as common stock. The former represent obligations of companies or government units to creditors. Stocks, on the other hand, are evidence of ownership of firms by stockholders. Although bondholders and stockholders have different legal status, it is often convenient to regard both bonds and stocks as securities, since capital may be obtained by firms through the issue of either type of instrument.

Securities may also be traded on the "floor" of a securities exchange or "over-the-counter" by personal or telephone contact with dealers and brokers. Although the New York Stock Exchange and the American Stock Exchange get most attention in newspaper articles, more securities are traded over-the-counter than on the exchanges.

### Money and Capital Markets

The third major way of classifying financial markets is to divide them into *money* and *capital* markets. "Money markets" refer to markets in which short-term instruments are traded. Usually we define a short-term instrument as one that has one year or less remaining until its maturity. "Capital markets" are those for longer-term debt instruments and stocks. However, the dividing line is arbitrary, and in some markets the one-year line may not be appropriate, but it is the one most often used. Capital market securities are, therefore, those that mature in more than one year or that have no maturity dates, as in the case of stocks.

Money markets are important for two reasons: (1) they provide a major means by which participants can adjust their liquidity positions, and (2) the Federal Reserve System, which is responsible for controlling the money supply, conducts most of its operations in the money market. Through these operations it seeks to achieve many of our nation's economic goals. Liquidity is important both to individuals and to institutions. Individuals and firms may have tax or other payments to make in the near future. By temporarily investing in money market instruments, they can earn interest and, when necessary, sell the money market assets to obtain money to make their payments. Banks and other financial institutions also buy money market instruments that mature shortly or can easily be sold to provide for withdrawals of funds by depositors or for making loans to customers.

The primary purpose of the capital markets is to channel saving into investment. This process, by adding to the nation's stock of capital goods, increases output per worker-hour and ultimately raises our standard of living. The capital markets facilitate this process in two ways. First, savers may buy newly issued long-term instruments that provide business firms with funds to finance capital expenditures. Second, financial institutions, such as savings and loan associations, commercial banks, life insurance companies, and others use the savings of individuals and business to acquire capital market securities, including mortgages. In both ways, savings are made available for investment purposes.

It is important to note that financial institutions borrow short-term funds when they accept savings because such funds may be withdrawn within a short time period. However, when financial institutions invest these funds in the capital markets, the funds are usually provided for longer periods of time. Thus the short-term and long-term markets are connected through the operations of the financial institutions.

## THE MONEY AND CAPITAL MARKETS

The money and capital markets are discussed in detail in later chapters. The following discussion is intended to familiarize the student with some basic elements of each market, including a brief description of the major participants and of the financial instruments that are traded.

### The Money Market

Short-term *loans* are negotiated and seldom sold; there is no active secondary market for them. Thus, we are concerned only with the interest rates that are negotiated when the loans are made. Short-term *securities*, however, are usually actively traded in a secondary market, and their prices and yields are closely related to those of newly issued instruments. Because their time to maturity is short, money market securities fluctuate very little in price when interest rates change. This, of course, is the primary reason for considering these instruments to be liquid assets. Investors can be assured that they can sell such instruments before maturity at close to their purchase price. The daily volume of transactions in these secondary markets is very large, involving in some cases billions of dollars. This trading is largely "over-the-counter" or, more precisely, "over-the-telephone" trading.

A list of principal money market instruments in the United States includes U.S. government Treasury bills, Federal funds, repurchase agreements (RPs), negotiable certificates of deposit (CDs), bankers acceptances (BAs), Eurodollars, and commercial paper. The market for each of these may be regarded as an individual part of the total money market.

The market for Treasury bills is perhaps the most important part of the U.S. money market. More than one-fifth of total U.S. government debt and more than one-third of the marketable government debt is in the form of Treasury bills.[2] Treasury bills are issued in maturities of three months, six months, and one year, and are sold at auction, in minimum amounts of $10,000. Banks, corporations, and individuals bid for these securities. Smaller investors may make noncompetitive bids that are filled at the average price bid by competitive bidders; the noncompetitive amounts are awarded first, reducing the amounts available for competitive bidders. This assures that smaller investors, such as small banks, can obtain *some* Treasury bills. The Federal Reserve System (the Fed) buys and sells large amounts of Treasury bills to control the money supply.

Federal funds are a unique money market instrument, and the market for them has special characteristics. Federal funds are deposits held (chiefly by banks) in Federal Reserve Banks. Banks with such deposits in excess of the amount required as reserves may lend the excess—Federal funds—to other banks simply by arranging by telephone or telegraph a transfer of funds from the lending bank to the borrowing bank. Banks may also lend their deposits in other commercial banks. Such loans are usually made for one to three days, often to banks that have insufficient reserves and wish to borrow to meet legal requirements. Average daily transfers in this market may be as much as $20 billion or more. The volume of funds traded is a better indicator of the importance of this market than is the amount of Federal funds held because only *excess* funds can be traded from deposits in the Fed. Interest rates in this market fluctuate with the needs of banks to borrow to meet reserve requirements.

Repurchase agreements (RPs) are sales of securities with an agreement to repurchase them in a short time. A bank can sell securities under such an agreement to another commercial bank, to a business firm, or to another institution. Business firms may find such purchases, with agreements by the banks to repurchase the securities, a convenient way to earn interest on funds for short periods of time. Otherwise, the funds might remain in checking accounts on which no explicit interest rate is paid.

---

[2] Some government debt, such as savings bonds and special issues of bonds sold only to government agencies and trust funds, is not marketable.

Negotiable certificates of deposit are a type of time deposit. Business firms may deposit funds in a commercial bank for a specified time—for example, 90 days—and banks issue certificates to the depositing firms. These certificates *may* be negotiable, and, if so, they may be traded to other firms or other purchasers in the secondary market for negotiable CDs. Thus, although the firm that deposited the funds cannot withdraw them prior to maturity, it can obtain money by selling the negotiable CDs.

Bankers acceptances are drafts drawn on banks and are accepted by banks, the acceptance indicating that the banks have agreed to pay the drafts at maturity.[3] Since bankers acceptances represent promises by banks to pay, they are usually regarded as having a high degree of safety. Bankers acceptances are used to finance foreign trade and sometimes to obtain loans. They are bought and sold by banks, other financial institutions, individuals, and the Fed in a market that is not extremely large but is an important auxiliary source of liquidity.

Eurodollars are a relatively recent addition to the list of money market instruments. They are dollars or some other convertible currency deposited in banks outside the country of origin of the currency.[4] Banks in England began to accept such deposits in the late 1950s, permitting depositors to withdraw funds in dollars, payable through New York, rather than in pounds sterling. Eurodollar deposits are time deposits rather than demand deposits. They are deposited usually for some specified period of time (although sometimes the period may be only overnight). Being time deposits, they are not used to make payments by check. Since they cannot be used directly for internal payments in the country in which they are held, they are usually not considered to be money when money is defined as what is used to make payments. Banks use most of the funds to make Eurodollar loans—loans to firms, other institutions, or governments that wish to borrow dollars. The loans are usually repayable in dollars. Transfers (depositing, lending, and use by borrowers for payments) are made through the U.S. bank clearing system.

Deposits counted as part of the Eurodollar market include some other currencies, such as Deutsche marks and Swiss francs, deposited in banks outside those countries. The total market could thus be termed a Eurocurrency market rather than a Eurodollar market; perhaps a better term is offshore market—a market for deposits *outside* (offshore) the country of the specific currency involved. One exception now exists: in 1981, international banking facilities (IBFs) were authorized in the United

---

[3] The distinction between a promissory note and a draft or bill of exchange is that a promissory note is a *promise* to pay and a draft is an *order* to pay—often to a third party, termed the payee. A draft is drawn on the debtor (termed the drawee) or on some other party who is to pay, for example, the debtor's bank. Of course, arrangements must be made in advance to draw such drafts; the debtor or buyer may arrange for the bank to issue a letter of credit or an acceptance agreement for this purpose.

[4] The term *currency* is used with two meanings. Within a country, currency means coins and paper money. Internationally, currency means financial assets denominated in the money of a certain country; the assets may be coins, paper money, bank deposits, or various short-term financial assets. Thus, the dollar may be referred to as a "strong currency," meaning that exchange rates for dollars (coins, paper money, bank deposits, and other financial assets) are trending upward or are remaining high. A *convertible* currency is one that can be exchanged into the currency of another country without any government restrictions.

States; IBFs accepted deposits *without* the usual requirements for reserves and deposit insurance, and the funds are used for international lending.[5]

Commercial paper consists of short-term corporate IOUs sold either directly or through dealers to a variety of investors. It is the only money market instrument that is traded in a secondary market and that is not an obligation of a government or of a bank. Regulations restrict commercial paper to a maturity of not more than 270 days. Most of the commercial paper outstanding in the United States has been issued by finance companies that provide funds for purchasing automobiles and other durable goods and for short-term personal and business loans. Because issues of commercial paper are often tailored to suit particular investors, the secondary market for commercial paper is not as large or significant as that for many other money market instruments.

Thus, the major participants in the money market are the government, banks, the Federal Reserve System, and business firms. Business firms participate to a small extent as issuers of commercial paper but to a large extent as suppliers of funds to banks by their purchases of certificates of deposit.

## The Capital Markets

Capital markets include those for long-term marketable government securities, corporate bonds, stocks, "municipal" bonds issued by state and local government units, and mortgages. Long-term government securities include Treasury notes and Treasury bonds. The market for government notes and bonds is important because these securities are relatively liquid and free of the risk of default.[6] Even if businesses and banks fail, the government can always redeem its securities for cash. Thus, both short-term and long-term government debt provide considerable liquidity and safety for financial institutions. The principal purchasers of government notes and bonds are banks, other financial institutions, the Federal Reserve System, foreign investors, and to some extent business firms and individuals.

The corporate bond market is an important source of long-term funds for business firms. Borrowing firms tend to rely more on debt issues than on equity financing for two reasons. First, interest payments on bonds are tax deductible, while dividends are not. Second, the issuance of additional bonds does not dilute the equity position of existing stockholders. The sale of additional shares of stock does have this effect, at least initially. The principal buyers of corporate bonds are nonbank financial institutions, such as insurance companies and pension funds, and individuals. These purchasers are attracted by the relative safety and high interest income of these debt instruments.

---

[5] The Eurodollar market is discussed in detail in Chapter 9.

[6] Technically, "bonds" may be issued with any maturity, but generally they have an original maturity of not less than 10 years. Government obligations that generally have shorter maturities than bonds (but longer than Treasury bills) are Treasury notes, which may be issued with maturities up to 10 years.

Municipal bonds are issued by state and local governments, usually to finance capital expenditures for projects such as streets, sewers, public buildings, and the like. Some of these bonds are *general obligation* bonds backed by the full taxing authority of the issuer. Some issues provide that certain specific tax revenues will be allocated to payment of interest and repayment of principal and are termed *revenue* bonds. Such bonds may be issued to be serviced by revenues from the specific projects they financed, for example, toll bridge bonds. Municipal bonds are unique in that interest income received by the bondholders is, on most such bonds, exempt from federal taxation. This legal provision stems from the doctrine of separation of powers of the federal government from those of state and local governments. Tax exemption enables state and local governments to borrow at lower rates of interest than they would otherwise have to pay and, therefore, these securities are attractive to lenders in high income tax brackets, including banks, individuals, and property and casualty insurance companies. Institutions such as mutual life insurance companies, pension funds, and certain others have little interest in these securities because the tax rates applicable to business corporations and banks do not apply to them.

Mortgages represent long-term financial commitments secured by liens on real estate.[7] Mortgages are the largest element in the capital markets in terms of amounts outstanding, but trading mortgages has until recent years been somewhat limited by their lack of uniformity and by the work involved in handling them to be sure that taxes on properties are paid, that properties are insured, and that regular mortgage amortization payments are made by the borrowers. In recent years mortgages have gained greater liquidity because of government efforts to develop a secondary market, especially for government-guaranteed mortgages.

The capital markets provide *some* degree of liquidity, but they are not as important in this function as the money markets. On the other hand, they are more important than the money markets in channeling funds into long-term investment projects. Money and capital market interest rates are determined by short-term business borrowing and, more important, by such factors as long-term investment, including expenditures on housing and spending by state and local government units for schools, roads, hospitals, and other institutions. The relationships between short-term and long-term interest rates are important for the economy, but analysis of these relationships is deferred until we have had an opportunity to analyze the role of financial institutions in allocating funds among the various sectors of the economy.

## THE ROLE OF GOVERNMENT IN FINANCIAL MARKETS

Government affects virtually every aspect of financial activity in the United States. Government's role is important and widespread, as borrower, insurer, regulator, and ultimate source of liquidity.

---

[7] Sometimes corporate bonds are secured by real estate mortgages. These issues are not counted as mortgage debt.

The U.S. government is the largest single borrower in the world. With federal budget deficits varying widely from year to year, it is difficult to say how rapidly U.S. debt will increase, but no doubt it will continue to rise. State and local governments also issue large amounts of debt, and such debt seems to increase rather steadily at a rate of about 8 percent per year. With continued urbanization, the role of state and local governments in the economy is bound to expand steadily in the foreseeable future.

Besides the various types of government debt, there exist a large number of debt issues of federal agencies (and of agencies originally sponsored by the federal government) that have credit programs of various sorts. Among these are the Veterans Administration, Federal Housing Administration, Federal National Mortgage Association, Small Business Administration, and Federal Home Loan Banks. Some of these agencies insure private loans, some lend directly, and some purchase private marketable securities. To finance their loans and purchases of securities, they issue debt instruments of their own (or "participation certificates" that give the buyer "ownership" of a part of a package of mortgages, say, that the agency holds). Through such agency activities the federal government again has significant effects on financial markets from both the supply side and the demand side.

But government involvement does not stop here. Besides participating directly in markets, government agencies regulate financial institutions to provide a secure financial system and to promote competition. Commercial banks and most other financial institutions are regulated either by the federal government or by the states that granted their charters. Three federal agencies—the Federal Reserve System, the Comptroller of the Currency (Treasury Department), and the Federal Deposit Insurance Corporation—are significant in regulating commercial banks.[8] Thus, one or more government agencies control the chartering of new banks, approve branching and merging of banks, insure deposits, and to some extent control rates that banks charge customers for various services offered. Mutual savings banks, savings and loan associations, credit unions, insurance companies, and small loan companies are also regulated. The Federal Savings and Loan Insurance Corporation insures share accounts (similar to deposits) in savings and loan associations in a manner similar to the insurance of demand and time deposits and savings accounts in commercial banks by the Federal Deposit Insurance Corporation. Through the Securities and Exchange Commission, the government also regulates the sale of new securities to the public and the operations of brokerage firms and securities exchanges.

Finally, government agencies have responsibility for implementation of monetary, fiscal, and debt management policies in the interest of economic stabilization. Monetary policy is concerned with changing the growth rate of the money supply and the terms and conditions of credit. Fiscal policy is concerned with taxes and expenditures of government. Debt management policy is concerned with the impact of the

---

[8] Many other governmental agencies, of course, regulate banks along with other firms; for example, there are regulations concerning hours of work, employment of minorities, and so forth.

government's debt-issue decisions on the financial markets. In carrying out these policy programs, government agencies exercise tremendous influence on the cost and availability of credit; this influence is felt throughout the entire structure of financial markets and institutions. Of special importance is the role of the Federal Reserve System as the ultimate source of liquidity for the banking system. The Fed has power to make funds available to banks and other government agencies on an almost unlimited scale if it were essential to do so in the public interest.

## SUMMARY

There are many interrelated markets for loanable funds. Market participants buy and sell both new and existing financial assets at prices determined in the markets. Borrowers have outstanding debt, and lenders acquire earning assets; debt and credit are *two sides of the same coin.*

For securities that vary in price, interest rates vary inversely with the prices of the securities. An increase in demand for funds leads to an increase in interest rates and at the same time a decline in prices paid for securities.

Financial markets perform both an economic and a financial function. Real economic resources are transferred to their most desired uses through provision of funds to borrowers and acquisition of earning assets by lenders.

Financial markets are diverse, with many types of loans and securities for many different purposes. But these markets are also closely interconnected; transactors move easily into and out of various market segments.

The role of government in financial markets is pervasive because of (1) direct government participation in the markets, (2) government regulatory activities, and (3) government responsibility for high employment and economic stability, attainment of which involves direct and indirect manipulation of financial markets for policy purposes. The government's influence extends beyond institutions and markets to all those who participate as borrowers or lenders and to individuals and businesses as buyers of goods and services, taxpayers, and citizens seeking a higher standard of living.

### Questions for Discussion

**1.** List a number of different types of financial assets. Which would you classify as money? Why?

**2.** Make an attempt to define the term "loanable funds." Try to make your definition carefully, to include precisely what is meant.

**3.** Distinguish between the economic function and the financial function of financial markets.

**4.** Refer to Figure 1–1 and assume that the supply of loanable funds increases (supply curve shifts to the right). What will happen to the rate of interest? How do we show this same result in the graph showing the supply and demand for securities? What will happen to the price of securities?

**5.** What is the present value (price) of a security that will guarantee payment of $1,100 a year from today if the interest rate is 10 percent? What is its present value if the interest rate is 5 percent?

**6.** Distinguish between bonds and mortgages. Some firms issue bonds secured by mortgages. In which category should these be classified? Why?

**7.** What grounds can you suggest for government participation in financial markets—for the establishment of agencies that make loans and issue bonds?

**8.** When the U.S. Constitution states that "Congress shall have the power to create money and regulate the value thereof," why is monetary policy in the hands of the central bank (the Federal Reserve System)?

**9.** Try to think of some institutions that are borderline, in that they might be classified as financial or as nonfinancial institutions. Indicate the basis for classification.

**10.** A very basic idea in finance is the discounting of future earnings or income to obtain the present value of that income. Does this discounting imply that people prefer present rather than future income?

## Selected References

The following texts provide extensive coverage of financial markets and institutions: *Financial Institutions and Markets*, 2nd ed., by Murray E. Polakoff, Thomas A. Durkin, and 33 contributors (Boston: Houghton Mifflin, 1981), is an unusual reference work that is a complete study of the loanable funds markets. Paul F. Smith's *Economics of Financial Institutions and Markets* (Homewood, Ill.: Richard D. Irwin, 1971) integrates descriptive materials on financial markets and institutions into economic theory. Smith's more recent book, *Money and Financial Intermediation* (Englewood Cliffs, N.J.: Prentice-Hall, 1978), follows similar lines.

As its title implies, *Financial Market Rates and Flows*, by James C. Van Horne (Englewood Cliffs, N.J.: Prentice-Hall, 1978), provides an intensive analysis of interest rates, including their role and determination, the relationships between various interest rates, and flows of funds. This book is an expanded and updated version of his *Function and Analysis of Capital Market Rates* (Englewood Cliffs, N.J.: Prentice-Hall, 1970).

In the field of money and capital markets, Roland I. Robinson and Dwayne Wrightsman, *Financial Markets: The Accumulation and Allocation of Wealth*, 2nd ed. (New York: McGraw-Hill, 1980), is a revision of the book by Roland I. Robinson, *Money and Capital Markets* (New York: McGraw-Hill, 1964); it deals at greater length than does our text with the money and capital markets and devotes a final section to the evaluation of the performance of financial markets. Another text in this area is J. C. Poindexter and Charles P. Jones, *Money, Financial Markets, and the Economy* (St. Paul, Minn.: West, 1980).

Many interesting empirical questions and theoretical issues are difficult to include in a conventional text. Moreover, there is no substitute for original writing in conveying the flavor of debates and the importance of policy issues that have arisen in the last two decades. Many important original articles are included in the following collections of readings:

The Federal Reserve System is a continual source of data, published monthly in the *Federal Reserve Bulletin*. In addition, the 12 Federal Reserve Banks offer the public free subscriptions to their economic and business reviews that report on staff studies, contain original articles on economic and financial affairs, and outline current developments in the economy.

Journals of special interest are the *Journal of Finance* and the *Journal of Money, Credit, and Banking*. On a day-to-day or week-to-week basis, the best coverage of financial developments is found in *The Wall Street Journal*, the *Journal of Commerce*, the *Commercial and Financial Chronicle, Barron's,* and the weekly issues of *Comments on Credit* issued by Salomon Brothers, New York. The weekly *Business and Financial Letter* (now the Federal Reserve Bank of San Francisco *Weekly Letter*), inaugurated in late 1972 by the Research Department of that bank, is also very useful. For regular coverage of developments in the international aspects of macrofinance, two very useful sources are the semimonthly *IMF Survey* issued by the International Monetary Fund and *World Financial Markets*, a monthly publication of the Morgan Guaranty Trust Company of New York.

Several texts have been published with coverage somewhat similar to that of our book; one example is Raymond E. Lombra, James B. Herendeen, and Raymond G. Torto, *Money and the Financial System* (New York: McGraw-Hill, 1980); another is Tim S. Campbell, *Financial Institutions, Markets, and Economic Activity* (New York: McGraw-Hill, 1982).

A book of readings, John R. Brick, ed., *Financial Markets: Instruments and Concepts* (Richmond, Va.: Robert F. Dame, 1981), covers many details concerning the financial markets, the instruments used in them, interrelationships, and innovations.

# SAVING AND INVESTMENT
# AND THE ROLE
# OF FINANCIAL INTERMEDIARIES

One of the most important relationships in economics is that between saving and investment. In examining the causes of business fluctuations, the process of economic growth, or the role played by financial institutions in these developments, we are always concerned with the meaning and significance of saving and investment and the relation between them. Of special interest are the processes of saving and investment in a modern enterprise economy and the role of financial institutions as intermediaries between lenders and borrowers.

In a modern economy, investment is carried out by one group of individuals and institutions, while much of the saving is done by another group. Financial institutions and instruments mediate between savers and producers who obtain funds in order to invest. These facts make it necessary, in examining saving and investment, to draw clear distinctions between (1) "real" and "financial" investment and (2) "ex ante" (planned) and "ex post" (realized or actual) saving and investment.

# SAVING, INVESTMENT, AND FINANCIAL INVESTMENT

Saving and investment are "flow" concepts as opposed to stock concepts.[1] Just as one may observe the water level in a lake at any time, or the flow of water into and out of a lake during a period of time, so one may measure the stock of capital goods existing in an economy at a time or the flow of investment spending during a period of time. Investment is the process of capital formation. The existing stock of capital depreciates over time as it is used in producing consumer goods or other investment goods, so the *net* investment is the net addition to the stock of capital (gross investment less depreciation and other capital consumption allowances) occurring over a period of time. These additions to the stock of capital are "real" investment.

Saving is a residual concept. It is that part of the output of an economy that is not consumed. Output (equal to income) is produced over a period of time; part of that output is consumed, another part is not consumed, but saved. That part that is saved is added to the stock of wealth (capital goods including inventories) and is available for use in the future. Thus, by *definition*, saving is identical to "real" investment. Both are flow concepts and refer to the *addition* to the stock of capital that occurs over a period of time.

Most "real" investment is undertaken by business firms. Business firms order newly produced capital goods—equipment, machinery, construction items, inventories. These capital goods are used in producing consumer goods and other capital goods in the future. Similarly, consumers invest in housing. Saving decisions, on the other hand, are made by consumers and government as well as by business managers. Consumers spend less than their income and thus save. Governments may spend less than the amount of tax revenue collected and thereby save. Business firms may hold undivided profits (retained earnings) or set aside, from earnings, depreciation allowances and save in these ways.[2] The actions of those who save result in real investment. They may also result in financial investment through the purchase of claims.

"Financial" investment refers to buying claims to wealth or repaying debt. In the acquisition of a claim to wealth, there is no immediate change in the stock of wealth of the economy. An asset formerly held by one person is simply transferred to another person's ownership. Purchase of a stock or a bond may precede or accompany real investment, but the purchase itself does not represent real investment. When saving and investment occur, there is an addition to the stock of wealth of the economy at large.

The term "financial investment" relates to individual consumers or firms or governments and their daily decisions about the forms in which they hold their claims to wealth. When referring to "real" investment, the analyst always has in mind the

---

[1] It is useful to distinguish the flow concept, "saving," from a stock concept, "savings." Savings are holdings of wealth in some form, usually claims (such as bank deposits, bonds, or stocks) or "real" assets (such as gold, houses, machinery, or factories). Saving is the addition to (flow into) such claims and real assets during a period.

[2] Technically, saving is the earnings set aside rather than the depreciation allowances, but, with some liberty, analysts pool the two accounting concepts under the heading of saving.

creation of productive tools or inventories of goods and materials that will be used in the production of consumer goods or other investment goods.

## Ex Ante and Ex Post Saving and Investment

The difference between ex ante and ex post saving and investment is that ex ante refers to plans or expectations about saving and investment, where ex post refers to actual, realized, past levels of saving and investment. In a modern economy, in which saving decisions are made principally by consumers and investment decisions are made principally by business firms, it would be rare indeed to find ex ante saving equal to ex ante investment, that is, to find planned or expected saving on the part of consumers to be the same in value as planned or expected investment by business firms. On the other hand, ex post saving must *always* equal ex post investment for the entire economy if all sectors of the economy are properly accounted for; this equality is a matter of definition.

In simple equation form we may write

$$\begin{array}{c} \text{planned (ex ante)} \\ \text{investment} \end{array} + \begin{array}{c} \text{unplanned} \\ \text{investment} \end{array} = \begin{array}{c} \text{actual (ex post)} \\ \text{investment} \end{array}$$

and

$$\begin{array}{c} \text{planned (ex ante)} \\ \text{saving} \end{array} + \begin{array}{c} \text{unplanned} \\ \text{saving} \end{array} = \begin{array}{c} \text{actual (ex post)} \\ \text{saving} \end{array}$$

Although by definition actual saving must equal investment, it is clear that planned saving and investment can differ. That is, there may be *unplanned* elements of saving and/or investment that, when combined with planned elements, make the actual or realized levels of saving and investment equal during a given period.

Investment in inventory may be used as an example of how there may be a discrepancy between ex ante saving and investment even though ex post saving and investment are necessarily equal. Let us assume that managers of a firm plan to increase inventories by 100 units. However, sales are less than expected so that actual inventories rise by 150 units, 50 of which are unplanned. At the same time, assume that consumers had planned saving of 150 units. Actual and planned saving are equal in this example, but actual and planned investment are not equal—inventories increase by more than the planned amount.

In the example, ex post saving and investment are both 150; ex ante saving is 150, but ex ante investment is 100, and unplanned investment in inventories is 50. The unplanned element—the discrepancy between ex ante saving and investment—is entirely on the investment side. Other examples could be given in which unplanned saving, perhaps because of changes in income, would occur rather than unplanned investment. In any event, whether ex ante saving and investment differ because of unplanned elements in saving or in investment, it is likely that subsequent adjustments by consumers or business firms will produce changes in spending and output.

**FIGURE 2–1**
**GNP, Saving, and Investment**

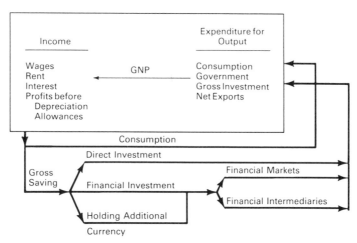

Net exports (net foreign investment) is often ignored, since, for the United States, it is relatively small and, in recent years, sometimes negative. Technically, saving equals total investment—domestic plus net foreign investment.

For this reason, the analysis of ex ante saving and investment is useful in explaining fluctuations in economic activity.

## Saving and Investment and the National Income Accounts

National income accounts measure the total value of goods and services produced for *final* use in a country during a given period.[3] The gross amount is usually referred to as gross national product (GNP). After deducting depreciation and other capital consumption allowances and certain other items from GNP, the resulting amount is termed national income. It is useful to consider briefly the relation between expenditures for GNP and the income received in the form of wages, rent, interest, and profits. Then the relationship between saving and investment can be examined in more detail because our discussion of financial markets is directly concerned with saving and investment.

Figure 2–1 shows these relationships in simplified form. One may view expenditures for final output as consumer expenditures, government spending, gross invest-

---

[3] The largest part of the gross value of transactions in an economy is not for the exchange of "final" goods but rather for (1) the exchange of "intermediate" goods and (2) the exchange of existing assets such as houses or financial claims. These latter transactions do not represent output, and our description of saving and investment is not directly concerned with them. One estimate is that these types of transactions, together with some others which do not involve purchase and sale of items in the current GNP, represent 96 percent of all transactions. See Guy E. Noyes, "The Multiple Flaws of the Monetary Base," *Morgan Guaranty Survey*, October 1981, pp. 6–10.

ment spending, and net spending by foreigners for exports. The same total amount may be viewed as income received by those who receive wages, rent, interest, and profits before depreciation allowances.

As noted on the lower left side of the figure, income may be used for consumption spending or may be saved. Saving may be used for direct investment, as for example when the owner of a single proprietorship business uses funds that he or she has saved to add new store equipment; it may also be used for financial investment, in the purchase of financial assets (stocks, bonds, promissory notes, and so forth); or it may simply be held in the form of additional money (assuming that the total money stock has been allowed to increase during the period).

Financial investment may go directly into loans and investments (purchase of corporate bonds, government bonds, stocks, etc.) or may be channeled through financial intermediaries such as banks, savings and loan associations, life insurance companies, and others. Funds received by such institutions may be channeled into business loans and investments, investments in government securities, or consumer loans. Amounts loaned to consumers may be used by them for consumption. Similarly, amounts loaned to government provide funds for the government to use for current spending.

Money is more carefully defined in Chapter 5, but at this point it may be noted that money is separated from other financial assets because of its special characteristics and importance. Moreover, in the United States, although interest or dividends are received by almost all those who own financial assets, those who hold money do *not* receive interest when they hold coins, paper money, or, in some cases, demand deposits. Interest is now paid on many checking deposits, and thus the presence or absence of interest payments cannot always be used to distinguish money from other financial assets.

Table 2–1 contains figures on saving and investment in billions of dollars for the year 1985 in the United States. The measures are taken from national income accounts prepared by the U.S. Department of Commerce and published in the *Survey of Current Business* (and also republished in several places, including the *Federal Reserve Bulletin* and *Economic Indicators*).

In 1985, as in any other year, gross investment in the economy equaled gross saving. Gross investment is the amount spent, in current dollar values, both for replacement of investment goods that have become obsolete or otherwise depreciated and for net new additions to the capital stock, including additions to business inventories. Reduction in inventories is treated as disinvestment. In addition to private domestic investment, there is a positive or negative amount of U.S. net foreign investment, which is measured by the excess of exports over imports of goods and services, including net transfer payments to foreigners. In 1985, as shown in the table, this amount was negative; that is, net investment in the United States by foreigners was greater than U.S. net investment abroad.

The gross saving figure includes saving of the household, business, and government sectors during the year. Government surplus (deficit) is the saving (dissaving) of federal, state, and local governments, as defined to fit the national income accounts. It

**TABLE 2–1**
**U.S. Gross Investment and Saving, 1985**
**(billions of dollars)**

| | | |
|---|---:|---:|
| Gross private domestic investment | | 669.3 |
| Net foreign investment | | −115.3 |
| Gross investment | | 554.0 |
| Gross private saving | | |
| Personal saving | 129.0 | |
| Undistributed corporate profits | 126.9 | |
| Corporate capital consumption allowances (chiefly depreciation) | 269.2 | |
| Noncorporate capital consumption allowances (chiefly depreciation) | 169.2 | 694.3 |
| Government surplus or deficit | | |
| Federal | −200.0 | |
| State and local | 59.0 | −141.0 |
| Gross saving | | 554.0 |

SOURCE: *Survey of Current Business,* July 1986, Table A-52.

is not the same as the amount of surplus (deficit) reported by the president each year in the annual government budget, because state and local government saving or dissaving is included and because of some differences in definitions of expenditures and receipts used in different budgets. Saving and investment in Table 2–1 are ex post.

The item "personal saving" is important. Two measures of personal saving are now commonly used. The measure used in Table 2–1 is derived by deducting current outlays of the personal sector for goods, services, and interest payments from the current disposable personal income. Disposable personal income (DPI) consists of after-tax wages and salaries, interest income, rent, dividends, and net transfer receipts. Capital gains, however, are not included. They are not income for the economy as a whole, since the economy does not have more real wealth simply because prices of houses, stocks, or other assets have increased.

This measure of personal saving gives no indication of the forms in which savings are held—it is simply a figure for total personal saving. Another measure, derived from what is termed "flow of funds" data, does show a breakdown of savings holdings, as in Table 2–2. There we see figures for holdings of savings in bank accounts, securities, insurance, and other financial assets, as well as holdings in the form of homes, durable goods, and other tangible assets. In this table, total personal saving is found by adding net increases in tangible assets to any net increase in financial assets and then subtracting any net increase in liabilities. An increase in assets minus an increase in liabilities equals an increase in net worth, or savings. This measure has resulted in larger figures for saving than the figures reported in the national income and product accounts (note the figures for personal saving, flow of

**TABLE 2–2**
**Amount and Composition of Individuals' Saving, 1984 and 1985**
(billions of dollars, seasonally adjusted annual rates)

|    |                                              | 1984   | 1985   |
|----|----------------------------------------------|--------|--------|
| 1  | Increase in financial assets                 | 535.3  | 537.9  |
| 2  | Checkable deposits and currency              | 23.4   | 48.9   |
| 3  | Time and savings deposits                    | 228.3  | 132.9  |
| 4  | Money market fund shares                     | 47.2   | −2.2   |
| 5  | Securities                                   | 78.7   | 160.2  |
| 6  | U.S. savings bonds                           | 3.0    | 5.3    |
| 7  | Other U.S. Treasury securities               | 44.5   | −27.9  |
| 8  | U.S. government agency securities            | 26.3   | 73.1   |
| 9  | Tax-exempt obligations                       | 41.7   | 89.1   |
| 10 | Corporate + foreign bonds                    | 15.3   | 3.1    |
| 11 | Open market paper                            | −10.8  | 33.2   |
| 12 | Mutual fund shares                           | 37.1   | 105.3  |
| 13 | Other corporate equities                     | −78.4  | −120.9 |
| 14 | Private life insurance residuals             | 5.0    | 7.6    |
| 15 | Private insured pension residuals            | 45.2   | 60.8   |
| 16 | Private noninsured pension residuals         | 26.0   | 36.9   |
| 17 | Government insurance + pension residuals      | 57.1   | 62.1   |
| 18 | Miscellaneous financial assets               | 24.5   | 30.7   |
| 19 | Gross investment in tangible assets          | 615.2  | 645.8  |
| 20 | Owner-occupied homes                         | 153.4  | 158.1  |
| 21 | Other fixed assets                           | 114.6  | 127.5  |
| 22 | Consumer durables                            | 331.1  | 361.5  |
| 23 | Inventories                                  | 16.2   | −1.4   |
| 24 | Capital consumption allowances               | 404.3  | 428.9  |
| 25 | Owner-occupied homes                         | 59.7   | 63.4   |
| 26 | Other fixed assets                           | 104.3  | 107.4  |
| 27 | Consumer durables                            | 240.4  | 258.1  |
| 28 | Net investment in tangible assets            | 210.9  | 216.9  |
| 29 | Owner-occupied homes                         | 93.7   | 94.7   |
| 30 | Other fixed assets                           | 10.3   | 20.1   |
| 31 | Consumer durables                            | 90.7   | 103.4  |
| 32 | Inventories                                  | 16.2   | −1.4   |
| 33 | Net increases in debt                        | 329.7  | 378.0  |
| 34 | Mortgage debt on nonfarm homes               | 130.4  | 154.7  |
| 35 | Other mortgage debt                          | 81.9   | 82.3   |
| 36 | Consumer credit                              | 94.8   | 96.6   |
| 37 | Security credit                              | −3.1   | 7.3    |
| 38 | Policy loans                                 | .4     | −.3    |
| 39 | Other debt                                   | 25.4   | 37.3   |
| 40 | Individuals' saving                          | 416.5  | 376.8  |

TABLE 2–2 (continued)

|    |                                                               | 1984  | 1985  |
|----|---------------------------------------------------------------|-------|-------|
| 41 | − Government insurance + pension residuals                    | 57.1  | 62.1  |
| 42 | − Net investment in consumer durables                         | 90.7  | 103.4 |
|    | − Capital gains dividends                                     |       |       |
| 43 |     from mutual funds                      | 6.0   | 4.9   |
| 44 | − Net saving by farm corporations                             | 1.3   | 1.8   |
| 45 | = Personal saving, flow of funds basis                        | 261.4 | 204.6 |
| 46 | Personal saving, national income and product accounts basis   | 172.5 | 129.0 |
| 47 | Difference                                                    | 88.9  | 75.6  |

SOURCE: Federal Reserve, *Flow of Funds Accounts*, First Quarter 1986.

funds basis and personal saving, national income and product accounts (NIPA) basis). The difference is shown in the last three lines of Table 2–2.

Reasons for the differences may be partly that capital gains are included in the flow of funds figures (an increase in asset values counts as an increase in net worth) and partly because durable goods are included as saving (and investment) in the flow of funds, whereas spending for durable goods is counted as consumption in the national income accounts. But even after adjusting for these items, flow of funds data have shown higher amounts of saving than have national income data.[4]

In the late 1970s, saving declined sharply. This was chiefly the result of a great increase in borrowing by consumers. Inflation was rising, and perhaps consumers believed they could borrow funds and repay them later when their incomes would be higher.[5]

Although both consumption and saving depend primarily on income, there are changes in the ratio of saving to income because consumers often do not increase their spending as rapidly as their incomes rise, and when incomes fall they are reluctant to reduce their spending. Hence, saving has risen as high as 8 or 9 percent of disposable personal income in some years of high business activity and has fallen as low as 5 or 4 percent, or occasionally even lower, in recessions. Nevertheless, in the long run, the ratio of saving to disposable personal income has been remarkably constant except in times of major wars.

---

[4] The Saving Rate: How Serious the Decline?" *Morgan Guaranty Survey*, February 1980, pp. 11–14. See also "Why the Saving Rate Has Its Own Biorhythms," Citibank, *Monthly Economic Letter*, April 1980, pp. 11–14. The national income accounts measure of saving is derived by subtracting one large figure (consumption expenditures) from an even larger one (disposable personal income); hence even a small error in one or both large figures results in a large percentage error in the figure for saving.

[5] Carol Corrado and Charles Steindel, "Perspectives on Personal Saving," *Federal Reserve Bulletin*, August 1980, pp. 613–625. See also Donald Cox, "The Decline in Personal Saving," Federal Reserve Bank of New York, *Quarterly Review*, Spring 1981, pp. 25–32.

## The Economic Significance of Saving and Investment

Economists use the concepts of saving and investment to help analyze two important aspects of macroeconomics: (1) fluctuations in economic activity between prosperity and recession and (2) the process of economic growth. Ex ante amounts are frequently used in analysis of causes of fluctuations that occur in the level of business activity; ex post saving and investment are significant factors affecting rates of economic growth. Both ex ante and ex post amounts, of course, vary cyclically and may affect long-run growth.

Why do business enterprise economies experience periods of expansion in output and employment, frequently accompanied by inflation, followed after some months or years by declines that we describe as "recessions"? Why, in other words, do we have business fluctuations? One approach suggests that discrepancies between what business firms plan to invest in capital goods and the amounts that they and members of the other sectors plan to withhold from the spending stream usually differ; that is, ex ante investment usually exceeds or falls short of ex ante saving. The level of income and spending rises when planned $I >$ planned $S$ and declined when planned $S >$ planned $I$. In this view, changes in economic activity occur when investment spending is greater or smaller than the amounts that would be saved at a given level of income. These discrepancies or differences between saving and investment may occur because of unplanned changes in sales and inventories or unplanned changes in income and spending. If planned investment and planned saving are not equal, it is because savers have different plans from those who determine the amount of investment or because of unplanned elements on either side that lead to subsequent changes in investment plans or saving plans and further increases or declines in spending and income.

The amount and percent of saving are important because saving provides funds for investment in capital goods, and such investment is necessary for economic growth. Growth may result, of course, from a larger, better trained, and better educated labor force; but in most cases an increase in capital is also needed. An increase in capital accompanying an increase in employment is sometimes termed "capital widening," while an increase in capital per unit of labor or output is often termed "capital deepening." Less developed countries generally recognize the need for increased capital to create growth, and saving, borrowing, or foreign equity investment (or some combination of these) are needed to provide funds for investment. A high rate of saving, characteristic of an economy such as that of Japan, is needed for rapid growth. Slow growth, however, may come from improper allocation of capital as well as from insufficient saving and investment.[6]

---

[6] An extensive study by the Federal Reserve System concluded that "one cannot say with any confidence that the United States saves too little or too much." The rate of saving and investment remained about the same during the slow growth of the 1970s as it had been during the period of much more rapid growth in the 1960s. See Jared J. Enzler, William E. Conrad, and Lewis Johnson, "Public Policy and Capital Formation," *Federal Reserve Bulletin*, October 1981, pp. 749–761, 753.

Along with growth, wider economic fluctuations also may result from a high rate of investment. Even a small decline in spending by consumers may result in a large percentage decline in the amount of new investment needed, and a rise in spending requires, at times, more investment because new factories and machinery are needed as well as the normal repair and replacement of old plant and equipment.[7]

# SAVING AND INVESTMENT IN BARTER AND MONETARY ECONOMIES

A "barter" economy is, by definition, one without money and having no other financial assets or liabilities. Hence there are no financial institutions. All trade of economic goods takes place "in kind." Only small amounts can be traded on any one occasion. Barter markets are almost always two-person markets, and there is no system of money prices. In theory, a system of relative prices could exist, but only if everyone engaged in trading knew the amounts of each good that could be traded for amounts of each and every other good—an unlikely state of affairs.

In a barter economy, all saving and investment decisions would be simultaneous; if one saved, one would thereby invest in real goods, and if one invested one would save to provide the real resources. Not only would saving be identical with investment in this sense, but all economic units would have balanced budgets at all times; there would be no external financing. In barter economies, savers invest in real capital goods; the saver-investor has but one source of finance: his or her own saving. Not only are the levels of income and capital formation low, but quite likely, the economy is inefficient. Investment/saving are tied rigidly to the distribution of current income and are not subjected to a yardstick of profitability. Capital formation takes place or not, depending upon the level of current income and the decision to consume.

In a barter economy, saving equals investment in the ex ante sense as well as in the ex post sense. The decisions or plans to save and invest occur simultaneously: they are both made by individuals. An example is a farmer who barters corn (which might have been consumed) for wood to build a fence.

The most elementary type of monetary economy is one with money as the sole financial asset (debt).[8] Fiat money (issued by the government to acquire goods and services from the private sector) may consist of coins and paper money that the community accepts as legal tender. It is a debt of the government and an asset of households and business firms.

The importance of money in the economy is twofold. First, money serves as a medium of exchange and helps circumvent the restrictions on exchange imposed by

---

[7] Because ex post $S$ equals $I$ at all times, the realized levels of $S$ and $I$ are always equal, but they both rise and fall during cyclical swings.

[8] Except for gold (and silver or similar monetary metals), all financial assets are also debt. Hence, if financial assets increase, debt increases. It should be noted that stocks are not technically debt, but they are evidences of *claims* held by stockholders.

the system of barter. Goods and services are exchanged for money, which in turn may be exchanged for goods and services. This promotes the development of markets, wider exchange, and specialization in production and distribution.

Second, money provides an additional asset for savers and an additional means of financing expenditures of investors. Savers may acquire real assets *or* accumulate cash balances; investors may finance expenditures from current saving *or* by drawing down previously accumulated money holdings. The rigid link between saving/investment and the distribution of current income is broken, and although all expenditures are financed internally, some flexibility has been introduced into the saving-investment process.

More complex and sophisticated financial systems simply extend the range of choices and alternatives available to suppliers and demanders of loanable funds. By increasing the number and variety of savings media and the techniques and means of raising funds, more sophisticated financial systems facilitate transfer of real resources from lenders to borrowers.

A sophisticated financial system is an essential feature of a highly industrialized economy. The mass production and distribution of goods and services and the high degree of specialization in product and factor markets are mirrored in the financial sector of the economy by a similar degree of complex interaction: an elaborate system of markets and institutions provides the mechanisms for bringing suppliers and demanders of funds together. The saving-investment process is facilitated by numerous institutions that offer savers a wide variety of substitutes for real capital or money, thus encouraging the flow and diversification of saving, and many methods of providing borrowers with funds to meet their requirements, thus promoting investment spending.

The transfer of real resources is made possible by a flow of funds from lenders through financial intermediaries to borrowing or deficit units. These funds are then available to bid for resources that are released from present consumption into the output of capital goods.[9]

Figure 2–2 depicts the process of intermediation.[10] In effect, Figure 2–2 is a blow-up of the part of Figure 2–1 that relates to transfers of funds rather than to real income. On the one hand there are the borrowers, who wish to supplement their current income and savings by acquiring funds to finance their expenditures. On the other hand there are the lenders, whose income and savings are in excess of their own internal needs. Positioned between these two groups are the financial institutions that serve as intermediaries ready to accommodate simultaneously both deficit and surplus sectors. The arrows indicate the direction of flow of securities and the net flows of loanable funds in the opposite direction. The nonbank financial institutions are discussed in detail in Chapter 4, but at this point it should be noted that the deposit-type

---

[9] At full employment, saving makes investment possible by releasing resources. At less than full employment, investment spending may raise the level of real income and make more saving possible and hence available.

[10] This diagram is based on that of John G. Gurley, *Liquidity and Financial Institutions in the Postwar Period*, Study Paper No. 4, Joint Economic Committee, 86th Cong., 1st sess., January 25, 1960, p. 21.

**FIGURE 2–2**
**Flow of Funds from Ultimate Lenders to Ultimate Borrowers**

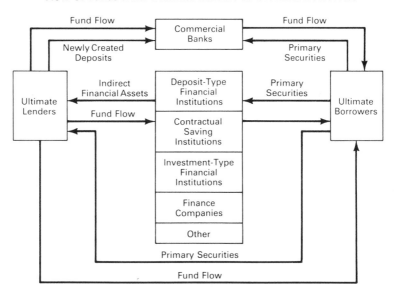

institutions include mutual savings banks, savings and loan associations, and credit unions; the contractual saving institutions include insurance companies and pension funds; the investment-type institutions include mutual funds and trust departments of commercial banks; and "other" consists chiefly of government agencies or agencies that were originally government agencies such as farm credit agencies and housing or mortgage market agencies (e.g., the Federal National Mortgage Association), together with conglomerates and nonfinancial companies that provide financial services.

We see that several sources of funds are available to borrowers. Households, business firms, or government units in need of funds may either borrow directly from savers, by selling their securities directly to them, or indirectly, by selling securities either to commercial banks (monetary intermediaries) or to nonmonetary intermediaries such as mutual savings banks, life insurance companies, or pension funds. The term "indirect borrowing" or "financing" thus implies the use of intermediaries as proximate lenders. However, the ultimate source of funds is the original lender because, as the diagram shows, the intermediaries acquire loanable funds from lenders and make them available to borrowers.

What is the process by which these financial intermediaries acquire loanable funds? Primarily it is by offering savers a more attractive alternative to the direct purchase of the borrower's debt. That is, by providing savers with assets that are either safe, more liquid, or have a higher net return—or, more likely, some attractive combination of these features—intermediaries induce lenders to exchange their loanable funds for claims against financial institutions rather than against primary borrowers. In essence, intermediaries buy borrowers' debt and sell their own liabilities to surplus units in exchange for loanable funds. An alternative way of viewing this process of intermediation is to visualize intermediaries as borrowing at one level of interest rates—those paid to lenders—and lending at another—the rates charged borrowers. The costs of serving as intermediaries, including a profit, are met by the excess of the lending rate over the borrowing rate.

Intermediation affects the saving-investment process in several ways. First, it facilitates the separation of the investment decision from the saving decision. Investment decisions can be made with no direct tie to any single saving decision. Second, intermediation encourages saving by providing diversification of assets available to lenders, diversified according to risk, yield, and liquidity. Third, intermediation encourages investment by providing a variety of available sources of funds that differ in regard to maturities of loans, interest charges, repayment provisions, and so on. Fourth, and of great importance, use of intermediaries reduces the risk of default to lenders and also assures borrowers that funds are generally available, whereas availability from individuals might be limited. Both of these cost-reducing functions mean lenders receive higher net returns and borrowers pay less for funds than in the absence of intermediaries. Specialization of activities increases productivity. Some individuals can specialize in the *management* of real resources, borrowing funds when necessary, while *owners* of such resources may continue their chosen activities. Labor and other resources involved in activities of intermediaries contribute to real productivity of the economy and to improving the standard of living because intermediaries are able simultaneously to satisfy portfolio preferences of borrowers and of lenders.

## Debts, Assets, and Financial Intermediation

Three important points are made in this section: (1) for every debt there is an asset; (2) most external financing is through debt issue rather than through equity issue;[11] and (3) the greater the reliance on debt and external finance, the more important is the role to be played by financial intermediaries.

**1.** It is well known that income and expenditures are two sides of the same coin: spending of one sector is income of another. Similarly, debts and assets are two sides of the same coin—one's debt is another's asset. This element of interdependence is often overlooked; for example, when we look favorably upon growth of assets but disapprovingly upon growth of debt, we are being inconsistent. Individuals, firms, or governments may deficit spend (borrow) to finance expenditures. Such spending units issue debt instruments—government securities, corporation notes and bonds, mortgages, and so on—that are all assets purchased either by ultimate lenders or by financial intermediaries.

Note, however, that, while all debts are also assets, the reverse is not true; all assets are *not* debts. Some assets are real assets (real capital or land or other earning source). In the United States, all *financial* assets are debt—even coins may be re-

---

[11] However, the existing *stock* of equity issues is very large.

garded as debt of the government. At this point no distinction is made between bonds (debt) and stock (equity) because their functions are basically the same.

Both assets and debts are created when credit is extended: "to obtain credit is to incur debt."[12] Although an individual may incur excessive debt, it is recognized that during prosperous economic times there is always a rapid increase in overall indebtedness, and during economic recessions there is always a slowdown in the rate of growth of outstanding debt. Debt performs a desirable function in any economy, and one should hesitate to condemn debt simply because, on some occasions, it is misused.

**2.** Most spending in our economy is financed out of current income. That is, it is financed "internally." The remaining spending is financed "externally" through debt creation or equity issue. Most "external" financing is undertaken by acquiring funds through issuance of debt instruments rather than equity (ownership) claims. For a variety of reasons both borrowers and lenders in recent years have preferred debt instruments to equities when engaged in external financing.

First, holders of debt instruments have prior claim to income and assets rather than the residual interest of ownership. Thus, debt instruments provide greater "safety" of principal (less risk of loss) than do equity instruments.

Second, current taxation rules give debt a privileged position. Interest charges on debt are deductible as business expenses. Even interest on home mortgages is generally deductible from personal income for tax purposes. In this way, much borrowing is "subsidized" by the government's system of taxation, and this alone gives great impetus to borrowing as opposed to equity issue as a means of financing expenditures.

Third, managers of business firms are often reluctant to dilute existing stockholders' equity because to do so will not only reduce control but also reduce earnings available to existing owners. If a firm is growing, current owners stand to share in the growth. If the growth is financed by debt, each shareholder retains control and ownership proportional to his or her number of shares of stock. On the other hand, if additional shares are sold, then each proportional interest in the growth is diminished. Thus, stockholders often do not approve of dilution of their pro rata share of ownership. Managers do not wish to offend existing shareholders because shareholders can vote to replace management if disillusionment is strong enough.

**3.** The third point to be emphasized in this section is that the greater the amount of spending financed externally through debt or equity issues, the greater will be the role played by financial institutions. If all our spending were financed out of current income, there would be no need for the services of such institutions. At the other extreme, if all spending were financed by issuance of debt or equity, then all increases in spending would have to be accompanied by concomitant charges in debt or equity, and the role of financial institutions would be maximized. In the U.S. economy, of course, internal financing out of current income is by far the most important source of funds, and we can say that, on average, budgets are far closer to being balanced (income financed) than they are to being totally debt financed.

---

[12] *The Two Faces of Debt*, Federal Reserve Bank of Chicago, 1972, p. 2. This pamphlet contains an excellent description of the role of debt in the economy.

## Growth of Debt and Equity Claims

Under present institutional arrangements that favor the use of debt instruments as a vehicle for transferring loanable funds, growth of debt is the financial side of growth in national income and output. Indeed, historically the ratio of debt to GNP in the United States has generally risen during prosperous times and declined during recessions. But it has averaged about 1.85; that is, $185 more debt is outstanding at the end of a year for every $100 worth of gross national product produced during an average year.[13] Continued expansion of economic activity would seem to require a continuation of the growth of debt, barring unforeseen institutional changes favoring, say, increased reliance upon international financing or equity financing.

Because for many purposes debt and equity claims are close substitutes, it is useful to include both when looking at the relationship between primary securities and total spending. Primary securities have increased, on average, about 2.5 times as rapidly as GNP in recent decades. Thus, for every $100 billion rise in GNP, primary securities increase by about $250 billion in a typical year. Of course, the relationship is not a precise one; in some years the increase is larger or smaller, reflecting changes in sources of funds and in the economy's growth rate. Implications of the increase in primary securities are most significant in the capital markets. In the years ahead, we should expect continued growth in net issues of bonds, mortgages, and equities as the economy continues to grow. Growth in real GNP should be accompanied by growth in both real capital and in financial assets.

In this section we have examined saving and investment and have stressed the importance of financial intermediaries in the saving-investment process. We have observed that financial assets and liabilities are two sides of the same coin and that financial transactions play an essential role in economic activity. In the next section we introduce flow of funds accounting. This framework enables us to measure various types of transactions between economic units. Flow of funds accounting provides a systematic way of integrating saving, investment, lending, and borrowing. In so doing, it brings together the real and financial sectors of the economy. For these reasons an understanding of flow of funds accounts is an indispensable tool of the financial analyst.

# FLOW OF FUNDS ANALYSIS

Although aggregate saving and investment must be equal, ex post, for the entire economy, it is unlikely that saving will equal investment for a particular sector during a given period. Saving may exceed investment; the surplus on current account will have been used for purposes other than financing capital expenditures. For example, the surplus funds may have been used to buy securities or to make loans. If a sector

---

[13] For a pioneering article that elucidated this relationship, see Marshall A. Robinson, "Debt in the American Economy," Reprint No. 31 (Washington, D.C.: The Brookings Institution, June 1959).

**TABLE 2–3**
**Sector Structure in Flow of Funds Accounts**

| | |
|---|---|
| Households | Credit unions |
| Total nonfinancial business | Life insurance companies |
| Farm business | Other insurance companies |
| Nonfarm noncorporate business | Private pension funds |
| Corporate nonfinancial business | State and local government employee |
| State and local governments | retirement funds |
| Foreign | Finance companies |
| U.S. government and credit agencies | Real estate investment trusts (REITs) |
| Banking system | Open-end investment companies |
| Savings and loan associations | Money market mutual funds |
| Mutual savings banks | Security brokers and dealers |

SOURCE: *Introduction to Flow of Funds,* Board of Governors of the Federal Reserve System, February 1975, p. 35.

has investment greater than saving, sources other than its own saving will have provided the funds necessary to finance these expenditures. Thus, saving is *one* source of funds; investment is *one* use of funds. The flow of funds accounts include *all* the sources and uses of funds for the various sectors of the economy, and by summation, for all sectors.

Flow of funds data for an economy are derived for a specific period of time by (1) dividing the economy into sectors, (2) preparing a source and use of funds statement for each sector, (3) summing the sources and uses for all sectors, and (4) placing the sector accounts side by side to form a table or matrix.[14] A simple matrix may consist of only a few sectors. For example, the entire economy can be divided into households, business firms, governments, and financial institutions. In a more complex matrix, these sectors may be subdivided with additional categories established for different types of business firms, government units, financial institutions, and so on. And, if foreign transactions are to be considered, it is necessary to include a sector for the rest of the world. The larger the number of sectors, the more likely it is that each sector will be composed of relatively homogeneous units. Ideally, each group's market behavior will be similarly influenced by the same set of economic variables. However, if the economy is divided into too many sectors, the model becomes cumbersome. Too much detail may obscure important relationships. The optimum number of groups depends ultimately on the purpose of the analysis and the degree of disaggregation necessary, on the availability of data, and on the time and effort required to collect and assemble the data. The Federal Reserve maintains data on the 21 sectors in Table 2–3.

---

[14] Our presentation of flow of funds accounting draws heavily upon two sources: Lawrence S. Ritter, *The Flow of Funds Accounts: A Framework for Financial Analysis,* New York University, Graduate School of Business Administration, *Bulletin,* No. 52, August 1968; and James C. Van Horne, *Function and Analysis of Capital Market Rates,* Foundation of Finances Series (Englewood Cliffs, N.J., Prentice-Hall, 1970), pp. 15–33.

The second step in constructing flow of funds accounts is to prepare a source and use statement for each sector. This is done by examining the balance sheets of the various sectors at the beginning and end of a quarter or a year. *Net* changes are noted in the stock of assets, liabilities, and net worth that occurred during the period.[15] Certain assets may have increased in value, others declined; some liabilities may be greater and some smaller than at the beginning of the period. The convention is to treat increases in assets as a use of funds and increases in liabilities or net worth as a source of funds. Sources and uses for a hypothetical sector are shown as follows:

### January 1, 19— to December 31, 19—

| Uses | Sources |
|---|---|
| Δ Real assets (investment or disinvestment) | Δ Liabilities (borrowing or debt repayment) |
| Δ Financial assets (lending or sale of securities) | Δ Net worth (saving or dissaving) |

A simple source and use statement for a given sector shows intersectoral flows on a new basis. That is, it does not record intrasector transactions; for example, a loan by one business firm to another would be excluded. Also, only *net* increases in assets are treated as a use of funds. Debt repayment or dissaving, which are in fact uses of funds, are treated as *negative sources* of funds. In the same way, disinvestment in real assets or the sale of securities, which are in fact *sources* of funds, are treated as *negative uses*. This characteristic of the accounts facilitates handling the data uniformly, but unfortunately it may also obscure some changes both within sectors and among different sectors.

For a given sector, and by summing all sectors, for the economy as a whole, the following equality is obtained:

$$\Delta \text{ net worth } + \Delta \text{ liabilities } = \Delta \text{ real assets } + \Delta \text{ financial assets}$$

or

$$\text{saving } + \text{ borrowing } = \text{ investment } + \text{ lending}$$

It follows that if, in a particular sector, saving > investment, then lending > borrowing. This sector is a surplus sector and a net lender to other sectors. If investment > saving, then borrowing > lending. In this case the sector is a deficit sector and a net borrower from other sectors.

---

[15] The Federal Reserve estimates flows and balance sheet positions separately and uses different valuation procedures. Bonds are reported at book value; equities are valued at market price in the figures for year-end outstandings and at book value in flow accounts where possible. The intent is to exclude capital gains and losses from the flow data, so that flow of funds accounts will be more compatible with national income and products data. For asset and liability data, market values, which include capital gains or losses, must be used.

In principle, an account is easily established for each of the several sectors that make up the economic system. Sources and uses of funds are identified as in the case of our hypothetical sector. If we place these statements side by side, we form a matrix to describe an interconnected system of flow of funds for, say, a year. As is shown in the hypothetical matrix in Table 2–4, not only does each sector's sources match its uses, but, by summation, total sources equal total uses. Furthermore, whereas $S \neq I$ for any sector individually, for the economy as a whole, $S = I$.

Table 2–4 is a simplified, hypothetical flow of funds matrix for an economy that has been divided into four sectors. Items in the cells of the matrix represent dollar flows that occurred during a period of time. In general, U stands for uses of funds and represents acquisitions or additions to assets, while S stands for sources of funds and represents additions to liabilities or to net worth.

We find that households saved $60 billion of their income during the period and used $10 billion of this to purchase real investment goods and the remaining $50 billion of this saving to purchase financial assets from financial intermediaries. The business sector saved $40 billion but also invested $80 billion during the period. This required business to obtain $40 billion in additional funds from financial intermediaries to have a total of $80 billion for investment spending. The government, by running a deficit in its budget, dissaved $10 billion and had to issue $10 billion of financial liabilities to cover this excess of spending over tax revenues. Finally, financial intermediaries experienced an increase in both assets and liabilities. They ac-

**TABLE 2–4**
**Flow of Funds Accounts for a Given Time Period**
**(billions of dollars)**

| | Sectors | | | | | | | | | |
|---|---|---|---|---|---|---|---|---|---|---|
| | Households | | Business | | Government | | Financial Intermediaries | | All Sectors | |
| | U | S | U | S | U | S | U | S | U | S |
| Saving (net worth) | | 60 | | 40 | | −10 | | | | 90 |
| Investment (real assets) | 10 | | 80 | | | | | | 90 | |
| Net change in financial assets | 50 | | | | | | 50 | | 100 | |
| Net change in financial liabilities | | | | 40 | | 10 | | 50 | | 100 |
| Totals | 60 | 60 | 80 | 80 | 0 | 0 | 50 | 50 | 190 | 190 |
| Sector surplus or (deficit) | 50 | | (40) | | (10) | | — | | — | |

U = Uses of funds.
S = Sources of funds.

cepted deposit liabilities to the households in the economy in the amount of $50 billion. At the same time, they used these deposits to purchase the debt of $40 billion that business offered in the market and $10 billion borrowed by government.

The column totals show equality of U and S for each sector, in keeping with the requirements that flow of funds statements always balance, so that net changes in uses equal net changes in sources for each sector.

The row totals show the overall equality of uses and sources of funds in the aggregate, for all sectors. Saving by households, business, and government totaled $90 billion, since the government actually dissaved $10 billion. This total saving also equals total investment of $90 billion, of which, in this simplified example, $80 billion was undertaken by business firms and $10 billion by households. The government's dissaving figure (−$10 billion) probably results from the fact that government spending is treated as being entirely for goods and services and not as representing additions to the stock of capital. In the United States, the federal government does not maintain a separate set of "capital" budget accounts as some other countries do. This is an arbitrary procedure. If, in fact, the government spent $10 billion on long-lived dams, perhaps it would be more appropriate to replace the −10 under sources with a +10 under uses in the investment row. Then total investment would be $100 billion and again equal to total saving. However, this is not the convention in the United States.

Households increased their holdings of financial assets by $50 billion, and this is reflected in the *sources* side of the financial intermediaries column, showing a $50 billion increase in financial liabilities. This $50 billion might be, for example, consumer demand or savings deposits at commercial banks or savings deposits at savings and loan associations—liabilities of financial institutions. The $50 billion, under uses, reflects the purchase of government and business securities. Overall, financial assets increased by a total of $100 billion, and liabilities also increased by $100 billion. Thus, in the "all sectors" column the total of $190 billion reflects the equality: saving + borrowing = investment + lending. In our example, saving and investment were both 90, while borrowing and lending were both $100 billion.

Along the bottom of Table 2–4 there is a row indicating the surplus or deficit that each sector realized during the period. Households had a surplus of $50 billion, whereas business firms and government both engaged in deficit financing part of their expenditures, $40 billion and $10 billion, respectively.

From the figures in the flow of funds matrix we can construct a credit market summary table that shows funds raised and advanced by sector. Table 2–5 provides this summary.

In Table 2–4 we did not include a separate row for money; rather, we pooled money in the row with other financial assets. Furthermore, we did not allow for the fact that business and government borrow funds directly from the household sector and from each other: all borrowing took the form of loans from financial institutions. We have also assumed that the nonfinancial sectors acquired financial assets *or* financial liabilities; that is, they loaned *or* borrowed funds. We know, of course, that they do engage in both borrowing and lending. These simplifying assumptions were made to acquaint the reader with the basic elements of flow of funds accounting. They will

**TABLE 2–5**
**Credit Market Summary**
**(billions of dollars)**

| | |
|---|---|
| Funds raised by sectors | |
|    Households | 0 |
|    Business | 40 |
|    Government | 10 |
|    Financial institutions | 50 |
|      Total | 100 |
| Funds advanced by sectors | |
|    Households | 50 |
|    Business | 0 |
|    Government | 0 |
|    Financial institutions | 50 |
|      Total | 100 |

be removed now as we turn to the accounting framework used by financial analysts. First, we examine the data and tables published by the Federal Reserve; then we conclude the chapter with a brief discussion of applications of flow of funds analysis.

## Federal Reserve Flow of Funds Matrix

The Federal Reserve has published flow of funds data in various forms since 1955.[16] A matrix that contains these data for 1984 and 1985 is shown in Table 2–6. It is far more elaborate than our earlier presentation, but most of the underlying principles are essentially the same. The table relates sources and uses, now labeled "funds raised in credit markets" and "credit market supply of funds" to the various sectors of the economy, and in some particular debt instrument forms. Table 2–6 shows funds raised by nonfinancial sectors, funds raised by financial sectors, and funds raised by major types of instruments.

Of total net borrowing of $883.8 billion in 1985, shown at the top of Table 2–6, some $223.6 billion was borrowed by the U.S. government, while private sector borrowing was the remainder, or $660.2 billion. Of this $660.2 billion, line 21 shows that households borrowed $297.7 billion.

The next section of the table shows borrowing by financial sectors, which amounted to $187.5 billion in 1985 as shown on line 31.

Total net borrowing for all sectors in 1985 was $1,070.9 billion, as shown on line 50. This amount could be contrasted with total new share issues that raised funds in the equity markets of $28.2 billion in 1985 on line 59. These figures clearly indicate

---

[16] The monthly *Federal Reserve Bulletin* includes tables showing sources and uses of funds in U.S. credit markets for recent years. These are expanded versions of our credit market summary (Table 2–3). Additional publications are given in selected references at the end of the chapter.

**TABLE 2–6**
**Summary of Funds Raised in Credit Markets, 1984 and 1985**
**(billions of dollars)**

| Transaction Category, Sector | 1984 | 1985 |
|---|---|---|
| *Nonfinancial Sectors* | | |
| 1   Total net borrowing by domestic nonfinancial sectors | 765.9 | 883.8 |
|     *By sector and instrument* | | |
| 2   U.S. government | 198.8 | 223.6 |
| 3       Treasury securities | 199.0 | 223.7 |
| 4       Agency issues and mortgages | −.2 | −.1 |
| 5   Private domestic nonfinancial sectors | 567.1 | 660.2 |
| 6       Debt capital instruments | 325.3 | 474.3 |
| 7         Tax-exempt obligations | 65.8 | 173.4 |
| 8         Corporate bonds | 47.1 | 67.9 |
| 9         Mortgages | 212.4 | 233.0 |
| 10          Home mortgages | 130.7 | 152.8 |
| 11          Multifamily residential | 20.7 | 25.7 |
| 12          Commercial | 62.0 | 59.0 |
| 13          Farm | −1.0 | −4.5 |
| 14      Other debt instruments | 241.9 | 185.9 |
| 15        Consumer credit | 94.8 | 103.6 |
| 16        Bank loans n.e.c.* | 79.5 | 30.7 |
| 17        Open market paper | 24.2 | 12.9 |
| 18        Other | 43.3 | 38.8 |
| 19      By borrowing sector | 567.1 | 660.2 |
| 20        State and local governments | 45.0 | 128.5 |
| 21        Households | 239.2 | 297.7 |
| 22        Farm | −.1 | −6.8 |
| 23        Nonfarm noncorporate | 90.8 | 84.0 |
| 24        Corporate | 192.3 | 156.9 |
| 25  Foreign net borrowing in United States | 2.8 | −.4 |
| 26      Bonds | 4.1 | 4.9 |
| 27      Bank loans n.e.c.* | −7.8 | −6.9 |
| 28      Open market paper | 2.5 | −1.0 |
| 29      U.S. government loans | 4.0 | 2.5 |
| 30  Total domestic plus foreign | 768.7 | 883.4 |
| *Financial Sectors* | | |
| 31  Total net borrowing by financial sectors | 138.2 | 187.5 |
|     *By instrument* | | |
| 32  U.S. government related | 74.9 | 99.4 |
| 33      Sponsored credit agency securities | 30.4 | 20.6 |
| 34      Mortgage pool securities | 44.4 | 78.8 |
| 35      Loans from U.S. government | — | — |
| 36  Private financial sectors | 63.3 | 88.1 |
| 37      Corporate bonds | 25.9 | 28.6 |

**TABLE 2–6 (continued)**

| Transaction Category, Sector | 1984 | 1985 |
|---|---|---|
| *Financial Sectors* | | |
| 38  Mortgages | .4 | −.2 |
| 39  Bank loans n.e.c.* | 1.0 | 4.2 |
| 40  Open market paper | 20.4 | 41.3 |
| 41  Loans from Federal Home Loan Banks | 15.7 | 14.2 |
| *By sector* | | |
| 42  Sponsored credit agencies | 30.4 | 20.6 |
| 43  Mortgage pools | 44.4 | 78.8 |
| 44  Private financial sectors | 63.3 | 88.1 |
| 45  Commercial banks | 4.4 | 3.8 |
| 46  Bank affiliates | 16.9 | 9.2 |
| 47  Savings and loan associations | 22.7 | 21.7 |
| 48  Finance companies | 19.3 | 54.4 |
| 49  Real estate investment trusts | .8 | −.1 |
| *All Sectors* | | |
| 50  Total net borrowing | 906.9 | 1,070.9 |
| 51  U.S. government securities | 273.8 | 323.1 |
| 52  State and local obligations | 65.8 | 173.4 |
| 53  Corporate and foreign bonds | 77.1 | 101.4 |
| 54  Mortgages | 212.7 | 232.8 |
| 55  Consumer credit | 94.8 | 103.6 |
| 56  Bank loans n.e.c.* | 72.7 | 28.0 |
| 57  Open market paper | 47.1 | 53.2 |
| 58  Other loans | 63.0 | 55.5 |
| *External Corporate Equity Funds Raised in United States* | | |
| 59  Total new share issues | −33.6 | 28.2 |
| 60  Mutual funds | 37.1 | 99.6 |
| 61  All other | −70.7 | −71.4 |
| 62  Nonfinancial corporations | −77.0 | −81.6 |
| 63  Financial corporations | 5.2 | 4.6 |
| 64  Foreign shares purchased in United States | 1.1 | 5.6 |

* n.e.c.—not elsewhere classified.
SOURCE: *Federal Reserve Bulletin,* June 1987, Table A42.

that, from the point of view of the financing of investment spending activity, the debt markets are far bigger than the equity markets in dollar terms. Although the debt markets are relatively more important to the economy, the stock markets tend to get far more coverage in the news. They seem to provide a bellwether on the economy for the general public.

Data for 1985 direct and indirect sources of funds are found in Table 2–7. Note that the total sources, $883.8 billion, just equals total uses (borrowing) reported in

**TABLE 2-7**
**Direct and Indirect Sources of Funds to Credit Markets, 1984 and 1985**
**(billions of dollars, seasonally adjusted annual rates)**

| | Transaction Category, or Sector | 1984 | 1985 |
|---|---|---|---|
| 1 | Total funds advanced in credit markets to domestic nonfinancial sectors | 765.9 | 883.8 |
| | *By public agencies and foreign* | | |
| 2 | Total net advances | 144.6 | 220.9 |
| 3 | U.S. government securities | 36.0 | 46.8 |
| 4 | Residential mortgages | 56.5 | 92.6 |
| 5 | FHLB advances to savings and loans | 15.7 | 14.2 |
| 6 | Other loans and securities | 36.6 | 67.3 |
| | Total advanced, by sector | | |
| 7 | U.S. government | 17.1 | 22.5 |
| 8 | Sponsored credit agencies | 73.3 | 103.9 |
| 9 | Monetary authorities | 8.4 | 21.6 |
| 10 | Foreign | 45.9 | 72.8 |
| | Agency and foreign borrowing not in line 1 | | |
| 11 | Sponsored credit agencies and mortgage pools | 74.9 | 99.4 |
| 12 | Foreign | 2.8 | −.4 |
| | *Private domestic funds advanced* | | |
| 13 | Total net advances | 699.0 | 762.0 |
| 14 | U.S. government securities | 237.8 | 276.4 |
| 15 | State and local obligations | 65.8 | 173.4 |
| 16 | Corporate and foreign bonds | 34.8 | 31.4 |
| 17 | Residential mortgages | 94.8 | 85.8 |
| 18 | Other mortgages and loans | 281.5 | 209.2 |
| 19 | Less: Federal Home Loan Bank advances | 15.7 | 14.2 |
| | *Private financial intermediation* | | |
| 20 | Credit market funds advanced by private financial institutions | 555.6 | 531.5 |
| 21 | Commercial banking | 181.7 | 170.8 |
| 22 | Savings institutions | 146.3 | 104.5 |
| 23 | Insurance and pension funds | 119.0 | 118.1 |
| 24 | Other finance | 108.6 | 138.1 |
| 25 | Sources of funds | 555.2 | 531.5 |
| 26 | Private domestic deposits and RPs | 298.8 | 201.5 |
| 27 | Credit market borrowing | 63.3 | 88.1 |
| 28 | Other sources | 193.5 | 241.9 |
| 29 | Foreign funds | 19.0 | 17.3 |
| 30 | Treasury balances | 4.0 | 9.8 |
| 31 | Insurance and pension reserves | 110.3 | 110.2 |
| 32 | Other, net | 60.1 | 104.5 |
| | *Private domestic nonfinancial investors* | | |
| 33 | Direct lending in credit markets | 206.7 | 318.6 |
| 34 | U.S. government securities | 125.8 | 155.3 |
| 35 | State and local obligations | 43.2 | 99.4 |
| 36 | Corporate and foreign bonds | 15.3 | 6.9 |

**TABLE 2-7** (continued)

| | Transaction Category, or Sector | 1984 | 1985 |
|---|---|---|---|
| | *Private domestic financial investors* | | |
| 37 | Open market paper | −1.4 | 30.9 |
| 38 | Other | 23.8 | 26.0 |
| 39 | Deposits and currency | 303.4 | 211.8 |
| 40 | Currency | 8.6 | 12.4 |
| 41 | Checkable deposits | 24.1 | 45.2 |
| 42 | Small time and savings accounts | 149.8 | 134.3 |
| 43 | Money market fund shares | 47.2 | −2.2 |
| 44 | Large time deposits | 83.6 | 14.1 |
| 45 | Security RPs | −5.8 | 10.1 |
| 46 | Deposits in foreign countries | −4.0 | −2.2 |
| 47 | Total of credit market instruments, deposits and currency | 510.1 | 530.3 |
| 48 | Public holdings as percent of total | 18.8 | 25.0 |
| 49 | Private financial intermediation (in percent) | 79.5 | 69.8 |
| 50 | Total foreign funds | 64.9 | 90.2 |
| | MEMO: Corporate equities not included above | | |
| 51 | Total net issues | −33.6 | 28.2 |
| 52 | Mutual fund shares | 37.1 | 99.6 |
| 53 | Other equities | −70.7 | −71.4 |
| 54 | Acquisitions by financial institutions | 10.3 | 47.4 |
| 55 | Other net purchases | −43.9 | −19.2 |

NOTE: Full statements for sectors and transaction types in flows and in amounts outstanding may be obtained from Flow of Funds Section, Division of Research and Statistics. Board of Governors of the Federal Reserve System, Washington, D.C. 20551.

SOURCE: *Federal Reserve Bulletin,* June 1987, Table A43.

Table 2–6. But several categories in the two tables differ. One group of accounts relating to deposits in financial institutions is of special interest, lines 39 through 46. There we see that $211.8 billion in funds were supplied to the economy in 1985 in the form of deposits and currency. These are created by banks and issued by government. Increases in the money supply constitute one of the sources of supply of funds in our analysis of the demand and supply of funds in Chapter 12.

The Federal Reserve System also publishes annual tables of total credit market debt outstanding for various types of debt: the U.S. government debt, home mortgage debt, consumer debt, and corporate debt.

Several private institutions—banks, brokerage houses, and insurance companies—also prepare their own statements of sources and uses of funds to focus more directly on those sectors that are of greatest importance to their planning.

## Interest Rate Forecasts and Other Applications

One method of forecasting interest rates begins with estimates of the supply and demand for funds in the period ahead.[17] The first step in preparing these estimates is to project the future level of business activity. A useful proxy for this purpose is the nation's GNP and its components: consumer, business, government, and net foreign spending. The economic forecast must then be used to derive estimates of sources and uses of funds. For example, the expected demand for residential construction is translated into a forecast of demand for mortgage loans. To do this one must make assumptions about interest rates in the period ahead since the demand for such loans depends in part on the interest rate charged the borrower. On the supply side, the same procedure is used to project sources of funds. Expected saving of each sector is converted into estimates of funds available to purchase various types of financial instruments directly or through financial intermediaries. Next, the sources of funds are added together and compared with total uses.

It is highly unlikely, of course, that the totals will balance on the first try when put in matrix form. Funds needed will exceed or fall short of those available. That is, there will be a gap between projected supply and demand for funds. Since the source-use approach to forecasting requires equality of supply and demand, adjustments must be made in these preliminary figures. The procedure used is to make changes in interest rates and, therefore, in sources and uses until a final balance is achieved. This procedure is one of iteration, of repeated changes or successive approximations.

Suppose, for example, that when source and use estimates are first compared, uses exceed sources. This implies that credit conditions will tighten and interest rates will rise. By allowing for a small increase in rates, prospective uses can be reduced and sources increased. Such adjustments in interest rates and in funds supplied and demanded can be made until the gap between the flows is closed. In this way the analyst will obtain reasonable and consistent estimates of financial flows and interest rates.

It is usually supposed that a large part of the adjustment in credit flows will take place on the supply side. A rise in interest rates, for example, will induce interest-sensitive investors such as individuals, foreigners, and others to supply more funds to the market. Individuals may buy additional financial instruments with idle funds, and foreign investors will be attracted to financial markets in the United States. Many analysts classify these purchases by households as a "residual" source of funds. Often foreign purchases are included as well. Some studies show that the "residual" component of supply is highly correlated with the level of rates. Changes in the size of the residual brought about by changes in rates is an important mechanism in balancing supply and demand for funds. Some evidence for this view comes from the fact that

---

[17] Other methods include excogitation (reflecting on the outlook), extrapolation of historical trends, and use of econometric-financial models. See William C. Freund and Edward D. Zinbarg, "Sources and Uses of Funds Analysis," in Murray E. Polakoff et al., eds., *Financial Institutions and Markets* (Boston: Houghton Mifflin, 1970), pp. 463–484.

the residual tends to be larger and to increase by a greater amount when interest rates are rising than when they are declining.

The investment behavior of individuals is of special interest to commercial banks and thrift institutions. When the yield on U.S. Treasury bills, for example, rises above those obtainable on savings accounts at these institutions, "disintermediation" may occur. Savings deposits may be withdrawn from financial intermediaries and used to purchase Treasury bills. Disintermediation generally results in less business activity and less income for these institutions. It also results in a smaller flow of funds to the borrower financed by these intermediaries. When interest rates fall, disintermediation is gradually halted.

Projections of the flow of funds are also used within the Federal Reserve System to aid in anticipating results of monetary policy actions. For example, if projections of flows of funds indicate that disintermediation is likely, actions may be taken to prevent it from being too pervasive. Perhaps the best example is disintermediation that results in a smaller flow of funds to those institutions that are mainly active in financing housing. If Federal Reserve System officials are concerned about the need for housing finance, they may take actions to avoid a large reduction in funds available for this purpose.

Further, flow of funds data are becoming more widely used in studies of portfolio choices of sectors of the economy. The relative preference of, say, households or business for money versus other financial assets may be studied using these data. More broadly, flow of funds accounts and source-use statements may be used to develop and test hypotheses concerning total spending in the economy. Recently, for example, one study suggested that changes in credit flows are the primary variables causing changes in total spending in an economy like that of the United States.[18] An important implication is that the Federal Reserve System might better attain its objectives by controlling credit rather than money. This remains, however, a topic of much debate, as we shall see later. Essentially, the question is whether bank loans, which result in creation of money, and at the same time generally lead to increased output of goods and services, have more effect on economic output than do bank investments, which create an equal amount of money but involve the purchase of securities by banks from those who hold securities. Bank investments do not *initially* lead to increased output of goods and services if the banks buy securities already outstanding.

## SUMMARY

Saving and investment are essential concepts in economics and finance. It is important, however, to distinguish among the various ways in which the terms are used. "Real" investment refers to capital formation and includes expenditures for plant and

---

[18] James S. Earley, Robert J. Parsons, and Fred A. Thompson, *Money, Credit and Expenditure: A Sources and Uses of Funds Approach*, New York University Graduate School of Business Administration, *Bulletin*, 1976–3.

equipment, residential and other construction, and additions to inventories. "Financial" investment means purchase of stocks, bonds, and other claims to wealth. Economists also distinguish between actual (ex post) and planned (ex ante) saving and investment. The former refers to amounts of saving and investment that actually occur during a given period of time. Measured this way, the nation's saving necessarily equals the nation's investment in capital during a given period. Ex ante saving and investment, on the other hand, are likely to differ because consumer (and other) plans to save or spend need not match business plans to invest in plant, equipment, and inventories.

In barter economies, the decision to save is a decision to invest in real capital. Financial investment is nonexistent because there are no financial assets. All current saving must be invested, and all investment is financed solely from current saving, out of current income. More sophisticated economies that use money and other financial assets have available a wider set of sources and uses of funds. Savers are not forced to invest in real capital, and investors are not limited to current saving as a source of funds.

In a modern economy, financial institutions act as intermediaries between ultimate lenders and borrowers. They facilitate the flow of real resources from surplus to deficit spending units. In essence, intermediaries buy borrowers' debt instruments with funds that they acquire from lenders who choose to hold claims against these institutions. To the extent that intermediation promotes the flow of saving into efficient investment outlets, it makes possible a higher and more productive rate of capital formation than would otherwise obtain.

Historically, most business spending has been financed internally rather than through debt creation or equity issues. The role of financial intermediaries has, therefore, been more limited than would be the case if most expenditures were financed externally. Most external financing has been through debt rather than through equity issue because of concern on the part of lenders for "safety" of principal, tax considerations, and managements' desire not to dilute stockholder equity.

Federal Reserve flow of funds accounts provide a useful framework for classifying and measuring the sources and uses of both internal and external funds. This framework shows clearly the relationships among various sectors of the economy. It provides historical data on each sector's saving, investment, lending, and borrowing. Source and use of funds statements published by certain private organizations provide complementary tabulations on the supply of and demand for loanable funds. Financial analysts use these data to make estimates of prospective financial flows, especially when forecasting interest rates. Other applications include the testing of hypotheses concerning the portfolio behavior of consumers and business firms and the relationships of credit flows to total spending on goods and services.

## Questions for Discussion

**1.** If saving is income that is not consumed, what about income held in the form of additional currency? What about holdings of additional demand deposits in banks? Relate to the $S = I$ discussion.

**2.** Show how ex post saving and ex post investment *must* be equal, by using balance sheets for individuals, totaling these for the economy, and eliminating items which are equivalent because one is the reverse of the other.

**3.** Indicate why items shown at the left side of the box in Figure 2–1 may be termed "gross national income." If profits after depreciation allowances were negative, what would be the situation of the economy?

**4.** Why does a country with a rapid rate of growth in income almost always have a high ratio of saving to GNP?

**5.** What reply can you make to those who argue that "debt is bad"? Comment on the relationship between this view and the view that credit is desirable.

**6.** On the basis of the ratios of debt securities and primary securities as a whole (debt plus equities) to GNP, project total debt for one year ahead and for five years ahead on the basis of projections of GNP. Show how you derive the projections.

**7.** Why do business firms in the United States rely more heavily on debt issues than on equity issues for external financing?

**8.** What is meant by "disintermediation"? When or under what conditions is it likely to occur?

**9.** Name as many individual types of financial institutions as you can, and classify each within the classification used in Figure 2–2.

**10.** Outline the procedure used in a source and use of funds approach to forecasting interest rates.

**11.** Find the table for flow of funds in a recent *Federal Reserve Bulletin*, and determine from it how much was borrowed (the amount of funds raised) by households (consumers) in a recent year.

**12.** Why is total spending so much greater (perhaps 25 times as much) as spending for current GNP? Discuss the significance of this for the control of GNP through control of spending.

## Selected References

The pioneering work of John Gurley and Edward Shaw in developing a theoretical framework that shows how "debt, financial assets, financial institutions and financial policies shape, and are in turn shaped by, general levels of prices and output" is found in their *Money in a Theory of Finance* (Washington, D.C.: The Brookings Institution, 1960) and numerous articles, including their "Financial Aspects of Economic Development," *American Economic Review*, September 1955, pp. 515–538; "Financial Intermediaries and the Saving-Investment Process," *Journal of Finance*, May 1956, pp. 257–276; and "The Growth of Debt and Money in the United States, 1800–1950; A Suggested Interpretation," *Review of Economics and Statistics*, August 1957, pp. 250–262.

Our simple presentation of the flow of funds accounts, like that of most recent texts, draws substantially upon the work of Lawrence S. Ritter in his *"The Flow of Funds Accounts: A Framework for Financial Analysis,"* New York University, Graduate School of Business Administration *Bulletin*, No. 52, August 1968. The Board of Governors of the Federal Reserve System publishes quarterly flow of funds data in the *Federal Reserve Bulletin;* once a year the data include estimates of financial assets and liabilities for each sector, by types of assets and liabilities.

# THE FINANCIAL
# SERVICES INDUSTRY:
# COMMERCIAL BANKS

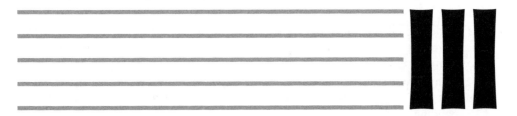

Supply of and demand for loanable funds are important because they determine interest rates. Interest rates influence the allocation of funds to the various sectors of the economy and thus affect the structure of industry, the availability of housing, the availability of funds to consumers who borrow, and other important parts of the economy. The total supply of loanable funds, from saving, creation of new money, and other sources (including foreign sources) is very significant for economic growth and for the maintenance of high employment. Investment, except that made directly by business firms, consumers, or government units from their own funds, cannot occur unless there is an equal supply of loanable funds.

As indicated in Figure 2–2 and in Table 2–7 in Chapter 2, much of the supply of loanable funds is channeled through commercial banks and other financial intermediaries.

Changes in the nature and functions of the intermediaries shown in Figure 2–2 have been so significant in recent years that it is now appropriate to refer to the *financial services industry* rather than simply to financial institutions. Many institutions that now provide financial services are now subsidiaries or integral parts of institutions which are nonfinancial. (Financial institutions are those that hold most of their assets in the form of financial assets—cash, loans, or investments.) The most obvious change is increasing provision of financial services by retail stores, credit card companies (such as American Express), and conglomerates and their subsidiaries. The nature of competition in the financial services industry is changing.

Nevertheless, commercial banks, discussed in Chapter 3, are still a very important segment of this industry and very important in providing funds to borrowers, both directly and through the financial markets.

Other institutions in the financial services industry are discussed in Chapter 4. Since additions to the money supply provide additional loanable funds, creation of money and the general way in which the money supply is controlled are discussed in Chapter 5; details of Federal Reserve policy for control of the money supply are deferred to Chapter 16. Finally, some current major problems and trends in the financial services industry are reviewed in Chapter 6.

Chapters 3 through 6 thus are concerned with activities of the financial services industry in channeling saving and newly created money to borrowers, both directly and through financial markets which form the subject matter of Part Three (Chapters 9 through 11).

Demand for loanable funds comes largely from (1) business firms, (2) the need for mortgage credit for purchase and construction of houses and other structures, (3) consumers (largely for the purchase of autos and other durable goods), (4) state and local government units, (5) the federal government, and (6) foreign borrowers. Private demand (the first three of these sources) is discussed in Chapter 7, while government and foreign demand for funds (and the supply of funds from foreign sources) are covered in Chapter 8. Major purposes of these chapters are to analyze ways in which demand for funds by these sources fluctuates. Such fluctuations are major causes of variations in interest rates, especially short-term interest rates.

## COMMERCIAL BANKS AND OTHER
## DEPOSITORY INSTITUTIONS

Depository institutions (institutions that accept funds as deposits or similar accounts—funds that may generally be withdrawn either on demand or after relatively short periods of time) constitute one major group within the financial services industry, as indicated in Figure 2–2. Depository institutions include commercial banks, savings banks and mutual savings banks, savings and loan associations, and credit unions.[1]

---

[1] Some mutual savings banks have recently changed to the corporate form, becoming savings banks. Mortgage banks, although called banks, are not depository institutions; they use borrowed and equity funds to make mortgage loans, and then sell those loans to other institutions such as insurance companies and use the proceeds to make more loans. Some other institutions whose names contain the word "bank" are also not depository institutions (they do not accept deposits): the Export-Import Bank, the World Bank, Federal Land Banks, and so on.

These institutions *must* be able to meet requests for withdrawals when appropriate, or close their doors—commercial banks must close immediately if they cannot meet justifiable requests for withdrawals. The distinction between the institutions mentioned and some others has been blurred in recent years by the development of new institutions, such as money market mutual funds, from which withdrawals may be made under some conditions by checks. The focus of this chapter is on commercial banks; the other depository institutions and the rest of the financial services industry are discussed in Chapter 4.

In the United States, a separate group of institutions provides or arranges for the obtaining of long-term funds. Sometimes this group is referred to as *investment banks*, sometimes as the "securities industry." Commercial banks have not been permitted, since 1933, to arrange for the sale of and/or underwrite (guarantee the final sale of) securities newly issued by business firms. Banks that were both commercial banks and investment banks were forced, by the Banking Act of 1933 (the Glass-Steagall Act), to choose to continue only one of these activities. Of course, commercial banks have for years made "term" loans, which may be intermediate term in length, and they also make possible the acquisition by business firms of equipment and other capital assets under leasing arrangements. They may also buy corporate bonds, although they do not buy large amounts. In many countries, all these activities can be carried out by commercial banks. Institutions that provide long-term funds have been termed *merchant banks*, although this term has also been applied to banks that provide short-term funds (an activity of commercial banks), intermediate-term funds (also provided by commercial banks), *and* long-term funds (an activity of investment banks).

The logic behind the restriction of commercial banks to short-term (or intermediate-term) lending is that long-term loans and the underwriting of securities issues may generally be presumed to involve more risk than short-term or intermediate-term loans—while commercial banks are expected to provide a high degree of safety for depositors' funds. In fact, as discussed later, commercial banks were thought by some to be institutions that should engage only in short-term lending for purchase of inventory and similar items, including imports, because of the presumed relatively high degree of safety of such loans.

Commercial banks are still the most important single group of financial intermediaries. They hold the bulk of the funds used by the public to make payments—checkable deposits. Such deposits constitute the bulk of the nation's money supply; currency (paper money and coins) is most of the remainder. Commercial banks are also a major holder of the public's savings. People deposit funds in savings accounts and other time deposits and thus provide funds for both business and government as well as for those consumers who borrow. Bank credit is used as the largest single source of borrowed funds for business (for investment), for the government (to meet deficits), and for consumers who need funds to buy houses, to buy appliances, and to make home repairs, or for other purposes, such as hospital expenses, travel, and so forth.

In this chapter we examine portfolio policies of commercial banks—the objectives and practices that determine the kinds and amounts of assets and liabilities banks hold. Management of a bank's liquidity and solvency is of special interest in our study of financial markets, and we review some of the innovative responses of bankers to dynamic changes in these markets in recent years. The chapter concludes with a brief discussion of the basis for and the purposes of government regulation and supervision of the commercial banking industry.

## COMMERCIAL BANKS AS BUSINESS FIRMS

Bank objectives and policies are similar to those of other financial institutions: all seek long-run profits by lending and investing funds at their disposal at as high a rate of return as is consistent with an appropriate degree of safety of principal. But, unlike many other lenders, banks must be prepared to meet the withdrawal of these funds virtually on demand.[2] Need for liquidity is therefore of utmost importance, and the central problem facing a bank's management is how to reconcile these often conflicting demands upon the bank's resources: safety, earnings, and liquidity. For perspective, let us examine business transactions of banks as shown in the balance sheet and the income statement.

### The Bank Balance Sheet

The balance sheet in Table 3–1 shows the major accounts of commercial banks.[3] In the table, the assets represent the uses of funds, and the liabilities and capital accounts are the sources of funds. On the asset side of the balance sheet are (1) cash assets, (2) earning assets, consisting of loans and securities, and (3) other assets. Liabilities are mainly demand and time deposits (including savings deposits), although borrowings are also important. The remaining item is the capital account, consisting of owners' equity and subordinated long-term debt.

### Cash Assets

Cash assets include vault cash and deposit balances held, directly or indirectly, at Federal Reserve Banks, balances at other commercial banks, and cash items in the process of collection. On December 31, 1985, cash assets totaled $211.6 billion, or 9 percent of total assets. Cash items in the process of collection, essentially checks that

---

[2] With the exception of certificates of deposit, which banks usually redeem only at maturity, most time deposits may in practice be withdrawn at any time even though, legally, notice of intent to withdraw may be required. Demand deposits are, of course, payable in currency or transferable on demand.

[3] At the end of 1986, there were approximately 14,200 insured commercial banks in the United States. Additionally, there are a small number of noninsured banks, most of them small in size. Data for all banks, rather than for banks that are members of the Federal Reserve System, are used here to provide better coverage. The distinction between member and nonmember banks is no longer important, since all banks must now keep the same reserves (in percentages) in the same form—vault cash and/or a deposit in a Federal Reserve Bank.

TABLE 3–1
**Balance Sheet for All Commercial Banking Institutions, December 31, 1985**
(billions of dollars)

| | Amount | Percentage of Total | Percentage of Subcategory |
|---|---|---|---|
| Assets | | | |
| Cash assets | $211.6 | 9% | |
| Currency and coin | 22.2 | | 10% |
| Reserves at Federal Reserve Banks | 27.6 | | 13 |
| Demand balances with depository institutions | 36.1 | | 17 |
| Cash items in process of collection | 79.3 | | 37 |
| Other cash assets | 46.5 | | 22 |
| | | | 100% |
| Loans, excluding interbank loans | 1,614.6 | 66 | |
| Commercial and industrial | 495.9 | | 31 |
| Interbank loans | 149.6 | | 9 |
| Other (consumer loans, real estate loans, etc.) | 969.1 | | 60 |
| | | | 100% |
| Investments | 413.6 | 17 | |
| U.S. government securities | 249.9 | | 60 |
| Other securities | 163.6 | | 40 |
| | | | 100% |
| Other assets | 189.4 | 8 | |
| Total assets | $2,460.3 | 100% | |
| Liabilities and capital | | | |
| Demand deposits (transactions deposits) | 536.4 | 22 | |
| Savings deposits | 450.0 | 18 | |
| Time deposits | 777.1 | 32 | |
| Borrowings | 361.5 | 15 | |
| Other liabilities | 178.5 | 7 | |
| Residual | 156.7 | 6 | |
| Total liabilities and capital | $2,460.3 | 100% | |

SOURCE: *Federal Reserve Bulletin,* May 1986, p. A18. Percentages may not add exactly to 100, because of rounding.

had been or soon would be presented to other banks for payment either through facilities of the Federal Reserve System or through "correspondent banks," totaled $79.3 billion.

Certain terms should be defined for clarity:

- *Legal reserves* are the *items* that may be counted to meet reserve requirements; with implementation of the Monetary Control Act of 1980, these include only vault cash (paper money and coins held in banks) and deposits held by banks and other depository institutions in Federal Reserve Banks.

- *Total reserves* are the total *amount* of reserves held by a bank or banks.
- *Required reserves* are the amounts held because of reserve requirements.
- *Excess reserves* are amounts held in excess of required reserves. Because of constant inflows and outflows of funds, banks find it difficult to hold *precisely* the required amount. They usually prefer to hold a little more than be penalized for holding less.
- *Borrowed reserves* are reserves borrowed from Federal Reserve Banks.
- *Nonborrowed reserves* are total reserves minus borrowed reserves.

The correspondent system is a unique feature of U.S. banking, acting as a linking mechanism among banks across the country.[4] Small banks associate with larger city banks, especially those in major financial centers, that provide them with a wide variety of services such as check collection facilities, investment advice, access to data processing equipment, the opportunity to participate in syndicated loans, and so on. Smaller banks would find it expensive and difficult to provide these services for themselves. In return, the smaller banks agree to carry deposits with their correspondents; these deposits provide the correspondent banks with additional funds. This network reduces the information and transactions costs of credit and is essential in the United States, where the banking system consists of more than 14,000 separate banking firms, the majority of which are quite small. Both the asset, due from banks (balances at other commercial banks), and most of the liability account, due to banks (interbank deposits), are the result of correspondent banking relationships.

## Bank Loans and Investments in Securities

Most bank funds are used to acquire earning assets, which provide the bulk of revenue and enable them to cover expenses, including the cost of capital and in most cases to earn a profit. Earning assets are classified as (1) loans or (2) securities. The former are usually negotiated on an individual basis with borrowers, whereas the latter are the obligations of governments and large, well-known corporations, usually sold on the open market and available to a wide variety of prospective buyers. In general, bankers prefer loans to securities because of the higher interest return and because a loan today usually opens the door to "repeat business" in the future, once a banker-borrower relationship is established.[5]

### Types of Bank Loans

Bank loans may be classified as (1) commercial and industrial, (2) real estate, (3) consumer, (4) agricultural, (5) securities, (6) loans to financial institutions, (7) loans of Federal funds, or (8) other loans. The first three are by far the most important. Commercial and industrial loans alone constituted 31 percent of all loans at the end of

---

[4] See "Correspondent Banking: Part I, Balances and Services," Federal Reserve Bank of Kansas City, *Monthly Review*, November 1970, pp. 3–14.

[5] See Edward J. Kane and Burton G. Malkiel, "Bank Portfolio Allocation, Deposit Variability, and the Availability Doctrine," *Quarterly Journal of Economics*, February 1965, pp. 113–134.

December 1985. The preferred type of loan for most banks is to business firms for working capital purposes. It is typically a short-term credit, subject to renewal, used by the business firm to carry accounts receivable and to purchase inventories; loans having an original maturity of one year or more ("term loans") are, however, a substantial part of business loans.

Loans for the purchase of residential property and consumer durables are the next largest categories, and for some "retail" banks located in small or medium-sized cities such loans may be as important as business loans. The real estate loans are either insured or guaranteed by the federal government (Federal Housing Administration or Veterans Administration) or are "conventional loans." Real estate loans are secured by residential property as specified in mortgages, which call for amortization of the loans over periods of, say, 20 or 30 years. Consumer loans help finance the purchase of automobiles, appliances, or other durables; in most cases loans, except for very small ones, are secured by durable goods such as automobiles or other acceptable property. Specific provisions as well as the relative importance of various loan categories vary from bank to bank.

### Investments

Banks also extend credit when they purchase securities, and this category of assets may be especially attractive when loan demand is slack, as a way for banks to invest loanable funds. A very high percentage of these securities represents the obligations of governmental units; the remainder is corporate notes and bonds. Over 30 years, from the early 1950s to the early 1980s, banks have added significantly to their holdings of the tax-exempt obligations of state and local governments (municipals), whereas their holdings of U.S. Treasury securities have remained quite stable in amount. The major reasons for the reduced importance of Treasury securities are the substantial increase in bank loans as business activity rises, the improved marketability of municipals, and the increasing number of alternative sources of liquidity available to larger banks (see Table 3–2).

TABLE 3–2
**Insured Bank Loans and Investments, 1952 and 1985**

|  | Percentage of Total Loans and Investments | |
|---|---|---|
|  | *December 31, 1952* | *December 31, 1985* |
| Loans | 45% | 80% |
| U.S. Treasury securities | 44 | 12 |
| Municipal securities[1] | 7 | 8 |

[1] Includes a small amount of corporate securities.

SOURCE: *Federal Reserve Bulletins.*

## Deposit Liabilities

The important source of bank funds for an individual bank is deposits, which in the 1980s made up over 70 percent of total liabilities and capital. Banks accept deposits from individuals, partnerships, and corporations (sometimes referred to as IPC deposits); they also accept deposits from state and local governments and the U.S. Treasury, and from other banks, as noted earlier in connection with correspondent banking.

### Demand Deposits and Reserve Requirements

Demand deposits, often referred to as "checking accounts," are essentially working balances that individuals, businesses, financial institutions, and governmental units use to make payments when they buy goods, services, and financial assets. Checks drawn on demand deposits are generally acceptable and convenient as a means of transferring deposits. Most demand deposits are held at banks that are insured by the Federal Deposit Insurance Corporation. Currently, up to $100,000 of each depositor's account is insured against loss.[6] Although these features make demand deposits an important source of bank funds, the prohibition against explicit interest payments in most of these accounts has led to a decline in this type of deposit relative to time and savings deposits on which banks may pay interest. In the 1970s, the upward trend of interest rates induced the public to economize with respect to demand deposits. Thus, demand deposits, which were about one-half of all sources of bank funds in the early 1970s, declined to about 22 percent of this total by the end of 1985.

One of the most important pieces of banking legislation in 45 years, the Depository Institutions Deregulation and Monetary Control Act of 1980 (DIDMCA), permitted banks and other deposit-type financial institutions to hold interest-bearing checking accounts, beginning January 1, 1981. Thus the 47-year period of prohibition on payment of interest on all checkable deposits in the United States ended, and, like many other countries, the United States now permits interest on such deposits.[7] Of course, banks paid *implicit* interest by providing services (collection of checks, etc.) at less than cost, but beginning in 1981 they were permitted to pay *explicit* interest. Highlights of this law are given in the appendix at the end of this chapter.

Under Federal Reserve regulations, "transactions accounts" in commercial

---

[6] A depositor's account in his or her name and a joint account with another party are considered as two accounts, both insured. However, two single-name accounts for the same person, even if in different branches of a bank, are added and are counted as one account.

[7] Interest still cannot be paid on ordinary demand deposits, but individuals (including certain nonprofit institutions) who wish to obtain interest can have accounts (termed NOW accounts) that pay interest and may also have arrangements for automatic transfers from their time deposits to their demand deposits. For practical purposes, NOW accounts are checking accounts on which interest is paid. For further discussion of these and other special accounts authorized for initial use in December 1982 and in January 1983, see Chapter 4; such accounts were authorized for other depository institutions as well as for commercial banks; and hence are discussed in the section of Chapter 4 on depository institutions.

banks and several other types of institutions are to be subject to reserve requirements shown in Table 3–3. Transactions accounts in essence means accounts *regularly* used for transfers or payments by check, telephone transfers, or other means.

It is important to note that prior Federal Reserve System reserve requirements applied only to *member commercial banks;* the requirements of the DIDMCA apply to transactions accounts and *nonpersonal* (chiefly corporation) time deposits in *all deposit-type financial institutions.* The law explicitly defined transactions accounts as demand deposits (checking accounts), NOW accounts (checking accounts on which interest is paid), and other accounts subject to written, automatic, or telephone transfer to third parties. The attempt was to make transactions accounts as nearly synonymous as possible with accounts used for final settlement of debts.

After a transition period, reserves are now held in cash and/or deposits in Federal Reserve Banks, but nonmember banks and other institutions may keep reserves in member banks or certain other institutions, on a passthrough basis: the institution in which reserves are placed by another bank in turn holds the same amount in the form of a deposit in the district Federal Reserve Bank, in addition to holding its own reserves. We present in Table 3–3 the requirements for depository institutions after implementation of the Monetary Control Act of 1980, without minor qualifications. Minor changes still occur, for example, because of changes in the amount of transactions accounts subject to the low reserve requirement of 3 percent.

A distinction between transactions accounts and other accounts is difficult to explain briefly. Some accounts authorized in the winter of 1982–1983 and discussed in Chapter 4 were difficult to classify. In essence, however, transactions accounts are those from which account holders can *regularly* make withdrawals by checks or similar

**TABLE 3–3**
**Reserve Requirements After Implementation of the Monetary Control Act**

| Type of Deposit or Other Liability | Percentage Reserve Requirement |
|---|---|
| Net transactions accounts | |
| $0 to $36.7 million[1] | 3% |
| Over $36.7 million[1] | 12 |
| Nonpersonal time deposits | |
| Original maturity less than 1½ years[2] | 3 |
| Original maturity 1½ years or more[2] | 0 |
| Eurocurrency liabilities[3] | 3 |

[1] These amounts of transactions accounts were effective December 31, 1985.
[2] These maturities were effective October 6, 1983.
[3] This reserve requirement was effective November 18, 1980.
SOURCE: *Federal Reserve Bulletin,* May 1986, p. A7, and Federal Reserve Bank of St. Louis, *U.S. Financial Data,* December 4, 1986. A small amount of total deposit or other liabilities, for which reserves would be required as above, has been exempt from the reserve requirement since 1982. This amount was $2.9 million in 1987; the amount is adjusted slightly higher each year.

instruments, by payment orders of withdrawal, and/or by telephone or preauthorized transfer, for the purpose of making payments to third parties or others. Two questions make classification difficult: (1) are withdrawals *regularly* made and how is "regularly" defined? and (2) are withdrawals generally for the purpose of making transfers to third parties, that is, are they for payments to *others* (a withdrawal by a depositor himself or herself is not a payment, nor is a transfer from a depositor's checking account to his or her savings account).

Effectively, total reserve requirements have been *reduced* for member banks, chiefly because the reserve requirement for personal time deposits is now zero instead of 3 percent. For nonmember banks and other institutions, effective reserve requirements have been generally *raised*, chiefly because reserves must now be held (directly or indirectly) in the Fed. Deposits in correspondent banks do not necessarily count, and items in process of collection (formerly counted as part of reserves in some states for state-chartered banks) do *not* count.[8]

Determination of the amount of *net* demand deposits (or net transactions accounts) requires (1) calculation of gross demand deposits or transactions accounts, including such items as officers' checks and certified checks, because these are demand obligations of the bank; and (2) subtraction from gross demand deposits of two items: (a) cash items in process of collection, because they have not yet been deducted from deposits in banks on which they were drawn, although they soon will be, and (b) demand deposits held *by* banks *in* other U.S. domestic banks, because these interbank deposits are not held by either the public or the government, and hence counting them involves counting deposits *not* held by the public.

For many years before 1984, the bank officer responsible for managing the bank's reserve position, often referred to as its "money position," knew in advance what the bank's daily average legal reserve (vault cash plus deposit in the Fed) had to be during the weekly reporting period (beginning Thursday and ending the following Wednesday for each period), because the reserve requirement was based on deposits held during the *second preceding* week. Moreover, vault cash held in that second preceding week was counted as part of the reserve, so that calculating required reserve as the appropriate percentage of deposits and subtracting vault cash held gave the amount of deposit the bank needed in the Fed, for the reporting week. These requirements are illustrated in the top part of Figure 3–1.

This method of determining reserve requirements, termed lagged reserve requirement accounting (LRA or LRR) was criticized by many on the grounds that it resulted in undesirable fluctuations in interest rates and in the money supply. Actions by the Fed, providing more deposits and reserves for banks or reducing their deposits and reserves, caused banks to adjust reserves. In doing so, they caused interest rates to fluctuate, sometimes widely, as they tried to borrow if they needed more reserves or to lend if they needed less. Then, if deposits changed again in amount, this affected the amount of reserves required two weeks later; again, banks had to adjust reserves,

---

[8] R. Alton Gilbert and Jean M. Lovati, "Bank Reserve Requirements and Their Enforcement: A Comparison Across States," Federal Reserve Bank of St. Louis, *Review*, March 1978, pp. 22–32.

## FIGURE 3–1
## Timing of Lagged and Contemporaneous Reserve Accounting Systems

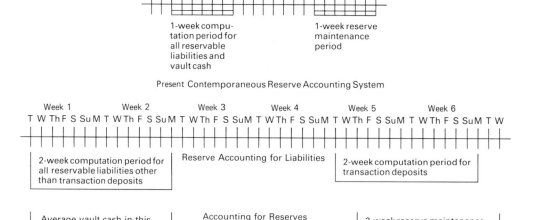

Lagged Reserve Accounting System, 1968 – 1984

Present Contemporaneous Reserve Accounting System

NOTE: A "reserve maintenance period" is a period over which the daily average reserves of a depository institution must equal or exceed its required reserves. Required reserves are based on daily average deposit liabilities in "reserve computation periods."

SOURCE: R. Alton Gilbert and Michael E. Trebing, "The New System of Contemporaneous Reserve Requirements," Federal Reserve Bank of St. Louis, *Review*, December 1982, pp. 3–7.

again causing interest rates to fluctuate. The Fed may then have felt that it had to supply reserves if needed—otherwise, interest rates might rise sharply.

The Board of Governors of the Federal Reserve System announced in the early 1980s that it would implement, for large banks which report weekly, a form of contemporaneous reserve requirement accounting (CRA or CRR).[9] The new system, somewhat different from the system in effect before 1968, involves timing provisions shown in Figure 3–1. Focusing first on the lower right-hand side of Figure 3–1, it shows, under Weeks 5 and 6, that transactions deposits are calculated as an average from a Tuesday through the second following Monday and that banks must maintain reserves (in the form of cash and/or deposits in the Fed) as the required percent of

---

[9] R. Alton Gilbert and Michael E. Trebing, "The New System of Contemporaneous Reserve Requirements," Federal Reserve Bank of St. Louis, *Review*, December 1982, pp. 3–7. See also Brian Motley, "Contemporaneous Reserve Accounting," Federal Reserve Bank of San Francisco, *Weekly Letter*, August 6, 1982.

such deposits. The reserve is calculated as an average from a Thursday through the second following Wednesday. There is an overlap of 12 of the 14 days of every 2-week period, but banks have 2 days after the end of each period for which they calculate average transactions deposits before they must calculate average reserves required for the period. This gives them 2 days after the end of a period to calculate the required reserves and to adjust reserves accordingly. Figure 3–1 as a whole indicates the following: (1) Reserve calculations for transactions deposits are for periods of 2 weeks, ending every other Wednesday. (2) Required reserves are to be held against average transactions account liabilities for the 14 days ending *two days before* the end of the current reserve period. Required reserves for time deposits and Eurodollar liabilities are based on an average for 14 days ending *30 days* before the end of the current reserve period. (3) Vault cash held during the same two-week period (ending 30 days before the end of the current reserve period) is counted as part of reserves. (4) Banks may carry over from one period to the next an amount equal to 2 percent of required reserves or $25,000, whichever is larger, using an excess to make up a deficiency (or part of it) or carrying over a deficit of that size without incurring a penalty.

The Fed notifies each bank before the beginning of each two-week reserve period how much reserves it must hold against liabilities other than transactions accounts and how much vault cash it held, which may be counted as part of the required reserve. The two days between the end of the reserve computation period for transactions account liabilities and the end of the reserve period give banks time to adjust—it takes them at least a day to measure such liabilities accurately. If banks wait until the ends of reserve periods to adjust reserves, there may be wide fluctuations in interest rates at those times, as banks borrow and lend to make adjustments. Alternatively, of course, the Fed might provide (or reduce) reserves, but this could mean that the Fed would miss its reserve targets. Implications of this for monetary policy are discussed in Chapter 16.

Counting vault cash on a lagged basis enables the Fed to know, at the beginning of each reserve period, exactly how much vault cash *was* available and hence will be counted in reserves. Lagged accounting for reserves for *non*transactions account liabilities also makes it easier for the Fed to know at the beginning of each reserve period the amount of reserves required for such liabilities. Only the amount of reserves required for *transactions accounts* is *not* known at that time; reserve management is easier for the Fed and for banks and other depository institutions.

At the same time, marketing of checking accounts is more complicated for banks, while consumers are provided with accounts suited to various groups.[10] For example, a bank may now offer "checkable" deposit accounts in the following forms: (1) a demand deposit account paying no interest (chiefly for corporations); (2) a

---

[10] Paul Calem, "The New Deposit Markets: Goodbye to Regulation Q," Federal Reserve Bank of Philadelphia, *Business Review,* November–December 1985, pp. 19–29. See also Michael C. Keeley and Gary C. Zimmerman, "Interest Checking and M1," Federal Reserve Bank of San Francisco, *Weekly Letter,* November 21, 1986. By 1986 interest was being paid on over 70 percent of *personal* checking account deposits. This 70 percent was about 30 percent of M1, a common measure of money supply that includes paper currency, coins, checkable deposit accounts, and certain travelers checks. Business firms cannot have checking accounts that pay interest.

checking account paying interest at a relatively low rate (sometimes referred to as a NOW account); (3) a Super-NOW account paying a slightly higher rate of interest (usually with a minimum balance requirement); and (4) accounts with special features such as no service fees if a specified minimum balance is maintained, accounts with a small charge for each check written (but no minimum balance requirement), accounts for "senior citizens" with no service fees, and others. Deposit market regulation in this area has almost ended, and product differentiation in this area makes decisions more complicated for consumers, while enabling banks to offer various accounts that may appeal more or less to different groups of consumers. Both marketing and pricing of bank services are now much more important for financial institutions.

One point should be emphasized: almost all deposit accounts for *individuals* must now be *attracted* (not created) by banks. The important activity of banks in *creating* deposits (money) exists chiefly in connection with business loans: a bank generally, in making a loan to a business firm, does not give cash to the firm, but simply creates a new (or additional) deposit for the firm. The bank's assets (loans) increase; demand deposits also increase. This "creation" of demand deposits (money) is very important and is discussed in detail in Chapter 5.

### Time Deposits

The time/demand deposit ratio is important because it influences the amount of loans a bank may make and the amount of deposits it may hold. With more time deposits, required reserves are lower, and it may well be possible to make more loans and create more deposits if, in making loans, borrowers are given deposit credits. If time deposits can be attracted, more of them can be held, given the same amount of reserves, than demand deposits. Of course, the cost to banks of acquiring time deposits may be greater, depending on whether the higher interest rate paid on time deposits more than offsets the costs of handling transactions accounts on which many checks are written. Different interest rate costs and different administrative costs affect profitability of banks when the deposit "mix" changes.

The term "time deposits" includes (1) savings deposits, (2) nonnegotiable time certificates of deposit (CDs), (3) negotiable CDs, and (4) "open account" time deposits. Savings deposits are predominantly held by individuals, generally in amounts of a few thousand dollars or less, although, in the mid-1970s, partnerships and corporations were allowed to own savings deposits not in excess of $150,000. Athough a 30-day notice of withdrawal may be required, banks ordinarily waive this requirement and pay out such deposits on demand to the depositor or to a properly designated third party. Sometimes banks try to enforce the notice requirement for the type of deposits discussed in the next paragraph.

Nonnegotiable time certificates of deposit (CDs) consist of a variety of instruments such as savings bonds, savings certificates, investment certificates, and so on. As the name suggests, these time deposits are not transferable; they are also not redeemable prior to maturity under usual circumstances, except with the loss of a substantial amount of interest. This category is often referred to as "consumer" time deposits, especially those in denominations of less than $100,000, to differentiate them from "business" time deposits, which are typically in denominations of $100,000 or more and are usually negotiable as well. Maturities of nonnegotiable CDs usually range from 1 month to 10 years.

Interest rates on nonnegotiable CDs were almost always fixed rates until June 1978, when commercial banks and thrift institutions were permitted to offer 6-month "money market certificates," on which interest rates varied with current money market rates. Minimum amounts for these certificates were $10,000, so that this provision could not be taken advantage of by small savers.

Negotiable CDs are issued by large banks and are bought mainly by nonfinancial corporations. At times, state and local governments, foreign interests, and non-bank financial institutions also purchase these short-term securities. Because the instrument is negotiable, it can be sold to other parties before maturity. This has encouraged the development of a secondary market that has become one of the most important parts of the money market. Most negotiable CDs, especially those traded in the New York market, are issued in minimum denominations of $100,000, with the most common denomination being $1,000,000. These and other aspects of negotiable CDs are discussed in Chapter 9.

The remaining category of time deposits is open account time deposits. These time deposits are "open" in that they do not, as a general rule, have a definite maturity date, but are automatically renewed unless the issuing bank or the depositor gives written notice of intent to terminate the contract. Such notice is usually required 10 to 30 days prior to termination. Mostly, these deposits are owned by business firms that agree to maintain them as a condition of acquiring a line of credit from the bank; they are similar in this respect to a "compensating balance," which is discussed shortly. Open account time deposits may be interest bearing, as, for example, when the deposit serves in lieu of a performance bond posted, say, by a contractor to ensure that he or she meets certain contractual requirements, or in the case of a Christmas account, which provides a means of setting aside funds for a definite time and need.

There is now no reserve required for *personal* time deposits. The purpose of required reserves is to give the Fed a focal point to control money creation. Since personal time deposits are seldom created, but are attracted either from cash held by the public or from deposits in other banks, there is no reason for required reserves. With demand deposits, if *excess reserves* exist, banks can create money. If reserves were below the required level, banks would be forced to reduce loans and deposits, and, in the process the nation's money supply would be reduced. Attracting deposits generally is not a basis for creation of money—if the attracted deposits came from other banks, one bank could make additional loans but others would lose deposits and reserves and have to tighten credit. Since the Fed controls excess reserves, it has the ultimate power to control growth of the money supply.

The importance of time deposits is that to obtain them, banks must pay attractive rates of interest or attract the deposits in some other way, such as a free service. Banks face a challenge to determine accurately their costs and to obtain interest on loans and investments sufficient to provide a satisfactory return on assets, ROA, and return on investment or equity, ROI or ROE.

## U.S. Treasury Tax and Loan Accounts

The federal government maintains a cash operating balance for the same reason that individuals and businesses do: current receipts seldom match disbursements in timing and amount. To provide for this, the U.S. Treasury holds its working balances at the 12 Federal Reserve Banks and pays for goods and services purchased by drawing down these deposits. Deposits are also held in thousands of commercial banks and savings institutions across the country that have qualified as special depositories. These are called Tax and Loan accounts because funds flow into them from two sources: (1) when individuals and businesses pay taxes (or withhold from employees' paychecks), these proceeds are deposited into Tax and Loan accounts at the various banks (and savings institutions), and (2) banks are *sometimes* allowed to pay for purchases of U.S. Treasury securities for themselves or on behalf of their customers by crediting their Tax and Loan accounts.

For many years it was assumed that the value of the Tax and Loan accounts to banks was approximately equal to the value of services that banks provided the Treasury, including collection of taxes, issuance and redemption of savings bonds, and cashing of government checks. It was, therefore, not a matter of concern that the Treasury received no explicit interest on these deposit balances. By 1974, however, the level of interest rates had risen substantially, and the Treasury's average cash balances at banks had increased in size; these developments led to a reexamination by the Treasury of its cash management policies. The Treasury's study in 1974 estimated that depository banks were earning over a quarter of a billion dollars a year more than the value of the services that banks were providing to the Treasury. The Treasury, therefore, reduced its balances at commercial banks and increased its deposits at Federal Reserve Banks. The transfer of funds to Federal Reserve Banks was expected to provide an additional return to the Treasury because most of the net earnings of the Federal Reserve System are remitted to the Treasury.

In 1977 legislation authorized the Treasury to invest in short-term obligations of depository institutions, including eligible thrift institutions as well as banks, and of the federal government. In turn, depositories were to be compensated by fees for handling federal tax deposits, issuance and redemption of savings bonds, and other financial services.[11] The new program was implemented in November 1978. Under this program, many banks that receive funds for the Treasury forward such funds to Federal Reserve Banks the following day, but large banks often choose to participate in the Treasury Tax and Loan (T & L) note program, under which the Treasury's funds are invested (for the Treasury) in the bank's interest-bearing callable notes. Thus the Treasury's earnings on its funds were increased.

In addition to the forwarding of funds to the Federal Reserve Banks for the Treasury's account daily by some banks, the Treasury's working balances at Federal Reserve Banks are augmented by "calling" the notes, in designated amounts or

---

[11] See Elijah Brewer, "Treasury to Invest Surplus Tax and Loan Balances," Federal Reserve Bank of Chicago, *Economic Perspectives*, November–December 1977, pp. 14–20. See also footnote 14 in Chapter 4.

proportions, ordering the banks to transfer the funds to the Treasury's accounts in the Federal Reserve Banks. Usually, calls are scheduled to coincide approximately with Treasury payments from its accounts in the Fed (calls add to such funds and reduce reserves, while payments reduce the funds and add to reserves), thus minimizing the impact on the banking system's reserves. Even so, individual banks may sometimes experience sharp changes in reserves as a result of discrepancies between Treasury receipts and expenditure differences and the calls to meet such differences. The handling of Tax and Loan accounts, callable notes, and "calls" are discussed in more detail in Chapter 5.

### Compensating Balances

Many large regional or national business concerns prearrange a "line of credit" with a bank that agrees to provide loan funds over a period of several months or more, and up to a certain limit, upon request. The line of credit is not a legally binding contract, but banks do not change the amounts agreed upon unless significant change occurs in relevant conditions. In return for this assurance of credit, the borrower usually is obliged to maintain an appropriate average level of deposits, often 10 to 20 percent of the line of credit, that "compensates" the bank for the costs of providing ready funds and any services associated with the credit agreement.[12] If, for example, the borrower must maintain deposits of 20 percent of a line of credit of $100,000 and loans have a 6 percent interest rate, full use of the line means $80,000 are available at an annual cost of $6,000, raising the effective interest rate to 7½ percent.

On the other hand, the "true" cost of the loan *to the borrower* may be lower than in this simple example if the balances the borrower would have held in the absence of the line of credit agreement were the same as or higher than with the agreement, if the rate of interest charged were lower because of the additional average balance held, or if additional services were provided to the borrower without further charge—if the bank considered itself to be compensated for these services by the balances held by the borrower. As is true of most bank practices, the compensating balance requirement is applied flexibly, and specific provisions vary from bank to bank and with respect to different borrowers under different sets of credit conditions. Compensating balances are usually part of the deposits held by business firms; usually they are demand deposits, but they may be time deposits, especially in cases of "link financing," in which a borrowing firm finds a financial institution that will deposit the compensating balance so that the borrowing firm may utilize the entire amount of the line of credit.

Banks may gain several advantages from compensating balances: (1) they may have more deposits, and thus more funds to lend, than otherwise; (2) they *may* obtain a higher effective interest rate than otherwise; and (3) they also have leeway, if borrowers' needs were underestimated, to permit customers to borrow more simply by permitting the compensating balance to decline, without the necessity of reviewing

---

[12] See Jack M. Guttentag and Richard G. Davis, "Compensating Balances," Federal Reserve Bank of New York, *Essays in Money and Credit*, 1964, pp. 57–61.

the approved amount of the loan and perhaps meeting objections from the senior loan committee.

## Borrowings and Capital Accounts

The term "borrowings" in Table 3–1 refers to the nondeposit liabilities of commercial banks and includes (1) borrowing from Federal Reserve Banks, (2) purchases of Federal funds, (3) borrowing of Eurodollars, (4) sale of bank promissory notes, and (5) sale of loans and securities under repurchase agreements. Long-term notes and debentures (capital debts) are, strictly speaking, also liabilities, but, under certain restrictions governing minimum maturities, banks are allowed to include them as part of bank capital. Thus, bank capital is defined somewhat differently from the capital accounts of nonfinancial business firms.

### Borrowings

The categories under "borrowings" that are of quantitative importance today are the first three and the fifth; bank sales of promissory notes called commercial paper were significant in the 1960s for a brief period, but these have been largely discontinued because of changes in Federal Reserve regulations that rendered them uneconomical sources of funds. Borrowing from the Federal Reserve, in the Federal funds market, and overseas in the Eurodollar market and acquisition of funds through sale of securities by banks under agreements to repurchase them (repos) remain important sources and are discussed in Chapter 5 and 9.

### Capital Accounts

The principal capital accounts are (1) capital stock, (2) surplus, and (3) undivided profits. Capital stock is mostly common shares that were sold when the bank was newly organized, issued later to raise additional long-term funds, or increased through stock dividends. The initial offerings of stock (at required 20 percent or more premium over par value in the case of national banks) created the surplus account. The surplus subsequently increases through retention of earnings and their transfer to this account. Undivided profits is the account that is credited with each year's earnings and later debited when cash dividends are declared, when (or if) assets fall in value (the surplus account may also be debited if necessary), or when the bank's directors transfer funds from undivided profits to the surplus account, thus earmarking earnings as relatively permanent capital rather than an amount available for dividend payments.

The reader should understand that reserves (assets) do *not* provide liquidity for depositors, except in very small amounts. For example, if depositors wish to withdraw $100,000 from a bank which has deposits of $1 million, if the reserve requirement is 10 percent, and if this amount is held, with the reduction of deposits from $1 million to $900,000, reserves can be reduced from $100,000 to $90,000. Only $10,000 of the amount needed to satisfy depositors' requests for funds can come from reserves. The rest must come from sale of other assets, such as short-term government securities held by the bank, or from borrowing by the bank.

Similarly, reserve requirements do little to provide safety. If loans turn bad and defaults seem likely, the bank must reduce the value of the loans on its books and at the same time reduce its capital accounts. Safety is provided either by making safe loans or by having enough capital that any probable losses on loans can be charged off against capital. Charges may be made against a special loan loss account in the capital accounts or against undivided profits and surplus; if charge-offs must be made against capital stock, a bank is insolvent and must close its doors unless a "rescue" can be arranged. It should be added there is an old saying: "no banker makes a bad loan, loans become bad after they make them." In many cases, this is true; the loans were safe when made, but the borrower's situation deteriorated, sometimes quite unexpectedly. Sometimes, however, bankers make loans on which losses are likely to be incurred. An example is some energy loans in the early 1980s.

The amount and structure of the capital accounts are important to commercial banks because the amount of capital is a measure of the cushion available to protect depositors against loss in the event of shrinkage in asset values and possible insolvency. The almost uninterrupted decline in the banking system's capital/deposit ratio led to increasing concern with the question of the "adequacy of bank capital."[13] Whether a particular bank's capital is sufficient depends upon much more than the capital/deposit ratio. Additional factors such as the risk structure of assets, the volatility of deposits, the overall liquidity position, and ultimately the quality of a bank's management are also important. If a bank's capital is deemed inadequate after an examination of these items, the regulatory authority may suggest to the bank's management that it increase the capital stock or surplus by following a more conservative dividend policy or by other means.

In recent years, the relative decline in capital accounts has heightened bankers' interest in senior securities as a source of long-term funds. Preferred stock and capital debt (capital notes and debentures), little used since the depression period of the mid-1930s, have been gaining favor, especially among bankers anxious to avoid possible dilution of the existing common shareholders' equity. Rulings by the Comptroller of the Currency have permitted national banks to include long-term capital debt as capital, for purposes of calculating lending limits. The most important limit relates to the size of a loan that may be made on an unsecured basis to an individual borrower— no more than 10 percent of its unimpaired capital and surplus. There are a number of exceptions to this rule for loans secured by suitable collateral. Similar restrictions

---

[13] Larry D. Wall, "Affiliated Bank Capital," Federal Reserve Bank of Atlanta, *Economic Review*, April 1985, pp. 12–19. Early in 1985 the regulatory authorities agreed upon capital standards—minimum capital to be a certain percent of total assets. See also his article "Regulation of Banks' Equity Capital," Federal Reserve Bank of Atlanta, *Economic Review*, November 1985, pp. 4–18. A new proposal was announced early in 1987 by the regulatory agencies in a joint suggestion with the Bank of England. This proposal related required capital to the riskiness of a bank's assets. See Janice M. Moulton, "New Guidelines for Bank Capital: An Attempt to Reflect Risk," Federal Reserve Bank of Philadelphia, *Business Review*, July–August 1987, pp. 19–33.

apply to real estate loans, which are limited to a certain ratio of a bank's capital and surplus or a certain proportion of its time deposits. Also, because they are exempt from reserve requirements and interest rate ceilings, capital debts may prove, under certain conditions, a more profitable source of funds than time deposits.

As bank failures began to increase in the 1980s, the regulatory authorities agreed in 1985 on minimum ratios: for primary capital (capital stock and surplus plus loan loss reserves and mandatory convertible debt items), 5½ percent of total assets, and for secondary capital (primary capital plus subordinated debt and limited life preferred stock), 6 percent. It was believed that depositors, perhaps because of deposit insurance, do not put pressure on banks to have as much capital as is needed. Bank holding companies *may* in some cases be willing to "spin off" their subsidiaries or let them fail; hence, adequate bank capital is necessary for both subsidiary banks and for bank holding companies.

The different ratio of required secondary capital from the ratio for required primary capital illustrates the increased importance of such items as subordinated debt. Debt has a tax advantage over equity, and shareholders of independent banks may try to obtain this tax advantage.[14] Banks that are subsidiaries of bank holding companies may be able to issue new capital stock and sell it to their holding companies; holding companies may be most interested in maximizing total profits of the system—hence, a bank holding company should let a subsidiary with a low cost of funds borrow and supply funds to a subsidiary with high marginal cost of funds and highest return on investments.

### Bank Income and Expenses

Our cursory examination of the balance sheet for a bank shows that, as a dealer in debt, most of the bank's income and expenses result from use of deposits and other borrowed funds. This is confirmed by the income statement for insured banks for 1981, presented in abridged form in Table 3–4. It shows the principal sources of revenue and expenses, most important of which is the interest received from loans and securities and interest paid on time and savings deposits, respectively.

By far the largest income item is interest from loans. This varies in importance from year to year as the composition of earning assets changes and as the general level of interest rates rises and falls with the level of business activity. Since the early 1950s, loans have exceeded securities and have increased at a faster rate of growth. Interest rates have also risen during most of this period; hence, interest from loans has become an increasingly important source of revenue, especially during periods of expansion of economic activity.

Generally, in recent years, interest paid on time deposits exceeded each of the other operating expenses, including wages and salaries. The amount of interest paid depends, of course, on the amount and composition of time deposits, the level of

[14] See Paul S. Nadler, "Time Deposits and Debentures: The New Sources of Bank Funds," New York University Graduate School of Business Administration, *Bulletin*, No. 30, July 1964, pp. 24–30.

**TABLE 3–4**
**Income and Expenses of Insured Commercial Banks, 1981**
(billions of dollars)

|  | Amount | Percentage of Subcategory |
|---|---|---|
| Operating income, total | $247.9 | 100.0% |
| Interest from |  |  |
|     Loans | 163.2 | 65.8 |
|     Balances with banks | 23.9 | 9.6 |
|     Federal funds sold and securities |  |  |
|       purchased under resale agreement | 12.2 | 4.9 |
|     Securities | 29.3 | 11.8 |
| Trust department | 3.2 | 1.3[a] |
| Service charges, fees, and other | 16.1 | 6.6[a] |
| Operating expenses, total | 227.7 | 100.0 |
| Interest on |  |  |
|     Time and savings deposits | 139.0 | 61.0 |
|     Federal funds and other borrowing | 30.3 | 13.3 |
| Salaries, wages, and benefits | 27.9 | 12.3 |
| Other operating expenses | 30.5 | 13.4 |
| Income before income taxes and securities |  |  |
|     gains or losses | 11.6 |  |
| Income taxes | 2.8 |  |
| Income before securities gains or losses | 8.8 |  |
| Net securities gains or losses | 0.1 |  |
|     Net income | 8.9 |  |

[a] These percentages, for all banks, are not representative for some large banks that have trust departments that are significant sources of income and for which international banking and assets abroad may provide from 20 to 70 percent of total income.

SOURCE: *Federal Reserve Bulletin*, August 1982, p. 463.

competing market rates, and the structure of interest rate ceilings imposed by the Federal Reserve under Regulation Q, until that regulation was phased out. With the rapid rise in interest rates in 1975 to 1982, interest paid as a percentage of total expenses increased sharply, from less than 50 percent to nearly 75 percent. Although not treated as an operating item, bank gains or losses on securities sold affect net income. Such gains or losses reflect conditions in the securities markets during the year. Banks gain in some years and lose in others. Net losses are usually incurred when banks liquidate securities on a large scale to provide funds for loan purposes.

## The Elements of Portfolio Policy

The central problem facing managers of commercial banks is to manage the banks' assets and liabilities so as to provide an adequate rate of return to stockholders, consistent with an appropriate degree of safety and liquidity. Earlier we expressed this goal in terms of reconciling the conflicting needs for safety, earnings, and liquidity. But safety and liquidity are not ultimate goals in themselves; they are necessary to achieve the long-run goal of managers—profitable operation of the firm. The bank must at least remain solvent (the realizable value of its assets must be equal to its legal liabilities plus the value of the "capital stock" account) in the long run and be able to ensure convertibility of deposits into currency in the very short run, if the expectation of profit is to be realized. There would, of course, be no "problem" if there were no risks or uncertainties. If the behavior of deposits were manageable, or at least predictable, and if there existed a collection of assets that were at the same time eminently safe and profitable, the banker's life would be simple indeed. But unfortunately, such is not the case. Assets are risky in varying degrees, deposits are volatile, and the promised rate of return on loanable funds varies directly with the degree of risk and inversely with its liquidity.

In short, safety of assets is of paramount importance because of the low capital/deposit ratio—that is, the thinness of the equity cushion; liquidity is necessary to meet the double-barreled demands of depositors and borrowers; earnings are essential if the bank is to compete successfully for customers, employees, and stockholders. In terms of managing the portfolio of assets, bankers must think in terms of "trade-offs" and recognize (1) that no single asset meets all their requirements and (2) that the cost of improved earnings is increased risk and reduced liquidity.

### Safety and Management of Bank Assets

Banks must seek safety in the choice of assets for their portfolios because bank failures have serious implications for the entire community. For this reason, banks in the United States are prohibited from investing in stocks, and stocks acquired as collateral for defaulted loans must be disposed of within a specified length of time. Another reason banks are not allowed to own stocks is to prevent the undue concentration of financial power in the economy, which such ownership may provide. Thus this prohibition is not simply a matter of reducing risk but is deeply rooted in the aversion to monopoly power. There are certain relatively minor exceptions to the prohibition. A member bank is obliged to buy stock in the Federal Reserve Bank of its district, and member banks are allowed to own, cooperatively, stocks in companies operating data processing facility centers. Banks may also own stock in bank-related subsidiaries such as safe deposit companies and, in certain cases, those engaged in foreign banking. Bank holding companies own their bank subsidiaries.

Similarly, relatively high standards of safety are imposed by law and/or tradition on loans and investments. Loans were for many years supposed to be "self-liquidating" assets, convertible into cash through sale of the short-term assets acquired by the borrower, using the loan proceeds.[15] Recognizing that not all bank assets were self-

---

[15] The prime example of the self-liquidating loan is one made to enable a firm to increase its inventory above normal levels for peak sales, such as at Christmas. Sales during the period provide funds to repay the loan plus profits for the business firm.

liquidating assets, it was later suggested that assets were safe if they were shiftable—if they could be sold, without significant loss, to another financial institution. Still later, it was recognized that loans might be relatively safe if anticipated income of the business firm seemed likely to be sufficient to repay the loan with interest.

Standards of safety in the acquisition of investment assets have been improved by regulations that in general prohibit banks from acquiring any but the highest grades of bonds and similar securities.

### Liquidity and Management of Bank Assets

Until the 1960s, the problem of bank liquidity was usually analyzed within the framework of adjusting the bank's asset portfolio. Accordingly, deposits were treated as an undependable source of funds subject to unexpected withdrawal and beyond the control of the bank's management. The maintenance of adequate liquidity was achieved by holding assets that had short-term maturities or that could be sold quickly and at minimum loss to meet these currency drains. From the time of Adam Smith (circa 1776) until the Great Depression of the 1930s, the "real bills" doctrine was prominent in the literature concerning appropriate bank behavior. According to this doctrine, because banks borrow short-term funds (deposits), they should also lend short-term funds. Their earning assets should be loans backed by "real" goods, such as inventory purchased with the borrowed funds. Thus, bank loans would not only be profitable and safe, but would provide a continual source of liquidity; as inventory was sold, loans could be repaid.

The "real bills" doctrine was eventually abandoned both in practice and in principle. First, under this doctrine bank lending policy often failed to accommodate the needs of bank customers. Business firms' investment programs required long-term as well as short-term financing, and consumers required installment loans and mortgage loans to finance their expenditures for durable goods and housing. Second, in accommodating the legitimate "needs" of business and commerce, the banking system contributed to business fluctuations by increasing business loans and deposits during prosperity and reducing them during recession. Even for the individual bank, the loans were often not "self-liquidating," especially during times of crisis. The "real bills" doctrine presumed that bankers could and would judge the appropriate amount of loans to meet the needs of increasing output, but would not make loans that would result in a potentially inflationary increase in demand. This judgment is difficult to make, and, if a recession occurs, "sound" loans may no longer be sound. Moreover, central banks began to be more active in efforts to control the economy, expanding bank reserves when they desired an increase in credit and money and reducing bank reserves when they felt this was necessary.

During the period following World War II, the resurgence of loan demand made it profitable for financial institutions, including banks, to reduce their substantial holdings of U.S. Treasury securities and replace them with loans to business and consumers. This was facilitated by the Federal Reserve's policy of buying government obligations at par, and large amounts of federal debt were shifted into the Federal

Reserve's portfolio. Under these conditions, "shiftability" became the hallmark of asset liquidity, and the provision of a protective or secondary reserve became the first line of defense in meeting the bankers' liquidity needs.

## The Schedule of Priorities

The secondary reserve is an important part of the concept of the "schedule of priorities," a significant development in the theory of management of bank assets.[16] Using this approach, bankers review the past behavior of their accounts and from this information prepare estimates of their near-term requirements. They then allocate their assets in such a way as to satisfy their most urgent prospective needs, according to their schedule of priorities:[17]

1. First priority: Primary reserves—cash and related items necessary to meet legal and operating needs of the bank for reserves and correspondent balances.
2. Second priority: Secondary reserves—short-term Treasury securities, commercial paper, and other readily marketable assets available to meet liquidity requirements.
3. Third priority: Customer loans—loans (to businesses and individuals) that usually provide the major part of a bank's earnings.
4. Fourth priority: Investment for income—U.S. Treasury, municipal, and corporate securities to supplement income from loans or to provide diversification, if necessary.

The value of establishing a schedule of priorities was that it encouraged bankers to quantify their anticipated requirements and at least implicitly to take them into account when making decisions about the allocation of bank funds. It also permitted clear recognition of the fact that most of the assets with the highest degree of liquidity (vault cash and balances with other banks) are *not* available to meet the possible demands upon the bank associated with deposit withdrawals and loan requests. That is, a bank must *maintain* legal reserves in an amount depending upon the size and composition of its deposits and the required reserve ratios applicable to these liabilities. In the event of deposit withdrawals, only a small portion of the legal reserve can be available to meet withdrawals. In addition, as an operating bank, correspondent balances must be treated as relatively frozen assets. Of course, reserves may be drawn down temporarily, and in an emergency, balances due from other banks may be called upon to meet currency requirements, but they must be restored to "normal" levels within a very short time if the bank is to continue to function as it did before the emergency arose. The primary reserve is not a long-run source of liquidity. Furthermore, the concept of a schedule of priorities rightly subordinates the need for current earnings to the short-run liquidity needs of the bank, while treating investment for

---

[16] The "schedule of priorities" is presented in Roland I. Robinson, *The Management of Bank Funds*, 2nd ed. (New York: McGraw-Hill, 1962), pp. 13–18.

[17] A more complete discussion of these priorities and their role in asset management is found in E. W. Reed, R. V. Cotter, E. K. Gill, and R. K. Smith, *Commercial Banking* (Englewood Cliffs, N.J.: Prentice-Hall, 1976), pp. 105–111.

income as a residual use of bank funds not held as primary reserves, secondary reserves, or loans.

## Management of Bank Liabilities

In the 1960s, developments in financial markets shifted bankers' attention to sources of funds other than demand deposits. First, relatively slow growth in demand deposits and continued reduction in the commercial banks' share of savings deposits forced banks to compete aggressively for savings and to reevaluate their loan policies. Increased expenditures on advertising, higher interest rates paid on savings deposits, and solicitation of real estate and consumer loans were the major steps taken to help reverse the outflow of funds and to attract new customers. Second, many of the larger regional and money market banks were experiencing withdrawals by corporate depositors, who found that money market instruments such as Treasury bills and commercial paper, which offered safety and liquidity plus an interest return, made demand deposits an undesirable form in which to hold short-term funds. In earlier years, business firms had been satisfied to hold excess demand deposits because the opportunity costs were very low and negotiable time deposits were unavailable to them. The gradual upward trend of market rates and the loss of business deposits posed a serious problem for banks, and several large banks responded by issuing negotiable time certificates of deposit, an important new money market instrument. In early 1961, a market developed for CDs, and the number of banks issuing certificates increased rapidly as business firms found certificates profitable for their excess funds.

Although the CD was an instant success and provided a new means of tapping the money market, for many banks it proved to be a mixed blessing: liquidity could be purchased by issuing CDs, but, if rising market rates later made them unattractive, the holder would invest the proceeds at maturity in other instruments, and the issuing bank faced a loss of deposits, termed disintermediation. This in fact occurred in 1966, 1969, 1973–1974, and 1979–1982. Rising market rates led to disintermediation with respect to those types of deposits that had interest rate ceilings (imposed by Regulation Q) below the rates in unregulated money markets.

The volatility of deposits intensified the search for other sources of liquidity. Bankers explored other markets and turned to Eurodollars, commercial paper, and older sources of funds—the Federal funds market and borrowing from the Federal Reserve—as alternative ways of meeting their need for funds. These sources are described in detail in Chapter 9. Suffice it to say here that management of liabilities represented a creative response by bankers to the changing financial environment in which they operate. Since these funds were not deposit funds, they were subject to reserve requirements only when the Fed imposed special provisions. Moreover, they could be increased or decreased in amount at the initiative of banks.

In the early 1970s, these developments were viewed with concern by the regulatory authorities. Many banks had relied heavily on borrowed, interest-sensitive funds for expanding their assets. This, in turn, reinforced the downward trend in bank capital ratios and led in some cases to a significant deterioration of asset quality. It also encouraged some banks to make generous advance commitments of funds to borrowers on the premise that these funds could be bought or borrowed by the bank when needed to make loans. In view of the failure of several large banks during this period, bankers were urged by some regulatory authorities to improve their capital positions and pay greater attention to liquidity and asset condition.[18]

### Emergence of Asset and Liability Management

Because of the rising trend and volatility of interest rates and the use of nondeposit liabilities as a source of funds, asset and liability management policies began to be developed by banks, replacing both the asset priority schedules and other asset management policies that had been common and replacing the management of liabilities as a separate policy. Financial management policy began to be integrated.

An important concept in asset and liability management is rate sensitivity management—identifying those assets and liabilities that are sensitive to changes in interest rates (i.e., assets and liabilities on which interest rates change significantly in short time periods, perhaps 90 days) and attempting to match the amount of rate-sensitive assets (RSA) and the amount of rate-sensitive liabilities (RSL). Obviously, if interest rates on liabilities rise and those on assets do not rise, profits are likely to fall. The ratio of RSAs to RSLs, unless it is 1 : 1, indicates a *gap*. It has been suggested by one author that this ratio should be between 1.0 : 1 and 1.6 : 1. Many banks have found substantial difficulty in forecasting interest rates.[19] If, however, interest rates can be forecast, a lower ratio is acceptable when interest rates are expected to fall. Clearly, if errors occur in interest rate forecasts, profits can be sharply reduced if interest rates rise when they are expected to fall and if the ratio of RSA to RSL is low. Interest rates have been very difficult to forecast in recent years; for example, with a slowdown in inflation from 1980 to 1982, interest rates might have been expected to decline, but this decline did not occur until the summer of 1982.[20]

An asset and liability management policy adopted by a bank may specify a desired rate of return on equity (capital accounts), or ROE and establish an asset and liability management committee or other group to review economic forecasts, interest rates, RSA/RSL ratios, and other important data and to develop plans for specified time periods during which desired spread between interest rates on assets and those on liabilities should be maintained, desired growth should be achieved, and desired

---

[18] Arthur F. Burns, "Maintaining the Soundness of Our Banking System," Federal Reserve Bank of New York, *Monthly Review*, November 1974, pp. 263–267; and Alfred Hayes, "Banking Supervision and Monetary Policy," Federal Reserve Bank of New York, *Monthly Review*, May 1975, pp. 99–102.

[19] James V. Baker, Jr., "Asset and Liability Management" (five parts), *Banking*, June, July, August, September, and October 1978.

[20] See "Forecasting Interest Rates: Some First Principles," *Morgan Guaranty Survey*, September 1981, pp. 1–7. In this article, it is suggested that traditional money demand/money supply analysis has had "decreased usefulness" and that "the link between interest rates and inflation sometimes comes apart." The latter seemed evident in 1981 and 1982 through June, but interest rates fell in the second half of 1982, as inflation had done much earlier.

ratios such as ROE, ROA (return on assets), RSA/RSL, and others should be maintained. Other desired amounts and ratios may be incorporated in such a plan. The plan may also include liquidity considerations, policy in offering time deposits (both small—less than $100,000—and large), policy in selling Federal funds, tax positions, loan loss reserve ratios, and dividend policy. Asset and liability management policy thus becomes the *core of financial management for banks*.

A more complete list of factors in asset and liability management, especially for very large banks that are involved in international banking, is (1) adequate capital, so that losses on loans and investments may be charged off without hurting either depositors or shareholders (the latter may be hurt, but should not be badly hurt); (2) adequate liquidity, to meet withdrawals and payments; (3) additional borrowing capacity, in case of need; (4) foreign currency position of such size as to limit risk; and (5) limited maturity mismatches. Maturity mismatches create liquidity problems—for example, if liabilities are short term and assets are long term, it may not be possible to liquidate enough assets to meet maturing liabilities. They also commit the banks to particular interest rates—if assets are longer in maturity than liabilities, and if interest rates rise, banks lose; if assets are shorter in maturity than liabilities and interest rates fall, banks lose.

Those who calculate maturity time accurately use the concept of *duration* of a financial asset rather than simply its term or time to maturity.[21] Duration reflects the average amount and time of all cash flows; time to maturity reflects only the time until repayment of principal at maturity. Since interest is usually received periodically, duration is normally less than time to maturity. The time until each expected cash flow (payment) is weighted by (multiplied by) its present value as a percent of the total present value of all cash flows; the result is a weighted average of the times until cash flows are received, and this weighted average is termed duration.

Examples are given in many standard investment texts. Assume that a 7 percent bond is issued at a premium to yield 6 percent to maturity; purchase price is $1,026.73. For simplicity assume maturity is three years and interest payments are made annually. Then cash flows are $70 at the end of each of the first two years, and $1,070 at the end of the third year, assuming no default. Present values of these amounts are $66.04, $62.30, and $898.39, respectively. As percentages of total cash flows, these amounts are 6.43, 6.07, and 87.5, respectively.[22] Using these percentages as weights for the cash flows, we obtain .0643, .1214, and 2.6250; these add to a total of 2.8107 years, the duration. The period of 2.8107 years reflects the amount and timing of every cash flow. The interest payments at the ends of the first and second years have the effect of shortening the weighted average time until cash flows are received.

[21] This concept was introduced by F. R. Macaulay, *Some Theoretical Problems Suggested by the Movement of Interest Rates, Bond Yields, and Stock Prices in the United States Since 1856* (New York: National Bureau of Economic Research, 1938).

[22] The above example is given in Jack Clark Francis, *Investments: Analysis and Management*, 3rd ed. (New York: McGraw-Hill, 1980), p. 204.

Thus the more interest paid before maturity and the sooner it is paid, the less the duration of a bond which is like another bond in other respects. Hence, duration is a measure of interest rate risk. Early cash flows cannot be affected adversely by a *subsequent* rise in market interest rates; cash flows already received can be invested at current market rates.

A perpetual bond has a limited duration because cash flows received after a certain number of years have infinitely small present values, and hence do not add significantly to duration. A bond sold at a premium has less duration (assuming the same maturity) than one sold at a discount. Bonds sold at discounts have longer durations, because a greater percentage of cash flows is received later (capital gain is received when the bond rises to par at maturity, assuming it is held to that date and there is no default).

Since bond prices fluctuate inversely with changes in interest rates on similar bonds, we can calculate *elasticities* of price changes with respect to interest rate changes. The greater this elasticity, the greater the fall in the bond price if interest rates rise. Elasticity increases as duration increases. A longer term to maturity or delayed interest payments add to duration and elasticity of price changes when interest rates change. Thus deferral of interest rate payments increases risk that bond prices will fall if interest rates rise.

Duration is, as we have seen, always shorter than time to maturity, in normal conditions. Matching duration of assets and liabilities should enable banks to avoid losses from mismatch. However, historical cost accounting ignores capital gains and losses until they are realized (until assets are sold). Inflation may seriously reduce the value of assets on which the interest rate is fixed, but accounting statements may not show this reduction. One alternative would be market value accounting—valuing assets, primarily loans and investments, and liabilities (deposits and borrowings) at the present values of the expected cash flows, using current estimates of interest rates expected to prevail over the lives of the assets. Using such valuation, net worth of many savings and loan associations would have been below zero in the recent period of high interest rates.

A problem arises in measuring *effective* maturities for both assets and liabilities—mortgage (and other) loans are often paid off before maturity, deposits are withdrawn before maturity of certificates of deposit, and so on. Obviously, market value accounting for financial institutions would involve judgmental problems. Some argue that such judgments are made every day in determining the prices of stocks, and are also made in valuing firms for mergers and acquisitions. Secondary markets for mortgage loans give some indication of market value for such loans. Market value accounting would reveal the effect of *expected* changes in interest rates on net worth. Such accounting might provide evidence that regulatory agencies could use to prevent bank and other failures before they occurred. Of course, the need for a change in accounting rules increases with inflation; if inflation moderates, the need is less obvious.

Problems faced by banks are less serious than are problems faced by other depository institutions because bank assets in some cases have variable interest rates, and in any case many bank loans are of shorter term (and duration) than many loans of the other institutions.[23]

### Global Asset and Liability Management

Large banks involved in international banking *may* take a global approach to the management of assets and liabilities: in *global asset and liability management*, all the markets in which the banks may raise funds and make loans and investments are considered together. A global approach may help a bank to obtain funds at the lowest possible cost and to lend at the highest rates consistent with the risk that the bank management feels justified in taking. With global management, a branch that needs funds and a branch that has surplus funds can net out these needs, without obtaining funds in a market or lending funds in a market. Costs may be reduced. Of course, global management means that personnel must recognize that they function in an overall plan and have less independence as branch managers or other officers than they would have in a bank that regards branches or regions as somewhat separate entities. Also, global management requires some personnel familiar with all functions of the banks. Hence some banks may opt for decentralization, some for global asset and liability management, and some for intermediate management positions, in which some operations may be relatively independent.

This brief review can do no more than give the reader a general perception of the problems involved in global asset and liability management. But the factors in decisions under such management should be remembered: enough but not too much capital, enough liquidity, room for borrowing if need be, foreign currency positions appropriate to the currency risk, and limited maturity mismatches.[24]

## Recent Expansion of Banking Services

Banks' search for profits has involved expansion of types and areas of service as well as asset and liability management. Banks have acted aggressively to serve new markets (when permitted) and to supply new services (again, when permitted) both domestically and abroad. Three developments during the period since 1960 deserve special mention: (1) the formation of bank holding companies and "nonbank banks," (2) the expansion of international banking, and (3) the growth and changes in form of "retail banking."

---

[23] For further discussion, see Jack Beebe and Matthew Blank, "Market Value—Part I" and "Market Value—Part II," Federal Reserve Bank of San Francisco, *Weekly Letter*, May 13 and 20, 1983.

[24] A convenient rather brief summary of the nature of global asset and liability management is Warren E. Moskowitz, "Global Asset and Liability Management at Commercial Banks," Federal Reserve Bank of New York, *Quarterly Review*, Spring 1979, pp. 42–48.

### Bank Holding Companies and "Nonbank Banks"

A bank holding company is a company that owns or otherwise controls one or more banks.[25] From 1970 to 1980, the proportion of banks controlled by holding companies rose from one-fifteenth to one-third; the proportion of deposits so controlled increased from one-sixth to nearly three-fourths. Although holding companies existed in the United States before 1900, their rate of growth began to accelerate in the mid-1960s. There are two types of bank holding companies: multibank and one-bank holding companies. They have been formed for different purposes, and they have grown at different rates throughout the country.

Multibank holding companies expanded to establish multiple office banking in states that had restrictive branching laws. In states in which they were permitted to operate—about four-fifths of all the states—holding companies could form new bank affiliates (de novo banks) or acquire existing banks. In those cases in which holding companies held affiliated banks in two or more states, the result was a step toward de facto interstate banking, an arrangement not permitted via branch banking. One bank holding company, with more than 20 banks in 11 states, has changed its name to First Interstate Corporation.[26]

In 1933 and 1935, federal legislation was enacted to limit the activities of holding companies and their affiliates, and the Bank Holding Company Act of 1956 and subsequent amendments in 1966 and 1970 now constitute basic regulation of multibank holding companies.

One-bank holding companies, as distinct from multibank companies, have been formed by banks to permit diversification into nonbanking activities such as leasing of personal property, factoring, and some types of insurance. One-bank holding companies grew rapidly during the 1960s. Because they were exempt from holding company legislation, they were an attractive vehicle for bank expansion, and between 1966 and 1970, about 900 new one-bank holding companies were formed; many of these owned very large banks. And, by 1970, this type of holding company held a larger share of total bank deposits than did the multibank companies.

In response to these developments, the Bank Holding Company Act was further amended in 1970 to cover one-bank companies. The 1970 amendment required *all* holding companies to register with the Board of Governors of the Federal Reserve System. In general, holding companies were also required to obtain Board approval

---

[25] For a comprehensive treatment of bank holding companies, see Harvey Rosenblum, "Bank Holding Companies: An Overview," Federal Reserve Bank of Chicago, *Business Conditions*, August 1973, pp. 3–13; Harvey Rosenblum, "Bank Holding Company Review 1973/4: Part I," Federal Reserve Bank of Chicago, *Business Conditions*, February 1975, pp. 3–10; Harvey Rosenblum, "Bank Holding Companies: Part II," Federal Reserve Bank of Chicago, *Business Conditions*, April 1975, pp. 13–15. See also Dale S. Drum, "MBHC's: Evidence After Two Decades of Regulation," Federal Reserve Bank of Chicago, *Business Conditions*, December 1976, pp. 3–15. An extensive bibliography is included. Finally, see Dale S. Drum, "Nonbanking Activities of Bank Holding Companies," Federal Reserve Bank of Chicago, *Economic Perspectives*, March–April 1977, pp. 12–21.

[26] This action lays the semantic groundwork for interstate banking, but not full interstate banking, because the separate banks owned by the holding company cannot act as one bank; for example, a depositor cannot tell one of those banks to transfer a deposit to another, as can be done easily between branches.

prior to acquiring additional banks or engaging in nonbanking activities, directly or through an affiliate.

In the past the Board has usually approved those activities it deems to be "closely related to banking" if their performance is expected to produce "net public benefits." Those activities that do not meet both of these tests are denied. The Board approves some cases by adding to the list of activities permitted under Regulation Y. It approves other activities by specific order for that case; another bank holding company seeking approval for such activities cannot assume that permission will be granted—review is on a case-by-case basis. The Board's classification of nonbanking activities for holding companies as of early 1983 is shown in Table 3–5.[27]

Applications to form holding company affiliates or to engage in nonbanking activities are closely examined by the Board. The Board considers such factors as the convenience and needs of the community, the expected effects on existing or potential competitors, and the financial condition of the banks and other holding company affiliates. To meet the test of net public benefits, the expected benefits to the public must outweigh possible adverse effects on competition and on the capital position of the affiliated firms.

The evidence to date is mixed concerning the net impact of holding companies on competition, concentration of financial resources, community welfare, and bank safety. As indicated, however, in terms of assets, the bank holding company has become the dominant form of organization. But assets of nonbank subsidiaries of holding companies are only about 5 percent of the total assets of commercial banks. Moreover, in recent years, concentration of banking in a few banks has been reduced slightly at the national and SMSA (standard metropolitan statistical area) levels.[28]

Further deregulation of financial institutions would probably benefit bank holding companies. They are in an excellent position to take advantage of any deregulation permitting branching in more than one state and/or engaging in activities not now permitted.[29]

The Bank Holding Company Act defined banks as institutions that hold demand deposits *and* make business loans. Bank holding companies that wanted to operate banks in other states, but could not do so because of regulatory actions, established what came to be known as "nonbank banks" in various states—banks that hold demand deposits *or* make business loans, but do not do both. Federal regulatory agencies approved a substantial number of these, but legal questions were raised in the courts. Early in 1986, the Supreme Court ruled that the regulatory agencies, including the Federal Reserve System, could not legally halt the expansion of non-

---

[27] In June 1986 the Board added financial counseling, tax planning, futures and options advisory services, operating a collection agency and a credit bureau and personal property appraisals to the list of permitted activities. See *The Wall Street Journal*, June 26, 1986, p. 4.

[28] Donald T. Savage, "Developments in Banking Structure, 1970–81," *Federal Reserve Bulletin*, February 1982, pp. 77–85. SMSAs are standard metropolitan statistical areas, basically areas of one or more counties containing one or more cities, each having a population of 50,000 or more.

[29] Thomas G. Watkins and Robert Craig West, "Bank Holding Companies: Development and Regulation," Federal Reserve Bank of Kansas City, *Economic Review*, June 1982, pp. 3–13.

## TABLE 3–5
### Permissible Nonbank Activities for Bank Holding Companies Under Section 4(c)8 of Regulation Y, February 1983

| Activities Permitted by Regulation | Activities Permitted by Order | Activities Denied by the Board |
|---|---|---|
| 1. Extensions of credit[2]<br>Mortgage banking<br>Finance companies: consumer, sales and commercial<br>credit cards<br>factoring | 1. Issuance and sale of travelers checks[2,6] | 1. Insurance premium funding (combined sales of mutual funds and insurance) |
| 2. Industrial bank, Morris plan bank, industrial loan company | 2. Buying and selling gold and silver bullion and silver coin[2,4] | 2. Underwriting life insurance not related to credit extension |
| 3. Serving loans and other extensions of credit[2] | 3. Issuing money orders and general-purpose variable denominated payment instruments[1,2,4] | 3. Sale of level-term credit life |
| 4. Trust company[2] | 4. Futures commission merchant to cover gold and silver bullion and coins[1,2] | 4. Real estate brokerage (residential) |
| 5. Investment or financial advising[2] | 5. Underwriting certain federal, state, and municipal securities[1,2] | 5. Armored car |
| 6. Full pay-out leasing of personal or real property | 6. Check verification[1,2,4] | 6. Land development |
| 7. Investments in community welfare projects[2] | 7. Financial advice to consumers[1,2] | 7. Real estate syndication |
| 8. Providing bookkeeping or data processing services[2] | 8. Issuance of small denomination debt instruments[1] | 8. General management consulting |
| 9. Acting as insurance agent or broker primarily in connection with credit extensions[2] | 9. Arranging for equity financing of real estate[1] | 9. Property management |
| 10. Underwriting credit life, accident, and health insurance | 10. Acting as futures commissions merchant[1] | 10. Computer output microfilm services |
| 11. Providing courier services[2] | 11. Discount brokerage[1] | 11. Underwriting mortgage guaranty insurance[3] |
| | 12. Operating a distressed savings and loan association[1] | 12. Operating a savings and loan association[1,5] |
| | 13. Operating an Article XII Investment Co.[1] | 13. Operating a travel agency[1,2] |
| | | 14. Underwriting property and casualty insurance[1] |
| | | 15. Underwriting home loan life mortgage insurance[1] |
| | | 16. Investment note issue with transactional characteristics[1] |
| | | 17. Real estate advisory services[1] |

| Activities Permitted by Regulation | Activities Permitted by Order | Activities Denied by the Board |
|---|---|---|
| 12. Management consulting for all depository institutions | 14. Executing foreign banking unsolicited purchases and sales of securities | |
| 13. Sale at retail of money orders with a face value of not more than $1,000, travelers checks and savings bonds[1,2] | 15. Engaging in commercial banking activities abroad through a limited purpose Delaware bank[1] | |
| 14. Performing appraisals of real estate[1] | 16. Performing appraisal of real estate and real estate advisor and real estate brokerage on nonresidential properties.[1] | |
| 15. Issuance and sale of travelers checks[1] | 17. Operating a Pool Reserve plan for loss reserves of banks for loans to small businesses[1] | |
| | 18. Operating a thrift institution in Rhode Island | |
| | 19. Operating a guarantee savings bank in New Hampshire[1] | |
| | 20. Offering informational advice and transactional services for foreign exchange services[1] | |

[1] Added to list since January 1, 1975.
[2] Activities permissible to national banks.
[3] Board orders found these activities closely related to banking but denied proposed acquisitions as part of its "go slow" policy.
[4] To be decided on a case-by-case basis.
[5] Operating a thrift institution has been permitted by order in Rhode Island, Ohio, New Hampshire, and California.
[6] Subsequently permitted by regulation.

NOTE: See also additions to this list, in 1986, indicated in footnote 27.

SOURCE: Federal Reserve Bank of Atlanta, *Economic Review*, May 1983, p. 11, from Federal Reserve Board data.

bank banks.[30] In 1987, Congress acted on this question, and its Competitive Equality Banking Act of 1987 was signed by President Reagan on August 10. This act prohibited new "nonbank banks" (also called limited service banks) and placed a temporary moratorium on bank expansion into the fields of insurance, real estate, and securities underwriting. Thus deregulation for banks with respect to the products or services they may provide has been at least delayed.

Meanwhile, state governments have been making regional agreements to permit bank holding companies from other states to own banks in a given state, on a reciprocal basis. It seems likely that interstate banking on a broad scale will become a reality sooner than was expected a few years ago. If so, banks will have obtained deposit interest rate deregulation and geographic deregulation, but face delay in expansion of services into the fields of insurance, real estate, and/or securities underwriting.

### Expansion of International Banking

International banking has become a major activity for many U.S. banks in recent years. Domestically, international banking activities of major banks have expanded, and even medium-sized banks outside financial centers have established international banking departments because of international activities of customers. Larger banks have also significantly increased loans to foreign business firms, governments, and financial institutions. Some of these loans have been made to less developed countries (LDCs) to help them finance necessary imports. In a few cases, LDC loans have had to be renegotiated, but outright defaults have not yet occurred on a large scale.

An important extension of international banking has been the growth of overseas offices.[31] U.S. banks have established foreign branches, Edge Act subsidiaries, and holding company subsidiaries.[32] They have also acquired equity interests in foreign financial institutions. There have been a number of reasons for these developments. First, major U.S. banks developed overseas branch and affiliate networks to meet needs of their corporate customers. Many had grown into multinational firms and banks often found that they could serve their customers best by maintaining branches or subsidiaries in countries where these firms conducted business. Also,

---

[30] For more details on nonbank banks, see Janice M. Moulton, "Nonbank Banks: Catalyst for Interstate Banking," Federal Reserve Bank of Philadelphia, *Business Review*, November–December 1985, pp. 3–18. The Supreme Court's decision relating to nonbank banks was reported in *The Wall Street Journal*, January 23, 1986, p. 3.

[31] In 1965, 13 U.S. banks had a total of 180 foreign branches. By 1975, 125 U.S. banks operated 732 branches abroad. Over the same period, assets of foreign branches rose from about $9.1 billion to over $150 billion. See Richard A. Debs, "International Banking," Federal Reserve Bank of New York, *Monthly Review*, June 1975, pp. 122–129.

[32] Edge Act corporations are bank subsidiaries whose activities are restricted to financial operations in foreign countries. A bank is allowed to have a maximum of five such subsidiaries, each of which may have an office in the United States. Although such offices are not permitted to make loans or investments within the United States or to accept domestic deposits, they may do everything but the final loan approval and, hence, in effect, carry on a form of de facto interstate banking.

during the period 1963 to 1974, government programs restricted the outflow of capital from the United States and put pressure on U.S. firms operating abroad to borrow abroad, and on banks to meet these needs through overseas facilities.

A second reason for the growth of overseas banking after 1965 was the effect of Regulation Q ceilings on banks' sources of funds. As noted earlier, during the credit crunches of 1966, 1967–1970, and 1980–1982, banks found it expedient to borrow funds (Eurodollars) through branches in London and other foreign financial centers.

Third, U.S. banks expanded their overseas operations to compete more effectively for loan and deposit accounts of foreign businesses. In the process, some banks engaged in activities that are not permitted for banks in the United States. An example is "merchant banking" activities whereby banks combine short-term and intermediate-term activities of banks as they operate in the United States with long-term financing through underwriting of business firms' bond and equity issues. Other activities were not as distinctive but perhaps merit mention, for example, syndicating Eurodollar loans and leasing. Banks in the United States syndicate loans when the credit is too large for safe incorporation in the portfolio of a single bank. Syndication of Eurodollar loans is somewhat complicated, however, because such loans are large, may be in a number of currencies, and may be made for operations in several countries. Leasing is also done in the United States, but international leasing activities are complicated by tax and legal differences among countries.

Finally, tax considerations have also contributed to the growth of foreign branches of U.S. banks. So-called "shell" branches in such places as Nassau in the Bahamas are "tax havens" because of low tax rates on business income. By channeling income into a shell branch, which is a "shell" because it does no local business, a bank may reduce its overall tax payments.

Wider fluctuations in exchange rates after early 1973 prompted many banks to increase their foreign exchange trading, sometimes with a view to avoiding losses in holding currencies that seemed likely to fall in value. Some losses were incurred, and these contributed to some extent to some widely publicized bank failures, such as that of Franklin National Bank, twentieth largest in the United States, and the Bankhaus Herstatt in Germany. Although such failures caused banks to exercise greater care in foreign exchange trading, the international banking system in general successfully weathered the difficulties caused by the oil price changes and the worldwide recession of 1973–1975.

New difficulties arose during the worldwide recession of 1980 to 1982, including possibilities of default and the necessity of restructuring debt (extending maturities, etc.) for countries such as Mexico and Poland. These difficulties created caution in international lending. There was also a tendency to close some branches in centers in which banking was less profitable, although new branches were being opened in some developing countries.

Thus, the period of rapid growth in overseas offices of U.S. banks may have come to an end in the mid-1970s. Risk in some countries has increased, the opportunity to participate in the Eurodollar market has been adequately met in some areas, and some·banks have begun to question the need to have branches in areas in which foreign correspondent banks can serve their purposes equally well. Future growth may continue at a slower pace.

Foreign banks have also been expanding their overseas operations, especially in the United States. For many of the reasons that U.S. banks went abroad, major banks in other countries have come to the United States. By mid-1982, there were 134 foreign banks operating in the United States. Foreign banking in the United States was still expanding. Although this was less than 1 percent of the total number of banks in the United States, foreign banks held about 5½ percent of total bank assets.

Until 1978, foreign banking operations in the United States were largely regulated by the individual states. Since only a few states allowed foreign banks to establish offices within their jurisdiction, most notably New York, California, and Illinois, foreign banking has been concentrated in a few geographical areas. However, foreign banks have been allowed to operate offices in more than one state, where state law permits. In May 1978, 63 banks with 122 banking offices operated in two or more states. This contrasts with the situation of U.S. banks, which are, with one exception, forbidden to engage in interstate banking.[33]

With the passage of the International Banking Act of 1978 (IBA), there was established for the first time a *national* policy for regulating foreign banks' activities in the United States. In brief, the act provides that, whereas the branch banking activities of foreign banks shall remain in the province of the individual states, these foreign-owned bank branches shall be restricted in their competition with domestic banks for loans and deposits not closely related to international finance. Further, although not requiring membership in the Federal Reserve System, the act provides that all branches and agencies of large foreign banks (worldwide assets of $1 billion or more) shall be subject to Federal Reserve reserve requirements. Finally, foreign banks are now subject to additional restrictions covering the underwriting and sale of stocks in the United States, an activity denied domestic banks since the 1930s by the Glass-Steagall Act. The intent of the new legislation was to provide more equal treatment for foreign and domestic banks while retaining the long-standing tradition of states' rights in commercial banking.[34]

Beginning in December 1981, banks and other depository institutions were permitted to establish international banking facilities (IBFs) for international financial transactions. Such facilities could engage in international banking activities without the reserve and deposit insurance requirements otherwise imposed, and without the interest rate limitations. Eurodollar deposits can be held in such facilities, and it was thought that these deposits might be attracted from the Bahamas, the Cayman Islands, and perhaps other places. The advantage is the presumed greater economic and political stability in the United States. Foreign banks saw an opportunity for international activity in the United States without reserve and deposit insurance require-

---

[33] The exception is the Bank of California, which had offices in California, Oregon, and Washington before such interstate banking was prohibited.

[34] Regulation of foreign banks in the United States under the IBA and other rules is described in Betsy Buttrill White, "Foreign Banking in the United States: A Regulatory and Supervisory Perspective," Federal Reserve Bank of New York, *Quarterly Review*, Summer 1982, pp. 48–58.

ments; Japanese banks, which had no offices in the Bahamas, established IBFs. In less than a year, about 400 banking institutions had established IBFs, and their total assets were nearly $160 billion. To be more active, IBFs needed permission to hold deposits smaller than $100,000, to issue negotiable CDs, and to accept overnight deposits from nonfinancial institutions.[35]

### Banking, the Payments Mechanism, and the Consumer

In domestic markets, there has been continued growth in "retail banking." Commercial banks, especially those outside money market centers, have moved aggressively into consumer lending and have expanded their financing of housing. More recently, banks of all sizes have increasingly participated in credit card plans that have enabled them to penetrate into new consumer and retailer markets and to promote fuller utilization of the banks' wide range of financial services.

In addition, the introduction of automatic transfer services (ATS) in 1978 provided consumers with, in essence, checking accounts that earn interest. Although these services differ from bank to bank, most are set up to transfer funds from a personal savings account to a checking account, to cover checks presented to the bank for collection. Thus, in such cases consumers are paid interest on what amounts to transactions-type balances. The Monetary Control Act of 1980 provided that automatic transfer services could be provided by insured banks and that NOW accounts could be offered for individuals and for certain nonprofit organizations by all depository institutions. Banks and other depository institutions were permitted to pay interest on NOW accounts.

Electronic funds transfer systems (EFTSs) are altering the nation's payments mechanism and are providing banks and other financial institutions with a means of offering new and improved consumer services at lower cost.[36] These electronic transfer arrangements are discussed in Chapter 6. There are now over 1,000 experiments being conducted throughout the country whereby individuals and businesses are able to receive and disburse funds through electronic credits or debits to their deposits rather than through the use of checks. Here are some examples of present-day applications of EFTSs: employers can pay workers by making electronic deposits to employees' checking accounts; individuals can preauthorize checkless payments of certain recurring bills, for example, mortgage payments, insurance premiums, utility bills; bills can be paid and funds transferred between accounts directly by telephone. In addition, point-of-sale terminals in retail establishments can be used to verify checks,

---

[35] Under the Depository Institutions Deregulation and Monetary Control Act (DIDMCA), foreign banks in the United States that hold deposits must in general meet the same reserve and deposit insurance requirements as U.S. banks; IBFs are excepted. For more details on the development of IBFs, see Hang-Sheng Cheng, "From the Caymans," Federal Reserve Bank of San Francisco, *Weekly Letter*, February 13, 1981; and Peter Koenig, "Whatever Happened to New York's IBFs?" *Institutional Investor*, April 1982, pp. 229–231.

[36] See Robert E. Knight, "The Changing Payment Mechanism: Electronic Funds Transfer Arrangements," Federal Reserve Bank of Kansas City, *Monthly Review*, July–August 1974, pp. 10–20.

transfer funds from customers to vendors, or dispense cash. Some of these services are also available at automated teller machines and cash dispensers. The continued growth of such facilities may, in the future, reduce the need for bank branches.

If these applications of EFTSs prove to be economically feasible and if they are accepted by the public, the payments mechanism will change dramatically in the years ahead. In the process, banks and other financial institutions will find it profitable to offer the public an increasing array of services made possible by the new technology. Some believe that a "checkless" society is not too far in the future, but some use of checks will no doubt continue for a long time. The technical and capital requirements for a nationwide EFTS are formidable. There is also considerable evidence that consumers are not as yet willing to participate on a scale that would ensure the profitability of such an enterprise. As one observer has noted, "most consumers will not willingly opt for EFTSs. That being so, it seems likely the EFTSs will either have to be forced upon them or will remain a marginal development, at least until the costs of the existing transfer system press heavily upon consumers and until ways are found to overcome some of the more undesirable features of EFTS."[37] These features include consumers' loss of control over certain financial decisions, such as which bills to pay and when; reduction or elimination of floating checks; overdrawing one's account in the expectation that a subsequent deposit will clear before one's check; loss of privacy under a system of computerized data; and elimination of canceled checks as proof of payment.

Some, perhaps most, of these undesirable features can be remedied in a carefully constructed EFTS. For example, the provision of overdraft facilities would enable qualified consumers to make purchases in excess of their existing deposit balances. The right to stop payment within a specified period would also permit some control over personal finances. Adequate records of payments might also be possible without the use of canceled checks. Nonetheless, the problem of personal privacy may prove to be more difficult to solve, and it is a matter of utmost concern to the most important element in any EFTS—the consumer.[38]

For some time, the expansion of bank services for consumers led to increase in the number and size of branches. But as an EFTS system comes into being, it is clear that many branches can serve the needs of most of the consumers in particular areas without being large or well staffed. In fact, in some areas an automatic teller machine (ATM) standing alone may suffice. Thus what began as expansion of branches is likely to continue in the future as reduction in the number of major branches and concentration of bank services in "hub" branches located in areas where consumers are likely to need a variety of bank services. The Bank of America alone has reduced the number of its branches in California by more than 200.

[37] Peter H. Schuck, "Electronic Funds Transfer: A Technology in Search of a Market," *The Economics of a National Electronic Funds Transfer System*, Federal Reserve Bank of Boston, October 1974, p. 163.

[38] See "EFT and Privacy," *Federal Reserve Bulletin*, April 1978, pp. 279–284.

# THE BASIS FOR AND THE PURPOSES OF REGULATION OF COMMERCIAL BANKS

Commercial banks are very heavily regulated, more so than most industries. In terms of government regulation and control, business firms in the United States fall into one of three categories. At one end of the spectrum are firms in the utilities area that are "vested with a public interest," accorded certain rights and responsibilities by government, and regulated as public utilities. At the other end are the vast majority of business enterprises that are much less subject to government control, except for broad guidelines and constraints imposed by the antitrust laws. Somewhere in between are the financial institutions, all regulated and supervised to one degree or another. The location of the banking industry in this spectrum of control has changed from one time period to another as new laws were passed governing its activities or new interpretations of existing laws were handed down by the courts or by the regulatory agencies.

Regulation over commercial banks is exercised at both the federal and state level, a historical result of our system of "dual banking," under which a bank is chartered by either the federal or a state government. A federally chartered bank is a "national" bank, subject to regulation and supervision by the Comptroller of the Currency. It must also be a member of the Federal Reserve System and must have deposit insurance coverage by the Federal Deposit Insurance Corporation, and is to some extent regulated by the banking authority of the state in which it does business. State-chartered banks may join the Federal Reserve System and may obtain insurance coverage from the FDIC. As shown in Table 3–6, most banks are state-chartered, nonmember, insured banks. In practice, to avoid duplication, the responsibility for the regulation of commercial banks is divided insofar as possible (see Table 3–7).

Some state banking authorities would object that they have more authority than may be inferred from Table 3–7, especially over insured nonmember banks. A council of regulatory agencies has been established to work out cooperation. It remains to be seen whether state authorities can halt the trend toward federal regulation, especially since *all* banks must now hold reserves at the Fed.

The scope of government regulation is very broad and affects both the *structure* of the banking industry and the *practices* of the individual banks. The number of banks and banking offices, their relative sizes, the geographical distribution of banking facilities—the structure of the industry—is partly the result of government decisions concerning proposed entrants, mergers, or branching of existing banks. Practices and policies of banks are also subject to a wide range of proscriptions that limit or prohibit certain types of assets or liabilities in bank portfolios or rates of interest charged borrowers or paid to depositors. Other regulations prohibit banks from buying stocks of private business firms and from holding corporate bonds that do not meet certain standards of quality.

**TABLE 3–6**
**Classification of Banks and Assets Held as of December 31, 1980**

| | Number of Banks | | Assets | |
|---|---|---|---|---|
| | Number | Percent | Amount (billions of dollars) | Percent |
| Charter | | | | |
| National | 4,425 | 30% | $  875 | 57% |
| State | 10,279 | 70 | 668 | 43 |
| Total | 14,704 | 100% | $1,443 | 100% |
| Membership in FRS | | | | |
| Member | 5,422 | 37 | 1,142 | 74 |
| Nonmember | 9,282 | 63 | 401 | 26 |
| Total | 14,704 | 100% | $1,543 | 100% |
| Membership in FDIC | | | | |
| Insured | 14,435 | 98 | 1,539 | 100 |
| Noninsured | 269 | 2 | 5 | * |
| Total | 14,704 | 100% | $1,544 | 100% |

* Less than ½ percent.
SOURCE: Federal Deposit Insurance Corporation, Annual Report, 1980, pp. 226, 243.

## The Basis for Regulating Banks

The particular set of laws now impinging upon financial institutions in the United States is the outgrowth of a long and interesting history.[39] Four very general observations can be made. First, the Constitution gives authority for control over the supply of money to the federal government.[40] For the several states to allow such power to rest in a central government was probably no less of a relinquishment of authority than was that allowing the federal government control over the army and navy. But the several states retained many rights, among them the right to charter corporations and regulate financial practices, inasmuch as these rights were not specifically vested in the federal government. Thus the struggle between federal and state governments for power and control has helped create a diversity of regulatory authority.

Second, U.S. history is replete with episodes of financial panic. Attempts to provide the country with a central bank after 1836 failed repeatedly to receive con-

[39] See the interesting chapter by H. E. Krooss and M. R. Blyn on "The Evolution of U.S. Money and Capital Markets and Financial Intermediaries" in Murray E. Polakoff et al., eds., *Financial Institutions and Markets* (Boston: Houghton Mifflin, 1970), pp. 62–82.

[40] Article I, Section 8, of the Constitution reads "The Congress shall have Power to . . . coin Money, regulate the Value thereof, and of foreign Coin and fix the Standard of Weights and Measures;."

**TABLE 3–7**
**Categories of Banks and Their Major Regulatory Agencies**

| Category of Bank | Major Regulatory Agency |
| --- | --- |
| National banks | Comptroller of the Currency |
| State member banks | Federal Reserve System |
| Insured nonmember banks | Federal Deposit Insurance Corporation |
| Uninsured banks | State banking authorities |

gressional sanction. Hence the Treasury exercised erratic control over the money supply by purchase of gold and silver and coinage of these metals, and later by issue of paper money in the form of silver and, later, gold certificates. Banks were chartered by states, which imposed inadequate regulations, and a period preceding the Civil War is now referred to as the "Age of Wildcat Banking." Banks in nearly every small community in the West began issuing their own notes, liabilities that circulated as currency. Failure was frequent, and public trust was shattered. After establishment of the national banking system at the time of the Civil War, a federal tax was levied on notes issued by state banks to stop their issue, and states began to exercise greater control over bank activities.

Third, a large set of regulatory controls grew out of the disaster of the Great Depression of the 1930s. The general failure of the economy and widespread failures of financial institutions led to a proliferation of laws and regulations and the establishment of a variety of supervisory agencies and government-operated financial intermediaries.

Fourth, election of President Reagan in 1980 began a period of deregulation of business. Controls over transportation services were relaxed, and banks and other depository institutions were given broader powers by the Depository Institutions Deregulation and Monetary Control Act of 1980 and the Depository Institutions Act of 1982. However, many still believe that banks should be regulated more than other businesses, even though this restricts competition.

Whatever the merits of the argument for restrictions on bank competition in the 1930s and for some time thereafter, it is difficult to support the argument today. Today, the competitive threat to banks is coming not so much from other banks, or even from other depository institutions, but from nonfinancial institutions and from conglomerates that include both financial and nonfinancial subsidiaries.

The problem is how to protect the *public*, without necessarily protecting banks from results of their own mistakes. Banks and other financial institutions often prefer regulation. For example, only a few years ago, savings institutions in California asked the state regulatory commission to restrict the value of a gift offered to customers for opening new accounts to $2 or less. In fact, one of the first acts of the Depository Institutions Deregulation Committee, established under the Depository Institutions Deregulation and Monetary Control Act of 1980, was to propose the prohibiting of the offering of premiums and gifts.

## Purposes and Effects of Regulation

The purposes of bank regulation may be classified under four general headings: (1) to provide safety for the public, especially for those with insufficient financial knowledge to judge safety of an institution into which they deposit funds, (2) to limit banks that must pay higher interest or offer higher premiums than they can "afford," (3) to limit ownership of risky assets by banks, and (4) to restrict concentration of banking (including merger and holding company activities) that might create monopoly or oligopoly and thus raise the costs of banking services to the public.

### Safety for the Public

The major provision intended to provide safety for the public is deposit insurance. A maximum limit per account is set because it is presumed that wealthier investors can judge for themselves whether banks are safe.

Clearly, the major reasons for regulating banks, to protect the public, are that (1) banks create money, which is needed for most transactions, and (2) banks operate the payments system (payments by check and by electronic transfer), which is essential at all times (when all banks were closed for a short period in 1933, payments could not be made in the usual manner—thus, for example, many people obtained groceries only because grocers extended credit).

Recently there has been discussion of another way in which banks may be unique or at least special: bank loans, among sources of borrowing, appear to have some special features. Banks are the major suppliers of short-term business loans, especially to medium-sized and small business firms. (Large, well-known firms can also obtain funds by sale of commercial paper.) Banks usually gather and maintain a large amount of information concerning firms to which they lend, and these firms also tend to be continuing depositors at the banks from which they borrow. There is evidence that bank loans to firms are followed by increases in prices of stocks of those firms, whereas this does not occur when firms borrow by issuing bonds or other debt. New bank loans or bank renewals seem to indicate that banks have examined the financial condition of the borrowing firms, and were willing to lend.

Other evidence comes from the market for negotiable CDs. Such CDs now require 3 percent in reserves; thus banks have increased cost when they issue such CDs—because reserves are nonearning assets. Thus negotiable CDs issued by banks might be expected to have lower yields than other money market instruments to compensate for the cost of holding increased reserves, but this does not seem to have been true. Banks could raise their loan interest rates to compensate for the added cost of issuing negotiable CDs, but this could be true only if bank loans are in some way "special"—i.e., have no close substitutes.

Thus it seems that bank loans *are* "special," and if this is true it can be argued that regulatory changes should take into consideration this special nature of bank business loans, and preferably should not adversely affect their cost and availability.[41]

---

[41] These comments draw heavily upon Christopher James, "Are Bank Loans Special?" Federal Reserve Bank of San Francisco, *Weekly Letter*, July 24, 1987.

### Regulation Q and Other Interest Rate Ceilings

The major provisions limiting interest payments have been the prohibition of payment of interest on demand deposits, the ceilings on interest rates under Federal Reserve Regulation Q and other regulations, and various limits on gifts and premiums.

Historically, interest rate ceilings were related to the opposition to usury, defined as "an exorbitant rate of interest." Opposition to usury originated in ancient times, when most lending was to consumers (usually poor people), and high interest rates were a heavy burden on the poor. The term "loan shark" was for a time applied to such lenders. With the industrial revolution, however, the basis for interest changed: business borrowing occurred because borrowing and spending for investment generated *increased* income. Business loans became more important than consumer loans. The ancient idea that "money is barren" or "money is not fruitful" was not valid for business lending. Nevertheless, the old idea that interest is somehow "wrong," especially if interest rates are high, still affects the thought of many people.

Usury laws have been imposed by many states, and rate limits vary. Even neighboring states have varying usury limits on various types of consumer loans. For larger business loans, mortgage loans, and loans made by national and state banks, savings and loan associations, and credit unions, usury ceilings were eliminated by the 1980 law, although they could have been reimposed by states during a limited time. The 1980 law also provided for the gradual elimination of the regulation of interest rates paid on time deposits; this meant, of course, elimination of the legal basis for payment of slightly higher interest rates by savings institutions than by commercial banks. Legislation in 1982 required the removal of this differential in 1984.

Research studies have found that usury laws have an adverse effect on the supply of credit. State laws can be circumvented by banks and other institutions conducting certain operations in other states.[42] Since ceilings normally have not applied to *all* lending, even uniform usury rates simply cause lending to be diverted to types of loans on which there are no ceiling rates.

Unregulated interest rates tend to rise by a percentage equal to, or slightly less than, the rate of inflation, for reasons discussed in later chapters. Unless inflation is judged to be acceptable, the best way to reduce interest rates is to reduce the inflation rate. As demonstrated in the period 1981–1986, when the inflation rate falls, interest rates also fall, although after considerable time lag.

Regulation Q has been eliminated (in 1986) and is no longer in effect.

### Limiting Ownership of Risky Assets by Banks

Bank ownership of risky assets has been limited by provisions making only federal government securities, municipal securities, and certain high-quality corporate securities eligible for bank investment. Moreover, banks in the United States are

---

[42] For a useful review of the results of economic studies of usury laws and interest rate ceilings, see Donna Vandenbrink, "The Effects of Usury Ceilings," Federal Reserve Bank of Chicago, *Economic Perspectives*, Midyear 1982, pp. 44–55.

forbidden to own stocks, and any stock that may be acquired (for example, in foreclosure on collateral for loans) must be disposed of within a relatively limited time period.[43]

Other restrictions have been imposed to prevent concentration of bank loans in single firms or industries. Diversification is a well-known means of reducing risk, and one long-established rule was that banks could not lend more than 10 percent of bank capital stock and surplus to one borrower, although there were a number of exceptions to this for secured loans and other cases in which risk was believed to be reduced. The Depository Institutions Act of 1982, however, recognized that this limit might well prevent small- and medium-sized banks from meeting the needs of business, and it provided that a national bank may lend up to 15 percent of its capital and surplus on an unsecured loan to a single borrower and 10 percent more than that on loans that required collateral.[44]

Since property and casualty insurance entails more risk than life insurance or credit life insurance, this act also prohibited banks from selling property and casualty insurance.[45] Risk is greater in property and casualty insurance because losses vary much more than deaths and because inflation made losses, even after allowing for depreciation, much larger. If inflation again became more serious, losses could mount.

### Restrictions on Concentration of Banking

Restrictions on concentration are another aspect of bank regulation. In this case the objective is prevention of monopoly or oligopoly that might create the opportunity for monopoly profits instead of reducing risk. In one sense this regulation is quite different—it is aimed at maintaining competition rather than at restricting competition. Banking law has been ambivalent—in some periods, regulation has tended to encourage competition, while in other periods it has tended to limit competition and thus provide conditions favorable to monopolistic practices. The ambivalence is well illustrated in the restrictions on entry into banking. In some countries banks may be started as easily as one might open a shoe store. In the United States, a bank charter can be obtained only if the organizers can persuade the authorities (state or federal) that the new bank is needed to serve the "convenience and needs" of the community and that it will not seriously harm existing banks.

The major legislation aimed at restriction of concentration in banking includes limitations on branch banking (on the basis that branches of large banks may compete with and harm smaller local banks), limitations on mergers, and the laws related to bank holding companies. Enforcement of the bank holding company legislation is

[43] Another method of discouraging excessive risk-taking might be to vary the premium charged for deposit insurance. See Ronald D. Watson, "Insuring Some Progress in the Bank Capital Hassle," Federal Reserve Bank of Philadelphia, *Business Review*, July–August 1974, pp. 3–18.

[44] For comments on the probable benefits to small- and medium-sized banks, such as regional banks, see *Business Week*, November 22, 1982, p. 103. The money center banks have such large amounts of capital and surplus that few borrowers are likely to need loans of 15 to 25 percent of those banks' capital and surplus.

[45] *Business Week*, October 18, 1982, p. 90.

primarily in the hands of the Board of Governors of the Federal Reserve System.[46]

Branch banking is still totally prohibited in a few states; in those states a bank may have only *one* office. In some states this results in many small banks, since small towns cannot support large banks. Many studies have shown some economies of scale in banking, at least up to some size of bank, and it is generally agreed that the very small banks common in some states are likely to be inefficient and may be prone to failure in adverse circumstances. In most states, branch banking is either allowed statewide or is gradually being extended. Maps showing the legal status indicate a gradual spread of more extensive branch banking, but, of course, only within a given state. There is no provision for branches outside a given state, although some offices may be established that perform some of the functions of branches (except taking deposits).

Limitations on bank mergers are imposed by the application of the Clayton Act to banks, most notably in the *Philadelphia National Bank* decision by the Supreme Court in 1963. In that case the Supreme Court noted that mergers are illegal if their effect "may be substantially to lessen competition" in a line of commerce (product or service market) in a section of the country (geographic area). The Court defined commercial banks as institutions that provide a single product or, rather, a unique cluster of products and services that together constitute a "line of commerce." Thus when a merger appears likely to increase the degree of concentration in a local market, so that the merged banks would have what the regulators deem to be an unduly large share, such a merger is not approved. Given this concept, competition of savings and loan associations and other institutions is ignored; it is presumed that they cannot provide the same "unique cluster of services" that banks provide. Recently, economists have begun to question the "single line of commerce" approach. They argue that although certain mergers might give the merged banks an undesirably large share of the total banking market if banking is viewed as a single line of commerce, this might not be true for a number of bank services if viewed individually. For example, a merger might give the merged banks a large share of total *bank* loans to small businesses in the area, but there might be other institutions in the area that could compete in making such loans. Thus the merged banks might *not* have a large share of the total market for *small business loans*.[47] In examining other areas of banking services, even a large share of loans to large business firms made in a given area might not matter, because large firms usually bank with and borrow from more than one bank—often from banks in several areas.

[46] The Bank Holding Company Act (BHCA) of 1956 defined banks as institutions chartered as banks or trust companies. Then it was modified to define them as institutions that accept demand deposits, with the explanation that savings banks and trust companies need not be included. In the 1970 amendments, the definition was changed to cover the acceptance of demand deposits *and* the making of commercial loans. In the Citicorp/Fidelity case (October 1982), the Board concluded the thrift institutions (in this case, a savings and loan association) are not "banks." With the power given to other depository institutions at the beginning of 1984 to place 10 percent of their assets in commercial loans (under the Garn-St Germain bill), it becomes increasingly difficult to separate banks from certain nonbank institutions. Modifications in the law attempting to clarify the distinction are quite likely to be offered. See John J. Di Clemente, "What Is a Bank?" Federal Reserve Bank of Chicago, *Economic Perspectives*, January–February 1983, pp. 20–31.

[47] See, for example, F. Jay Cummings, "Commercial Banking as a Line of Commerce: Time for Change?" Federal Reserve Bank of Dallas, *Economic Review*, September 1982, pp. 11–20.

Regulation of bank holding companies has been intended to prevent monopoly or oligopoly positions similar to those obtained by mergers. Also, the 1970 amendment of the Bank Holding Company Act restricted subsidiaries of bank holding companies to "activities which are closely related to banking or managing and controlling banks." As we discuss in Chapter 4, competition is now facing banks from retail stores and conglomerates, which are not limited to any single area (geographic or product). As such institutions continue to expand their financial services, banks find themselves regulated, whereas their competitors are much less regulated.

### Effects of Bank Regulation

Regulation of banking affects efficiency in banking, growth of banking, and ability of the banking industry to compete with nonbank and nonfinancial institutions. Regulation of banking that protects small banks may not promote efficiency. If there are significant "economies of scale" in the production of banking services, then larger banks are able to provide services at lower unit costs. Some observers believe that significant economies of scale do exist. The manager of a branch of a large bank may offer more services to a customer than may the manager of a unit bank the same size as the branch office. This is because a branch can tap the resources of its head office. Thus, to insist on an all-unit bank system, as was the case in the state of Illinois, for example, may deny customers services they otherwise might have obtained. Allowing banks to penetrate their rivals' markets may be the best way of promoting competition. At present, most unit banks are small, *and* most communities are served by fewer than three banks; therefore, merging of small banks and allowing large banks to branch into each other's territory (perhaps by branching across state lines), but not allowing large banks to expand inside of their own market areas, might increase competition among banks.

Except for special offices, such as the U.S. offices of Edge Act subsidiaries of banks and loan production offices authorized by the Federal Reserve System to permit banks to generate (but not finalize) loans outside the states in which they operate regular banking offices, no commercial bank in the United States can operate offices in more than one state (with one exception: a bank that had such offices long ago). A state bank may branch only within the state that chartered it, and the McFadden Act limited national banks to branching no more extensive than that permitted for state banks. The McFadden Act was under review by the president in 1980, but thus far no legislation has made changes that would explicitly permit interstate branching. Studies have been made of the competitive effects of interstate banking.[48] Elimination of the McFadden Act restriction on interstate banking would probably increase concentration in larger banks in the banking industry, but would also increase competition among the larger banks.[49]

---

[48] Stephen A. Rhoades, "The Competitive Effects of Interstate Banking," *Federal Reserve Bulletin*, January 1980, pp. 1–8.

[49] See "Interstate Banking Laws," special issue, Federal Reserve Bank of Atlanta, *Economic Review*, March 1985.

The question of how a growing economy is to provide growth of banking services—through *more* banks or through banks of *larger size*—depends primarily upon the stance taken by regulatory authorities.

Issues concerning safety and efficiency and just how to obtain the optimum banking system are unresolved. Many economists and financial market observers agree that certain changes in our regulatory framework are desirable. Some argue that many parts of the present system of regulation are disruptive of banking practices and expensive in terms of wasted resources and tend to promote a misallocation of resources. They are disruptive of banking practices because they arbitrarily interfere with bank portfolio policies, and there is often an implicit assumption that banking supervisory personnel know better than bankers what income-risk positions are best. Regulations are also often expensive in terms of resources, not only because of direct costs of conforming to them, but also because they induce banks to devote effort in search of alternative sources and uses of funds.[50]

Finally, regulations often promote a misallocation of resources by preventing market forces and relative cost considerations from determining the final allocation. An obvious example is the interest rate ceilings of time deposits, which for a time made it possible for financial institutions to make mortgage loans at relatively low interest rates but then, when market interest rates rose, severely restricted their ability to make such loans at any rates. "Too much" funds for housing at one period became "too little" funds for housing later. (The terms "too much" and "too little" are used only to mean more or less funds than would have been obtained in a free market.)

As more banking services are provided by nonbank and nonfinancial institutions that are able to provide nationwide services, restriction of bank services to branches within one state seriously limits their ability to compete. As is often the case, legislation is slower to change than are markets and technology. But legislation has made it possible for banks to compete more effectively in some ways. The entire financial services industry is changing significantly, with new institutions entering the field, new legislation changing the powers of various institutions, and events causing regulatory authorities to permit activities that under other circumstances they might have denied.[51]

---

[50] An example is the Community Reinvestment Act of 1977 (CRA), designed to encourage federally insured commercial banks, mutual savings banks, and savings and loan associations to help meet the credit needs of the local communities in which they are chartered. One evaluation indicated that after three years, it appeared that costs of the CRA were heavy and benefits not clearly present. Thus the value of this regulation was doubtful; see Norman N. Bowsher, "The Three-Year Experience with the Community Reinvestment Act," Federal Reserve Bank of St. Louis, *Review*, February 1982, pp. 3–10.

[51] An example is the permission of the regulatory authorities for the purchase of Fidelity Savings, a savings and loan association in San Francisco, by Citicorp, the holding company that owns Citibank, located in New York. A new competitor thus entered the California financial market, and this was one step toward the "halting but inexorable birth of interstate banking," although Citicorp signed an agreement pledging to continue to operate Fidelity as a savings and loan association, so that it is not yet a commercial bank. For more details, see Gary Hector, "Citicorp Goes West," *Fortune*, November 29, 1982, pp. 83–90.

## SUMMARY

Commercial banks are probably still the most important intermediaries in the financial markets. They provide a wide range of services to both depositors and borrowers.

Banks hold cash assets to meet reserve requirements, daily transactions needs, and the need to keep balances in correspondent banks through which they clear checks. Most bank funds, however, are used to acquire earning assets, primarily loans to business firms and consumers and investments in federal and in state and local government securities for both liquidity and income reasons.

Demand and time deposits are the most important sources of funds for banks, but in recent years banks have increasingly turned to other sources, such as borrowing Fed funds, borrowing from the Eurodollar market, and issuing negotiable CDs, as well as borrowing from the Fed.

Interest earned on loans is the major source of income for banks; interest paid on time deposits is now the major expense. A bank's net income depends on the size and composition of its assets and its liabilities, on the level and structure of interest rates, and on various government regulations. Asset and liability management has thus become the key policy area in bank financial management.

Long-run profitability is the main objective of a bank's portfolio policy. But to be profitable a bank must maintain an appropriate degree of safety and liquidity. Safety of assets is of paramount importance because banks have a relatively low capital/deposit ratio (equity/debt ratio). Liquidity of assets is necessary because of the short-term nature and volatility of many bank liabilities.

Over the years there have been changes in banking theory and practice concerning the management of a bank's liquidity position. The "real bills" doctrine, widely held prior to the 1930s, was replaced by the "shiftability" theory of liquidity that stressed the marketability of assets. Since the 1960s banks have found it profitable to manage their liabilities as well as their assets in meeting liquidity needs and in attempting to increase profits. Several new techniques and markets have developed, among them the market for negotiable CDs, Eurodollars, commercial paper issued by bank holding companies, and others.

Regulation of commercial banks is exercised at both the federal and state levels. Regulations affect the structure of the banking industry and the practices of individual banks. Some of the restrictions and controls were imposed to assure a "safe" banking system; others were imposed to promote efficiency, mainly by encouraging competition among banks. Many believe that these goals may at times be inconsistent with one another. Although views differ as to *what* changes ought to be made in bank regulation, many favor more liberal regulation of branching, mergers, and portfolio practices.

Commercial banks have become "department stores" of finance, engaging in many types of lending, some types of investing, and many activities closely related to lending and investing. In previous decades, government regulation limited these activities. But bank innovations in recent years, including the issue of negotiable CDs, broadened the role of banks in the U.S. financial structure. The development of the one-bank holding company, with a holding company owning a bank and also owning subsidiaries engaging in activities closely related to banking, has caused further change. Amendments to the Bank Holding Company Act passed in 1970 may have seemed restrictive. But the fact that Congress gave the Board of Governors of the Federal Reserve System the authority, subject to court review, to determine permissible activities of bank holding companies and their subsidiaries has opened the possibility of a broadening scope of activities. Some new and innovative services have been declared permissible, and the fact that one-bank and multibank holding companies control over two-thirds of all commercial bank deposits is significant.

## Appendix: Highlights of the Depository Institutions Deregulation and Monetary Control Act of 1980[52]

***Monetary Control Act.*** To facilitate control of the monetary aggregates, the Board of Governors can require all depository institutions (commercial banks, savings banks, savings and loan associations, and credit unions) to submit directly or indirectly reports of assets and liabilities.

Each depository institution must maintain reserves against transaction accounts—demand deposits, negotiable order of withdrawal (NOW) deposits, share draft deposits, and deposits subject to automatic and telephone transfer—in a ratio of 3 percent for amounts of $32 million or less and, initially, 12 percent for amounts in excess of $32 million. The statutory range for amounts in excess of $25 million is 8 percent to 14 percent. Reserves on nonpersonal time deposits must be held initially at a ratio of 3 percent. The legal range is 0 to 9 percent.

The $32 million level of transaction accounts is adjusted annually by the Board depending on the growth of the total level of transaction accounts nationwide.

If five Board members find that extraordinary circumstances exist, the Board may, after consultation with congressional banking committees, alter reserve ratios from the statutory ranges for renewable 180-day periods.

Five Board members also may impose a supplemental reserve requirement of up to 4 percent on an institution's transaction accounts.

The supplemental reserves may be held as vault cash or placed in an "earnings participation account," which will earn interest at a rate not exceeding what the Federal Reserve System open market account portfolio earned during the previous calendar quarter. No interest will be earned on supplemental reserves in the form of vault cash.

The Board may impose reserves on any depository institution's borrowings from its foreign offices, loans to U.S. residents by its foreign offices, and assets purchased by its foreign offices from its domestic offices.

Reserve requirements for nonmember depository institutions have been phased in evenly over seven years. Starting September 1, 1987, all nonmember depository

---

[52] Source: Federal Reserve Bank of New York, *Quarterly Review*, Summer 1980, pp. 12–13.

institutions, except those in Alaska and Hawaii, are subject to full reserve requirements. But reserves were required immediately for any new types of deposits or accounts authorized by Federal law after April 1, 1980. The necessary adjustments in reserve requirements for member banks were phased in over a three-year period.

Reserves must be in the form of Reserve Bank balances, but also, with Board consent, may be vault cash. Nonmembers may keep balances with correspondents, a Federal Home Loan Bank, or the National Credit Union Administration Central Liquidity Facility, if those institutions maintain balances at Reserve Banks.

Depository institutions with transaction accounts or nonpersonal time deposits are entitled to the same discount window privileges as member banks.

The Board published for comment a set of pricing principles and a proposed schedule of fees for Reserve Bank services before September 1, 1980. By September 1, 1981, the Board began to put a schedule of fees for services into effect.

*Depository Institutions Deregulation Act.* The act provides for the phase-out of limitations on interest and dividend rates paid by depository institutions by extending the authority to impose such limitations for six years, subject to specific standards designed to ensure their replacement by market rates. During the six-year period, the ¼ percent interest rate differential payable on certain accounts by commercial banks and thrift institutions continues.

A new Depository Institutions Deregulation Committee (DIDC) was created to assume authority to prescribe rules for payment of interest.

Voting members of the DIDC are the secretary of the Treasury, the chairman of the Board of Governors, the chairman of the board of the Federal Deposit Insurance Corporation (FDIC), the chairman of the Federal Home Loan Bank Board, and the chairman of the National Credit Union Administration (NCUA) Board. The Comptroller of the Currency is a nonvoting member.

The DIDC was required to exercise its authority to provide for the phase-out and ultimate elimination of interest and dividend rate ceilings as rapidly as permitted by economic conditions. It was also required to increase all interest and dividend rate ceilings to market rates as soon as feasible during the six-year period following March 31, 1980.

Within 18 months of March 31, 1980, the DIDC had to vote on at least a ¼ percent increase in the passbook account limit, and to vote on a ½ percent increase in the limit on all accounts not later than the end of the third, fourth, fifth, and sixth years after March 31, 1980.

*Consumer Checking Account Equity Act.* Member banks and FDIC-insured nonmember banks may continue to provide automatic transfers from savings to checking accounts.

NOW accounts were permitted nationwide December 31, 1980 at all depository institutions for individuals and certain nonprofit organizations.

Federally insured credit unions are authorized to offer share draft accounts.

Federal deposit insurance at commercial banks, savings banks, savings and loan associations, and credit unions is increased to $100,000 per account.

Federal credit unions can make residential real estate loans on residential cooperatives.

A federal credit union can charge up to 15 percent annually on loans. The NCUA Board may establish a higher loan interest ceiling for periods not to exceed 18 months.

***Powers of Thrift Institutions.***   Federal savings and loan associations may invest in shares or certificates of open-end investment companies registered with the Securities and Exchange Commission, if the portfolio of the investment company is restricted to certain investments that savings and loan associations may invest in directly.

Up to 20 percent of the assets of a federal savings and loan association may consist of consumer loans, commercial paper, and corporate debt securities.

Federal savings and loan associations may make real estate loans without regard to the geographic area, as well as acquisition, development, and construction loans.

Federal savings and loan associations may issue credit cards.

Federal savings and loan associations may exercise trust and fiduciary powers.

A federal mutual savings bank may have up to 5 percent of its assets as commercial, corporate, and business loans, if the loans are made only within the state where the bank is located or within 75 miles of the bank's home office.

A federal mutual savings bank may accept demand deposits in connection with a commercial, corporate, or business loan relationship.

***State Usury Laws.***   Effective April 1, 1980, state residential first mortgage real property, co-op, and mobile home usury ceilings were rendered inapplicable, unless prior to April 1, 1983 a state adopted a new usury ceiling or certified that its voters voted in favor of or to retain a state constitutional provision imposing a usury ceiling.

A state may adopt a law placing limitations on discount points or other charges on residential real estate, co-ops, and mobile homes.

Federally insured state-chartered commercial and mutual savings banks, branches of foreign banks, savings and loan associations, credit unions, and small business investment companies may charge interest on loans at a rate equal to 1 percentage point above the basic Federal Reserve discount rate. This excludes any surcharge imposed by a Reserve Bank.

## Questions for Discussion

**1.** Would you expect causes of the growth of time deposits to be different from causes of the growth of demand deposits? If so, what differences do you see?

**2.** Do banks prefer to make business loans (if possible) rather than consumer loans, mortgage loans, other loans, or investments? If so, what reasons can you suggest for this preference?

**3.** What reasons can you suggest for the higher reserves required for deposits in excess of certain amounts?

**4.** The negotiable CD was "invented" in the early 1960s. Indicate the reasons for this development and the effects it had on banks—their balance sheets, their earnings, their costs, and their competitive position vis-à-vis other institutions.

**5.** Of the three major sources of nondeposit debt funds (borrowing from the Federal Reserve System, purchasing Federal funds, and borrowing Eurodollars), which do you think banks prefer? Why? Does it depend on conditions? If so, what conditions?

**6.** Why is safety more important for bank portfolio selection than for most other institutions?

**7.** How has liquidity changed as a determinant of bank portfolio selection with the increase in nondeposit sources of debt funds?

**8.** Since most depositors are covered by FDIC insurance, why is a bank's capital position a matter of concern to bank customers? To the bank's management?

**9.** What is meant by the term "liability management" as applied to commercial banks? Why has the increased reliance on borrowed funds led to concern over the adequacy of bank capital?

**10.** Why are banks more closely regulated and supervised by government than most nonfinancial business firms? Why is it sometimes said that the goals of bank regulation are frequently inconsistent with one another?

## Selected References

An introduction to commercial bank portfolio policy is presented in Roland I. Robinson, *Management of Bank Funds*, 2nd ed. (New York: McGraw-Hill, 1972). This traditional view of banks as relatively passive lending institutions has been modified in recent years as the competition for funds has become more intense and as new markets and management techniques have developed.

A more sophisticated treatment of some aspects of portfolio policy is found in Howard Crosse and George H. Hempel, *Management Policies for Commercial Banks* (Englewood Cliffs, N.J.: Prentice-Hall, 1976), especially Chapters 8 and 9. The bases for policy decisions by bank managers are examined in George H. Hempel and Jess B. Yawitz, *Financial Management of Financial Institutions* (Englewood Cliffs, N.J.: Prentice-Hall, 1977), Chapter 5.

A plethora of articles on the regulation of commercial banks has ranged from description and appraisal of the regulatory framework to an evaluation of Regulation Q. The first two suggested readings are broad in coverage and are reprinted in several books of readings. The other articles deal with topics of special interest to students of financial markets.

Almarin Phillips, "Competition, Confusion, and Commercial Banking," *Journal of Finance*, March 1964, pp. 32–45.

Paul M. Horvitz, "Stimulating Bank Competition Through Regulatory Action," *Journal of Finance*, March 1965, pp. 1–13.

Robert Lindsay, *The Economics of Interest Rate Ceilings*, New York University Graduate School of Business Administration, December 1970.

Competition between banks and bank holding companies and nonfinancial business firms is discussed in a booklet by Cleveland A. Christophe, *Competition in Financial Services* (New York: First National City Corporation, 1974).

For rather detailed discussion, see Charles R. McNeill, "The Depository Institutions Deregulation and Monetary Control Act of 1980," *Federal Reserve Bulletin*, June 1980, pp. 444–453.

For a discussion of the extent of interstate banking activity and the ways in which it may expand in the future, see Federal Reserve Bank of Atlanta, *Economic Review*, March 1985. It is interesting to note that, because of the Douglas amendment to the Bank Holding Company Act of 1956, BankAmerica Corporation (holding company) could acquire Seattle-First National Bank in 1983 only after passage of a law, by the Washington state legislature, explicitly permitting this.

For a discussion of "nonbank banks," see Janice M. Moulton, "Nonbank Banks: Catalyst for Interstate Banking," Federal Reserve Bank of Philadelphia, *Business Review*, November–December 1985, pp. 3–18.

For a discussion of the end of Regulation Q (in 1986), see Paul Calem, "The New Bank Deposit Markets: Goodbye to Regulation Q," Federal Reserve Bank of Philadelphia, *Business Review*, November–December 1985, pp. 19–29.

For a discussion of the pricing of its services by the Federal Reserve System, see Anatoli Kuprianov, "An Analysis of Federal Reserve Pricing," Federal Reserve Bank of Richmond, *Economic Review*, March–April 1986, pp. 3–19.

For an analysis of the effects on commercial banks of the rise in inflation in the 1970s and its fall in the early 1980s, see G. J. Santoni, "The Effects of Inflation on Commercial Banks," Federal Reserve Bank of St. Louis, *Review*, March 1986, pp. 15–26.

For discussion of bank holding companies, see Charles S. Morris and Katherine M. Hecht, "Do Multibank Holding Companies Affect Banking Market Concentration?" Federal Reserve Bank of Kansas City, *Economic Review*, April 1986, pp. 19–30; and John H. Boyd and Stanley H. Graham, "Risk, Regulation, and Bank Holding Company Expansion into Nonbanking," Federal Reserve Bank of Minneapolis, *Quarterly Review*, Spring 1986, pp. 2–17.

For a comparative historical analysis of private versus Federal Reserve activity in the check handling and collection system, see James N. Duprey and Clarence W. Nelson, "A Visible Hand: The Fed's Involvement in the Check Payments System," Federal Reserve Bank of Minneapolis, *Quarterly Review*, Spring 1986, pp. 18–29.

For a technical analysis of regulation of bank capital, see Frederick T. Furlong and Michael C. Keeley, "Bank Capital Regulation and Asset Risk," Federal Reserve Bank of San Francisco, *Economic Review*, Spring 1987, pp. 20–40.

A general framework for reform of regulation of the financial system was suggested in 1987 by the president of the Federal Reserve Bank of New York; see E. Gerald Corrigan, "A Framework for Reform of the Financial System," Federal Reserve Bank of New York, *Quarterly Review*, Summer 1987, pp. 1–8. The guiding principles and specific changes suggested could be a basis for interesting discussion of the issues and problems involved.

# THE FINANCIAL SERVICES INDUSTRY: OTHER INSTITUTIONS

IV

There are many financial services, and if related activities are included, the list becomes very long. Even financial activities permissible for bank holding companies constitute a rather long list (see Table 3–5). Financial institutions other than banks provide many financial services; in recent years, nonfinancial institutions have begun to provide more such services.[1] Moreover, with changing technology, new services related to finance have become important: telecommunications and data processing are examples.

As a result, the financial services industry now includes many companies that are not purely financial institutions. Such firms as Sears, Roebuck and Company, American Express, Gulf & Western, Greyhound, Avco, General Electric, National Steel, and others are among those providing financial services. Take Sears as an example: it provides insurance through Allstate Insurance, it now sells securities

---

[1] Financial institutions are those in which financial assets constitute a majority of total assets.

through Dean Witter Reynolds, it provides real estate brokerage services through Coldwell Banker, it has its own extensive credit card system, and it provides thrift institution services through the offices of California-based Allstate Savings and Loan. Sears offers a money market fund and opportunities to invest in IRA accounts.

To analyze financial institutions without taking into account such major providers of financial services would be nearly ridiculous. Hence, the focus of our attention is on the financial services industry, which includes many types of financial institutions but also includes many institutions that are in large part nonfinancial.

What Sears plans for the future is even more significant: opportunities to borrow on home equities, electronic fund transfers, capacity to accept and disburse funds in all outlets, a financial card capable of handling nearly all household financial transactions, and two-way communications with homes through both computers and telephones, for both financial transactions and consumer products.[2]

# A CLASSIFICATION OF INSTITUTIONS IN THE FINANCIAL SERVICES INDUSTRY

With many additional institutions providing financial services and with changing activities and advancing technology, no classification of institutions in the financial services industry is entirely satisfactory. However, some classification is needed to reflect similarities in groups, to compare relative size when possible, and to reflect the wide diversity involved.

The classification used does not consist entirely of mutually exclusive groups. Just as individuals may be both producers and consumers, institutions may be active in more than one of the groups listed.

Some institutions are quite specialized; some are heavily regulated; and some are active in many fields, and much less regulated.

In examining various groups of institutions, our concerns include (1) what types of services do they provide? (2) are they specialized, and if so, is this advantageous or disadvantageous? (3) are they heavily regulated? (4) do they affect the amount of saving by consumers and others? (5) do they create money? (6) to which financial markets do they supply funds? (7) what types of credit do they create? and (8) are there any obvious trends in growth, profitability, or significance?

We use chiefly the classification in the flow of funds data, discussed in Chapter 2, but modified to recognize the additional institutions now providing a significant amount of financial services.

Our classification of institutions providing financial services is, then, as follows:

- The central bank (in the United States, the Federal Reserve System), discussed at appropriate points in this book.

---

[2] "Meeting the New Realities of the American Marketplace," Edward R. Telling, Chairman and Chief Executive Officer, Sears, Roebuck and Company, at the Economic Club of Chicago, February 25, 1982. Banks are also developing electronic banking for use in homes; see "Home Banking Moves off the Drawing Board," *Business Week*, September 20, 1982, p. 39.

- Commercial banks, domestic and foreign, discussed in Chapter 3.
- Other depository institutions: mutual savings banks, savings banks, savings and loan associations, and credit unions, together often referred to as the "thrift institutions" or "thrifts," for short. We also include in this group money market mutual funds and government savings bonds. Characteristics of all of these include relatively high safety, relatively great liquidity (through redemption), and use as precautionary balances by individuals.
- Contract saving institutions, which provide future payments under specified conditions (specified in an agreement or policy)—insurance companies and pension funds. Such institutions have liabilities that lack liquidity, have regular inflows of funds under premium or contribution payments, and can, because of predictability of future payments, invest in long-term capital markets.
- Investment-type institutions, which receive funds at varying times but which, like contract saving institutions, invest chiefly in stocks, bonds, real estate, and mortgages. Among institutions in this group are mutual funds or investment companies, trust funds managed by trust departments of commercial banks or, in some cases, by trust companies, real estate investment trusts (REITs), and foundations and endowments.
- Finance companies, which use borrowed funds and equity to make business and consumer loans. Business finance companies provide loans for businesses, often when firms cannot obtain loans from banks; sales finance companies provide funds for purchases of autos and appliances; and personal finance companies, or small loan companies, provide small loans to consumers, usually at high interest rates. Finance companies are among the institutions that obtain funds in both the short-term market (for example, by selling commercial paper) and in the long-term market (by issuing bonds and stocks).
- Miscellaneous institutions:
  Government and quasi-government lending agencies, most of them in the fields of housing and farm lending
  Retail stores
  Conglomerates (including some general manufacturing companies, transportation companies, general conglomerates, and communications companies)
  Investment and brokerage houses, which facilitate financial investment, assisting borrowers to obtain funds by issuing securities and/or assisting lenders to buy or sell securities (these institutions, as a group, are sometimes known as the "securities industry")
  Some minor institutions such as pawnshops

Creation of money should be distinguished from the provision of credit. Creation of money generally means the creation of some form of debt that is generally used by the public to make payments and to settle debts. Since, except for paper money and coins, the only other form of money has been, until recently, demand deposits created by commercial banks, it has been generally agreed that commercial banks have had the special privilege of creating money. Recently, negotiable order of withdrawal (NOW) accounts, on which interest is paid, have been offered by other depository institutions as well as by banks, but these institutions generally had to *attract* funds into the accounts rather than simply create the accounts.

Provision of credit means granting loans or making investments. Business loans by commercial banks generally involve simultaneously the provision of credit to business firms and the creation of money in accounts for them. Loans and investments made by other institutions involve the provision of credit, but generally without any creation of money.[3]

The volume of credit is thus much larger than the volume of money. Commercial banks may provide credit by buying securities, and they may or may not create money when they do this. Other institutions, as noted, until recently did not create money. If they are permitted to make business loans, they *may* create money in the same manner as commercial banks.

The volume of credit is much larger than the amount of saving, since savings deposited in banks may be withdrawn and deposited in other institutions, which in turn may redeposit the funds in banks which can then lend them. In turn, the borrowers (or those to whom they pay funds) may again redeposit the funds in banks. The volume of credit is obviously also much larger than is the volume of money.[4] Thus comparisons of borrowing and saving, or borrowing and money, are misleading.[5]

These distinctions are important because questions are raised as to whether it is important, or sufficient, to control the amount of money or whether instead credit should be controlled. The question is also raised as to whether interest rates should be controlled.

In the early 1980s, commercial banks held about 30 percent of total financial assets held by all these institutions, "thrifts" held about 25 percent, contractual saving institutions held about 20 percent, and investment institutions held about 15 percent. The securities industry (security brokers and dealers) were, of course, much more important in providing financial services than in the percentage of total financial assets held. Nevertheless, in many ways commercial banks were the most important group of financial institutions.

The chief financial assets of commercial banks were business loans, mortgage loans, consumer loans (including home improvement and automobile purchase loans), and investments in federal government and federal government agency securities. Their holdings of "municipal" securities (issued by state and local government authorities) and of miscellaneous loans (to other financial institutions, churches, etc.) were also important.

---

[3] We shall find in Chapter 5 that there are additional ways of defining money in which institutions other than commercial banks are involved. For example, if savings or time deposits are counted as money, then mutual savings banks, savings and loan associations, and other institutions are involved. But generally such funds have been *attracted* rather than created—the attraction generally being the rate of interest paid, combined with safety and liquidity.

[4] It was noted in Chapter 2 that the volume of credit grows more rapidly than does GNP, whereas money, narrowly defined, tends to grow more slowly than GNP. The ratio of the growth of credit to the growth of GNP has been, in the long run in the United States, about 1.85 to 1 if only debt instruments are counted as credit but about 2.5 to 1 if stocks are counted as credit. (Keep in mind that what lenders view as credit provided by them is viewed by borrowers as debt owed by them. Stocks may be considered as debt owed to stockholders.)

[5] Some pointed with alarm to the fact, as they termed it, that government deficits in the early 1980s were nearly as large as personal saving. But this is an improper comparison; deficits should be compared with total lending in the financial markets, which is several times as large as personal saving. Personal saving was $130 billion in 1981, while total funds available for borrowing in the credit markets were estimated at $390 billion.

In contrast, almost all the assets of "thrifts" consisted of mortgage loans, federal government agency securities, corporate bonds (held chiefly by mutual savings banks), and consumer loans (held chiefly by credit unions and savings and loan associations). Money market mutual funds held chiefly commercial paper (promissory notes issued by corporations), U.S. government securities, and time deposits (generally CDs—certificates of deposit).

Liabilities of commercial banks consisted almost entirely of time deposits (CDs), demand deposits, and negotiable CDs, whereas liabilities of "thrifts" consisted almost entirely of time deposits (passbook savings accounts and CDs).

Let us now examine more carefully the characteristics, objectives, and problems of "thrifts," including also U.S. government savings bonds and money market mutual funds.

## DEPOSIT-TYPE FINANCIAL INSTITUTIONS

Deposit-type financial institutions have liabilities that are very similar to those of commercial banks: they are deposits or similar claims that may be withdrawn, in most cases, in a relatively short time, although in recent years the amount of liabilities having longer maturities (and hence that can be withdrawn only with a penalty, losing some interest) has increased.

Those who desire *legal* precision may object that in some cases the claims are not deposits. A depositor is a *creditor,* not a part owner. As a creditor, the depositor has first claim on the assets if the institution is liquidated. Holders of accounts in mutual savings and loan associations and in credit unions are not creditors—they are part owners. Each one who holds an account is a part owner of the institution. But in most cases, this technical legal distinction is not important, since few institutions are liquidated. Funds deposited in mutual savings and loan associations may be termed "accounts" or "share accounts" by those desiring to be precise. Under the 1980 law, mutual savings banks may have demand deposits for corporations in connection with business loans, as well as time deposits, which they have always had. Savings and loan associations may have "NOW" accounts—demand deposits on which interest is paid. Hence it is logical to treat depository institutions (including commercial banks) as a single group—institutions that hold time deposits or similar accounts and that hold and may create demand deposits. This significant characteristic distinguishes them from other financial institutions. Deposits and other accounts are fixed-value redeemable claims—they have a fixed value and do not change in value as stocks and bonds do (except, of course, that interest as earned may be added). They can be redeemed either on demand or after short notice. Although the "fine print" concerning time deposits reads that the institutions may require holders to give notice (for a month, perhaps) before withdrawing funds, this requirement is almost never enforced on passbook accounts. In practice, on other time deposits, a penalty is imposed if funds are withdrawn before maturity.

Time deposits are *near-money;* that is, they are financial claims that may be converted into money on demand, and hence are "near-money." Use of this concept emphasizes the idea that near-monies are close substitutes for money.[6]

Another concept is also helpful—*velocity of money*. Money may be spent quickly, slowly, or not at all. The rate of turnover (spending) of money is termed velocity. Velocity is discussed in more detail in later chapters, but clearly velocity is zero as long as money is hoarded and velocity of time deposits (near-money) is less than that of demand deposits (money).

The distinction between "creation" of demand deposits and "acceptance" of time deposits is crucial. Banks generally *create* demand deposits when they make business loans and give the borrowing firms increases in their demand deposit accounts. These increases represent new deposits that did not exist before. Since they can be used to make final payments, they are money. Other liabilities represent funds that are *attracted* by paying interest, or in other ways.

In some loans made by banks, and in most loans made by other depository institutions, there is no money creation. The institutions make some loans by providing borrowers with currency, from the institutions' cash holdings. They make many loans by transferring funds to designated parties—in the case of mortgage loans, usually to the parties selling houses. Time deposits must be acquired before such institutions can lend. To acquire them, institutions usually must offer competitive interest rates, although sometimes premiums of various sorts are offered to acquire additional funds. The distinction between money creation and the making of loans by institutions that do not directly create money may be diagrammed as follows:

| Bank | | Savings and Loan | |
|---|---|---|---|
| | ↗ *Deposit* + | − Cash (or deposit in bank) | |
| + Loan ↗ | | + Loan | |

Banks create deposits in the process of making business loans and to some extent in making consumer loans. Other institutions usually make loans by reducing their own deposits in banks or by reducing their own cash holdings. This is usual in mortgage loans, whether made by banks or by thrifts. The institution pays to sellers of real property amounts equal to the mortgage loans, and at the same time reduces its cash or its deposit in a bank.

There is nothing mysterious about the process of creating money. An individual can create a mortgage by obtaining a mortgage loan, and a company can create a bond and thus obtain funds from those who buy the bonds. The only unique characteristic of money is that, unlike most other financial assets, it is *regularly used to make final payments*, or, if we wish to define money more broadly, it also includes financial claims easily, quickly, and, with little cost or loss, convertible into whatever is so used.

---

[6] For a review of evidence that seems to indicate that near-monies are good substitutes for money, see T. H. Lee, "Substitutability of Non-Bank Intermediary Liabilities for Money: The Empirical Evidence," *Journal of Finance*, September 1966, pp. 441–457. For a review of evidence that seems to indicate that they are *not* very good substitutes, see E. L. Feige, *The Demand for Liquid Assets: A Temporal Cross-Section Analysis* (Englewood Cliffs, N.J.: Prentice-Hall, 1964).

People who deposit funds in banks are guaranteed that, unless banks fail, they can withdraw that money whenever they wish (demand deposits) or within a short time or at an agreed date not too far in the future (time deposits of various kinds). Every day, some people deposit funds in a bank and others withdraw funds. A bank needs to keep only enough cash to meet the *net* excess of outflow over inflow. Some have remarked that what banks "bank on" is not having to pay their depositors or, more correctly, on not having to pay all their depositors at one time.

Let us look at part of the balance sheet of a bank that is able to meet all requests for withdrawals:

**Bank**

| Assets | Liabilities and Capital |
|---|---|
| Cash, immediately salable securities, and loans collectible in the near future | Deposits, payable on demand or in the near future |
| Other assets (chiefly short term) | Capital |

If a bank's liabilities are short term (as most of them are), the bank should keep a large part of the assets in the form of short-term financial claims. Doing so is one form of hedging.

The balance sheet just shown is a hedged balance sheet. The bank makes its profit by charging more interest on loans than it pays on deposits (enough more to more than cover its costs). It gambles less. A gambler may bet $100 that A will beat B in a race. But if the gambler has only $50, he or she may wonder how to pay his or her bet if A loses. One way to do so would be to make a second bet, this time $50 that B will beat A. If the gambler wins the first bet, he or she wins $100 but has to pay $50 on the second bet. Winnings are reduced, but so are losses. By hedging, if losses occur, they are smaller than if hedging were not done.

Banks hedge their positions with respect to interest rates when they match the maturity of their assets with the maturity of their liabilities, as was indicated in the discussion of asset and liability management by banks in Chapter 3. Individuals hedge when they budget monthly mortgage payments to coincide (or occur slightly later than) the receipt of monthly paychecks.

Institutions that have liabilities maturing far in the future, such as insurance companies, usually purchase long-term bonds and mortgages so that they can earn a known rate of interest until they must pay death or other benefits.

Thus loans and investments that are suitable for one type of financial institution are not necessarily suitable for another type.[7]

---

[7] Because the future is uncertain, everyone gambles—everyone who buys a bond is gambling that serious inflation will not occur. If inflation occurs, bonds fall in price; if held to maturity, their face maturity value is not worth as much as it was when the bonds were purchased. Everyone who holds a time deposit for, say, six months, or a share in a money market mutual fund, gambles that short-term interest rates will not fall during that time or, if they do, that it will be possible at the end of six months to find other investments with satisfactory yields.

## Mutual Savings Banks and Savings Banks

Mutual savings banks are an unusual type of institution. They have no stockholders, yet their depositors are not part owners, as is the case for those who have accounts in mutual savings and loan associations. Mutual savings banks date back to the early part of the nineteenth century, when civic-minded individuals wished to establish institutions to encourage thrift on the part of workers by providing safe depositories for small amounts saved. A mutual savings bank has been defined by the U.S. Supreme Court as

> an institution in the hands of disinterested persons, the profits of which, after deducting the necessary expenses of conducting the business, inure wholly to the benefit of the depositors, in dividends, or in a reserved surplus for their greater security.

The "disinterested persons" are trustees, who are self-appointed at the time of organization and who perpetuate themselves by electing successors to fill vacancies. Large profits are not envisaged in organizing mutual savings banks. Few have been organized in recent years, although some have come into existence as a result of conversion of savings and loan associations into mutual savings banks.

Mutual savings banks are state chartered and exist in only one-third of the states and in Puerto Rico. The states are largely in the northeastern part of the United States, although Washington, Oregon, and Alaska are western states in which mutual savings banks exist. Proposals for federal chartering of mutual savings banks have been made in several studies of the U.S. financial system. Because mutual savings banks and savings and loan associations specialize in real estate mortgage lending, it was felt that federal chartering and the possible resulting spread of mutual savings banks to states in which they are not now established would strengthen the residential mortgage market and encourage competition between mutual savings banks and savings and loan associations in states in which such competition cannot now occur. It is also argued that, on grounds of equity, mutual savings banks should have the privilege of seeking either state or federal charter, as this privilege is available to commercial banks and to savings and loan associations. Legislation effective in March 1979 finally provided for shifts to national charters by mutual savings banks. The first major mutual savings bank to apply for such a charter did so in February 1980. Wider branching privileges available under national charters enable savings banks to branch out from areas having little growth prospect to areas where opportunities are more favorable, and the additional capital available through sale of stock also provides funds for expansion. By the early 1980s a number of mutual savings banks were making this change, becoming nationally chartered (stock) savings banks.

Safety of deposits is evident in the historical record of mutual savings banks. Only about 1½ percent of the total number of mutual savings banks in existence suspended operations in the four-year period 1930–1933, whereas about 16 percent of the total number of commercial banks in operation at the beginning of 1930 suspended operations in that period. In spite of this excellent safety record, many mutual savings banks have joined the Federal Deposit Insurance Corporation, giving depositors the same protection as insured commercial banks give their depositors. Mutual savings banks in the state of New York organized a commercial bank, the Savings Bank Trust Company, to perform for the mutual savings banks in that state the central function of making loans to them in an emergency. The Savings Bank Trust Company can obtain emergency funds by borrowing from the Federal Reserve System because it is a member bank. Mutual savings banks in Massachusetts have created their own deposit insurance system. Thus about 90 percent of the total deposits in mutual savings banks are insured up to the maximum per account ($100,000).

Liquidity of the deposits in mutual savings banks is supported by holdings of cash and government securities, by the ability of those mutual savings banks that are members of the Federal Reserve System to borrow from Federal Reserve Banks, and by other factors such as the regular inflow of amortization payments on mortgage loans.

Mortgage loans normally constitute about 60 percent of the total assets of mutual savings banks. Government and corporate bonds are of some importance in their asset portfolios, and small amounts of state and local government securities, stocks, consumer loans, and other assets are also held.

Mutual savings banks, especially in New York (where more than one-third of the total assets of such banks are held), were hard hit by the inflation of the 1970s. Strict usury laws, limiting the interest rates charged on mortgage loans to 10 percent or less in some cases, created an additional problem. The fact that some parts of New York have not been growing in population, and the fact that many mortgages held were old, with low interest rates, were additional problems. Social pressure to lend locally and to avoid "redlining" (refusing to lend in certain areas) added to difficulties. As depositors finally began to shift from savings passbook accounts to other time deposits on which higher interest rates were paid, the problem of high costs and low income was exacerbated.[8]

As the rate of inflation fell, from a peak of about 18 percent (annual rate) in early 1980 to about 5 percent toward the end of 1982, the situation of mutual savings banks improved somewhat. Their interest costs fell. But mortgage loan rates were still too high to generate much demand for mortgage loans.

There is some disagreement as to whether the continued high level of interest rates was caused by lack of sufficient saving to meet the demand for loanable funds or by tight money policy exercised by the Fed, limiting the creation of additional money to fight inflation. Certainly interest rates remained relatively high during 1981 and 1982, when the rate of inflation was falling. Figures for saving as a percent of disposable personal income do not show unusually low rates of saving, but these figures are notoriously subject to error. As the rate of inflation fell, people should have begun (at some point) to anticipate lower rates of inflation. Presumably, this would lead them to be willing to hold larger amounts of money (on which no interest or a low rate of interest is obtained). As more money is held, unless GNP rises rapidly, the velocity of

---

[8] For more details, see Sanford Rose, "How the Savings Banks Can Save Themselves," *Fortune*, January 28, 1980, pp. 76–81.

money should fall—as it did. If checkable deposits (the major part of the money supply) earn market interest rates, such rates would fall as more money is held, thus moderating the shift to holding larger money balances and moderating the decline in velocity (as people held more money, some of which they did not need for transactions purposes, the velocity or rate of turnover of money fell). This is one interpretation of the events of 1982.

During the period of high inflation, persons who received about 5½ percent interest on time deposits and were taxed at 70 percent (the top marginal rate) were receiving an after-tax rate of about 1.65 percent. Wealthy investors could easily shift to other forms of investment. Those with low incomes could not easily do so and often had insufficient information concerning other investments. The result was to penalize low-income and middle-income savers. Consumption was being rewarded and saving was being penalized, for these people.

The legislation of 1980 and 1982 made it possible for mutual savings banks to diversify their assets to a somewhat greater degree and to pay higher rates on deposits when necessary to attract funds. Nevertheless, as short-term interest rates rise in any business recovery, mutual savings banks will find that they must pay market-level interest rates and that unless they have made provisions for a rise in mortgage interest rates (through variable-rate mortgages or other means), they may again face a period of difficulty or even crisis.

Because of problems encountered, some mutual savings banks (and many mutual savings and loan associations) converted into either state or federal savings banks, issuing stock. Issuing stock enabled them to obtain funds for expansion into areas suited to additional mortgage lending, and immediately raised their capital-to-asset ratios. Management of savings banks was likely to be more aggressive and innovative than trustees of mutual savings banks, who had no compensation to give them incentive for expansion.[9]

## Savings and Loan Associations

Savings and loan associations, also called building and loan associations, date back to before the middle of the nineteenth century. The building and loan associations were originally intended to be associations pooling the funds of members to make mortgage loans to members; gradually a difference developed between the borrowing group and the saving group, and the institutions began to solicit savings from the general public. Savings and loan associations may now be either federally chartered or state chartered. They are managed by boards of directors; the extent to which share account holders actively participate in election of directors varies. Federal savings and loan associations must be members of the Federal Savings and Loan

---

[9] Although conversion provides the foregoing benefits, there are problems: stock issued may be a more risky investment than many mutual owners wish to buy, costs of conversion may be high, so that many mutual owners receive little compensation, and so on; for a discussion, see Constance R. Dunham, "Mutual-to-Stock Conversion for Thrifts: Implications for Soundness," Federal Reserve Bank of Boston, *New England Economic Review*, January–February 1985, pp. 31–45.

Insurance Corporation rather than of the Federal Deposit Insurance Corporation. Maximum insured amounts and general insurance provisions are similar, but a commercial bank, having demand deposits, must close its doors immediately if it cannot meet depositors' requests for withdrawals. Savings and loan associations, on the other hand, could in the past go "on notice" for a time, and payments to share account holders could be delayed. In practice, this has not often occurred. Safety of commercial deposits in a commercial bank and in a savings and loan association seem comparable, if insured by the FDIC and the FSLIC. The FSLIC has a smaller fund, but it seems likely that ways will be found to protect insured deposits.[10] In a few states, such as Ohio, Maryland, and some others, deposits are insured by state funds. Difficulties have been encountered in some of these states.

Banks are now almost all incorporated, while savings and loan associations have, until recently, been mostly mutuals, owned by the depositors. Mutual savings banks are not technically owned by the depositors, but in the event of liquidation, any surplus after payment of liabilities would be divided among the depositors. Technically, the return on deposits in both mutual savings banks and savings and loan associations should have been termed dividends, not interest. This technical distinction has been largely ignored by the public.

In recent years, a number of savings and loan associations have converted from mutuals to corporations, and a number of mutual savings banks have incorporated as savings banks. One advantage is that they can sell additional stock, thus increasing their capital; as mutuals, they could increase their capital only by retaining earnings. With additional capital, they can establish new branches in areas favorable for mortgage lending. New mortgage loans can be made at prevailing mortgage loan interest rates, generally raising the average return on mortgage loans.[11] In the early 1980s, over 200 savings and loan associations failed and over 300 appear to have avoided failure through mergers arranged by the authorities. By mid-1985, nearly 500 had negative equity under generally accepted accounting principles (GAAP), which overstate equity because mortgages are carried at book value even if their market value has fallen. Regulatory accounting principles (RAP) and Federal Home Loan Bank Board (FHLBB) net worth certificates provided to them enable them to overstate equity even more. Even by these measures, over 800 savings and loan associations have capital of less than 3 percent of total assets, whereas it was noted in Chapter 3 that

[10] See, for example, *The Wall Street Journal*, July 15, 1986, p. 60. A 1987 law permits the FSLIC to issue over $10 billion of bonds (over a number of years) to strengthen its financial situation; see *The Wall Street Journal*, August 4, 1987, p. 2.

[11] In early 1972, after almost a decade with no conversions, a federal mutual savings and loan association converted into a state-chartered stock savings and loan association, perhaps with the encouragement of the regulatory authority. Since that time there have been a number of such conversions. Stock associations tend to be more aggressive than mutuals, making more construction loans, more loans with high ratios of loan to value, and generally more profits, although they also at times incur sizable losses because of the types of loans they make. For an interesting discussion of efforts to stimulate changes that might result in longer-term liabilities and shorter-term assets for savings and loan associations, see Sanford Rose, "The S & Ls Break Out of Their Shell," *Fortune*, September 1972, pp. 152–170.

authorities regulating banks have set a minimum standard of a 5½ to 6 percent ratio of capital to assets for banks.[12]

Liquidity of savings and loan associations is provided by holdings of cash and government securities and by their membership in the Federal Home Loan Bank System. Savings and loan associations that are members of the system may borrow from the Federal Home Loan Banks under specified conditions, just as commercial banks may borrow from the Federal Reserve Banks.

Savings and loan associations have an even larger proportion of their assets in the form of mortgage loans than do mutual savings banks—over four-fifths. Although recent legislation has permitted both to diversify somewhat by allowing them to make certain types of consumer loans, the heavy concentration of assets of these two institutions in mortgage loans means that, when flows of funds into these institutions were heavy, as in 1976 and 1977, availability of funds for mortgage loans increased. When that flow was reduced, however, as it was after 1978, the mortgage market tightened.

The high inflation and high interest rates of the late 1970s affected savings and loan associations as adversely as they did mutual savings banks. The Federal Home Loan Bank Board approved funds to aid the industry and permitted federally chartered savings and loan associations to issue variable-rate mortgages, so that mortgage interest rates could be readjusted every three, four, or five years. The fluctuating nature of inflation in the past decade and a half has been especially difficult for savings and loan associations. If inflation remained at a steady rate, even if that rate were high, the institutions could adjust by gradually making only mortgage loans with high interest rates. A fluctuating rate of inflation has put serious pressure on the savings and loan associations for a time and then the pressure has eased; then it has returned again, and eased again.

In the early 1980s the problems inherent in a mismatched (unhedged) balance sheet came home to roost. Mutual savings banks and savings and loan associations had liabilities that were essentially payable, in large part, on demand, but their assets were largely long-term fixed-rate mortgages. Many of the mortgage loans had been made at relatively low interest rates. Some had many years remaining until maturity. Assets were in some cases earning only 6 to 9 percent, while deposit liabilities that formerly had paid only 5½ percent were in some cases paying as high as 16 percent. The predictable result was losses, in some cases heavy.

The Depository Institutions Act of 1982 was the government's response to the situation. It expanded the powers of both commercial banks and thrifts and provided for FDIC authorization for takeovers of troubled banks, mutual savings banks, and savings and loan associations by (1) institutions of the same type in the same state, (2) institutions of the same type in different states, (3) institutions of different types in the same state, and (4) institutions of different types in different states. The last case had

---

[12] The data on failures are from a study by George J. Benston, *An Analysis of the Causes of Savings and Loan Association Failures*, Graduate School of Business Administration, New York University, Monograph Series in Finance and Economics, Monograph 1985–4/5.

already occurred when Citicorp (the large New York City bank holding company) was permitted to acquire a savings and loan association in the San Francisco area with authorization of the Federal Home Loan Bank Board and the Federal Reserve Board.[13]

Another provision of the law permitted the government to provide net worth in the form of certificates, up to 70 percent of operating losses where necessary. The law also authorized a "money market account" with no interest rate ceiling, deposit insurance, a maximum of six third-party transfers (checks) per month, no reserve requirements for individuals' accounts, and a minimum amount to be set by the Depository Institutions Deregulation Committee, which was also to work out other details. The minimum set was $2,500.[14] Incidentally, all interest rate differentials on all deposits, between commercial banks and thrifts, were to be eliminated by January 1, 1984.

The new money market deposit accounts (MMDAs), as they were often termed, were authorized initially for December 14, 1982. At about the same time the DIDC also authorized, effective January 5, 1983, another account with no interest rate ceiling and with unlimited transfer powers by checks and other means. This account was limited to individuals and nonprofit institutions. It came to be referred to as a Super-NOW account—a NOW account paying a higher interest rate (interest on NOW accounts was limited to 5¼ percent for banks and 5½ percent for thrift institutions until elimination of the differential January 1, 1984).

The law also permits changes in interest rates on mortgage loans when properties are sold—with certain exceptions. The loans are due when the properties are sold, and those who assume the mortgages in effect acquire new mortgage loans at a new interest rate.[15]

As might have been expected, the money market mutual funds, discussed in detail later in this chapter, wanted interest rate limits on the money market accounts, suggested that the DIDC consider withholding deposit insurance from such accounts, and suggested a higher minimum balance. The funds argued that deposit insurance is government subsidized and that without any interest rate ceiling, banks would have an unfair advantage because of the large resources of the major money center banks.[16]

The details of these challenges are less important than the evident fact that, even with short-term interest rates falling in 1982, the money market accounts attracted a substantial amount of funds from the money market mutual funds. They could be

[13] *The Wall Street Journal*, September 29, 1982, p. 3. The question could be raised whether a holding company owning one or more savings and loan associations is a "bank holding company." However, the Garn-St Germain bill specifically excluded savings and loan associations (in spite of their expanded powers) from regulation under the Bank Holding Company Act.

[14] *The Wall Street Journal*, November 26, 1982, p. 7. Reserve requirements, the same as for checking accounts, were to be imposed if more than six transfers per month to third parties were permitted. For nonpersonal accounts (those held by corporations), the reserve requirement was to be 3 percent. For more details concerning provisions of the Depository Institutions Act of 1982, see the appendix to this chapter.

[15] For more details, see Federal Reserve Bank of San Francisco, *Weekly Letter*, October 15, 1982; *The Wall Street Journal*, October 4, 1982, p. 10; and *The Wall Street Journal*, October 7, 1982, p. 3.

[16] *The Wall Street Journal*, October 26, 1982, p. 12.

even more significant when short-term rates rise, as might be expected in a period of rising business activity.

A provision in the law authorized mutual savings banks and savings and loan associations to place up to 10 percent of their assets, after January 1, 1984, in commercial and farm loans and to offer related demand deposits. It would be difficult for many thrifts, especially small ones, to make many business loans because of the expertise needed, and competing with commercial banks to make such loans would be relatively difficult. Yet the long-term trend may well be for thrifts to become more and more similar to commercial banks; certainly more short-term (or even medium-term) business loans would be more advantageous than the very high percentage of mortgage loans now held. Table 4–1 shows a comparison of asset, deposit, and other powers now available to the three major categories of federally chartered depository institutions (national banks, savings banks, and federal savings and loan associations).

Provisions in the Depository Institutions Deregulation and Monetary Control Act of 1980 already had permitted savings and loan associations to issue credit cards and extend credit on them, to exercise trust powers (for which they would charge fees), and to invest up to 20 percent (increased to 30 percent by the 1982 law) of their assets in consumer loans and in various forms of corporate debt. These activities are also likely to be helpful in diversifying their assets into short-term credits on which rates can be raised when new loans are made, if inflation necessitates such a change.

Clearly, the future for savings and loan associations lies in some diversification of assets, the offering of competitive short-term "money market" accounts, and increasing expertise in the various phases of providing financial services. The wrong kind of specialization came close to causing their failure in massive numbers. Changing from mutual associations to stock companies, so that they can increase their capital, is likely to be helpful for some. Variable-rate mortgages may also be advantageous, if consumers will accept them. Finally, the slowdown in the rate of inflation from 1980 to 1987 has laid a foundation for profitable operation again for many of them. A rise in the rate of inflation could, nevertheless, bring back the same problems for many.

The financing of housing is essential, although some might argue that subsidization through low interest rates and tax benefits has financed more expensive housing than would have been possible in a free market economy. In the 1980s, the more successful savings and loan associations can become family financial service companies: consumer banks that offer NOW accounts, other certificates and money market accounts to attract savings, credit card services, bill-paying services, trust services, and financial counseling services.[17] These associations must define their appropriate markets in terms of geographic areas, population characteristics, and present and likely future competitors. They may need to establish employee training programs, especially for activities not previously handled.

---

[17] This list of services adds one or two to that provided by Glenn C. Hansen, "What a Savings and Loan Can Learn from General George Armstrong Custer," Federal Reserve Bank of Chicago, *Economic Perspectives*, Fall 1982, pp. 33–35.

**TABLE 4–1**
**Federally Chartered Depository Institutions**

| Banking Powers | National Banks | Savings Banks | Savings & Loan Associations |
|---|---|---|---|
| *Loan Powers* | | | |
| Real estate loans | May not exceed 100 percent of time and savings deposits except for government-insured loans. | No aggregate limit on residential real estate loans, not more than 40 percent of assets to be loaned on nonresidential real estate. | Same as savings banks. |
| Commercial and industrial loans | No aggregate limit. | Up to 7½ percent of assets.[1] | Up to 5 percent of assets.[1] |
| Loans to individuals (includes credit cards) | No aggregate limit. | May invest up to 30 percent of assets in consumer loans and commercial paper combined. | Same as savings banks. |
| Leeway provision | None. | Up to 5 percent of assets may be invested in loans secured by real estate that do not conform to specific provisions. This 5 percent may not be added to existing provisions. | Same as savings banks. |

| Deposit Powers | | | |
|---|---|---|---|
| **Demand Deposits** | | | |
| Personal | No restrictions. | Prohibited. | Prohibited. |
| Corporate | No restrictions. | May accept business demand deposits in conjunction with a loan relationship. | Same as savings banks. |
| **NOW accounts** | | | |
| Personal | No restrictions. | No restrictions. | No restrictions. |
| Corporate (NINOW) | Prohibited. | Prohibited. | Prohibited. |
| Time and savings deposits | No restrictions. | No restrictions. | No restrictions. |
| **Other Powers** | | | |
| Trust services | Full powers. | Full powers. | Full powers. |
| Service corporations | Up to 10 percent of capital and surplus. | May invest up to 3 percent of assets in corporations wholly owned by thrift institutions. | Same as savings banks. |
| International banking facilities (Edge Act) | Up to 10 percent of capital and surplus. | Prohibited. | Prohibited. |

[1] The limitation on thrift investment in commercial loans increased to 10 percent of assets on January 1, 1984.

SOURCE: Joseph Gagnon and Steve Yokas, "Recent Developments in Federal and New England Banking Laws," Federal Reserve Bank of Boston, *New England Economic Review*, January–February 1983, pp. 18–27.

Finally, savings and loan associations must be watchful for a possible return of inflation. With mortgage loans probably continuing to be their major asset, they cannot afford to ignore the interest rate risk inherent in fixed-rate, long-term assets and demand or short-term liabilities that are necessarily variable in the interest rate paid on them when inflation occurs.

## Credit Unions

Credit unions date only from the early twentieth century. They are state or federally chartered nonprofit cooperative institutions designed to provide credit to members. Members must usually have a common bond of some type—they must be employees of a certain company or industry, or they must live in a particular geographic area. Over 90 percent of all credit unions have members with some form of occupational bond. The major differences between credit unions and the other institutions just discussed lie in this requirement of a bond of association among members of a credit union and in the fact that most of the loans made by credit unions are consumer loans rather than mortgage loans.

Cost of operation of credit unions is low because in many cases some work is performed by volunteers and because office space and utility services are often provided by the employer of members of the union. Credit unions are in effect subsidized, to aid in providing credit to members who otherwise might have to pay high interest costs.

For most of the other deposit-type institutions, safety has been assured since the 1930s by deposit insurance, but credit union accounts were not insured until 1970 (although some credit unions obtained insurance through private agencies). It was recommended in the *Economic Report of the President,* 1956, that Congress "consider the desirability of establishing a self-supporting federal program of share-account insurance for credit unions." In 1970, this was finally implemented by the establishment of a national credit union insurance fund, following the establishment of the National Credit Union Administration as an independent agency. Accounts in federal credit unions are insured to a maximum of $100,000 per account, as bank deposits are, and accounts in state-chartered credit unions may be insured. Some states now require that any state-chartered credit unions that are not insured by the National Credit Union Administration (NCUA) must obtain state insurance.

On the asset side, credit unions compete with commercial banks (consumer loan departments), sales finance companies, personal finance (small loan) companies, and retailers in making loans to finance the purchase of automobiles or appliances, to repay other debts, to pay for medical services or other special expenses, such as those for vacations, or for other purposes.[18]

Cash and government securities provide liquidity; credit unions also sometimes borrow from commercial banks to meet peak loan demand and may do so to meet part

---

[18] Competition with sales finance companies was strong in 1986 as auto manufacturers' subsidiary sales finance companies offered low interest rates: *The Wall Street Journal,* June 24, 1986, p. 31.

of their liquidity needs. They may also obtain funds by issuing certificates of indebtedness, either to their members or to outsiders. No ceiling is imposed on the interest rate that they may pay on such certificates.

In a sense, the credit union has two inconsistent goals: to pay high rates to its members who have credit union accounts and to charge low rates to borrowers, who are part of the same group of people. Savings and loan associations had a similar inconsistency in goals in their early history, but with the rise in market interest rates in the 1970s, they were forced to pay as much as they legally could, to retain accounts. Because of this, mortgage loan interest rates rose. Credit unions have traditionally been the lowest-cost source of consumer credit, with commercial banks charging slightly higher rates and the consumer finance companies (personal loan companies) charging much higher rates. Consumer credit is inherently high-cost credit, partly because fixed costs are incurred in making any loan and the small size of the average consumer loan means that these fixed costs are spread over fewer dollars.[19]

Credit unions do have some advantages in keeping loan interest rates low. Some are provided with office space, and in some cases utilities are paid for them, by business firms. Part of the work is sometimes done by volunteer labor. They have smaller loan losses than do commercial banks (on consumer loans) and much smaller losses than do consumer finance companies. The common bond of association means that credit unions can get some information about borrowers rather easily. Finally, loan repayments are sometimes handled through payroll deduction plans, minimizing defaults.

Perhaps in part because of these advantages, credit unions had the fastest growth rate from 1960 to 1980 of all the depository institutions thus far discussed.[20] They could legally pay interest rates that were often a little higher than those that could be paid by the other institutions, and credit union members tended in any event to have some allegiance to the credit unions to which they belonged.

Recognizing that use of funds to pay bills is important to accountholders, some credit unions began to offer "share draft" privileges—accountholders could draw drafts, cleared through commercial banks, to pay bills from funds in their accounts. Costs were reduced by sending periodic itemized statements but not returning canceled checks.

It is also of value to credit unions to be tied into electronic funds transfer networks as these are completed. Direct deposit of checks, both for wages and for such receipts as Social Security benefits, is likely to become more popular, and unless credit unions are tied into the electronic networks, they cannot receive such direct deposits.

---

[19] It has been estimated that a rate of over 100 percent interest on the outstanding balance would be required to cover costs on a $100, one-year loan repaid in monthly installments. Cost of making such a loan is about $25, cost of handling and recording monthly payments is about $25, and cost of interest paid to account holders on the average of $50 outstanding is about $5, including some allowance for bad debt losses. See Mark J. Flannery, "Credit Unions as Consumer Lenders in the United States," Federal Reserve Bank of Boston, *New England Economic Review*, July–August 1974, pp. 3–12.

[20] "Tearing Off the Plain Brown Wrapper," Chase Manhattan Bank, *Business in Brief*, August 1976.

Credit unions generally cannot make mortgage loans because they generally cannot make loans with maturities over 10 years. They cannot, generally, make business loans. They cannot invest in stocks or bonds, in general. They have not issued many credit cards because, frequently, each amount used from a line of credit must be separately approved by the credit union loan committee.

Do credit unions have economies of scale that have consistently been found, at least to some degree, for other financial institutions? This is controversial. Flannery did not find them and has argued that perhaps this was because donated office space and volunteer labor were generally not available as credit unions increased in size.[21] Koot claimed to find *dis*economies of scale, even after correcting for the effects of volunteer labor.[22] On the other hand, Wolken and Navratil argued that Koot assumed that the amount of volunteer labor is proportional to costs, an unjustified assumption, and that both Koot and Flannery failed to include in costs a measure of wages (for nonvolunteer labor), although clearly wages differ in different areas.[23] When the assumption was changed and a measure of wages was included, they found some, though not major, economies of scale.

Legislation may provide additional powers for credit unions and thus permit further growth. But limits of size, the required bond of association, and the probable limit of providing chiefly consumer credit may well mean that the period of rapid growth for credit unions has ended.[24]

## Money Market Mutual Funds

High interest rates in the 1970s and the difficulty for many investors of buying individual money market instruments (because of minimum amounts, for example) led to the emergence of a wide variety of what have been termed short-term investment pools (STIPs).[25] Investors desired liquidity, in view of the danger of investing in long-term securities in a period of inflation. Short-term interest rates reached very high levels and remained high for a long period of time—an unusual event, since short-term rates usually have reached peaks when short-term business demand for loans reached high levels (at peaks of business activity), but have fallen as a recession began. Although a recession occurred in the first half of 1980 and another recession

---

[21] M. J. Flannery, *An Economic Evaluation of Credit Unions in the United States*, Research Report No. 54, Federal Reserve Bank of Boston, 1974.

[22] Ronald S. Koot, "On Economies of Scale in Credit Unions," *Journal of Finance*, September 1978, pp. 1087–1094.

[23] John D. Wolken and Frank J. Navratil, "Economies of Scale in Credit Unions: Further Evidence," *Journal of Finance*, June 1980, pp. 769–777.

[24] Credit unions have reduced consumer loans as a percentage of assets, they can now make more mortgage loans and can offer credit cards, and the "common bond" requirement for membership has been loosened. They also now have *direct* access to Fed services. They are probably still the fastest-growing group among depository institutions. See Douglas K. Pearce, "Recent Developments in the Credit Union Industry," Federal Reserve Bank of Kansas City, *Economic Review*, June 1984, pp. 3–19.

[25] Timothy Q. Cook and Jeremy Duffield, "Short-Term Investment Pools," in *Instruments of the Money Market*, 5th ed. (Federal Reserve Bank of Richmond, 1981).

(or was it a continuation of the first?) began in mid-1981, short-term interest rates did not begin any substantial decline until late summer of 1982. In such an environment, it is not surprising that various institutions began offering numerous forms of shares in pools of various short-term financial assets.

The most well publicized of these STIPs were the money market mutual funds (MMMFs). Most MMMFs require an initial investment of from $500 to $5,000, and most invest chiefly in bank certificates of deposit (CDs), commercial paper, and Treasury bills (short-term government securities).

Assets held in MMMFs grew from less than $1 billion in 1974 to more than $200 billion in mid-1982, as short-term interest rates rose and remained high. Investors often could write checks on these money market funds, usually with minimum amounts of $500. Thus these became transactions accounts, but they could not be used for regular small payments or for most other spending. They were near-money, but close to being money.

Brokerage and investment houses (discussed later) offered cash management accounts in which investors could place minimum amounts of stocks and cash, with the understanding that all cash would be constantly invested in short-term (money market) assets. Cash obtained from sales of stocks and from receipt of dividends would be invested with other cash.[26] Investors could borrow against the stocks. The investment of cash in short-term assets assured high returns as long as short-term interest rates remained high.

A wide variety of STIPs came into existence—tax-exempt funds for those desiring tax-free income, short-term investment funds for trust departments of commercial banks, local government STIPs for state and local government units, credit union pools for credit unions, and others.

STIPs for individuals, like Merrill Lynch's Cash Management Account, are for high-income investors. A person must hold a minimum of $20,000 in securities and/or cash in the account. Since Merrill Lynch is not a bank, it cannot legally accept "deposits" or have checks on itself cleared through the banking system. A bank serves as the institution on which checks are written. Merrill Lynch has an account at the bank, and that account has a zero balance at the end of each day (Merrill Lynch pays or receives payment). Thus this account does not appear in the demand deposit (money supply) figures.[27] Cash is invested in some form of money market fund (earning interest).

It is important to understand the causal factors that gave rise to STIPs: inflation, which stimulated both individuals and institutions to gain more liquidity (why hold long-term financial assets when money is losing its value?), the technology of com-

---

[26] The name Cash Management Account is the trademark name registered by Merrill Lynch for its account. Other brokerage and investment houses offered similar accounts. For details on such accounts, see for example, Merrill Lynch's brochure, "Cash Management Account." In Merrill Lynch's account, an investor can choose from among a money market fund, a tax-exempt fund, or a government securities fund.

[27] For more details, see Martin Mayer, "Merrill Lynch Quacks Like a Bank," *Fortune*, October 20, 1980, pp. 135–144.

puters and electronic funds transfers, the ingenuity that is stimulated by new conditions, and the widespread use of plastic cards.

It is difficult to judge whether STIPs, including MMMFs, are a temporary phenomenon, likely to decline in importance when short-term interest rates fall and long-term rates again are higher, or whether they may have a more permanent place. Corporations, which might be expected to invest surplus cash in STIPs, often obtain services from banks in which they hold demand deposits, inducing them to retain the demand deposit accounts (the services constitute a form of implicit interest).[28] Moreover, corporations can exchange deposits for government securities under repurchase agreements (the banks agreeing to repurchase the securities after a designated time). These considerations argue that if inflation is subdued, MMMFs and other STIPs will at best continue as minor factors in the financial scene.

With the 1982 permission for banks and savings and loan associations to offer money market accounts, competition of these institutions with the MMMFs increased.[29] Both money market accounts and MMMFs are attractive for some investors who desire a high degree of liquidity and are unwilling to invest in bonds and stocks even if yields on such investments exceed those on MMMFs. In the competition between money market mutual funds on the one hand and banks and savings and loan associations on the other, the authorization for money market deposit accounts and Super-NOW accounts was of significant benefit to the banks and savings and loan associations. From a peak of over $220 billion in late 1982, funds in MMMFs dropped to about $185 billion in early 1983. Presumably the fact that MMDAs and Super-NOW accounts were insured by the FDIC and the FSLIC was a major factor enabling them to gain funds. MMDAs were much more popular than Super-NOW accounts, reaching $319 billion in mid-March 1983 while deposits in Super-NOW accounts reached only $27 billion, according to Federal Reserve System figures. Obviously, only a small amount of the MMDAs came from MMMFs; one estimate was about $20 billion. MMMFs may be able to regain some funds if they find a way to provide insurance or other desirable features; by 1986, MMMFs totaled $266 billion, while MMDAs totaled $525 billion (including accounts in commercial banks and in thrifts).

---

[28] See Timothy Q. Cook and Jeremy G. Duffield, "Money Market Mutual Funds," Federal Reserve Bank of Richmond, *Economic Review*, July–August 1979, pp. 15–31, and "Average Costs of Money Market Mutual Funds," ibid., pp. 32–39. Cook and Duffield try to assess whether the funds are a temporary institution or a permanent one according to the extent to which the funds are merely a means of providing access to money markets for those who cannot invest in them otherwise, at a time of very high short-term interest rates, versus the extent to which the funds provide an intermediary specializing in investment in short-term financial assets—a type of intermediary not existing until recently, yet of value at almost all times to those who have short-term funds to invest and desire a high degree of liquidity.

[29] These accounts were discussed earlier in this chapter, in the section on savings and loan associations. The need to permit those institutions to offer more competitive accounts was obvious. To maintain a "level playing field," these types of accounts were authorized for other government-regulated depository institutions as well. Of course, MMMFs may be expected to attempt new activities in competition with banks; for actions taken by one MMMF (Dreyfus), see Gary Hector, "How Dreyfus Plans to Beat the Banks," *Fortune*, March 21, 1983, pp. 64–72. They may also try to provide insurance to compete with the insured deposits in banks; for one example, see *Business Week*, April 4, 1983, p. 89.

### U.S. Savings Bonds

Although not an institution in the brick-and-mortar sense or even in the sense of being an incorporated organization, U.S. savings bonds should be mentioned at this point because they serve the same purpose as depository institutions do—they have a high degree of safety and liquidity (after a short initial time).

The inflation of the 1970s created problems in marketing savings bonds, since the interest rate on them was relatively low. Moreover, the interest they earned was not constant—it was quite low in the first years and much higher in the later years of the holding period. In 1980 and 1981, net redemptions of savings bonds were $6 billion in each year.

The Treasury's reason for selling savings bonds is that many are purchased by people who otherwise would not buy bonds. Thus the Treasury is able to sell part of its debt to people who would not otherwise buy it and who generally hold it for a lengthy period. Part of the national debt is held in a nonmarketable form. Presumably, this reduces the supply of debt otherwise available to the market, thus tending to raise prices and lower yields (debt costs).

An important issue concerning savings bonds is the question of whether or not "constant purchasing power" bonds should be issued, as has been done in some countries. Commissions that have studied the financial system have recommended against this.[30] It has been argued that issuing such bonds would (1) single out a certain group for protection against harmful effects of inflation, (2) tend to lead to acceptance of the inevitability of inflation, and (3) compete unfairly with other liquid assets. Other economists have argued that low-income and medium-income consumers who save are often badly hurt by inflation, as their savings lose value, and should have available a form of protection—a hedge against inflation.

With the slowdown of inflation in the 1980–1982 period, it did not seem likely that constant purchasing power bonds would be given serious consideration. Instead, the Treasury attempted to stimulate demand for savings bonds by offering 85 percent of the average return for the preceding six months on 5-year Treasury securities, with a guaranteed minimum rate of 7½ percent, reduced to 6 percent as interest rates were falling in the mid-1980s, compounded semiannually. On outstanding savings bonds, the guaranteed rate was set at 7½ percent or the rate promised when the bonds were issued, whichever was higher. Complexity of the method of determining the redemption value may be a deterrent for some potential purchasers—redemption value is to be determined by the average of the six-month rates, so that some calculation is needed to find redemption values. At maturity in 10 years, purchasers are guaranteed that values of the bonds will have doubled (with the minimum 7½ percent rate), and

---

[30] See, for example, the *Report of the Commission on Money and Credit* (Englewood Cliffs, N.J.: Prentice-Hall, 1961), p. 107. See also Alicia H. Munnell and Joseph B. Grolnic, "Should the U.S. Government Issue Index Bonds?" Federal Reserve Bank of Boston, *New England Economic Review*, September–October 1986, pp. 3–21. These economists report the success of index bonds in Britain and argue that index bonds could provide fully inflation-indexed pensions for retirees.

they may be worth more. After 5 years, the 10 semiannual average rates to that point are to be added, averaged, and compounded to determine the yield.[31] Then bonds held for longer periods (that is, renewed) earn more.

Given the method of calculation of interest, much depends on whether yields on 5-year securities are higher for a 5-year period than are yields for short-term securities. This depends on the nature of the yield curve, discussed in Chapter 13.

The features of savings bonds that attract purchasers are their safety (including the fact that they are replaced by the Treasury if lost, stolen, or destroyed), the fact that they can be redeemed at any time after the first six months, the fact that initial investment can be as small as $25, and the fact that they can often be purchased under payroll deduction plans. They are also exempt from state and local income taxes, and payment of federal income tax on the interest can be deferred until redemption; in the past, this was often decades, because after 10 years they were automatically renewed.

It remains to be seen whether interest rates at 85 percent of the average return on 5-year Treasury securities will be attractive. Consumers, after a long period of inflation, are more sophisticated than before. In early 1986, net sales of savings bonds exceeded redemptions, and the rate of return on them seemed rather attractive in comparison with other money market rates. But in 1986 the inflation rate was extremely low, and if the rate of inflation increases (and interest rates rise), this situation may change. Bonds bought when the variable rates were first introduced (1982) have yielded an average rate of return over 9 percent thus far.[32] This sounds attractive compared with other money market rates in mid-1986, but compare it with the 35 percent yield in 1985 on stocks in a fund yielding a rate (dividends plus price gain) comparable to that of the S & P 500 stocks.

As a financial investment in a period of inflation, perhaps the best that can be said for savings bonds, without a constant purchasing power clause, is that psychologically, some lower-income persons may be induced to buy savings bonds when otherwise they might not have saved at all. This is especially true when payroll deductions are made for the purchases of savings bonds.

### Inflation and Deposit-Type Institutions

Clearly, the rise in the rate of inflation in the 1970s to a peak in early 1980, and its subsequent fall, were disastrous to many savings and loan associations. Commercial banks suffered less, but could be harmed if this process were repeated, especially if they make long-term loans and investments—to retain deposits, they would have to pay higher rates on time deposits, but could raise rates only on variable rate loans, before maturity. What could banks do to be profitable? One thing would be to sell (broker) some of their long-term loans to investors able to make long-term investments. This would mean a larger volume of loans *handled* with the same assets and capital, but profit would come in part from brokerage fees. Banks would become more

---

[31] *The Wall Street Journal*, November 15, 1982, p. 48.
[32] *U.S. News and World Report*, July 28, 1986, p. 44.

service oriented, and less asset oriented.[33] This may occur if more services are demanded by consumers—financial counseling, cash management, travel agency and car rental services, and others. A transition from primarily an asset-holding industry to a service oriented industry may be a major trend in this part of the financial services industry in the 1980s and beyond.

# CONTRACTUAL SAVING INSTITUTIONS

Contractual saving institutions such as life insurance companies and pension funds receive a steady inflow of funds in the form of premiums for insurance policies and regular contributions to pension plan programs. Except during a serious depression, such as that of the 1930s, few persons fail to pay premiums or to make their regular contributions, and thus liquidity is not a problem for these institutions. At the same time, most of these institutions are able to predict relatively accurately the amounts of insurance and pension benefits to be paid. Since their liabilities are long term, maturing many years, in most cases, after the purchase of an insurance policy or the beginning of a pension plan, the major activity of these institutions is the appropriate long-term investment of their funds. They desire an adequate return to meet their obligations when insurance policies mature and when pensions must be paid to beneficiaries.

The growth of "variable annuities," still in its infancy, may gradually change this situation, because variable annuities provide fluctuating benefits, depending on changing income and changing values of the assets in which the funds are invested. At present, however, both the inflow of funds and the amounts of payments to be made are closely predictable. Moreover, the rate of return guaranteed in insurance policies has been relatively low. Thus insurance companies have had less need for a high rate of return than most of the other nonbank institutions.

## Life Insurance Companies

The importance of life insurance companies in the money and capital markets arises largely from the fact that much of the insurance sold has been in forms that combine both insurance and saving. Pure life insurance—term insurance policies are close to this—provides protection (for beneficiaries) against the risk of death of the insured. There is little or no saving, and when the term is ended, the policies have no value. Insurance policies that provide both insurance and a means of saving provide maturity values for the policies. Those who buy insurance are buying not only insurance protection but are also saving amounts that can be obtained later.

Term insurance policies are usually written for specified terms: 1, 5, or 10 years. They are often renewable, but at higher premiums, since the risk of death is higher as people grow older. Premiums cover operating costs of the insurance companies and

---

[33] See Sanford Rose, "The Future Competitive Environment: Strategic Planning for the 1990s," Federal Reserve Bank of Chicago, *Economic Perspectives*, Fall 1982, pp. 28–29.

provide for some addition to surplus for mutual companies or for dividends to stock-holders of stock companies. Thus no large sums are available for investment by the insurance companies.

Other types of policies, however—whole life policies, endowment policies, and others—provide for payments to policyholders (if living) at some future dates. Thus they combine insurance protection (payments to beneficiaries in the event of death) with saving for the future (payments to policyholders or beneficiaries at specified future dates). With constant premiums for these policies, the premiums in early years must be high enough to meet the future payments. The premiums during early years provide substantial sums for investment by the insurance companies.

Insurance companies have a need for adequate yields on their investments (but, in the past, not very high yields because rates of return guaranteed to policyholders were not high). They have little need for liquidity, however, because they can predict quite accurately the amounts of payments that they must make in the future. There-fore, their investments have been largely in corporate bonds, government bonds, mortgages, and real estate, with a small amount of funds invested in common stocks. Because mutual life insurance companies, which provide about half of the insurance in force, are usually subject to relatively low rates of taxation, they are generally not much interested in the tax-exempt feature of the income on municipal securities. During World War II, when government securities were plentiful, insurance compa-nies invested heavily in them; then, after the war, their holdings of government securities declined.

Insurance companies have used what is termed "direct placement" for much of their investment in corporate bonds, negotiating directly with the borrowing corpora-tion for purchase of a large block of bonds. Because regular inflows of funds are expected, life insurance companies often make forward or future commitments for investment of substantial sums. Borrowers can avoid some underwriting and registra-tion costs, and terms can be flexible, with special provisions agreed upon by both parties.

Insurance companies were legally restrained from investment in stocks for many years because it was believed that investments in stocks involved greater risks than did investment in bonds. Recognition of the higher average yields on stocks and the growth of "variable annuities" has resulted in increased investment in stocks; laws have been liberalized somewhat to permit this.

Nearly 30 percent of all financial assets held by life insurance companies consists of mortgages. The largest portion of these are conventional, but a large part also consists of FHA-insured or VA-guaranteed mortgages. Because life insurance compa-nies operate over wide territories and cannot have large offices in every local area, they frequently obtain mortgages by arranging with mortgage companies for purchase from those companies of groups or packages of mortgages, in sizable total amounts. Forward or future commitments of several months are usually made for such pur-chases, as they often are for purchases of directly placed bond issues. Mortgage companies usually know in advance when mortgages will be sold to insurance compa-nies. Thus, some lag may be anticipated between the time of any change in mortgage rates or regulation and the effect of such change on purchases of mortgages by insurance companies.

Total assets of life insurance companies have grown more slowly since World War II than before that time. The slower growth may be attributed either to (1) the fear that inflation reduces the value of insurance policies or to (2) increased competition by other financial institutions. There has been somewhat more rapid growth in term insurance than there has in other forms, suggesting that some persons may be buying term insurance but investing the remainder of the funds (that would otherwise be paid in higher premiums for other forms of insurance) in another type of financial asset. Presumably the assets they invest in would, to some extent at least, provide some hedge against inflation. Insurance companies' growth rate increased somewhat in the late 1970s through sale of annuities. Popularity of annuities increased as people with limited savings bought annuities to obtain the highest income for later years. Annuities pay out to beneficiaries both the interest and a portion of the principal each year. Moreover, taxes on the income are deferred until benefits begin. If this is after retirement, beneficiaries may be in lower tax brackets.[34] Some insurance companies have begun to sell variable insurance policies, with benefits rising according to some formula. In 1973, the Securities and Exchange Commission exempted life insurance from regulation under the Investment Company Act, making it easier for life insurance companies to sell variable life insurance policies. Since reserves are only a fraction of the face values of policies, capital gain on invested reserves provides only a small increase in the face values of policies. Nevertheless, a $10,000 policy bought in 1935 might have provided from $50,000 to $100,000 of insurance in 1972, if a variable policy had been bought in 1935.[35]

Life insurance companies have become more active as managers of pension funds. As inflation fell and stock market prices rose in the 1980s, many companies that had "defined benefit" plans (plans providing specified benefits) replaced them with "defined contribution" plans; increases in stock (and bond) prices had resulted in defined benefit plans having more funds than needed. In managing pension funds, life insurance companies can invest more heavily in stocks.

At least four factors have adversely affected life insurance companies in the recent inflation years. (1) Tax rates for mutual life insurance company income rise as rates of interest earned rise; if companies earn 12 percent interest, they *may* pay a *marginal* tax rate high enough to take all the earnings yielding that rate. (2) Some people have always advised buyers of insurance to buy term insurance and invest the difference in cost (the cost of a whole life policy minus the cost of a term policy), on the ground that individuals can thus earn more than insurance companies would pay them—and this advice seemed better and better as interest rates rose. (3) Because funds invested by life insurance companies for policyholders earn relatively low rates, when interest rates rose, some policyholders surrendered their policies and asked for

[34] See Mary Greenebaum, "Why Annuities Are Taking Off," *Fortune*, August 27, 1979, pp. 121–123, for a more detailed analysis.

[35] See *Fortune*, March 1973, pp. 51–56.

cash, and others sought policy loans at low interest rates (provided for by policy clauses)—in effect, "disintermediation" for insurance companies. (4) Life insurance companies dealt more with groups and less with individuals because (a) they obtained some money from pension funds to invest in fixed-income securities (whereas previously the pension funds were investing more heavily in stocks), and (b) employers more often provided group life insurance (usually term insurance) for employees. Groups usually bargained more vigorously than individuals, and term insurance was less profitable than whole life insurance. Taxes on life insurance companies were reduced in 1984, and new types of policies have reduced the disadvantage of other forms of insurance compared with term life insurance and investment of remaining funds elsewhere.

Future growth of life insurance companies clearly depends in part on trends in inflation and in interest rates. If interest rates rise significantly, people will terminate older cash-value life insurance policies, but if interest rates fall or remain stable, life insurance companies will grow more rapidly. Pension fund management by life insurance companies will increase in either case. In the long run, life insurance companies will try to improve their competitive position, offering new types of policies and probably working with other institutions in providing for sale of insurance company services to the public.[36] The rise in required contributions to Social Security is a negative factor—people are likely to have less funds available for other uses.

Finally, mention should be made of policy loans. Most policyholders have clauses in their policies permitting them to borrow specified amounts at relatively low interest rates compared with rates on other consumer loans. At times, especially when other sources of consumer loans were limited, policyholders have turned in increasing numbers to their life insurance companies for loans. In 1966 and again in 1969, for example, periods of "credit crunches," this resulted in some reduction in the volume of funds available for investment by life insurance companies in the long-term capital markets. The same thing occurred in the late 1970s and early 1980s.

## Pension Funds

Pension funds include the funds held by the Old Age, Survivors, Disability, and Health Insurance System OASDHI (or Social Security) and by some federally supervised pension funds such as the Railroad Retirement fund and the Civil Service pension fund, corporate pension funds, and the employee retirement funds of state and local governments.

Social Security funds and the federally supervised pension funds are invested in special classes of government securities; this "locks up" a small portion of the national debt and reduces the supply of *marketable* government securities.

Social Security programs are unique because of their large size, their dependence on congressional actions, and the fact that the "fund" is relatively small. Most

---

[36] Timothy Curry and Mark Warshawsky, "Life Insurance Companies in a Changing Environment," *Federal Reserve Bulletin*, July 1986, pp. 449–460.

benefits are paid from the current contributions required from workers; they are "transfers" from workers to retirees. Thus Social Security contributions are not "saving" that provides funds largely for investment; much (perhaps most) of the transferred funds provide money for consumption spending by retirees. Some economists, such as Martin Feldstein and Michael Boskin, believe that the existence of Social Security benefits has for years held down the rate of saving in the United States, because people who anticipated Social Security benefits saved less in other forms of assets held for retirement years. Most saving goes into banks, stocks, bonds, and the like and provides (mostly) funds for investment, whereas a very large part of Social Security contributions provides funds for consumption. Pension funds are normally invested during working years, providing funds for "real" investment—in factories, equipment, and so on. But even if the Social Security fund is increasing in size (as it is in the 1980s), it is invested in special government securities and does not provide funds for "real" investment.

Economists such as Boskin find other defects in Social Security: if a couple both work and pay Social Security contributions, the amounts they receive in the future may be far less than the present value of the contributions they make; on the other hand, a couple with only one working (at the same salary as one of the persons in the former case) may receive more than the present value of the contributions made.[37]

In spite of such criticisms, there is broad public support for Social Security, and major changes are not very likely in the near future, although Congress might "index" the income level at which half of Social Security benefits becomes taxable.

Corporate pension funds have become important recently—indeed, largely in the second half of the twentieth century, although some corporate pension funds began as early as World War I. Pension agreements usually provide for a pension of a certain number of dollars each month, often calculated as a multiple of the number of years worked, with variations. Although unions may negotiate for increases in pension amounts, once these are agreed upon, the amounts of pension payments are fixed for a period of time. Because contributions are usually made by employers, sometimes solely by employers, and because payments are fixed until terms of the agreement change, it is in the interest of employers to obtain high rates of return on investment of pension funds, so that the same dollar amounts of pensions may be obtained with smaller contributions. As pension funds became more common, the desire for a higher rate of return led to some shift, from the bonds most pension funds were first invested in, to stocks on which the combined return of dividends and capital gain exceeded the average rate of return on bonds. At the end of 1982, pension funds had 58 percent of their assets in stocks and only 35 percent in bonds.

Because accounting valuation of assets is discretionary and most funds carry assets at cost, fluctuations in market values of stock do not create difficulties. Because much pension fund income is exempt from taxation, pension fund managers have little interest in tax-exempt securities.

Assets in pension funds grow over long periods because most of the employees

---

[37] "Blasting Away at Social Security," *Fortune*, August 4, 1986, pp. 233–236.

who come under a newly formed pension plan are a number of years from retirement. For many years, contributions made by those who are employed exceed the payments to those who have retired. Moreover, inadequate provisions for "vesting" have meant that many employees who are discharged or who seek other employment lose their pension rights. Thus, pension funds generally can look forward to a long period of growth. Any legislative or other encouragement that would make possible the growth of funds in areas not now generally covered would obviously lead to further growth of total pension fund assets for some period of time. The major area for such growth is that of medium-sized and small business firms.

Many corporate pension funds are managed by trust departments of banks, some by corporations themselves, and some by life insurance companies. Pension funds constitute over 35 percent of the assets of the trust departments of banks, and about 60 percent of this amount is invested in common stocks.[38] There is intense competition among financial institutions for the business of management of these large sums.

Congress became concerned because of many cases in which workers with long years of service failed to receive pension benefits because they were forced out of employment before retirement age. It also became concerned about safety in the investment of pension funds. The Employee Retirement Income Security Act of 1974 (ERISA) provided minimum standards for vesting (giving employees irrevocable rights to pensions) after certain time periods. The act also increased the requirement for funding pension liabilities (paying in sufficient funds to meet the expected benefit payments) under certain conditions. Further, a number of rules were prescribed to ensure that those who manage pension funds must invest those funds in the interest of the beneficiaries, must exercise prudence in such investment, and must diversify investments to minimize losses. Some firms terminated their pension plans because of the greater burden of maintaining them under ERISA, and the number of new plans initiated dropped markedly.

Some companies now permit an increasing percentage of the retirement pension to be vested each year. Employees know the amount of pension funds already available to them, although final pension amounts may be somewhat less because they are usually based on average career earnings instead of on the last five years of employment.[39]

Based on the increasing numbers of persons expected to live beyond 65 years of age and on a belief that Social Security benefits may not be sufficient to provide a comfortable living, other plans for retirement investment have become popular. These include individual retirement accounts (IRAs), Keough plans for those who are self-employed, and 401(k) plans, to which companies usually contribute. Under IRA and Keough plans, individuals contribute amounts up to an allowed maximum each year; taxes on the contributions and on the interest earned are deferred until with-

---

[38] Edna E. Ehrlich, "The Functions and Investment Policies of Personal Trust Departments," Federal Reserve Bank of New York, *Monthly Review*, October 1972, pp. 255–270.

[39] *The Wall Street Journal*, March 26, 1986, p. 31.

drawals begin, in the case of IRAs at age 70½. IRAs became very popular, although 401(k) plans, where they exist, have the advantage that contributions are usually made by employers as well as by employees. Since IRA and Keough investments may be made in a wide variety of forms (CDs, stocks, bonds, mutual funds, etc.), investors may shift such funds as returns appear to be better on one type of investment than on others. CDs were very popular when interest rates on them were as high as 16 percent or more, but as rates on CDs fell to 7 percent and less by 1986, other forms became more popular. Under 1986 legislation, amounts that can be put into IRAs with deferral of taxes vary, depending on income and on coverage under a Keough or 401 (k) plan.[40]

## State and Local Government Employees' Retirement Funds

State and local government employees' retirement funds, in contrast to corporate pension funds, are hedged about by many specific restrictions on investment. When such restrictions are not limiting, the asset portfolio depends on the sophistication of the investment officer. In many jurisdictions this individual's investment training may be very limited. Hence it is not surprising that until recently most of the funds were invested in state and local government and U.S. government securities. These funds now have nearly half of their assets invested in corporate and foreign bonds and about 25 percent in stocks. The shift to investment in corporate bonds and stocks came as the need for higher yields was recognized and as education of the investment officers increased.

The chief importance of the contractual saving institutions, both the life insurance companies and the pension funds, is that they are an important conduit through which savings regularly flow into designated parts of the money and capital markets. Although growth rates change over time, the contractual saving institutions usually do not have the wide fluctuations that characterize deposits in depository-type institutions. Unlike the depository-type institutions, life insurance companies are not usually important in attracting funds at certain times, such as periods of very high short-term interest rates (1980–1982).

## Property and Casualty Insurance Companies

Property and casualty insurance companies are quite different in their investment policies from life insurance companies and pension funds, but they are discussed here to complete the coverage of insurance companies. Payments that have to be made by such companies are not nearly as easily predictable as are those of life insurance companies; if inflation occurs, many payments of property and casualty insurance companies rise because costs of repairs and replacements are greater. Hence property and casualty insurance companies have both a greater need for liquidity and a greater need for higher return than do life insurance companies, leading them to invest in

---

[40] Tax on interest earned on an IRA is still deferred until retirement.

government securities for liquidity and in stocks for higher return. Because many of them are stock companies, subject to the regular corporate income tax, they also invest in municipal securities because of the tax-exempt feature. Property and casualty insurance companies invest rather heavily in stocks. They had, in the early 1980s, nearly half of their assets in state and local government securities and about 20 percent in stocks. When stock market values rise, dividend yields *appear* to decline.[41] Nevertheless, net investment income provides a supplement to net underwriting income (premiums minus underwriting expenses and loss claims paid). In recent years, when net underwriting income has been negative (losses), net investment income has allowed the companies to continue to show profits.

# INVESTMENT-TYPE INSTITUTIONS

The major investment-type institutions include investment companies, real estate investment trusts, personal and common trust funds managed by trust departments of commercial banks, and foundations and endowments. Specified commitments are agreed upon for payments of income from these funds to beneficiaries, although some mutual funds provide for automatic reinvestment of dividends and capital gains distributions.

## Investment Companies

Mutual funds, one category among investment companies, regularly sell shares to investors and invest the funds in stocks and/or bonds. Their advantages to small investors are that they permit diversification, not possible in direct investment of small amounts by individuals in specific stocks and/or in individual bond issues, and that they may provide more expert management than small investors could generally give to their own portfolios. Mutual funds may be bond funds, stock funds, or mixed funds. In the early 1980s, the total value of stocks held amounted to approximately 70 percent of the total assets held by all such funds, while the value of corporate bonds was only about 15 percent and the value of government securities held in the funds was quite small.

Mutual funds grew rapidly after World War II, as stock prices generally rose. With the poor performance of the stock market in the 1970s, however, mutual funds experienced excesses of redemptions of shares over new sales. Emphasis on performance—substantial short-term capital gains—in the 1960s led some mutual funds to engage in rapid turnover of stocks held in their portfolios and thus may have contributed to the volatility of the market. The fact that mutual funds concentrated attention on a limited number of favorite stocks may also have caused the prices of such stocks to rise more than would otherwise have been the case. There is disagreement concerning both the effect of mutual funds on volatility of stock prices and the management expertise of mutual funds. Such questions are outside the scope of this book, but the

---

[41] Net yields before taxes are relatively low because of the relatively large investments in tax-exempt securities, which have low yields.

attitude of investors toward mutual funds is an important factor affecting stock prices. If investors are hesitant to buy mutual fund shares and instead place their funds in other financial institutions, stock prices may remain lower in relation to earnings than they were in the 1960s. Much depends on the extent to which investors feel a need to invest in assets that can rise in price, to hedge against inflation. Such factors affect both the rates of growth of various financial institutions and the money and capital markets to which individuals and institutions supply funds.

A new type of mutual fund appeared after passage of the Tax Reform Act of 1976. This is the tax-free bond fund, which is permitted to pass through to fund shareholders the tax-free interest earned on municipal (state and local government) securities. Small initial investments, sometimes as low as $100, are permitted. Although the advantage of investing in tax-free bonds is greater for investors in higher tax brackets, there may be some advantage for moderate-income investors. As inflation occurs, more people find themselves in higher tax brackets. Of course, bonds may fall in price if interest rates rise with continuing inflation, and, if investors must sell their holdings, they lose. There is also some default risk in municipal securities. Hence, small investors, who often invest in mutual funds or keep their savings in institutions such as savings and loan associations, may not find the tax-free bond funds as appealing as they may at first seem. This is indicated by the relatively small size of such funds.

Another type of mutual fund gained some popularity in recent years when short-term interest rates were high—the money market mutual fund. Money market mutual funds, discussed in an earlier section in this chapter, are a type of mutual fund. But, since their assets are held in short-term securities rather than in long-term investments, and their liabilities are liquid rather than long-term, they were discussed separately.

Closed-end investment companies are a special type; they issue shares that are not redeemable and new shares are not sold regularly. Thus for considerable periods of time, no new shares may be sold, whereas mutual funds regularly sell new shares and endeavor to expand. Closed-end investment companies offer the possibility of leverage: investors may obtain higher returns because the fund issues debt instruments, such as debentures, as well as capital shares. Purchasers of capital shares may obtain higher returns if returns on assets that funds are invested in are higher than interest rates that must be paid on the debentures. A number of closed-end investment companies were organized before the stock market crash of 1929; their shares have continuously sold at discount in recent years. Thus there is little incentive to form new companies, and closed-end investment companies may continue to be an investment medium for only a small group of investors.

## Real Estate Investment Trusts (REITs)

Real estate investment trusts are another institution that became important in the 1970s. The Real Estate Investment Act of 1960 authorized the establishment of institutions that, if they had 75 percent or more of their assets in real estate, derived

75 percent or more of their income from real estate, and distributed 90 percent or more of their income to their stockholders, were exempt from income tax. Stockholders, of course, are taxed on the income received, as usual. But they, too, receive a tax advantage because each of them is allowed a pro rata share of the depreciation allowances permitted on the property owned by the trust.

Numerous REITs were created in 1969 and 1970, as the end of one stock market boom shifted speculation to other types of assets. Some were independently organized, some were sponsored by banks, and some by life insurance companies and other financial institutions. Some were equity investors in real estate, some engaged in real estate development, almost entirely of income property, and made construction loans, and some were mainly long-term mortgage lenders. REITs had, in addition to equity capital, long-term debt in the form of bonds and usually short-term debt in the form of bank borrowings.

In the 1973–1975 period, many REITs encountered severe financial difficulties because of a combination of inflation, which pushed up construction costs and other expenses, and high interest rates that led to a decline in the amount of real estate demanded. These difficulties in turn caused losses for banks that had invested in them. When the real estate market weakened, REITs that were making construction loans were especially hard hit. Some projects could not be completed, and some were so high in cost that obtainable rental income could not cover expenses. Because of these difficulties, it appears that REITs may not become a major type of financial institution, but, if a number of them recover from their adverse positions, they will constitute a small institutional subsector within the group of institutions that lend in the mortgage and real estate market.

Rising values of real estate in the late 1970s, accompanying the serious inflation, improved the situation of many REITs, but left them vulnerable to takeovers, acquisitions, or mergers. This situation increased the probability that REITs will not become a major financial institution, but might survive on a small scale. The rise in real estate values without a corresponding rise in the values of stocks left shares in REITs undervalued (perhaps in common with many other stocks). For some REITs, the damage inflicted by the 1973–1975 recession seems to have been offset.[42] However, they are in total size relatively small.

## Personal Trust Funds

Personal trust funds managed by trust departments of banks are highly safety oriented, preservation of capital being a major goal. One general guideline for investments in many states is the "prudent man rule," which specifies that managers of trusts must invest "only in such securities as would be acquired by prudent men of discretion and intelligence in such matters who are seeking a reasonable income and

---

[42] See, for example, "REITs Try to Dodge the Takeover Sharks," *Business Week*, October 29, 1979, pp. 85–86.

the preservation of their capital." There is wide leeway for interpretation of this rule. Most of the funds are invested in common stocks (about 60–65 percent), corporate bonds (about 15 percent),[43] government securities, state and local government securities, and real estate and real estate mortgages (a little over 5 percent in each category).

Both the contractual saving institutions and the investment-type institutions have a dual importance in the capital markets: they are important because of the inflows of funds to them, which they largely invest in long-term assets, and they are important as holders and managers of large amounts of wealth. Markets for long-term financial assets involve purchases and sales in amounts that, in any given year, are small fractions of the total held by individuals and institutions. Although individuals still hold a majority of the total value of all stocks, individuals as a group were net sellers for a number of years. Because of this selling pressure, prices of stocks would tend to fall if they were not purchased in sizable amounts by institutions such as pension funds, personal trust funds, and mutual funds. The existence of such institutions provides a substantial demand for stocks and thus generally has helped stock prices to rise over long periods of time, in spite of temporary declines. Moreover, if corporations had to attract individual investors in larger numbers, they might well have to pay out more funds in dividends. Purchases of stocks by institutions that desire both dividends and capital gains, and for whom capital gains are relatively attractive when the institutions are growing in size, permit corporations to retain large amounts of earnings, rather than having to seek a flow of funds for investment financed by sales of newly issued securities in the capital markets.

## Foundations and Endowments

Foundations and endowments have become significant enough to warrant special mention. Their assets are chiefly invested in stocks (nearly 60 percent) and bonds (about 22 percent). Income provides funds for the charitable, educational, or religious purposes for which most foundations and endowments were established.

Both investment-type institutions and contractual saving institutions have rather long investment horizons. Since their inflows of funds usually exceed their outpayments because they are growing, they need not be concerned about sale of stocks or bonds on account of temporary needs for funds. Temporary fluctuations in values of stocks and bonds can be overlooked. If long-run prospects for higher values for stocks look bright, only institutions with shorter investment time horizons are more concerned about short-term price fluctuations.

Thus the investment-type financial institutions are important participants in the capital markets. They provide funds that have helped maintain the general long-term rise in stock prices, and they make it possible for corporations to retain large amounts of earnings for use in investment.

---

[43] Corporate bonds constitute a significant percentage of total assets held by trust departments because of their importance in pension funds managed by these departments.

## FINANCE COMPANIES

Finance companies include three types of institutions: sales finance companies, which finance purchases of automobiles and other durable goods on the installment plan; consumer finance or small loan companies, which specialize in making small loans to consumers; and business or commercial finance companies, which specialize in loans to business firms, usually loans that could not be obtained from commercial banks because banks regard the risks as higher than they wish to incur at the rates of interest they are permitted to charge. Finance companies have a quite different liability and capital structure from that of other financial institutions. Unlike banks and other deposit-type institutions, they have a relatively large proportion of equity capital, averaging about one-third of their total funds. To obtain the rest of the funds they need, they borrow in the short-term money market and in the long-term capital market, by obtaining bank loans and by issuing commercial paper (promissory notes) and debentures (bonds not secured by specific assets). A large part of all outstanding commercial paper has been issued by finance companies; often they place this commercial paper directly with institutions such as life insurance companies and banks. Life insurance companies need *some* liquid assets, and banks often wish to invest some funds in commercial paper because of its unusually high degree of safety and high liquidity.[44] Commercial paper is not renewed at maturity, and its maturity is relatively short—never more than 270 days—because longer maturity would necessitate its issue in compliance with the rather burdensome regulations governing the issuing of long-term securities. Liquidity results from the short maturity, often tailored to investors' desires, although there is some repurchase of commercial paper by issuers, which provides some additional degree of liquidity.

Finance companies, because they borrow in both the short-term money market and the long-term capital market, provide one of the links between these markets and are thus important in the relationship between long-term and short-term interest rates.

About half of finance company funds go into consumer finance. Thus, sales finance companies and personal finance companies compete with the consumer loan departments of commercial banks and with credit unions. They assist nonfinancial institutions such as retailers in extending consumer credit for the purchase of goods and services. Utilities and professional people such as doctors and dentists are, of course, other sources of consumer credit.

The other half of finance company lending now goes to business firms, providing short-term and intermediate-term credit, chiefly to small- and medium-sized businesses. Bank loans now provide less than three-fourths of the short-term and intermediate-term credit obtained by business firms; finance companies provide about

---

[44] It was most unusual, in 1970, that the Penn Central Transportation Co. had $82 million in commercial paper outstanding when the Penn Central went into bankruptcy, because prior to that time there had been almost no defaults on commercial paper since 1936. For an interesting story of the 1970 crisis and how it was met, see Carol J. Loomis, "The Lesson of the Credit Crisis," *Fortune*, May 1971, pp. 141–143, 274–286.

20 percent and sale of commercial paper provides an increasing amount. Many finance companies are "captives" of manufacturing firms, financing sales of products to dealers and retailers.[45]

## MISCELLANEOUS

The other categories of institutions in the financial services industry are much more difficult to discuss in terms of types of assets and liabilities held and owed. These other institutions include (1) institutions that originated as government agencies and are still government-supervised in many cases, but that are now largely privately owned; (2) retail stores that see an opportunity to serve both the goods and services needs and the financial needs of consumers and recognize the increased amounts of both discretionary spending and saving and financial investment that are likely with rising income levels; (3) conglomerates that see an opportunity to provide a great variety of financial services, although they may be excluded from certain areas reserved for commercial banks; (4) brokerage and investment houses that have constituted the "securities industry," buying and selling securities for customers (brokerage) and underwriting and distributing securities for firms that borrow in the bond market and that issue new issues of stocks; and (5) some miscellaneous institutions, such as mortgage companies, that make some mortgage loans with their own funds but in general serve to make mortgage loans on a temporary basis until they can sell a group or package of mortgage loans to other institutions (chiefly insurance companies); pawnshops; and others.

We consider first the quasi-government lending agencies, which exist chiefly in the fields of farm credit and housing finance. The government has entered the field of business credit only in a limited way, the chief agencies being the Small Business Administration for credit to small business firms, and the Export-Import Bank to finance exports (and theoretically imports). The government has also done very little in consumer lending (which is normally defined so as to exclude loans to buy or build houses).

### Government Lending Agencies

As indicated in Chapter 1, the government has important financial roles as a borrower, an insurer of deposits, a regulator of the financial services industry, and an ultimate source of liquidity (government securities have a high degree of safety and liquidity, even when private institutions fail and losses may be incurred on deposits and other liabilities). Here we examine its role in sponsoring lending agencies.

The first government institutions were established in agriculture; the Federal Land Banks were organized to provide agricultural mortgage credit. Much later Federal Intermediate Credit Banks and Production Credit Associations were formed.

---

[45] For more details, see Maury Harris, "Finance Companies as Business Lenders," Federal Reserve Bank of New York, *Quarterly Review*, Summer 1979, pp. 35–39.

In the field of housing, the first significant effort of the government was directed toward insurance of mortgage loans, to encourage private lending institutions to make such loans. The insurance and guarantee programs of the Federal Housing Administration (FHA) and the Veterans Administration (VA) have significantly aided the mortgage market. The government also established agencies to provide housing for low-income groups; the Public Housing Administration (PHA) and the Farmers' Home Administration are evidence of the government interest in subsidizing such housing. The Rural Electrification Administration (REA) was very important in subsidizing the distribution of electricity. Finally, a group of agencies has been created to aid in developing a secondary market for mortgages—the Federal National Mortgage Association (FNMA, or Fanny Mae), the Government National Mortgage Association (GNMA, or Ginny Mae), and the Federal Home Loan Mortgage Corporation (Freddy Mac). Many of these agencies are now privately owned.

The historical details of the establishment of these and other agencies are interesting, but beyond what we can discuss at this point. However, the existence of a number of privately owned agencies that still are or formerly were government agencies is significant in the money and capital markets. Securities of these agencies compete with Treasury securities and private securities, and some significant effects in yield fluctuations result from such competition. The fact that most of these agencies (those that are privately owned) are not now included in the federal government budget removes them from scrutiny when the budget is being curtailed—in effect influencing the flow of funds into the housing and agricultural credit fields.[46]

## Retail Stores

Retail stores have provided some financial services for many years. Many offered charge accounts (department stores) or, more recently, plastic cards for charging purchases (stores like Sears, Roebuck and J. C. Penney). Sears has had a subsidiary, Allstate Insurance, to sell insurance policies. What is new is that some of these retail stores are now moving ahead with vigor to gain a more prominent place as a part of the financial services industry.

Officials such as Edward R. Telling, Chairman and Chief Executive Officer of Sears, recognized that the shift in government policy in 1980 meant that the government was taking steps to shift the choice between consumption and saving in the direction of saving. Lower taxes, especially marginal rates, leave more income for saving; lower inflation means less fear of loss of the value of savings; IRAs and other new forms of accounts encourage saving, whereas the growth of Social Security

---

[46] Concern about the rapid growth of government lending (both that which is included in the budget and that which is not included in the budget because it is by institutions which are now privately owned) has been expressed by some; see, for example, "The Sugar Daddy of Federal Credit," Citibank, *Monthly Economic Letter*, July 1980, pp. 5–7. On the other hand, some are concerned about problems some of these agencies, such as the Farm Credit System, are encountering in the 1980s in providing needed credit; see, for example, Kerry Webb, "The Farm Credit System," Federal Reserve Bank of Kansas City, *Economic Review*, June 1980, pp. 16–30.

benefits must be slowed unless taxes (Social Security contributions) are raised. Telling recognized this shift toward saving, and realized that this means somewhat slower long-run growth in consumption. He therefore argued that Sears should participate in the provision of financial services needed both because small savers were not well served in the past and because additional saving will require additional services.

Telling commented that "if multistate banking and interstate banking are not permitted, then firms like American Express and Sears, with electronic fund transfers, will do the job banks should do."[47]

Sears has Allstate Insurance, it has acquired Dean Witter Reynolds, a large brokerage firm, it has acquired the largest independent real estate broker in the country (Coldwell Banker), it has a large credit card system, and it now owns a large California-based thrift, Allstate Savings and Loan. It plans, according to its chief executive officer, to lend to its customers on the security of their home equities, provide electronic transfers throughout the country, provide a facility for acceptance and disbursal of funds in every Sears store, have a more widely useful credit card, develop two-way communications with homes so that many more financial transactions can be undertaken without people leaving their homes, and support further deregulation of the financial services industry.

If Sears is able to effect these changes, a retail sales firm will become an *important* element in the financial services industry. The competitive pressure on other elements of the industry will be great.

## Conglomerates

Conglomerates such as Shearson Lehman Brothers (a subsidiary of American Express) are also becoming quite significant as elements in the financial services industry. It might seem that conglomerates, large retail stores, and large commercial banks have the resources to dominate the future financial services industry. But the industry provides services to all kinds of consumers and to all kinds of business firms, it provides many different financial services, and it uses many distribution systems. There is room for small- and medium-sized institutions providing financial services, just as there is room for large airlines and small ones.

We need to reconsider the economic advantages that conglomerates may be presumed to have. Size enables them to take advantage of economies of scale, as far as these exist. "Synergy" may enable a conglomerate to be more efficient than any of the component companies could be by themselves. But conglomerates also have disadvantages. Too great a size leads to problems of management and control. It is not possible for one firm to possess superior expertise in a very wide variety of activities.

The most significant single statistic is the relatively *low* profit in banking: return on equity (ROE) in 1980 was about 13 percent on book value of equity, whereas for Standard & Poor's 500 stocks and for life insurance companies, it was over 15 percent,

---

[47] Edward R. Telling, "Meeting the New Realities of the American Marketplace," address to the Economic Club of Chicago, February 25, 1982 (mimeographed).

and for investment brokerage companies (discussed shortly), it was 22 percent.[48] There are probably too many banks and too many bank offices. With the advent of more offices of retail stores and conglomerates, all providing many financial services, the need for consolidation is apparent.

In view of this need, it is unlikely that the financial services industry will be deregulated as much as other industries. Nevertheless, a change in many of the laws hurriedly imposed in the 1930s is needed. So a *change* in regulation, with *some* deregulation, may be expected. Since financial institutions *can* be subject to manipulation and fraud, probably more than commodity-selling institutions, government is likely to continue to regulate the industry. And government cannot overlook the possibility of a financial collapse, such as occurred in the period 1931 to 1933.

In the long run, with the advent of retail stores and conglomerates that have no reserve requirements, it is possible that reserve requirements for banks may be reduced. As indicated in Chapter 3, such requirements serve no significant purpose of safety or liquidity; they are in effect simply a tax and a way of providing a fulcrum (leverage point) for controlling bank reserves and thus controlling the money supply. This leverage point could be provided with a much lower reserve requirement, but of course lowering reserve requirements drastically is not appropriate while the danger of inflation continues.

## Investment Houses and Brokerage Firms

Investment houses and brokerage firms specialize in aiding firms in selling new securities (bonds or stocks) and in providing a means whereby individuals and institutions can trade stocks and bonds. If they specialize more in the former, they are investment houses; if in the latter, they are brokerage firms. Actually, most such firms carry out both functions to some extent.

The chief difference between these firms and most of the other financial institutions thus far discussed is that these firms have much smaller assets, relative to the volume of their business. They are indeed primarily selling *services* rather than holding assets for customers, although of course they hold some assets—as is evident to anyone who has a brokerage house hold stocks for him or her, in "street" name.

The services that these firms sell are those involved in marketing securities for business firms (new issues) and in providing information, research, and other services for investors, as well as handling transactions for them.

Legislation of the 1930s has prevented banks from performing most of these functions of the securities industry, as it is called. But some banks have positioned themselves to conduct investment house and brokerage services if the law is changed. Bank of America, for example, bought a discount brokerage house as a subsidiary of Bank of America's holding company. In autumn 1982, Bank of America began bro-

---

[48] These figures, and some of the ideas that follow, were contained in Alex J. Pollock, "The Future of Banking: A National Market and Its Implications," Federal Reserve Bank of Chicago, *Economic Perspectives*, Fall 1982, pp. 30–32.

kerage services at six branches as a pilot program, even though Federal Reserve approval was not expected until early 1983.[49] Other banks have offered telephone brokerage services, and some banks have established small "merchant banking" divisions to advise business firms on issuing securities, even though the banks cannot underwrite and distribute such securities unless the law is changed. Return on equity in the brokerage activity is, as noted, higher than in banking, and these actions may increase the profitability of banking.

A decision by a federal appeals court in 1982 seemed to have cleared the way for banks to compete with investment houses in distributing (selling) commercial paper, under certain conditions. However, a Fed opinion, also favorable, was reversed by a court decision in early 1986 that prohibited banks from selling commercial paper, arguing that this constituted an activity prohibited by the Glass-Steagall Act of 1933. The concern, then and now, is potential conflict of interest—for example, might a bank make a loan to facilitate sale of commercial paper? Could it sell paper to its trust department? Prospects for wider bank activity in areas now covered by investment and brokerage houses are uncertain.[50]

### Others

There are a number of other financial or semifinancial institutions, such as mortgage banks, pawnshops, investment affiliates of foreign banks, and others, but they are not discussed because they are generally of minor importance in the financial system.

## SUMMARY

Institutions in the financial services industry may be classified on the basis of (1) the nature of their liabilities; (2) the liquidity, maturity, and yield of their assets; and (3) the types of services they provide.

Deposit-type financial institutions, or depository institutions, have demand or relatively short-term liabilities and fluctuating inflows and outflows of funds (although fluctuations are usually less than those for commercial banks). The deposit-type financial institutions compete for savings (and to a minor extent, now, transactions) balances. They invest large percentages of their assets in housing (mortgage) loans, a much smaller percentage in consumer loans, and in recent years have been permitted to make business loans as a small percentage of their total assets. The chief distinction between commercial banks and other deposit-type institutions used to be that com-

---

[49] *The Wall Street Journal*, October 21, 1982, p. 33. That discount brokerage house became independent again in 1987; see *Business Week*, August 17, 1987, p. 77.

[50] For background and further details, see *The Wall Street Journal*, June 5, 1985, p. 2, and February 5, 1986, p. 2. For a more general analysis, see Anthony Saunders, "Securities Activities of Commercial Banks: The Problem of Conflicts of Interest," Federal Reserve Bank of Philadelphia, *Business Review*, July–August, 1985, pp. 17–26.

mercial banks held *demand* deposits and created money. Money was created because (usually) banks made loans to business borrowers and in doing so created new or increased demand deposit accounts for them. The other deposit-type institutions usually reduced their own cash or deposits held as assets when they made mortgage loans. In the 1980s, as these other deposit-type institutions were granted more power to make consumer loans and to make some business loans, they gained the power to create money if in making such loans they create new or additional demand deposits for the borrowers. In order to create money, an institution must have "excess reserves" (more reserves than required). Thus, fundamentally, control of the size of the money supply rests with the Federal Reserve System and its power to create (or reduce) excess reserves. Details are discussed in Chapter 5.

Contractual saving institutions have quite regular inflows of funds (in policy premiums or pension fund contributions); having little need for liquidity, they have usually invested most of their assets in long-term bonds, stocks, and mortgages, and sometimes in real estate.

Investment-type institutions have generally long-term liabilities but not the regular inflows of funds experienced by contractual savings institutions. They also have little need for liquidity and invest chiefly in stocks, bonds, and real estate.

Finance companies have both long-term liabilities (often debentures) and short-term liabilities (commonly commercial paper). They finance both consumers and business firms, usually business firms that find it difficult to obtain loans from banks.

Finally, miscellaneous institutions, which formerly included mainly government-sponsored agencies in housing and farm financing, together with investment and brokerage houses, now also include retail stores and conglomerates as major participants. Some retail stores recognize the opportunity to attract savings as government policy shifts toward encouragement of saving. They also see an opportunity to provide one-stop service for many consumer needs in financial services. Conglomerates have seen the value of participation in such activities as investment and brokerage services and have acquired major investment and/or brokerage houses. Both retail stores and conglomerates also have recognized the need to participate in some form of provision for acceptance of payments and disbursement of funds, probably (in the long run) an electronic funds transfer system.

Major causes of the changes in the financial services industry are the inflation of the 1970s and the policy change in the early 1980s that has already reduced inflation, reduced interest rates, and to some extent encouraged saving. These developments and the completion of electronic funds transfer networks are basic factors in causing fundamental change in the financial services industry.

## Appendix: Major Provisions of the Depository Institutions Act of 1982 (the Garn-St Germain bill)

Major purposes of this legislation were to provide some means of assistance for savings and loan associations, which had been very adversely affected by economic conditions, to provide assistance for banks, and to make all depository institutions more competitive with each other and with other institutions having somewhat similar liabilities, such as money market mutual funds. The law directed the DIDC to specify details for a new type of deposit account, later termed the money market deposit account (MMDA), with a minimum initial deposit of not more than $5,000 (the DIDC set the minimum at $2,500 and made December 14, 1982 the effective date), with no required reserves but with deposit insurance and with limited transfer privileges. All depositors, including trust depositors, were eligible. No more than six transfers out of an account could be made per month (meaning either a calendar month or a bank statement cycle period). Transfers included preauthorized transfers, automatic transfers, and telephone transfers, as well as checks; of the six, no more than three could be by third-party checks. Checks made out to "cash," to the accountholder, or to the bank holding the account are regarded as second party checks, and may be used in unlimited numbers. Unlimited numbers of over-the-counter withdrawals or transfers can be made, in person, by request of a personal agent, by letter request, or through automatic teller machines (ATMs). There was to be no interest rate ceiling.

(Although not part of the Garn-St Germain bill, another type of account was also authorized by the DIDC, effective January 5, 1983. This account is limited to individuals and to nonprofit institutions if treated as such by the Internal Revenue Service (partnerships and corporations do not qualify). Unlimited numbers of checks, ATM withdrawals, automatic transfers, and "sweeps" into other accounts are permitted. With unlimited numbers of transfers, costs for banks are higher than for the MMDAs, and hence, as might have been expected, interest rates paid are generally lower. The MMDAs have been much more popular than the Super-NOW accounts, as these second accounts came to be known.)

The FDIC is empowered to arrange loans to buy the securities of, assume the liabilities of, or make contributions to any insured bank experiencing severe financial difficulties. Financial institutions may issue net worth certificates backed by the FDIC or FSLIC, as appropriate, if net worth falls below three percent of assets. To obtain such aid, an institution must have at least 20 percent of its portfolio in residential mortgages—obviously, savings and loan associations are more likely to meet this requirement than banks. The regulatory authorities also may merge a failing savings and loan association with one in another state or with a commercial bank.

Financial institutions are permitted to offer NOW accounts and share draft accounts to state and local government units.

Insurance activities by bank holding companies are prohibited unless already being conducted before May 1, 1982. Commercial banks may not sell property and casualty insurance.

"Due on sale" clauses found in many mortgages can in general be enforced—this means that a buyer of a house, assuming an existing mortgage, may have to pay a higher interest rate. In June 1982, the Supreme Court had authorized this for federal savings and loan associations, and the law extended this to national banks and to state-chartered savings and loan associations.

Federally chartered savings and loan associations can increase nonresidential real estate lending up to 40 percent of their assets, and can make consumer loans up to

30 percent of their assets. They, and also federally chartered savings banks, can (after January 1, 1984) make commercial loans in amounts not exceeding, in total, 10 percent of their assets.

Differences between banks and savings and loan associations in interest rates paid on deposits or share accounts had to be eliminated by January 1, 1984.

The act also provided that the first $2 million of liabilities requiring reserves, for each depository institution, be exempt from reserve requirements. This amount is adjusted slightly by the Federal Reserve System each year. The exemption was set at $2.1 million for the first year (beginning December 9, 1982) and an order was established for types of accounts to be exempt from reserve requirements. It has been estimated that this will eliminate reserve requirements for over 20,000 credit unions, savings and loan associations, and commercial banks—more than half of all such institutions—but that this accounts for less than 2 percent of total deposits. Small institutions are benefited by elimination of the cost (and effort of calculation) of required reserves, but the ability of the Federal Reserve System to control required reserves and thus control total deposits for all depository institutions as a group is not materially affected.

Issues not dealt with by this law include the McFadden Act restrictions on branch banking (which do not apply to thrift institutions or money market funds) and the Glass-Steagall Act restrictions on security subsidiaries (which apply only to national banks and state banks which are members of the Federal Reserve System).[51]

## Questions for Discussion

**1.** Cite reasons for classifying all deposit-type financial institutions in one group. What similarities do they have in the nature of their assets, the nature of their liabilities, and their need for liquidity?

**2.** Is deposit insurance equally needed for deposits in commercial banks, deposits in mutual savings banks, accounts in savings and loan associations, and accounts in credit unions? Why or why not?

**3.** Why do commercial banks invest such small amounts of funds in corporate bonds?

**4.** Why do savings and loan associations invest almost no funds in corporate bonds?

**5.** Why is there usually no change in size of money supply (M1) when funds are shifted from demand deposit accounts in commercial banks to accounts in or claims on nonbank financial institutions?

**6.** What are the arguments for permitting federal charters for mutual savings banks? Were there any arguments against this change?

**7.** Would you expect life insurance companies to grow as rapidly in the next decade as commercial banks or nonbank deposit-type institutions? Why or why not?

[51] For further discussion of the background of this act, see Verle Johnston, "Sero Sed Serio" ("late but earnest"), Federal Reserve Bank of San Francisco, *Weekly Letter*, October 15, 1982.

**8.** What factors may permit greater growth of private pension funds in the next decade, and what factors may tend to restrict such growth?

**9.** Why are finance companies such important issuers of commercial paper? What factors may tend to affect the rate of growth of commercial paper in the next decade?

**10.** Why did government-sponsored financial institutions become so important in the fields of housing and agriculture? Why are retail stores and conglomerates becoming important in providing many financial services?

## Selected References

Financial institutions discussed in this chapter are discussed in more detail in Robert O. Edmister, *Financial Institutions, Markets, and Management* (New York: McGraw-Hill, 1980). Another useful source of information is *Nonbank Financial Institutions* (Federal Reserve Bank of Richmond, 1975).

Statistics concerning major financial institutions may be found in the *Federal Reserve Bulletin* (monthly), the *Life Insurance Fact Book* (annually), the *Savings and Loan Fact Book* (annually), and the *International Credit Union Yearbook* (annually). The *NCUA Quarterly*, published by the National Credit Union Administration, provides relatively current information on credit unions, and the *Journal* published by the Federal Home Loan Bank Board does the same for savings and loan associations.

An interesting history of various types of financial intermediaries is that of Herman E. Krooss and Martin R. Blyn, *A History of Financial Intermediaries* (New York: Random House, 1971). A useful, rather brief discussion of the Employee Retirement Income Security Act of 1974 (ERISA) and its effects on pension funds is "Private Pensions: Adapting to ERISA," *Morgan Guaranty Survey*, October 1976, pp. 6–13.

Information on personal trust funds is available in Edna E. Ehrlich, "The Functions and Investment Policies of Personal Trust Departments," Federal Reserve Bank of New York, *Monthly Review*, October 1972, pp. 255–270, and January 1973, pp. 12–19.

For a comprehensive study of mutual funds, see Irwin Friend, Marshall Blume, and Jean Crockett, *Mutual Funds and Other Institutional Investors: A New Perspective* (New York: McGraw-Hill, 1970).

A historical study of mutual savings banks is that of Weldon Welfling, *Mutual Savings Banks: The Evolution of a Financial Intermediary* (Cleveland, Ohio: Case Western Reserve University Press, 1968).

Analytical materials on credit unions are relatively scarce, but see John T. Croteau, *The Economics of the Credit Union* (Detroit: Wayne State University Press, 1963). See also Gary G. Heaton and Constance R. Dunham, "The Growing Competitiveness of Credit Unions," Federal Reserve Bank of Boston, *New England Economic Review*, May–June 1985, pp. 19–34.

For a very readable account of the adverse effects of inflation on life insurance companies, see Carol J. Loomis, "Life Isn't What It Used to Be," *Fortune*, July 14, 1980, pp. 86–100. On indexing life insurance policy death benefits to compensate for inflation, see Mary Greenebaum, "Cost-of-Living Insurance Costs Too Much," *Fortune*, June 16, 1980, pp. 205–208.

The history leading to passage, the provisions, and the impact on various institutions of the Garn-St Germain bill (the Depository Institutions Act of 1982) are covered in *Economic Perspectives*, Federal Reserve Bank of Chicago, March–April 1983.

A summary analysis of innovative forces let loose by inflation in the 1970s and improved technology is provided by Alfred Broadus, "Financial Innovation in the United States—Background, Current Status, and Prospects," Federal Reserve Bank of Richmond, *Economic Review*, January–February 1985, pp. 2–22.

# MONEY: DEFINITIONS, MEASURES, CREATION, AND CONTROL OF SUPPLY

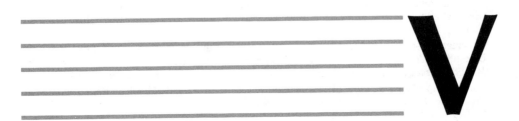

This chapter is concerned with money: definitions and measures of money, the creation of money, and the money controls used by the Federal Reserve System.

In the first section, we present some of the alternative ways of defining and measuring the money supply, and we distinguish between money and credit. In the second section, we review the process by which financial institutions create money on the basis of reserves they are required to hold against their deposit liabilities. In the third section, we discuss the process of money creation. In the fourth section, we examine the sources of reserves, developing the "reserve equation," which indicates determinants of the "monetary base" (reserves plus currency). In the fifth section, we present an analysis of the relationship of the monetary base to the money supply, indicating the role played in the determination of the money supply by banks and related financial institutions, the public, the Treasury, and the Federal Reserve System. Finally, in the sixth section, we present a brief overview of Federal Reserve policy tools for control of the money supply. Details of Federal Reserve policy are reserved for discussion in Chapter 16.

# DEFINING MONEY

We can distinguish between the process of *defining* something and the process of *measuring* something. Usually, definitions come first, for it is generally impossible to measure something unless one knows what it is.[1]

## A Definition of Money

Definitions are often expressed in terms of functions; thus an automobile is a means of transportation. What is money? What is it used for? Money is what people use as a medium of exchange in an exchange economy. A medium of exchange is what people use to pay for goods and services, and to discharge debt. In a very real sense, paying for goods and services is the discharge or liquidation of debt. For example, when you buy something, a clerk may give you a bill as evidence of the debt you have incurred. When you pay the bill you discharge that debt. Thus, the simplest definition of money is that money is anything people use to discharge debts. More precisely, money is what is used for *final* discharge of debt. Suppose you use a credit card to pay for a coat or a restaurant meal. Is the credit card money? No—you still must pay the issuer of the credit card. Hence, credit cards are not money.

Money also serves other functions. It may be used as a store of value, that is, one may hold wealth in the form of money. Money is not unique in performing this function; gold, bonds, stocks, and real estate are also held as wealth or stores of value.

The monetary unit (the dollar in the United States) also serves as a unit of account, as when businesses and individuals keep books in terms of dollars. The unit of account, sometimes called a standard of value, is also used in contracts that provide for future payments. Sometimes, therefore, it is said that money performs four functions: it functions as (1) a medium of exchange, (2) a store of value, (3) a unit of account, and (4) a standard for deferred payments. But the distinguishing characteristic of money is that it serves as a medium of exchange and as a means of *final* settlement of debt.

Throughout recorded history many different things have served as money—cattle, salt, beads, sea shells, gold, and silver are examples. Coins and paper money have been used for centuries, while the use of checking accounts is more recent. When money is clearly defined, things used as money may change, although the definition remains the same. As the things used as money change, *measurement* of money must change.

## Alternative Definitions of Money

Some economists have defined money so that its measurement includes some assets that cannot themselves be used for final discharge of debt but that can easily, quickly, and with little loss or cost be converted into money. For example, $200 in a

---

[1] Of course, one can observe and measure something and then give it a name, so that naming and measuring occur simultaneously. But naming is not defining.

noncheckable savings account might be counted as money, in addition to currency and checking accounts. But if a savings account *is* money, what can it mean to say that it must be converted into money before being spent? A definition of money that includes close money substitutes is an ambiguous definition. The ambiguity becomes more pronounced when one tries to measure the assets that can easily and quickly, and with little loss, be converted into money. Should savings accounts, other time deposits, government securities, and gold be included in measuring money?

To focus our question, we may ask: Why do we want to define and measure money in the first place? One answer is that, since money is what people use to buy goods, services, and financial assets, if money can be defined, measured, and *controlled*, spending can be controlled. Since spending equals the value of what is bought, this means that the quantity of output can be controlled, at least in the short run. In the long run, the general level of prices can be controlled by letting increases in money be no greater than possible increases in output. Thus, long-run control of money is necessary for long-run control of inflation.

If our goal is to control the level of economic activity as measured by gross national product (GNP) in the short run, and to control inflation as measured by changes in the average level of prices in the long run, then we want to control the total of that group of items, or monetary aggregates, that correlates best with GNP. An economist who asks for control of money might prefer to define money as that monetary aggregate that functions best in controlling spending and inflation, that is, whatever monetary aggregate is best correlated with spending as measured by GNP.

But a fundamental problem arises: if your thesis is that control over money enables us to control GNP, and if money, defined as whatever is used for payments and for final discharge of debt, is *not* well correlated with GNP, then your thesis is weak. But if you find a monetary aggregate that *does* correlate well with GNP, and define that aggregate as money, rather than test your theory, you have simply chosen a definition and measurement of money that supports your thesis best.

Because one monetary aggregate may not correlate with GNP better than others in all time periods, and because characteristics of some assets change (e.g., savings accounts may become checking accounts), it is difficult to know whether correlations of a particular monetary aggregate with GNP are measuring the same thing. Hence, economists have become cautious in trying to find an appropriate monetary aggregate to use as a definition and measurement of money.

Nevertheless, there is merit in the idea that if the goal is to control real GNP and the price level, then the appropriate monetary aggregate to control would be that which has the closest correlation with GNP. We do not need to define that aggregate as money to justify the policy. Recent evidence shows that the relation between money and income has changed in the 1970s and 1980s.[2] With that change, control of different monetary aggregates may have been appropriate.

[2] Diane F. Siegel, "The Relationship of Money and Income: The Breakdowns in the 70s and 80s," Federal Reserve Bank of Chicago, *Economic Perspectives*, July–August 1986, pp. 3–16. See also Bryon Higgins and Jon Faust, "NOW's and Super NOW's: Implications for Defining and Measuring Money," Federal Reserve Bank of Kansas City, *Economic Review*, January 1983, pp. 3–18. For the view that the

# MEASURES OF THE MONEY SUPPLY OR MONEY STOCK

It is not easy to measure money, especially in a country such as the United States, which has a complex financial system.

## Measures Published by the Federal Reserve System

The Board of Governors of the Federal Reserve System publishes measures of monetary aggregates: M1, M2, and M3. Table 5–1, from its weekly statistical release, shows seasonally adjusted averages of daily figures. The table also includes two broader measures: L and total domestic debt of nonfinancial sectors.

The first column of the table, labeled M1, best fits our definition of money as a medium of exchange. M1 includes currency (coins plus paper money outstanding), travelers checks issued by nonbank institutions, demand deposits, and other checkable deposits. Travelers checks issued by banks are included in demand deposits.

Currency means all coins and paper money issued by the Treasury and the Federal Reserve System *less* any held in bank vaults. The net amount is termed "currency in circulation" or "currency in the hands of the public." Amounts held by the Treasury, by the Federal Reserve, or in bank vaults are not counted, since this currency is not available for spending. If a person deposits currency in a bank, then at that moment currency in circulation decreases but bank deposits increase; M1 does not change.

Demand deposits are *private* demand deposits *adjusted*. Private means that federal government deposits in banks are not included, because federal government spending does not depend on the amount of such deposits, but on the federal government budget. Adjusted means that interbank deposits and checks in the process of being collected are excluded. A deposit by one bank in another bank is an asset for one bank but a liability for the other; for all banks, these items offset each other. Checks being collected are those deposited but not yet collected from banks on which they were drawn. When checks are deposited, depositors' accounts increase. Checks still in the process of collection have resulted in increases in some depositors' accounts, but have *not yet* resulted in decreases in the deposits of those who wrote the checks. Thus, counting checks that are being collected counts some deposits twice: for the depositor and for the writers of the checks.

Other checkable deposits (OCD) principally include negotiable order of withdrawal (NOW) accounts, automatic transfer service (ATS) accounts, and credit union share draft (USD) accounts. These accounts are checkable, but depositors receive

---

decline in velocity of M1 in 1982 (which was admittedly unusual) could have been expected because, with the reduction in inflation, all financial assets became more desirable, see Michael W. Keran, "Velocity and Monetary Policy in 1982," Federal Reserve Bank of San Francisco, *Weekly Letter*, March 18, 1983. Velocity also declined in 1985 and 1986; we discuss this later.

**TABLE 5–1**
**Money Stock, Liquid Assets, and Debt Measures, 1985–1986**
**(billions of dollars, seasonally adjusted, averages of daily figures)**

| Date | M1 (sum of currency, travelers checks, demand deposits and other checkable deposits[1]) | M2 (M1 plus overnight RPs and Eurodollars, MMMF balances (general purpose and broker/dealer), MMDAs, and savings and small time deposits[2]) | M3 (M2 plus large time deposits, term RPs, term Eurodollars and institution-only MMMF balances[3]) | L (M3 plus other liquid assets[4]) | Debt (debt of domestic nonfinancial sectors[5]) |
|---|---|---|---|---|---|
| 1985 | | | | | |
| July | $596.2 | $2,496.2 | $3,112.2 | $3,683.3 | $6,389.8 |
| August | 604.8 | 2,515.6 | 3,130.5 | 3,711.5 | 6,460.3 |
| September | 611.5 | 2,529.9 | 3,150.8 | 3,739.7 | 6,525.3 |
| October | 614.2 | 2,538.9 | 3,165.7 | 3,761.6 | 6,592.0 |
| November | 620.1 | 2,551.4 | 3,181.2 | 3,799.2 | 6,680.5 |
| December | 626.6 | 2,566.5 | 3,201.1 | 3,838.2 | 6,810.0 |
| 1986 | | | | | |
| January | 627.2 | 2,569.9 | 3,224.4 | 3,860.5 | 6,913.9 |
| February | 631.0 | 2,577.6 | 3,241.3 | 3,878.9 | 6,964.1 |
| March | 638.4 | 2,592.3 | 3,262.2 | 3,892.4 | 7,012.4 |
| April | 646.1 | 2,622.4 | 3,293.2 | 3,916.2 | 7,070.5 |
| May | 658.7 | 2,649.7 | 3,311.6 | 3,949.3 | 7,133.3 |
| June | 666.8 | 2,670.9 | 3,332.9 | 3,967.1 | 7,194.6 |
| July | 676.2 | 2,698.9 | 3,369.0 | | |

[1] Consists of (1) currency outside the Treasury, Federal Reserve Banks, and the vaults of commercial banks; (2) travelers checks of nonbank issuers; (3) demand deposits at all commercial banks other than those due to domestic banks, the U.S. government, and foreign banks and official institutions less cash items in the process of collection and Federal Reserve float; and (4) other checkable deposits (OCD) consisting of negotiable order of withdrawal (NOW) and automatic transfer service (ATS) accounts at depository institutions, credit union share draft accounts, and demand deposits at thrift institutions. The currency and demand deposit components exclude the estimated amount of vault cash and demand deposits, respectively, held by thrift institutions to service their OCD liabilities.

[2] Consists of M1 plus overnight (and continuing contract) RPs issued by all commercial banks and overnight Eurodollars issued to U.S. residents by foreign branches of U.S. banks worldwide, MMDAs, savings and small-denomination time deposits (time deposits—including retail RPs—in amounts of less than $100,000), and balances in both taxable and tax-exempt general-purpose and broker/dealer money market mutual funds. Excludes IRA and Keogh balances at depository institutions and money market funds. Also excludes all balances held by U.S. commercial banks, money market funds (general-purpose and broker/dealer), foreign governments and commercial banks, and the U.S. government. Also subtracted is a consolidation adjustment that represents the estimated amount of demand deposits and vault cash held by thrift institutions to service their time and savings deposits.

[3] Consists of M2 plus large-denomination time deposits (in amounts of $100,000 or more) and term RP liabilities issued by commercial banks and thrift institutions, term Eurodollars held by U.S. residents at foreign branches of U.S. banks worldwide and at all banking offices in the United Kingdom and Canada, and balances in both taxable and tax-exempt institution-only money market mutual funds. Excludes amounts held by depository institutions, the U.S. government, money market funds, and foreign banks and official institutions. Also subtracted is a consolidation adjustment that represents the estimated amount of overnight RPs and Eurodollars held by institution-only money market mutual funds.

[4] Consists of M3 plus the nonbank public holdings of U.S. savings bonds, short-term Treasury securities, commercial paper and bankers acceptances, net of money market mutual fund holdings of these assets.

[5] Debt of domestic nonfinancial sectors consists of outstanding credit market debt of the U.S. government, state and local governments, and private nonfinancial sectors. Private debt consists of corporate bonds, mortgages, consumer credit (including bank loans), other bank loans, commercial paper, bankers acceptances, and other debt instruments. The data are derived from the Federal Reserve Board's flow of funds accounts. All data on debt of domestic nonfinancial sectors are presented in month-average form, derived by averaging month-end levels of adjacent months. These data have also been adjusted to remove statistical discontinuities that may arise in the underlying flow of funds statistics. The presentation of debt data in this release differs, therefore, from the quarterly flow of funds statistics contained in the Federal Reserve releases 2.7 and 2.1. In those releases, published levels of credit market debt are measured on a quarter-end basis and include discontinuities.

SOURCE: *Federal Reserve Bulletin*, October 1986, p. A13.

interest. On demand deposits, narrowly defined, no interest can be paid. Most demand deposits now are those of business firms. Some individual depositors also receive no interest on checking account deposits, often if the balances in the accounts are small.

Components of the money stock as measured by M1 are shown in Table 5–2. Of a total of about $675 billion in money (M1) outstanding in 1986, about $175 billion consisted of currency; the remaining $500 billion consisted of demand deposits, other checkable deposits, and travelers checks issued by nonbank institutions.

Table 5–1 showed two broader measures of money, M2 and M3. M2 includes *M1 plus* overnight repurchase agreements (RPs) at banks, certain overnight Eurodollar deposits, certain money market mutual fund (MMMF) deposits, money market deposit accounts (MMDAs) at banks, and savings accounts and "small" time deposits

**TABLE 5–2**
**Components of the Money Stock, 1985–1986**
**(billions of dollars, seasonally adjusted)**

| Date | Currency[1] | Travelers Checks[2] | Demand Deposits[3] | Other Checkable Deposits[4] |
|------|-----------|---------------------|--------------------|-----------------------------|
| 1985 | | | | |
| July | $165.3 | $5.8 | $260.4 | $164.8 |
| August | 166.9 | 5.9 | 263.1 | 169.0 |
| September | 167.7 | 5.9 | 266.4 | 171.5 |
| October | 168.7 | 5.9 | 266.0 | 173.7 |
| November | 169.8 | 5.9 | 267.8 | 176.7 |
| December | 170.6 | 5.9 | 271.5 | 178.6 |
| 1986 | | | | |
| January | 171.9 | 5.9 | 268.9 | 180.5 |
| February | 172.9 | 5.9 | 269.2 | 183.1 |
| March | 173.9 | 6.1 | 273.2 | 185.2 |
| April | 174.4 | 6.1 | 275.7 | 189.9 |
| May | 175.8 | 6.1 | 281.6 | 195.1 |
| June | 176.7 | 6.2 | 284.9 | 199.0 |
| July | 177.6 | 6.4 | 288.3 | 203.9 |

[1] Currency outside the U.S. Treasury, Federal Reserve Banks, and vaults of commercial banks. Excludes the estimated amount of vault cash held by thrift institutions to service their OCD liabilities.
[2] Outstanding amount of U.S. dollar-denominated travelers checks of nonbank issuers. Travelers checks issued by depository institutions are included in demand deposits.
[3] Demand deposits at commercial banks and foreign related institutions other than those due to domestic banks, the U.S. government, and foreign banks and official institutions less cash items in the process of collection and Federal Reserve float. Excludes the estimated amount of demand deposits held at commercial banks by thrift institutions to service their OCD liabilities.
[4] Consists of NOW and ATS balances at all depository institutions, credit union share draft balances, and demand deposits at thrift institutions. Other checkable deposits seasonally adjusted equals the difference between the seasonally adjusted sum of demand deposits plus OCD and seasonally adjusted demand deposits.
SOURCE: *Federal Reserve Bulletin,* October 1986, p. A13.

(under $100,000). These items are all quickly available for spending, although savings and other time deposits cannot in most cases be spent directly.

M3 includes *M2 plus* large (over $100,000) time deposits, usually held by corporations as temporary investments, and money market mutual fund balances held by institutions. These items presumably are not commonly used for spending.

L includes *M3 plus* U.S. savings bonds held by the public, short-term securities issued by the government (T-bills and others), commercial paper, bankers acceptances, and "term" Eurodollar deposits (Eurodollars deposited for a "term," not overnight).

## Technical Points

There are disagreements concerning the inclusion or exclusion of certain items from the measures of money. For example, some economists argue that some erratic movements in the money supply would be smoothed out if government deposits were included; changes in size of these deposits cause erratic movements not related to spending by the public. As another example, M1 formerly included foreign demand deposits at Federal Reserve Banks, on the grounds that these funds could be spent to purchase goods and services. However, economists who studied this matter recommended that these deposits be excluded, on the ground that they were held chiefly as "precautionary" rather than "transactions" balances and were not usually converted into deposits used for spending—so that they did not belong in either M1 or M2.

The careful reader may have noted that Table 5–1 is headed "Money *Stock* . . . Measures." The terms "money stock" and "money supply" are often used interchangeably, and we follow this practice. Technically, "money stock" might be preferred on the ground that "supply" in economics generally means the amount offered for sale at various prices, not the total amount (stock) available.

Finally, some believe that certain figures included in M2 should be included in M1. Let us assume that a corporation has an account at a bank and decides at 3:00 P.M. to put the funds into securities overnight, under a repurchase agreement with the bank. The money in the account can certainly be spent the following day, because the bank automatically repurchases the securities and puts the funds back into the account, and does this the next day. In essence, the funds remain spendable. Treatment of such items as these may be even more important in the future, as there is increased automation of fund transfers.

Use of checks drawn on MMMF balances and on MMDAs, and use of RPs for payments, together with other new practices in the future, may well mean that old measures of money understate the money supply by our definitions. Such procedural and institutional innovations are increasing with the aid of developing technology.

Measurement of "money" is clearly complicated. One suggestion might be to let M1 be *the* measure of money and label the following columns in Table 5–1 as L1, L2, L3—monetary aggregates consisting of M1 *plus* the several categories of liquid assets as noted. But even this suggestion raises problems. M2, M3, and L are all measures of money available for spending (M1) *plus* various liquid assets that may relatively easily and quickly be converted into M1. But the ease, quickness, and frequency of such conversion varies widely.

Moreover, *some* of the items, especially some in M2, can be used directly for payments. For example, one large business firm may pay another large business firm with an RP payable in Fed funds (Federal Reserve funds) with no effect on M1.[3] It should be evident that the usefulness of M1 or any other measure of money as a means of controlling the amount of spending depends on a stable ratio of money thus measured to nominal GNP.

Even if the items to be included in M1, M2, or M3 are carefully specified, financial innovations may cause items included in one measure or another to be somewhat inappropriate. For example, as indicated, NOW accounts and Super-NOW accounts have been included in M1. But they may not be *extensively* used for payments; hence an increase in their amount may not mean an equivalent increase in payments. "Other checkable deposits" (which includes these accounts) grew very rapidly in 1981 and 1982. From this it could be inferred that there was likely to be too much spending, causing more inflation. But this would be wrong if many of these accounts are not used, or are very seldom used, for spending. Perhaps people were simply fast in transferring funds from regular demand deposit accounts to NOW accounts in 1981 and 1982; perhaps people regarded "other checkable deposits" as relatively normal transactions balances; or perhaps uncertainty about the economy caused people to put precautionary savings funds into NOW accounts and other checkable deposits. If interest is paid on what are presumably transactions balances (as NOW accounts, Super-NOW accounts, and similar accounts were often assumed to be), are they *used* as transactions balances? Should an alternative definition of money as a liquid store of value (probably measured by M2, although M3 or L could be used) be the focus of attention rather than M1? Two researchers concluded that "the liquidity approach to defining money may be preferable to the transactions approach in the emerging financial environment."[4] Other measures could be developed to include other assets—one government committee in Britain argued that *all* assets are money, because all can be converted into what is used to make payments. This extreme position was not generally accepted.

## THE PROCESS OF MONEY CREATION

The student may recall from an introductory course in economics the elements of money creation under a fractional reserve banking system. When a bank makes a loan, the banker often simply increases the borrower's demand deposit account balance; the borrower now has more deposits than he or she had before and, since the

[3] Guy E. Noyes, "The Multiple Flaws of the Monetary Base," *Morgan Guaranty Survey*, October 1981, pp. 6–10. If payments occur without a transfer of M1, then surely the ratio of M1 to total payments (and probably to GNP) must change. Thus, the stability of this ratio, termed the velocity ratio, is crucial.

[4] See Higgins and Faust, "NOW's and Super NOW's." See also Howard L. Roth, "Has Deregulation Ruined M1 as a Policy Guide?" Federal Reserve Bank of Kansas City, *Economic Review*, June 1987. Roth concluded the usefulness of M1 was at least damaged, if not ruined.

borrower can now use these to buy things, we say that money has been created. Of course, the bank also acquires an asset—the customer has an obligation to repay the bank at a future date so the asset item "loans" shows an increase that balances the increased liability. The money supply may decrease when the loan is repaid.

Because bank credit policy is so important in its effects on the money supply, we must emphasize again that when banks extend credit, they usually *create* new deposits; they do *not* simply lend out depositors' funds. From the individual banker's point of view, the ability to lend does depend upon a net inflow of deposits, the major source of funds. Therefore, bankers may object to the assertion that they can create more deposits whenever they wish to increase their loans. How can we reconcile the two views: that bankers create money—deposit money—rather than lend their depositors' funds, even though their ability to create money does depend upon the value of deposits that they receive? The first step is to distinguish *primary* from *derivative* deposits. The former arise from deposits of cash or checks drawn upon other commercial banks; the depositors receive credits to their checking accounts or time deposits, and the bank adds to its vault cash or sends the checks to the local Federal Reserve Banks for credit to the banks' reserve accounts.[5] To the individual bank a *primary* deposit is a source of bank reserves and if the bank's reserves are greater in amount than its required reserves—required against demand and time deposits—the "excess" reserves enable the bank to make loans (grant credit) and "create" deposits in the process. These deposits are *derivative* deposits, so called because they are derived from extension of bank credit.

Thus, a single bank can create money to the extent of its excess reserves. If it makes loans and creates deposits beyond this amount, it may face an adverse balance of payments (clearinghouse balance) vis-à-vis other banks when the checks drawn against these deposits are presented for payment, and its reserve position may fall below the level required. If the bank does not expand its loans and security holdings to the extent of its excess reserves, perhaps because of inadequate loan demand or a generally conservative loan policy, the bank will have reserves available for future use.

When viewing the entire banking system, it is important to note that, for any given primary deposit, a *multiple* of that amount in new deposits may be created by all banks. In other words, an increase in excess reserves will permit all banks together to add to loans and deposits by a multiple of the original excess reserves.

A simple example may help to clarify this important point. Assume that all banks hold reserves in the Federal Reserve System and that the reserve requirement for demand deposits is 20 percent. Also assume that the public chooses to hold all new money as demand deposits rather than as currency, and does not shift any funds from demand deposits to time deposits. If Mr. Jones deposits $10,000 in currency in his bank in exchange for a demand deposit receipt of $10,000, the bank's total cash reserves have increased by $10,000. These actions appear as items (1) and (2) in the bank's balance sheet shown as Table 5–3. If the bank has exactly the required amount

---

[5] To simplify, we assume at this point that all commercial banks must hold their legal reserves as vault cash or as deposits with the Federal Reserve Bank of their district.

### TABLE 5–3
### Balance Sheet of a Commercial Bank

| Assets | | Liabilities | |
|---|---|---|---|
| Cash and deposits at the Fed | $\begin{cases} +10,000(2) \\ -\ \ 8,000(6) \end{cases}$ | Mr. Jones' demand deposit (primary deposit) Mr. Smith's demand deposit (derivative deposit) | $\begin{cases} +10,000(1) \\ +\ \ 8,000(3) \\ -\ \ 8,000(5) \end{cases}$ |
| Loan to Mr. Smith | $+\ \ 8,000(4)$ | | |

### Balance Sheet of a Second Bank

| Assets | | Liabilities | |
|---|---|---|---|
| Cash and deposits at the Fed | $+8,000(7)$ | Mr. Henry's demand deposit | $+8,000(8)$ |
| Loan to Mr. Wells | $+6,400(9)$ | Mr. Wells' demand deposit | $+6,400(10)$ |

of reserves at the time, $2,000 must be held as required reserves because of the 20 percent legal reserve requirement. Thus, excess reserves increase by $8,000. Items (3) and (4) are entered in the bank's balance sheet when Mr. Smith borrows from the bank and when he spends the $8,000, the person, Mr. Henry, receiving the check will deposit it in his account in, say, a second bank. The first bank honors the check drawn upon it, and currency, or more likely a reserve balance at the Federal Reserve, is transferred to the second bank. This withdrawal of funds by Mr. Smith is shown by items (5) and (6).

The second bank now has increased deposits of $8,000 and excess reserves of $6,400 as shown by items (7) and (8) on the balance sheet of the second bank. If the second bank in turn makes a loan of $6,400 as shown by items (9) and (10), and the funds are transferred to a third bank, further lending and deposit creation may occur until the banking system has no remaining excess reserves—until the additional required reserves total $10,000, new loans total $40,000, and total deposits have risen by $50,000. Each bank manager may view the process as one in which the individual bank acquires deposits and then makes loans equal to 80 percent of the acquired deposits. The net effect is that each extends credit and creates deposits to the extent of its excess reserves. But the *system* of banks creates deposits by a multiple of any original primary deposit.

This power to create money results from the so-called "fractional reserve" system that permits banks to hold reserves equal to some fraction of their demand deposits. In our example, the theoretical limit to the expansion of deposits, when $r$ is the required reserve ratio, $R$ is total reserves, and $D$ is deposits, is given by $D = (1/r) \times R$. Because $r$ was assumed to be .2, $1/r = 5$, so that $D = 5R$. This theoretical "money multiplier" of 5 is only an approximation to the actual value that might exist; the actual value is smaller because there are some "leakages" in the process of money creation, which we deal with in a later section. The reader should note that the creation of money by banks does not occur *because of the existence of a system* of banks, but *because deposits do not leave the system.* If all checks were redeposited in the same bank, the same amount of deposit creation could occur with only a single bank.

## Sources of Reserves

We have seen that banks, individually and collectively, must have excess reserves to expand their earning assets and create new deposits. How do banks acquire these reserves?

### A Single Bank

Let us first examine the sources of increased reserves for a single bank. First, reserves of a bank are increased if members of the public deposit currency. The bank can hold the currency as vault cash or deposit it in its reserve deposit in a Federal Reserve Bank.

Second, loans may be repaid in currency. The result is shown in Table 5–4; items (1) and (2) show the deposit of currency by Mr. Smith and the resulting increase in cash held by the bank; items (3) and (4) show the cancellation of his loan and the corresponding reduction in his deposit account. A more common means of repayment of a loan might simply be for Mr. Smith to agree with the bank that it could reduce his deposit account to cancel the loan. This provides excess reserves because, with fewer deposits, less reserves are required. But if borrowers ask for loans, the bank is likely to make loans until its reserves are again close to the required level.

Third, reserves of a bank are increased if members of the public deposit checks and similar instruments. But checks deposited in one bank must have been drawn on other banks, so there is no net increase in deposits (or reserves) for all banks.

Fourth, banks might have additional excess reserves if reserve requirements are reduced—if required reserves are less, and banks have the same reserves, more of the reserve is excess. However, reserve requirements are not reduced frequently.

Fifth, a bank may obtain reserves by borrowing. If it borrows Fed funds, it gains reserves but the lending bank loses reserves.

Sixth, a bank may sell securities that it held. If the purchaser is a depositor of the bank, his or her account is reduced, and securities held by the bank are reduced,

**TABLE 5–4**
**Balance Sheet of a Commercial Bank**

| Assets | | Liabilities | |
|---|---|---|---|
| Cash | +8,000 (2) | Mr. Smith's deposit account | +8,000 (1) |
| Loans to Mr. Smith | −8,000 (4) | | −8,000 (3) |

**TABLE 5–5**
**Balance Sheet of a Commercial Bank**

| Assets | | Liabilities | |
|---|---|---|---|
| Securities held | −1,000 (2) | Mr. Brown's account | −1,000 (1) |

as shown in Table 5–5. Banks often sell securities, but when they do so, their purpose is usually to make more loans, which would immediately use up (as required reserves) any excess reserves obtained by selling securities.

What can we conclude? We can conclude that there are a number of ways for a single bank to obtain additional excess reserves, but that most of them are not likely to provide very large amounts of excess reserves, some are not likely to occur frequently, and some add to excess reserves of the bank but result in a loss of reserves by another bank.

There is one source of reserves that we have not discussed. The Fed may make open market purchases of securities, paying for them by check. If such a check is deposited in the bank we have been discussing, it can be sent to the Fed for collection, but the Fed, normally, would not give the bank cash—instead, it would give the bank an increase in its deposit balance (reserve). This is the *major* source of additional reserves.

### The Banking System

Many sources of reserves discussed earlier involve transfers of funds from one bank to another; they do not result in additions to total reserves of all banks. The purchase of securities by the Fed is an exception; it does add to reserves of the banking *system*.

The banking system does not face one problem that is faced by an individual bank: if an individual bank makes a loan and creates a deposit, it *may* face withdrawal of that deposit by checks written to individuals or businesses that deposit the checks in other banks. Check payments do not result in a loss of funds for the banking system as a whole.

One final point: can the public withdraw funds from other depository institutions and deposit them in a bank, thereby providing the banking system with added funds? No, because such a transfer usually reduces deposits that other depository institutions held in banks. Deposits of the public in banks are increased, but deposits of other depository institutions in banks are reduced.

In conclusion: reserves of the banking system are increased or reduced primarily as a result of actions of the Fed in open market operations. However, actions of the Treasury, of the public, and of banks themselves may also affect the size of deposits and reserves to some extent. To examine this conclusion carefully, we need a framework for analysis. One such framework is an analysis of the factors affecting the "monetary base." We then analyze the factors affecting the money supply (M1, M2, or another measure) as a ratio of money to the monetary base—a ratio which is termed the "money multiplier."

## Reserves, the Monetary Base, and the Money Supply

Reserves are created and destroyed by various Federal Reserve and Treasury actions and by some actions of individuals, business firms, and banks. The level of currency in circulation is also the result of decisions by these units. The money supply that exists at any time is the net outcome of a variety of policy decisions by monetary authorities and of portfolio decisions by individuals and firms. To capsulize the nature of the interaction of factors that determine the money supply, we use the concept of the "monetary base." But first let us review briefly a few of the most significant factors that affect the level of bank reserves and the level of currency in circulation.

### Currency and Reserves: The "Monetary Base"

Years ago the paper money supply was "backed" by silver and/or gold. In those days we could have said that the Treasury's stock of these precious metals was the monetary base. When the Treasury bought silver, it paid for the silver bullion and issued silver certificates, redeemable in silver bullion. These certificates then circulated as currency and were said to be "backed" by silver. The Treasury no longer issues these certificates, but this is a good example of one way in which currency could enter the economy in the years before the Federal Reserve System was established. During the Civil War, Congress authorized the Treasury to issue currency without regard to "backing" in bullion; these certificates were called "greenbacks." As a liability of the Treasury, these greenbacks were used as currency and as reserves for commercial banks. They constituted part of the monetary base, even though not "backed" by metal. (Some still circulate; for example, they used to be found in the form of two-dollar bills popular at race tracks, but nowadays the two-dollar bills are usually Federal Reserve notes.) Gradually, almost all paper currency in the United States has come to consist of Federal Reserve notes issued by the Federal Reserve System.

The Treasury also may buy gold and issue gold certificates or credits payable in gold certificates to Federal Reserve Banks in exchange for deposit credit. To pay for its purchase of gold, it writes a check on its deposit with the Federal Reserve. When the individual selling the gold receives the check, he or she deposits it with a commercial bank. The bank then collects by sending the check to the Federal Reserve, and ownership of the deposit passes from the Treasury to the bank; hence bank reserves increase, and the potential money supply increases as lending power of banks expands. But, to assist in understanding this process more clearly, let us show changes in the balance sheet of the Federal Reserve that bring about the increase in bank reserves when the Treasury buys gold.

## How the Fed and the Treasury Affect
## the Monetary Base

The 12 Federal Reserve Banks that make up the Federal Reserve System each hold the reserve deposits of institutions in their regions. That is, banks and some other institutions do their banking at the Federal Reserve just as ordinary citizens do their banking at banks. In addition, the Federal Reserve is the bank that the U.S. Treasury uses to hold its deposits for the most part. Thus, Treasury deposits and reserve deposits are two of the most important liabilities of the Federal Reserve.

On the balance sheet shown in Table 5–6, we see that item (1) is the deposit balance that the Treasury receives when it deposits the gold certificates it has had printed. These certificates are held by the Federal Reserve as an asset as in item (2). But the Treasury must pay whoever sold the gold to it, and so it writes a check drawn on its account at the Fed. Whoever sold the gold will take the check to a bank or other institution and deposit it in his or her account. The institution, seeing that the check is drawn on the Fed, will deposit the check in its account at the Fed, item (3). When the Fed sees the check is written on the Treasury account, it will reduce the Treasury's balance, item (4).

The final result is that the institution now has $100 more reserves than it had earlier—reserves that can be used to expand loans and deposit money as we described earlier. Thus, the Treasury's purchases of gold add to the reserves of the system as a whole.

If the Treasury had printed and issued greenbacks and had deposited them with the Fed, and then spent the deposited funds, the effect on bank reserves would have been the same. Then, if institutions needed currency, they could draw down their accounts at the Fed and the Fed might send them the greenbacks that the Treasury had deposited. In this way the greenbacks eventually become a circulating medium in the hands of the public. The point is that the Treasury has the power to issue liabilities against itself within certain limits, and these liabilities serve either as currency in circulation (e.g., greenbacks) or as reserves of Federal Reserve Banks (e.g., gold certificates) and also usually result in an increase in reserves of banks.

Federal Reserve Banks also have the power to issue liabilities against themselves. Paramount among the procedures for doing so is the creation of a demand deposit in favor of a financial institution. For example, assume that a depository institution finds its legal reserve position deficient and goes to the Federal Reserve to borrow funds. The Fed gives the bank a deposit. The Fed also acquires an asset in the

## TABLE 5–6
### Balance Sheet of the Federal Reserve System

| Assets | | Liabilities | |
|---|---|---|---|
| Gold certificates | +100 (2) | Treasury deposits | +100 (1) |
| | | | −100 (4) |
| | | Reserve deposits | +100 (3) |

**TABLE 5–7**
**Balance Sheet of the Federal Reserve System**

| *Assets* | *Liabilities* |
|---|---|
| Government securities   +100 (2) | Reserve deposits                    +100 (1) |

form of a loan to the institution. Deposits with the Fed are, of course, reserves—sometimes called "high-powered" money because upon the base provided by these reserves, banks and some other institutions can expand loans and deposits and hence the money supply. When the Fed was first established in 1913, the borrowing mechanism was the principal tool of control over the supply of money exercised by the Fed. As a central bank it was labeled the "lender of last resort," a source of funds available for tapping if a financial panic were to threaten.[6]

But the borrowing mechanism is no longer the Fed's principal tool of control over the level of reserves. Today, "open market operations" play this role, as the Fed buys and sells government securities on the open market. When the Fed buys a government security on the open market, it pays for the security by issuing a check drawn on itself and payable to the seller. This individual will collect his or her money by depositing the check in his or her account. The financial institution will collect by sending the check to the Fed and reserve deposits rise as shown in item (1) in Table 5–7. Item (2) records the asset in the form of government securities that the Fed now holds. In this manner the reserves of the financial system as a whole are *increased* when the Fed makes *open market purchases* of government securities. Open market *sales* of government securities have the *opposite* effect—reducing the Fed's holdings of government securities and also reducing member bank reserves. These open market purchases and sales of government securities—open market operations—represent the principal tool of control over bank reserves and, therefore, over the supply of money now being used.[7]

The Fed also issues circulating currency in the form of Federal Reserve notes, which now constitute about 90 percent of all currency in circulation. If individuals wish to hold more currency, they usually go to a financial institution, draw down their deposits, and receive either Federal Reserve notes or Treasury currency (coins). If the institution finds its supply of currency running low, it asks the Fed to reduce its deposit and send either Federal Reserve notes or Treasury currency. The effect of sending Federal Reserve notes is shown by items (1) and (2) on the Fed's balance sheet in Table 5–8. Thus the Fed again has created a liability against itself in the form

---

[6] Under the National Banking System, which preceded the Federal Reserve System, individual national banks around the country had the authority to issue their own notes. These were printed by the government and were identical except for the name of the individual issuing bank printed on the face of the note. Frequent money panics occurred when there were not enough such notes to meet the demand for currency, and this and other defects of the system led to the creation of the Federal Reserve System.

[7] The Federal Reserve has also bought and sold bankers acceptances as part of its open market operations, but such buying has been reduced since 1977.

**TABLE 5–8**
**Balance Sheet of the Federal Reserve System**

| Assets | Liabilities | |
|---|---|---|
| | Federal Reserve notes outstanding | +100 (1) |
| | Reserve deposits | −100 (2) |

of a note outstanding, and this currency can be used either as hand-to-hand cash or as reserves held by a depository financial institution.[8]

It is, therefore, by the creation of deposit and note liabilities against itself that the Fed supplies reserves to financial institutions and currency to the public. The Treasury has only limited power to create liabilities against itself that are accepted as money or which add directly to bank reserves. The combination of the decisions of these two authorities provides the mechanism for control over the money supply. In recent years, since the Treasury does not print and issue paper money and has not been buying gold, its contribution is almost entirely the minting of coins.

Although decisions of the Fed and the Treasury to issue liabilities determine the total volume of reserves plus currency in circulation, decisions by others in the economy help to determine the size of the major part of the money supply (demand deposits) that some financial institutions create through their lending activities.[9]

First, the decisions of business firms and individuals in the aggregate help to determine the ratio of currency to deposits and, thus, the volume of bank reserves.

Second, if an individual holds funds in the form of time deposits rather than as demand deposits, this also affects the volume of reserves that can be used to create demand deposits. This is because there is no reserve requirement for personal time deposits. Again, decisions of individuals and businesses regarding the proportion of deposits held in time deposits affect the lending power of banks and the volume of money that banks create; there is a small reserve requirement against *business* time deposits.

Third, commercial banks and other institutions that may create demand deposits or similar accounts have some leeway in deciding to lend or not to lend. Because excess reserves are not earning assets, most depository institution managers attempt to keep excess reserves very close to zero. If excess reserves are zero, we sometimes say that the system is "fully loaned." In this case the actual reserve ratio is equal to the legally required reserve ratio. If, however, for whatever reason, managers maintain excess reserves, then the actual reserve ratio is somewhat greater than the legally

---

[8] When the Federal Reserve System needs more coin, coins are obtained from the mints, and the Treasury's deposit account at the Fed is increased just as you or I may increase our bank accounts by depositing coin. When financial institutions obtain the coins from the Fed, their deposit accounts are reduced.

[9] The term "currency in circulation" does not include currency held by the Fed, by the U.S. Treasury, or in the vaults of commercial banks.

required ratio, and the volume of money created by the system is somewhat less than it otherwise would be.

Finally, the Treasury makes decisions about the volume of deposits that it holds in its Tax and Loan accounts. These accounts were described in Chapter 3. There we saw that U.S. government demand deposits in commercial banks are referred to as Treasury Tax and Loan (TT&L) accounts because the funds in them come chiefly from withholding of taxes and balances created when commercial banks make loans to (buy securities of) the government. Here we wish to emphasize that, when the Treasury calls the funds for transfer from commercial banks to its account with the Fed, reserve deposits with the Fed fall as the Treasury's account with the Fed rises. The result is a reduction in the volume of reserves and in the ability of banks to lend and create money.

The holding of Treasury funds in TT&L accounts created some controversy in 1975. When the Treasury made deposits, it, in effect, gave the banks money to lend and the Treasury received no interest earnings on the deposited funds. Therefore, the Congress directed the Treasury to send the funds directly to the Federal Reserve.[10]

To see how this makes a difference to the taxpayer, let us trace through the steps. The Treasury collects a tax or sells a bond, and someone writes a check on a bank and gives it to the Treasury. When the Treasury deposits this check in a commercial bank, its TT&L account is increased, and the individual's account is reduced. Then, the Treasury tells the bank to send the money on in to the Fed for deposit to the Treasury's account. So the Treasury's account in the bank goes down and its account in the Fed goes up, but the bank's account with the Fed goes down. This decline in bank reserves would mean that if the Fed wished to keep the size of the money supply the same, it would have to use open market operations, buying government securities to replenish the reserves of financial institutions. This means that the Fed would hold government securities that individuals in the private sector used to hold. The Fed now gets the interest that the Treasury used to pay to the individuals. But the Fed earns so much money from the Treasury, on Fed holdings of government securities, that it simply gives about 90 percent of its gross earnings back to the Treasury at the end of each year. That is, it only uses about 10 percent of its gross earnings to pay its operating costs. Thus, as a practical matter, the Treasury doesn't end up having to pay interest on the securities that the Fed holds. Of course, this is as it should be, because the Fed is, in essence, an agency of the government and not a private institution.

The result is that the larger the Treasury's balance at the Fed, the lower the amount of debt in the hands of the public and the lower the net interest payments that the Treasury must pay on its debt. By shifting deposits to the Fed, therefore, the

---

[10] See Joan E. Lovett, "Treasury Tax and Loan Accounts and Federal Reserve Open Market Operations," Federal Reserve Bank of New York, *Quarterly Review*, Summer 1978, pp. 41–46; and Richard W. Lang, "TTL Note Accounts and the Money Supply Process," Federal Reserve Bank of St. Louis, *Review*, October 1979, pp. 3–14.

Treasury can save hundreds of millions of dollars a year in interest payments that it would otherwise have to make to citizens if they held government securities.

But a problem arose out of this procedure. Treasury receipts and payments were often made in sizable amounts. For example, large receipts came in on quarterly tax dates. Thus, the Treasury's balance at the Fed fluctuated widely, making it difficult for the Fed to control banks' overall reserve position. The Fed could not know what the amount of bank reserves would be, because of the erratic behavior of the Treasury's account.

Therefore, in late 1978 Congress passed legislation permitting commercial banks to create a new type of "open-ended note" liability so that they could pay the Treasury interest on Treasury funds. Without going into extensive detail, the program works something like this. The Treasury deposits money with a commercial bank; the next day the bank puts the funds into an open-note account, against which it does not have to hold reserves; the notes are also exempt from interest rate ceilings, so that the commercial bank (or other depository such as a thrift institution) can pay interest on weekly average balances at a rate ¼ or ½ percent below the weekly average yield on Federal funds. When the Treasury wants its money transferred to its account at the Fed, it simply uses the usual call procedure. The commercial bank charges the Treasury certain service fees for sales and redemptions of savings bonds.

Thus, the 1978 program attempts to save interest for taxpayers, reward commercial banks and others with specific fees for the services they provide to the Treasury, and even out the flow of deposits to the Fed, so that the Fed's job of steadying the volume of bank reserves can be accomplished more easily.

In summary, various actions of the Treasury and the Federal Reserve have effects on the reserves of deposit-type financial institutions. The Treasury and the Fed are also responsible for issuing currency—the Treasury for coins and the Fed for paper money. Currency could be issued and pass right through financial institutions if it were sent to them and immediately, or very quickly, withdrawn by the public. Thus, reserves and currency are referred to as the monetary base; upon this base, depository institutions may create demand deposit money, in lending to individuals and businesses. Thus, this base supports the money supply.

## THE RESERVE EQUATION AND THE MONETARY BASE

To bring together the diverse activities of the Fed, the Treasury, and the public, as these activities affect the money supply, we begin by looking at a balance sheet for the Federal Reserve Banks as a group. Then we add relevant Treasury monetary items (being careful to add the same amounts to the asset side and to the liability and capital side), and simplify the result to obtain a "reserve equation" in which the asset-side items are the sources for funds for reserves and other purposes, and the liability-side items include reserves and items that constitute *other* uses of such funds.

Principal items in the combined balance sheets of the 12 Federal Reserve Banks include the items shown in Table 5–9.

**TABLE 5–9**
**Principal Items in Balance Sheet for Federal Reserve Banks**

| *Assets* | *Liabilities* |
|---|---|
| Currency | Federal Reserve notes outstanding |
| Gold certificates and foreign exchange (foreign currencies)[1] | Reserve deposits |
| | Treasury deposits |
| Government securities | Foreign and other deposits |
| Discounts and advances (loans to borrowing institutions) | Other liabilities and capital |
| Float (cash items in process of collection less deferred availability items) | |
| Other assets[1] | |

[1] SDRs ("paper gold" issued by the International Monetary Fund) are also included in other assets. If gold becomes less important as an international reserve asset, SDRs are likely to be larger in amount and in importance. For many central banks in other countries, foreign exchange is also an important asset.

## Federal Reserve Assets

Under assets, "currency" includes chiefly coins minted by the Treasury and held by the Federal Reserve Banks plus Federal Reserve notes of one Federal Reserve Bank held by other Federal Reserve Banks. Gold certificates are issued by the Treasury after a gold purchase to replenish the Treasury deposit account that was depleted when the Treasury wrote a check to pay for the gold. Since the Treasury is neither selling nor buying gold, gold certificates are now stable in amount. The Federal Reserve System buys foreign exchange (Deutschemarks, etc.) when it wishes to affect exchange rates or needs foreign currencies for other reasons. Government securities are U.S. government securities that the Federal Reserve has either bought outright or holds temporarily under repurchase agreements. Discounts and advances are simply loans to depository institutions, as discussed earlier.

"Float" arises out of Federal Reserve check-clearing activities. Institutions that deposit checks with the Fed for collection may not receive deposit credit immediately if the checks are drawn on institutions some distance away. Instead, the Fed credits a liability account, called "deferred availability items," and debits an asset account called "cash items in process of collection." On a scheduled time basis, not more than two days, the Fed reduces the deferred availability account and increases the deposit account of the depositing institution. But the institution on which the check was drawn may not yet have been presented with the check to be paid by it, and so the Fed does not reduce its reserve balance by the amount of the check until the check is received. Thus, for a day or two, depending upon location and transportation conditions, the account "cash items in process of collection" is larger than the account "deferred availability items"; this difference is the "float." The institution that deposited the check with the Fed has had its reserves increased, but the one on which the check was drawn has *not* had its reserves decreased. Thus an increase in float represents a *net* increase in available reserves. Float is not peculiar to the Federal Reserve System; it exists whenever two agencies or individuals keep records and there is a time difference. Thus, if Mr. Jones writes a check to Mrs. Smith, Jones' checkbook shows a lower balance, but Smith's does not show a higher balance until she receives and deposits the check. Federal Reserve float is especially important because of the key role of bank reserves in the economy. In effect, Federal Reserve float is a short-term interest-free loan by the Fed to depository institutions.[11]

When the check is finally received by the institution on which it was drawn and the Fed is notified, the Fed reduces that institution's deposit with the Fed and also reduces the item "cash items in process of collection" by the same amount; thus float is eliminated. But check clearing is a continuous process, and some float is always outstanding. The float varies widely from day to day and is increased when weather or strikes disrupt normal communication and transportation channels. It also has regular daily, weekly, and monthly variations arising from the regularity in payment procedures institutionalized in the economy.[12]

Clearly, it is simpler to have a definite schedule for availability of funds than it is to try to determine the actual clearing time for each check and count the proceeds of that check as available at that time. Thus the Fed float is essentially a service that increases convenience. Similarly, depository institutions provide the same service for checking account customers when they give immediate credit for checks deposited instead of waiting until those checks have been collected.

The Depository Institutions Deregulation and Monetary Control Act of 1980 required the Fed to charge for its nongovernmental services; it also required the Fed either to eliminate the float or to charge for it. The float reached a peak of about $6 billion annually on average during the late 1970s; if banks had had to borrow these funds (instead of being provided with them) at the Fed funds rate, the cost to the banks would have been nearly $800 million.[13] Float could be reduced (and perhaps eliminated) by (1) speedier collection of checks, (2) slightly longer time before the funds are credited to bank reserves, or (3) changing the latest hours at which banks can deposit checks with the Fed for credit on given days and the latest hours at which the Fed must present checks for collection from banks on which they are drawn. Some combination of these alternatives is possible, and actions taken have reduced float, generally, to below $1 billion by the mid-1980s.

---

[11] The reason for the existence of float is that banks, like individuals, want credit as soon as possible for checks they deposit or send for collection.

[12] See Irving Auerbach, "Forecasting Float," *Essays in Money and Credit*, Federal Reserve Bank of New York, 1964, pp. 7–12; and Thomas A. Gittings, "Sinking Float," Federal Reserve Bank of Chicago, *Economic Perspectives*, May–June 1980, pp. 19–23. See also *The Wall Street Journal*, August 21, 1980, p. 12, for a discussion of the Fed's plans to reduce float. Ways to reduce float were discussed in Benjamin Wolkowitz and Peter R. Lloyd-Davies, "Reducing Federal Reserve Float," *Federal Reserve Bulletin*, December 1979, pp. 945–950. Introduction and expansion of an electronic funds transfer system will reduce float; this is discussed in Chapter 6.

[13] It is estimated that total cost of all other Fed services for which the Fed must set prices is not more than $400 million to $500 million; see Jack H. Beebe, "Float," Federal Reserve Bank of San Francisco, *Weekly Letter*, December 3, 1982.

### TABLE 5–10
#### Treasury Monetary Items

| *Assets* | *Liabilities* |
| --- | --- |
| Gold stock<br>Treasury currency outstanding<br>Treasury cash (except free gold) | Gold certificates plus free gold (gold against which no certificate has been issued)<br>Treasury currency outstanding<br>Treasury cash (except free gold) |

Charging for float provides more revenue for the Fed and, hence, assuming Fed costs do not rise, more revenue after costs is transferred from the Fed to the Treasury. Just as reserve requirements are essentially a tax on banks, float is a subsidy offsetting *part* of that tax.[14]

## Federal Reserve Liabilities

On the liability side of the balance sheet, principal items are Federal Reserve notes outstanding and reserve deposits. These two items form the bulk of the monetary base. Federal Reserve notes are almost the only kind of paper money now held by the public, although a number of kinds were formerly issued by the Treasury and the Fed. The other items are Treasury deposits and other deposits, a few other liabilities such as dividends payable, and capital of Federal Reserve Banks.

## Treasury Monetary Items

To this Federal Reserve composite balance sheet, we must add the appropriate Treasury monetary items to show *all* sources of money. Then we rearrange the items to simplify. Additions made to bring in Treasury actions are shown in Table 5–10. Treasury *currency* is now coins minted for the Treasury and put into circulation, while Treasury *cash* is simply cash (coins and paper money) *held by* the Treasury. We have now added equal amounts to both sides of the Federal Reserve balance sheet; hence totals on both sides are still equal. Now we make four changes, to simplify:

1. Because gold certificates are both Treasury liabilities and Federal Reserve Bank assets, they appear on both sides of the equation and may be deleted from both sides, leaving gold stock on the left.
2. Free gold and Treasury cash (except free gold), on the right side, may be combined to form total Treasury cash—free gold and currency held by the Treasury.

---

[14] For details of the rise in float in the 1970s because of inflation and high interest rates, and its reduction in the first half of the 1980s, through cost-effective operational improvements and charging banks for the remaining float, see John E. Young, "The Rise and Fall of Federal Reserve Float," Federal Reserve Bank of Kansas City, *Economic Review*, February 1986, pp. 28–38.

3. Federal Reserve notes outstanding plus Treasury currency outstanding on the right side of the equation, minus currency and Treasury cash (except free gold) on the left side, may be combined to form a single item—currency in circulation.

4. Vault cash may be subtracted from currency in circulation and added to reserve deposit balances, to form total reserves (the subtraction of vault cash leaves currency outside depository institutions).

## The Reserve Equation and the Monetary Base

With these changes, the remaining items are shown in Table 5–11; they show the *sources* of reserves and currency in circulation (together termed the monetary base) and the items (including the monetary base) absorbing such funds.

Increases in the gold stock, increases in Treasury currency outstanding, and increases in Federal Reserve credit are three sources of increases in reserves and currency in circulation. These items increase the monetary base unless there are offsetting changes in other items. Federal Reserve credit is the main source, especially since gold is no longer bought or sold in significant quantities by the government.

Table 5–12 shows the amounts of these items (with a few minor items added) as of September 1986. Table 5–12 should be interpreted as follows: an increase in any item on the left side will increase the monetary base unless there is an increase in one of the items *other than the base* on the right side. Such an increase could partly (or perhaps entirely) offset the effect on the base. Since changes in most of the items (on both sides) other than Federal Reserve credit and the monetary base items are small, the Fed can anticipate such small changes and even if some error occurs, a change in the amount of Federal Reserve credit will result in approximately the desired change in the monetary base.

How could another item on the right be affected? Suppose that checks used by the Fed to pay for open market purchases (purchases of government securities from the public) were deposited but immediately used to pay income taxes. Instead of an increase in the monetary base, there would be an increase in Treasury deposits in Federal Reserve Banks. The Federal Reserve attempts to forecast such changes. By

### TABLE 5–11
### Sources of Reserves and Uses of Funds Available

| Sources of Bank Reserves | Uses of Funds Available |
| --- | --- |
| Gold stock and SDRs | Reserves of depository institutions |
| Treasury currency outstanding | Currency in circulation |
| Federal Reserve credit | Treasury cash |
| Government securities | Treasury deposits in Federal Reserve Banks |
| Discounts and advances | |
| Float | Foreign and other deposits in Federal Reserve Banks |
| | Other Fed liabilities and capital minus other Fed assets |

**TABLE 5–12**
**Sources and Uses of the Monetary Base**
**End of Month Figures for September 1986**
**(billions of dollars)**

| *Sources of the Base* | | *Uses of the Base* | |
|---|---|---|---|
| Federal Reserve credit | 202.3 | Reserves | 35.1 |
| U.S. government and agency | | | |
|    securities | 200.6 | Currency held by the public | 200.6 |
| Discounts and advances | 0.9 | | |
| Float | 0.8 | | |
| Gold stock | 11.1 | Treasury cash holdings | 0.5 |
| SDR certificates[1] | 5.0 | Treasury deposits at Fed | 7.5 |
| Treasury currency outstanding | 17.4 | Other deposits at Fed | 0.3 |
| Other Fed assets | 17.0 | Required clearing balances[2] | 2.3 |
| | | Other Fed liabilities and capital | 6.5 |
| Equals: | | Equals: | |
|    Sources supplying reserve funds | 252.8 |    Items absorbing reserve funds | 252.8 |

[1] These were distributed to all member countries, at certain times, by the International Monetary Fund (IMF).
[2] We ignore this small item in our discussion.
SOURCE: *Federal Reserve Bulletin,* December 1986, p. A4.

doing so with reasonable accuracy, and by making desired changes in Federal Reserve credit, the Fed can control with reasonable accuracy the growth of the monetary base.

The next question is: Given an increase in the monetary base, how much increase is likely to occur in the money supply? We now turn to this question.

## THE MONETARY BASE AND THE MONEY SUPPLY[15]

Let the money supply, consisting of demand deposits and currency in circulation, be some multiple, $m$, of the "monetary base," $B$. Thus $M = mB$.

The monetary base, $B$, is the net monetary liabilities of government—in particular those of the Fed and the Treasury—held by certain financial institutions and by the nonbank public.

At the outset of this chapter we discussed how certain financial institutions were able to create money (demand deposits) up to some multiple of their reserves as determined by the legal reserve ratio. Demand deposits were some multiple of reserves, and we wrote $D = (1/r)R$. In our hypothetical example, $r$ was the legal reserve ratio of 20 percent and $D = 5R$. Thus, $5 of demand deposits could be created on

---

[15] This section draws on the presentation found in Jerry L. Jordan, "Elements of Money Stock Determination," Federal Reserve Bank of St. Louis, *Review,* October 1969, pp. 10–19. Also see a descriptive presentation of the base in Ross M. Robertson and Almarin Phillips, "Optional Affiliation with the Federal Reserve System for Reserve Purposes Is Consistent with Effective Monetary Policies," Conference of State Bank Supervisors, 1974.

every $1 of reserve provided by the Fed. But this multiple is, in fact, too large because of what might be called "leakages" in the system. In developing the concept of the multiplier, we take explicit account of these leakages and attempt to view the entire money supply (demand deposits *and* currency in circulation) as some multiple of the monetary base (rather than only demand deposits as some multiple of reserves alone):

$$M = mB$$

## The Money Multiplier

The relation between $M$ and $B$ is $m$, the money multiplier. The value of $m$ is the result not only of the legally required reserve ratio, but also of the portfolio decisions of depository institutions, the public, the Treasury, and the Federal Reserve System. To clarify the nature of these decisions, let

$R$ = reserves

$C$ = currency in circulation

$D$ = private demand deposits and other checkable accounts

$T$ = time deposits

$G$ = government deposits

With these definitions let us now consider four ratios that we will call the $r$-ratio, the $k$-ratio, the $t$-ratio, and the $g$-ratio:

1. The $r$-ratio:

$$r = \frac{R}{D + T + G}$$

or

$$R = r(D + T + G)$$

The $r$-ratio is the ratio of reserves, $R$, to total deposits, $D + T + G$. Principally, the value of $r$ depends upon the legal requirements. Of course, the ratio is some weighted average figure because legal reserve requirements differ between time and demand deposits and between institutions with different amounts of deposits. It is also affected by the voluntary action of depository institutions when they establish their excess reserve position and when they decide whether or not they will borrow from the Federal Reserve.

2. The $k$-ratio:

$$k = \frac{C}{D}$$

or

$$C = kD$$

The $k$-ratio is the ratio of currency to demand deposits and other checkable accounts. It reflects the desire of the public to hold money in one or the other of the two forms. Seasonally the $k$-ratio varies considerably. At Christmastime shoppers need more currency than usual and retailers also need more change in their cash registers. Similar currency needs arise at Easter and during the August "vacation" season. Moreover, in recent years the $k$-ratio has sometimes risen over a long run, whether because of hoarding currency, "black market" transactions, tax evasion, or other factors.

3. The $t$-ratio:

$$t = \frac{T}{D}$$

or

$$T = tD$$

The $t$-ratio is the ratio of time deposits to demand and other checkable deposits. Again, this ratio is determined by the preferences of the consuming public to hold their deposits in one of two forms—as demand and other checkable deposits or as time deposits. Of course, they might be induced to increase the $t$-ratio (raise $T$ relative to $D$) if interest rates paid on time deposits rise while demand deposits continued to pay no interest at all, or to pay a low interest rate.

4. The $g$-ratio:

$$g = \frac{G}{D}$$

or

$$G = gD$$

Government deposits are not part of the money supply as it is currently defined; however, reserves must be held against these deposits.[16] The $g$-ratio indicates the ratio of government deposits (Tax and Loan accounts) to private demand and other checkable deposits.

With these four ratios defined, let us again look at

$$M = D + C \quad \text{(money is demand deposits and other checkable deposits plus currency in circulation)}$$

---

[16] They are not, however, required to hold reserves against the open-end notes that the banks and other depository institutions sell to the Treasury. The Treasury can earn interest on the funds it leaves in note form; notes were first issued in November 1978.

$B = R + C$    (the monetary base consists of reserves, including cash in bank vaults and deposits in the Fed, and currency in circulation)

Since $M = mB$, the money "multiplier," $m$, is

$$m = \frac{M}{B}$$

and by substitution

$$m = \frac{D + C}{R + C}$$

$$= \frac{D + kD}{r(D + T + G) + kD} = \frac{D(1 + k)}{D[r(1 + t + g) + k]}$$

Since the Ds cancel, we have remaining

$$m = \frac{1 + k}{r(1 + t + g) + k}$$

The money multiplier is not a constant, but a variable, determined by all the factors other than $B$ that affect the money supply. In Table 5–13, the checkmarks indicate which sectors' decisions directly affect the determinants of the money supply. As we see in the table, portfolio decisions of depository institutions are reflected in the value of $r$, which results from depository institutions' willingness to hold not only legally required reserves but also some excess reserves, and the value of $t$, which reflects willingness or ability of banks to attract time deposits, as they might through, say, raising interest rates they pay for time deposits. Portfolio decisions of the public are reflected in $k$, which results from decisions to hold currency rather than checkable deposits, or vice versa. Portfolio decisions of the Treasury are reflected in $g$, which

**TABLE 5–13**
**Sectors That Affect Specific Determinants of M1**

| Determinants of M1 | Sector | | | |
|:---:|:---:|:---:|:---:|:---:|
| | Depository Institutions | Nonbank Public | Treasury | Federal Reserve |
| $B$ | | | ✓ | ✓ |
| $r$ | ✓ | | | ✓ |
| $k$ | | ✓ | | |
| $t$ | ✓ | ✓ | | |
| $g$ | | | ✓ | |

results from decisions by the government to hold deposits with depository institutions rather than at the Federal Reserve Banks, or vice versa. And, of course, the Fed determines $B$, with some influence from the Treasury (which the Fed may offset if it wishes).

If M2 (or M3) is used as the measure of the money supply instead of M1, the formula for the multiplier changes slightly. The additional items included in M2 (or in M3) must be included in the numerator. The denominator does not change. Thus for M2, the numerator will include not only $D$ (demand deposits) plus other checkable deposits at banks and at thrift institutions, but also overnight RPs at commercial banks, overnight Eurodollars held by U.S. nonbank customers in Caribbean branches of U.S. banks, money market mutual fund shares, money market deposit accounts, and savings and small (less than $100,000) time deposits at commercial banks and thrift institutions. Because the denominator is reserves plus currency (i.e., vault cash plus deposits at the Fed plus currency outstanding), the denominator does not change. Since the numerator is larger while the denominator is unchanged if M2 (or M3) is used as the measure of money, the money multiplier is larger.

Many refinements of the multiplier have been made, but their description would require more pages than are appropriate for our survey.[17]

Several statistical series for the monetary base are now published; major differences merit brief comment. The Federal Reserve Bank of St. Louis has published one series since 1978; this series is adjusted when reserve requirements change, that is, when the required reserve percentage is changed. The reason for adjustment is that, if, for example, reserve requirements rise, either the Fed must provide more reserves so that institutions can meet the higher requirements, or institutions must reduce assets and deposits. It is likely that the Fed will provide additional reserves. If so, the monetary base will rise. But the situation is different from a rise that occurs when there is no change in reserve requirements. A rise in the base with no change in reserve requirements indicates that depository institutions can increase the money supply, but a rise in the base when reserve requirements are increased simply means that actual reserves rise to approximately the level required by the higher requirements. If the statistical series were not adjusted, it might appear that there was a rapid rise in the base in the latter case, and observers might assume (wrongly) that depository institutions can increase the money supply rapidly.

After the 1976 report of the Advisory Committee on Monetary Statistics recommended publication of data on the monetary base, the Board of Governors began such publication. The Board now publishes both an unadjusted series and an adjusted series. The adjusted series is slightly different from that published by the Federal Reserve Bank of St. Louis, and there are minor differences in the base figures before adjustment.[18]

---

[17] The interested reader may wish to examine Chapters 5 and 6 of William R. Hosek and Frank Zahn, *Monetary Theory, Policy, and Financial Markets* (New York: McGraw-Hill, 1977).

[18] For an explanation of differences among the three series and of the method used by the Federal Reserve Bank of St. Louis to adjust for changes in reserve requirements, see Albert E. Burger, "Alternative Measures of the Monetary Base," Federal Reserve Bank of St. Louis, *Review*, June 1979, pp. 3–9.

## Empirical Values of the Base and Multiplier

Figures 5–1(a), (b), and (c) show data for the monetary base ($B$), the money supply ($M$), and the money multiplier ($m$) for the last half of 1985 and the first half of 1986.[19] At the end of July 1986 the money supply was about $677 billion. With a base of $246.5 billion, $m$ was about 2.75. Approximate values of the ratios used in calculating $m$ were

$$r = .03, \quad k = .36, \quad t = 2.37, \quad g = .03$$

These ratios are obtained using the formulas given in preceding pages.

In Figure 5–1(a) we see that the base ($B$) moved up and down from month to month, but showed a fairly steady upward trend of about 8 percent for the year. The money supply ($M$) rose more rapidly, at a rate of over 13 percent for the year, as shown in Figure 5–1(b). This growth in money was related to the growth in the multiplier ($m$) as shown in Figure 5–1(c), from about 2.6 to 2.75.

Looking at the chief factors determining $m$ ($k$, $t$, and $g$), principal reasons for the more rapid growth in $M$ can be inferred. First, the $k$-ratio declined from about .39 to about .36 in the year. A decline in currency holdings of the public relative to their holdings of checkable deposits increased the multiplier. This contrasted with a rise in $k$ from .29 in 1970 to .38 in 1980.[20]

Second, the $t$-ratio declined from about 2.57 to about 2.37; a decline in any ratio in the denominator of the formula for $m$ increases $m$. Thus over the year from mid-1985 to mid-1986, declines in $k$ and $t$ were largely responsible for an increase in $m$, and therefore for a more rapid increase in $M$ than in $B$ (given the increase in $B$ which was directly controlled, for the most part, by Federal Reserve actions).

Can monetary managers of the Treasury and the Fed count on $m$ to be stable; that is, can they control $M$ relatively quickly by policy moves designed to set a particular value for $B$? The answer to this question is yet to come, and many economists are actively engaged in examination of evidence to see just how stable $m$ is over time.

Lest readers assume, because we have written a definite formula $M = mB$, that somehow the relation represented by $m$ is established, we urge them to understand that the value $m$ is *not* independent of actions designed to alter $B$. In other words, the formula is a way to put some pieces of a puzzle together, but it is not the complete picture by far. For example, if $B$ increases when the Fed buys short-term securities and this leads to reduced yields on these securities and the yields on time deposits

---

[19] See Jane Anderson and Thomas M. Humphrey, "Determinants of Change in the Money Stock, 1960–1970," Federal Reserve Bank of Richmond, *Monthly Review*, March 1972, pp. 1–8, for a detailed examination of changes in $m$ over the decade of the 1960s.

[20] Why this occurred in a period when inflation was reducing the value of money is somewhat of a puzzle. See "The Growing Appetite for Cash," Federal Reserve Bank of Chicago, *Business Conditions*, April 1971, pp. 12–16; and the later discussion by Paul S. Anderson, "Currency in Use and in Hoards," Federal Reserve Bank of Boston, *New England Economic Review*, March–April 1977, pp. 21–30.

**FIGURE 5–1(a)**
**Adjusted Monetary Base, 1985–1986**
**(averages of daily figures, seasonally adjusted by this bank)**

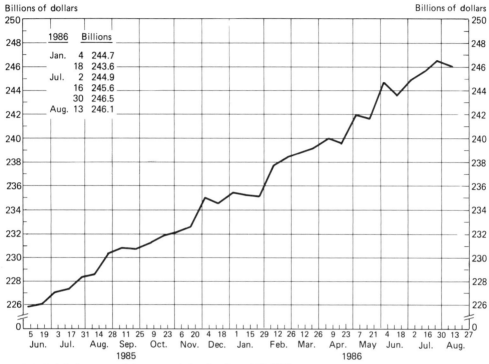

Latest plotted reserve maintenance period ending August 13, 1986.

The adjusted monetary base is the sum of reserve accounts of financial institutions at Federal Reserve Banks, currency in circulation (currency held by the public and in the vaults of all depository institutions), and an adjustment for reserve requirement ratio changes. The major source of the adjusted monetary base is Federal Reserve credit. Data are computed by this Bank. A detailed description of the adjusted monetary base is available from this Bank.

Recent data are preliminary.

| | Compounded Annual Rates of Change, Average of Two Maintenance Periods Ending | | | | | | | |
|---|---|---|---|---|---|---|---|---|
| | 8/14/85 | 11/6/85 | 1/15/86 | 2/12/86 | 3/12/86 | 4/9/86 | 5/7/86 | 6/18/86 |
| To the average of two maintenance periods ending | | | | | | | | |
| 1/15/86 | 7.2 | | | | | | | |
| 2/12/86 | 7.0 | 7.2 | | | | | | |
| 3/12/86 | 7.8 | 8.4 | 9.5 | | | | | |
| 4/ 9/86 | 7.5 | 7.9 | 8.2 | 9.1 | | | | |
| 5/ 7/86 | 7.4 | 7.7 | 7.8 | 8.3 | 6.1 | | | |
| 6/18/86 | 8.2 | 8.7 | 9.2 | 9.8 | 9.0 | 10.4 | | |
| 7/16/86 | 8.0 | 8.4 | 8.7 | 9.1 | 8.3 | 9.1 | 10.1 | |
| 8/13/86 | 7.8 | 8.1 | 8.2 | 8.6 | 7.8 | 8.3 | 8.8 | 5.7 |

SOURCE: Federal Reserve Bank of St. Louis, *U.S. Financial Data*, August 21, 1986.

**FIGURE 5–1(b)**
**Money Stock (M1), 1985–1986**
**(averages of daily figures, seasonally adjusted)**

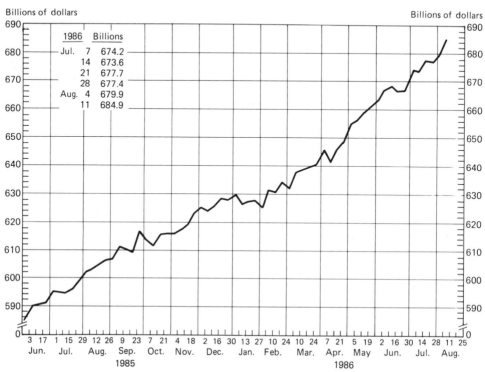

Billions of dollars

| 1986 | Billions |
|------|----------|
| Jul. 7 | 674.2 |
| 14 | 673.6 |
| 21 | 677.7 |
| 28 | 677.4 |
| Aug. 4 | 679.9 |
| 11 | 684.9 |

Latest data plotted week ending August 11, 1986.

Current data appear in the Board of Governors H.6 Release.

M1 is the sum of currency held by the nonbank public, demand deposits, other checkable deposits and travelers checks.

| | Compounded Annual Rates of Change, Average of Four Weeks Ending | | | | | | | |
|---|---|---|---|---|---|---|---|---|
| | 8/12/85 | 11/11/85 | 1/13/86 | 2/10/86 | 3/10/86 | 4/14/86 | 5/12/86 | 6/9/86 |
| To the average of four weeks ending | | | | | | | | |
| 1/13/86 | 11.4 | | | | | | | |
| 2/10/86 | 9.5 | 7.9 | | | | | | |
| 3/10/86 | 9.9 | 9.0 | 5.9 | | | | | |
| 4/14/86 | 10.6 | 10.2 | 9.1 | 13.6 | | | | |
| 5/12/86 | 11.6 | 11.8 | 11.8 | 15.8 | 17.3 | | | |
| 6/ 9/86 | 12.8 | 13.4 | 14.2 | 17.9 | 19.5 | 22.9 | | |
| 7/14/86 | 12.8 | 13.4 | 13.9 | 16.7 | 17.7 | 19.0 | 18.1 | |
| 8/11/86 | 13.4 | 14.1 | 14.8 | 17.3 | 18.2 | 19.3 | 18.8 | 16.3 |

SOURCE: Federal Reserve Bank of St. Louis, *U.S. Financial Data*, August 21, 1986.

**FIGURE 5–1(c)**
**Money Multiplier,\* 1985–1986**
**(averages of daily figures, seasonally adjusted)**

| 1986 | | Ratio |
|------|----|-------|
| May | 19 | 2.722 |
| Jun. | 2 | 2.706 |
| | 16 | 2.742 |
| | 30 | 2.722 |
| Jul. | 14 | 2.744 |
| | 28 | 2.748 |

Latest data plotted: two weeks ending July 28, 1986.

\* Ratio of money stock (M1) to adjusted monetary base.

SOURCE: Federal Reserve Bank of St. Louis, *U.S. Financial Data*, August 7, 1986.

seem attractive by comparison, then the public may shift into $T$ out of $D$, causing an increase in $t$ and a decrease in $m$. Thus, $B$ and $m$ would not be independent of each other; a rise in $B$ would lead to a decline in $m$ as well. If an expansion of $B$ and a subsequent expansion of $M$ leads to increased demand for currency, then $k$ would be affected and so would $m$. Other examples could be given.

Furthermore, $r$, $k$, $t$, and $g$ are not necessarily independent of each other. A change in $T$ and $t$ will affect $r$, because $r$ is a weighted average of excess and legal required reserve ratios for demand and time deposits, and $r$ falls when $t$ rises, because the reserve ratio required for time deposits (on average) is much less than the ratio required for demand deposits.

Thus, the formula should not be interpreted in a mechanistic fashion; rather, it should be looked upon as a convenient frame of reference. In particular, it points up the necessity of understanding portfolio decisions of individuals as they choose among instruments of the financial markets if we are to understand fully the process of money creation, spending, and resulting changes in GNP and in the price level.

# MONETARY CONTROLS

In this concluding section, we review briefly the instruments of control Federal Reserve officials have at their disposal and point up the connections between these instruments and conditions in those financial markets that are the focal points of this book. Our concern with the money supply and the institutional mechanism for controlling it stems from the belief that changes in the money supply lead to changes in the level of aggregate demand. Economists differ in opinions about the precise mechanism by which changes in the supply of money affect spending. Some believe that an increase in the supply of money will lead directly to spending by consumers and businesses. Others believe that increases in the money supply lead to purchases of bonds, which drive bond prices up and interest rates down. Lower interest rates, in turn, induce spending on the part of consumers and business. Whichever view one holds about the mechanism, it follows that money supply changes affect demand. If the rate of growth in the money supply over the long run is too great, inflation and its undesirable effects will result. If the rate of growth is too slow, the likely result will be reduced demand, deflation, and unemployment. It is important, therefore, to control the money supply so that it grows rapidly enough but not too rapidly. We now outline briefly the policy tools of the Federal Reserve that are used to regulate growth of the money supply; in later chapters on theory and policy we examine the impact of changes in the money supply on the economy and discuss in more detail the methods used by the Fed to control growth of the money supply.

## Open Market Operations

The 7 members of the Board of Governors of the Federal Reserve System and 5 of the 12 presidents of the 12 regional Federal Reserve Banks constitute the 12-member Federal Open Market Committee (FOMC). Four of the 5 bank presidents are members on a rotating basis, while the fifth, president of the Federal Reserve Bank of New York, is a permanent member of the committee. Open market operations are carried out by a trading desk in New York, and the manager for domestic operations is an officer of the Federal Reserve Bank of New York. Records of the FOMC are released to the public about one month following each meeting and are published in the *Federal Reserve Bulletin*. The FOMC gives instructions of a general nature to the manager. Instruction may be "to promote ease" or "to maintain prevailing conditions" or "to accommodate greater growth in the monetary aggregates." They may be, and have in recent years been, somewhat more specific. Open market operations are the major means of controlling the money supply.

When the manager buys U.S. government securities, it is useful to assume that the manager pays for these with a check drawn on the Fed. When this check is deposited and then returned to the Federal Reserve, that depository institution's account at the Fed is increased (reserves are increased) and $B$ is increased. Sizable purchases by the Fed may drive up the prices of government securities and drive yields down. Furthermore, because depository institutions have gained excess reserves, the immediate impact may be observed in the Federal funds market. Excess reserves may be loaned to institutions that wish to enlarge their reserve positions. With large amounts of excess reserves, the supply of Federal funds increases, and yields on Federal funds fall. The market for Federal funds reflects from day to day the ease or tightness of reserves.

Open market operations are sometimes termed "defensive" and sometimes "dynamic." For example, if a snowstorm delays forwarding of deposited checks, float may increase dramatically. The manager of the account then sells government securities to absorb some of the reserves supplied to member banks by the increased float. Thus, although the manager may wish to *add* reserves to the system, nevertheless some government securities must be sold, for otherwise the float will create a large volume of reserves and increase the base by more than the desired amount. "Defensive" operations, therefore, are housekeeping operations designed to offset various influences on reserve positions, whereas "dynamic" operations are those designed to promote changes in the money supply as dictated by policy.[21]

Similarly, when currency flows out of banks on a large scale, as it does before holiday periods, the Fed may buy securities to replenish what would otherwise be depleted reserves. The procedure is reversed as currency flows back in to depository institutions in the aftermath of these periods of high spending. Thus, on a seasonal basis the Fed uses defensive open market operations to offset changes in $m$ that follow from seasonal changes in $k$.

## Discounting (Borrowing) from the Fed

Insofar as the Fed lends directly to banks or other institutions, the base is increased and so is lending power. However, since it is typically the case that the Fed has already created tight conditions by open market sales, reserves are reduced and institutions finding themselves short of reserves may obtain reserves by borrowing from the Fed. Thus, when the Fed lends, it is often in a sense undoing with its left hand what its right hand did somewhat earlier. Many economists feel that this tool of monetary policy is an abomination and should be suspended, especially in view of the thoroughly developed market for Federal funds. However, others feel that, with the U.S. system of many individual banks and other depository institutions, there is need to retain the discount window as a "safety valve" for individual institutions caught in a difficult position.

In 1973 Regulation A was revised to allow an estimated 2,000 small banks in agricultural and resort areas to borrow from the discount window on a seasonal basis.[22] Federal Reserve Banks are able to make loans for up to 90 days if application is made in advance for the borrowing privilege and proof is offered that borrowers

---

[21] For a description of "defensive" and "dynamic" responsibilities of the Fed and a description of activity on the trading desk, see Paul Meek, *U.S. Monetary Policy and Financial Markets*, Federal Reserve Bank of New York, 1982, pp. 99–104 and 105–109.

[22] Actually, there is no window as such; borrowings are negotiated in an office.

must satisfy a seasonal demand for funds for at least an 8-week period. They must also show that they lack reasonably reliable access to national money markets. This requirement is surely difficult to meet, inasmuch as modern communications enable the immediate transfer of funds and immediate borrowing in the market for Federal funds. Nevertheless, the institution of this "seasonal" borrowing privilege indicates that discount window activity will remain strong in the near future.

Many economists argued, even in the early days of the Federal Reserve System, that the discount rate should be a *penalty* rate. If it is not, there is a temptation for banks to borrow at low rates from the Federal Reserve System and lend at higher rates, thus making profits on the borrowed funds. If the discount rate were a penalty rate, banks could not do this, and the "discount window" would be used only when funds were urgently needed. Effects of borrowing through the discount window are discussed in more detail in Chapter 16.[23]

## Changes in Required Reserve Ratios

The power of the Fed to set legal required reserve ratios helps to determine the size of *r* in the money multiplier formula. Of course, *r* is also partly determined by decisions of managers of financial institutions to maintain excess reserves in smaller or larger amounts. As noted in Chapter 3, 1980 legislation reduced reserve requirements for banks and required the phasing in of reserve requirements for thrift institutions that offered checkable deposits. Reducing reserve requirements reduces bank costs (since reserves generate no earnings) and permits additional money to be created on the basis of a given volume of reserves.

## Interest Rate Ceilings and Other Controls

In addition to the foregoing tools that affect the monetary base and/or the money multiplier directly, the Fed has other powers that affect financial markets. Regulation Q, before it was phased out in the spring of 1986, allowed the Fed to establish a maximum interest rate that institutions could pay depositors on time deposits.[24] Payment of interest on "demand deposits" is prohibited by the Banking Act of 1933, which is still effective. In 1980 NOW accounts (checkable accounts on which interest is paid) were authorized for all depository institutions. In other countries banks often pay interest to individuals holding demand deposits. In the United States, service charges may be reduced or eliminated if individuals maintain certain balances or under some other conditions. Thus, depositors who maintain sufficient balances make little or no payment, directly, for the checking services provided. In

---

[23] Gordon H. Sellon, Jr., and Diane Seibert, "The Discount Rate Experience Under Reserve Targeting," Federal Reserve Bank of Kansas City, *Economic Review*, September–October 1982, pp. 3–18. Since 1980, there has been a discount rate surcharge for large banks that borrow frequently. This article also contains a theoretical and an empirical analysis of effects of the surcharge.

[24] For a detailed analysis of Regulation Q, see R. Alton Gilbert, "Requiem for Regulation Q: What It Did and Why It Passed Away," Federal Reserve Bank of St. Louis, *Review*, February 1986, pp. 22–37.

effect, such persons are receiving the equivalent of interest on their accounts, in comparison with those who pay service charges.[25]

On passbook savings deposits, the maximum interest rate payable was 5¼ percent for banks and 5½ percent for savings and loan associations and other institutions, until the end of 1983. On time deposits of larger amounts and longer term to maturity, maximum rates ranged from 5½ to 8 percent. For the special category of negotiable CDs of $100,000 and over, with maturity from 30 to 90 days, the ceiling was suspended on January 21, 1970. Later, in mid-May 1973, the decision was made to suspend rate ceilings on all these large negotiable CDs without regard to maturity. In 1980 the Congress passed legislation to phase out ceilings altogether over a period of several years. The rate at which this occurred was determined by the Depository Institutions Deregulation Committee, as indicated in the appendix to Chapter 3.

Regulations G, T, and U, prescribed in accordance with the Securities and Exchange Act of 1934 and its amendments, limit the amount of credit that a bank, broker, dealer, or others can extend to someone wishing to purchase and carry securities, by prescribing a maximum loan value that is a specified percentage of the market value of the security at the time that credit is extended. These percentages are called margin requirements. In early 1970, on margin stocks the requirement was 80 percent. By December 1971, it was reduced to 55 percent, and late in 1972 it was raised again to 65 percent. In January 1974 it was again reduced, this time to 50 percent, and it remained there in the mid-1980s. Thus, a purchaser of $100 of stock could borrow $50 from a bank and put up $50 cash, pledging the securities as collateral against his or her loan. On convertible bonds the ratio was also 50 percent. These requirements have a direct impact on the availability of funds in the market for equities and convertible bonds.

During periods of severe economic stress, the Fed has been given direct controls over terms of lending to consumers for mortgages and for all forms of installment credit. By "terms" we mean the down payment required and the length of time over which repayment must be made. For example, such controls were exercised during World War II and in several periods after that war. The Fed no longer has such power, but could easily be given it again; from time to time the suggestion is made that such power be available on a standby basis.

"Moral suasion" is also a policy tool. Federal Reserve memoranda sent to commercial banks can induce them to restrict "speculative" or other types of loans, and bank examiners often look at the "quality" of the loan—noting whether it is more or less speculative. Although these procedures are not clearly defined, bank managers are sensitive to the overall examination procedure and the availability of funds for certain types of loans can be influenced. On September 1, 1966, a letter from each Federal Reserve Bank president to member banks in his district stated that the "System believes that the national economic interest would be better served by a

---

[25] Questions that may be raised are rather complex: for instance, what service charge would just compensate the bank for its cost of handling checking accounts? What does a specified deposit balance (for example, $300) contribute to offsetting the cost of handling the account by providing for the particular bank funds that may be loaned out at interest?

lower rate of expansion of bank loans to business" and that "this objective will be kept in mind by the Federal Reserve Banks in their extensions of credit to member banks through the discount window." In October 1979, Board Chairman Paul A. Volcker told banks to restrict the extent of their "speculative" lending. He said in a speech, "Banks should take care to avoid financing essentially speculative activity in commodity, gold, and foreign exchange markets." Occasions such as this, when the Federal Reserve System feels impelled to supplement its usual credit control powers with special pronouncements, usually come in times of "crisis," or at least severe strain, in the money market.[26]

It is important to note that the controls that affect the monetary base and the money supply are *general* controls—they affect the total supply of funds available for spending or saving. The other controls, however, are *selective*—they affect particular types of spending or particular forms of saving. Thus interest rate controls affect spending for categories of goods and services for which interest rates are controlled, or they affect saving in the particular forms or channels on which rates are controlled. Similarly, consumer credit controls are selective—they affected, in the past, consumer purchases of durable goods when the purchases were made on credit.

The problem that arises when selective controls are used is that other (uncontrolled) interest rates may rise, for example, thus leading to a shift of saving to forms on which interest rates are higher and a significant reduction in the supply of funds for the types of loans made by institutions for which interest rates are subject to control. In wartime such controls may be necessary; when autos cannot be produced because of a need for production of tanks and other military goods, purchases of autos may need to be controlled. But it must be recognized that both interest rate and credit controls have effects on particular segments of the economy which may not be desired and which sometimes are not expected.

## SUMMARY

Money is important in a modern economy because almost all purchases involve money and because there are significant correlations between rates of increase in the money stock and GNP. Problems in defining and measuring money, however, complicate analysis. Money consists of currency plus liabilities of certain financial institutions. In the present institutional environment, measures of money always include currency and demand deposits. But broader measures of money are becoming more important now that checks can be written, and telephone payment orders taken, against deposits

---

[26] In May 1973 strong inflationary pressures led Arthur F. Burns, then chairman of the Board of Governors, to send a letter to all banks somewhat similar to the letter sent by Federal Reserve Bank presidents in 1966. Although the Bank of England has statutory powers over bank lending, it still prefers to operate informally through "moral suasion." Moral suasion can be used more easily in a country such as Great Britain, with a very small number of banks. In the United States, although moral suasion is occasionally used, as in the two instances cited, specific lending controls on particular types of lending are more common. See the discussion of credit controls in Chapter 7, and, on the British procedures, see "Public Control of Bank Lending," *Midland Bank Review*, August 1976, pp. 12–21.

of various types. The new measure of money most generally quoted, M1, includes checkable deposits in nonbank institutions.

Banks create money by making loans and giving borrowers deposit credits or currency. Most countries have banking systems consisting of a number of banks, from fewer than a dozen in some countries to many thousands in the United States. In a banking system, the money creating process involves creation of deposits on the basis of reserves, with the limitation that banks may not hold less than the required amount of reserves. Other institutions that have checkable deposits are subject, in the United States, to the same reserve requirements.

The authorities now define reserves to be deposits in the Fed and cash in bank vaults except that nonmember institutions may keep reserves in the form of balances at certain institutions that keep reserves at the Fed *both* for themselves and for other institutions.

A variety of actions can change the actual amount of *reserves;* for example, if the public decides to hold less cash, they deposit it in depository institutions and reserves increase. If the Treasury buys gold and pays for it with a check on its account at the Fed, when the institution deposits the check with the Fed, reserves increase. When the Fed buys government securities (or anything else, for that matter), it pays with a check drawn on itself and whoever receives that check deposits it in a bank or other depository institution. This institution gains reserves. A variety of actions changes the level of *required* reserves even if the actual level is unchanged. For example, people can shift funds from demand to savings deposits. Since personal savings deposits carry no reserve requirement, this shift of funds reduces the level of required reserves. Thus, a given level of total reserves now can support a larger volume of money than before, if money consists of both demand and time deposits. The Fed can lower the required reserve ratio, and again the existing volume of reserves can support a larger volume of deposits.

Currency plus reserves, with appropriate adjustments, have been termed the "monetary base" on which deposits are created. The "reserve equation" shows the factors affecting the monetary base; amounts of items in the equation can be controlled or allowed for by the Fed.

A formula used recently shows the factors affecting the size of the money stock, given the size of the monetary base. This formula is termed the "money multiplier" ($M/B$, or $m$). Examining this formula, it is seen that the public, the government, and the depository institutions, as well as the Federal Reserve System, play roles in determining the size of the money stock.

However, the Federal Reserve System has the ability to control the size of the money stock over a period of time, although it may not be able to do so as quickly as may be desired or as precisely. The tools it has used include open market operations, lending to eligible institutions, changes in required reserve ratios, interest rate ceilings, and moral suasion. The major tool in the United States is open market operations, but in other countries, where financial markets are less well developed, the other types of control are more often used, and sometimes open market operations are not used.

## Questions for Discussion

**1.** Overnight RPs and money market mutual funds are included in M2 but not in M1 (see Table 5–1). Do you think they should be included in M1? Why or why not?

**2.** List arguments for the use of M1 as the money supply; then list arguments for using M2. Which is the better measure? Why?

**3.** Some economists prefer the term "stock of money" rather than the term "money supply." Why?

**4.** Would it be possible for a single commercial bank, if isolated, for example, in Alaska, without communications, to create money?

**5.** Show in skeleton balance sheet form, for the Federal Reserve Banks, and for depository institutions, the effects of open market purchases by the Fed.

**6.** Show how the reserve equation is used to demonstrate what factors determine the size of the monetary base.

**7.** Derive the equation for the money multiplier. Derive it when time deposits are included in the measure of money. Why is the money multiplier quite volatile in the short run?

**8.** Contrast "defensive" and "dynamic" open market operations.

**9.** Evaluate each of the other tools now used, or used in the past, by the Fed to control the money supply and/or credit. How useful is each? What defects do you find in each?

**10.** Why is it necessary at certain times to restrain bank loans to business firms? Why has the Fed at certain times indicated that whether banks restrain such loans or not will be kept in mind when banks apply to the Fed for borrowings?

## Selected References

To gain a better understanding of the money creation process and the effects of various participants on the money supply including the Federal Reserve's policy tools, the student should study through *Modern Money Mechanics*, Federal Reserve Bank of Chicago. This publication is free upon request.

Because of the importance of money in economic and financial affairs, the student would find it rewarding to survey the controversy over the definition and measurement of money. An excellent introduction is provided in David Laidler's "The Definition of Money," *Journal of Money, Credit and Banking*, August 1969, pp. 508–525, reprinted in William F. Gibson and George G. Kaufman, eds., *Monetary Economics: Readings on Current Issues* (New York: McGraw-Hill, 1971). A comprehensive analysis of the many problems of money measurement is found in Thomas D. Simpson et al., "A Proposal for Redefining the Monetary Aggregates," *Federal Reserve Bulletin*, January 1979, pp. 13–42, and his "The Redefined Monetary Aggregates," *Federal Reserve Bulletin*, February 1980, pp. 97–114.

For an important committee report on defining and measuring money, see *Improving the Monetary Aggregates*, Report of the Advisory Committee on Monetary Statistics, Board of Governors of the Federal Reserve System, Washington, D.C., June 1976.

The monetary base and multiplier model, which has become widely used to integrate the roles played by the commercial banks, the public, the Treasury, and the Fed in determination of the money supply, is presented in Jerry L. Jordan's "Elements of Money Stock Determination," Federal Reserve Bank of St. Louis, *Review*, October 1969, pp. 10–19 (reprinted in *Monetary Economics: Readings on Current Issues*). Also see Albert E. Burger, "Alternative Measures of the Monetary Base," Federal Reserve Bank of St. Louis, *Review*, June 1979, pp. 3–8.

The weekly Federal Reserve statement provides information about the monetary base presented in terms of the sources and uses of member bank reserves. A useful pamphlet is *Statfacts*, published by the Federal Reserve Bank of New York (1981), which describes and explains the terms used in all major Federal Reserve statistical releases. Current values for the base and the monetary multiplier are published weekly in the Federal Reserve Bank of St. Louis, *U.S. Financial Data. Monetary Trends* by the same bank includes data on the rates of change of money supply measures, bank credit, and the base.

In addition to references cited in this chapter, one other useful discussion of the redefined measures of the money supply is R. W. Hafer, "The New Money Aggregates," Federal Reserve Bank of St. Louis, *Review*, February 1980, pp. 25–32.

For a useful discussion of possible reasons for the increasing demand for currency, see Norman N. Bowsher, "The Demand for Currency: Is the Underground Economy Undermining Monetary Policy?" Federal Reserve Bank of St. Louis, *Review*, January 1980, pp. 11–17.

# SOME CURRENT ISSUES CONCERNING THE ROLE OF THE FINANCIAL SERVICES INDUSTRY IN FINANCIAL MARKETS AND IN THE ECONOMY

In this chapter we examine six issues that have been widely discussed because of changes in the nature of the financial services industry and of regulations affecting that industry. First, we discuss two issues that were greatly affected by the Depository Institutions Deregulation and Monetary Control Act of 1980 and the Depository Institutions Act of 1982. These issues are (1) Are commercial banks unique as creators of money and as institutions that provide a wide variety of banking services? (2) Was the declining membership of banks in the Federal Reserve System harmful, especially if it diminished the ability of the Fed to control the money stock?

Then, we discuss effects of developments in the financial services industry on the economy: (3) competition among financial and nonfinancial institutions in the financial services industry, (4) the problem of handling payments and records of payments, (5) the long-run effect of the development of financial institutions on saving, and (6) the appropriate place in the economy for government lending and government lending agencies.

# THE UNIQUENESS OF COMMERCIAL BANKS

Commercial banks were at one time considered to be unique and so significant that university courses in "Money and Banking" were widely offered. While other parts of the financial services industry, the financial markets, and the theory of interest were given little attention, the history of banking was discussed in detail.

Banks have been considered to be a unique institution both by economists and by the U.S. Supreme Court. Let us examine the viewpoint of economists first.

## Economic Uniqueness of Commercial Banks

Special emphasis has been given to *money* because it is the means for making final payments and because it may be used as a "temporary store of purchasing power." Much attention has been focused on M1 or M2 as measures of money for these uses. Banks have been considered as unique by many economists who assert that banks alone, among private financial institutions, create money.

We have noted that when banks make loans or buy securities they create money when they create, or add to, the demand deposits of the borrowers. The process is essentially the same whether loans are for business purposes, for consumers, for home buyers, for foreigners, or for government units (except that, as noted, U.S. federal government deposits are not counted as a part of M1).

What is significant here is that the banks are creating money *and credit* in these types of financial transactions. They acquire both an earning asset (creating credit) *and* a checking account liability (money). Most nonbank lending institutions, on the other hand, acquire an earning asset *in exchange for* another asset—in the past, usually, a claim on a deposit that they held in a commercial bank. In such cases no new demand deposits (money) are created. There is simply a transfer of an amount from an existing deposit held by a lending institution to the borrower or to someone designated by the borrower.

Especially since the 1980 legislation authorizing NOW accounts and other checking (or checkable) deposits, commercial banks and some savings banks and savings and loan associations offer checking accounts to their customers. These are not "demand deposits" as defined in the law, since "demand" deposits so defined cannot pay interest. Both commercial banks and savings banks may create, or they may accept, these "other checkable deposits" (OCDs).[1] If created, they add to the money supply (M1). If they are attracted by offering desirable interest rates, the money supply (M1) is increased, but the phrase "creation of money" does not seem appropriate.

The individual bank or nonbank lender is, of course, limited in the amount of

---

[1] The M1 measure of the money supply is now composed of (1) currency ($186.2 billion); (2) travelers checks issued by nonbank issuers ($6.0 billion); (3) demand deposits ($319.5 billion); and (4) other checkable deposits, OCDs ($235.0 billion). Amounts are those reported at the end of 1986 (*Federal Reserve Bulletin*, June 1987, p. A13).

credit it can extend or the deposits it can create. It can lend *safely* only to the extent of its excess reserves. Banks compete among themselves and with other types of institutions, such as insurance companies, pension funds, and others.

There is, however, an important difference between the *system* of commercial banks and the system of nonbank institutions with respect to money and credit creation. When banks make loans, although individual banks lose reserves, the *system* typically does not—even if borrowers use the funds to make payments to others, the others typically deposit the funds, at least initially, in *some* banks. Thus the banking *system* has the potential to increase total loans and deposits by a multiple of the system's excess reserves. The extent of ultimate expansion of deposits depends on the public's decisions with respect to holdings of financial assets in the forms of currency, checkable deposits, time deposits, and other financial assets.

In the case of nonbank lenders, it was in the past highly probable that if they made loans, these institutions lost funds held in commercial banks. For example, a savings and loan association might make a mortgage loan and transfer funds to the seller of property by a draft on the S and L's deposit in a commercial bank. The seller was likely to deposit the funds in a commercial bank.

A reduction in bank reserve requirements—or an increase in bank reserves as a result of open market operations by the Federal Reserve System—permits additional credit and money creation by banks. If the public then shifts funds to savings and loan associations, for example, to restore the previous ratio of savings and loan account holdings to demand deposit holdings, it permits additional credit creation by the savings and loan associations. But now assume that savings and loan associations have reserve requirements and that these are reduced. Additional credit creation by the savings and loan associations is then possible. But this does not lead to any further credit creation by banks. Borrowers from savings and loan associations receive title to deposits in commercial banks, and they transfer such title to those to whom they make payments. Velocity of money increases, but there is no reason to anticipate a change in the size of the money stock. Even if the amount of share accounts in savings and loan associations was much larger than the amount of demand deposits in banks, the credit creation by banks *and* by savings and loan associations, resulting from a reduction in reserve requirements for banks, would be larger than the credit creation by savings and loan associations *alone*, resulting from a reduction in reserve requirements for savings and loan associations. Of course, the larger the nonbank financial institutions (NBFIs) become, the less important the difference is, for the ratio of bank credit creation plus NBFI credit creation to NBFI credit creation alone will fall as the importance of NBFIs increases.[2] But the principle remains: banks have a greater importance than do NBFIs, as long as NBFIs keep deposits in banks as a major part of their reserves. Such bank deposits are money, a means of settlement of debts, exchanged among sectors of the public, including the NBFI sector, but usually neither increased nor decreased in amount by such exchange.

---

[2] To the extent that NBFIs obtain checkable deposits and redeposit the funds in commercial banks, the NBFIs participate in the process of money creation—demand deposits in banks are not reduced, and at the same time checkable deposits in NBFIs increase.

This conclusion hinges on the fact that NBFIs hold reserves largely in the form of deposits in commercial banks, and these deposits are payments media for them as well as for the public. The foundation of the greater importance of commercial banks in credit creation is the special status of commercial banks because demand deposits in such banks are used for final settlement of debts. As other institutions offer checking accounts and these are used to settle debts, these institutions become more like commercial banks. Commercial banks begin to lose their uniqueness. If the nonbank deposit-type institutions make loans and create deposit accounts (or add to existing accounts) for borrowers, they too will be creators of money. It will be interesting to watch this process during the late 1980s and into the 1990s.

Especially since the legislation of 1980 permitting interest on checkable deposits, the temporary store of purchasing power aspect of money, as measured by M1, has become more important. M1 increased very rapidly—over 11 percent in 1985 and over 16 percent in 1986. (M2 increased only 8 percent and 9 percent in those years.) Within M1, "other checkable deposits" increased over 24 percent from September 1985 to March 1987, while demand deposits increased only 8 percent.[3] Why? One suggestion is that the shift to "other checkable deposits" may have occurred because of a change in the "opportunity cost" of holding a checkable deposit compared to holding another relatively liquid asset. As interest rates in the money market fell from 1984 to 1987, rates on other checkable deposits did not fall very much—thus the opportunity cost of holding such deposits fell, and they became relatively more desirable. In this view, the increase in other checkable deposits reflected a shift in *demand* for that type of money, not a shift in its supply (creation).

To conclude, economists have debated for years whether the central bank should focus its effort on control of the money supply (and if so, on which measure of the money supply), or on credit, or on interest rates. We return to these questions in Chapter 16. At this point, it is enough to say that the answer rests in large part on the *predictability* of the velocity of whatever measure of money is used. If changes in velocity are predictable, the central bank can control total spending by controlling the money supply and allowing for changes in velocity of money. Control of total spending for GNP should constitute control of GNP as measured by income or output, since spending must equal income obtained by output (effort of labor, use of capital to produce more goods, etc.).

## Legal Views on the Uniqueness of Commercial Banks

In the early 1960s, the Supreme Court stated, in a bank merger decision, that "the cluster of products [various kinds of credit] and services [such as checking accounts and trust administration] denoted by the term 'commercial banking'" was sufficient to define commercial banking as a distinct line of commerce, within the meaning of antitrust legislation (the Clayton Act) that declares mergers illegal if their

---

[3] *Monetary Trends*, Federal Reserve Bank of St. Louis, April 1987, p. 1.

effect is "substantially to lessen competition" in any line of commerce.[4] Provisions of the Depository Institutions Deregulation and Monetary Control Act of 1980 make it possible for other institutions to offer more of these services, perhaps as a package or cluster, and to reduce incentives for consumers to obtain all the services in one place. Since the Fed will now charge for services formerly provided free of charge, banks will have more incentive to charge their customers separately for those services.

Certainly banking cannot be regarded as unique if time deposits alone are considered as a separate product. Commercial banks, mutual savings banks, savings and loan associations, and credit unions all have time deposit accounts or similar accounts, and they all compete with each other and with such institutions as money market mutual funds, for example.

Another emerging problem is presented by retail stores and conglomerates: if they begin to offer most of the services offered by commercial banks (which savings and loan associations, for example, generally do *not* do), are they competitors of banks in the line of commerce defined as commercial banking? In the 1980s it may be time for reexamination of the definition of commercial banking as a line of commerce.

In the Supreme Court's view, in a later case, it was indicated that other institutions need not have *all* the powers held by commercial banks to be considered as part of the commercial banking line of commerce, but they would have to offer enough variety of services for both individual *and* business customers to make them competitive alternatives to commercial banks. As other institutions gain legal power to offer additional services, or offer such services because no legal provision prevents them, it may become significant to reexamine the line drawn in the foregoing decisions of the Supreme Court.

The institution that is closest to commercial banking in legal powers is the mutual savings bank or savings bank. (Some mutual savings banks have become savings banks, issuing stock to obtain capital.) Federal savings banks, authorized in 1980, are permitted to have demand deposits of business firms. (For a comparison of the powers of national banks and savings banks, see Table 4–1 in Chapter 4.) State regulations vary, but even if demand deposits for business firms are permitted, until recently such accounts were not very useful because mutual savings banks could not provide services such as check collection. In New England, an area in which mutual savings banks are relatively important, they were not important competitors of commercial banks in the group of services provided by commercial banks as a whole, but in individual services they were becoming significant in the early 1980s.

As indicated later in this chapter, the fundamental question that must be faced in the late 1980s and beyond is: Are lines to be drawn separating the various participants offering financial services? And if so, where? Both economically and in the ways significant for legal decisions, the financial services industry as a whole is becoming more homogeneous; yet at the same time, individual institutions are finding niches as specialists in one or several types of financial service.

---

[4] *United States* v. *Philadelphia National Bank*, 374 U.S. 321, 1963. The Supreme Court affirmed the judgment of the district court that had heard the case earlier, *United States* v. *Philadelphia National Bank*, 201 F. Supp. 348, 1962.

# THE FED MEMBERSHIP ISSUE

In recent years many state banks withdrew from membership in the Federal Reserve System. National banks, of course, cannot withdraw. But the percentage of total commercial bank deposits held by member banks fell from about 80 percent to about 70 percent. The Fed was concerned that a further decline in membership might make it difficult for the Fed to control the size of the money stock, since the Fed directly controls only the reserves of institutions that hold reserves at the Fed. If a large percentage of banks did not hold reserves at the Fed, those banks could expand the money supply before the Fed could react—Fed control of the money supply would, at best, be irregular.

A number of alternatives were available as inducements to member banks to remain members and to new state banks to become members. Reserve requirements could be reduced, to make them comparable to or lower than reserve requirements of state banks. Interest could be paid on reserves held in the Fed. Or other inducements could have been offered. Each had drawbacks. To be effective, the reduction in reserve requirements would have had to have been sizable, and to do this in a period of inflation seemed to be wrong. Interest payments would be costly, and the Treasury would lose revenue (remember, after expenses, 90 percent of Fed revenue is paid to the Treasury). In a period of government budget deficits, this seemed undesirable.

The Depository Institutions Deregulation and Monetary Control Act of 1980 adopted a different alternative—it required all banks, whether members of the Fed or not, to keep their reserves in vault cash and/or in deposits in the Fed. It went beyond this—it required all institutions holding demand deposits or NOW accounts to keep reserves in these forms. It mandated the same reserve requirements for all such institutions, except that on the first $25 million of net demand deposits, the required reserve percentage was only 3 percent, whereas on deposits above $25 million, it was set at 12 percent and could be varied down to 8 percent or up to 14 percent. Later, the Depository Institutions Act of 1982 exempted the first $2 million of checkable deposits from reserve requirements, for a given institution. Both the $25 million figure and the $2 million figure are varied slightly each year.

Since the Fed would hold all reserves except those held in vault cash, the question of membership in the Fed became immaterial. For banks, there might be some small advantage in being members (prestige, power to vote for directors of the local Federal Reserve Banks, and so on), but these were relatively insignificant. The important result was that the Fed's control of the money supply would not be diminished if banks left the System or if new banks did not join the System.

The Depository Institutions Deregulation and Monetary Control Act of 1980 also provided that the Federal Reserve System charge for services provided to institutions and that the same charge be made for each institution for the same service. Thus there was no advantage in this respect to be obtained by being a member. Services could not be obtained by members at any lower cost than for nonmembers, and there was no advantage in being a nonmember, since both members and nonmembers could obtain certain services either from the Fed or elsewhere, such as from correspondent banks.

A significant core of member banks remained because of the provision that all national banks must be members (this provision of the National Banking Act was unchanged). Whatever advantages might exist in being national banks (prestige, ease of obtaining charters in some cases, and so on) remained.

It is no wonder that the Depository Institutions Deregulation and Monetary Control Act of 1980 was termed "landmark legislation." It relegated the Fed membership problem to relative insignificance, it specified reserve requirements for all transactions balances (except possibly for some borderline items), it removed reserve requirements for personal savings accounts and other personal time deposits, and it made many other changes: increasing the powers of depository institutions other than commercial banks, providing for the phasing out of interest rate ceilings on time deposits, and legalizing the payment of interest on NOW accounts for individuals and nonprofit institutions. The provision of the Banking Act of 1933 prohibiting payment of interest on demand deposits remained in effect, so that explicit interest is still not paid on demand deposits held by business firms. (Firms may receive services that constitute implicit interest, however.)

This one law alone has made commercial banks less unique than hitherto; provided for market-level interest rates, after a period of time, for all depository institutions; and effectively solved the Fed membership problem by giving control of reserves for checkable deposits to the Fed.

# COMPETITION AMONG INSTITUTIONS IN THE FINANCIAL SERVICES INDUSTRY

Even those who emphasize the uniqueness of commercial banks do not deny that commercial banks compete with other financial institutions, especially the nonbank deposit-type institutions. Competition occurs both in efforts to attract funds of savers and in the investment of such funds. Effects of this and other competition among financial institutions may be viewed from the perspective of the institutions themselves, the effects on velocity of money and total spending, and the effects on various types of loans and spending.

## Competition Among Depository Institutions

Competition among deposit-type institutions has been widely discussed. Liabilities of all institutions in this group are held as liquid assets by the public, and characteristics of the various assets are sufficiently similar to induce shifts from one to another with changes in yields.

### Recent Competitive Trends

In the 1950s, growth of savings and loan associations was relatively rapid, and some concern was expressed over the competition of these institutions with commercial banks. Growth of savings and loan associations in this period was more rapid than that of commercial banks, in part because slow growth of the money supply (a result of Federal Reserve policy) did not permit rapid growth of demand deposits of banks. In part, however, the slower growth of commercial banks occurred because they did not take sufficient initiative in seeking new sources of funds in additional time deposits and other forms. In the 1960s, the position was reversed; commercial banks entered a period of rapid growth as they were permitted to raise interest rates paid on time deposits, and they actively sought and attracted large amounts of deposit funds plus nondeposit funds obtained by borrowing.

In this competition, commercial banks have one major advantage and several small disadvantages. Their major advantage is that they need not pay as high a rate of interest (by about ¾ percent, according to one study)[5] as do savings and loan associations. Their disadvantages, which are less significant, include the following: (1) they must keep slightly more funds in nonearning assets as reserves; (2) they may have a slight disadvantage in net return on loans because savings and loan associations specialize in higher-interest conventional mortgage loans, and they have a disadvantage because they must pay somewhat higher rates of income tax than do savings and loan associations; and (3) they must pay a return to stockholders, which mutual savings and loan associations need not do. Both types of institutions must, of course, add to capital accounts as their deposits and share account liabilities grow, to maintain an appropriate capital/deposit ratio or capital/share account ratio.

Although total commercial bank profits rose in the 1960s, commercial bank profit margins narrowed as higher marginal costs were incurred when rates of interest paid on time deposits rose. The average "spread" between rates paid by savings and loan associations and those paid by banks fell from 1½ percent or more in the early 1950s to about ½ percent in the mid-1960s, whereas the ratio of bank net income to bank capital accounts—a measure of the rate of total profit on capital—did not fall significantly. This reduction in interest rate spread led to a rapid rise in savings accounts in commercial banks; from the end of 1965 to the end of 1971, household savings accounts in commercial banks nearly doubled, whereas household share accounts and deposits in savings and loan associations and mutual savings banks increased by only about 60 percent. Concern over welfare of the commercial banks in the 1950s was replaced by concern over the welfare of the nonbank deposit-type institutions.

As inflation became worse and worse in the 1970s, and as market rates of interest (rates on bonds, money market funds, and so on) reached levels much higher than the interest rates that either banks or savings and loan associations could, under the law, pay on time deposits and savings accounts, "disintermediation" became more and more serious—individuals shifted funds out of banks and savings and loan associations and into market instruments. The situation for savings and loans became much worse than the situation for banks because of the relatively short-term liabilities of both, and the relatively long-term assets of the savings and loans. Some view savings

    [5] Jack R. Vernon, "Competition for Savings Deposits: The Recent Experience," *National Banking Review*, December 1966, pp. 183–192.

and loan associations as obsolete, not viable as financial institutions. They must at the very least diversify their loans and make variable-rate mortgage loans.[6] Many economists predict considerable shrinkage in the savings and loan industry, with many institutions failing and/or being taken over by other institutions. On the other hand, many savings and loans are viable and some are moving to improve their situations.

### Competition and the Effectiveness of Monetary Control

Concern over the competitive position of the different institutions is not the only reason for examining the competition in this field. There is also concern that nonbank deposit-type institutions, by attracting funds from commercial banks, might expand credit even when monetary policy was restrictive on commercial banks. Gradual long-run growth did not give rise to concern, as this could be allowed for in policy decisions; the concern was that cyclical fluctuations might create a problem.[7]

Evidence in the studies of Milton Friedman and others that velocity of money generally rose when the money supply increased and fell when the money supply declined, in cyclical fluctuations, threw some doubt on whether changes resulting from shifts of funds to and from nonbank financial institutions might change velocity in a direction contrary to that desired for monetary policy.[8] The possibility was still open that control of bank credit might not be sufficient to control credit expansion by the nonbank deposit-type institutions or that, if it were, restraint on bank credit might have to be unduly restrictive. Some argued, however, that the commercial banks, as shown, contribute far more to changes in velocity than do the nonbank financial institutions because of commercial bank shifts from investments, which may involve purchase of existing securities and hence no rise in income velocity of money, to loans, which provide funds for the purchase of goods and services and, hence, usually a rise in income velocity. Moreover, in the credit crunches of 1966 and 1969, it became evident that the nonbank deposit-type institutions might suffer much more than the commercial banks when tight monetary policy caused interest rates to rise sharply. Thus concern over control of the nonbank deposit-type institutions diminished. The gradual rise in income velocity of money (M1) after 1945 and the more rapid rise in periods of rising business activity (1961–1966, 1971–1973, and after

---

[6] For a negative view of the situation, see Bert Ely, "This Savings and Loan Mess Won't Go Away," *The Wall Street Journal*, July 17, 1986, p. 22.

[7] This problem was emphasized in the writings of John G. Gurley and Edward S. Shaw (see, for example, *Money in a Theory of Finance*, Washington, D.C., The Brookings Institution, 1960), although it is not clear to what extent they concurred in the policy recommendation that could be inferred—that nonbank financial institutions as well as commercial banks should be subject to controls by the monetary policy authorities.

[8] Friedman found that in the period prior to World War II, when the trend of velocity was downward, velocity sometimes declined both in recovery phases and in declining phases of business activity. However, after World War II velocity increased in periods of business expansion and declined slightly in recessions. Since periods of business expansion have been longer than have periods of recession, the trend of velocity has been upward. Milton Friedman and Anna J. Schwartz, "Money and Business Cycles," *Review of Economics and Statistics*, February 1963, Supplement.

FIGURE 6–1
Income Velocity of Money
(annually, 1910–1946; seasonally adjusted, quarterly, 1947–1976)

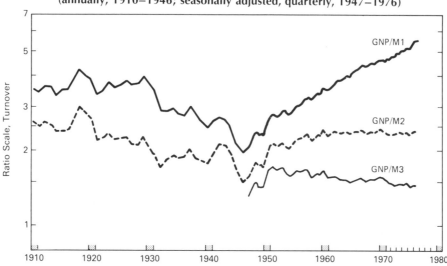

SOURCE: Federal Reserve Bank of Boston, *New England Economic Review,* March–April 1977, p. 10.

1975) is shown in Figure 6–1. Note that income velocity of M2 was very stable from 1960 to 1976, whereas the velocity of M3 declined somewhat.[9]

Analysis of the effect of total spending on prices and output begins with the equation of exchange: $MV$ equals $PT$ (money times its velocity or rate of turnover equals prices times total transactions).[10] In modern analysis, $PT$ is replaced by $PY$— $T$, total transactions, is replaced by $Y$, total currently produced goods and services. $T$ is much broader than $Y$: $T$ includes purchases of old houses and used autos, gifts, and, most important, financial assets (stocks, bonds, bank CDs, etc.) as well as purchases of current output of goods and services.

Monetarist analysis is expressed in the well-known quantity theory of money. Monetarists begin with the equation of exchange, a *truism:* total spending *must* equal the total value of what is purchased. Development of the quantity theory of money involves two steps based on this equation: (1) $PT$ is replaced by $PY$, and therefore, $V_t$

[9] Paul S. Anderson, "Behavior of Monetary Velocity," Federal Reserve Bank of Boston, *New England Economic Review,* March–April 1977, pp. 8–20, indicated that velocity of M1 held by businesses and by state and local governments rose fairly rapidly, whereas velocity of M1 held by households rose very little. For a review of theories concerning the velocity of M1, see Bryon Higgins, "Velocity: Money's Second Dimension," Federal Reserve Bank of Kansas City, *Economic Review,* June 1978, pp. 15–31.

[10] A more accurate formula would be $MV$ equals $\Sigma pt$—take average price of oranges per dozen ($p$) multiplied by the number of dozens of oranges sold ($t$), average price of autos multiplied by the number of autos sold, and so on, and then add. It is impossible to add oranges and autos meaningfully, but the *values* (quantities times average price of each) can be added.

must be replaced by $V_y$—velocity of money in all transactions is replaced by velocity of money in transactions involving purchases of goods and services produced during the current period. (2) It is then argued that (a) velocity is either stable or predictable, and (b) $Y$ cannot increase in the short run once full employment is reached, that is, once available labor is fully employed and capital resources (factories and equipment) are fully utilized. Even at full employment, *some* unemployment of labor exists: (1) some people have quit their jobs but have not yet found new jobs and some graduates of high schools and universities are seeking employment, and (2) there may not be enough people trained for available jobs and too many people in lines in which employment is being reduced. The first is termed "frictional" unemployment, and the second is termed "structural" unemployment.

The quantity theory of money then concludes that an increase in the money supply causes a rise in the price level, under the foregoing conditions. But two problems arise: (1) although transactions velocity of money and income velocity of money can both be measured ($V_t$ is total bank debits plus an estimate of cash spending, divided by $M$, and $V_y$ is $GNP/M$), $V_t$ is much greater than $V_y$, and past trends do not necessarily enable us to predict future trends. If, for example, financial transactions (purchase of stocks and bonds, etc.) increased rapidly, while purchases of GNP increased slowly, $V_t$ would be increasing and $V_y$ might be declining. (2) Both $V_t$ and $V_y$ might become more rapid or might slow down. As Figure 6–1 indicates, income velocity generally declined from 1920 to 1945; after World War II, this trend was reversed, using M1 as the measure of money supply. After 1960, income velocity of M2 was quite stable, which might have been expected—savings accounts (a large part of M2) are likely to have slower turnover, or velocity, than cash and checking accounts, the components of M1.

A major change occurred again in the 1980s: income velocity of M1 declined in 1981–1982, rose almost as much in 1983–1984, and declined very sharply again in 1984–1986.[11] With stable velocity, a stable money supply should result in relatively stable prices. But with declining velocity, more money is needed to prevent a decline in prices and perhaps in real GNP also.

It is clear that the volume of credit (the supply of loanable funds) is much greater than the volume of money measured by any of the usual measures. It is also clear that credit is used for many other actions than purchase of items composing GNP; people buy used autos, stocks and bonds, and many other things on credit. Do we wish to control total credit, or spending on the basis of credit, rather than to control money? We have so little research indicating whether control of such an aggregate would better stabilize the economy and lead to economic growth that results are difficult to predict. Casual observation suggests that several credit or debt measures have been remarkably stable in relation to GNP, more so than M1, especially since 1980. These relationships are shown in Figure 6–2. Proposals to use credit aggregates as a focus for monetary and credit control cannot be ignored, but it seems

---

[11] "Monetary Policy Report to the Congress," *Federal Reserve Bulletin*, April 1986, pp. 213–228, esp. pp. 225–226. See also "Monetary Policy and Open Market Operations in 1985," Federal Reserve Bank of New York, *Quarterly Review*, Spring 1986, pp. 34–53, esp. pp. 37–38.

FIGURE 6–2
Income Velocities of M1 and Various Credit Aggregates

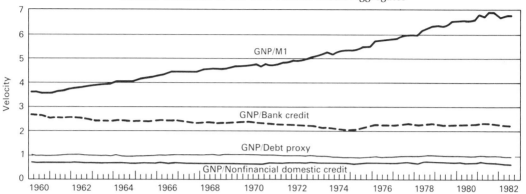

SOURCES: Board of Governors of the Federal Reserve System; United States Department of Commerce, Bureau of Economic Analysis; Federal Reserve Bank of New York, *Quarterly Review*, Winter 1982–1983, p. 5. Bank credit is total bank loans plus investments in federal, state, and local government securities; the debt proxy is, in general terms, total debt of government (all units) and of financial institutions to private domestic nonfinancial investors; and nonfinancial domestic credit is borrowing by government and nonfinancial private sectors. For details, see source.

unlikely that a drastic change would be made when results cannot be predicted because little research has been done on these proposals. This is especially true since the policy changes indicated by one of these measures in the past were often not the same as those indicated by another measure.

Moreover, there is another possibility: attempt might be made to control *payments*, rather than controlling money because it is the means used to make payments. This was discussed by economists as long ago as the late 1920s. It was evident that a huge volume of payments was involved in buying stocks in the stock market boom of 1927–1929, and some economists suggested that control was appropriate. Of course, debits (reductions in transactions accounts, whether by check or by withdrawal) could also occur if financial panic occurred, and people hurried to withdraw funds from financial institutions in fear of failures of such institutions. There is also no way of measuring with any accuracy the payments made in currency rather than from transactions accounts.[12]

The tremendous rise in debits to transactions accounts is quite evident, for the period since about 1965, in Figure 6–3. Partly, debits increased as inflation caused people to transfer funds from transactions accounts to keep money balances low.

[12] For a discussion of recent proposals to use credit or debt aggregates as monetary policy targets, and the idea that control of payments might be more appropriate than control of money, see James Fackler and Andrew Silver, "Credit Aggregates as Policy Targets," Federal Reserve Bank of New York, *Quarterly Review*, Winter 1982–1983, pp. 2–9; Marcelle Arak, "Control of a Credit Aggregate," ibid., pp. 10–15; John Wenninger, "Reserves Against Debits," ibid., pp. 16–23; Benjamin Friedman, "Time to Reexamine the Monetary Targets Framework," Federal Reserve Bank of Boston, *New England Economic Review*, March/April, 1982, pp. 15–23; and Richard G. Davis, "Broad Credit Measures as Targets for Monetary Policy," Federal Reserve Bank of New York, *Quarterly Review*, Summer 1979, pp. 13–22.

## FIGURE 6–3

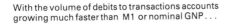

With the volume of debits to transactions accounts growing much faster than M1 or nominal GNP...

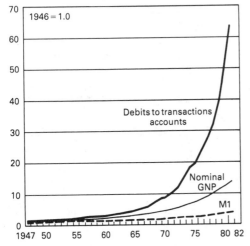

...the velocity of M1 measured in terms of debits has increased much more rapidly than velocity measured in terms of GNP.

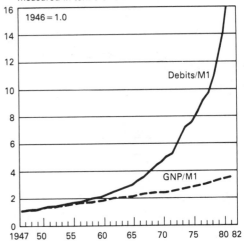

SOURCE: Board of Governors of the Federal Reserve System; Federal Reserve Bank of New York, *Quarterly Review,* Winter 1982–1983, p. 17.

In conclusion, the monetary approach, which we discuss in later chapters, rests on the stability of velocity. The case for such stability in the long run is strong; evidence from research of monetarist economists is plentiful. But in short-run periods, velocity may vary. One such period was the depression years of 1929–1933; another has been the first years of the 1980s. If velocity varies, short-run damage may occur. If velocity increases significantly, inflation is likely to be the result. If velocity decreases, less total spending occurs. This could result in less inflation (slower increase in prices), a fall in prices (as in 1929–1933), or a fall in the amount of real goods and services purchased. Without more evidence of the causes of short-run instability in velocity, it is risky to assume that velocity will stabilize itself. When velocity is unstable, many economists are hesitant about maintaining a steady increase in the money supply. If velocity increases, it may be desirable to slow down the increase in the money supply, to avoid inflation. If velocity decreases, it may be better to increase the rate of growth of the money supply, to avoid recession.

### Proposals and Actions to Permit Increased Competition

In the 1950s, there was concern over the competitive advantages of other depository institutions over commercial banks; in the 1960s and 1970s this shifted to concern over their ability to compete with commercial banks and to a belief that more competition was desirable.

Both the Commission on Money and Credit report (1961) and the Hunt Commission report (1971) made many suggestions for increased competition among depository institutions, and to eliminate various restrictions that gave advantages to one type of institution or another, so that competition might be "on a level playing field."

Without discussing details, it was clear that the *mutual* form of organization made expansion based on increase of capital difficult, that mutual savings banks and savings and loan associations were too limited to one type of loan (mortgage loans), and that fixed interest rates on such loans could cause problems if market interest rates fluctuated widely. On the other hand, if competition were free, there would be no basis for the lower interest rate ceilings on time deposits in commercial banks than on similar accounts in the other depository institutions. Other problems facing the nonbank depository institutions were the need for trained personnel for broadening the scope of their loans and investments, the need for some type of facilities to permit their integration into electronic funds networks (otherwise direct electronic deposit of Social Security and many other checks into those institutions would be impossible), and, above all, the threat that inflation created—rising costs of their funds (liabilities) and fixed yields on their assets.

Automatic teller machines (ATMs) can be staffed (in an institution's branch offices or in retail stores, for example) or unstaffed—fully automated electronic devices, operated by special cards given to customers, located almost any place, and operating 24 hours a day, 7 days a week, 365 days a year.

Should nonbank institutions offer transactions accounts? Demand deposits are costly. Special checking accounts (small accounts that average $300 or less per account) cost commercial banks about 5 cents per year, per dollar of such deposits, in excess of service charge income. If service charges were not imposed, the cost would be almost 10 cents a year per deposit dollar. If commercial banks compete by offering "no service charge" accounts, it will be difficult for savings institutions to compete on a cost basis. Moreover, entry costs are high. The cost per dollar of deposit for an institution handling 1,000 accounts is about 50 percent higher than it is for an institution handling 50,000 accounts.[13] Because thrift institutions entering the business of handling demand deposits are likely to have only a small number of accounts initially and for some time, their entry costs will be substantial.

An interesting innovation began in New England in 1972. Mutual savings banks, followed by savings and loan associations, began offering what they termed negotiable order of withdrawal (NOW) accounts on which interest was paid but on which checks could be written. Actually, checks were drawn on accounts held by these institutions in commercial banks and cleared through those accounts, but the effect was to offer interest-bearing demand deposit accounts to customers. In 1976 Congress made it possible for all federally regulated institutions in all New England states, including commercial banks, to offer NOW accounts, and this was later ex-

---

[13] See Paul S. Anderson and Robert W. Eisenmenger, "Structural Reform for Thrift Institutions: The Experience in the United States and Canada," Federal Reserve Bank of Boston, *New England Economic Review*, July–August 1972, pp. 3–17. See also *Policies for a More Competitive Financial System*, Proceedings of a Conference held in June 1972, Federal Reserve Bank of Boston.

tended to New York. In the same year, Illinois-chartered savings and loan associations were permitted to offer noninterest-bearing NOW accounts—sometimes referred to as NINOWs. Also, in Maine, Connecticut, and New Hampshire state-chartered thrift institutions were permitted to offer checking accounts. Thus in New England and New York, an experiment has been in progress in which interest-bearing checking accounts were offered by commercial banks and by thrift institutions. As might be expected, various combinations of practices in handling the accounts and of pricing policies were tested. Some institutions offered free NOW accounts at first, to promote their acceptance. Required minimum balances, charges for drafts drawn, and recording methods have varied.[14]

With the passage of the Depository Institutions Deregulation and Monetary Control Act of 1980, NOW accounts were authorized throughout the United States, beginning January 1, 1981. Payment of interest on accounts on which checks can be written finally was made possible in all states, and the prohibition of payment of interest on demand deposits had little remaining significance for individuals.

The Board of Governors of the Federal Reserve System had at first opposed the spread of NOW accounts, on the grounds that it was inequitable to permit thrift institutions, which are subject to lower tax rates and lower reserve requirements, to offer payments mechanism services; that the monetary authorities need to control all institutions that provide such services; and that those institutions should all share in the costs of providing and improving such services.[15] The 1980 law changed the whole situation—it made reserve requirements the same for all institutions having transactions accounts, it required all reserves to be held in vault cash and/or as deposits in the Fed, and it provided for Fed services to be offered to all depository institutions, and at prices (the same to all), rather than free.

Several changes were made so that savings and loan associations and mutual savings banks can have greater diversification in their assets. The 1980 law permits federal savings and loan associations to invest up to 20 percent of their assets in consumer loans, commercial paper, and corporate debt securities (bonds, etc.) and to invest in certain shares of mutual funds that make investments that savings and loan associations may make directly. Federal mutual savings banks are authorized to make *business* loans up to 10 percent of their total assets (beginning January 1, 1984) but only within the state in which the bank is located or within 75 miles of the bank's home office.

Consumer loans would help to diversify the asset portfolios of thrift institutions, making them less vulnerable to withdrawals of short-term deposit liabilities than they now are (because their assets are now nearly all long-term assets). But consumer loans,

---

[14] For more detail, see Ralph C. Kimball, "Recent Developments in the NOW Account Experiment in New England," Federal Reserve Bank of Boston, *New England Economic Review*, November–December 1976, pp. 3–19; and Ralph C. Kimball, "The Maturing of the NOW Account in New England," Federal Reserve Bank of Boston, *New England Economic Review*, July–August 1978, pp. 27–42. See also Donald Basch, "The Diffusion of NOW Accounts in Massachusetts," ibid., November–December 1976, pp. 20–30.

[15] *Federal Reserve Bulletin*, April 1973, pp. 276–280.

although they have high gross yields, have processing costs that total about 4 percent per year, in contrast to processing costs of only about ½ percent for mortgage loans. Thus mortgage loans at 7½ percent may be just as profitable as consumer loans at 11 percent.

Permitting thrift institutions to acquire more corporate bonds simply substitutes one long-term asset for another. Corporate bonds might be somewhat more attractive than mortgages at certain times, but the advantage would be relatively small. Fundamentally, diversification through additional holdings of corporate bonds does not reduce the basic difficulty—that thrift institutions have relatively short-term liabilities but long-term fixed-rate assets.

Savings institutions might protect themselves against periods of tight money by increasing their capital reserves to a point that they could pay high current market interest rates on their deposits when necessary, without being technically insolvent. Unfortunately, this would require reserves much higher than at present. To meet the standard used by the Federal Reserve System to measure adequacy of bank capital, for example, savings and loan associations would need to have capital approximately twice as high (in relation to share accounts) as at present.

Variable-rate mortgages (VRMs), widely used in some foreign countries, such as Finland, Great Britain, The Netherlands, and Sweden, clearly benefit the thrift institutions. Use of variable-rate mortgages with appropriate safeguards was one of the recommendations of the Hunt Commission. It was suggested that borrowers should be offered fixed-rate alternatives, the variable rate should be fully explained, the maximum movement for any five-year period should be only 3 percent, the index that determines rate changes should be agreed upon, and mortgagees should be given the option of continuing or of arranging new financing after five years. Combined with some incentive, borrowers may accept variable-rate mortgage loans. Whether the "returns" to thrift institutions would be large enough to warrant incurring these costs to strengthen their position in case of rising interest rates is questionable. In conclusion, it appears that most measures to help savings institutions in periods of tight money are not very likely to be of significant value, with the possible exception of variable-rate mortgage loans.

The most widespread experience with VRMs is in California. This experience suggests that the VRM is a complex instrument and has some unexpected results. It was difficult to find an appropriate average interest rate to which the interest rate on VRMs could be tied. The rate used as an index in California was a weighted average cost of savings, borrowings, and Federal Home Loan Bank Board (FHLBB) advances to California federal savings and loan associations. Since this index is published only semiannually, there is a lag. Another difficulty arose from the provision limiting increases in VRM interest rates to not more than 2½ percent. Third, although some argued that, with VRMs, mortgages could easily be assumed by new purchasers of properties, some lenders imposed assumption restrictions because old VRM mortgages were not always equivalent to new mortgages. Fourth, when lenders permitted borrowers to pay higher rates by making more payments of the same amount rather than by making higher payments, liquidity problems arose for some lenders when rates fell again and lenders did not shorten the total length of the mortgage payment period, but simply permitted borrowers to pay less each month. Borrowers may not fully understand VRMs, and it is not clear from the California experience how useful VRMs may be.[16] Nevertheless, persistent inflation has made it likely that VRMs will spread. The FHLBB authorized federal savings and loan associations to offer VRMs beginning July 1, 1979, and there are indications that VRMs may become popular in many areas if inflation continues. Changes in the nature of VRMs may occur, and new terms may be used. The term "renegotiated rate mortgage" (RRM) has been used, indicating that the rate of interest is subject to renegotiation at specified times. Whatever the specific form, the underlying basis for the new instruments is the need to change stated or specified interest rates as inflation results in rising market interest rates. Renegotiable rate mortgages were authorized for federal savings and loan associations in April 1980. Interest rates may be adjusted up or down every three, four, or five years, based on the interest rate on purchase of previously occupied homes, published in the FHLBB *Journal*.[17]

Another type of change occurred with the introduction of graduated payment mortgages (GPM) instead of fixed payment mortgages (FPM). With GPMs, the interest rate is fixed, but the monthly payments are small in early years and are increased later. Thus young couples and others who might have difficulty in making heavy mortgage payments in the early years may benefit; as years go on and their incomes rise, they may be able to pay the higher payments. Mortgage payments are tailored to expected growth of income of home buyers. GPMs address the life-cycle problem, whereas VRMs address the rising (or falling) interest rate situation. If interest rates and home prices remain relatively high, the life-cycle variation in income may be a problem even if inflation is reduced from the level it reached by 1980.[18]

Are thrift institutions able, because of various regulations and conditions, to obtain *more* funds from savers than might be predicted from economic theory?[19] Perhaps housing is obtaining more funds than it would in an economy where the assumptions of classical economic theory were more nearly valid. A very important question of policy goals can be raised: How important is "better" housing as a goal? One view, quite widely held, is that a high-priority goal is a rapid increase in the growth of per capita real income and that, if income rises rapidly, consumers can spend on housing if they wish or, at the other extreme, they may live in very modest homes and devote much more funds to travel and other forms of recreation or to various types of consumer goods and services other than housing.

[16] See George G. Kaufman, "Variable Rate Residential Mortgages: The Early Experience in California," Federal Reserve Bank of San Francisco, *Economic Review*, Summer 1976, pp. 5–16; see also William C. Melton and Diane L. Heidt, "Variable Rate Mortgages," Federal Reserve Bank of New York, *Quarterly Review*, Summer 1979, pp. 23–31.

[17] See United States League of Savings Associations, *Washington Notes*, April 4, 1980, pp. 3–4.

[18] William C. Melton, "Graduated Payment Mortgages," Federal Reserve Bank of New York, *Quarterly Review*, Spring 1980, pp. 21–28.

[19] Paul A. Samuelson, "The Current State of the Theory of Interest Rates, with Special Reference to Mortgage Rates," *Proceedings of the 1960 Conference on Savings and Residential Financing*, May 1960, p. 25; reprinted in James A. Crutchfield, Charles N. Henning, and William Pigott, eds., *Money, Financial Institutions, and the Economy: A Book of Readings* (Englewood Cliffs, N.J.: Prentice-Hall, 1965).

On the other hand, the inflation accompanying the war in Vietnam and the wide fluctuations in interest rates that occurred since the late 1960s created special stringencies for the thrift institutions. Housing finance was hard hit in 1973–1975 and again in 1979–1986.[20]

Housing is almost certain to be adversely affected during any recession. But, over the long term, demand for homes is likely to continue to be strong. If inflation moderates somewhat and interest rate ceilings on thrift deposits are gradually removed (as with a process completed in the spring of 1986), mortgage interest rates may remain relatively high, and savers may obtain higher returns on savings. As long as inflation continues, even if its rate is more moderate, demand for housing is likely to be sustained by a belief (confirmed thus far) that house prices will probably rise with inflation.[21] Houses may remain attractive as an inflation hedge, especially if other assets are not very attractive for this purpose. The attractiveness is increased by the tax change that now permits persons over age 55 to pay no capital gains tax on sales of homes in which they have lived, for capital gains up to $125,000.[22]

However, if houses are regarded as investments, their value must be measured, like that of other capital assets, in terms of the expected or current earnings and the relationships of price to earnings. If the price is 10 times current earnings, current earnings are being discounted (in the formula used in Chapter 1) at a 10 percent rate; but if the price is 20 times current earnings, those earnings are being discounted at only a 5 percent rate—a buyer can expect to earn, currently, only 5 percent on the investment he or she makes in buying the house. Is 5 percent a high enough return to satisfy investors (as distinct from those who buy homes *primarily* to live in them)? We return to this question later, when discussing bonds in Chapter 10 and stocks in Chapter 11.

In summary, the proposals made in the Hunt Commission report, designed to increase competition among the commercial banks and the thrift institutions and partially to deregulate this industry, bore little fruit until, in 1979, the problem of Fed membership became acute. At the end of that year, it appeared that some large banks might withdraw from Fed membership. It was evident that unless something were done, Fed membership would seriously decline. Magically, all fell into place upon the enactment of the Depository Institutions Deregulation and Monetary Control Act of 1980. This act required all banks (and other institutions, if they hold checkable deposits) to keep reserves in vault cash and/or with the Fed, gave all the institutions access to the Fed's lending and other services, and provided that interest rate ceilings on time deposits were to be phased out over a period of time. About 17,000 institu-

---

[20] For a savings and loan association view of the 1973 episode, see *Savings and Loan News*, November 1973, pp. 16–17.

[21] This was much more true in the West than in other sections of the country in the late 1970s. See Lynn E. Browne, "From Boom to Bust in the Housing Market," Federal Reserve Bank of Boston, *New England Economic Review*, May–June 1982, pp. 28–50.

[22] It should be noted that during inflation, after-tax interest rates are often negative in real terms. If there is no inflation, an interest rate of 4 percent taxed at a marginal tax rate of 30 percent is equivalent to an after-tax rate of 2.8 percent. If the rate of inflation is 12 percent, the after-tax interest rate is .7 × 16 percent, or 11.2 percent. It is assumed that with inflation at 12 percent, the interest rate would rise to 16 percent. The rate of 11.2 percent is less than the inflation rate of 12 percent; in real terms, it is negative.

tions are subject to the new reserve requirements, with 9,000 nonmember banks being added to the 5,400 member banks, together with about 3,400 savings and loan associations and mutual savings banks and some credit unions.

Savings and loan associations gained the right to issue credit cards and to extend credit on them and to invest up to 20 percent of their assets in consumer loans and in various types of corporate debt, so that they will no longer necessarily be strictly mortgage lending institutions. Mutual savings banks were given the right to offer checking accounts for business firms and to put up to 10 percent of their assets into commercial loans to firms in the local market areas, so that they can make some business loans. Credit unions gained the right to charge 15 percent interest, with higher rates to be permitted by the Credit Union National Administration (CUNA) when required by money market conditions. State usury ceilings on mortgage loan interest rates were overridden by this national legislation, and on business and agricultural loans, the law permits interest rates of not more than 5 percent above the Fed's discount rate (including the surcharge permitted for lending to large banks that are frequent borrowers).[23]

Thus, as a crisis seemed possibly imminent, major legislation changed many rules for the whole financial system, especially for the deposit-type financial institutions. The results of this major change will become apparent as the 1980s end.

Since the reserve requirement for nonpersonal time deposits is only 3 percent (and there is no reserve requirement for personal time deposits), vault cash may be sufficient to satisfy reserve requirements for many of the thrift institutions. Institutions that have checkable deposits will have to meet the reserve requirement of 3 percent on the first few million dollars of such deposits and 12 percent on amounts above that level. Vault cash needed by institutions is not likely to be sufficient to meet this requirement, and such institutions are likely, therefore, to have to hold deposits at the Fed, in addition to vault cash. Control over the money supply by the Fed is strengthened, and its powers over financial institutions are broadened.

In conclusion, the *long run* competitive position of the depository institutions other than commercial banks ought to improve in the years ahead if inflation is under control. But in the *short run*, high interest rates may hurt them. Competition from other institutions will increase in the long run, and depository institutions will face threats from both nondepository financial institutions and from institutions that in large part are nonfinancial.

## Competition for Saving Among All Institutions in the Financial Services Industry

We have examined in some detail the competition between commercial banks and other depository institutions because the two groups are direct competitors for deposits and in making certain types of loans. But in a sense, all participants in the financial services industry compete for the saving generated in the economy.

[23] The landmark nature of this legislation is emphasized in Verle Johnston, "Historic Legislation," Federal Reserve Bank of San Francisco, *Weekly Letter*, April 4, 1980.

Business firms save (as indicated in Chapter 2) by retaining some of their profits, but they invest most of those savings in plant, equipment, and inventories. They also borrow large sums to finance additional investment. The government in recent years has been a major borrowing sector, also. Thus, business firms, government, and participants in the financial services industry compete for the net saving of consumers.[24]

Because of the existence of the financial services industry, total credit is much larger than total savings. Because some institutions in the financial services industry hold reserves (deposits) in other institutions, and simply transfer these deposits to borrowers or to persons designated by borrowers, these institutions can make loans and investments without reducing the amount of loans and investments made by banks (usually the institutions in which deposits of other institutions are held).

Saving by consumers, when measured by net increase in net worth, may be divided into three parts: (1) housing, (2) consumer durables, and (3) net financial saving. In the late 1970s, there was a shift from net financial investment to investment in housing and consumer durables. Moreover, the ratio of saving to disposable personal income fell, and net financial investment fell to very low levels, as consumers borrowed heavily. The result was that the financial services industry was competing with the government (and, to some extent, with corporate issues of bonds and other debt) for a *very* limited amount of personal saving.[25] No serious problem arose because private borrowing was low during the recessions of 1980 and 1981–1982.

As inflation was reduced in the early 1980s, and as interest rates paid to savers rose (at least until the summer of 1982), the volume of saving began to revive.

At the same time, however, relatively new participants in the financial services industry began to compete for a larger share of the saving. In addition to depository institutions, contractual saving institutions, investment-type institutions, and finance companies, retail stores and conglomerates began providing a greater number of financial services and competing more strongly for funds. This competition occurs both in the provision of services and in the attempt to acquire funds.

Retail stores and conglomerates provide some services through third parties, such as banks. They may pay interest on deposits of some types, provide checking facilities, make loans, make mortgage loans, issue credit cards, sell securities, sell insurance, act as brokers to enable people to buy and/or rent real estate, operate travel agencies, operate car rental offices, and provide facilities for investing in money market mutual funds. These institutions do not as yet make large amounts of business loans, nor are their demand deposit facilities large. But they now offer or can offer most of the facilities provided for consumers by thrift institutions. It is likely that competition will force many consolidations in the thrift industry (many have already occurred).

---

[24] The term "net saving" is used because some consumers borrow. This borrowing is subtracted from gross saving to obtain net saving of the consumer sector.

[25] For more details on the trend in saving and the composition of saving, see Carol Corrado and Charles Steindal, "Perspectives on Personal Saving," *Federal Reserve Bulletin*, August 1980, pp. 613–615.

Given the relatively low level of personal saving, and especially of net *financial* investment, what prompts the expanded competition for savings? The major forces are four. (1) Both increased investment and (concomitantly) increased saving are essential if the United States is to retain its position as a high-income country and regain its position as a net exporter. (2) If inflation remains at a low level, the ratio of saving to personal income is likely to be higher than it was in the late 1970s and early 1980s, offering opportunity for various institutions to compete for new saving. (3) The technology of an electronic funds payments system is developing and improving, and participants in the financial services industry should be able to provide electronic funds transfer services and offer other financial services, such as information, through interactive video screens and computers. Minicomputers in households are spreading rapidly, so that financial institutions have much less need for branch offices that consumers may visit. (4) Finally, the outlook for rising stock prices became favorable in the early 1980s, for several reasons: (a) stocks were very much undervalued, in terms of the ratio of their prices to the replacement cost of the underlying net assets; (b) increased saving was making more funds available for various types of investment; and (c) as interest rates on short-term investments fell after mid-1982, both bonds and stocks began to look more attractive. Some observers capsulized the situation as follows: stock prices would rise because stocks were cheap, because there was plenty of money to buy them, and because rates of return on short-term investments were falling. The Dow-Jones average of stock prices more than tripled from 1982 to 1987.

All the foregoing factors made the retail stores and the conglomerates appear to have significant competitive strength in the new era, especially when one also considered the wide geographic spread and the minimum of regulation for these institutions.

# THE PROBLEM OF HANDLING PAYMENTS

The threat that the growing volume of checks to be cleared will swamp the banks' payments-handling mechanism has prompted many efforts to find a means to reduce paperwork connected with payments. Some have anticipated rapid progress toward a less check (not a checkless) society, in which a system of automatic payment transfers would reduce the paperwork load substantially.

Technological developments have resulted in the gradual installation of systems to process financial data electronically, transmit financial information, and transfer funds between financial institutions and their customers. Three major elements are involved in this broad system.

## A Communications Network

The first element is a communications network to make possible speedy communication of financial information between banks and cities. The Federal Reserve wire system, first established to permit communication among the Federal Reserve Banks, branches, and Board of Governors, has been extended and modernized so that it connects all elements of the Fed, the U.S. Treasury and other government agencies, a number of regional check-processing centers, and 200 member commercial banks. There are also Bank Wires I and II that provide similar services for a large segment of the banking community, and the Society for Worldwide Interbank Financial Tele-communications (SWIFT) provides for bank-to-bank international transfers. The Federal Reserve System took the lead in providing a nationwide communications network for interregional settlements between financial institutions. Although there are other networks, as indicated, they are more limited in scope. Concern has been expressed about the potential infringement on privacy if all transactions flow through one network, whether public or private.

## Automated Clearinghouses

The second element consists of automated clearinghouses that permit paperless exchanges between financial institutions in a city or region. Thirty-two automated clearinghouses (ACHs) are now in operation; two are privately owned (in New York and Chicago), and the others are operated by the Fed at no charge for use of the facilities. The issues raised by the existence of ACHs are the questions of whether or not they are natural monopolies and, if so, whether and how they should be con-trolled; how prices should be set for their services, who should be charged, and who should bear initial losses that are likely to occur; and the question of whether all interested financial institutions should have access to them. Justice Department offi-cials have taken the position that it has not been proven that ACHs are natural monopolies, partly because average transactions costs decline quite quickly as volume rises. Thus market demand may be large enough for several ACHs to operate in a market and still achieve minimum average costs. Minimum long-run average cost as a pricing criterion is suggested by economic theory. It also suggests charging the initia-tor of a transaction, thus giving that party an incentive to select the least cost means of making the transaction. Thus far, thrift institutions that have third-party payment powers have direct access to ACHs operated by the Fed; others must use a "passthrough" process, processing items through accounts of member institutions.[26]

## Customer Terminals

The third element is a variety of electronic terminals to link consumers to financial institutions. These include automated teller machines (ATMs), which may be located on bank or other financial institution premises or elsewhere (in which case they are sometimes called "satellites"). The simpler varieties are simply cash dis-pensers, but the more complicated ones can verify checks, take deposits, permit

---

[26] For a discussion of reasons for the relatively slow growth in use of ACHs, in spite of their obvious advantages if a sufficient volume of transactions passes through them, see "The Automated Clearinghouse Alternative: How Do We Get There from Here?" Federal Reserve Bank of Atlanta, *Economic Review*, April 1986.

withdrawals, transfer funds from savings accounts to checking accounts and vice versa, and provide other services.

Another variety of electronic terminal is termed a point-of-sale (POS) terminal. POSs are frequently located in retail establishments and provide the services offered by ATMs and also make transfers of funds directly from consumers to the retail establishments. POSs operated by banks have been termed customer bank communication terminals, while those operated by savings and loan associations have been termed remote service units (RSUs).

It appears that most electronic terminals are not yet being used sufficiently to achieve the lowest possible costs per transaction. Thus there is some incentive for institutions to share their use. It is likely that large institutions will initiate their use and then offer sharing, at a price, to smaller institutions. Independent banks have been concerned about the cost of operation of terminals and also about large banks' economies of scale advantages. On the other hand, terminals cannot open accounts, nor can they approve new loans. With NOW accounts or checking accounts, thrift institutions can deploy terminals and thus compete more directly with commercial banks.

The regulatory environment has been more favorable for such activities by thrift institutions than for commercial banks. The Federal Home Loan Bank Board authorized off-premise terminals, and its authority seems to have been upheld. The unlikely locale of a significant test was Lincoln, Nebraska. A system installed by First Federal Savings and Loan Association in Hinky Dinky Food Stores withstood several court tests and was well received by consumers. Use of the system was later shared by the Omaha National Bank.

Commercial banks faced a somewhat different regulatory environment. The McFadden Act of 1927 defined branches as any facilities making possible deposits, cash withdrawals, or loans. When the Comptroller of the Currency authorized national banks to establish remote terminals without obtaining branch authorization, the decision was challenged. The U.S. Circuit Court of Appeals ruled that banks in Illinois, an important state since it prohibits branch banking, could not operate remote terminals without their approval as branches. The U.S. Supreme Court refused to review this decision; hence, under court decision, terminals are branches under the McFadden Act. Branching is permitted for national banks only to the extent that it is permitted in a given state for state banks. A number of states have adopted laws declaring terminals *not* to be branches. The Comptroller of the Currency authorized new "CBCT (customer bank communication terminal) branch" procedures to permit easier establishment of such branches where permitted. It is also possible that banks may contract with outside parties to establish terminals, which might then not be regarded as bank branches.

Spread of "satellites" is a part of the much broader issue of interstate banking. It appears that expansion of interstate banking is occurring more rapidly than was expected by many, with the help of regional agreements among states, need for takeovers of potentially failing banks, and the establishment of "nonbank banks," which are probably a transition form of organization.

It is evident that the entire issue of bank branching has been opened up by this development. The In-Touch service offered for a time by Seattle-First National Bank, which permitted subscribers with touch telephones to use them for computing services, bill paying, and family budgeting is an illustration of the logical problem that arises. Had this service been maintained, or if a similar service is established and continued, a consumer's telephone is in effect a terminal. For many transactions, even ATMs would not be needed.

## Progress Toward an EFTS (Electronic Funds Transfer System)

The view that EFTS is here to stay, partly because unit automation costs appear to decline each year about as much as labor costs rise, is generally accepted. Many believe that banks and other institutions should be permitted to cross state lines with terminals where market areas justify this; many also favor statewide branching for all institutions.

There seems to be no doubt that technological and other forces are creating, slowly, a national simplified payments system, at the same time forcing the much greater standardization of powers for all depository institutions.

Although experiments take time, it seems likely that during the next decade substantial progress will be made in handling many types of payments through "checkless" transfers. To the extent that commercial banks act more swiftly than nonbank financial institutions in providing such facilities, banks may be able to increase their advantage. They may also find it less necessary to provide additional fully equipped banking offices, as customers will be able to obtain many services by telephone, in retail stores, or in "satellites" (automated facilities).

Aside from the mechanical elements involved and the psychological factors related to consumer acceptance, this change is significant for financial markets and the economy because it will bring a substantial increase in the transactions velocity of money. Instead of the usual several days or more of "float" time, payments will be made more quickly, and changes in money balances held will occur promptly. The increase in transactions velocity will probably be accompanied by an increase in income velocity of money, as more rapid transactions generate income more quickly. Thus, a slower rate of growth of the money supply may be required to attain a given increase in total spending without significant inflation.

Questions arise in connection with the access of commercial banks and thrift institutions to EFTS. If commercial banks have access and thrift institutions do not, one can visualize paychecks being automatically deposited by such transfers into commercial banks; if so, the placement of funds by consumers in thrift institutions might be much reduced, especially since Regulation Q ceilings on payment of interest on time deposits have been removed and commercial banks are permitted to pay as much interest on such deposits as thrift institutions. On the other hand, if thrift institutions have access to an efficient system for "checkless" transfers, and commercial banks, or some of them, do not, the situation might be reversed. If "satellite banking," in the form of unstaffed automated teller stations, either in retail establishments or in such places as parking lots, is engaged in extensively by one type of institution and not by the other, significant changes can be envisaged, especially if in some way the public comes to have a preference for carrying out as many financial transactions as possible through such stations rather than in banking or thrift institution regular offices.

Perhaps the most revolutionary development of all is the use of the telephone in connection with an EFTS system. An example is Farmers and Mechanics Savings Bank of Minneapolis, which cannot branch into the suburbs, but has used a "Pay-by-Phone" system not only to retain customers but to attract new ones, many of them from suburbs. Some readers may have seen the many advertisements in *Business Week* and other publications indicating how easy it is to dial direct to cities in Europe, Asia, or South America. The day is coming when individuals who wish to do so can bank with an institution in Tokyo or London as easily as with one in their home city in the United States. This means increasing world competition for banks. As home computers come into wider use, banking from home will increase.

Long ago it was argued in the United States that reserve requirements were necessary because reserves provide liquidity for banks. That view was largely abandoned when it was recognized that required reserves do *not* provide much liquidity; banks must hold *secondary* reserves (such as short-term government securities) for this purpose. It can be argued that reserve requirements are needed to prevent banks from obtaining "rent" (the layperson would say "profit") from the creation of money or that reserve requirements should be low to permit a country's banks to compete with banks in other countries that have low reserve requirements. As long as there is *some* level of *required* reserves, the central bank has a level through which it can control the creation of money by raising or lowering the *actual* reserves of banks above or below the required level. In fact, it could be argued that because common sense requires that banks have *some* reserves, there is a level of reserves required because of the need for vault cash, even if no *legal* reserve requirement were imposed.

Spread of an EFTS would make it possible for banks in any area of the country, or indeed of the world, to compete with banks in any other area, not only in lending, but in accepting deposits. Thus the question would be which banks can provide the best services the most efficiently, at the lowest costs. If institutions other than banks could do this, they would be strong competitors.[27]

## EFFECT OF GROWTH OF FINANCIAL INSTITUTIONS ON SAVING

Thus far it has been assumed that the ratio of saving to income will continue to be relatively constant in the long run. The question may now be asked, "Is there any evidence that the growth of financial institutions tends to affect the ratio of saving to

---

[27] For a review of the way in which banks made successful efforts to cross the geographic barriers established in the McFadden Act of 1927 and the Banking Act of 1935, see Joanna H. Frodin, "Electronics: The Key to Breaking the Interstate Banking Barrier," Federal Reserve Bank of Philadelphia, *Business Review*, September–October 1982, pp. 3–11.

income? If so, such influence would be significant, for a small change in the ratio of saving to income would produce a large change in the amount of saving within a few years.

## The Income-Saving Relationship

It is widely agreed that income is the major factor affecting consumption. Because saving equals income minus consumption, and income is the major factor affecting consumption, it must also be the major factor affecting saving. If so, there may be little room for any effect on saving resulting from changes in rates of growth of financial institutions. And many financial institutions are best viewed as conduits for financial investment of saving that has already resulted from decisions concerning the disposition of income.

The long-run stability of the ratio of personal saving to personal disposable income, found in empirical studies, has led to a general belief that this ratio would not change significantly in the long run, although it might vary during business fluctuations.[28] On this basis, it was generally presumed that factors such as growth of financial institutions would not significantly affect the volume of saving—that their major effects would be on the velocity of money and the sectors into which loanable funds were channeled.

## Effect of Growth of Pension Funds and Social Security on Saving

One study has found that persons covered by pension plans saved higher fractions of their income than did persons of comparable income levels who were not under pension programs. Not only did they save more in the form of pension contributions, but they saved more in other forms as well.[29] In a period of rapid growth of pension plans, this should have resulted in a rise in the long-run ratio of saving to income, but there was little evidence that this occurred.[30] However, the growth of pension funds is recent, and some evidence of their effect may show up as time passes.

Several plausible hypotheses may be advanced to account for the increase in saving when individuals participate in pension programs. People may not regard the funds contributed to pension plans as available for other purposes and hence may save

---

[28] Incidentally, it also raised some questions about the consumption function, or relationship of consumption to income. For if in the long run savings/income is a relatively constant ratio, the long-run consumption function must be a straight line rising from the origin (income zero, consumption zero) at less than a 45° angle. Thus it cannot intersect the 45° line, as the short-run consumption function was presumed to do. There are various ways of reconciling this divergence; one is to assume that the short-run consumption function shifts upward over time.

[29] Phillip Cagan, *The Effect of Pension Plans on Aggregate Saving* (New York: National Bureau of Economic Research, 1965).

[30] For example, in the 10 years 1955 to 1965, saving averaged 6.7 percent of disposable personal income, and there was no discernible tendency for the ratio to rise. At the same time, pension saving as a fraction of total personal saving rose from 30 percent to over 40 percent. Data for years after 1965 are not very useful because they are distorted by the effects of the inflation during the Vietnam conflict.

in other forms to provide for planned expenditures. Or the expectation of pension income may create an awareness of the need for other saving. These hypotheses have neither been proved nor disproved with present evidence.

Alicia Munnell advanced the hypothesis that Social Security has two opposite effects on the ratio of saving to income. First, the prospective availability of Social Security benefits tends to discourage saving for retirement purposes, but, second, the earlier retirement that has occurred under Social Security has probably encouraged saving to provide for the greater number of prospective retirement years.[31] Her data were consistent with these hypotheses. They are criticized, however, partly on the grounds that earlier retirement reduces the labor force, income, and saving, but it does not necessarily change the *ratio* of saving to income. It was also pointed out that Social Security contributions by workers, a form of saving, are offset by spending of benefits by retirees (dissaving).[32]

A later study suggested that, while Social Security contributions may have caused the young, especially, to reduce their ratio of saving to income, this may have been offset by increasing saving, in relation to income, by the elderly—saving by those receiving Social Security benefits.[33] With present Social Security benefits and tax provisions, it may be possible for more retired persons to save rather than, as formerly, to use previous savings to live. How long this may be possible depends on inflation and on whether or not incomes are indexed.

Income tax provisions clearly affect saving. Individuals can spend income today or save it and spend the income plus the interest on that income in the future. If interest rates are lower than inflation rates, people have less real income to spend in the future. Moreover, the interest return is taxed, so that after-tax return is still smaller than the amount needed to maintain real income. Thus income taxes together with inflation militate against saving; the effect may be offset in some cases by efforts to save more. When saving is for retirement, it may be possible to eliminate the current effect of taxes by deferring such taxes on both the income saved and on the interest or dividend return. Although taxes on income must eventually be paid, people may be in lower tax brackets when they receive pension income and pay tax on it. Some saving for retirement may have been induced by the extension, under ERISA, of tax deferral to individuals not covered by company pension plans, provided that they place their savings in individual retirement accounts (IRAs) and the subsequent authorization of IRAs for everyone with at least $2,000 in earned income (that amount or less can be placed in an IRA). Saving may also have been stimulated

[31] Alicia H. Munnell, *The Effect of Social Security on Personal Saving* (Cambridge, Mass.: Ballinger, 1974), and "The Impact of Social Security on Personal Saving," Federal Reserve Bank of Boston, *New England Economic Review*, January–February 1975, pp. 27–41.

[32] Michael R. Darby, review of the book by Munnell, *Journal of Finance*, March 1976, pp. 186–187.

[33] Laurence J. Kotlikoff, "Testing the Theory of Social Security and Life Cycle Accumulation," *American Economic Review*, June 1979, pp. 396–410. Social Security involves little saving; it consists now almost entirely of *transfers* from those working and paying in contributions to those receiving benefits (some who made contributions for many years, but also others who contributed very little). People retiring at a time when their salaries are high relative to their past salaries may receive relatively high benefits.

by the increase in limits on contributions made by self-employed individuals to their retirement plan funds, termed Keogh plan funds.

Since those who contribute are providing funds for benefits, no aggregate saving occurs; what occurs is a transfer of income from current workers to Social Security beneficiaries. Whether Social Security taxes should be higher so that the Social Security system can accumulate savings is controversial. Some economists, such as Martin Feldstein, argued for this.[34] But Social Security funds would probably be invested in government securities, and government spending is largely for consumption rather than for investment.

Probably the most serious effect of the recent rise in benefits under Social Security is the competition between Social Security contributions (which are *not* saving) and the contributions to private pension funds (which, in general, *are* saving). Social Security benefits now replace about 45 percent of the wages earned by the median male worker retiring under Social Security. Not being taxed, for those below a certain level of income, these benefits have a much larger value in comparison with an equal amount of pretax income of workers. Benefits for those who had median earnings come close to providing an amount equal to the "intermediate budget" specified by the Bureau of Labor Statistics. Thus there was concern that median- and lower-income workers may feel little incentive to contribute to private pension funds, which may be largely restricted to supplementing income for higher-income workers. Reduced saving by workers, even if compensated for by greater saving by retirees, could restrict the growth of pension funds,[35] and hence reduce funds available for investment.

Developments in the early 1980s, however, *may* tend to stimulate saving, especially later in the decade. The Economic Recovery Tax Act of 1981, in addition to providing for tax cut, authorized each worker to put a maximum of $2,000 ($2,250 for a worker and a spouse or $4,000 for a two-income family) from earned income into an individual retirement account (IRA). Tax on the interest on these accounts is deferred until the individual begins to withdraw funds, not earlier than when he or she reaches 59½ years of age. Withdrawal must begin at age 70½. The tax on capital gains was reduced to an effective rate of 20 percent, encouraging the seeking of capital gains.[36] Thus the authorization of IRAs and changes in taxes *may* tend to increase saving in the 1980s. Increase in saving and investment, essential to long-run economic growth, was a major goal of what quickly came to be termed "Reaganomics."

---

[34] Martin Feldstein, "Social Security: A Saving Depressant?" *Morgan Guaranty Survey*, November 1976, pp. 3–7.

[35] See Alicia H. Munnell, "Are Private Pension Funds Doomed?" Federal Reserve Bank of Boston, *New England Economic Review*, March–April 1978, pp. 5–20.

[36] For a number of other features of this tax law that encourage saving (counting capital gains as saving or additions to wealth), see Karen W. Arenson, *Guide to Making the New Tax Law Work for You* (New York: Times Books, 1981). The Tax Reform Act of 1986 limited the tax-deferred deposit of funds in IRAs by people who already have company pension plans and have incomes above a specified level. The advantage of deferral of taxes on interest, as it accumulates, remains. This law also provided for taxation of capital gains at the same rate as other income.

Social Security contributions by workers are currently needed to provide benefits. In fact, in autumn 1982, the Old Age benefit fund was nearly exhausted, and legislation finally passed in March 1983 was needed to "rescue" Social Security. Most of the change involved an acceleration of payroll tax increases already scheduled; taxation of high income individuals, on one-half of their Social Security benefits, was also provided. On the benefit side, cost-of-living increases, normally given July 1 of each year, were delayed until January 1 of following years. Many other minor changes were made, but the system remains essentially a transfer of funds from current workers to beneficiaries, involving neither saving nor investment.

# THE PROPER PLACE OF GOVERNMENT LENDING

A final topic for consideration in our review of nonbank financial institutions and their growth is the proper place of government lending, a particularly appropriate topic because of the recent rapid growth of government and quasi-government agencies and of agency securities.

## Reasons for Government Lending

Government lending has generally been justified on one or both of two grounds: (1) government lending will improve the allocation of resources, and (2) government lending will aid in redistributing income in a desired manner. Misallocation of resources may occur if there is a degree of monopoly in lending, if there is less than sufficient information available concerning borrowing opportunities, if there are legal restrictions that distort lending, or if there are external economies and/or diseconomies in lending (because external economies or diseconomies may not affect lenders—they affect society as a whole or groups other than the lenders). Thus, student loans may not be made in sufficient amounts because private lending agencies do not recognize the benefit to society arising from a better educated population.

The government agencies mentioned in Chapter 4 were established largely on the basis of arguments that special conditions existed in certain fields—that agriculture could not obtain sufficient credit, especially because legal restrictions prevented the long-term lending necessary for farmers to buy land and pay for it over many years out of income; that special agencies were needed to lend to small business firms and to exporters; and that institutions were needed to create a secondary market for mortgages to improve their liquidity. It was also argued that special agencies were needed to make housing loans to low-income persons on a subsidized basis.

The special needs of agricultural credit (long-term mortgage loans and relatively large amounts of credit, for the sizes of the communities involved, at certain times in the agricultural production cycle) and the desire for more adequate housing led to establishment of most government agencies in these two fields. Very few government lending agencies operate in other areas—the Export-Import Bank is almost the exception that proves the rule.

## Results of Government Lending

Because housing and farming are markedly sensitive to changes in credit conditions, it should perhaps be expected that the government attempts to moderate the effects of changes in cost and availability of credit on these sectors.

The direct lending activity of government agencies in these fields does not seem to have prevented growth of private lending. For example, farm mortgage credit extended by life insurance companies and banks has grown rapidly, in spite of the existence of Federal Land Banks. *Perhaps* private institutions would have played a more active role in the absence of government activity, but this remains debatable. If widely accepted social goals do not seem to be adequately served by private financial institutions, government agencies are likely to be established to shift the flow of funds in the desired direction.

The growth of the government lending agencies has resulted in growth of what are termed "agency securities," bonds and other securities issued by these agencies in the capital markets. Interest rates (yields) on these securities are usually somewhat higher than on comparable Treasury issues (since the agency issues have somewhat less liquidity) but somewhat lower than yields on corporate bonds. The result of this process is a larger flow of funds to the mortgage market and the field of agricultural credit, a preempting of funds that otherwise might go to other sectors. Investors prefer agency securities over purely private securities because of their status as securities of quasi-government agencies; yet they do not obtain the full advantage of the lower rate of interest on Treasury borrowing. Those who favor these programs argue that the funds supplied through these agencies mitigate the effects of credit stringency on housing and to some extent on agriculture. Those who question these programs argue that the desired actions could be accomplished at less cost through direct Treasury borrowing and that agency borrowing means that this activity escapes budget scrutiny, thus changing the allocation of national resources without explicit consideration in the budget decision process. Basically, proponents argue that funds obtained through the issue of agency securities are helping to protect the mortgage and agricultural credit markets from the effects of credit stringency; opponents argue that this is being done at the cost of creating programs subject to review neither by the private credit market mechanism nor by the budget decision process.[37] The agencies have become major factors in the capital markets. In fact, there is some evidence that they may lower mortgage rates relative to other long-term rates, thus increasing the difficulties of savings and loan associations in earning rates high enough to pay rates on their share accounts sufficient to attract savings.

[37] See, for example, the views of R. Bruce Ricks and of Murray Weidenbaum in the Federal Home Loan Bank Board, *Journal*, September 1971, pp. 7–16.

# SUMMARY

In this chapter, we have discussed six issues concerning the financial services industry: (1) the uniqueness of commercial banks, (2) the problem of the decline in Fed membership, (3) competition in the financial services industry, (4) the problem of handling a mountainous volume of payments and records of payments, (5) the long-run effect of financial institutions on saving, if any, and (6) the appropriate place in the economy for government lending and lending agencies.

Commercial banks have been considered to be unique because they have liabilities that are money—means of final settlement of debts—and because they have greater importance for credit creation than do other financial institutions, especially as long as the other institutions keep deposits in banks and make loans and investments by transferring these deposits. The Depository Institutions Deregulation and Monetary Control Act of 1980 (DIDMCA) made it possible for banks and other depository institutions to hold NOW accounts (in effect, demand deposits that pay interest). *If* institutions other than banks begin to make loans and give borrowers increases in their accounts, or new accounts, in making the loans, they can create money. The limited extent to which they can make business loans, and the likelihood that they will continue present practices in making mortgage and consumer loans, makes it unlikely that they will become significant creators of money. As long as this is true, commercial banks will probably continue to be more important than other financial institutions in creating credit as well as being the only *significant* creators of money.

Interest rate ceilings in a period of inflation had one clear effect and another effect that is debatable: (1) they hurt small savers, who had difficulty in investing in the financial markets and as a result had to be limited to the relatively low interest rates obtainable on deposits and similar assets; and (2) they *may* have tended to reduce saving as a proportion of total income. The DIDMCA provided for gradual elimination of ceilings on interest rates, thus gradually eliminating any problems caused by these ceilings. Ceilings finally ended in spring 1986.

The DIDMCA also made the problem of declining membership in the Fed of little significance, since DIDMCA required that *all* depository institutions hold the same reserves (for the same size and types of accounts) *in vault cash and/or in the Fed*. Thus the Fed increased its control over reserves and thus probably improved its ability to control the money supply. However, shifts in *velocity* of money complicated the Fed's task.

More institutions are competing in providing financial services. An appropriate term now is the financial *services* industry, since many institutions now providing financial services are not primarily financial institutions. New major participants, such as retail stores and conglomerates, with advantages of broad geographic markets and less regulation, are likely to cause the government to move toward some further deregulation of the financial services industry, especially in geographic market limitations and in limitations on permissible services. The term *services* should be emphasized: assets are becoming less important in comparison with services, and some institutions may sell (broker) some long-term loans to achieve better balance in maturities of assets as compared with maturities of liabilities. Also, as institutions become more similar in their activities, the Supreme Court's designation of commercial banking as a single line of commerce providing a unique bundle of services is becoming outmoded.

The financial services industry is progressing toward an electronic funds transfer system that will reduce the work load of processing checks (although substantial use of checks will continue). With this progress, there will be less need for customers to visit bank offices; such visits may be necessary only for applications for business loans, seeking financial advice on relatively complex matters, such as trust services, and other special circumstances. Need for branches, especially large branches, will diminish, and need for cash machines (ATMs) in various places will expand.

The long-run effect of changes in the financial services industry on the saving-income ratio is controversial at best. If Social Security, for example, negatively affects the saving ratio, this may have been offset by the tax legislation of 1981 and 1986, which provided tax benefits for savers. The low rate of saving in earlier years may have been a temporary phenomenon; increasing saving may occur in the coming decade.

Finally, the place of government lending agencies seems likely to continue as it is: limited almost entirely to two fields, farm and housing credit. Whether government lending in these fields has adversely affected private lending is debatable. It *is* clear that government lending agencies and tax laws have to some extent subsidized housing. Whether this is desirable is a policy question, considered in Chapter 15. It is also clear that federal government agency securities have gained an important place in financial markets and are likely to remain significant.

## Questions for Discussion

**1.** What are the arguments for and against the view expressed in the British Radcliffe report—that what is important is the liquidity of the economy, not the size of any single class of financial assets, such as M1 or M2?

**2.** Develop a numerical example to show how banks have had a greater effect on spending than other financial institutions have had. Show how your conclusions depend on the fact that nonbank financial institutions have held deposits in commercial banks and those deposits were media for transfers of funds by NBFIs as well as by individuals, business firms, and government.

**3.** Why were NOW accounts opposed by some authorities?

**4.** Develop arguments for and against variable-rate mortgage loans.

**5.** Trace the effects of inflation on financial institutions, financial assets, and interest rates.

**6.** What are the major factors determining the growth rate of commercial banks? Do the same factors affect the rate of growth of other financial institutions?

**7.** What are some of the factors that must be considered in introducing a system of paperless entries for payments recording?

**8.** Note in Figure 6–1 that, although the velocity of the new M2 measure varied, it was just about the same at the end of the 1970s as at the end of the 1950s. What does this suggest concerning the new M2 measure of money as an indicator of the aggregate that should be controlled to affect GNP?

**9.** Do you think that the Depository Institutions Deregulation and Monetary Control Act of 1980 finally solved the Fed membership problem? Why or why not?

**10.** Why is the possible effect of pension funds on the ratio of saving to personal disposable income such an important question for research?

**11.** If financial institutions (with the possible exception of pension funds) do not significantly change the ratio of saving to disposable personal income, why are the growth and development of financial institutions essential in the process of economic development of less developed countries?

**12.** Do you believe that government lending agencies should be included in the federal government budget to facilitate a consideration of the desirability of their activities in relation to other possible uses of funds? Have many of these agencies gained a special position by being government-sponsored agencies, yet not subject to government budget scrutiny?

## Selected References

The potential importance of nonbank financial institutions in affecting spending and economic growth and development was emphasized in a series of writings by John G. Gurley and Edward S. Shaw. For relevant works, see the selected reference list following Chapter 2.

For a good discussion of problems related to the definition of money, see Carl M. Gambs, "Money—A Changing Concept in a Changing World," Federal Reserve Bank of Kansas City, *Monthly Review*, January 1977, pp. 3–12. See also "Improving the Monetary Aggregates: Report of the Advisory Committee on Monetary Statistics," *Federal Reserve Bulletin*, May 1976, pp. 422–426.

The "new view" that there is no very clear line of demarcation between commercial banks and other financial institutions was set forth by James Tobin, "Commercial Banks as Creators of 'Money,'" in Deane Carson, ed., *Banking and Monetary Studies* (Homewood, Ill.: Richard D. Irwin, 1963).

See also Joel M. Yesley, "Defining the Product Market in Commercial Banking," Federal Reserve Bank of Cleveland, *Economic Review*, June–July 1972, pp. 17–31. This article examines opposing viewpoints in economic literature, court decisions, and statistical studies concerning the question whether or not commercial banks compete significantly with other financial institutions.

The study by Phillip Cagan, *The Effects of Pension Plans on Aggregate Saving* (New York: National Bureau of Economic Research, 1965), provided evidence of the effect of pension plan saving on total saving.

The article by Donald Shelby, "Some Implications of the Growth of Financial Intermediaries," *Journal of Finance*, December 1958, pp. 527–541, was significant in showing the multiplication of credit (and thus the increase in velocity of money) concomitant with growth of various types of financial institutions.

A very interesting analysis of trends is presented in The Future Structure of the Financial Services Industry, Economics Department, Rainier National Bank, Seattle (mimeographed), March 1982.

The question of payment of interest on demand deposits is reviewed in Bryon Higgins, "Interest Payments on Demand Deposits: Historical Evolution and the Current Controversy," Federal Reserve Bank of Kansas City, *Monthly Review,* July–August 1977, pp. 3–11.

For one view of the Federal Reserve membership issue, see George J. Benston, *Federal Reserve Membership: Costs, Benefits, and Alternatives* (Chicago: Association of Reserve City Bankers, 1978).

For an analysis of potential progress in use of POSs and ATMs, see Steven D. Filgran, "From ATM to POS Networks: Branching, Access, and Pricing," Federal Reserve Bank of Boston, *New England Economic Review,* May–June 1985, pp. 44–61.

For a view that argues that the Social Security system will face a serious crisis in future decades, see Michael J. Boskin, *Too Many Promises: The Uncertain Future of Social Security* (Dow Jones–Irwin, 1986).

# PRIVATE DOMESTIC ECONOMIC ACTIVITY AND DEMAND FOR LOANABLE FUNDS

# VII

The *supply* of loanable funds was discussed in Chapters 2 through 6. We surveyed saving and the role of various financial institutions in channeling saving to borrowers, often through financial markets, and in creating money, thus adding to the supply of loanable funds.

Short-term fluctuations in the supply of loanable funds are usually rather minor. To the extent that saving is related primarily to income, it presumably rises and falls only as income rises and falls, and it does not change much with changes in interest rates. The Fed may, of course, permit more or less creation of money, and the velocity or rate of turnover of money may change. If additional money is created and then spent (whether for GNP or for purchases of financial assets), velocity may also increase.[1] But such variations in the supply of loanable funds are usually small.

---

[1] If, as possibly occurred in the last half of 1982, people are willing to hold more money because they perceive that the rate of inflation is falling, and if they do not spend that money very rapidly, velocity may *fall* rather than rise—producing the unexpected phenomenon of increase in the rate of growth of money but a fall in the rate of growth in GNP. For this type of analysis, see Michael W. Keran, "Velocity and Monetary Policy in 1982," Federal Reserve Bank of San Francisco, *Weekly Letter*, March 18, 1983.

Having discussed saving and the financial institutions industry through which much of the saving flows to investment in Chapters 2 through 6, we now turn to what is often termed the "real" side of the economy and its fluctuations. The effects of monetary and fiscal policy on the real economy are important, as monetarists and Keynesians have argued, but the real economy is also moved by growth of the labor force, increased or declining productivity, and certain cyclical factors that create fluctuations in the economy and long-term growth or lack of growth. This is the so-called "supply side" of the economy. Long ago, early "supply-side" economists argued that "supply creates its own demand"—if people work and produce more goods and services, the income they receive is sufficient to buy what they produce, assuming that they produce goods and services for which there is demand. Incentives for work, education and training to improve the effectiveness of work, and improved technology to cause greater output per worker-hour are the significant factors. This type of analysis goes back at least as far as Adam Smith's *Wealth of Nations* (1776). In modern times, rapid economic growth has been demonstrated by such countries as South Korea, Taiwan, Hong Kong, and Singapore (sometimes referred to as "the four tigers").

In this chapter we examine the impact of fluctuations in the "real" economy on the financial services industry and on monetary and fiscal policy. Saving, monetary policy, and fiscal policy affect the real economy, but the number of people who want to work (to "join the labor force"), increased education and training, and technological improvements affect saving and monetary and fiscal policy decisions. Since this book is focused on financial markets, the discussion relates chiefly to the effect of "real" changes on financial institutions and markets.

A rise in economic activity usually requires borrowing by business firms to add to inventories and to factories and equipment—a rise in the *demand for loanable funds*.

The *demand* for loanable funds fluctuates quite widely and is the *chief* cause (except in periods of inflation) of variations in average interest rates. As a business recovery begins, for example, changes in the rate of growth of GNP result in increased demand for loanable funds. As sales rise, business firms at some point decide to hold more inventory, and usually they borrow to obtain funds for this purpose. Later, they may decide that they should invest in more machinery and perhaps in additions to factories or new factories. Although interest rates may fall for a time after recovery begins, at some point they begin to rise as the demand for loanable funds increases.

Of course, a recession must have had a cause, or several causes. Examples are (1) monetary policy changes (as Friedman argued was the case in 1930 to 1933, when the money supply fell by nearly one-third), (2) fiscal policy (e.g., a reduction in government spending not offset by a rise in private spending, as was probably the case in 1957 to 1958), (3) a slowdown in the rate of increase (not necessarily a decline) in consumer spending, for whatever reason, that leads to an accumulation of excess inventory and then inventory reduction and a fall in production (a major factor in most of the recessions since World War II), or (4) a rise in the cost of important imports (as in the 1973 rise in oil prices) that, unless exports rise, reduces *net* exports (exports minus imports) and leads to a flow of income out of the country. These examples are illustrative, but they may indicate that sometimes causes are *external* to the private economy (monetary policy changes, fiscal policy changes, and oil price increases) and sometimes *internal* (a slowdown in the rate of increase in consumer spending).

As sales decline, business borrowing falls, and in most cases short-term interest rates at some point begin to fall. In some cases the fall in these interest rates may be much delayed, as in 1981 to 1982, when the economy began to decline in mid-1981 and short-term interest rates did not begin to fall until after mid-1982. Consumers generally reduce spending rather reluctantly, and some recessions are quite mild (in the first quarter of 1967, for example, decline was so small and the period so short that it was not classified as a recession by the National Bureau of Economic Research, which has over the years made these classifications and determined turning points).

If a recession is extensive enough that business fixed investment (investment in machinery and factories) declines, the fall in GNP is likely to be greater. Unemployment may then rise significantly, as GNP falls below its potential level. This relationship is known as Okun's law, which was first formulated in the early 1960s to state that a decline of real GNP of 3 percent below potential would lead to a rise of 1 percent in the unemployment rate. The relationship is still useful today, although the precise ratio is somewhat different.

When a turning point is reached, and business activity begins to increase (as in early 1983),[2] it can be expected that at some point an increase in demand for loanable funds will cause short-term interest rates to rise. The upturn may occur when business managers feel that they have reduced inventories sufficiently; the cessation of inventory reduction removes a *negative* element in GNP. Or, consumers may begin to buy more, as incomes cease to fall. Or, of course, an increase in government spending may occur, or an increase in money supply may lead to increased spending.

Demand for loanable funds comes from the business sector, the consumer sector, the government sector, and from foreigners. In this chapter we consider variations in business and consumer borrowing; in Chapter 8 we consider government and foreign borrowing. We also discuss the supply of loanable funds from foreign countries, because neither foreign lending nor foreign borrowing was considered in Chapters 3 to 6.

Recall Figure 2–2 in Chapter 2. In that figure, the flow of loanable funds was shown as a flow to ultimate borrowers—business firms, consumers, government, and foreigners—and also a flow of funds to financial institutions, from which a flow of funds was shown to the ultimate borrowers. To borrow, business firms, consumers, government, and foreigners issue "primary securities"—promissory notes, bonds, short-term government securities, and others. Financial institutions issue passbooks

---

[2] Real GNP rose at an annual rate of 6.9 percent during 1983 and the first part of 1984; growth in the latter part of 1984 and during 1985 was only about 2 percent (annual rate), in spite of the fact that M1 continued to increase at 12 percent during 1985 after rising at a 13 percent rate during much of 1983. M2 rose at about an 8 percent rate during this entire period.

(for savings accounts), time certificates of deposit, and other instruments. These are not ultimate securities because they are not issued by the ultimate borrowers.

An analysis of the demand for loanable funds should begin with the factors affecting the issue of primary securities. In particular, we must ask what factors affect the issue of primary securities by those sectors that vary their borrowing with variations in economic conditions and in interest rates. Although government may be a large borrower, its borrowing is determined by the difference between tax and other revenues and the budgeted expenditures, and is not varied, in most cases, because of any change in interest rates. Consumers also are somewhat insensitive to changes in interest rates unless rates get very high. Thus we properly focus attention on business borrowing. Business firms borrow because they need funds to purchase inventory, buy machinery, and build factories. If they calculate correctly, they will be willing to pay interest rates only if they are less than the rate of return the business firms expect to earn with the use of the borrowed money. Thus the fundamental basis of the demand for loanable funds by business firms—generally the marginal borrowers—is the fact that capital is productive, that with factories and machinery firms can earn enough to repay loans, pay interest, and retain some profit.

## FLUCTUATIONS IN DEMAND FOR LOANABLE FUNDS

In general, both business and consumer demand for loanable funds fluctuate directly with rise and fall in business activity. Most industrialized countries and some less developed countries (especially those in the process of industrialization) experience these fluctuations in income and in business activity, sometimes called business cycles.

Because there is considerable variation in the length of both downturns and recoveries—for example, although the average downturn since World War II has been 10 or 11 months, the 1981–1982 decline lasted approximately 18 months—the term business *cycles* has been less used. But business forecasting has increased as an activity of business economists. Both "judgmental" forecasts and forecasts based on complex econometric models are made.[3] These forecasts usually attempt to predict, often for a year or a year and a half, GNP (output and income), employment or unemployment, industrial production, prices, interest rates, and other economic variables.

It is useful to note that eight such declines, followed by periods of rising business activity, have occurred since World War II. Declines have averaged about 11

---

[3] There does not seem to be much difference in the accuracy of forecasts that are sometimes termed judgmental and those made with the aid of large-scale econometric models, using computers. See Thomas B. Fomby, "A Comparison of Judgmental and Econometric Forecasts of the Economy: The Business Week Survey," Federal Reserve Bank of Dallas, *Economic Review*, September 1982, pp. 1–10. Both methods of forecasting have been relatively accurate for such variables as real GNP, industrial production, and unemployment; both have been quite inaccurate in forecasting inflation and often inaccurate in forecasting interest rates.

months (although the decline of 1973–1975 was longer); periods of rising business activity have averaged about 30 months. Variation is evident, however, when it is noted that the period of rising business activity beginning in 1961 lasted for 8 years (over 100 months). The rise beginning in summer 1982 had lasted for 4½ years by the end of 1986, longer than any *peacetime* expansion since World War II.

As we consider the various sources of demand for loanable funds, we relate them to these periods of declining and rising business activity—the declines often being termed recessions.[4] We also discuss reasons for inaccurate forecasts of both inflation and interest rates and relate interest rate movements (especially those for short-term interest rates) to movements in income, employment, and production.

For convenience, demand for loanable funds is analyzed in terms of business demand, demand for mortgage credit, consumer demand, government demand, and foreign demand. Businesses borrow for plant and equipment spending, inventory increases, and increasing their liquidity ratios. Demand for mortgage credit arises both from residential and other construction. Consumer demand for loanable funds is chiefly for the purchase of automobiles and other durable goods, but to some extent for current consumption.[5] State and local government demand for loanable funds is chiefly for utilities, bridges, and highways. Federal government demand is based on the need to meet deficits that arise when expenditures exceed taxes and other revenues by more than the amount that can be met by drawing down cash balances. Finally, foreign demand for loanable funds arises from foreign business and government spending in excess of their own available domestic funds. The first three sources of demand for loanable funds are discussed in this chapter; federal government, state and local government, and foreign demand for loanable funds are discussed in Chapter 8.

## BUSINESS DEMAND FOR LOANABLE FUNDS

Business firms demand loanable funds because they expect to earn, from investment in various assets, more than the cost of the loanable funds, including an allowance for the risk involved in investment in real capital assets. The assets of business firms consist largely of plant and equipment, inventories, accounts receivable, and a relatively small amount of liquid assets to meet current payments. When business firms believe that an increase in any of these assets—but especially plant, equipment, and inventories—will yield enough return to warrant the allocation of funds, they will

---

[4] Although jokes are often made about a recession being a time when your neighbor is out of a job and a depression being a time when *you* are out of a job, there is a difference in terms of quantitative measures: the 1929–1932 decline is usually termed a depression because real GNP fell about 50 percent. The decline in real GNP in 1937–1938 was also quite large. In contrast, the recessions since World War II have never been accompanied by declines in real GNP of as much as 10 percent.

[5] Spending for automobiles and other durable assets is treated as consumption spending in the national income accounts, but is treated as investment in the flow of funds accounts described in Chapter 2. If the flow of funds treatment were followed, it could be stated that most consumer borrowing, as well as most business borrowing, is for investment.

allocate to this use either funds already available or funds obtained by borrowing or selling equities.[6]

The *fundamental* rate of return, or interest rate, is therefore based on the expected return on assets held by business firms, chiefly real capital assets. Business firms, by investing funds in a type of activity in which they have acquired or can develop expertise, can earn enough in an average year to pay the cost of borrowed funds and still obtain a margin of net profit sufficient to compensate them for the risks they take. At the margin, business firms can afford to pay in interest almost the same rate they are earning on their investment of funds in real capital assets. Firms that have higher rates of return than the marginal firm earn an additional amount, which compensates them for risks that they incur.[7]

In this analysis, the basic rate of interest is related to productivity. If productivity increases by 3 percent and if inflation is 4 percent, so that GNP in nominal terms increases by 7 percent a year, with the same assumptions the return to business firms also increases by 7 percent a year. Business firms at the margin pay up to 7 percent as interest for borrowed funds. The nominal rate of interest is thus based upon the "real" rate of interest; it may increase by an "inflation premium" when the price level is rising.[8]

During any given period, business firms need funds for investment in plant and equipment. The amount of such investment depends on expected yields. Investment, in turn, leads to an increase in income, and increase in consumption, and a further increase in income. The concept of the investment multiplier (often termed simply "the" multiplier) should already be familiar; it is the relation of the increase in income to the increase in investment.[9] If the multiplier is, for example, 2½, then the increase in GNP would be 2½ times the increase in investment. It should be recognized that

---

[6] John Maynard Keynes discussed this in Chapter 12 of his most famous book (*The General Theory of Employment, Interest, and Money*) but argued that such decisions were based more on what he termed "animal spirits" than on analysis. He therefore focused attention chiefly on other topics.

[7] It is assumed at this point that the relative shares of labor, capital, and land in total national income (or GNP) remain the same. If the share obtained by capital falls, business firms may not be able to pay quite as high a rate of interest as is mentioned. Based upon the assumption that real GNP increases by 3 percent a year, capital, labor, and land can each receive returns that increase 3 percent a year without causing inflation. This was the basis of the wage-price guidelines, given some publicity by the government in the early 1960s; thus capital can receive interest or profits of 3 percent, and labor can receive its current wage rate plus an increase of 3 percent, without danger of causing further inflation. For further details on the guideposts, see *Economic Report of the President*, January 1962, pp. 185–190.

[8] This view is based upon Irving Fisher's analysis. For a review of the evidence, see Stephen F. LeRoy, "Interest Rates and the Inflation Premium," Federal Reserve Bank of Kansas City, *Monthly Review*, May 1973, pp. 11–18. See also William D. Jackson, "Federal Deficits, Inflation, and Monetary Growth: Can They Predict Interest Rates?" Federal Reserve Bank of Richmond, *Economic Review*, September–October 1976, pp. 13–25, and the extensive references cited in that article.

[9] To refresh the reader's memory, the multiplier is $\Delta Y/\Delta I$. Because $Y$ (income, or GNP) equals $I$ (investment) plus $C$ (consumption) if government and foreign spending is ignored, $Y/Y$ equals $I/Y$ plus $C/Y$ (dividing all items in the equation by $Y$). Thus $I/Y$ equals 1 minus $C/Y$, or $Y/I = 1/(1-C/Y)$. The multiplier can be expressed in terms of *increases* in income, investment, and consumption, so that $\Delta Y/\Delta I = 1/(1 - \Delta C/\Delta Y)$. As is apparent, if consumption were a stable fraction of income, the multiplier would be a constant. Since consumption varies to some extent as a fraction of income, the multiplier also varies.

this direct multiplier is augmented by an indirect effect, or feedback, from consumption to investment; this is often termed the accelerator. The two effects together give the net result in increasing GNP. In any calculations, investment must be measured on a net basis—that is, depreciation and other capital consumption allowances must be deducted from gross investment (often referred to in the statistics as gross private domestic investment, or GPDI) to obtain net investment.[10]

Because the use of capital increases output, investment in plant and equipment is obviously related to growth of GNP. Paul Samuelson has pointed out that, in economic development, certain ratios have remained constant for long periods of time in given countries, with some exceptions during special periods such as that of the Great Depression and possibly that of the 1970s, in which rapid inflation occurred. One such ratio is that of the value of plant and equipment to GNP; in the United States this ratio has been approximately 3:1 for a century.[11] If the labor force increases 1½ percent a year and if productivity also increases 1½ percent a year, the increase in output resulting from labor is 3 percent a year. Since all productivity is ascribed to labor, capital must also increase 3 percent a year if its output is to rise at the same rate as that of labor. This would maintain a constant ratio of capital ($K$) to output (GNP). Investment, or the increase in capital during a year, must be 3 percent of capital, and, since capital is three times GNP, investment must be 3 percent of three times GNP, or 9 percent of GNP, to assure a growth of 3 percent a year in real income.[12] Attempts have been made to estimate how much higher than 9 percent the ratio of fixed investment spending to GNP must be to achieve higher rates of growth, but this leads us into the theory of economic growth, which is not our concern at this point. Moreover, factors other than the amount of investment—for example, technological improvement, education of workers, and application of technological advances—are determinants of the rate of growth.

Business firms must also add to their inventory holdings. Inventory is held because sales do not coincide with output, and sufficient stock must be kept in

---

[10] GPDI includes additions to inventory and to the stock of housing as well as investment in plant and equipment, but, in this and the following paragraph, the reference is to investment in plant and equipment.

[11] For an early discussion of these elements in growth theory, see Robert M. Solow, "Technical Progress, Capital Formation and Economic Growth," *American Economic Review*, Papers and Proceedings, May 1962, pp. 76–87. For discussion of the slowdown in the growth of productivity in the 1970s, see Paul Bennett, "American Productivity Growth: Perspectives on the Slowdown," Federal Reserve Bank of New York, *Quarterly Review*, Autumn 1979, pp. 25–31.

[12] More accurately, the factors determining the potential rate of growth in an economy can be expressed in the following formula: the growth rate, $g$, is $\Delta Y/Y$, and

$$\frac{\Delta Y}{Y} = \frac{\Delta T}{T} + s_K \frac{\Delta K}{K} + s_L \frac{\Delta L}{L}$$

where $T$ indicates technology, $s_K$ the share of capital in national income, $K$ the stock of capital, $s_L$ the share of labor in national income, and $L$ the labor force. This formula can be applied to the economics of different countries, and it is clear that in various countries the shares of labor and capital in national income and the sizes of the stock of capital and of the labor force differ sufficiently that the same ratios will not be applicable. For an excellent discussion, see Hang-Sheng Cheng, "Investment Ratios and Economic Growth Rates," Federal Reserve Bank of San Francisco, *Business Review*, Spring 1974, pp. 9–20.

inventory to avoid losses of sales and costs of frequent reordering. The optimum amount of inventory is that which balances the costs of holding inventory (capital costs, warehousing or storage costs, service costs, and costs arising from risks involved in holding inventory when styles may change) with the costs of lost sales and frequent reordering. Quantitative models have been developed to determine the cost-minimizing levels of inventories, and the widespread use of computers may permit a lower ratio of inventories to sales than was possible when it was more difficult to calculate amounts needed at various places. In any event, some ratio of inventory to sales is desirable, and, as sales increase, inventories must generally increase also. In aggregate terms, this is why figures for "final" total demand (GNP minus additions to inventories) are an indicator of the projected trend in GNP—as final demand rises, inventories must also rise, and hence GNP will usually rise even if it has been falling because of reductions in inventories.

Finally, business firms borrow at certain times to add to their liquid financial assets. Business firms must hold some liquid assets to meet excesses of current payments over current receipts, which may occur from time to time. At times the liquidity of business firms may be of critical importance, as in the "liquidity crisis" in the spring of 1970, when some firms could not pay promissory notes, or commercial paper, as they came due, and those who evaluate credit began to wonder whether many firms had enough liquidity to meet other current liabilities. Fortunately, at that time the Federal Reserve System made additional reserves available to banks, and banks were able to extend loans to many business firms that were in some difficulty. In the period that followed, business firms rebuilt their liquidity positions to some extent.[13]

## Funds for Plant and Equipment Spending

The major need for funds for business firms is usually for replacement or expansion of plant and equipment. A major source of funds is the internally generated retained earnings and profits against which depreciation was charged. Both inflation and taxes are significant in affecting the proportions of spending for plant and for equipment.[14]

### Internally Generated Funds

Business firms generate a sizable amount of funds internally because they make depreciation and other capital consumption charges against earnings but do not make corresponding cash outlays, and because they retain a sizable portion of their earnings after depreciation and taxes. The ratio of dividends paid to total earnings after taxes,

---

[13] The ratio of corporate financial assets to short-term liabilities fell from 1.025 in early 1966 to approximately .85 in late 1970, as business firms continued for some time to borrow to finance investment. Efforts to improve the ratio resulted in a rise to nearly .9 by late 1972. See "Corporate Financing and Liquidity, 1968–1972," Federal Reserve Bank of Richmond, *Monthly Review*, November 1972, pp. 12–15.

[14] See Patrick J. Corcoran, "Inflation, Taxes and the Composition of Business Investment," Federal Reserve Bank of New York, *Quarterly Review*, Autumn 1979, pp. 13–24.

termed the payout ratio, is usually about 50 percent on the average, although ratios vary, being considerably higher for most utilities and lower for new and rapidly growing firms. Internally generated funds remaining after dividends have been paid are available for investment; they constitute *gross business saving*. They are likely to be used for internal investment purposes because they are not likely to have any alternative use that can produce a higher yield. Normally, rates of return on real capital assets are higher than bond yields and other yields on financial assets, and presumably the firm could not invest its money in some other line of business at a higher yield, since the firm has expertise in its own field.

What is the cost of such funds? Investors presumably invested in a given firm because it was earning, say, 10 percent on its capital, and investors could not find other companies with comparable risk that earned a higher rate. Thus the company must earn, or expect to earn, at least 10 percent on its capital so that those who purchased stock will be satisfied with their investment. If stock prices reflected accurately the discounted expected earnings of the firm, one could say that the firm should earn a high enough rate on new investments to maintain the price of its shares at the current level. If such prices fall, it means that investors expected a lower rate of return, and holders of stock in that firm would suffer in comparison with other investors. Thus the cost of equity capital in the form of funds from depreciation[15] and retained earnings is the same 10 percent rate that the company has been earning on its capital.[16] Growing firms whose earnings are increasing tend to retain much or all of their earnings after taxes; utilities, which are permitted to earn a specified rate of return by the regulatory agencies, usually pay out most of their earnings and borrow funds as needed.

In a country in which economic growth is occurring, it is not likely in most years that funds available because of depreciation charges and from retained earnings will be sufficient to meet investment needs. As is explained in macroeconomic theory, investment fluctuates more widely than does the level of general business activity.[17] Hence it usually happens that, although internally generated funds may be sufficient in the early months of a period of rising business activity to provide for investment for many firms, the need for external funds rises as business activity continues to in-

---

[15] The reader probably recognizes that the term "funds from depreciation" is a shorthand expression and not precisely accurate. Funds are, of course, not supplied by depreciation, but by earnings against which depreciation was charged. In some cases, earnings may not be sufficient to cover these charges, and hence less funds are supplied in such cases.

[16] Essentially this is an opportunity cost concept; if investors received all earnings in the form of dividends, they would be free to reinvest or not; presumably they would reinvest in firms with comparable risk that earn comparable rates of return. For further discussion, see any standard text on corporate finance; for example, J. Fred Weston and Eugene F. Brigham, *Managerial Finance*, 3rd ed. (New York: Holt, Rinehart and Winston, 1969), pp. 344 ff.

[17] In part, this is simply because real capital assets are used for long periods of time. Because of this fact, only a tenth or a twentieth of their value may be lost by depreciation in a single year. If in that year demand should increase by 10 percent, it may be necessary to invest enough funds to replace worn-out equipment (10 percent of the equipment, say) and also to add enough new equipment to produce 10 percent more output (perhaps 10 percent more equipment), to meet the additional demand. This "acceleration" principle, as it is known, is a "feedback" from consumption to investment.

**FIGURE 7–1**
**Marginal Cost of Funds for Business Firms**

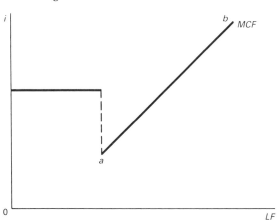

crease. Some firms, such as utilities, pay out a large part of their earnings in dividends and engage regularly in a large volume of construction. They borrow significant amounts even in years of relatively low total business demand for loanable funds. Hence some firms are borrowing even during recessions. On the other hand, borrowing may continue to be heavy near the end of a period of rising business activity, as firms find that they have used up most of their excess capacity and must build new facilities. Thus borrowing was especially heavy in the years 1969–1970, even though business activity began to decline in late 1969 and profits before that.

### The Marginal Cost of Funds

In a growing economy, investment normally exceeds the amount of internally generated funds. When prices rise in inflation, funds available from depreciation and other capital consumption allowances are generally not sufficient to cover replacement cost of worn-out plant and equipment.[18] Some and perhaps all of the retained earnings have to be used to maintain the current level of the stock of capital. Thus some borrowing is likely to occur, and the relevant marginal cost of funds is that of borrowing (or issuing equity) in the money and capital markets, as indicated in schematic form by the rising part of the marginal costs of funds curve *ab* in Figure 7–1.

---

[18] If firms used replacement cost values for fixed assets in their accounting records, depreciation charges could approximately equal replacement costs. This is done by some firms in some countries, for example, in The Netherlands. See Gerhard G. Mueller, *Accounting Practices in The Netherlands* (Seattle: Graduate School of Business Administration, University of Washington, 1962); and Abram May, *On the Application of Business Economics and Replacement Value Accounting in the Netherlands* (Seattle: Graduate School of Business Administration, University of Washington, 1970). See also the report of the British committee chaired by F. E. P. Sandilands; this report is summarized in *Inflation Accounting*, Cmd 6225 (London: Her Majesty's Stationery Office, 1975).

The flat portion of the marginal cost of funds curve in Figure 7–1 indicates the cost of internally generated funds; the portion of the curve designated as *ab* indicates the cost of borrowed funds and of funds raised through new issues of equity securities. This cost is presumed to rise as additional amounts are borrowed because additional amounts of loanable funds will be supplied, it is generally assumed, only at higher interest rates. Borrowed funds are likely to be cheaper than internally generated funds when interest rates are low, but as interest rates rise, borrowing (through loans, bonds, etc.) becomes more costly.

### Borrowing for Plant and Equipment Spending

Borrowing by business firms may provide funds for investment in plant and equipment, for additions to inventory, or for increase in liquidity of firms. In a period of inflation, internally generated funds may be less adequate for inventory replacement, just as depreciation charges may be less than the cost of replacing worn out plant and equipment. Firms that use first-in, first-out (FIFO) inventory accounting may show profits that are in part illusory, because the inventory used up (and shown as a cost) is less expensive than that which must be acquired to replace it. Use of last-in, first-out (LIFO) inventory accounting shows much smaller profits. The inventory valuation adjustment made in the national income accounts results in reduced profits, closely approximating the reductions that would occur if all firms used LIFO. Retained earnings shown in the national income accounts are thus a more accurate indication of funds available for additional investment than are retained earnings reported by firms that use FIFO inventory accounting.

In theory, the amount of funds borrowed should be the amount needed for that quantity of investment at which the marginal efficiency of investment equals the marginal cost of funds. The total amount of investment is indicated by the point at which marginal efficiency of investment equals marginal cost of funds; the amount borrowed is the *additional* amount needed to supplement internally generated funds. A considerable amount of the internally generated funds—usually more than the amount of funds equal to depreciation charges, and perhaps in some cases more than total internally generated funds—is needed simply to replace worn-out or obsolescent plant and equipment. Additional investment, beyond that amount, is *net* investment.

The term "marginal efficiency of investment" requires brief explanation. The term "marginal efficiency of *capital*" is frequently used and is found in Keynes' famous work, *The General Theory of Employment, Interest, and Money*. But, more accurately, what is significant is the marginal efficiency of *investment*—not the return on a marginal addition to the country's stock of capital, regardless of time, but the return on a marginal addition to investment *in the current time period*.[19] The difference between the marginal efficiency of capital and the marginal efficiency of investment is illustrated in Figure 7–2. The value of the stock of capital is the total value of real

---

[19] Some of the considerations involved are presented clearly in Gardner Ackley, *Macroeconomic Theory* (New York: Macmillan, 1961), pp. 481 ff. See also Abba P. Lerner, *The Economics of Control* (New York: Macmillan, 1944), Chapter 25, for a much earlier presentation.

**FIGURE 7–2**
**Marginal Efficiency of Capital and Marginal Efficiency of Investment**

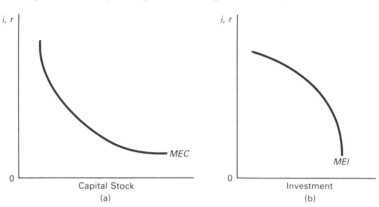

capital assets in the economy. At present this is roughly equivalent to three times one year's GNP. Investment in plant and equipment in a year is normally not more than 3 percent or 4 percent of the value of the capital assets; total investment is about 5 percent, adding inventory and housing investment.

The term "efficiency" is used rather than marginal rate of *return* on investment (or capital) because two different investments might have the same average rates of return, but one may have a higher "efficiency." As explained earlier, income to be received in the future is discounted by some rate of interest in obtaining the present value of such income. Thus the present value of a bond is found by the formula

$$PV = \frac{Y_1}{(1 + r)} + \frac{Y_2}{(1 + r)^2} + \frac{Y_3}{(1 + r)^3} + \cdots + \frac{Y_n}{(1 + r)^n} + \frac{F}{(1 + r)^n}$$

in which $PV$ is present value, $Y_1 \ldots Y_n$ are the interest payments to be received in the future, and $F$ is the final maturity value to be paid to the bondholder. Similarly, the present value of a real capital asset is found by the same formula. In this case, $F$ represents the scrap or resale value of the capital asset at the end of whatever period is being considered. Use of this formula does not imply that people prefer present goods to future goods but simply that, because a return is obtained over a period of time, the value of a capital asset at the beginning of any period is less than the value at the end of the period by an amount based on the return to be obtained.

Using this formula, suppose that one investment were expected to yield nothing the first year, 5 percent the second year, and 10 percent the third year, whereas another investment was expected to yield 10 percent the first year, 5 percent the second year, and nothing the third year. The two investments would have the same average rate of return (5 percent), but the second investment would have greater efficiency, because the first year's return (10 percent, compared with nothing on the first investment) would be discounted for only one year to obtain its present value.

The 10 percent yield in the third year, returned by the first investment, would have to be discounted for three years to obtain its present value.

In making a decision on a new investment, a firm should examine the probable returns expected in future years minus expected costs (net cash inflows expected), the appropriate rate of interest at which to discount such expected returns, and the resulting present value of the proposed investment. If this present value is higher than the estimated cost of the investment, the decision logically is to proceed with the investment. The appropriate rate of discount is either (1) the current rate of interest that the firm would have to pay to borrow the funds for investment, plus a premium to compensate for the additional risk of investing in plant and equipment as compared with risk encountered by those who invest in bonds, or (2) the cost of internally generated funds, which presumably includes such a risk premium.

Marginal investment would be made if it were expected to yield a rate of return equal to the marginal cost of funds. The average investment, however, would be made at a rate sufficiently higher to compensate for the risk perceived in average investments. This risk of course varies as managements of business firms perceive changes in risks because of business cycles, government regulation, costs of antipollution equipment, variation in consumer demand, and so on. In a period of inflation the risk may be quite great, explaining why investment may be delayed during such a period.

The marginal efficiency of investment curve is likely to be concave toward the axes and the marginal efficiency of capital convex toward the axes because an attempt to make a very large amount of investment in a *single* period is likely to cause the rate of return to fall sharply, whereas additions to the country's stock of capital over a longer period of time are likely to be at rates of return only slightly less than those obtained on previous additions to the stock of capital. In a short period of time it is not possible for necessary additional labor to become available except at rising costs, and additional investments are likely to yield sharply lower rates of return if investment spending is unusually great. There are barriers to an extremely large amount of investment in a given period that probably do not exist for additions to capital stock over long periods of time.

Considering a period of time in which there is rising business activity, internally generated funds may provide for necessary replacement, or perhaps be sufficient to provide for some net investment, as diagrammed in Figure 7–3. As time passes, the curve indicating the marginal efficiency of investment, which at the beginning of the period of rising business activity provided for only a modest amount of net new investment, shifts to the right as prospects for profits on investment appear brighter. This is also shown in Figure 7–3. The same amount of investment has a higher expected yield or "efficiency," and additional investment appears to be profitable at a given level of return and cost. The marginal cost of funds rises as more funds are borrowed to provide money needed for more real investment, as shown in Figure 7–3.

Much controversy has arisen concerning the response of investment to changes in the interest rate (i.e., the interest elasticity of the *MEI* curve). But this is largely a waste of time. The significant question is not elasticity but, rather, the *shift* of the *MEI* curve to the right as earnings are expected to be higher—perhaps because consumer demand is increasing, perhaps because innovations are leading to lower

FIGURE 7–3

Marginal Efficiency of Investment and Marginal Cost of Funds
with Rising Business Activity

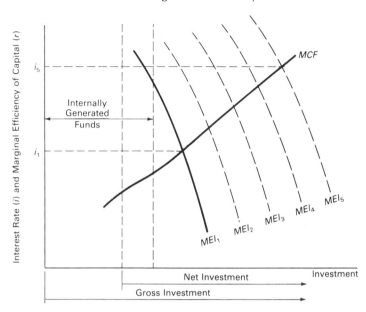

costs, or for other reasons. This shift generates more investment, regardless of the interest rate. Additional investment may, of course, be generated by a fall in the interest rate, which reduces the cost of borrowing funds. But the major factor in an increase in investment is the expectation of earnings.[20]

*The cyclical rise and fall of interest rates, as distinct from long-run trends, is largely explained in terms of changes in the marginal efficiency of investment, that is, of expectations of yields.* These expectations are not necessarily based on precise mathematical calculations of quantitative yields multiplied by the probabilities of those yields.[21]

### The Role of the Debt/Equity Ratio

If investment continues to increase over a number of periods of rising business activity, business borrowing usually increases, although there may be some rise also in internally generated funds and therefore some increase in investment that can be financed without borrowing.

[20] Keynes, in *The General Theory of Employment, Interest, and Money*, Chapter 12, called attention to "the extreme precariousness of the basis of knowledge on which our estimates of prospective yield have to be made" (p. 149). He also noted that the value of an investment, as indicated in the stock market, may be determined largely in the short run by individuals' expectations of the value that other individuals may place on a stock.

[21] Again, it is relevant to remember Keynes' words: that probably most "of our decisions to do something positive . . . can only be taken as a result of animal spirits—of a spontaneous urge to action rather than inaction" (*The General Theory of Employment, Interest, and Money*, p. 161).

As business borrowing increases, it is likely that at some point corporations begin to have debt/equity ratios that are higher than desired. Some corporations may encounter this point relatively quickly, others after a longer time. Suppose that the marginal efficiency of investment curve shifts to the right, as innovations or prospects of higher rates of return for other reasons result in higher expected marginal efficiency of investment at given levels of investment; there is, therefore, an increase in investment. In such a situation, more firms find, as time passes, that, to maintain what is believed to be an appropriate debt/equity ratio, they must obtain additional equity. As more firms reach such a point, the volume of new issues of stock increases, and the mix of funds obtained by business firms may shift somewhat in the direction of a higher proportion of funds obtained through issues of stock.

The debt/equity ratio is important because it is one measure of the risk incurred by those who lend funds to business firms. If the debt/equity ratio is low, the firm has a relatively large amount of its own funds with which to repay debt if necessary. Such a firm can easily repay debt by liquidating assets and reducing its equity. As the debt/equity ratio rises, the risk incurred by lenders increases. Firms must liquidate larger fractions of their total assets to repay debt, and the resulting reductions in their equities become larger relative to the remaining equity.[22]

Cost of capital obtained through stock issues is generally higher than that for debt issues because new stock must yield the same return that is now being obtained on investment, or higher, plus the cost of issuing new stock (flotation costs). Moreover, earnings from which dividends are paid are taxable income, whereas interest is paid on bonds before taxable income is calculated. Hence the marginal cost of funds generally may be assumed to continue to rise. At some point the *MEI* curve may cease to shift to the right—higher returns for additional investments are no longer expected. If at such a point conditions lead to lower expected returns, the *MEI* curve may shift to the left, and a business recession may follow.

An amount of investment less than the amount needed to replace worn-out and obsolete assets results in a declining economy. An amount of investment less than the amount provided by internally generated funds is not likely. If the marginal cost of funds were high enough to discourage retention of earnings, bond yields would be nearly as high as, or possibly higher than, returns on some real capital assets. This would mean that little or no return, or perhaps a negative return, was being obtained for the additional risk involved in holding real capital assets rather than financial assets such as bonds. If bond yields were as high or higher than common stock dividend yields plus capital gains, investment in real capital assets through retention of earnings would be discouraged, and industries would be contracting rather than expanding. This may occur for an individual firm, and some firms may go out of business, but it is unlikely for the economy as a whole. Thus, except for temporary periods, dividends plus capital gains should be higher than bond yields. If, for exam-

---

[22] Some economists are concerned about the rapid rise in debt in the United States in the 1980s. Debt must be repaid from income. Sharp rise in the ratio of debt to income, as occurred in the United States in the first half of the 1980s, means that borrowing exceeded domestic loanable funds. For the United States, the difference has been made up by an inflow of loanable funds (investment) from abroad.

ple, average bond yields are 7 percent, dividends plus capital gains arising from retained earnings should be higher; if dividends average 3 percent, capital gains must average *at least* 4 percent, in the long run. Whether or not stock market prices rise and thus provide such capital gains is a point to which we return in Chapter 11.

## Borrowing to Finance Additions to Inventories

In addition to borrowing for plant and equipment spending, business firms need to borrow funds to increase their inventories when this is necessary. Basically, inventories are required in a certain ratio to sales, this ratio depending upon the efficiency with which inventories can be supplied to the points of sale, the time required for obtaining additional inventories, and the degree of fluctuations in sales. When inventory/sales ratios are relatively low, business firms need to add to inventories, especially if sales are rising. Borrowing for this purpose is likely to be short-term borrowing, largely from commercial banks or from commercial finance companies for some marginal firms or firms that have borrowed as much as they can from banks.

Percentage fluctuations in inventory borrowing are likely to be very great, as in some years business firms reduce inventories and may need no funds for inventory purchases on a net basis. In other years, with rapidly rising sales, business firms need large additions to inventories. For this reason, demand for short-term borrowing is likely to fluctuate more (in percentage terms) than long-term borrowing. This is a second reason why short-term interest rates are likely to fluctuate more than long-term interest rates. They also fluctuate more with a given change in demand for securities because a very small change in the price of a short-term financial asset causes a large change in its yield, since the yield is obtained over a short period.

There is no absolute dividing line between short-term inventory borrowing and long-term borrowing for plant and equipment spending. Even plant and equipment spending may at times be financed by short-term borrowing, especially in the early stages of a business recovery. Until a business recovery has proceeded for some time, business managers may not clearly perceive that a significant increase in investment and hence in long-term borrowing will be needed, and they may attempt, for a time, to meet needs for replacement of equipment and maintenance through short-term borrowing. Moreover, short-term borrowing often becomes longer-term borrowing as loans are renewed by banks. At times, moreover, loans may be negotiated with banks in the form of term loans with an original maturity of more than one year, at lower interest rates than those that would have to be paid on bond issues or even on short-term loans.

Moreover, although certain normal inventory/sales ratios may serve as guidelines in forecasting inventory accumulation or reduction, these ratios are not fixed, and inventory changes may not occur as expected. An example is the recession of 1969–1970, in which inventory ratios were not reduced for some time; for this reason, buildup of inventories was also delayed as business activity rose in 1971 and 1972. The ratio usually falls as business activity rises and rises as a recession occurs. Fluctuations

FIGURE 7–4
Inventories Compared with Monthly Sales
Manufacturing and Trade, 1972–1986*

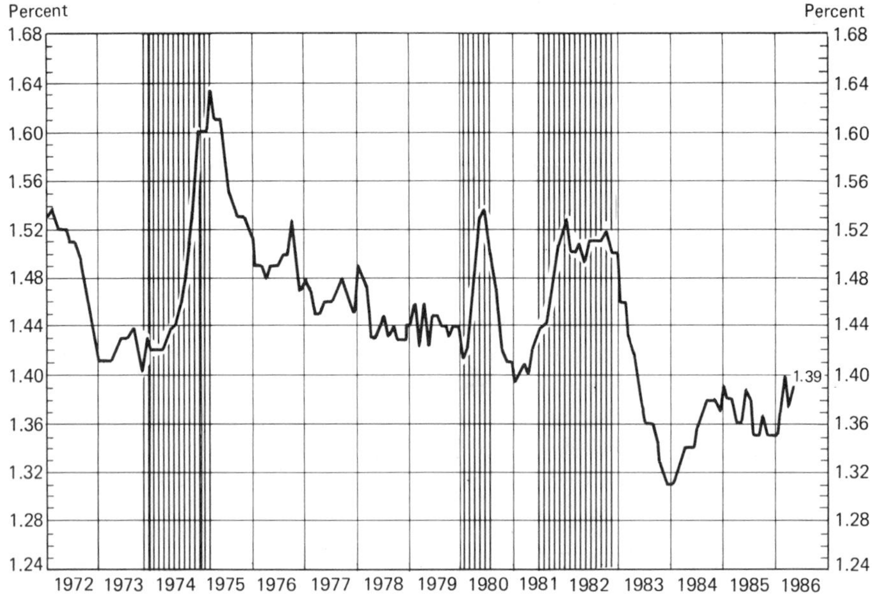

*Ratios based on seasonally adjusted data. Shaded areas represent periods of business recession.
Latest data plotted: May preliminary.

SOURCE: Federal Reserve Bank of St. Louis, *National Economic Trends,* July 1986, p. 18.

in the inventory/sales ratio are shown in Figure 7–4; note that inventories have usually fluctuated between 1.36 and 1.56 times monthly sales.

It must be noted that inflation, combined with the use of different methods of valuation of inventories that are considered to be sold, and hence included as part of the cost of goods sold, distorts figures on values of inventories that remain. Shifts from FIFO to LIFO (or vice versa) also make it very difficult to judge, especially in a period of rapid inflation, whether inventories are excessive or not.

## Borrowing to Increase Liquidity

Finally, business firms may borrow, either short term or long term, to improve their own liquidity ratios if these are relatively low. One reason for such borrowing is the concern that low liquidity ratios (low ratios of liquid financial assets to current liabilities) may be looked upon unfavorably by lenders or may lead to situations in which payments due on current liabilities cannot be met. Another reason is the fear that, if borrowing should become necessary, there might be occasions when commercial banks might not lend: they might already have become "loaned up," reaching a loan/deposit ratio as high as they wish to maintain. Business owners might foresee, or think that they foresee, actions by the Federal Reserve System to tighten credit. Memories of such actions, for example, in 1966, 1969, 1974, and again in 1980, might reinforce their beliefs.

If the borrowed funds are held in the form of cash or other liquid assets, they clearly increase the amount of liquid assets held by firms, but they may or may not improve the liquidity ratio. If a firm has more current liabilities than current assets, short-term borrowing will improve the liquidity ratio slightly; if it has more current assets than current liabilities, the liquidity ratio will worsen slightly with short-term borrowing. Intermediate-term or long-term borrowing, of course, will improve the liquidity ratio in either case, since it adds to current assets, at least temporarily, without adding to *current* liabilities.

## Forecasting the Demand for Loanable Funds by Business Firms

The demand for loanable funds by business firms is the sum of their borrowing plus their issue of new equity securities for investment spending, for increases in inventories, and for improvement of their liquidity position. Surveys of the investment spending plans of business firms, made by government agencies and by private firms, aid in forecasting borrowing for investment in plant and equipment;[23] analysis of trends in inventory/sales ratios, their current level, and the forecast level of sales aids in forecasting borrowing to finance increases in inventories; and analysis of liquidity ratios aids in forecasting liquidity borrowing.

The amount of borrowing for these purposes cannot be adequately forecast, however, until an estimate has been made of the amount of funds likely to be available from depreciation and other capital consumption allowances and from retained earnings, as these funds will generally be used before borrowed funds are sought. Of course, in every year *some* firms need funds, but more firms begin to borrow as internally generated funds become insufficient to meet planned investment. The amount of depreciation may be affected by any changes in rules governing depreciation rates, and the amount of retained earnings may be affected not only by profit margins but also by any change in corporate tax rates.

For individual firms, the need for external funds may be forecast by estimating the required increase in assets minus any expected increase in current liabilities and minus expected internally generated funds. One way of estimating these items is to use a forecast of next year's sales and forecast other items according to their percentages of last year's sales. Since our primary interest is in total demand for loanable funds by business firms, the surveys of plans for investment spending by firms are the

---

[23] The Commerce Department-Securities and Exchange Commission (usually referred to as the Commerce-SEC) surveys and the McGraw-Hill surveys of intentions to spend for business fixed investment have been quite successful in forecasting expenditures. Errors have been substantially less than the average annual variations in expenditures. See Arthur M. Okun, "The Predictive Value of Surveys of Business Intentions," *American Economic Review*, Papers and Proceedings, May 1962.

best beginning point, but adjustments are necessary for errors believed to exist in such surveys and for the possibility in some years that plant expansion cannot always be carried out because of commodity shortages or because of insufficient supply of funds available at "reasonable" interest rates.

With these estimates made for total funds needed and for internally generated funds, the analyst is ready to estimate the demand for loanable funds by business firms. In general, because amounts for the preceding period are known, the task of the analyst is to estimate *changes* in plant and equipment spending, inventory accumulation, liquidity, and internally generated funds. Although borrowing for plant and equipment spending is generally long-term borrowing, and other funds are generally obtained through short-term borrowing, there is no precise dividing line for the separation of borrowing into long-term and short-term markets.

In conclusion, it may be noted that fluctuations in loans by banks to business firms are determined largely by *demand*. One study showed that, when demand fell, loans declined, even though the supply of funds banks could have used to make loans remained ample.[24] In the late 1950s and in the early 1960s, New York banks had sufficient funds to make a substantial additional volume of business loans, but loans increased only 2½ percent a year; on the other hand, loans increased at over 20 percent a year in the mid-1950s and in the mid-1960s, when demand was strong. Business firms borrowed to finance capital expenditures, as reflected in the high proportion of term loans, nearly two-thirds of all business loans outstanding. Bank loans are also obtained as interim financing in the early stages of capital projects, when the amount of funds that will ultimately be needed is not necessarily known. The second major factor affecting loan demand was the availability of internal financing relative to fixed investment and changes in inventories. When cash flows were less than these needs for funds, bank borrowing increased sharply.

## Agricultural Demand for Credit

Farms are usually both homes and business operations, and agricultural credit can be treated as both business and consumer credit. As there are only a relatively small number of corporations engaged in agriculture, most farmers must borrow from financial institutions or individual lenders rather than in the bond market. The need for credit has become increasingly important with more extensive use of farm machinery, chemical fertilizers, and other manufactured products. Because farmers have *relatively* heavy debt—largely as a result of their need to purchase long-lived assets in the form of farmland and machinery—and relatively few liquid assets, their demand for credit fluctuates rather widely with the need for purchases of equipment, seed,

[24] George Budzeika, *Lending to Business by New York City Banks,* New York University, Institute of Finance, *Bulletin,* Nos. 76–77, September 1971. Inventory financing was less significant in this particular study than it might have been in other studies because it was conducted in New York City, where there is a concentration of financing by banks of utilities and petroleum companies, neither of which carry large inventories relative to their size. Thus in New York inventory financing is less important than in most centers.

feed, fertilizers, and land. At the same time, risks of lending in agriculture are greater than in business, generally because of the small size and usually noncorporate form of farm businesses, the sometimes inadequate record keeping, and the risks generally peculiar to agriculture: crop and livestock diseases, weather changes, insect pests, and other sources of risks, plus the risk of widely fluctuating prices because of relatively inelastic demand for many farm products and relatively wide fluctuations in supply.

The demand for credit in agriculture has the same origin as the demand for credit in other business, recognition of the productivity of land and capital. The agricultural revolution since the mid-1930s led to great increases in output per worker-hour, with increased use of equipment and fertilizer. The increased return permitted borrowing. Increase in output per worker-hour is often referred to as productivity of labor; it can be referred to, as in this paragraph, as productivity of capital. Perhaps the best phraseology would be "the increase in productivity of labor using more (or better) land and capital."

One significant problem in demand for agricultural credit has been that of gaining access to institutions and markets that could provide credit at rates comparable to those charged to other forms of business, with perhaps some adjustment because of the risks peculiar to agriculture. The establishment of government-sponsored agricultural credit agencies, mentioned in Chapter 4, gave farmers an improved position. First, it gave them alternative sources of borrowing, and in some cases *a* source of borrowing, by creating credit agencies that could supplement lending by commercial banks, life insurance companies, and individuals. Second, by establishing institutions that could obtain funds for loans to agriculture by issuing bonds, it gave noncorporate farms access to the bond market. Incidentally, the bond could be issued at relatively low rates of interest because the agencies were government sponsored and government regulated, and the securities, as agency securities, had nearly the same status as Treasury securities.

Demand for agricultural credit is a relatively small factor in an economy such as that of the United States, in which a very small percentage of GNP is produced by the agricultural sector. Nevertheless, the need of agriculture for loanable funds has increased rapidly since the mid-1930s, and the importance of credit for agriculture in providing the marginal funds needed cannot be overlooked.

Most of the long-term demand by the agricultural sector for credit is for mortgage credit, used in buying land and sometimes to obtain funds on the security of land already owned. Although the direct demand is for mortgage credit, if the funds are obtained from a government agency—for example, a Federal Land Bank—the Federal Land Bank obtains its funds primarily from the issue of bonds. Thus the level of bond interest yields has relevance for farmers, and high bond interest rates may indirectly affect farm credit.

Most of the short-term and intermediate-term demand for credit by the agricultural sector is met by commercial banks and by government-sponsored agencies such as the Production Credit Associations, which in turn can obtain funds from another government-sponsored agency, the Federal Intermediate Credit Banks. These institutions, in turn, issue bonds to obtain funds, so that both long-term and short-term credit depend to some extent on bond interest rates.

Rise in the foreign exchange value of the dollar in the early 1980s made it difficult to export farm products, and the farm sector suffered greatly.[25]

# THE DEMAND FOR MORTGAGE CREDIT

Mortgage credit means credit secured by mortgages on real estate. Most housing is constructed and purchased with the aid of mortgage credit, and a substantial amount of nonresidential construction also makes use of mortgage credit. Construction by public utilities and by many industrial firms, however, is usually financed by bond issues, and such demand is not considered as mortgage credit even if the bonds are secured by mortgages. Construction undertaken by nonprofit institutions, such as college buildings, hospitals, and religious structures, and some commercial and industrial buildings, including office buildings, is often financed by loans secured by mortgages on buildings being constructed and is a factor in mortgage credit demand. Thus mortgage credit demand comes from consumers, nonprofit institutions, and to some extent from business firms.

A substantial amount of mortgage credit is used to finance purchases of existing houses, existing offices, and other buildings. As inflation occurred, prices of homes frequently rose by more than enough to offset depreciation, and as mortgages were paid off, new purchasers found that larger mortgages were needed to buy homes. Demand for such credit does not depend directly on the current volume of construction and, hence, may be more difficult to forecast than the volume of mortgage credit needed to finance new construction. Sometimes homeowners borrow by increasing the amounts of existing mortgages, or by obtaining new mortgages, to use the funds for other purposes.

## Nature and Growth of Mortgage Credit

Mortgage debt differs from other debt because the collateral consists of mortgages on land and buildings. Hence, although attention should always properly be given to ability of borrowers to repay, some weight is inevitably placed on property values. Emphasis is given to such things as loan/value ratios and to methods of appraising values of properties on a cost basis, on a market sale basis, or on a capitalization of prospective income basis. None of these bases is completely satisfactory, as costs cannot be accurately adjusted to reflect current values, sales prices of similar properties are not entirely accurate indexes of potential sales prices of particular properties because properties vary, and prospective income cannot be accurately foreseen.

Mortgage debt also differs from much other debt because mortgages are heterogeneous. They differ in amounts, in descriptions and characteristics, and in quality in

---

[25] More rapid economic growth in the United States than in Europe in the first half of the 1980s, farm aid programs that probably set price support levels too high, and relatively slow domestic growth in such countries as Australia and Canada, leading them to export more farm products, combined to create problems for U.S. agriculture. See Mark Drabenstott and Kim Norris, "Competing in the World Marketplace: The Challenge for American Agriculture," Federal Reserve Bank of Kansas City, *Economic Review*, February 1986, pp. 3–13.

terms of assurance of clear title and other factors. Hence, unlike corporate and government bonds, which have broad secondary markets based on continuous sale of homogeneous securities, mortgages have a much less adequate secondary market and much less liquidity. It should be noted, of course, that mortgage loans are not as heterogeneous as other business loans and that there is some secondary market for mortgages, whereas there is almost no secondary market for business loans. Liquidity of mortgages is intermediate between that of bonds and of business loans.

Mortgage credit (mortgage debt outstanding) has increased very rapidly; the increase in mortgage credit since World War II has been greater than the increase in government and corporate securities combined. Even this comparison understates the volume of mortgage lending; because repayment of mortgage debt is usually on an amortized basis, the amortized part of such mortgage debt is repaid every year, and the funds are normally loaned out again.

Mobile homes—which some say are neither mobile nor homes—are now included in national income accounts under the heading of construction, if they are over 30 feet in length. Their purchase is generally financed by finance companies or commercial banks, and in some ways the mobile home dealer operates like an automobile dealer. Nevertheless, mobile homes must be considered as part of the housing picture; they are financed by what is termed consumer credit rather than mortgage credit, however.[26]

## Sources of the Demand for Mortgage Credit

Demand for mortgage credit depends on the volume of residential and nonresidential construction, just as business demand for credit depends on spending for plant and equipment and inventories. It may be argued that the volume of construction depends in part on availability of mortgage credit. If mortgage credit is readily available builders may be induced to expand operations more than they otherwise would. It is difficult to determine whether availability of mortgage credit is a significant independent factor determining the volume of construction. Maisel included the interest rate on conventional mortgages as one factor in a regression equation used to predict the number of housing starts.[27] Certainly, high interest rates and restricted availability of credit frequently have curtailed an increase in housing starts.

Demand for mortgage credit for residential construction also depends upon the number of housing units being constructed, the land and building costs involved, and the loan/value ratios used by lending institutions or individual mortgage lenders. The

---

[26] See the interesting article by Lawrence A. Mayer, "Mobile Homes Move into the Breach," *Fortune*, March 1970, pp. 126–130, 144–146.

[27] See Sherman Maisel, *Financing Real Estate* (New York: McGraw-Hill, 1965). Housing starts may be assumed to be a function of interest rates on conventional mortgages, vacancies, the ratio of rental costs to housing construction costs, the change in the number of houses and apartment buildings under construction, and the number of removals. Housing starts may be related to some of these variables with lag; for example, they may be related to the average level of mortgage interest rates in several previous quarters. Removals may be related to the previous period's stock of housing. With estimates of the lags involved, a regression equation can be developed. Such a forecasting equation is not suitable for continued use without modification because conditions change. However, like computer models used in forecasting general business activity, such a partial model of one sector of the economy has definite usefulness.

number of housing units being constructed depends in turn on the number of new households being formed and the number of houses demolished for slum clearance, highway construction, and so on. Both the number of households to be formed and the number of houses to be demolished are relatively accurately predictable, although at times certain factors may create problems for those who attempt to analyze housing demand; for example, after a wartime period in which many families were forced to live together, newly married couples often living with their parents, there may be a demand for new housing arising out of "undoubling," the amount of which may be difficult to estimate. Construction costs vary with price levels, number of rooms per house, and features included in construction (built-in appliances, etc.). Land costs also vary with price levels, but depend to some extent on the relative numbers of single-family and apartment dwellings being built; land on which apartment houses are built is usually more expensive per square foot, but the number of square feet per household is smaller. Finally, loan/value ratios depend partly upon the amount of financing being handled by particular types of institutions. The major types of institutions making mortgage loans are commercial banks, savings and loan associations, mutual savings banks, and life insurance companies (which frequently purchase mortgage loans already made by mortgage companies). Each of these institutions is subject to regulations that limit maturities of mortgage loans and in many instances limit loan/value ratios. Loan/value ratios have been raised in recent years; they are usually higher on FHA-insured or VA-guaranteed loans than on so-called conventional mortgage loans. FHA-insured and VA-guaranteed loans are insured or guaranteed by a federal government agency, the Federal Housing Administration or the Veterans Administration, in return for payment of a specified premium. Although financial institutions may suffer some losses because of repossession and other costs, they are insured against loss of principal and interest on such loans. FHA-insured and VA-guaranteed loans are more common when funds are more readily available because lending institutions make them at such times although at other times they prefer the higher rates and less red tape of conventional loans.

The demand for nonresidential mortgage credit is based largely on the amount of construction of commercial, religious, educational, and hospital buildings. The amount of such construction is more difficult to forecast and is likely to be a source of error in any forecast of demand for mortgage credit. Although almost all increases in residential construction are financed by mortgage credit, a substantial part of an increase in nonresidential construction may be financed by other means. Utilities finance construction through bond issues, and this is frequently true for other industrial firms. Construction by state and local governments is usually financed by municipal bond issues. Hence even an accurate forecast of the trend in total nonresidential construction does not assure an accurate forecast of the nonresidential demand for mortgage credit.[28]

---

[28] Robinson Newcomb emphasized the impact of the acceleration principle on construction: because construction may add only perhaps 3 percent to the total stock of buildings and other structures in a year, small variations in demand for utilization of structures can cause larger changes in the amount of construction. See Robinson Newcomb, "Construction Forecasting," in William F. Butler and Robert A. Kavesh, eds., *How Business Economists Forecast* (Englewood Cliffs, N.J.: Prentice-Hall, 1966), pp. 186–220.

## Short and Long Cycles in Construction Activity

Construction activity is cyclical, exhibiting both short-term and long-term cycles. Short-term cycles in construction activity tend to exhibit a pattern different from that of cycles in general business activity: construction activity generally rises during the latter part of a decline in general business activity, continues to rise as general business activity begins to rise, and begins to decline some time before the peak in general business activity. Like most forms of investment, construction activity tends to fluctuate more widely than does general business activity. One factor causing the difference in pattern is the sensitivity of construction activity to interest rates and availability of credit. Interest rate costs constitute a large part of total costs of financing construction, and hence a rise in interest rates during an upswing tends to inhibit construction, especially residential construction. As general business activity declines and as interest rates fall, the lower interest costs and greater availability of credit encourage an increase in construction activity.

Long cycles are also found in construction activity; these long cycles have typically been about 20 years from trough to trough, the most recent clearly identifiable trough being in the period 1942–1944, probably because of the war. Shorter cycles are superimposed on the long cycles, and both must be kept in mind in forecasts of cyclical activity. The evidence for the existence of long cycles and the length of long cycles is not entirely satisfactory. Thus after the trough in 1942–1944, the next trough should have occurred in the late 1950s or in the early 1960s. No clear trough at that time is identifiable, although housing activity did not rise significantly.

It is generally presumed that there is a "normal" level of vacancies in housing, related to size, mobility, income level, and rate of growth of the population and to tax and other costs of holding property vacant. There is also presumed to be a "normal" demand for housing, composed of the number of net households formed, the increase in "normal" vacancies, and demolitions. As construction activity rises and housing starts begin to exceed the level of normal demand, vacancies begin to rise. When builders begin to recognize that their activities are outrunning demand, the number of housing starts begins to fall, but the number of vacancies may continue to rise as long as housing starts still exceed the normal demand for houses. When they fall below that level, vacancies begin to fall; they may continue to fall as long as housing starts are below the level of demand. Fluctuations in the number of housing starts are generally rather wide because of the time required for developing real estate subdivisions and because of the large number of small builders, many of whom have relatively little knowledge concerning general market conditions.

## Flow of Mortgage Funds

Because the amount of mortgage loans demanded in any area does not usually equal the amount of mortgage lending available in the area, mortgage market facilities are needed to permit funds to flow in greater volume to areas in which there is greater demand and to permit resale of at least some mortgages when lending activity is greater than the inflow of funds permits. Many lending institutions, especially in recent years, have been active in lending in areas outside of their own localities, and government agencies have been established to increase the market for mortgages by being ready to buy and sell mortgages. Institutions located in areas where mortgage loan demand is heavy have solicited savings deposits from out-of-state savers, although restrictions have been imposed on the extent of such solicitations. Such deposits may be more volatile than other share accounts, as they are often made in response to advertising of interest rates higher than those paid in other states. In recent years thrift institutions have not been very successful in attracting such funds from other areas. The Federal Home Loan Bank system has sometimes restricted savings and loan associations that have obtained more than a specified proportion of their savings from other states.

The share of housing in total credit increased from 19 percent in the 1960s to 20½ percent in the 1970s; much of this increase was dependent on government institutions, which provided funds for more than one-fourth of all home mortgages. The number of households increased by more than 20 percent in the 1970s, yet the number of people per household fell. In 1978, the average household consisted of only one or two persons. Nevertheless, the average size of homes increased. Probably more funds went into housing than would have been possible in the absence of inflation and government subsidies. Mortgage borrowing became a means of acquiring an equity in an asset that rose in value.

At the same time, housing has been a volatile industry, with severe cyclical fluctuations. The traditional major source of mortgage funds is the thrift institutions; they have been hurt, at times of high market interest rates, by interest rate ceilings on accounts in thrift institutions. Some help should be afforded by the phasing out of such interest rate ceilings under the Depository Institutions Deregulation and Monetary Control Act of 1980. Development of new types of mortgages, with either variable interest rates or variable monthly payments, should also help thrift institutions meet the problem of rising and falling interest rates. However, other changes may hurt the flow of funds into housing; the deregulation act permits savings and loan associations to invest more funds in consumer loans and in corporate debt. Moderation in the rate of inflation would moderate fluctuations in interest rates, and perhaps moderate the cyclical volatility in the housing industry.

## Forecasting the Demand for Mortgage Credit

Forecasting the demand for mortgage credit involves combination of a forecast of the demand for residential mortgage credit with one for the demand for nonresidential mortgage financing. Maturities of mortgages are limited, although the number of years to maturity has been increasing in recent years. Although some increase in maturity may be possible, to keep the annual interest rate from rising too much, when demand for mortgage loans is heavy, the rate of interest rises rather sharply. Above certain interest rate levels, demand for mortgage credit may be responsive to changes in interest rates. Borrowers find that high interest rates cause monthly payments to be much greater, and normally their income is not rising sufficiently to enable them to make such payments easily. When interest rate ceilings are imposed, as they have been on FHA-insured and VA-guaranteed loans, demand cannot be satisfied at rates above the ceilings. Unless mortgages are discounted to the sellers, such mortgage loans cannot be made. Thus the burden of interest cost may be shifted in part to sellers.

## CONSUMER DEMAND FOR LOANABLE FUNDS

Consumer demand for loanable funds could be ignored by treating the supply of loanable funds from consumers as a net supply, subtracting consumer borrowing from gross saving. However, it is preferable to begin with the gross supply of loanable funds by consumers and to treat consumer demand for loanable funds as a part of total demand. This is in accord with the reality of the market for loanable funds and facilitates analysis because it separates consumer increases in tangible and financial assets from consumer borrowing. Consumer saving, of course, is the increase in net worth—the increase in tangible and financial assets minus the increase in consumer debt.

### Consumer Saving and Borrowing

At least since the advent of Keynesian theory in the 1930s, it has been generally assumed that consumer saving depends primarily on consumer *income*. Whether the correlation was made between personal saving and GNP or between personal saving and disposable personal income, relatively high correlations were obtained with annual data. This led to the presumption that consumer saving is not very sensitive to interest rate changes. Because saving by business firms (depreciation and retained earnings) is also not very sensitive to changes in interest rates, the conclusion was reached that saving could be treated as a function of income, not as a function of interest rates. Whatever the factors that determined how much income was saved, it seemed that interest rates played a small role.

However, there was some variation in the rate of saving out of income over the course of a business cycle. Moreover, the marginal rate of saving did not (with the possible exception of a year or two in the Great Depression) become negative for the population as a whole, as might have been expected from a long-run consumption function of the same form as the original formulation of short-term Keynesian theory.[29] These facts led to the elaboration of more sophisticated theories of the relationship between saving and income.

---

[29] In the original formulation of Keynesian theory of the consumption function, based on his statement that "men are disposed, as a rule, and on the average, to increase their consumption as their income increases, but not by as much as the increase in their income," $\Delta C/\Delta Y$ was assumed to be greater than zero but less than one. It was usually presumed, moreover, that $\Delta C/\Delta Y$ was sufficiently less than unity that, at some low level of income, consumption would equal income, and there would be no saving. If it were assumed that the long-run consumption function had the same form, the implication was that at some time in the past there was no saving. The fact that in the long run $C/Y$ was relatively constant (instead of falling as income rose) led to reconsideration of the relationships.

Arthur Smithies suggested that the shift might be related to changes in the proportions of certain groups in the population and to the continual introduction of new commodities that competed for consumer spending. Cross-section studies show that farmers save more than do urban residents with the same levels of income; the shift of population from farms to cities might tend to raise consumption and reduce saving. Older persons have usually consumed more and saved less of their income; the relatively greater proportion of older persons in the population thus might also tend to raise consumption. Finally, the introduction of new commodities might tend to have the same effect.[30]

James Duesenberry suggested that cyclical fluctuations in the rate of saving might be explained by the fact that income fluctuates over the cycle; as income rises, consumption rises, but with a lag, so that, at high levels of business activity, there is more saving. Then, as business activity declines in a recession, consumers reduce their spending, but not as much as the decline in income; they are reluctant to reduce consumption from the peak attained in the period of peak income. Hence, the rate of saving declines.[31]

Milton Friedman introduced the view that consumption is proportional, not to measured income (as measured in GNP accounts) but to "permanent" income—long-run expected income, which may be estimated by extrapolation of a weighted average of past incomes, the most recent income being given the greatest weight. He argued that consumption is not related to "transitory" income, unexpected windfalls. A considerable number of attempts have been made to test the permanent income hypothesis, with varying results. Both Kuznets' data on GNP and Friedman's hypothesis suggested that $\Delta C/\Delta Y$ was approximately equal to $C/Y$ (not less, as had been assumed).[32] However, some tests found that $\Delta C/\Delta Y$ *was* less than $C/Y$, although the difference was not as great when permanent income was used for $Y$ as it was when income as measured in GNP was used.[33]

With any of the theories other than that of Friedman's, there was no basis for a theory of consumer borrowing, except borrowing that might be done by those with low incomes, who might spend more than their total incomes. Such borrowing does occur, but it does not constitute the major portion of present-day consumer borrowing. Most present-day consumer borrowing is done by middle-income consumers and is related to purchases of automobiles or appliances, or to the remodeling and improvement of homes.

A theory of consumption similar to Friedman's, that can account for this common type of consumer borrowing quite easily, is that developed by Modigliani and

[30] Arthur Smithies, "Forecasting Postwar Demand: I," *Econometrica*, January 1945, pp. 1–14.

[31] James Duesenberry, *Income, Savings and the Theory of Consumer Behavior* (Cambridge, Mass.: Harvard University Press, 1949).

[32] Kuznets' data were reported in Simon Kuznets, *National Product Since 1869* (New York: National Bureau of Economic Research, 1946), and the permanent income hypothesis was presented in Milton Friedman, *A Theory of the Consumption Function* (Princeton, N.J.: Princeton University Press, 1957).

[33] See, for example, Thomas Mayer, "The Propensity to Consume Permanent Income," *American Economic Review*, December 1966, pp. 1158–1177.

Brumberg and further amplified by Modigliani and Ando.[34] This theory hypothesizes that in any year consumption is proportional to the present value of total resources accruing to the individual or head of household over the rest of his or her life. Total resources accruing to the person over the rest of his or her life are the sum of net worth from previous periods plus the present value of income that the person expects to earn. With this hypothesis, young married couples, because they can look forward to a long period of discounted expected income, could be expected to spend much of their total current income, and perhaps more than the total. If the previous peak income is regarded as a proxy for wealth or net worth, the Ando-Modigliani formulation is similar to that of Duesenberry, mentioned previously.

The theory of the consumption function is still in the process of development, and no firm final conclusion can be reached at this point. A related question is the impact of stock market prices on consumption, as rising prices of stocks and resultant capital gains add to net worth of those who invest in stocks.[35] The evidence to date is consistent with the life-cycle hypothesis and the presumption that changes in prices of assets such as stocks can significantly affect consumption, but the evidence is not such that there is a consensus on these points.

## The Growth of Consumer Credit Demand

Consumer credit has grown rapidly in the twentieth century, as new institutions have developed in this field and existing institutions such as commercial banks have found it attractive. The growth of consumer debt has two significant effects: (1) it permits increased consumer spending and thus indirectly tends (through a feedback effect) to increase business investment spending, and (2) it creates a volume of liabilities that compete with liabilities of other sectors, thus causing interest rates to be somewhat higher than they would be otherwise. To some extent, therefore, it may also tend to reduce investment spending based on borrowing; it is difficult to evaluate the overall effect on investment.

The growth of consumer debt, especially consumer installment debt, is largely the result of the growth of the automobile and appliance industries. Borrowing to purchase these types of assets, especially automobiles, can be justified on the ground that the assets provide services for a number of years, and it is therefore reasonable to pay for them over a period of years.

Since 1920, consumer credit increased very rapidly in three periods: in 1920–1929, it grew at 15 percent per year; in 1936–1941, it grew at 11 percent per year; and in 1947–1955, it grew at 19 percent per year. It decreased in the depression of the 1930s and during World War II, but it did not decline significantly in the postwar recessions. Installment credit constitutes over 80 percent of total consumer credit; the

[34] Albert Ando and Franco Modigliani, "The 'Life Cycle' Hypothesis of Saving: Aggregate Implications and Tests," *American Economic Review*, March 1963, pp. 55–84. For a review of further developments in the theory of consumer spending, saving and borrowing, see Robert Ferber, "Consumer Economics, A Survey," *Journal of Economic Literature*, December 1973, pp. 1303–1342, esp. pp. 1304–1312.

[35] See Robert H. Rasche, "Impact of the Stock Market on Private Demand," *American Economic Review*, Papers and Proceedings, May 1972, pp. 220–228.

remainder, noninstallment credit, is composed of single-payment loans (chiefly from banks), charge accounts (including bank credit cards), and service credit from utilities and professional people such as doctors and dentists.

As the ratio of consumer credit to personal income rose, some concern developed that continued rise in this ratio might create problems. One economist attempted to explain the trend of this ratio. He assumed that a "life-cycle" theory of saving and borrowing was valid and that most borrowing would be done by young household heads acquiring durable goods. Therefore he argued that the increase in the number of households and the increase in average income per household would be the major determinants of the size of consumer installment debt. From this reasoning he derived the result that the ratio of consumer installment credit outstanding will tend to approach a limiting constant equal to $k(1 + r)/r$, in which $k$ is the increase in consumer installment debt as a fixed proportion of personal income and $r$ is the annual rate of growth of personal income.[36] A later study used personal income, the square of personal income, the number of income-receiving units, and the level of liquid assets held by the household sector of the economy as the determinants of the ratio.[37] The two models predicted, or explained, the growth of consumer installment credit rather well. The second model may have been slightly more accurate, but this model assumed an inverse relationship between liquid asset holdings and consumer debt, which seems to be incorrect. Probably it is best to assume the simplest case—the rapid rise in consumer debt in the decade after World War II was caused largely by the shortage of durable goods during the war; after the war consumers tried to "catch up."

Neither model explained very well the deceleration in the growth of consumer installment credit relative to personal income in the late 1960s and early 1970s. It is quite possible that the factors responsible were the general rise and wide fluctuations in interest rates and the onset of relatively rapid inflation. Although it might be assumed by some that inflation would tend to increase consumer installment credit by inducing people to buy more before prices rise, within certain limits inflation seems to have the opposite effect. One hypothesis is that consumers try to save more and borrow less because they feel that asset holdings may not be sufficient to provide for future expenditures. Liquid assets held by families in the $5,000- to $15,000-a-year income bracket, which did most of the installment credit buying, dropped in 1965–1970, and it may well be that future trend in the consumer installment debt/personal income ratio depends on the trend in interest rates and inflation.[38]

There was some concern in the late 1970s about the rise in consumer credit, the fear being expressed that consumer debt might rise so high that the growth of con-

[36] Alain Enthoven, "The Growth of Installment Credit and the Future of Prosperity," *American Economic Review*, December 1957, pp. 913–929. See also his later supplementary article, in response to criticism, "On a Debt-Income Model of Consumer Installment Credit Growth: Reply," *American Economic Review*, June 1964, pp. 415–417.

[37] Helen M. Hunter, "A Behavioral Model of the Long-Run Growth of Aggregate Consumer Credit in the United States," *Review of Economics and Statistics*, May 1966, pp. 124–131.

[38] Michael J. Prell, "The Long-Run Growth of Consumer Installment Credit—Some Observations," Federal Reserve Bank of Kansas City, *Monthly Review*, February 1973, pp. 3–13. Prell regarded the factors restraining the growth of consumer credit in the late 1960s and early 1970s as chiefly cyclical factors.

sumption would subsequently be slowed and delinquency on consumer debt would rise. Although the ratio of consumer debt outstanding to disposable personal income was slightly higher than levels reached in earlier cyclical peaks, the trend was not significantly out of line with the long-term level. The ratio fell sharply during the recession of 1973–1975 and then rose again relatively rapidly in the subsequent recovery period. The ratio of liquid assets to debt actually shows a rise from the level of the 1960s. Since stocks are probably not important holdings of lower-income and middle-income families, which are those most likely to be forced to reduce consumption or become delinquent on debt if debt is too high, the conclusion seems justified that consumer debt was not much more of a problem in the late 1970s than in the 1960s.[39]

## Consumer Credit Demand and Economic Stabilization

The question has been raised many times whether or not consumer credit contributes to increasing the amplitude of business fluctuations. With the possible exception of the period 1954–1955, consumer credit was not the *main* factor in business upswings, but such credit has amplified fluctuations. Cases can be found, however, in which cash sales fluctuated more than credit sales, for example, automobile sales in 1950–1953.

Selective regulation of consumer credit may be necessary if consumer credit is *destabilizing* and if *general* control of money and bank credit does not significantly affect consumer credit. It has been argued that consumer credit is slow to react to general control of money and credit, or perhaps is little affected, because (1) consumers are not very sensitive to changes in the interest rates they must pay and such rates do not change much and (2) banks and other consumer lenders are slow to restrict consumer credit because they find consumer lending quite profitable. Profitability of consumer lending, of course, varies with the level of other interest rates; when other interest rates are high, consumer lending may have a smaller advantage, or possibly no advantage, in profit potential.

Evidence from the period 1955–1956, a period of credit restraint by the monetary authorities, indicates that both large banks and medium-sized banks restricted consumer credit in this period when their deposit experience was unfavorable—when they either lost deposits or had a smaller increase in deposits than the average bank.[40]

---

[39] For two analyses, see Citibank, *Monthly Economic Letter*, February 1979, pp. 6–9; and Maury Harris and Karen Bradley, "Are Households Financially Overextended?" Federal Reserve Bank of New York, *Quarterly Review*, Autumn 1977, pp. 22–26.

[40] Paul Smith, "Response of Consumer Loans to General Credit Conditions," *American Economic Review*, September 1958, pp. 649–655. Smith's data were obtained from banks that had more than one-third of their total loans in the form of consumer loans. Data from this period are used because the policy of restraint after the 1957–1958 recession prevented output from again reaching its potential level until 1965, and the credit crunches of 1966 and 1969 provide somewhat different conditions. More recently, Thomas Mayer, "Financial Guidelines and Credit Controls," *Journal of Money, Credit, and Banking*, May 1972, pp. 360–373, argued that tight monetary policy has a direct impact on consumer installment credit; he simply observed a positive correlation between rates of nominal money stock growth and installment credit or debt/income ratio growth. It should be remembered that, although most interest rates rose in the late 1960s, consumer installment loan rates did not, in general, because they are limited by statutory ceilings.

There was some evidence that medium-sized banks in the sample, banks with deposits of $10 million to $50 million, were somewhat slow to restrict consumer credit, but both groups of banks restricted consumer loans more than commercial loans. Large banks, especially those with unfavorable deposit experience, sold government securities to continue to expand business loans.

Evidence also indicates that tightening credit leads banks to increase compensating balances required for finance companies, to apply general restrictions on lines of credit to such companies, and to reduce purchases of commercial paper offered by finance companies. Finance companies are able to offset such restriction to some extent by shifting from bank borrowing to capital market borrowing through the issuing of debentures and through directly placed commercial paper, commercial paper sold directly to insurance companies and other institutional lenders. Such borrowing in these circumstances may be at relatively high cost, and hence there is some restraint. To the extent that business firms and other institutions are willing to reduce their liquidity in the form of cash and to purchase commercial paper, velocity of money may increase and consumer credit may be less affected by restraint.

"Tight" money has comparatively little effect on terms of loans to consumers, but rates charged to dealers are raised and floor-plan credit used to finance dealers' inventories of automobiles and appliances is tightened.

Selective control of consumer credit was used during four recent periods: during World War II, briefly in 1948–1949, again in 1950–1952 as a part of emergency measures for the Korean war period, and briefly again in 1980. Regulation W, issued by the Federal Reserve System, specified minimum down payments and maximum loan maturities. Enforcement involved many administrative problems: it was difficult to control installment sales credit without controlling consumer installment loan credit; the use of large "balloon payments" at the end of repayment periods, as a device to extend maturities, had to be guarded against; and regulations had to be very carefully worded to prevent escape from control by breaking sales into parts. Objections were raised by some who argued that Regulation W discriminated against lower-income consumers. The Federal Reserve System has desired to avoid such controls unless they seemed essential, as they did during World War II when automobiles were not being manufactured. After extensive study, the Board of Governors of the Federal Reserve System did not recommend that they be given even a standby power to impose such control and concluded that fluctuations in consumer installment credit, with some exceptions, were "generally within limits that could be tolerated in a rapidly growing and dynamic economy."[41] The arguments leading to the conclusion that consumer credit control is not needed except in emergencies may be summarized as (1) consumer credit may not again grow as rapidly as it did just after World War II, when consumers made large purchases of durable goods; (2) changes in consumer credit have not been *significantly* destabilizing, as they have amounted to only about one-seventh of total changes in GNP in recent years; (3) pressure for credit control can be exerted through other means; (4) there is no assurance that money not spent on

---

[41] *Federal Reserve Bulletin*, June 1957, p. 648.

durable goods would be spent in "better" ways; and (5) consumer credit control may not prevent loan delinquencies because reasons for such delinquencies are many, delinquencies often occurring when consumers are young, transient, and inexperienced, rather than when down payments are too small and maturities too long.[42]

A peak in demand for credit was reached in the early spring of 1980. Consumer demand and business demand both increased rapidly. Only mortgage demand had fallen, as very high interest rates adversely impacted the housing industry. President Carter used the Credit Control Act of 1969 to authorize the Federal Reserve System to restrict both business and consumer credit and to impose a reserve requirement of 10 percent (instead of 8 percent imposed in October 1979) on *increases* in certain managed liabilities of *both* member and nonmember banks. By making acquisition of funds by banks more costly it was hoped to reduce the acquisition of funds, and thus reduce ability of banks to increase loans.

It is evident from experience in 1966, 1969, 1973–1974, and 1979–1980 that monetary policy aimed at slowing inflation causes short-term interest rates to rise sharply, and that this is very adverse in its effect on the housing industry and on purchases of durable goods, especially automobiles. These two industries were very hard hit.

The rise in the cost of obtaining funds needed by banks to extend consumer credit, combined with the usury law limits on interest rates that could be charged consumers, caused many banks to raise the cost and restrict the amount of consumer credit. With a reserve requirement of 15 percent for every increase in consumer credit, there was added incentive for such action. Hence many issuers of credit cards began to charge annual fees for them, to cease encouraging applications for new credit cards, to increase monthly repayment of debt by consumers, and to make efforts to reduce delinquencies. Banks that could do so raised interest rates on outstanding credit card debt; national banks could charge 1 percent above the Fed discount rate.

As might have been expected, consumers sought other lower-cost sources of credit; insurance company policyholder loans, often obtainable at low interest rates (under insurance policies written when interest rates were much lower than in 1980), increased.[43]

Short-term interest rates reached a peak in the spring of 1980. Real GNP fell in the second quarter, and the first two quarters were classified as a recession. In retrospect, it appears that consumer credit controls might better not have been imposed. There seems to be no reason to change the conclusion reached by the Fed in 1957: consumer credit controls are desirable in wartime, because many consumer goods are being produced in small quantities or not at all, and some means of restraining consumer demand are needed. But except for such special conditions, changes in consumer debt do not seem to be sufficient to necessitate special credit controls.

Economic expansion after 1982 brought with it a rise in consumer debt and in

---

[42] These conclusions were reached in a study by Paul W. McCracken, James C. T. Mao, and Cedric Fricke, *Consumer Installment Credit and Public Policy* (Ann Arbor: Bureau of Business Research, Graduate School of Business Administration, University of Michigan, 1965).

[43] *The Wall Street Journal*, March 19, 1980, p. 19.

consumer debt/income ratios. An increase was predictable from the life-cycle model (because younger age groups were increasing in size). Longer maturities of loans for the purchase of autos were also a factor. Another factor was increasing use of credit cards by "convenience" users—people who use credit cards but pay the amounts at the end of each month; such people are simply using credit cards and writing checks a few days (or weeks) later. One analyst concluded that except in the event of a *general* economic downturn, consumer debt was not likely to limit consumer spending.[44]

## SUMMARY

This chapter has analyzed the demand for credit by the business sector, the demand for mortgage credit, and consumer demand for loanable funds.

Business demand for loanable funds, based upon rates of return that are expected to be earned on investment in real capital assets, constitutes a major source of fluctuations in private borrowing. These fluctuations have significant impact on interest rates. Because of relatively high productivity of capital, demand for business loans tends to persist in periods of high economic activity, even when interest rates rise sharply. Because of the profitability of business loans, commercial banks and occasionally some other financial institutions tend to satisfy business loan demand if they can, even at the expense of other types of loans, and certainly at the expense of investments. Inventory loans rise as business activity rises. Short-term interest rates rise even if inflation does not occur. Thus a basic cause of fluctuations in interest rates is the demand for business loans. This is based on (1) expected rates of return on investment in real capital assets (machinery and factories) and (2) changes in accumulation or reduction of inventories.

Far too much emphasis has been placed on the interest elasticity of such demand and on the need for monetary and fiscal policy actions to push interest rates down to increase investment spending. If expected rates of profit are relatively high, demand for business loans will rise and short-term interest rates will also *rise*. Of course, at *certain times* policy actions to cause a drop in interest rates may be appropriate.

Demand for mortgage credit is based primarily on factors such as household formation, demolition of houses, and interest rates. Because long-term mortgage loans are required generally for buying houses, mortgage loan demand is greatly affected by the level of long-term interest rates. Long-term interest rates are higher when inflation occurs, to compensate for the loss of purchasing power of money while the loan is outstanding. Hence demand for mortgage credit need not rise and fall at the same time as business demand for short-term loans. Both long-term and short-term interest rates remained at very high levels even as the inflation rate began to fall from 1980 to 1982. Demand for mortgage loans was therefore much reduced.

Consumer demand for loanable funds is a relatively small percent of the total. Business demand has exceeded $100 billion in many years, and mortgage credit

---

[44] Douglas K. Pearce, "Rising Household Debt in Perspective," Federal Reserve Bank of Kansas City, *Economic Review*, July–August 1985, pp. 3–17.

exceeded $150 billion in 1978 and 1979 (admittedly peak years). Consumer credit, on the other hand, usually is less than $50 billion, in extension of new credit. Businesses, including the housing industry, are the chief private borrowers of funds.

Economists have gradually come to accept a permanent consumption or life-cycle hypothesis of consumer spending and saving, rather than the early Keynesian explanation that spending by consumers was based on current income. Young married couples, looking forward to a long period of discounted expected income, may spend their total income and go into debt. Thus consumer credit demand is likely to be increasing when the population in the 20- to 44-year age bracket is increasing. Consumer credit demand is also affected by the desire to purchase durable goods that have long useful lives, providing service over many years. Consumer credit may contribute to increasing the amplitude of business fluctuations, because consumers are not very sensitive to increases in interest rates and banks are somewhat slow to restrict consumer credit. Nevertheless, evidence led most economists to conclude that overexpansion of consumer credit in boom periods is not likely to be serious enough to justify special controls on consumer credit. Fluctuations in consumer credit are generally within limits that can be tolerated in a dynamic, growing economy. Except in wartime, there does not seem to be enough justification for consumer credit controls. Perhaps 1980 was an exception, because the rate of saving fell to an abnormally low level. Even so, some questioned the need for credit controls, and many thought they would be temporary, which proved to be correct.

Changes in money supply and in velocity of money affect prices and GNP; we examined channels through which these effects occur in Chapters 2 through 6. Changes in GNP likewise have an impact on supply of and demand for money and loanable funds. This chapter has covered changes in GNP arising from activities of business and consumers.

In summary,

1. Pure "inventory recessions" occur, but are minor unless other segments of GNP are involved.
2. Changes in consumer borrowing do not seem to be a major cause of economic fluctuations.
3. Construction has cyclical fluctuations, but construction is *one* industry or industry group and hence is usually not a major cause of GNP fluctuations.
4. Thus changes in business fixed investment (BFI—business spending for plant and equipment) are the main cause of fluctuations in real GNP.
5. There are several models for forecasting such investment spending, but the "neoclassical" and cash flow models seem generally to be the best. In the neoclassical model, BFI is affected by expected sales and prices, interest rates, and tax changes. In the cash flow model, business cash flow (expected profits minus taxes plus depreciation minus dividend payments) is assumed to be the chief determinant of investment spending because businesses generally rely on cash flow for financing first; if more funds are needed, they borrow, making interest rates, availability of credit, and other factors significant.[45]

[45] For more detailed discussion, see Richard W. Kopcke, "The Determinants of Investment Spending," Federal Reserve Bank of Boston, *New England Economic Review*, July–August 1985, pp. 19–35.

In Chapter 8, we examine effects of changes in government spending and borrowing, and of international factors affecting exports and imports, but also affecting capital inflows and outflows and hence interest rates.

## Questions for Discussion

**1.** Present the argument that relates the interest rate that can be paid by business firms to the rate that they expect to obtain by investment in real capital assets.

**2.** Why is it generally presumed that business firms use internally generated funds for investment purposes before they borrow external funds for such needs?

**3.** What is the role of the debt/equity ratio in determining the extent of business borrowing for investment purposes?

**4.** Is long-term investment ever financed by short-term borrowing? Under what conditions may this occur?

**5.** Why is borrowing to finance investment in inventories likely to be from commercial banks or business finance companies? Show how commercial bank lending is important in inventory fluctuations.

**6.** Why may business borrowing for liquidity purposes occur even after a long period of increasing capital investment has ended?

**7.** Why were government-sponsored financial institutions that obtained funds by selling bonds important in providing additional credit for agriculture?

**8.** Evaluate the argument that, in contrast to business demand for loanable funds, the demand for mortgage credit may be a dependent variable, the independent variable being the *supply* of mortgage credit.

**9.** How does the life-cycle theory of the consumption function differ from the theory of the consumption function originally presented by John Maynard Keynes and early Keynesian economists?

**10.** Why are measures to control the availability of credit generally relied upon to control expansion of business and mortgage credit, whereas direct control of consumer demand for loanable funds is sometimes urged?

## Selected References

This chapter involves some integration of the theory of business finance with part of macroeconomic theory. Hence a text on business finance, such as Lawrence D. Schall and Charles W. Haley, *Introduction to Financial Management*, 2nd ed. (New York: McGraw-Hill, 1980), is a useful reference.

Relevant macroeconomic theory is discussed in detail in Gardner Ackley, *Macroeconomic Theory* (New York: Macmillan, 1961).

Much more detailed coverage on some points relative to demand for loanable funds is provided by Polakoff and others, *Financial Institutions and Markets* (Boston: Houghton Mifflin, 1970), Chapters 12–15.

An interesting discussion of corporate borrowing and the "liquidity crisis" of 1970 is found in Carol J. Loomis, "The Lesson of the Credit Crisis," *Fortune*, May 1971, pp. 141–143, 274–286.

For statistical data and projections, see the annual *Supply and Demand for Credit* (Salomon Brothers) and *Credit and Capital Markets* (Bankers Trust Company) as well as the *Federal Reserve Bulletin*.

For comments on the illusory nature of part of retained earnings in a period of inflation, see Henry C. Wallich and Mable I. Wallich, "Profits Aren't as Good as They Look," *Fortune*, March 1974, pp. 126–129, 172.

A good summary of the consumer credit controls imposed by the Federal Reserve System in 1980 may be found in the Federal Reserve Bank of New York, *Quarterly Review*, Spring 1980, pp. 32–33.

For an analysis of the brief credit restraint program of spring 1980 and its phase-out that summer, see Randall C. Merris and Larry R. Mote, "The Credit Restraint Program in Perspective," Federal Reserve Bank of Chicago, *Economic Perspectives*, July–August 1980, pp. 7–14.

On recent trends in agricultural credit, see Marvin Duncan, "Financing Agriculture in the 1980s," and Dean W. Hughes, "Financial Condition of Agricultural Lenders in a Time of Farm Distress," Federal Reserve Bank of Kansas City, *Economic Review*, July–August 1983, pp. 3–12, 13–31.

On the rise in debt in the 1980s, see Paul A. Volcker, "The Rapid Growth of Debt in the United States," Federal Reserve Bank of Kansas City, *Economic Review*, May 1986, pp. 3–12.

# GOVERNMENT AND FOREIGN ECONOMIC ACTIVITY AND DEMAND FOR LOANABLE FUNDS

# VIII

As with changes in business and consumer spending discussed in Chapter 7, changes in government spending and in taxes do not in and of themselves affect the money supply, except perhaps in indirect ways. An increase in taxes reduces the amount of money available to business and consumers, but when government spends the funds obtained from taxes, the money returns to business and consumers. If government spending exceeds tax revenues, the government must borrow. This affects the demand for loanable funds. Of course, government *can* create money, as it did in the form of greenbacks at the time of the Civil War, but such money creation by the U.S. government has not occurred in the twentieth century.

Government spending does shift funds from one part of the economy to another. A large part of total government spending is for Social Security (including Medicare); as a result, Social Security beneficiaries have more funds to spend, and there is in general a shift from investment spending to consumer spending.

It is important to note that government spending does not necessarily increase total demand for loanable funds, even if government must borrow heavily. If business and consumer demand for loanable funds is falling (as in a recession), government spending may simply cause total demand for loanable funds to decline less than it might have declined otherwise. For this reason, the common reaction that "government borrowing raises interest rates" is too simple; at times it may simply slow a decline in interest rates. Moreover, of course, if the rate of inflation is falling, interest rates are likely to fall (as in 1982–1986), whether government spending rises or falls. Many studies have shown no significant correlation between government spending and interest rates.

Government demand for loanable funds includes both demand by state and local government units and demand by the federal government. State and local government units borrow because, like private sectors of the economy, their planned or unplanned expenditures frequently exceed their receipts, at least temporarily. State and local government units have no way of creating money to meet their needs; hence their demand is similar in many respects to that of the private sectors (business and consumers) discussed in Chapter 7.

Foreign demand includes borrowing by foreign firms and official agencies from American individuals and financial institutions, marketing of foreign securities in U.S. money and capital markets, and also the direct investment made by U.S. firms and individuals in branches and subsidiaries abroad. Because direct foreign investment, like domestic direct investment, does not channel funds into a money or capital market, direct investment may be excluded when the market for loanable funds is discussed.

Foreign countries constitute sources of *supply* of loanable funds as well as sources of demand. Foreign individuals, institutions, firms, and governments invest in the U.S. money and capital markets and supply funds to certain types of financial institutions. Because neither foreign demand nor foreign supply of loanable funds has been discussed thus far, both are treated in this chapter.

Government and foreign demand for loanable funds are important because they frequently fluctuate widely, sometimes tripling in one or two years, and then decline again to small fractions of the peak amounts. For example, in 1969 it was estimated that government and foreign demands for loanable funds totaled only $9.9 billion, whereas in 1971 it was estimated that they totaled $44.4 billion and in 1976 it was estimated that they totaled $68 billion. (These figures exclude foreign demand in the form of sales of equities, for which data are not readily available.) Thus government and foreigners are important elements in demand, having a more than proportionate effect upon interest rates because of their wide fluctuations.

# STATE AND LOCAL GOVERNMENT DEMAND FOR LOANABLE FUNDS

Like other sectors, state and local government units borrow because available receipts are not sufficient to meet desired expenditures, and future receipts must be expected to provide the funds to repay debt over a period during which assets purchased with the aid of borrowing will continue to provide services.

## Why State and Local Government Units Borrow

State and local government units have provided in increasing amounts services that require capital expenditures—highways, schools, water supply facilities and sewers, electric utilities (except where these are supplied by private companies), airports, parks, and others. Of course, in connection with these facilities there are also current expenditures: highway maintenance, salaries of teachers and school administrators, and so on. The ratio of capital expenditures to total expenditures of state and local government units was quite stable, at approximately 26 percent since World War I; both have grown at an annual rate of about 5½ percent in real terms. This is somewhat higher than the average annual growth of real GNP because the growth of the automobile and airplane industries, the trend toward urbanization, and the trend toward a greater number of years of education for the average person have caused state and local government expenditures to increase at a rapid pace.[1]

Until the mid-1970s, state and local government spending, and hence their borrowing, could be forecast by simple time series trend extrapolation. Complex theory and regression formulas were hardly worthwhile. But after the mid-1970s, the increase in spending by state and local governments was less. One formula included the following as basic determinants of state and local government spending: real spendable earnings of the average worker times average annual employment, federal grants-in-aid to state and local governments in real terms, and Moody's Aaa municipal bond yield adjusted for the inflation rate. Real take-home pay times the average employment was used instead of total real disposable personal income because the latter includes items such as food stamps that are not likely to be related to ability and willingness to pay for services of state and local governments (either through taxes or through user fees). Correlation of spending with the interest rate was positive, perhaps because rising interest income enables people to buy more services, and this offsets the negative effect of rising interest costs on spending by state and local governments.[2] Clearly, reduced federal taxes would tend to increase state and local spending, reduced federal grants-in-aid would tend to reduce it, and inflation would tend to increase nominal spending.

Borrowing by state and local governments suddenly began to accelerate in the mid-1970s, and in the early 1980s it increased sharply. Most of the increase was in revenue bonds rather than in general obligation bonds. General obligation bonds have traditionally been issued for capital purposes such as construction of schools, hospitals, and prisons—generally, public institutions. But revenue bonds have been used for power generation, housing, and in some cases, industrial development. Revenue bonds usually have not been subject to voter approval, because revenues from the

---

[1] Occasionally, expenditures other than construction expenditures—such as veterans' bonuses, welfare benefits, and disaster relief—have been financed by borrowing, but the long-run average of such borrowing is small.

[2] Dale Allman and Dan M. Bechter, "State and Local Governments: Their Stake in Federal Budget Reform," Federal Reserve Bank of Kansas City, *Economic Review*, November 1981, pp. 20–27.

projects have been expected to provide the funds for repayment. (An initiative in the state of Washington, requiring voter approval for further issues of bonds by the Washington Public Power Supply System, is an exception.) At the same time, groups that traditionally have purchased "municipal" (state and local government) bonds have been somewhat less numerous (for example, tax cuts reduced the number of persons in the highest tax brackets, who have traditionally bought large amounts of municipal bonds to obtain the tax exemption). The result has been fewer buyers and more issuers, and hence a rise in municipal bond yields relative to those on taxable bonds. The problem is discussed more thoroughly in Chapter 10.

## Debt Limitations

State and local government units defaulted on debts on a number of occasions in depressions in the 1830s, 1870s, 1890s, and 1930s and on some other occasions. In many cases there was poor planning of capital expenditures. These defaults resulted in limitations on bases for borrowing, amounts of debt, and/or terms and conditions of borrowing; frequently these limitations were incorporated in state constitutions and other basic legislation.

Efforts to avoid the debt limitation provisions, as they could not easily be eliminated from state constitutions, were made by creating special agencies to construct and operate certain facilities. Revenues from use of these facilities were to constitute the source of repayment of the debt and payment of interest on the debt. Nonguaranteed debt has also been issued, partly to avoid debt limitations, since courts often ruled that the limitations applied only to fully guaranteed debt. In many cases, however, nonguaranteed debt is in effect guaranteed: the state is likely to provide aid for a facility before the agency defaults on its debt, or it is likely to make good on defaulted issues. Thus, the use of agency debt and nonguaranteed debt has resulted in higher interest costs, but the debt could be issued in this manner where it could not otherwise be issued because of the debt limitation provisions.[3]

## Interest Elasticity of Borrowing by State and Local Government Units

Recent periods of high interest rates have provided some evidence that borrowing by state and local government units is sensitive to changes in interest rates. The borrowing process is rather lengthy. After an initial decision to borrow, it may be necessary to have a vote by the legislature or a referendum vote by the citizens, and thereafter bids may be sought from investment bankers for the authorized issue of securities. These are cumbersome procedures that take considerable time. Credit crunches in 1966 and again in 1969 resulted in reduction or abandonment of planned

---

[3] See William E. Mitchell, "The Effectiveness of Debt Limits on State and Local Government Borrowing," New York University, *Bulletin*, No. 45, October 1967.

borrowing in a number of cases, although it is not entirely clear whether financing of the projects was prevented or simply delayed by these conditions.[4]

Demand for loanable funds by state and local government units may be influenced by anticipated availability of the supply of loanable funds. State and local government securities have the almost unique feature that the interest income on them is exempt from federal income tax.[5] Because of this feature, their yields are relatively low, and hence they are sold almost exclusively to those who pay relatively high rates of federal income tax—high-income individuals, commercial banks, and property and casualty insurance companies (many of which are stock companies, not mutuals, and hence pay a high tax rate) constitute the major sources of demand for these securities. All other holders hold less than 10 percent of the total outstanding. Demand from these groups may vary; in some years, banks may have had enough tax-exempt income from other sources, or demand for loans may be so great that they may not wish to or be able to buy many municipals. Hence yields on municipals have tended to vary.

State and local governments in the past have generally had balanced budgets, or budgets close to being balanced. But in recent years, the situation has varied. In some years, and especially in some states and cities, financial problems have been serious—New York City in the early 1970s was one such example. In other years, state and local governments, taken as a whole, have had surpluses (Table 2–1 in Chapter 2 shows that in 1981 they had a surplus of nearly $32 billion, offsetting a little more than half the federal government deficit).

With the increase in the issue of revenue bonds has come a change in interest elasticity: state and local governments have been willing to pay higher interest rates on revenue bonds because they are not often limited by specific provisions of state laws or constitutions and partly because, since the revenues are used for revenue-producing projects, the rates that can be paid nearly approach the higher rates that corporate borrowers would pay.

It should be evident that the changed conditions have created a new situation: average yields on municipals have been rising and rising, not only absolutely (as has been true of most interest rates), but relative to Treasury securities yields. This rise has occurred for long-term issues only; yields on short-term issues have risen, but no more than have yields on Treasury securities.

The problem of the rapidly rising cost of financing cost of state and local government debt, and its apparent lack of the once normal interest rate sensitivity, is discussed in more detail in Chapter 10.

---

[4] John E. Petersen, "Response of State and Local Governments to Varying Credit Conditions," *Federal Reserve Bulletin*, March 1971, reported surveys indicating that about one-third of planned state and local government long-term borrowing was canceled because of tight money in 1969–1970. However, more than half the funds they had planned to raise through long-term borrowing was raised through short-term borrowing, not subject to legal interest rate ceilings.

[5] For special reasons, stocks issued by some private utilities have had this characteristic, in whole or in part, but this situation is changing and the number of such stocks on which dividends are not fully taxed is declining sharply.

# FEDERAL GOVERNMENT DEMAND FOR LOANABLE FUNDS

Government lending agencies were mentioned in Chapter 4, in discussion of the various institutions that act as intermediaries in *supplying* loanable funds. The major impact of the government, however, is in its role as a *demander* of loanable funds. There is presumed to be no interest elasticity in government demand; government does not vary its borrowing as interest rates rise and fall, but borrows whatever is needed to meet any gap between spending based on authorizations and appropriations and revenues based on current tax rates. Government borrowing is based on budget plans that combine decisions to continue present government programs, decisions based on the desirability of new programs as viewed by Congress, and fiscal policy decisions to spend more or less than is expected to be received in tax and other revenues. Because tax and spending decisions are not fully coordinated, results may be less than optimum. Questions of fiscal policy are explored in Chapter 17. The present concern is with how the process works and how the amount to be borrowed is determined.

## The Budget Process

The budgetary cycle in the United States is far from simple. It has been estimated that the total time elapsing from budgetary planning in agencies and departments to the final development of the budget is about 27 months.[6] The president's budget message is usually delivered to Congress in late January of each year, presenting the proposed budget for the fiscal year beginning the next October 1. The government's fiscal year, which formerly began on July 1, was changed in 1976 to begin on October 1, so that Congress might complete action on appropriations and its own final budget resolution prior to the beginning of the fiscal year. The period from January to July 1 was hardly long enough for this to occur.

Any new activity for which spending is proposed must be authorized by legislation, passed by appropriate committees of the House and Senate and approved by the president or allowed by him to become law without his signature. Legislation authorizing an activity is customarily followed by a bill appropriating money for the activity, although authorization and appropriation may be included in the same legislation. Tax bills must, under the Constitution, originate in the House of Representatives, and by custom appropriation bills also originate there. They are first considered by the Appropriations Committee of the House. Some programs are long term or permanent and do not require annual authorization, whereas others require authorization and appropriations each year. Sometimes authority is given to spend money from borrowed funds. Authority to spend money, enter into contracts, or borrow money is given in legislation providing what has been termed "new obligational authority." If

---

[6] Jesse Burkhead, *Government Budgeting* (New York: John Wiley, 1956), p. 106.

the authorization is to spend borrowed money, no further legislation is needed. Some government loan programs operate in this way. It is expected that the funds used will be borrowed and will then revolve as loans are made and repaid. Often Congress authorizes spending greater amounts than are actually spent in a given year, and there is often a carryover of obligational authority.

Authorizations and appropriations are considered singly or in groups, but until recently there was no mechanism to force Congress to consider the entire process and its result. Legislation in 1974 established a Congressional Budget Office and Budget Committees in the House and Senate. It also specified that Congress must enact a preliminary resolution specifying budget targets on May 15 of each year and a final resolution on September 15.[7] The result has been and, it is hoped, will continue to be better control by Congress over total spending and taxing and, thus, over borrowing. Before 1975, Congress often voted specific tax or spending changes, which then almost precluded other changes that might have been more desirable but were not acted upon because Congress had no process of overall review of taxing, spending, and borrowing. For example, Social Security benefits were increased approximately 20 percent in 1972 and another 11 percent in 1974. The accompanying increase in Social Security contributions meant, in effect, an increase in taxes, the proceeds to go for increased Social Security benefits.

Government departments and agencies make expenditures, subject to controls established in the legislation. Actual payment is often made after goods have been delivered and found to meet specifications, although progress payments are also common. Departments and agencies, in purchasing goods and services, usually award contracts; this is termed "incurring obligations." There may be a substantial time lag, after funds are authorized and appropriated, before funds are spent or obligations incurred. There may be another time lag before such spending affects spending by other sectors of the economy. Thus the importance of cash flow data as well as budget data is evident.

Almost all government spending takes the form of issuance of checks on the government's General Account, maintained in Federal Reserve Banks. Thus government spending reduces government deposit balances in those banks and increases private deposits in commercial banks. Because these latter are part of the money supply, the stock of money is thereby increased. Of course, it was probably previously reduced when funds were transferred from government deposits in the commercial banks to the government's General Account, to provide enough funds for expenditures.

---

[7] For further details on this process, see Joseph Scherer, "New Directions for the Federal Budget?" Federal Reserve Bank of New York, *Quarterly Review*, Spring 1977, pp. 1–10. Whether these resolutions are good indicators of final tax receipts, spending, and deficits depends to some extent on changes in real GNP and in inflation as well as on actions of Congress. See, for example, James R. Capra, "The First Concurrent Resolution and the Budget Outlook," Federal Reserve Bank of New York, *Quarterly Review*, Summer 1982, pp. 32–40.

## Measurement of Need for Borrowing:
## The Unified Budget

A preliminary measure of the need for borrowing may be gained from the unified budget that is presented to Congress, modified by congressional action, and reviewed thereafter in the midyear review.[8] The unified budget presented by the president in January and reviewed in midyear includes all government receipts and spending, including those of trust funds such as the Social Security fund. These were not included in regular budgets before 1970, and their exclusion meant that budgets presented very incomplete pictures of the fiscal situation. Lending activities are shown in a separate section of the unified budget, but only lending by government-owned agencies is included; the agencies originally established by the government but now privately owned are not included.[9] Third, it was planned that after a transitional period the unified budget would, insofar as possible, be on an accrual basis, receipts and expenditures being recorded when the obligation to pay taxes is incurred or when the obligation to spend funds is incurred.[10] Although this procedure is in accord with generally accepted accounting procedures, it makes the unified budget less than fully satisfactory as an indicator of need for borrowing, because accrued receipts do not provide a current inflow of funds and the timing of actual spending and of actual receipts may differ. For some purposes, therefore, it may still be necessary to refer to figures for government cash flows, and for some comparisons with other parts of the national income it may be necessary to refer to what has been termed the NIPA budget—national income and product account budget. Nevertheless, the unified budget figures provide a starting point for evaluating the demand for loanable funds by the federal government.

## Cash Flows, Cash Balances, and Debt

When a cash flow deficit occurs, the Treasury may draw down its cash balances or it may borrow. Historically, the government could print money (noninterest-bearing government debt), but this power is now restricted.[11] Because spending of receipts from borrowing from the Federal Reserve System has effects similar to those resulting from printing and spending of money, this type of borrowing also is re-

---

[8] The midyear review (actually late in the summer, usually), although not nearly as much publicized as the January budget, is a better indicator of the fiscal situation of the government, because it incorporates both the actions by Congress (or most of them) and the changes that occurred in the economic situation, which may not all have been anticipated in January.

[9] These privately owned credit agencies represent another category of institutions constituting a demand for loanable funds, but they are not separately discussed in this chapter.

[10] Not all items are on an accrual basis, because of some difficulties encountered in estimating accruals.

[11] The last time that the government was authorized to print fiat money was in the Thomas amendment to the Agricultural Adjustment Act in 1933; this act authorized the issue of a maximum of $3 billion in "greenbacks," but the power was not used.

stricted to special circumstances. Thus the government generally must borrow whether from the general public, including nonbank financial institutions, or from commercial banks. Effects may differ. If the Treasury sells new securities to commercial banks, commercial banks may be permitted to pay for the securities by crediting Tax and Loan account deposit balances of the government, rather than by reducing their own cash holdings. The banks may even be excused in wartime from holding reserves for the increased deposits. In such cases, an automatic supply of loanable funds exists to meet the demand for loanable funds by the government, and effects in the loanable funds market on interest rates and on other borrowers do not occur directly. If the Treasury sells new securities to commercial banks, but the banks must pay for these by reducing cash balances, the ultimate effects depend upon the monetary policy of the central bank, to be discussed in Chapter 16. Excluding these special cases, Treasury borrowing from the general public means that an additional demand is added to the demand of the private sectors, or perhaps causes some shifts in their demand. Because the Treasury must borrow what is needed to meet the budget deficit, except for such adjustments as it may make in its cash balances, it is presumed that the amount of borrowing by the federal government is not affected by interest rates.

## The Debt Ceiling and the Interest Rate Ceiling

In an effort to control the volume of federal debt, Congress has imposed a ceiling on the public debt. This has had little effect, however; unlike the ceilings on debt of state and local governments, which forced them to use other means of raising funds, the ceiling on the federal debt has simply been raised by Congress when necessary. This is because Congress recognizes that it is responsible for tax receipts and appropriations and therefore also is responsible for any deficit that arises when receipts fall short of expenditures. The chief effect of the ceiling has been to increase the burden on the Treasury, since action to raise the debt limit is seldom taken until the limit is nearly reached, and the Treasury may have problems in determining amounts and types of debt to be issued at such times.

Congress also imposed a ceiling on the coupon interest rate on bonds at the time of World War I. At first 3½ percent, it was raised to 4¼ percent in 1918.[12] Bonds may be of any maturity, but are typically issued with a maturity of at least five years. The maximum permissible coupon rate, 4¼ percent per year, has been too low in recent years to permit issue of such bonds, unless they were to be sold below par so that the effective yield could be more than 4¼ percent.[13] The rise in yields on long-term bonds above the 4¼ percent ceiling rate beginning in 1965 is shown in Figure

[12] On the details of the debt and bond interest rate ceilings, see Michael J. Prell, "The Treasury Debt and Bond Rate Ceilings," Federal Reserve Bank of Kansas City, *Monthly Review*, April 1971, pp. 9–16.

[13] Some exemptions were made so that some bonds have been issued at higher coupon rates. But bonds now constitute less than one-eighth of marketable federal government debt and less than one tenth of total federal government debt.

FIGURE 8–1
**Yields on Selected Long-Term Securities, 1950–1973; Monthly Averages of Daily Interest Rate Figures**

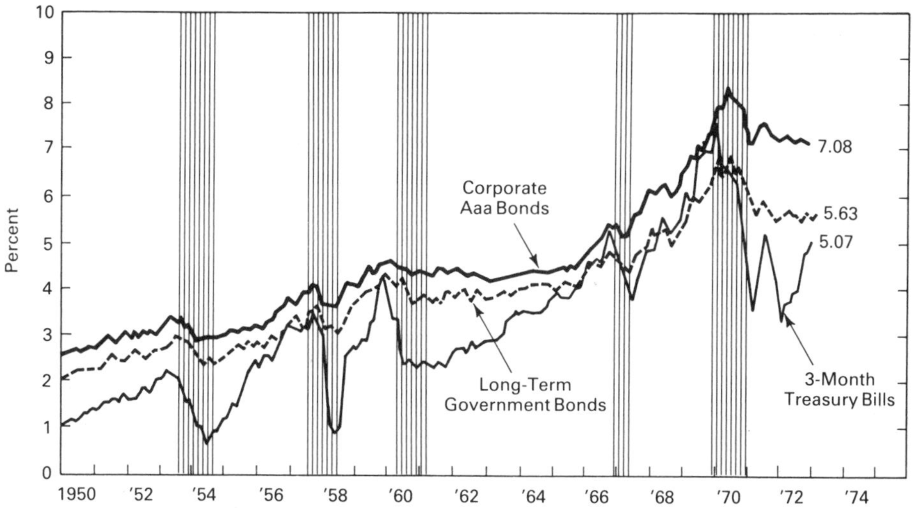

SOURCE: Federal Reserve Bank of St. Louis, *Review,* January 1973, p. 3.

8–1. That figure shows the gradual rise of yields on corporate Aaa bonds from about 4 percent in the early 1960s to about 7 percent in the early 1970s, as inflation continued. Some, including Robert Kennedy when he was attorney general, argued that bonds could be issued at a discount, but in general the Treasury has preferred not to do this because it would be against the spirit, if not the letter, of the law. Thus the practical effect of the interest rate ceiling was to cause the Treasury to issue types of securities other than bonds. In 1971, Congress authorized the Treasury to issue $10 billion in bonds without regard to the 4¼ percent ceiling and by 1982 this amount had been raised to $110 billion. The first issue under this authorization was a 10-year 7 percent offered in July 1971. By 1982, $75.6 billion of outstanding bonds carried coupon rates exceeding 4¼ percent, but total bonds outstanding constituted less than one-seventh of total marketable government debt, in contrast to nearly half such debt in 1965.

Congress also redefined notes so as to change their maximum maturity, which had been 5 years, to 10 years. Subsequently, a number of issues of notes were offered by the Treasury. Treasury bills and notes now constitute the major U.S. government debt instruments. Thus the major effect of the interest rate ceiling has been to shift more borrowing so that it is carried out through the issue of short-term and intermediate-term securities. This has resulted in definite shortening of the average maturity of the federal debt and some problems in "rolling over" a large amount of such debt every year.

Readers should note in Figure 8–1 a regular pattern usually present before the high inflation of the late 1970s and early 1980s. Short-term interest rates (such as the rate on Treasury bills, shown in that figure) were usually below long-term rates, but rose above them at peaks of business activity, especially after 1960. Yields on both corporate and government bonds rose to nearly 13 percent; short-term rates rose much higher—the Treasury bill rate to over 16 percent and the prime rate to 20 percent.

As short-term rates fell in the spring of 1980, it was generally agreed that recession, forecast by many as early as the spring of 1979, had indeed begun. It also seemed that a third decline in the rate of inflation was beginning (inflation had declined from 6 percent to about 3 percent in 1969–1971, and from about 12 percent to about 6 percent in 1974–1976). The third time was the charm! The change in Federal Reserve policy from a money supply target affected through interest rates to a money supply target affected through bank reserves, announced in autumn 1979, was beginning to be effective, and inflation gradually fell to a very low level in the mid-1980s.

# FOREIGN DEMAND FOR AND SUPPLY OF LOANABLE FUNDS

Foreign demand for and supply of loanable funds remain to be considered. In the absence of barriers to international capital movements, funds would presumably flow into foreign financing on the same basis that they flow into domestic use: relative yields in relation to safety and liquidity. Thus foreign countries and their residents compete for loanable funds on the same basis as sectors of the domestic economy; that is, interest rates paid or rates of return earned must be comparable with U.S. domestic rates, commensurate with the degrees of risk and liquidity in the types of loans and investments made in foreign securities and industries.

Much foreign investment is direct investment. An American firm builds a branch plant abroad, buys a controlling interest in a foreign company, or establishes a new foreign subsidiary by direct investment. In a sense this may be considered to be a foreign demand for loanable funds, and certainly it is likely to reduce the supply of loanable funds otherwise available in the U.S. domestic markets. However, such investment is usually made at the initiative of the investing firm, which sends funds overseas in making the investment. Such flows of funds are not directly reflected in supply or demand in the loanable funds market in this country. Although the volume of direct investment is significant and has important effects, it is not part of foreign supply of and demand for loanable funds in the U.S. money and capital markets.

Foreign demand for long-term loanable funds is expressed directly in sales of foreign stocks and bonds in the American market. Purchases of these securities represent long-term portfolio investment by American investors; part of the supply of loanable funds is thus diverted to meet foreign demand.

If, for the moment, it is assumed that imports and exports of goods and services are equal in value, it is evident that any net direct or portfolio investment in foreign capital assets or securities provides funds to foreign countries or their residents. They hold these funds for the moment in the form of short-term dollar balances. An increase in such balances represents an increase in current liabilities in the U.S. balance of payments.[14] Such an increase and/or a loss of international reserve assets such as gold was termed a deficit in the balance of payments because it represented a reduction in the ratio of reserve assets to current liabilities and, thus, reduced ability to meet such current liabilities if foreigners asked for other reserve assets instead of dollar deposits. The decline in this ratio, when it occurred, was regarded as undesirable and measures were often taken to limit such deficits when they continued or were sizable.[15]

The shift from fixed parities for exchange rates for the major industrial countries to "floating" rates in 1973 changed the situation with respect to deficits. Presumably, if exchange rates are permitted to float upward or downward, deficits or surpluses in the balance of payments may be rectified by such changes, and therefore countries need not give much attention to such imbalances. In recent years, moreover, it has become increasingly difficult to make some of the distinctions necessary in determining the amounts of deficits or surpluses. For example, long-term investments, nonliquid short-term loans and investments, and private loans and investments are generally regarded as being motivated by desire for income and, hence, not settlement items and not constituting either surpluses or deficits. On the other hand, short-term liquid loans and investments and government holdings of foreign assets have been regarded as settlement items, made for the purpose of settling balances due. But short-term loans are frequently renewed, becoming long-term loans; liquid loans may become illiquid; and funds deposited in the United States by OPEC governments may well be held for income purposes rather than simply being held as balances received in settlement of oil payments.

For the foregoing and other reasons, the President's Advisory Committee on the Presentation of Balance of Payments Statistics suggested in the spring of 1976 that traditional deficit and surplus figures no longer be published. Even the so-called "basic balance" should not be published, this committee held. Although some of these balances can still be calculated from published figures, their omission from publication presumably leads readers to put less emphasis on them.[16]

## Controls on Foreign Loans and Investments

Because both direct and portfolio investment increased rapidly in the 1960s, foreigners acquired large amounts of dollar holdings. Because foreign individuals and private foreign institutions were not permitted to convert their dollar holdings into

---

[14] It is useful to think of the balance of payments as being in three main parts: (1) imports and exports of goods and services, (2) flows of loans and investments out of and into the country, and (3) the net flow of settlement items or reserve assets (gold, dollar bank balances, etc.) necessary to balance total flows.

[15] The precise nature of a deficit must be specified, however, and it must be shown that that particular deficit is detrimental before there is justification for such actions. See John Pippenger, "Balance-of-Payments Deficits: Measurement and Interpretation," Federal Reserve Bank of St. Louis, *Review*, November 1973, pp. 6–14.

[16] See Janice M. Westerfield, "A Lower Profile for the U.S. Balance of Payments," Federal Reserve Bank of Philadelphia, *Business Review*, November–December 1976, pp. 11–17. The basic balance is the balance of current account items plus long-term investment items.

gold, official holdings of dollars were deemed more significant as a potential claim on U.S. gold holdings. During the 1960s, efforts were made to reduce foreign demand for loanable funds (or alternatively the supply of loanable funds to foreign investment) by (1) placing an interest equalization tax (IET) on purchases of foreign securities to reduce the amount of such investment, (2) introducing a voluntary program of controls on bank loans to foreign companies and residents, and (3) starting a mandatory program of control to limit direct investment by American firms.[17]

These controls remained in effect for some time, but in early 1974 they were all eliminated. Thus the United States returned to its traditional position of relative freedom from controls on international loans and investments. The action followed readjustments of currency values, discussed in the following paragraphs, and was expected in the long run to encourage both an outflow of loans and investment from the United States and investment in the United States by foreigners. With removal of controls, foreigners would have less need for concern that at some time controls might prevent them from withdrawing funds that they had invested.

In late 1979, when the U.S. embassy in Teheran was seized and personnel were held hostages, the U.S. government "froze" assets of the Iranian government and of Iranian government agencies held in the United States. There was some concern that this might be regarded as a precedent for other similar actions, thus changing the traditional policy of free flow of capital into and out of the United States, except for enemy nations in wartime. However, the special circumstances in this rather unusual case were recognized by most outside observers.

## A New International Monetary System

In spite of these programs, foreign holdings of dollars continued to rise, and, as these holdings were transferred to foreign governments, U.S. gold holdings declined when foreign governments converted dollar holdings into gold. A sharp outflow of gold in August 1971 and a concomitant rise in foreign official dollar holdings triggered the closing of the "gold window," the announcement by President Nixon that gold would no longer be available to foreign official holders of dollars.[18] Foreign governments, therefore, as well as foreign individuals and private institutions, had to decide whether or not, in view of this action, they wished to continue to accumulate dollar balances. As individuals sold unwanted dollar balances, foreign official holdings of

---

[17] The IET was enacted in 1964, the VFCR (voluntary foreign credit restraint) program was begun in 1964, and the mandatory control on direct investment was instituted in 1968. Controls on bank lending to foreign countries and business firms were again being discussed in the early 1980s. For a discussion of some of the problems of such lending (and the need for it) see William J. Gasser and David L. Roberts, "Bank Lending to Developing Countries: Problems and Prospects," Federal Reserve Bank of New York, *Quarterly Review*, Autumn 1982, pp. 18–29.

[18] Mention should be made of the role played in this episode by the holdings of Eurodollars abroad. Eurodollars are dollars held outside the United States, for example, in the form of Eurodollar deposits in European banks. Those who held such deposits, including multinational firms, could quickly and easily transfer them into a currency they felt might appreciate in value, and those who received dollars in excess of desired holdings sold them to central banks.

dollars increased. The only solution was the refusal to purchase dollars—which meant that the values of foreign currencies, in countries in which this occurred, rose relative to the value of the dollar. Thus the result was the upward revaluation of a number of European currencies and of the Japanese yen.[19]

When total U.S. foreign spending for goods, services, loans, and investments exceeds similar spending by foreigners in the United States, foreigners accumulate liquid assets in the form of dollar balances. Under some circumstances, such as those existing for a time after World War II, foreign countries may desire to accumulate liquid assets in the form of dollar balances, because they may feel that their reserves of such assets are insufficient. When liquid balances exceed desired amounts, however, foreigners either spend such balances for U.S. exports or try to convert them into some basic international reserve assets such as gold, or into other currencies such as marks.

Early in 1973, dollar balances held by foreigners again were used to purchase marks, gold, and other assets that seemed likely to rise in value. After acquiring a substantial amount of dollars, the German central bank felt that further effort to hold down the mark was not warranted. After international consultations the dollar was again devalued, the price of gold being raised to $42.22 per fine ounce. The German mark was revalued upward, in terms of gold, by 3 percent, and major currencies were permitted to float in relation to the dollar. The pound sterling and the lira were also permitted to float relative to other major currencies, but the other Common Market currencies were to be kept within limits of 2¼ percent relative to each other.

Further reform of the international monetary system was obviously needed. Without discussing in detail the many specific problems, it is clear that arrangements were needed with respect to coordination of financial policies of major nations, the degree of flexibility to be permitted in exchange rates, the need for surplus nations as well as deficit nations to make adjustments, the specific events that might trigger such adjustments, the role of gold and "paper gold" as international reserve assets, and the question of convertibility of dollars into gold, paper gold, or some other asset.[20]

One stage in reform was completed and formalized in the Jamaica agreement reached by a committee of the IMF in early 1976. In this agreement, a new section was authorized for the IMF charter. The new section provided that countries might use floating rates of exchange or other policies instead of being required to establish

---

[19] Countries were pressured to revalue their currencies upward by a U.S. tax on most imports, but this tax was removed when upward revaluations occurred.

[20] "Paper gold," or more technically "special drawing rights" (SDRs) were created in 1970–1972 by the International Monetary Fund (IMF) and distributed to member countries in accordance with quotas. SDRs, at first fixed in value in terms of gold, added to world liquidity, which was believed to be insufficient because of the rapid rise in world trade and payments and the slow rise in monetary gold holdings. A second series of SDR allocations was made in 1979–1981, this time partly because of maldistribution of reserve assets. SDRs are used primarily for settlements among central banks and are not used by the public. However, a private market in SDR-denominated instruments has developed in recent years. For SDRs to be widely used in private markets, if this were permitted, they must be attractive to hold in reducing risk, having stable value and in other ways. See Dorothy Meadow Sobol, "The SDR in Private International Finance," Federal Reserve Bank of New York, *Quarterly Review*, Winter 1981–1982, pp. 29–41.

fixed par values for their currencies. It also provided that the IMF should exercise surveillance over such policies and over internal policies when funds were loaned by the IMF, to ensure their appropriateness. At the same time, steps were taken to enlarge the lending ability of the IMF. Finally, it was provided that member countries of the IMF, by an 85 percent majority vote, might at some date vote to reestablish a stable but adjustable par value system for exchange rates.[21]

Thus, for the time being, countries were to be permitted to adopt separate policies, but fixed par values remained as a future possibility. Essentially, the question is whether floating exchange rates for major currencies will prove disruptive or can be managed through central bank intervention so that they will not disrupt international commerce and finance. In any event, the changes resulting in the later 1970s from the huge oil price increases of 1973 were so great that it was not clear what par values would have been appropriate, even had it been decided to restore stable but adjustable par values at that time.

Essentially, excessive creation of U.S. dollars and their shift to holders outside the United States, together with rapid growth in real output and moderate inflation in such countries as West Germany and Japan, led to a need to change the international monetary system. With the great rise in oil prices, it was not clear that correct new par values could be identified, and a period of floating exchange rates was therefore agreed upon. At the same time gold was reduced in importance as a reserve asset, leaving somewhat of a vacuum. Dollars were plentiful, but, with rapid inflation in the United States, dollars were not very satisfactory as a store of value. Gold became again a store of value for some of the public.

European countries did not like the instability in exchange rates among their countries. If the European Community (EC) was one large market, it really should have one currency. A step in that direction was taken in 1979 with the establishment of the European Monetary System. A European currency unit (ECU) was devised, a bookkeeping unit with a value determined by that of a basket of the various EC currencies. A European Monetary Cooperation Fund (EMCF) was established to promote stabilization of rates among the EC currencies. Credit facilities were also provided for the same purpose. The intent was to coordinate policies of EC countries and stabilize exchange rates among them, with only small fluctuations.[22] Fluctuations among the EC currencies, the U.S. dollar, the yen, and other major currencies would not be eliminated, but regional stability might be attained.

## Problems in the Mid-1980s

In the 1980s, the U.S. current account deficit increased dramatically. This deficit had to be, and was, offset by a large capital account surplus, arising as foreigners were willing to invest in the United States. The United States was able to

---

[21] Text of the new section, or article, of the IMF agreement or charter is found in the *IMF Survey*, January 19, 1976, pp. 20–21.

[22] *IMF Survey*, March 19, 1979, Supplement.

finance a huge current account deficit and at the same time have a strong rise in the dollar until the mid-1980s. Foreigners' willingness to invest in the United States was caused in part by relatively high interest rates in the United States for a time (as people seemed to fear continued or renewed inflation) and in part by the attitude of foreigners that the United States was a relatively safe place for investment.

A fundamental cause of problems was the fact that United States saving was not sufficient to finance the rise in business activity in the United States and the huge budget deficits simultaneously.

When the dollar began, in the mid-1980s, to fall in relation to the yen and to major European currencies, foreigners still seemed to be willing to acquire dollar investments. In part, this may have been caused by the dramatic rise in both bond and stock markets in the United States, as the fall in inflation after 1980 led investors to shift from "real" investments (land, houses, gold, etc.) to financial assets.

The dollar, however, did not decline vis-à-vis all currencies. It *appreciated* against the Canadian dollar and against currencies of Latin American and Asiatic LDCs (less developed countries). Such LDCs—Mexico is the obvious example— have serious problems. Some fall in the dollar was desirable, since increased U.S. exports were desirable. More U.S. saving was needed, more rapid growth in other major industrial countries was needed, and many LDCs needed current account surpluses to permit them to reduce their international debt.

### The Long-Run Outlook

Direct controls on imports or on foreign loans and investments are not desirable; such controls could make the problems of trade imbalances, international debt, and currency fluctuations worse. Yet some are likely to favor such controls if problems continue.

Signs of improvement—the fall in the dollar if it does not go too far, an increase in U.S. saving, continued decline in U.S. interest rates (moderately), signs of increased economic growth in major European countries, and less exposure of U.S. banks to defaults on international loans relative to U.S. bank capital—all tend to suggest that over time the imbalances are likely to moderate.

The long-run outlook depended on avoidance of supposed "quick cures" such as import controls and continuation of patient attempts to achieve progress in reducing U.S. budget deficits relative to saving, encouraging growth in Europe, and helping LDCs in economic readjustment (aided by *some* additional financing).

## SUMMARY

State and local government units borrow primarily to finance capital expenditures for construction. At the end of World War II, state and local government units were, on a *net* basis, out of debt. Past defaults resulted in strict limitations on state and local government borrowing. The limitations, in turn, led to efforts to evade them, by creating special agencies to operate facilities and to borrow funds for construction.

Because interest income on state and local government securities is exempt from the federal income tax, these securities are bought chiefly by high-income individuals, commercial banks, property and casualty insurance companies, and some other less important groups. When interest rates are high, commercial banks and some other purchasers are likely to be relatively short of funds. The market for state and local government securities may be "thin."

Federal government borrowing, unlike that of state and local government units, is presumed *not* to be interest elastic. Government borrowing need not weigh cost versus expected return, although the Treasury may try to reduce cost of debt. A preliminary measure of the need for government borrowing is to be found in the unified budget. Cash flows are a more accurate indicator of need, but the government may to some extent vary its cash balances. Congress imposed a ceiling on federal debt, but this has simply been raised when necessary. It has had little effect except to create inconveniences when debt approached the ceiling. Congress also imposed a ceiling on the coupon interest rate on bonds, although later a significant amount was exempted from the ceiling. This ceiling could be evaded by selling bonds at a discount, but the Treasury has disliked this alternative. Instead, the Treasury has issued some intermediate-term debt at rates higher than the ceiling rate on bond interest and has financed heavily through short-term issues.

Foreign demand for *loanable funds* has generally been a relatively small part of total demand, although much *direct* investment by American firms abroad has occurred. Because the investment outflow was not matched by corresponding increase in net U.S. exports or by net foreign long-term investment in the United States, foreign countries accumulated large dollar balances and substantial amounts of gold until President Nixon "closed the gold window" on August 15, 1971. Increases in gold and dollar balances held by foreigners are termed a "deficit" in the U.S. balance of payments. Various measures were taken in the 1960s to reduce deficits by restricting investment and payments abroad. Two devaluations of the dollar followed, raising the official price of gold. The free market price of gold in foreign countries soared far above the official price level. Major foreign industrialized countries permitted values of their currencies to "float" upward, to reduce dollar balances held by their central banks.

It was anticipated that changes in exchange rates and international monetary reform would result in increased U.S. exports and increased long-term investment in the United States by foreign countries. Increase in supply of loanable funds in the United States would follow. Slower increase in liquid dollar balances held by foreign countries would permit a more orderly functioning of the international monetary system. Large accumulations of gold and dollars by oil producing nations, arising from the energy crisis and actions of such nations, added a complicating factor. Major central banks agreed that they were free, beginning in late 1973, to sell gold, thus potentially reducing the role of gold in the international monetary system. However, adverse effects of the energy crisis on Europe and Japan and resulting declines in values of their currencies made gold and dollars again seem to be of continuing importance. The huge rise in foreign central bank holdings of dollars in the period

1971–1973, as foreign private holders sold dollars to their central banks once it was clear that dollars could not be converted into gold, made it unlikely that SDRs could become a major international reserve asset. It seemed probable that, for some time to come, dollars would be the chief such asset, with gold diminishing in importance as the IMF and some countries sold some part of their gold holdings.

The importance of gold in its role in the international monetary system has in fact been much reduced by these actions. But the continued inflation, reducing the purchasing power of many currencies, has led to a search by some among the public in various countries for a hedge against inflation. Some have found it in gold, and, by the late 1970s, the demand for gold had pushed its price well above $400 per ounce, in contrast to the $35 an ounce of the 1947–1971 period. The price of gold was very volatile, rising above $800 per ounce at one time, then falling below $500, then rising above $600 again, then falling to about $400.

More rapid inflation in a particular country, such as the United States, means more rapid loss of purchasing power for the dollar and, therefore, in the long run, a decline in its value in the foreign exchange market. Two other factors affect this value: changes in relative interest rates lead to capital flows to countries in which interest rates are relatively higher, and anticipation of developments affecting purchasing power and interest rates leads to speculative purchases and sales of currencies in the foreign exchange market. A decline in the value of the U.S. dollar, resulting from these factors, is much more serious than a decline in the values of some other currencies, because so many dollars are widely held as stores of value. Yet they are not good stores of value if their values fall drastically. In the late 1970s competition raged between gold and dollars as stores of value. The dollar won as inflation in the United States was slowed down.

Speculative factors led to a sharp decline in the foreign exchange value of the U.S. dollar in late 1978. The U.S. Treasury and Federal Reserve System announced a series of actions designed to stabilize the value of the dollar, and, as actions were taken and trade deficits declined somewhat, the dollar did for a time stabilize. But in the autumn of 1979, after rapid inflation in the United States all year, the dollar declined again. At that point the Federal Reserve System announced major policy changes, discussed in Chapter 16, designed to control inflation. The major change was the announcement that greater attention would be given to money supply figures and to bank reserves that are the major part of the monetary base supporting the money supply. *Finally* a *real* effort was made to control U.S. inflation; this effort succeeded more quickly than many anticipated, reducing inflation rates to moderate levels by 1982.

Nevertheless, serious international economic problems continued in the mid-1980s, as indicated.

## Questions for Discussion

**1.** Why does the federal government depend heavily on short-term borrowing, whereas state and local government units use short-term borrowing only rarely?

**2.** Why are commercial banks so important as purchasers of state and local government securities?

**3.** What are the arguments for and against the exemption of income on state and local government securities from the federal income tax?

**4.** Households and commercial banks are the major purchasers of federal government debt. Why?

**5.** Show how divergence between federal government receipts and expenditures has an impact on bank reserves.

**6.** What might be the effects if Congress repealed the ceiling on interest rates on government bonds?

**7.** Evaluate the program of controls of U.S. foreign lending and investment; did it eliminate the problem it was designed to solve?

**8.** Show how the U.S. government actions of August 15, 1971 forced an upward "float" of major foreign currencies.

**9.** Do you think that "floating" of major foreign currencies (the situation since 1973) is desirable in the long run? Why or why not?

**10.** Why is it apparently desirable for the United States to have less inflation (a lower rate of inflation) than other major industrialized countries, so that the international monetary system may work smoothly?

## Selected References

An historical review of the desirability and value of the income tax exemption for income from municipal bonds may be found in Roland I. Robinson, *Postwar Market for State and Local Government Securities* (Princeton, N.J.: Princeton University Press, 1960).

The unified budget concept is discussed in the *Report of the President's Commission on Budget Concepts* (Washington, D.C.: Government Printing Office, 1967). See also Joseph Scherer, "The Report of the President's Commission on Budget Concepts: A Review," Federal Reserve Bank of New York, *Monthly Review*, December 1967, pp. 231–238.

On federal debt and interest rate ceilings, see Ira O. Scott, Jr., *Government Securities Market* (New York: McGraw-Hill, 1965), and his bibliography on these topics, pp. 192–193.

For a relatively nontechnical discussion of the balance of payments and the international monetary mechanism, see Leland B. Yeager, *The International Monetary Mechanism* (New York: Holt, Rinehart and Winston, 1968). For a discussion of the role of short-term capital movements in creating or escalating international monetary crises, see Donald L. Kohn, "Capital Flows in a Foreign Exchange Crisis," Federal Reserve Bank of Kansas City, *Monthly Review*, February 1973, pp. 14–23. Proposals for reform of the international monetary system are discussed in Norman S. Fieleke, "International Economic Reform," Federal Reserve Bank of Boston, *New England Economic Review*, January–February 1973, pp. 19–27; and in "The International Economic System in Transition," *Economic Report of the President*, January 1973, Chapter 5. The U.S. proposals for reforms, presented to the IMF in September 1972, are set forth in a supplement to Chapter 5, *Economic Report of the President*, January 1973, pp. 160–174. A convenient relatively nontechnical discussion of the situation in the early 1970s is Francis Cassell, *International Adjustment and the Dollar*, rev. ed., April 1973, Ninth District Economic Information Series, Federal Reserve Bank of Minneapolis.

For a thoughtful consideration by a leading economist of the longer-run outlook for international transactions, see Paul A. Samuelson, "International Trade for a Rich Country," *Morgan Guaranty Survey*, July 1972, pp. 3–11.

Changing interpretations of the data shown in balance-of-payments accounts may be appreciated by reading four successive articles: Norman S. Fieleke, "Accounting for the Balance of Payments," Federal Reserve Bank of Boston, *New England Economic Review*, May–June 1971, pp. 2–15; Christopher Bach and Anatol Balbach, "The New Look for the Balance of Payments," Federal Reserve Bank of St. Louis, *Review*, August 1971, pp. 8–11; John Pippenger, "Balance-of-Payments Deficits: Measurement and Interpretation," Federal Reserve Bank of St. Louis, *Review*, November 1973, pp. 6–14; and Janice M. Westerfield, "A Lower Profile for the U.S. Balance of Payments," Federal Reserve Bank of Philadelphia, *Business Review*, November–December 1976, pp. 11–17.

Exchange rate policies which now exist, since the change to floating rates by major countries in 1973, are clearly described in Nicholas Carlozzi, "Pegs and Floats: The Changing Face of the Foreign Exchange Market," Federal Reserve Bank of Philadelphia, *Business Review*, May–June 1980, pp. 13–23.

For one view of major international financial problems in the mid-1980s, see E. Gerald Corrigan, "Reducing International Imbalances in an Interdependent World," Federal Reserve Bank of New York, *Quarterly Review*, Spring 1986, pp. 1–5. For a view stressing the increasing internationalization of financial markets, see Preston Martin and Bryon Higgins, "The World Financial Scene: Balancing Risks and Rewards," Federal Reserve Bank of Kansas City, *Economic Review*, June 1986, pp. 3–9.

# THE MONEY MARKET

**IX**

Financial markets exist for initial issue and purchase of financial assets and for secondary trading. Although the term "market" may suggest trading of assets, some loans and investments are not traded or are seldom traded after the initial transaction. Interest rates on such loans and investments are interrelated with secondary market rates, and both are analyzed in this part of the book, Part Three.

The money market in which short-term funds are obtained by borrowers and in which many types of short-term financial assets are exchanged is discussed in Chapter 9. Short-term interest rates are determined in this market, and most intervention of the central bank for the purpose of implementing monetary policy also occurs in this market.

The capital markets in which bonds, mortgages, and stocks are issued and traded are discussed in Chapters 10 and 11. Chapter 10 is devoted to debt issues—bonds and mortgages—that have important primary and secondary markets. Chapter 11 is devoted to the market for stocks, or equities (securities representing *ownership*), where the focus must be on the important secondary market, because addition to the outstanding supply of equities in any year is relatively very small.

*Primary* markets enable borrowers to obtain funds, whereas *secondary* markets provide liquidity for lenders and thus induce them to lend at lower rates than they would probably require if they knew that they would be forced to hold securities or promissory notes to maturity. Not all types of financial assets have secondary markets, but, in general, secondary markets are important. In some cases, development of a primary market would be difficult if a secondary market were not developed simultaneously.

Capital markets facilitate *long-term* investment and provide a degree of liquidity for financial assets that, being long term, would not otherwise be liquid. The money market facilitates short-term financing and assures the liquidity of short-term financial assets. The money market is also the main focus of central bank activities in implementing monetary policy, although central banks do occasionally deal in the long-term government securities market. Finally, the money market is significant in indicating changes in short-term interest rates, monetary policy, and availability of short-term credit.

## DEFINITION AND NATURE OF THE MONEY MARKET

The money market is the place or mechanism whereby funds are obtained for short periods of time (from one day to one year) and financial assets representing short-term claims are exchanged. As with the capital markets, there is a primary money market, where short-term funds are obtained at varying rates, depending on the source of funds, the credit standing of the borrowers, and so on. There is also in most cases a secondary market, where financial assets representing short-term claims are traded, at rates determined by demand for and supply of short-term financial assets. Table 9–1 shows the various instruments traded in the money market.

The money market has no specific place of operation; it consists simply of the total activity of all those who lend and borrow short-term funds. Often, "money market" refers primarily to the secondary market in these assets, but the interrelationship between the secondary market and rates established in the primary market for short-term loans cannot be ignored.

The money market, at least in terms of the secondary market, is largely an over-the-telephone market. The heart of the market machinery consists of about 25 to 30 "money market" commercial banks that trade heavily in money market instruments; over three dozen government securities dealers, some of which are banks; a few commercial paper dealers and a few bankers acceptance dealers; some brokers who specialize in aiding borrowers to obtain funds and placing funds for lenders; and the Federal Reserve Bank of New York, which intervenes in the market to implement monetary policy.

Money market obligations traded in the secondary market are characterized by a very high degree of safety and are issued by borrowers of very high credit standing.

**TABLE 9-1**
**Instruments in the Money Market**

| Instruments | Typical Maturities | Principal Borrowers | Secondary Market |
|---|---|---|---|
| Federal funds | Chiefly 1 business day | Banks | None |
| Negotiable certificates of deposit (CDs) | 1, 2, 3, and 6 months | Banks | Active |
| Bankers acceptances | 90 days | Financial and business enterprises | Active |
| Eurodollars | | | |
| Time deposits (nonnegotiable) | Overnight, 1 week, and 1 to 6 months | Banks | None |
| CDs (negotiable) | 1 to 6 months | Banks | Moderately active |
| Treasury bills | 3 to 12 months | U.S. government | Very active |
| Repurchase agreements | 1 day, 1 week, 3–6 months | Banks, securities dealers, other owners of governments | Very active primary market for short maturities |
| Futures contracts (Treasury bills, CDs, and Eurodollars) | 3–18 months | Dealers, banks (users) | Active arbitrage with cash market |
| Federal agencies | | Federally sponsored agencies | |
| Discount notes | 30–360 days | Farm Credit System Federal Home Loan Banks | Limited |
| Coupon securities | 6–9 months | Federal National Mortgage Association | Active |
| Commercial paper | 30–270 days | Financial and business enterprises | Limited |
| Municipal notes | 30 days to 1 year | State and local governments | Moderately active for large issuers |

SOURCE: Paul Meek, *U.S. Monetary Policy and Financial Markets* (New York: Federal Reserve Bank of New York, 1982), p. 57.

274

Although the secondary market has no specific location, its ready accessibility by telephone makes it possible for lenders and borrowers in all parts of the country to lend and borrow funds quickly. Thus both safety and liquidity are nearly always assured. In a liquidity crisis, of course, safety and liquidity may come into question, as some types of money market instruments may not be paid at maturity, leading to questioning of the liquidity and safety of others.

The "average" or "representative" short-term interest rate on money market instruments is significant in several ways: (1) it indicates the return obtainable on those funds that lenders feel they must keep in liquid form, and its fluctuations may affect the flow of funds into liquid assets; (2) it indicates the cost of borrowing for those who need short-term funds, and, although fluctuations may not be as vital as fluctuations in the long-term rate, because short-term borrowing may be possible even at high interest rates, the cost of short-term borrowing is of some significance as an indicator of borrowing ease or difficulty; and (3) conditions in the money market are of some significance for monetary policy discussed in detail in Chapter 16.

Rates in the money market fluctuate much more widely than capital market rates. Figure 8–1 (in Chapter 8) showed the movement over time of both the average of corporate Aaa bonds (a representative capital market rate) and the average rate on three-month Treasury bills (a representative money market rate). Short-term rates usually rise when business activity rises and fall when business activity declines. A fall in sales means less need for business borrowing. However, in recent years other factors have caused interest rates to be both higher and more volatile.[1]

## ROLE OF THE MONEY MARKET

Both risk of capital losses and risk of default are minimized in the money market. Risk of capital losses is often termed *money* risk. Money risk is minimized because the financial assets are short term; hence a change in interest rates cannot affect their prices very much because the assured maturity value is discounted for only a short period. Risk of default, often termed *credit* risk, is minimized because instruments in the market, especially in the secondary market, are for the most part liabilities of the government, the central bank, and commercial banks—credit risk is small.

The importance of the money market arises from two facts: (1) the existence of an efficient money market means that short-term financial assets can almost instantly be converted into money, to make payments, and (2) the central bank operates in the money market to increase or reduce bank reserves and incidentally affects the short-term interest rates.

---

[1] In business forecasting, forecasting real GNP changes has been relatively accurate, but especially in recent years forecasting of inflation and interest rates has been much less accurate. For a discussion of the role of changes in business activity, changes in the inflation rate, changes in central bank policy, and changes in velocity of money, see "Forecasting Interest Rates: Some First Principles," *Morgan Guaranty Survey*, September 1981, pp. 1–7.

Major borrowers include the Treasury, commercial banks, securities dealers, and some nonbank financial institutions and business firms. The Treasury can obtain funds easily and often inexpensively in the short-term market.[2] Finance companies and some business firms can issue commercial paper to obtain funds for operations and inventory accumulation. Commercial banks can issue CDs and thus obtain funds for lending. Federal Reserve Banks have deposit liabilities that are traded by those owning such deposits; such trading is referred to as lending and borrowing Federal funds. Government securities dealers must borrow to finance their holdings of securities. Those who borrow on bankers acceptances because they need funds for short periods of time can usually obtain funds relatively cheaply in this manner, although high rates may be paid when it is difficult to obtain funds in other ways, such as by direct loans. Finally, commercial banks may need to borrow, temporarily, from Federal Reserve Banks.

Major lenders are commercial banks, corporations and other business firms, nonbank financial institutions, state and local governments, foreign governments, central banks, and private institutions and the Federal Reserve System. Commercial banks place funds temporarily not needed, but that may be needed to meet deposit withdrawals or bank loan demand, in money market instruments. Corporations and other business firms hold money market instruments to meet payments such as taxes, to provide for unexpected payments, or to hold temporarily funds borrowed in long-term markets for later use for investment. Nonbank financial institutions hold such instruments for the same purposes. State and local governments may have funds from taxes or borrowings that are temporarily not needed. Foreign governments, central banks, and private institutions accumulate funds from sales to U.S. firms and resident individuals and from other sources, such as sales of their own currencies to purchase dollar instruments in the foreign exchange market. Finally, the Federal Reserve System holds short-term securities, chiefly Treasury bills, but also government agency securities and bank acceptances, as a result of open market purchases.

Individuals usually did not lend significant amounts in the money market, partly because it was inconvenient for them to buy money market instruments and partly because rates frequently dropped far below long-term rates. In the 1970s, because of the very high return on money market instruments and their high degree of safety, individuals found them attractive. Many of the instruments must be purchased in relatively large amounts, but recently it has been possible for small investors to purchase money market instruments indirectly by buying shares in money market mutual funds.

A large part of total payments for dealings in the money market is made in "immediately available" funds. These are funds on deposit in Federal Reserve Banks and certain liabilities of commercial banks. The speedy transfer of such funds from the account of one bank or one customer's bank to another bank or participant in the money market is essential to the very short-term transfers involved.

---

[2] An extreme example is the low cost of short-term government financing during World War II; the yield on Treasury bills was pegged at ⅜ percent per annum.

# INSTRUMENTS AND RATES IN THE MONEY MARKET

Instruments in the money market are chiefly liabilities of government (including the federal government, government-sponsored agencies, and state and local government units), of the central bank (the Fed), and of banks. Bankers acceptances, for which financial and business enterprises are listed as the principal borrowers in Table 9–1, are the *direct* liabilities of banks. The only money market instrument that consists wholly of liabilities of nonbank financial institutions and of business enterprises is commercial paper.

Interest rates on all these instruments as a group are termed money market interest rates. In addition to such rates, several other rates are significant in relation to the money market: the "prime" rate on short-term bank loans to customers with high credit ratings, the dealer rate on loans to U.S. government securities dealers, and the discount rate on funds borrowed by financial institutions from the Federal Reserve Banks.

Most money market interest rates are quite volatile in comparison with capital market yield rates such as those on bonds and mortgages. Money market rates generally drop substantially below capital market yield rates (normally during periods of recession) but rise with rising business activity, and often reach peaks above capital market yield rates at periods of high business activity.

Our discussion begins with government money market instruments (Treasury bills and the Treasury bills futures markets), the government agency securities market, and the municipal notes market. We then discuss the market for central bank liabilities (Fed funds) and the related repurchase agreements market. Next, we discuss the markets for domestic bank liabilities (bankers acceptances and negotiable CDs) and the market for Eurodollar bank liabilities (nonnegotiable time deposits and negotiable CDs). We conclude this part of the chapter with discussion of the commercial paper market.

## Government Securities: Treasury Bills

In both Great Britain and the United States, a large part of the short-term debt of the government (sometimes called "floating debt") is in the form of Treasury bills, an instrument invented at the suggestion of the famous financial economist, Walter Bagehot, in 1887. When federal government debt was small in the United States, Treasury bills were not used, but in 1929 they were issued because it was believed (1) that their use could eliminate errors of judgment in pricing bond or certificate issues and (2) that their use could permit close matching of maturities with fund needs, thus avoiding the payment of interest on funds not needed. Treasury bills now constitute almost 35 percent of the total outstanding marketable public debt.

Treasury bills have been issued with maturities of 3 months, 6 months, 9 months, and 1 year. There have also been issues referred to as tax anticipation bills, or TABs, designed to attract funds held temporarily for payment of income taxes.

Treasury bills are sold at auction, on a discount basis. Because the bills are worth face value at maturity, the interest is the amount of discount.[3] Noncompetitive offers may be made in an amount up to $500,000 by any one bidder. Thus small banks that may not have the sophistication to submit an appropriate bid can obtain Treasury bills.[4] These are allotted first and carry a yield equal to the average yield on those competitive bids that are accepted. The rest of the bills are allotted to those offering the highest bid prices. The lowest accepted bid price is termed the stop-out price. Formerly, the smallest units in which bills were sold was $1,000 face value. But high yields on bills in the late 1960s led many individuals to withdraw their savings accounts and buy bills. So the Treasury raised the minimum purchase to $10,000 to exclude the small investor from this market and to prevent funds from being diverted away from the mortgage and housing markets.[5] The principal groups that hold Treasury bills are individuals, commercial banks, foreigners, and the Federal Reserve System.

A number of economists have argued that the Treasury could obtain more revenue from a competitive bidding auction in which all bids accepted would be accepted at one price—a price low enough, and hence a yield high enough, to result in sale of all bills offered. In the present type of auction, each bid accepted is accepted at the bid price. The argument is that a competitive bidding auction in which everyone ends up paying the same price would probably have more participants and hence probably higher prices and lower yields. One study showed that, on the basis of a model of the demand for Treasury bills, as little as a 1 percent increase in participation would result in more revenue.[6] To obtain this result, noncompetitive bids must still

---

[3] A 360-day year is used in calculating rates on Treasury bills. The formula for the discount rate is

$$d = \frac{360}{n} \left( \frac{100 - P}{100} \right)$$

where $d$ is the discount rate, $n$ is the number of days to maturity, and $P$ is the price. For the yield on a bond issue with the same maturity, the formula would be

$$i = \frac{365}{n} \left( \frac{100 - P}{P} \right)$$

where $i$ is the yield in percent. The Treasury bill rate is a *discount* rate on *par*, using a *360-day* year, whereas for bonds a *yield* rate on *purchase price* and a *365-day* year are used.

[4] Individuals also submit noncompetitive offers. Often a large number of offers, but a much smaller percent of the total *amount* is from individuals. See Charles M. Sivesind, "Noncompetitive Tenders in Treasury Auctions: How Much Do They Affect Savings Flows?" Federal Reserve Bank of New York, *Quarterly Review*, Autumn 1978, pp. 34–38.

[5] Most of the other money market instruments discussed in this section have minimum amounts of $100,000 so that Treasury bills were, until recently, about the only money market instrument available to be bought by any individuals except the most wealthy. For more details on Treasury bills, see Timothy Q. Cook and Jimmie R. Monhollon, "Treasury Bills," in *Instruments of the Money Market* (Federal Reserve Bank of Richmond, 1981), pp. 7–19. See also Federal Reserve Bank of Dallas, *Roundup*, March 1983, for details.

[6] Steven Bolten, "Treasury Bill Auction Procedures: An Empirical Investigation," *Journal of Finance*, June 1973, pp. 577–585. His bibliography provides a guide to the various arguments. See also Margaret E. Bedford, "Recent Developments in Treasury Financing Techniques," Federal Reserve Bank of Kansas City, *Monthly Review*, July–August 1977, pp. 12–24. The uniform price or "Dutch" auction has been used several times in issuing long-term bonds, but never for Treasury bills.

be accepted, and noncompetitive demand must remain constant or at least not decline sharply. Noncompetitive bids account for about 20 percent of all bids, and their elimination would mean a loss of participants who pay the average accepted bid price.[7] Although the results seem plausible, it is not certain that participation would increase if competitive biddings with all bids accepted at one price were used.

Government securities dealers (about a dozen banks plus 20 to 25 nonbank dealers) make a market for all outstanding issues of Treasury bills, so that bills have a high degree of liquidity. Yields on outstanding issues tend to be higher when maturities are longer, but there have been times, especially in the late 1960s, when 9-month and 12-month bills had lower yields than did 6-month bills.

The importance of individuals as purchasers of Treasury bills has been a result of the high short-term interest rates and the fact that until the late 1970s, Treasury bills were the only money market instruments that could be purchased by individuals, except the most wealthy. In 1978, depository institutions were permitted to offer 6-month money market certificates on which interest rates were tied to Treasury bill rates. Also in the 1970s, there was a great growth in money market funds, which are invested in money market instruments, as described in Chapter 4. Finally, in December 1982, depository institutions were permitted to offer money market accounts on which there is no interest rate ceiling, as indicated in Chapter 6.

Treasury bills are probably the single most important type of money market instrument. They are also the chief instrument through which the Federal Reserve System carries out monetary policy—increasing bank reserves by buying Treasury bills and reducing reserves by selling them.

## The Treasury Bill Futures Market

There are futures markets for many types of financial instruments. We use the Treasury bills futures market as an example to illustrate how futures markets work and to explain their usefulness.[8]

First, there are two broad classes of futures markets: (1) commodities futures markets and (2) financial futures markets. Commodities futures markets for wheat, soybeans, coffee, plywood, orange juice, pig iron, pork bellies, and the like are very well known among the farming community and the foreign trade community. Financial futures markets are less well known, but they have grown dramatically since 1970.

There are also two broad classes of financial futures markets: (1) foreign exchange futures markets for Canadian dollars, German marks, Japanese yen, and the British pound, for example, and (2) interest rate futures markets for Treasury bills, Treasury bonds, certificates of deposit, and Eurodollar deposits, for example.

---

[7] From the viewpoint of noncompetitive bidders, they avoid paying the highest accepted bids (the lowest yields) and at the same time avoid the possibility that they may bid too low and obtain no Treasury bills.

[8] Details concerning operation of the Treasury bill futures market and some discussion of principles involved can be found in Albert E. Burger, Richard W. Land, and Robert H. Rasche, "The Treasury Bill Futures Market and Market Expectations of Interest Rates," Federal Reserve Bank of St. Louis, *Review*, June 1977, pp. 2–9.

To explain what a futures market is, it is useful to begin by explaining what a spot market is and what a forward market is, and then draw the contrast between a forward market and a futures market.

A spot market is simply a market where trades of goods or securities take place "on the spot." The transaction is completed at the instant goods or securities are exchanged for money. A forward market exists when people who trade agree to make the exchange of goods or securities, not instantly, but at some date in the future, at a price agreed upon when the trade is agreed upon.

It is common, for example, for an importer to know that he or she will want foreign exchange at some date in the future to pay foreign suppliers. Rather than buying Deutsche marks on the spot market today, the importer may go to a bank and draw up a contract with the bank to buy from the bank a certain number of Deutsche marks for a specified price in dollars on a specific date in the future. The price of foreign exchange is locked in as part of the contract. By making these kinds of forward contracts, people are participating in what we call a forward market for Deutsche marks rather than the spot market for Deutsche marks. The bank agrees to deliver marks at a set price in, say, 60 days.

The distinction between a futures market and a forward market can now be clarified: a futures market in marks is not a market where marks are traded on future dates; it is instead a market where *contracts* to trade marks in the future are themselves traded—it is a market for trading *futures contracts*. The importer who has a contract to buy marks can sell his contract to someone else. Futures contracts for foreign exchange are bought and sold in a futures market.

*Contracts* to buy and sell Treasury bills are bought or sold in the interest rate futures market. Treasury bills are sold at a discount. A bill's face value is $10,000, and it may sell for, say, $9,800. The price of the bill determines its yield to maturity. Therefore, if an investor enters into a contract to buy a Treasury bill at a specified price on some future date, the future yield on the bill is locked in. This is why futures contracts for Treasury bills and other securities are called interest rate futures contracts. They are traded by people who want to be certain of the interest rate they will earn when they buy a security on some future date.

The contracts that people arrange with banks in the forward market are inappropriate for a well-developed futures market because each contract is unique in its amount and date, and in provisions for delivery. Thus, to develop a futures market, the first thing to establish is a set of *uniform* contracts that can be traded. Contracts are, for example, for a given uniform amount of T-bills, say $1 million worth. Dates of expiration are also uniform. Contracts may expire quarterly in, say, March, June, September, December, and the following March.

Besides uniformity in the contract it is important to establish an exchange, like a stock exchange, where buyers and sellers of contracts are brought together. Indeed, it is difficult to imagine how a futures market could develop at all without a centralized exchange. The reason is that on a futures market exchange, *all* contracts are made with the exchange itself. Contracts do not exist between individuals, only between individuals and the exchange. For example, assume it is now June and a business knows it will want to borrow $1 million next December, some 6 months from now. The business will call the futures market broker, and a message will be sent to the broker on the floor of the exchange to sell one contract. The contract provides that the seller will sell and the buyer will buy a $1 million T-bill on the specified date for a given price. Let us think of brokers on the floor of the exchange as A, B, C, . . . . Broker A receives the order to sell a contract and yells around to other brokers the offering price. In a moment, broker B waves to broker A and accepts the offer by offering to buy the contract for the given price. Then broker A notes the sale of a contract on a slip of paper. Broker B notes the purchase of a contract, also on a piece of paper. Runners come by continuously during trading to take the pieces of paper to the Exchange desk where the Exchange *itself* agrees to buy one contract from A and sell one contract to B.

The fundamental question remains. Why would a business want to sell a contract to sell a $1 million T-bill at a given price on a specified date in the future? The reason is that it wants to lock in the interest that it will have to pay next December when it plans to borrow $1 million for three months. Let's see how this works by elaborating on the example.

Assume that the business involves the construction of a building. It is now June and financing the construction has already been arranged for 6 months through December. But it will take another 3 months after December before construction will be completed and the building sold. Therefore, an extra 3 months of borrowing from the bank will be required, starting in December. What interest rate will banks be charging next December? If the rate rises, the construction firm may find that higher interest costs may eat up the firm's profits. If the rate falls, the firm may realize higher profit. The extent of profit variability is a measure of risk. To reduce the risk, the firm will hedge; that is, it takes a position so that it will neither gain nor lose.

The firm sells a T-bill contract at a certain price. If interest rates go up, the price of T-bills will fall. So, if interest rates go up between now and December, the business firm can buy a contract through the exchange at a lower price. It originally sold a contract at a higher price and now it buys a contract at a lower price and erases its position. It made a profit. But, with interest rates higher, the 3-month bank loan will carry higher interest charges. So the profit on the futures is eaten up by the higher interest on the bank loan. The firm has neither gained nor lost from the movement in interest rates during the 6 months. It has hedged its interest rate risk.

Broker A has sold a contract for his client to the exchange, *not* to broker B. By playing this go-between role, the exchange provides an important market function— adding liquidity to the market for futures contracts. To see this, assume that the business wants to get out from under its contract to sell T-bills. It contacts broker A and says to buy a contract. Broker A does not need to find broker B. Rather, A simply calls around the floor and perhaps broker C agrees to sell a contract to A. After the trade is completed, the business has *both* bought and sold *identical* contracts with the exchange so its position is wiped out. Nearly everyone who uses the futures market wipes out his or her position before the specified date for delivery of T-bills. Therefore, only very rarely is there any actual delivery of T-bills under the contracts.

The exchange is always in a balanced position with respect to contracts to buy and contracts to sell—it is almost completely unexposed to risk of default on contracts. Brokers A, B, and C do not need to own any T-bills, to speak of. When A agreed to a contract to sell a T-bill, neither A nor A's business client actually owned any T-bills. Indeed, B probably did not have a client asking him to buy a T-bill contract; instead, B was speculating on the likelihood that contracts would go up in price so that later in the day B could sell a contract to someone else for more money and clear his own position at a profit.

The upshot is that, essentially, those who trade in futures markets for wheat, orange juice, Deutsche marks, T-bills, and so on do not actually own and trade these commodities or securities. They only trade contracts under the supervision of the exchange.

The hedge may not be perfect. The *difference* between the T-bill rate and the rate banks charge on loans is called the *basis*.[9] If the basis stays the same over the intervening 6 months, the hedge will be almost perfect. But, if the basis changes, then the profit made in the futures market may not fully offset a loss, for example, in higher interest charges levied by the bank. Thus, potential changes in the basis will leave the business open to some risk.

Notice that the construction firm is not in the business of dealing in T-bills at all. It is because the rate on T-bills and bank loan rates move roughly together that it is appropriate to use the T-bill futures market.

In the example, the firm was a borrower. An opposite example would be the case of a bank or a savings and loan firm that has an outstanding commitment to make a loan at a given interest rate. The bank may say the rate is good for 2 weeks. But, what if rates rise and the bank finds itself making the loan at lower than market rates? It might lose. To protect itself from loss, the bank may buy a T-bill contract; the hedging process follows (the bank is protected from loss provided T-bill rates and loan rates change in a parallel manner). Regulatory agencies allow financial institutions to use financial futures contracts only for hedging purposes.

A sale of futures is often referred to as a short hedge, because the seller is selling something he or she does not own (a short sale); purchases of futures are referred to as long hedges (a long position is one of buying or owning something).

Futures markets are useful when prices of commodities or foreign currencies or securities are highly variable. Commodities prices may vary partly because of the effects of the vagaries of weather on production. Exchange rates of the currencies of major countries have varied greatly since 1973 when governments let foreign exchange rates float. Also, since 1965, the interest rates have become highly variable. Thus, markets in financial futures have become more and more in demand.

By 1986, financial futures contracts were being traded on the Chicago Board of Trade, for Government National Mortgage Association (GNMA) certificates and for

---

[9] For a sophisticated analysis of basis changes, see Martin L. Leibowitz, *The Analysis of Value and Volatility in Financial Futures*, Monograph 1981–3, Salomon Brothers Center for the Study of Financial Institutions, Graduate School of Business Administration, New York University, 1981.

Treasury bond futures contracts. Trading occurred on the International Monetary Market of the Chicago Mercantile Exchange for Treasury bill and certificate of deposit (CD) futures as well as for futures in various currencies. Financial futures are also traded on the American Stock Exchange (AMEX), the New York Stock Exchange (NYSE), and other exchanges in such places as Kansas City, Philadelphia, Tokyo, Singapore, and Hong Kong. Details of the various contracts and their uses are obtainable directly from the exchanges in materials used to advertise their offerings.[10] The stock exchanges trade futures contracts based on stock market indexes; these are discussed in Chapter 11. A London International Financial Futures Exchange (LIFFE) opened in autumn 1982. Trading began in Eurodollar deposit contracts, short-term deposit contracts, and British government bond contracts, the last two priced in sterling.

Regulatory agencies in the United States allow financial institutions to use financial futures contracts only for hedging purposes. Dealing in futures also occurs because people wish to speculate—hoping to profit from changes in prices, interest rates, or exchange rates. If a savings and loan association has a large volume of fixed-rate mortgage loans and obtains funds by offering money market certificates of deposit, it incurs risk—if money market interest rates rise, its costs rise while a large part of its income does not rise. It has a negative maturity gap (as discussed in Chapter 3).[11] It might appropriately hedge to offset this risk. It can hedge by selling T-bill futures and buying T-bill futures for the same delivery date at a lower price. The two agreements cancel, and no delivery is needed. Of course, if interest rates fall, the hedger loses, but there is also a profit because cost of money market CDs also falls.[12]

## Short-Term Government Agency Securities

Government agency securities have recently become an important factor in the secondary money market, with the growth of government lending agencies described at the end of Chapter 4. Many of these securities, when issued, were long-term securities, but, as time passed, they became short term in nature. However, short-term instruments are also issued by the government-sponsored agencies; more than one-fifth of their debt had an original maturity of one year or less. These short-term

---

[10] An abundance of information is available on financial futures markets: *Sources of Financial Futures Information*, a bibliography, and other booklets, such as *An Introduction to the Interest Rate Futures Market*, are available from the Chicago Board of Trade. On LIFFE, see *The Wall Street Journal*, September 29, 1982, p. 42. A management bulletin on the financial futures market is available from the United States League of Savings Associations.

[11] A negative gap (as explained in Chapter 3) means that it has a mismatch of assets and liabilities, in this case more fixed-rate assets than fixed-rate liabilities. Many of the fixed-rate assets are funded by liabilities on which rates vary, and are apt to rise if inflation occurs (hence a *negative* gap).

[12] For relatively nontechnical discussions of financial futures, see Howard Keen, Jr., "Interest Rate Futures: A Challenge for Bankers," Federal Reserve Bank of Philadelphia, *Business Review*, November–December 1980, pp. 13–24; and Donald L. Koch, Delores W. Steinhauser, and Pamela Whigham, "Financial Futures as a Risk Management Tool for Banks and S&Ls," Federal Reserve Bank of Atlanta, *Economic Review*, September 1982, pp. 4–14.

issues include both coupon bonds and discount notes. Discount notes are more flexible, since they can be sold whenever the need for cash arises. Discounts (and hence yield rates) can be easily changed.

As indicated in Chapter 4, most of these agencies provide either farm credit or housing credit; in the housing field, they are for the most part secondary market agencies for mortgage loans. Major agencies are listed in Table 9–1. These agencies, although government sponsored, are now privately owned.

Only a few of these securities are government guaranteed, but most have some government support. For some issues, purchase by the Treasury is authorized in case of need for market support; some agencies can borrow from the Treasury. Some agency issues can be used as collateral for borrowing by financial institutions from the Federal Reserve System. For a number of years, the Fed has bought and sold agency securities as part of its open market operations.

Because they are regarded as quasi-government securities, agency securities generally carry lower yields than do private securities. Yet, since most of the agencies are now privately owned, their lending and borrowing has not been included in the government budget, and their operations are not subject to review when the budget is prepared by the administration and passed by Congress.

One might ask why there is any difference between yields on these securities and yields on comparable Treasury securities, yet a difference (sometimes negligible, sometimes ¼ percent or more) does exist.[13] Since there is little difference in risk, marketability is a likely factor causing the difference. Treasury issues are larger in amount, in most cases. Regressions of yields involving four variables that might cause differences in yields—issue size, issuing agency, maturity, and coupon rate—have indicated that issue size is an important determinant: the smaller the size of the issue, the higher the yield (by a small amount, of course).

Many small government agencies borrowed directly in the financial markets in the past. Many issues of securities were quite small. Because of this, the Federal Financing Bank was established in 1974 to consolidate such borrowings. Since that time, all federally *owned* agencies raise funds through that bank. Except in one case, the Federal Financing Bank has always obtained its funds by borrowing from the Treasury.[14]

## Municipal Notes[15]

State and local government units now issue "municipal notes" to finance short-term cash needs; the notes are issued in anticipation of receipt of tax or other revenues or in anticipation of sale of bonds. The federal government also auctions notes every

---

[13] Federal Reserve Bank of Richmond, *Instruments of the Money Market*, 5th ed., 1981, p. 28. In certain years, larger differences have existed—about ¾ percent in 1974, for example.

[14] For more details about the government lending agencies, see Donna Howell, "Federally Sponsored Credit Agency Securities," in *Instruments of the Money Market*, 5th ed. (Federal Reserve Bank of Richmond, 1981), pp. 20–29.

[15] This section is based on Paul Meek, *U.S. Monetary Policy and Financial Markets* (New York: Federal Reserve Bank of New York, 1982), pp. 86–87.

month on behalf of communities, to finance federally sponsored low-cost housing. Income on both is exempt from federal income taxes, and the housing notes are also backed by the U.S. government and their income is exempt from state income taxes.

Local government units sometimes borrow from banks on a negotiated basis while at other times they issue municipal notes, usually on a competitive bid basis. Moody's classifies issuers into four classes (MIG 1 to 4) to help those buying the notes; some banks and dealers make secondary markets for larger issues.

As is the case with municipal bonds, investors are usually those to whom the tax-exemption feature is important. Commercial banks, property and casualty insurance companies, and high-income individuals are the major buyers, but business firms are also buyers.

## Fed Funds and Repurchase Agreements

Because the federal government, member banks and foreign banks, and certain other institutions have deposits in Federal Reserve Banks, it is not surprising that such deposits were traded by commercial banks as early as the 1920s. With the depression of the 1930s and the large amount of unused bank reserves, trading in Federal funds dried up, but in the post–World War II period and especially after 1955, Federal funds trading revived and grew in importance.

Commercial banks, agencies of foreign banks, securities dealers, and some other institutions now participate in the market. Securities dealers obtain bank loans in Federal funds to carry inventories of government securities. Because most trading is done by major banks, the Federal Reserve System confines collection of daily data to a relatively small number of large banks.[16]

### The Fed Funds Market

Several factors contributed to rapid growth of the Federal funds market. First, the Comptroller of the Currency, in 1963, eliminated restrictions on the amount that a national bank could lend to another bank, permitting small banks to be more active in the market. Then, in 1965, the Fed ruled that member banks could purchase correspondent balances held in those member banks by nonmember banks and that these purchases would be regarded as purchases (or borrowings) of Fed funds. Third, the spread of "liability management" among banks meant that banks were more willing to expand various types of borrowing when loan demand was strong. Fourth, a change in Regulation D (which specifies details of reserve requirements) in 1970 made it clear that borrowings of Fed funds were not subjected to reserve requirements. This was already true when the lender was a U.S. commercial bank, but it was now clear that it was also true if the lender was a U.S. government agency, a savings and loan association, a mutual savings bank, or an agency or branch of a foreign bank. This meant

---

[16] The reader should not infer that small banks do not participate in the Federal funds market—in fact, dealing in Federal funds by banks is almost universal. See Carl M. Gambs and Donald V. Kimball, "Small Banks and the Federal Funds Market," Federal Reserve Bank of Kansas City, *Economic Review*, November 1979, pp. 3–12.

that banks could obtain funds from selected *nonbank lenders*, the borrowing being termed the acquisition of Fed funds. Thus several ways were open to banks to obtain funds not subject to reserve requirements.

How can nonbank lenders lend Fed funds? At this point we should define a new term: *immediately available funds*. Member banks have reserves in the Fed, and these are immediately available funds, since they can be transferred almost instantaneously. All banks have certain collected liabilities (that is, deposits and certain other funds that have been collected)—either the funds were deposited in the form of currency or (more likely) the checks deposited were collected from the banks on which they were drawn. Rapid collection is possible by use of the "Fed wire," an electronic communications network connecting member banks and Fed banks and their branches. Banks permit the collected part of deposits to be used for immediate payments or for lending.

If banks wish to borrow Fed funds, they may do so by borrowing deposits that other banks have in the Fed *or* they may borrow from either their own depositors or depositors in other banks, from immediately available funds. In borrowing Fed funds, banks may borrow only from other commercial banks, federal government agencies, savings and loan associations, mutual savings banks, agencies and branches of foreign banks, and government securities dealers. Borrowing reduces the deposits and increases the nondeposit liabilities (borrowings) of banks. If a bank borrows deposits from its own depositors, no wire network transfer is needed; if it borrows from depositors who hold accounts in other banks, a wire network transfer is needed to reduce the deposits of the other banks in the Fed and to increase the reserves of the borrowing bank. About one-fifth of the Fed funds borrowed by the 46 large banks that do most of the Fed funds trading are now borrowed from nonbank lenders. Daily outstanding borrowings of Fed funds by these large banks are *larger* than their *total* reserves.

Most borrowing is for one day, repayment being made the next day; essentially, these borrowings are one-day unsecured loans. Secured Fed funds borrowing is done by smaller banks. Purchasing (borrowing) banks place government securities in custody accounts for the selling (lending) banks for one day. Some Fed funds lending is for periods longer than one day; such lending has been called "term Fed funds" lending. Most lending is unsecured, and most of the transactions are interbank transactions. Of course, banks could obtain funds, if needed to meet reserve requirements, by selling Treasury bills, but such sale could be costly. Turnaround costs for a bank that sold bills and then bought them back a day later would be perhaps as high as one one-hundredth of 1 percent of the value of the bills, or 3.65 percent a year, plus the loss of interest on the bills.[17]

Because banks make heavy use of Federal funds to adjust reserve positions, those that have excess reserves early in a reserve period tend to sell funds toward the

---

[17] See Federal Reserve Bank of Richmond, *Instruments of the Money Market*, 2nd ed., 1970, p. 19. Of course, if the funds were needed for a longer period, turnaround costs would, in most cases, be less as a percentage of the amount sold and repurchased.

end of the period, thus reducing the rate on Federal funds.[18] In recent years, some banks have borrowed Federal funds continuously to maintain balance sheet positions and to accommodate smaller correspondent banks that may have funds to lend or may need reserves.

Also, because Federal funds are used by banks—especially major money market banks—to adjust reserve positions, the rate is very volatile. The Federal funds rate is thus quite useful as an indicator of pressure on bank reserves and hence on the base for creating money (see Chapter 5).

The major suppliers of Federal funds formerly were banks that had excess reserves. But Fed funds trading now involves trading "immediately available" funds between member banks (in which case they may be trading reserve balances), between member and nonmember banks, or between member banks and other financial institutions and government agencies. Some banks borrow amounts in the Fed funds market that are several times as large as their required reserves. When banks borrow "Fed funds" from correspondent banks that have deposits in the borrowing banks, the entries on the borrowing banks' books may show shifts from "deposits of correspondent banks" to "Fed funds borrowed" on the liability side of the balance sheet.[19]

### Repurchase Agreements

Repurchase agreements provide for the purchase of securities by a lender, usually with payment in immediately available funds. Repurchase agreements, or RPs or repos as they are often known, have different uses. They can be used as a means of investing funds on a very short-term basis, and they can be used by the Federal Reserve System to provide funds to banks *temporarily*. The market for RPs, as it has developed, is very similar to the market for Fed funds described earlier in this chapter. In both cases banks are the temporary recipients of funds; other banks, nonbank private institutions, or the Fed may supply funds. Although the receipt of funds is temporary, the continuous use of RPs may provide continuing funds to banks.

RPs are a more flexible source of funds for banks than are CDs. CDs cannot be issued with a maturity less than 14 days. But RPs can be for one day, or they may be "continuing contracts," or they may be fixed neither in time nor in amount. Corporations, for example, may agree with banks that, each day, any amounts in their accounts above certain minimum amounts may be converted into RPs. This flexibility caused a dramatic growth in RPs during the 1970s, so that by the late 1970s the relatively small number of large commercial banks that do most of the trading in the Fed funds market (as described earlier) were obtaining only somewhat less funds from

---

[18] There is an entertaining "diary" of the money desk of a large bank for a week in Wesley Lindow, *Inside the Money Market* (New York: Random House, 1972), pp. 97–103. At one point during the week, it was estimated that reserves might be $240 million below requirements, although at the close of the week they were $1 million above requirements.

[19] For more details, see the very significant article by Charles M. Lucas, Marcos T. Jones, and Thom B. Thurston, "Federal Funds and Repurchase Agreements," Federal Reserve Bank of New York, *Quarterly Review*, Summer 1977, pp. 33–48.

RPs than from Fed funds borrowing. In effect, RPs are (or may be) interest-earning demand deposits. Even thrift institutions can and do provide funds to the Fed funds market or the RP market or both, thus bringing the funds of small-income savers to this liquid market. As inflation and rising interest rates made it costly to leave funds in demand deposit accounts, those holding such funds sought ways of obtaining interest. Even state and local governments that had revenue-sharing receipts from the federal government were investing such funds, until needed, in RPs.[20]

Some have suggested that RPs and Fed funds purchased represent, in effect, interest-earning demand deposits that should be added to the currently reported figures for demand deposits to obtain a more correct figure of money (M1). Indeed, it has been suggested that the trend in demand deposits since 1974 can be forecast reasonably accurately if immediately available funds (roughly, RPs and Fed funds purchased) are treated as part of demand deposits. Otherwise, the forecast of the amount of demand deposits that people and business firms would hold is too high. Incidentally, this analysis can also explain the rise in the *k*-ratio (currency to demand deposits) discussed in Chapter 5. When immediately available funds are added to demand deposits, the ratio of currency to that total does not show any substantial rise.[21] It seems quite possible that holders now consider demand deposits, currency, *and* immediately available funds such as RPs and Fed funds purchased as funds that can be used for final settlement of debts and, hence, as money.

Borrowers (banks, securities dealers, business firms, and others) pay interest on RPs at rates negotiated with the lenders. The securities may be viewed as collateral for a loan instead of being viewed as a temporary sale. Suppose that government securities dealers need funds to finance their inventory of government securities; they may sell some securities to a bank, agreeing to repurchase the securities after a short period. Is it a sale to a bank or a loan from a bank? The view that it is a loan has been taken by the Internal Revenue Service. Many participants in financial markets, however, feel that RP transactions are sales/purchases. Legally, the difference is important because if the government securities dealer ("seller") is really obtaining a collateralized loan, the "buyer" may not own the securities (and hence may not be able to sell them if the securities dealer goes into bankruptcy).

Until recently, most RP transactions were for amounts of $1 million or more. Payment is made in immediately available funds (deposits in Federal Reserve Banks or collected liabilities of financial institutions) that can be immediately withdrawn in cash if desired. Customers of financial institutions can make such funds available to other financial institutions than those in which they have deposits by transfers through the Fed wire transfer network. Government securities dealers use RPs to help

---

[20] For more details, see Norman N. Bowsher, "Repurchase Agreements," in *Instruments of the Money Market*, 5th ed. (Federal Reserve Bank of Richmond, 1981), pp. 52–58; and Barbara Bennett and Gary C. Zimmerman, "Retail RPs," Federal Reserve Bank of San Francisco, *Weekly Review*, November 12, 1982.

[21] See Gillian Garcia and Simon Pak, "The Ratio of Currency to Demand Deposits in the United States," *Journal of Finance*, June 1979, pp. 703–715.

finance their portfolios of government securities (banks or other financial institutions purchase the securities under the RP agreements).

Since RPs are backed by government securities, can be for any maturity, and can be dealt in by anyone, they are an excellent money market instrument—low risk, variable maturity, flexibility, and liquidity.

In the early 1980s, a new form of RPs, termed "retail RPs," became fairly common. Since financial institutions could use "wholesale" RPs to obtain funds from corporations and other institutions, why not use retail RPs to obtain funds from individuals? For retail RPs, the financial institutions sell shares in pools of government (or agency) securities. RPs do not have deposit insurance, but they are backed by government securities. However, a legal question may be asked: Do investors in RPs have a *"perfected security interest"* in those securities? Did the financial institution take the steps necessary to ensure that investors had such a proper legal claim? If not, as may have been the case in some failed banks, investors may lose. It is also possible that the value of the securities may fall (if interest rates rise); if a financial institution is not able to repurchase those securities, are the investors likely to lose?

Repurchase agreements are also made by the trading desk of the Federal Reserve Bank of New York, acting for the Federal Reserve System.[22] These RPs are used for monetary policy purposes rather than for profit. When the Federal Reserve System wishes to provide bank reserves on a long-term basis, it usually engages in direct open market purchases. When it wishes to provide reserves on a temporary basis, it may use RPs. When RPs are used, participants in the market know that the transaction will be reversed in the near future. Hence it is believed that any decline in yields will be less than would accompany the same volume of open market purchases; thus the use of RPs may tend to stabilize yields.

Since 1966 matched sale-purchase transactions (or reverse RPs) have also been used.[23] It is agreed that the Federal Reserve System, in selling securities, will repurchase them within a short time. One reason for this type of arrangement rather than direct sales followed later by purchases is that banks may have acquired a large volume of temporary excess reserves. For example, an increase in the float that temporarily increases reserves may result when transportation facilities are halted by a snowstorm. The excess reserves may be temporarily reduced by reverse RPs.

## Bank Liabilities

Two types of bank liabilities are traded in the secondary money market: bankers acceptances and negotiable certificates of deposit. Because bankers acceptances and negotiable CDs are issued almost entirely by very strong banks, they have a low risk of default.

---

[22] Fed use of RPs predates their extensive private use; Fed use began as early as 1917. However, this use became more significant after World War II.

[23] Sometimes these transactions are termed RPs, if arranged at the initiative of dealers, and matched sale-purchase agreements, if arranged at the initiative of the Fed.

### Bankers Acceptances

In commercial law, there are two major types of negotiable instruments: (1) promises to pay, such as promissory notes and bonds, and (2) orders to pay. Technically, orders to pay are termed drafts or bills of exchange. Most of us are familiar with one kind of bill of exchange—the check. Checks are orders to pay, drawn on banks by people who have deposit accounts in the banks. Drafts is simply a general term for all orders to pay. They may be drawn by any person or institution on any person or institution, although clearly, unless there is a reason to pay, the person or institution on which the draft is drawn will refuse to pay. A bankers acceptance is a draft drawn on a bank by a drawer, often by an exporter or another seller of merchandise, but sometimes by importers and other buyers. Such drafts may call for immediate payment, in which case they are termed "sight drafts." If they call for payment at some future date, they are called "time drafts." Since drafts might be drawn without proper justification, time drafts are "accepted" by the person or institution (bank) on which they are drawn, to indicate both that they are legitimate and that the date on which payment is due can be determined by the acceptance date. Drafts often say "60 days after sight, pay . . ."—the date of sight is the date of acceptance, indicated by stamping the draft with the date and signing it across the face. Under prearranged agreements, often letters of credit and sometimes acceptance agreements, such drafts are "accepted" by banks, indicating that payment will be made at the appropriate time.

The drafts are then termed bankers acceptances. Since the accepting banks are almost always large, well-known banks, the acceptances can be sold in the secondary money market. Anyone purchasing them can present them to the accepting banks for payment at the appropriate time.

Many of these drafts are drawn in foreign trade transactions. Exporters could, of course, simply bill the importers, but at times they find this risky. They could also, of course, draw drafts on the importers, but if the importers' government prohibited payment, the exporter would be unable to require payment.[24] Hence, arrangements are often made under what are termed letters of credit, for banks to pay the drafts. Governments are not likely to force banks to refuse to pay, since this destroys the credit of the country's banking system. Bankers acceptances can also arise from acceptance agreements between banks and importers. In both cases, there is also an agreement for the importers to reimburse the banks at the appropriate times. Acceptances may be used to finance trade between third countries, also, and they may also be used to finance domestic shipment and storage of goods. There are also acceptances that are simply alternatives to loans—a firm can draw on a bank, the draft is accepted and sold in the money market, and the firm has obtained a loan. When the draft comes due, the bank must pay, and, of course, the firm must reimburse the bank.

When bank loan interest rates are low, bank acceptances are used less frequently; it may be cheaper simply to obtain bank loans, although in international

---

[24] Drafts drawn on importers or on other business firms or individuals and accepted by the importers or others on whom they are drawn are known as trade acceptances.

trade, bankers acceptances may be used even at such times. As loan interest rates rise, acceptance rates may not rise proportionately, for two reasons: (1) the fee for creating acceptances, which is part of the cost, is a flat fee, seldom changed; and (2) because of the minimum risk on bank acceptances, rates on them may rise less than on loans. Thus in a period of high interest rates, such as the late 1960s, use of bankers acceptances increases; there is also, of course, some secular trend increase with increase in world trade.[25] Use of acceptances may also increase in a period of credit tightness because banks may have lent as much as they can, or as much as they wish, either to individual borrowers or to borrowers as a whole, but may still be able to accept drafts, perhaps selling the accepted drafts in the money market.

A very small amount of acceptances is created to provide "dollar exchange." Some countries, chiefly in Latin America, have marked seasonal fluctuations in exports. When exports are low, not many drafts are drawn and few bank acceptances are created, but the need for dollars to pay for imports may be strong. In such circumstances it is permissible for U.S. banks to accept drafts for the purpose of providing dollars for the Latin American countries, with the understanding that the funds to pay the drafts at maturity can be provided from funds obtained from the more numerous drafts drawn when exports of the Latin American countries are seasonally large. This use of acceptances has diminished in recent years as industries in a number of Latin American countries have become more diversified, and it is now of little importance.

Regulations governing creation of bank acceptances are strict because, since no funds need be paid out at the time of creation of acceptances, banks might otherwise be tempted to create too many acceptances.[26] Bank acceptances may be eligible for discount at Federal Reserve Banks or for purchase by the Federal Reserve System under certain conditions; regulations require evidence that the acceptances were used to finance import, export, storage, or shipment of goods, or to create dollar exchange.

Before World War I, "finance" bills were drawn by U.S. banks on financial institutions in London to obtain funds to pay for imports in the spring and summer. The U.S. banks were, of course, required to provide funds in London so that holders of accepted drafts could be paid when the acceptances matured. These funds were provided by selling documentary drafts drawn on London financial institutions pursuant to more plentiful U.S. exports in the autumn.[27] Recently, some large banks in money market centers have been accepting drafts drawn on them by customers who

---

[25] In the mid-1970s, the volume of bankers acceptances outstanding in the United States was less than $20 billion; by 1980, it exceeded $50 billion. See Jeremy G. Duffield and Bruce G. Summers, "Bankers Acceptances," in *Instruments of the Money Market*, 5th ed. (Federal Reserve Bank of Richmond, 1981), pp. 114–122.

[26] The rule has been that banks may not accept drafts for more than 10 percent of the bank's paid-up and unimpaired capital and surplus for any one borrower on an unsecured basis. Further, no bank may accept drafts for a total amount equal to more than 50 percent of its paid-up and unimpaired capital and surplus, except that with special permission from the Federal Reserve System a bank may increase the limit to 100 percent (but domestic acceptances in any event are limited to a total of 50 percent).

[27] Benjamin M. Anderson, *Economics and the Public Welfare* (New York: Van Nostrand, 1949), p. 19.

desired to obtain funds for working capital purposes.[28] Such acceptances are similar in many respects to finance bills and are not eligible for discount at Federal Reserve Banks. They enable business firms to obtain funds even when money is tight and loans from banks might be impossible to obtain. The accepted drafts can be sold in the money market; if they are not purchased by banks, bank funds are not used and remain available for other purposes. Nor are total deposits in the banking system reduced, as payment for the acceptances purchased, usually by check, reduces deposits in one bank but increases deposits in another bank. Because of this situation, the Federal Reserve System imposed a basic 5 percent reserve requirement on finance bills in June 1973, after business activity had been rising rapidly and money was becoming quite tight. An additional 3 percent reserve requirement was imposed on additional finance bills outstanding. Even with such control, finance bills may become more common as banks seek additional sources of funds.

The difference between bank acceptances that are eligible for rediscount at Federal Reserve Banks and those that are not eligible is that the former finance trade in some form. It may be international or domestic trade. The acceptances are "real bills" in the sense in which that phrase was used in Chapter 3, whether the goods constitute collateral or not. Finance bills and other ineligible acceptances, on the other hand, do not finance trade, but provide a means for borrowers to obtain funds. The borrowers may be business firms or banks. While the eligible acceptances are usually drawn under letters of credit or acceptance agreements to provide credit for exporters or for importers, the ineligible acceptances provide credit for any purpose. Hence the Federal Reserve System is cautious about their expanding use.

Banks may buy their own acceptances at a discount that provides a yield. Banks are likely to buy their own or other acceptances when their reserves are relatively high and to reduce holdings when reserves are declining and are close to required levels. Because investors in foreign countries are familiar with bank acceptances and recognize their high degree of safety, high rates on bank acceptances may attract foreign funds for their purchase, thus providing additional funds for foreign trade and other types of business activity traditionally financed by acceptances.

When the Federal Reserve System was first established, it purchased bankers acceptances as well as government securities, but it now buys them chiefly for foreign correspondents. They are a safe, liquid investment. The rules of eligibility of acceptances for purchases and for rediscount at the Fed are still in the regulations. "Ineligible" acceptances sold in the market make it necessary for banks to keep reserves against the proceeds.[29] "Eligible" acceptances are easily sold in the acceptance market, through dealers. Money market mutual funds and even individuals buy bankers acceptances, especially when their yield rates are relatively high.

The Bank Export Services Act (BESA), passed by Congress in 1982, raised the limit on the amount of eligible acceptances that may be issued by an individual bank

---

[28] *Money Market Handbook for the Short-Term Investor*, 3rd ed. (New York: Brown Brothers Harriman & Co., 1970), p. 38.

[29] To encourage their use, "eligible" acceptances are not subject to reserve requirements.

from 50 percent of capital (or 100 percent with explicit permission) to 150 percent of capital (or 200 percent with explicit permission of the Board of Governors).

Before 1980, most acceptances were used to finance U.S. imports and exports, but from 1980 to 1985 there were more acceptances used to finance trade between third countries. The overall market for acceptances declined in 1984–1985, probably because attractive alternative sources of credit existed in the Eurodollar CD market. A market for bankers acceptances denominated in yen opened in mid-1986 as part of the process of deregulation of financial institutions in Japan.[30]

At times, yields on bankers acceptances exceed yields on Treasury bills by significant percentages. For example, when oil prices were raised substantially in 1973–1974, bank acceptances were widely used for oil imports, not only by the United States but also by other countries. Thus, the supply of bankers acceptances was large. Demand was also great because the rates were relatively high, especially compared with rates on Treasury bills, and although investors perceived *some* risk in acceptances, they purchased them in large amounts because the relatively high yields seemed to compensate for the risk—which was probably not great, because most bank acceptances are drawn on very large, sound banks.

### Negotiable CDs

Time deposits include both savings accounts and certificates of deposit, which specify a period of time for the deposit. In 1961, banks began to issue certificates of deposit in negotiable form, so that a holder could sell a certificate to another holder at any time. With the existence of a secondary market, negotiable CDs increased rapidly in amounts outstanding. These CDs were in amounts of $100,000 or more; nonnegotiable CDs, in smaller amounts for each certificate, are discussed later in this chapter. There are four groups of negotiable CDs: (1) those issued by U.S. banks; (2) those issued in dollars by banks abroad, termed Eurodollar CDs or Euro CDs; (3) those issued by U.S. branches of foreign banks, termed Yankee CDs; and (4) those issued by depository institutions other than commercial banks.

*Domestic Bank CDs.* Domestic CDs were issued to attract funds of business firms; firms were trying to hold less cash and invest in Treasury bills and other short-term money market instruments. Reserves are required for CDs, but since they are time deposits, the required reserve percentage is low (see Chapter 3). Federal Reserve Regulation Q limited interest rates on all kinds of CDs, but eventually the ceiling on interest rates on large negotiable CDs was eliminated. By 1980, the amount of outstanding negotiable CDs issued by large commercial banks that report to the Fed weekly exceeded $100 billion. The Regulation Q ceiling on interest rates on short-term negotiable CDs was removed at the time of the commercial paper crisis in 1970

---

[30] For recent history of the acceptance market, see Frederick H. Jensen and Patrick M. Parkinson, "Recent Developments in the Bankers Acceptance Market," *Federal Reserve Bulletin*, January 1986, pp. 1–14.

(short-term meant 30 days to 89 days). Thirty days was the minimum maturity of any time deposits except savings accounts for a long time, but in 1980 the minimum maturity was reduced to 14 days.

Investors have developed preferences for CDs of certain banks, with the results that the yield on these CDs is slightly lower. Investors *may* be able to get a slightly higher yield by buying CDs of sound banks that are not in the "top tier."

In the 1960s, Regulation Q still restricted interest rates on most CDs, and Citibank's London branch in 1966 began to issue Eurodollar CDs. Eurodollar banks are free of interest rate regulation.[31]

*Yankee CDs.*   Yankee CDs are issued by U.S. branch offices of large foreign banks. Loan customers of those branches were familiar with those banks and were willing to buy their CDs; others also bought them. For a time, issue of Yankee CDs may have been discouraged because of reserve requirements on amounts issued above a specified base amount. Foreign branches just beginning to issue Yankee CDs had low base amounts.

*Thrift Institution CDs.*   Thrift institutions, especially savings and loan associations, have large volumes of time deposits as well as savings accounts. Most of the time deposit certificates have been nonnegotiable, but savings and loan associations began to issue negotiable CDs to obtain funds.

When business firms buy CDs, they often hold them to maturity; sometimes they buy them because they expect to have to pay income taxes at certain dates and hold the CDs until those dates. For this reason, and because CDs lack homogeneity—they differ by issuer, maturity date, interest rate, and other features—they are not traded as widely as Treasury bills are. Credit risk exists because deposit insurance does not cover amounts over $100,000, and CDs have, as indicated, somewhat less marketability than do Treasury bills. Moody's has begun to rate CDs, based on the issuing institutions; Standard & Poor's has begun to rate CDs issued by savings and loan associations (primarily long-term CDs). Changes in supply of CDs, as well as risk and marketability, can be a cause of changes in yields on CDs.

*Variable-Rate CDs.*   Some negotiable CDs are variable-rate CDs—they may be for, say, four years, but are "rolled over" every six months, say, with a change in the interest rate. The interest rate is higher than that on other CDs, since the maturity is longer. On the other hand, risk of investing for a long period in fixed-rate instruments is greater; demand for variable-rate CDs (or VRCDs) has been heavy.

From the preceding paragraphs, it should be evident that varying regulation and the force of competition have changed the nature of CDs and have caused the growth of the outstanding amount of negotiable CDs to vary.

---

[31] For further details, see Bruce G. Summers, "Negotiable Certificates of Deposit," in *Instruments of the Money Market*, 5th ed. (Federal Reserve Bank of Richmond, 1981), pp. 73–93.

## Offshore Bank Liabilities: The Eurodollar Market

In international finance, certain currencies have importance as reserve assets held by central banks for final settlement of international debt and as vehicle currencies held and used by commercial banks and business firms to finance trade between the country concerned and among other countries. The wide use of the U.S. dollar, both as a reserve asset or reserve currency and as a vehicle currency, means that it has been in wide demand. Its generally greater stability than other currencies, evidenced by its devaluation only three times in this century—in 1933, in 1971, and in 1973, in contrast to the numerous and larger devaluations that have occurred for most other major currencies—makes it a desirable asset to hold. Dollar assets held for such purposes are generally kept in deposits in U.S. banks or in U.S. government securities (often Treasury bills), in the custody of the Fed.

In contrast, "Eurodollars" is a general term used to refer to dollars (and other currencies) on deposit in banks *outside* the countries that issue those currencies. An exception is U.S. dollar deposits in international banking facilities (IBFs) located in the United States, mentioned earlier. Because some of these currencies are marks, Swiss francs, and so on, as well as dollars, the term "Eurocurrencies" is perhaps more appropriate. But since the market exists in many areas, including the Caribbean islands and countries in Asia, a still better term might be "offshore" deposits.[32]

Banks that accept Eurodollar deposits agree to redeem the deposits in U.S. dollars at the specified time (or in whatever other currency was deposited). This is significant because deposits in any country are normally denominated in the currency of that country and are redeemed in that currency.

Eurodollar accounts are time deposits, and even those that are overnight deposits are paid through the New York clearing system, as in the case of domestic U.S. dollar payments. Thus Eurodollar deposits have not generally been considered to be part of a country's money supply. Nor are they generally considered to be part of the U.S. money supply, except for overnight Eurodollar deposits held by U.S. residents in Caribbean branches of U.S. banks (as noted in Chapter 5).

### Origin of the Market

In the 1950s, European banks, especially British banks, were anxious to expand their activities and increase their profits. Those who wished to have dollar accounts, including some Eastern European governments, but did not necessarily wish to have them in the United States, were induced to deposit funds in Eurodollar banks by the fact that these were dollar accounts and by the fact that attractive interest rates were offered. With the decline in the role of the pound sterling in financing world trade, as Britain's economic position was weaker than that before World War II, British banks especially sought deposit funds to maintain their share of international financing.

---

[32] As noted, IBFs (since they are located within the United States) are an exception.

Origin of the Eurodollar market is often wrongly attributed to the fact that the United States had continued balance-of-payments deficits.[33] With deficits (more imports plus outflow of loans to foreigners and investments in foreign countries than exports plus inflow of capital from foreign countries), the United States had an outflow of reserve assets (especially gold) and an accumulation of dollar deposits in the hands of foreigners. But such dollar deposits would have been retained in the United States had not interest rates on Eurodollar deposits been more attractive. It should also be remembered that U.S. residents also can shift funds from deposits in U.S. banks to Eurodollar deposits. The key factor is interest rates, although other factors, mentioned in the paragraphs that follow, also exist. (A favorable factor is that the funds are in U.S. dollars or another strong currency; a possible unfavorable factor is country risk.)

Foreign central banks have at times encouraged commercial banks in their countries to place funds in the Eurodollar market. When central banks were accumulating large amounts of dollars, they sometimes encouraged commercial banks to do this by making forward cover (future conversion of dollars into a bank's home currency) available cheaply. This presumably meant that the dollars lent by banks would not contribute to an increase in that country's money supply at that time, as they would have done if the country's central bank had to purchase and hold them, paying for the purchase with domestic funds, which add to commercial bank reserves and hence to their ability to create money.

Since very little currency is transferred internationally, transfers of funds adding to the amount of Eurodollar deposits must come from dollar deposits in the United States. As long as U.S. citizens were prohibited from making such transfers, they were made almost entirely by foreigners who held funds in the United States. What happened may be illustrated as follows. Suppose that a foreigner has a time deposit in the United States and believes that a higher interest rate can be obtained on a Eurodollar deposit. He or she transfers funds out of the time deposit and into a demand deposit (1); then he asks his bank to transfer those funds to a Eurodollar deposit (2). This may be illustrated as shown in Table 9–2. Note that the Eurodollar bank receives a deposit credit in the U.S. bank for the funds, so that in the United States, funds have been transferred from ownership by a foreign individual to ownership by a Eurodollar bank. Note that the size of the U.S. money stock is *not* changed

---

[33] In any balance of payments, total debits equal total credits, as the balance of payments is based on double-entry accounting. Items below an arbitrary line are designated as "surplus" or "deficit" items. In balance-of-payments accounting, losses of reserve assets such as gold or foreign currencies, together with increase in certain short-term liabilities (dollar deposits held by foreigners), were treated as deficits. Inflows of gold and reductions in the designated short-term liabilities were surpluses. Losses of gold reduce a country's ability to meet its liabilities; an increase in liabilities means that more liabilities may have to be met by the holdings of gold and other reserves. Beginning in the spring of 1976, figures for U.S. deficits and surpluses were no longer published, on the grounds that such single figures were apt to be viewed without reference to other balance-of-payments data and hence to be misleading. For convenient explanations of the accounting problems, see Norman S. Fieleke, "Accounting for the Balance of Payments," Federal Reserve Bank of Boston, *New England Economic Review*, May–June 1971, pp. 2–15; and John Pippenger, "Balance of Payments Deficits: Measurement and Interpretation," Federal Reserve Bank of St. Louis, *Review*, November 1973, pp. 6–14.

**TABLE 9–2**
**Balance Sheets Showing Transfer of Funds from U.S. to Eurodollar Account**

| U.S. Bank | | Eurodollar Bank | |
|---|---|---|---|
| | Foreign demand + (1) <br> deposit − (2) <br> Eurodollar bank de- <br> mand deposit + (2) <br> Foreign time <br> deposit − (1) | (2) + Deposit in U.S. <br> bank | Eurodollar <br> deposit + (2) |

by the creation of Eurodollar deposits. Transactions velocity of deposits $(T/M)$ may increase, however. But whether income velocity of money $(Y/M)$ increased or not is a question requiring further analysis.

If the Eurodollar bank does not have an immediate use for the funds in making loans, it may, if interest rates are favorable, redeposit the funds in another Eurodollar bank, perhaps in another country. Assume that the original Eurodollar bank was in London and that it finds that interest rates on Eurodollar deposits are slightly higher in Paris. What occurs may be illustrated as shown in Table 9–3. If the French bank wishes to hold its deposit in a different U.S. bank, a transfer of Federal funds (reserves) is required from the one U.S. bank to another.

At some point, Eurodollar banks no doubt find that some borrowers are anxious to obtain Eurodollar loans. At that point they may make such loans, and what happens may be illustrated as shown in Table 9–4. If at some point Eurodollar borrowers use the funds to make payments to U.S. exporters or other U.S. firms or institutions, the funds "leak" out of the Eurodollar market because at that point the deposit transfer is to a U.S. resident and the funds are no longer available in the Eurodollar banking system. It is for this reason, among others, that many economists believe that leakages out of the Eurodollar system are probably large, so that there is not much

**TABLE 9–3**
**Balance Sheets Showing Interbank Transfer of Eurodollar Funds**

| British Bank | | French Bank | |
|---|---|---|---|
| (3) − Deposit in U.S. <br> bank <br> (3) + Eurodollar de- <br> posit in Paris | | (3) + Deposit in <br> U.S. bank | Eurodollar <br> deposit + (3) |

| U.S. Bank | |
|---|---|
| | Deposit of British <br> bank − (3) <br> Deposit of French <br> bank + (3) |

TABLE 9–4
Balance Sheets Showing Loan of Eurodollar Funds

| Eurodollar Bank | | | | U.S. Bank |
|---|---|---|---|---|
| − Deposit in U.S. bank | | | | Deposit of Eurodollar bank − |
| + Loan of Eurodollars | | | | Deposit of borrower + |

chance of a large multiplier such as that for domestic demand deposits. Additional Eurodollar deposits must, it is now generally believed, come from dollar deposits in the United States, and growth of Eurodollar deposits depends on efficiency of the Eurodollar banking system in attracting deposits and making loans at rates attractive to borrowers on the one hand and depositors on the other.

### Significance of the Market

Because Eurodollars initially originate in the transfer of a demand deposit in a U.S. bank to a Eurodollar deposit in a European bank or another bank *outside* the United States, payments to foreigners and transfer of foreign funds already on deposit in U.S. banks can make possible an expansion of the amount of Eurodollars.

Since Eurodollar deposits received by one bank are often redeposited in other banks, size of the Eurodollar market can be measured as the gross amount of Eurodollar deposits, the amount held by other banks, the amount held by nonbank institutions and by individuals, and the amount held by central banks. These data for years 1978–1985 are shown in Table 9–5. It is not clear what portion, or whether any portion, should be included in the money supply. First, these are all time deposits and, hence, are not included in M1 as M1 is measured in the United States. Second, they were all attracted by interest rates paid by Eurodollar banks and, hence, were not created by Eurodollar banks. Finally, Eurodollars are not used for payments in the countries in which the deposits exist and, hence, are *not* transactions balances in those countries. Clearly, there is an expansion of *credit*—when a bank receives Eurodollar deposits, it is able, in the same way as if it received ordinary time deposits, to make loans.

Maturities of Eurodollar deposits range from overnight to several years, but most such deposits are in the range from one week to six months. Negotiable Eurodollar CDs were introduced in 1966 and had reached an amount of about $50 billion by 1980. With rising interest rates in the 1970s, Eurodollar floating rate CDs (FRCDs) and Eurodollar floating rate notes (FRNs) were issued.

An important rate in the Eurodollar market is the London Interbank Offer Rate (LIBOR)—the rate paid by major banks to deposits from other banks, for 1, 2, 3, 6, and 12 months. Other rates, both deposit and loan rates, are generally tied to the LIBOR rate. Rates on overnight deposits in the Eurodollar market are generally slightly above the Fed funds rate in the United States, while rates on 3-month Eurodollar CDs are slightly above 3-month CD rates in the United States.

**TABLE 9–5**
**Eurocurrency Market, 1978–1985***
**(billions of dollars at end of period)**

| | 1978 | 1979 | 1980 | 1981 | 1982 | 1983 | 1984 | 1985 June | 1985 Sept. | 1985 Dec. |
|---|---|---|---|---|---|---|---|---|---|---|
| **Gross liabilities to** | | | | | | | | | | |
| Nonbanks | $187 | $ 219 | $ 278 | $ 372 | $ 432 | $ 479 | $ 497 | $ 520 | $ 546 | $ 572 |
| Central banks | 86 | 122 | 128 | 112 | 91 | 88 | 96 | 106 | 109 | 112 |
| Other banks | 673 | 904 | 1,172 | 1,470 | 1,645 | 1,711 | 1,793 | 1,845 | 1,986 | 2,112 |
| Total | 946 | 1,245 | 1,578 | 1,954 | 2,168 | 2,278 | 2,386 | 2,471 | 2,641 | 2,796 |
| Eurodollars as a percentage of total gross liabilities in all Eurocurrencies | 73% | 72% | 76% | 79% | 80% | 81% | 82% | 80% | 77% | 75% |
| Dollar liabilities of foreign branches of U.S. banks as a percentage of total gross liabilities in all Eurocurrencies | 24% | 22% | 20% | 19% | 18% | 17% | 15% | 15% | 13% | 13% |

* Based on foreign liabilities of banks in major European countries, the Bahamas, Cayman Islands, Panama, Canada, Japan, Hong Kong, and Singapore.
SOURCE: *International Economic Conditions*, Federal Reserve Bank of St. Louis, August 1986, p. 8; compiled from data provided by the Board of Governors of the Federal Reserve System and by Morgan Guaranty Trust Company.

Eurodollars have special elements of risk. First, there is the risk that the government of the country in which the Eurodollar bank is located might prevent withdrawal of funds and their transmission to the depositors in other countries. U.S. residents might see this as a risk, whereas residents in some other countries might see more of this type of risk in deposits held in the United States.[34]

Second, there is the risk of possible international legal disputes and some uncertainty about legal settlements in various countries in the event of bank failures.

Third, Eurodollar deposits do not have deposit insurance, whereas deposits in the United States do have this protection. Moreover, while U.S. banks can obtain assistance from the Fed, it is not certain that foreign banks can obtain such aid from their central banks.

Finally, depositors probably have more knowledge about the financial condition of U.S. banks (or at least can obtain such information) than about foreign banks.

Since the Eurodollar market is essentially an unregulated market, interest rates are set competitively. Countries have competed for Eurodollar deposits by offering little regulation, and other incentives. If, however, the risks mentioned begin to be perceived as increasing, the phenomenal growth of the Eurodollar market may slow, or growth may even cease.

Interest rates on Eurodollar loans must be higher than those on Eurodollar deposits to provide a spread to cover costs and profit. Loan interest rates have commonly been expressed as LIBOR plus some percentage, the percentage depending on the risk perceived by the banks in making the loans and on some other factors, such as competition.

Banks in the United States borrow Eurodollar deposits regularly as a temporary source of funds—an alternative to borrowing Fed funds, selling Treasury bills, or attracting more time deposits (CDs). The borrowed deposits might be deposits already in the foreign branches of the U.S. banks, or might be created by those branches (just as any bank or branch creates a deposit for a borrower), or might be in other Eurodollar banks. For a time, the Fed imposed reserve requirements against such borrowed funds, above certain minimum amounts. The 1980 law made this requirement 3 percent against total Eurocurrency liabilities.

The Eurodollar market has been quite significant in a number of ways. First, it has tended to reduce interest rate spreads among countries. Second, it provides an alternative borrowing source for business firms, and especially for multinational firms, as well as for governments and government agencies if they can qualify for borrowing in the Eurodollar market. Most Eurodollar loans to less developed countries (LDCs) have been to those that have had good records of economic growth—countries such as South Korea and, until recently, Brazil and Mexico. Third, since it is relatively easy to transfer funds from one offshore market area to another, movement of such funds has at times contributed to volatility of exchange rates, in response to varying government policies.

---

[34] For a rather technical discussion, see Gunter Dufey and Ian H. Giddy, *The Legal Risks of Eurocurrency Deposits,* Working Paper No. 326, Division of Research, Graduate School of Business Administration, University of Michigan, Ann Arbor, January 1983.

Recent analyses have generally agreed that, since most Eurodollar deposits are time deposits, they must be attracted; banks do not create them as they create demand deposits in the process of making loans. Efficiency of operation of the banks in the Eurodollar market, restrictions on interest paid on time deposits by U.S. banks, desire to hold dollar deposits, and desire by some depositors to hold those deposits outside the United States have all contributed to the growth of the Eurodollar market. Perception of risks existing for holders of Eurodollars is also a factor. The elimination of restrictions on interest paid on time deposits in U.S. banks and the possibility of increased risks for depositors in the Eurodollar market are factors that tend to slow down further growth of the market.

Eurodollar deposits by OPEC countries provided funds for loans, and banks "recycled" such funds to lend them especially to countries that had to pay larger amounts for oil imports. Thus in the 1970s the Eurodollar market performed a valuable service. Its role in the 1980s is somewhat changed, as country risk seems to have increased.

## Commercial Paper

Commercial paper consists of short-term unsecured promissory notes. It is now issued by industrial firms, public utilities, bank holding companies, finance companies, and other institutions. To obtain exemption from the Securities and Exchange Commission requirements for registration of securities, the maximum maturity of commercial paper is 270 days. The average maturity of outstanding commercial paper is only about 30 days.[35]

Denominations of commercial paper can be as small as $25,000 or $50,000, but most offerings are in multiples of $100,000. They may be sold directly to investors or through dealers. If firms sell large amounts of commercial paper, it may be cheaper to maintain a sales force and sell directly; otherwise, it may be cheaper to use dealers, who usually charge one-eighth of 1 percent commission.

Unlike the other money market instruments already discussed, there is no significant secondary market for commercial paper (see Table 9–1), partly because it is short-term and partly because investors sometimes buy it to hold until a specific date.

Moody's, Standard & Poor's, and Fitch rate commercial paper on the basis of the financial position of the industry, the company and its management, its financial structure, and other factors. This is another reason why commercial paper would be difficult to trade in a secondary market—it is not homogeneous.

In addition to the interest cost, firms issuing commercial paper must pay for backup lines of credit issued by commercial banks. These are necessary to be sure that commercial paper can be paid off when it matures. Banks also charge fees for serving as issuing and paying agents for the commercial paper. And the rating agencies charge fees for the ratings.

---

[35] This entire section draws heavily on Peter A. Abken, "Commercial Paper," in *Instruments of the Money Market*, 5th ed. (Federal Reserve Bank of Richmond, 1981), pp. 94–113.

Those who purchase commercial paper include banks, state and local governments, pension funds, foundations, individuals, and savings and loan associations (recently given authority to invest more of their assets in commercial paper).

Commercial paper has a long history, relative to that of most of the other instruments already considered. It was used in the nineteenth century by firms that could not obtain bank loans. Gradually it became a better quality instrument. As automobiles and other consumer goods began to be sold on credit, finance companies developed, and they issued large amounts of commercial paper. The Great Depression caused a decline in the use of commercial paper, but after World War II, it expanded again. Finance companies were the major issuers, and most commercial paper was directly placed. Banks bought less commercial paper, buying Treasury bills instead, but business firms began to buy commercial paper instead of holding demand deposits, as interest rates began to rise and demand deposits still paid no interest.

The commercial paper market was hurt by the Penn Central crisis in 1970, when that firm defaulted on more than $80 million of its outstanding commercial paper. This led investors to be more selective in quality of commercial paper. Bank holding companies also found some difficulty in issuing commercial paper after the failure of Franklin National Bank in 1974.

Inflation, especially in the late 1970s, led to a great increase in the issue of commercial paper. Firms were hesitant to borrow at the very high rates that had to be paid, because of inflation, on long-term debt; hence they issued more short-term debt instruments. Investors also were cautious in buying long-term financial assets because of uncertainty about long-term inflation. Even at high interest rates, long-term financial assets would not be worth much in purchasing power in the future if inflation worsened.

Because commercial banks more and more were forced to resort to issuing CDs to obtain funds, and CD rates were rising because of inflation, bank loan rates (including the prime rate) rose sharply. Banks had to keep reserves against CDs, and since no interest was obtained on reserves, this increased the rate that banks charged on loans.

Large finance companies have continued to be major issuers of commercial paper. Bank holding companies have issued commercial paper to finance their banking-related activities. Foreign firms and banks have begun to issue commercial paper to finance activities in the United States, introducing another complicating factor—country risk. Foreign firms and banks may be financially strong, but will countries permit payoffs in dollars at all times? Savings and loan associations and mutual savings banks have recently been allowed to issue commercial paper. The financial difficulties of both groups of institutions in the period of inflation hindered their use of this permission. Moreover, the Depository Institutions Deregulation and Monetary Control Act of 1980 requires 3 percent reserves against commercial paper, which is classified with nonpersonal time deposits. (Commercial banks cannot issue commercial paper.) Some commercial paper has been issued by state and local government units and by nonprofit institutions; income from this paper is tax-exempt. The commercial paper market is likely to continue to expand rapidly, although its growth may be slow in any period of financial difficulties.

# RELATED SHORT-TERM FINANCIAL ASSETS
# AND INTEREST RATES

In addition to the short-term financial assets thus far discussed, for which there are generally secondary markets and which have fluctuating interest rates, there are some related short-term financial assets on which rates change much less frequently, in general. These include bank loans (for which the "prime rate" has become well known as an announced rate); funds borrowed by depository institutions from the Fed; special loan rates for securities dealers; repurchase agreements under which funds are obtained by sale of securities with an agreement to repurchase them at a specified later time; and savings accounts and nonnegotiable CDs, on which interest rates have been fixed in the past by regulation, with these regulations being terminated in the mid-1980s.

## Bank Loans: The Prime Rate
## and Other Loan Rates

Bank loans are normally not traded in any secondary market; whatever liquidity exists in a loan portfolio exists because many business loans are short-term loans, so that a certain portion of the loan portfolio matures almost every day, and, unless loans are renewed, they are repaid. The interest rates on business and other loans are, however, significant for the money market for several reasons. First, some borrowers have the alternative of borrowing through issues of commercial paper, and some have the alternative of borrowing in the Eurodollar market. Second, the rate on business loans indicates the cost of short-term borrowing by business firms and thus is a useful indicator of demand and supply of short-term borrowing by business firms, a major part of demand and supply of short-term funds. Third, the publicity given to the prime rate has tended to focus attention on changes in that rate. Although the degree of attention may have been unwarranted, the rate could not be ignored.

An announced prime rate was first established in the 1930s to prevent interest rates from going too low. Banks had large amounts of excess reserves, business activity was at a low level, and it was feared that rates on business loans might go below the 1½ percent believed to be the administrative and servicing cost of business loans. This rate of 1½ percent remained as the prime rate until 1947. Since that time the prime rate has increased as interest rates generally rose and declined when they fell; adjustments were normally made in "steps" of at least ¼ percent at a time.

When interest rates are high and credit availability is limited, a higher proportion of all business loans is made at the prime rate, although this may seem surprising. Customers who have been issuing commercial paper may turn to banks for loans when the rate on commercial paper rises significantly above the more slowly adjusted prime rate, and banks may accommodate such prime customers ahead of other customers.

The prime rate for some years was a lagging rate, being adjusted upward (or downward) only when banks were satisfied that the demand for loans had increased (or decreased) and was likely to remain at its current level or move further in the same direction. The prime rate was thus one of the last short-term rates to be changed. As the prime rate had become the base rate or anchor rate for other loan rates, this was significant.

Changes in the prime rate were usually initiated by a New York bank, and an element of gamesmanship may have been present. Which bank would change its rate first? Would it suffer a loss of loan demand if others did not follow a rate increase? Would it receive a flood of loan applications if it lowered the rate? The prime rate remained unchanged from 1960 to 1965 but was changed several times a year in the second half of the decade of the 1960s. As might be expected, changes were generally upward from 1965 through 1969, as the prime rate followed the rising demand for funds in the latter stages of a period of rising business activity.

As might be anticipated, the increases in the prime rate in the late 1960s were both unpopular and distasteful for the banks. Being announced in newspapers and other media, they were especially evident to the public. Although they were simply following previous upward movements of other short-term rates, the attention given to them suggested to some banks the idea of using a "floating" prime rate, adjusted upward or downward in accordance with some rate in the secondary money market. The rate chosen was generally the commercial paper rate, because (1) it is a market rate, set by impersonal forces; (2) it is an alternative to bank borrowing, at least for some borrowers; and (3) the maturities of commercial paper are comparable to those of short-term business loans. One bank has also used the rate on 89-day CDs as a determinant of the floating prime rate. Bankers believed that by using the commercial paper rate as a determinant of the prime rate, they could avoid outcries that they were unjustly raising loan rates, that they could make more frequent and more timely adjustments in the prime rate, and that they could raise the prime rate (and other loan rates) sufficiently to meet the costs of borrowing funds. The rate on CDs represents the cost of one part of borrowed funds. Because CD rates move with commercial paper rates and one bank used CD rates directly in its determination of the prime rate, loan rates should move reasonably proportionately with the cost to banks of borrowing funds. A floating prime would rise more rapidly and somewhat higher in periods of rising interest rates than the prime rate had in the past and would drop more rapidly and somewhat farther in periods of falling rates.

In early 1973 banks were urged by monetary authorities not to raise the prime rate and to modify or abandon floating rate formulas that would have resulted in rate increases. It seemed that "floating" prime rates might disappear for a time. Obviously a rise in the announced prime rate was also undesirable from the viewpoint of those who feared that rising interest rates might revive or continue inflationary expectations and thus make the control of inflation more difficult.[36]

The Committee on Interest and Dividends, established by President Nixon as part of the mechanism for control of inflation, pressured banks to establish dual prime

---

[36] It was reported that Bankers Trust Company, Mellon Bank, and Irving Trust Company suspended the use of automatic formulas to determine their floating prime rates, leaving only Citibank among large banks with a floating rate. *The Wall Street Journal*, January 26, 1973, p. 13.

rates: one, a rate, which might float, for large business borrowers; the other, which should be more stable, a rate applicable to small business and farm borrowers, mortgage borrowers, and consumers. The desire was to permit the rate charged to large business firms to rise consistently with the increase in the cost of borrowing by such firms from alternative sources such as commercial paper. Banks could thus charge rates on large business loans adequate to compensate them, in general, for the marginal cost of funds obtained through issues of CDs and/or commercial paper. At the same time, it was desired to restrain increases in interest rates charged small business firms, farmers, mortgage borrowers, and consumers, to avoid sharp cutbacks in funds available to them. As usual, in a period of business expansion, the most rapid rise was occurring in business borrowing, and it was desired to restrain this without necessarily imposing heavy restraint on other borrowing.[37]

The commercial paper rate is not necessarily the best guide for a "floating" prime rate. Sometimes the commercial paper rate is out of line with other secondary money market rates. At such times the floating prime rate, based on the commercial paper rate, will not adequately reflect the cost of funds borrowed by banks that have floating prime rates. With liability management as well as asset management an important part of bank portfolio policy, this is a significant feature.

The prime rate reached an all-time high to that date of 12 percent the summer of 1974, as interest rates continued to rise after business activity turned downward in the autumn of 1973. Inventory borrowing was heavy, as firms tried to obtain inventory despite shortages. Business managers seemed to feel that it was essential to build up inventories because of such shortages and because of the inflation, which meant that prices for inventory replacement would be higher as time passed. The normal drop in the prime rate finally occurred with further decline in business activity in late 1974. Firms finally reduced inventories. Perhaps of most significance, the prime rate remained at a relatively low level in the last part of 1975 and during 1976. Business demand for loans was abnormally low. Banks apparently perceived that demand for business loans was quite inelastic with respect to the interest rate on such loans. Clearly demand for borrowing funds is a factor in interest rate setting, along with the cost of supplying funds.

Relatively low profits, after allowances for depreciation and replacement cost of inventories, and the many uncertainties of a continued period of inflation and a period of some political turmoil made business hesitant to expand investment. Combined with a rapid increase in the labor force, resulting largely from efforts of increased numbers of teenagers and of women to find jobs, this caused the unemployment rate to remain relatively high in a period of some inflation. The combination of unemployment and inflation seemed difficult to combat.

As business recovery continued to occur from the spring of 1975 until the first quarter of 1980, and as inflation became more and more severe after 1976, the prime

---

[37] A succinct discussion may be found in the Federal Reserve Bank of San Francisco, *Business & Financial Letter*, April 27, 1973, pp. 1–3. See also "The Dual Rate Structure: A New Plan for the Banks," Chase Manhattan Bank, *Business in Brief*, April 1973, pp. 2–3.

rate rose again, reaching an all-time peak of 20 percent in the spring of 1980. Real GNP, after rising in the first quarter of 1979, fell in the second quarter but rose again in the third quarter and also in the fourth quarter, raising questions as to whether a recession was beginning. Actions of the Federal Reserve System, beginning in early October, aimed at slowing inflation, are discussed in Chapter 16. Those actions, if successful, could be expected to be followed by a rather sharp fall in the prime and other short-term interest rates. This fall occurred in the spring of 1980, as the long-expected recession began early in 1980, but the prime rate later rose again and remained relatively high until the summer of 1982. Thus there was a long delay after the beginning of the fall in the inflation rate until substantial declines finally occurred in short-term interest rates.

The prime rate may no longer be as significant a barometer as it may once have been. In 1986, more than two-thirds of commercial bank business loans were being made to borrowers with good credit at interest rates *below* the prime rate. Of these, 74 percent were fixed-rate loans and about 19 percent were floating rate loans. Business firms are also relying to a greater extent on other sources for funds—foreign banks, the commercial paper market, and other sources. Also, there has been some trend in the United States to use an interest rate that covers total cost, whereas the common practice until recently was to charge a prime rate *plus* a requirement for compensating balances, the amount of which might vary. An all-inclusive rate is used in the Euro-dollar market, as noted earlier in this chapter—LIBOR plus 1 percent, LIBOR plus 1½ percent, and so on, with no compensating balance requirement.[38]

## Borrowing from the Fed: The Discount Rate

When the Federal Reserve System was first established in 1913, it was patterned to a considerable extent after the Bank of England. An important feature of Bank of England policy was use of the discount rate, the rate at which financial institutions could borrow from it to obtain funds. It was believed that the discount privilege and the discount rate would be the primary tools of the new central bank in determining how much, and at what cost, banks could borrow, and therefore how much credit they could create. Early critics of Federal Reserve policy, such as Benjamin Anderson, argued that the discount rate should be a penalty rate, above the prime loan rate, so that banks would discount at the Fed only if they badly needed funds.[39] Later, it was suggested, for example, by Robert Turner, that since banks could sell Treasury

---

[38] For a comment, see "The Prime: A Bellwether No More," *Business Week*, December 10, 1979, pp. 99–100. See also Randall C. Merris, "Prime Rate Update," Federal Reserve Bank of Chicago, *Economic Perspectives*, May–June 1978, pp. 14–16, and Brian C. Gendreau, "When Is the Prime Rate Second Class?" Federal Reserve Bank of Philadelphia, *Business Review*, May–June 1983, pp. 13–23. On 1986 rates below the prime rate, see Federal Reserve Bank of St. Louis, *U.S. Financial Data*, November 28, 1986.

[39] Benjamin M. Anderson, *Economics and the Public Welfare* (New York: Van Nostrand, 1949), pp. 58, 86. Anderson was economist for the Chase National Bank, and his argument was stated in *The Chase Economic Bulletin*, 1, No. 5 (July 20, 1921). Anderson did not believe that the central bank should undertake management of the money supply but believed that it should simply serve as a "lender of last resort" in cases of emergency.

bills to obtain funds, it was only necessary for the discount rate to be above the Treasury bill rate for it to be a "penalty" rate.[40] In fact, the discount rate has seldom been a penalty rate in the United States; the discount rate has usually been lower than other rates it might logically be compared with.

Over the years, the task of the Federal Reserve System, as it was viewed by economists inside and outside the system, changed from primarily that of supplying funds in emergencies to that of controlling the money (and credit) supply. The role of discounts and advances also changed. Discounts and advances became a means of supplying funds to banks with temporary needs, sometimes because monetary policy actions had impinged too heavily on them. The discount privilege came to be regarded as a "safety valve," needed because, in a country of more than 14,000 separate banks, some were more likely to be adversely affected by monetary policy changes than others, and those so affected would need emergency funds.

Borrowing mechanics also changed. Most borrowing occurred in the form of advances with collateral rather than discounts, borrowing by banks on the basis of their own promissory notes rather than discounting notes of business firms already held by banks. The most common collateral is government securities. In the absence of "eligible paper" for discounts or government securities as collateral for advances, advances based on any collateral satisfactory to the Federal Reserve System may be made under a section of the law added in 1932, at a rate currently ½ percent above the normal discount rate. Documentation was made easier by execution of a continuing lending agreement, thus avoiding execution of new promissory notes and borrowing resolutions for a series of borrowings. Borrowing can be done by telephone, with immediate credit to the borrowing bank's reserve account.

In the 1960s, the Federal Reserve System made an extensive study of the discount mechanism and concluded that modifications were needed. It was suggested that banks should have a "basic borrowing privilege" that would vary with required reserves of banks; smaller banks would be able to borrow more, relative to their required reserves, than larger banks. A seasonal borrowing privilege was also suggested, to permit borrowing by banks, especially those in rural areas, that experienced seasonal losses of deposits and seasonal increases in loans, both of which cause drains on reserves. The earlier philosophy had been that banks should be able to forecast such seasonal needs and could borrow only when needs were unexpectedly large. This facility was intended primarily to be of use to about 2,000 banks that have marked seasonal loan and deposit changes, most of these banks being not over $50 million each in deposits. Such banks, the Federal Reserve System officials concluded, have more difficulty in gaining access to the national money market to meet temporary needs. A decline in available funds (deposits minus loans) of 5 percent of the previous year's average deposits, for a period of at least eight weeks, is sufficient to qualify a bank for seasonal borrowing. In implementing this change, the readiness of the Federal Reserve System to lend in emergencies, even to nonbank financial institutions and to business firms, was restated.

---

[40] Robert C. Turner, *Member Bank Borrowing* (Columbus: Ohio State University Press, 1938).

Changes made in the discount rate have "announcement" effects in much the same way as changes in a fixed prime rate. It is not clear, however, whether these effects are always the same. An increase in the discount rate is usually interpreted as a signal that the Federal Reserve System intends to pursue a more restrictive monetary policy, but in fact such an increase may only indicate that the Federal Reserve System has adjusted the discount rate in line with other money market rates to prevent undue borrowing from the Fed by banks that could obtain funds in other ways. A rise in the discount rate can do little to slow the expansion of money and credit if at the same time the Federal Reserve System injects new funds into bank reserves by open market purchases.

Because the discount rate is determined administratively by the Federal Reserve System, it does not respond immediately to money market supply and demand.[41] The discount rate is significant for the amount of borrowed reserves and, therefore, for the portion of bank reserves that must be repaid to the Fed in the near future. The role of the discount rate in monetary policy is less significant.[42] Suffice it to say at this point that the discount rate is of relatively minor importance in monetary policy but is of some importance in determining the role of borrowing from the Fed as a source of commercial banks funds and may be of some value as a lagging indicator of both general money market conditions and Federal Reserve System policy. In its suggestions for modification of the discount mechanism, the Federal Reserve System proposed that the discount rate be changed by small amounts more frequently or otherwise become more flexible. In fact, the discount rate has been changed quite frequently in the period since 1970.

In recent years the discount rate has sometimes widely diverged from other rates. An example is short-term interest rates in 1974, a year of rapid inflation. On a monthly basis, the peak rates that summer were prime rate, 12 percent; commercial paper rate, almost as high; Eurodollar rate for three-month deposits, nearly 14 percent; Federal funds rate, nearly 13 percent. Yet the rate on three-month Treasury bills was only 9 percent, and the discount rate was only 8 percent. Thus, there was what was termed a "quality spread." Interest rates on riskless government securities remained at relatively low levels whereas interest rates on private debt instruments rose sharply. In the spring of 1980, the peak reached by the discount rate was 13 percent, whereas the Treasury bill rate rose to about 14 percent, the commercial paper

---

[41] Some central banks have experimented with a "floating" discount rate. For example, late in 1956 the Bank of Canada announced that until further notice its minimum lending rate (discount rate) would be ¼ percent above the average Treasury bill rate, making the discount rate clearly a market-determined rate rather than a policy rate. See Peter G. Fousek, *Foreign Central Banking: The Instruments of Monetary Policy* (Federal Reserve Bank of New York, 1957), pp. 18, 20. Also, see footnote 27.

[42] An indication of the declining importance of the discount rate in monetary policy is the abandonment of the traditional fixed "bank rate" (discount rate) of the Bank of England, a tradition for about 270 years. It was announced that a "last resort rate" would be based on the interest rate on Treasury bills. This policy officially recognized that the discount rate, or bank rate, is no longer a policy instrument, but simply a rate at which banks may borrow from the central bank, at somewhat higher cost than if they sold Treasury bills, when emergencies arise. The discount rate thus becomes a market rate rather than a fixed rate. See *The Wall Street Journal*, October 10, 1972.

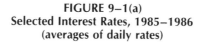

### FIGURE 9–1(a)
### Selected Interest Rates, 1985–1986
### (averages of daily rates)

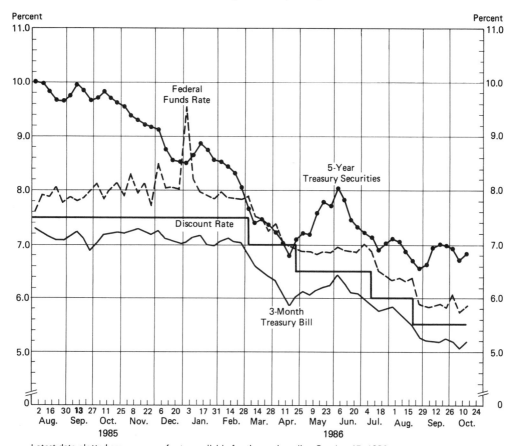

Latest data plotted are averages of rates available for the week ending October 17, 1986.

SOURCE: Federal Reserve Bank of St. Louis, *U.S. Financial Data,* October 16, 1986.

rate to about 17 percent, the 90-day CD rate to about 18 percent, and the prime loan rate to 20 percent. These short-term interest rates did not begin to fall until the summer of 1982, in spite of the recession from mid-1981 to the end of 1982. But by 1986 all these rates (both short-term and long-term) were substantially lower, as shown in Figures 9–1(a) and 9–1(b).

In the 1980s the Fed was charging the "regular" discount rate [see Figure 9–1(a)] for basic borrowing and a higher rate for "extended borrowing," thus in effect charging a penalty rate to *some* borrowers, whose period of borrowing was longer.[43]

[43] For more details, see David L. Mengle, "The Discount Window," Federal Reserve Bank of Richmond, *Economic Review*, May–June 1986, pp. 2–10, esp. pp. 3–4.

**FIGURE 9–1(b)**
**Yields on Selected Securities, 1985–1986**
**(averages of daily rates)**

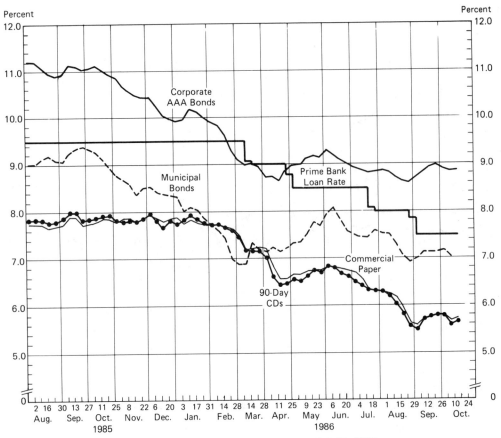

SOURCE: Federal Reserve Bank of St. Louis, *U.S. Financial Data,* October 16, 1986.

## Dealer Loans and the Dealer Rate

Government securities dealers and other dealers in the money market make heavy use of borrowed funds to finance inventories of securities. These funds are generally obtained from commercial banks, but in some cases from corporations, either under dealer loans or what are termed repurchase agreements. Dealer loans are made to dealers by commercial banks at designated rates. These loans are usually made by banks in New York City, which post interest rates daily for dealer loans. Dealers obtain additional needed financing from repurchase agreements (RPs). RPs are also used by dealer banks to obtain financing not supplied by the banks themselves, in allotments to the securities or investment department. Dealer loans are collateralized by the securities being financed. The Federal Reserve System also makes repurchase agreements with dealers.

## Savings Deposits and Nonnegotiable CDs

While banks were able to obtain funds by offering negotiable CDs, borrowing from the Eurodollar market, and other means involving variable interest rates, they still had sizable deposits in savings accounts and in nonnegotiable CDs. The other depository institutions had large percentages of their deposit liabilities in such accounts, on which interest rates were limited by Regulation Q. Rates on savings accounts (passbook accounts from which funds could, in practice, be withdrawn at any time) were limited to 5¼ percent for banks, and 5½ percent for the savings and loan associations. Although daily compounding of interest by many institutions increased the effective rate to 5.73 percent, this was far below market rates as the rate of inflation rose.

Although rates as high as 8 percent could be offered on nonnegotiable CDs with maturities of 8 to 10 years, there were significant penalties for early withdrawals, and as inflation worsened, people began to question whether funds should be invested for long periods of time at fixed interest rates.

In 1978, banks and thrift institutions were authorized to issue six-month money market certificates at rates based on the most recent Treasury bill auction rates. The authorization made it possible for banks and thrift institutions to retain more of their time deposit funds as rates on Treasury bills and other money market instruments were rising. Use of 365-day years for calculating interest in one case and 360-day years in the other case, the fact that interest is calculated on a discount basis for Treasury bills, and the fact that interest rates on money market certificates may be compounded daily (whereas interest on six-month Treasury bills is compounded only semiannually) complicate rate comparisons somewhat. The money market certificates had some advantages: they could be purchased in any amounts above the minimum amount of $10,000, whereas Treasury bills could be purchased in only $10,000 amounts, and they could be obtained at local banks or the institutions with which individuals were accustomed to dealing. Money market certificates proved to be very popular. Of course, this forced the institutions to pay much higher interest rates than they had been paying on savings accounts and other time deposits. At one point, money market certificate rates exceeded 16 percent.

In 1982 a new three-month money market certificate was authorized; ceiling interest rates were tied to three-month Treasury bill auction rates, but the minimum amount was $7,500.

A special type of CD termed an All Savers Certificate was authorized in September 1981 for sale through the end of 1982. Those interested in availability of funds for housing were very much concerned about the outflow of funds from thrift institutions and the threatened failure of many such institutions. Interest rates authorized were 70 percent of the rates on Treasury bills, but the interest income was exempt from income tax—hence, the after-tax return was higher. Many people invested in such certificates (maximum $1,000 for a person, $2,000 for an individual and spouse) to reduce taxes, if for no other reason.[44] It seems doubtful whether availability of funds for housing was significantly increased; in any event, mortgage interest rates were so high as to discourage demand for mortgage loans.

Money market mutual funds, another alternative for investment for individuals desiring short-term investments, were already described in Chapter 4. Money market mutual funds usually invest in Treasury bills, CDs, and commercial paper, so that the interest rates obtained are those available in the money market.

Finally, as noted in an earlier chapter, legislation in autumn 1982 authorized money market deposit accounts (MMDAs) for depository institutions, insured but without reserve requirements. No interest rate ceiling was specified for these accounts, nor for a Super-NOW account authorized for early 1983.

The basic cause underlying these changes must not be forgotten: inflation was increasing until 1980, and hence risks of investing in long-term instruments were greater and borrowers were willing to pay high short-term interest rates but were discouraged by high long-term rates in view of the uncertainty of the future. If inflation moderated, long-term rates would, after a time, fall. It was preferable to pay high short-term interest rates in view of a possible fall in long-term interest rates.

Federal Reserve System authorities felt compelled to raise interest rate ceilings on time deposits to enable banks to compete for interest-sensitive funds and to avoid large outflows of funds from banks. At the same time, they worried about the effect of these increases on deposit-type institutions, which have difficulty paying interest rates much higher than those of recent past years because they are locked into holdings of long-term financial assets with specified yields, as explained in Chapter 6. Many economists believe that interest rate ceilings are undesirable because they discriminate against those who have insufficient knowledge and insufficient funds to invest in the money and capital markets directly.[45]

# INTERRELATIONSHIPS OF SHORT-TERM INTEREST RATES

Since both borrowers and lenders in the short-term money market are primarily the Treasury, the central bank, commercial banks, corporations, finance companies, and government securities and other money market dealers, rates on different money market instruments are usually highly correlated with one another.

---

[44] One survey estimated that, although the All Savers Certificates reduced interest cost for thrifts slightly, every dollar of such benefit was more than balanced by two dollars of loss in tax revenue to the Treasury. See Donald L. Koch, B. Frank King, and Delores W. Steinhauser, "Is the All Savers Certificate a Success? Evidence from the Southeast," Federal Reserve Bank of Atlanta, *Economic Review*, December 1981, pp. 4–12.

[45] For example, see Robert Lindsay, *The Economics of Interest Rate Ceilings*, New York University *Bulletin*, Nos. 68–69, December 1970. The history of rate ceilings was reviewed in Charlotte E. Ruebling, "The Administration of Regulation Q," Federal Reserve Bank of St. Louis, *Review*, February 1970, pp. 29–40.

## Normal Relationships

The most usual relationship is that Treasury bill rates are the lowest rates, with agency securities rates, bankers acceptance rates, and commercial paper rates in ascending order. Negotiable CD rates have averaged somewhat above rates on government agency securities and slightly below rates on bank acceptances. Eurodollar rates have generally been higher than rates on CDs. Federal funds rates fluctuate widely because banks that borrow in the Federal funds market may urgently need funds and may be willing to pay a high rate. Until the mid-1960s, the Federal funds rate was seldom higher than the discount rate because banks could always borrow from the Fed as an alternative to borrowing Federal funds. In the mid-1960s, however, banks began to borrow Federal funds more regularly, and the Federal funds rate rose above the discount rate. Later, borrowing from the Fed *did* increase when spread of the Fed funds rate above the discount rate increased, and vice versa.

The announced prime rate is generally above the rate on commercial paper, although changes in the announced prime rate lag, and sometimes the commercial paper rate rises before the prime rate is raised sufficiently to equal the commercial paper rate.

As commercial banks can obtain funds either by discounts or advances from the Fed, borrowing in the Federal funds market, or selling bills, as well as in some other ways, it used to be generally believed that the discount rate and the Treasury bill rate would be relatively close together. However, these and other short-term rates have fluctuated widely in more recent years, and relationships have varied.

## Significance of the Treasury Bill Rate

If any single rate is to be selected as representative of money market rates, it should probably be the Treasury bill rate because this is the rate on the major money market instrument, and the market for Treasury bills is broad and sensitive.

Second, most open market purchases by the Federal Reserve System, and virtually all open market sales, involve Treasury bills. Prevailing conditions in the Treasury bill market are considered in open market policy decisions, and open market operations affect Treasury bill yields.

Third, except for the Federal funds rate, which fluctuates widely, the Treasury bill rate is usually the lowest rate in the money market. Levels of other rates may be explained in terms of factors causing them to be higher than Treasury bill rates by varying amounts.

## Role of the Federal Funds Rate

The fact that banks can quickly dispose of excess reserves and obtain reserves if they are deficient means that effects of monetary policy actions are transmitted through the banking system more quickly than they otherwise might be. If actions of the Federal Reserve System supply reserves to New York banks, these banks can normally quickly dispose of the reserves. Thus banks in the aggregate may remain more fully invested. The effect of a change in reserves in New York is quickly transmitted to banks elsewhere in the system.

When pressure for funds is strong, the Federal funds rate tends to be above the discount rate. Formerly, the discount rate was a ceiling rate for the Federal funds rate, but in recent years, as explained earlier, the Federal funds rate has risen to approximate yields banks can obtain on the loans for which there is heavy demand, or on certain investments that have high after-tax yields. When pressure for funds is slack, the Federal funds rate fluctuates more closely with the Treasury bill rate, as banks can obtain funds either by selling Treasury bills or by borrowing Federal funds.

The Federal funds rate is closely watched as a barometer of the money market, although its volatility and the fact that it may be associated with several other rates make interpretation of changes in it difficult.[46] One approach is to determine the "basic reserve position" of the large money market banks—their excess reserves minus their borrowings from the Fed and their net purchases of Federal funds. This indicates how large excess reserves or reserve deficiencies would have been without borrowing from the Fed and without purchases of Federal funds. Because these are temporary means of adjusting reserve positions, large reserve deficiencies are likely to mean heavy demand for Federal funds; large amounts of excess reserves mean light demand. This analysis, combined with other information such as the strength of bank loan demand, is helpful in appraising money market positions of the key large banks and thus in interpreting movements of the Federal funds rate. As explained in Chapter 16, this and other information is used in determining appropriate discretionary monetary policy.

## The Discount Rate, Dealer Rates, and Other Money Market Rates

The money market is the first point of impact in the transmission of effects of Federal Reserve System policy actions. Federal reserve transactions in U.S. government securities affect bank reserves on the one hand and portfolios of government securities dealers on the other. Bank reserve positions affect bank management of money market assets first and of other credit somewhat later. Portfolios of government securities dealers affect money market conditions because dealers increase or reduce their borrowing as their inventories of securities rise or fall. Money market conditions are reflected in the level of Treasury bill rates, the level of the Federal funds rate in relation to the discount rate and to Treasury bill rates, the volume of Federal funds flows, and the volume of and rates on dealer loans. Money market changes in turn affect bank deposits, which are also affected by bank management of money market assets. Refer to Figure 9–2 and trace these effects.

---

[46] The Fed funds rate was especially volatile after the Fed policy change in early October 1979; on some nonreserve settlement days the range in one day was from 12 percent to 18 percent, whereas on some reserve settlement days it was from 12 percent to 20 percent and even greater in one case. See Federal Reserve Bank of St. Louis, *U.S. Financial Data*, week ending October 24, 1979.

**FIGURE 9–2**
**First Steps in the Monetary Process**

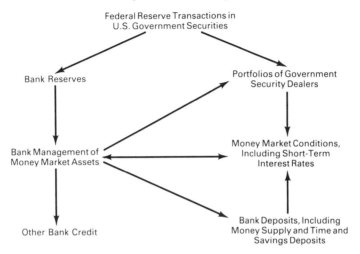

Federal Reserve Transactions in
U.S. Government Securities

Bank Reserves

Portfolios of Government
Security Dealers

Bank Management of
Money Market Assets

Money Market Conditions,
Including Short-Term
Interest Rates

Other Bank Credit

Bank Deposits, Including
Money Supply and Time and
Savings Deposits

**Major Remaining Steps in the Monetary Process—**
**with Some of the Main Interactions Noted**

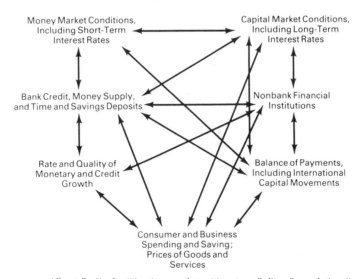

Money Market Conditions,
Including Short-Term
Interest Rates

Capital Market Conditions,
Including Long-Term
Interest Rates

Bank Credit, Money Supply,
and Time and Savings Deposits

Nonbank Financial
Institutions

Rate and Quality of
Monetary and Credit
Growth

Balance of Payments,
Including International
Capital Movements

Consumer and Business
Spending and Saving;
Prices of Goods and
Services

SOURCE: Albert R. Koch, "An Approach to Monetary Policy Formulation,"
Federal Reserve Bank of Philadelphia, *Business Review*, February 1965.

Since demand for money and bank credit is very volatile in the short run, it has been the Fed's aim for a long time to permit short-term changes in such demand to be accommodated. If this demand were not accommodated, money market conditions would be quite unstable. Such instability may, of course, be necessary, in the interest of other objectives, and this question is discussed in some detail in Chapter 16.

The key position of money market conditions may be appreciated by viewing, in bird's-eye fashion, some of the steps in the monetary control process. These are shown in tentative fashion in Figure 9–2. Although Figure 9–2 somewhat oversimplifies the relationships, and although different economists emphasize in varying degrees specific relationships shown in the diagram, the bird's-eye view can be used as a framework for integrating various elements of the situation of the financial markets vis-à-vis the economy at any particular time. The reader should examine each relationship shown in Figure 9–2.

## FLUCTUATIONS IN MONEY MARKET RATES

Until 1965, wide fluctuations in money market rates were rather unusual. Rates might not change more than 25 basis points (¼ percent) from one month to the next, and rates on acceptances and finance paper might not vary for several months. Since 1965, there has been much greater fluctuation in rates. Monthly yield changes of 50 basis points or more are common. The reasons are varied and may stem from the variety of economic problems faced by the United States and accentuated by the economic pressures of the war in Vietnam. There has been uncertainty about monetary policy and wide swings in the rate of change in the money supply, uncertainty about fiscal policy and wide change in federal deficits, and uncertainty about the international monetary system and several crises involving sterling, marks, francs, and finally the dollar, and there has been uncertainty concerning the trend of many developments in society—inflation, productivity, desire for environmental improvement instead of increased output, and government corruption, among others.

Yield spreads also increased after 1965, both yield spreads between three-month and six-month maturities of the same type of instrument and spreads of yields on other instruments over yields on Treasury bills. Desire for liquidity may have been a significant factor explaining the first spread and perhaps the second. In connection with spreads of yields on other instruments over yields on Treasury bills, however, it should be noted that although the volume of Treasury bills increased sharply, the amount held by the Federal Reserve System and by government trust funds increased both absolutely and relative to amounts held by the public. Limited supply available to the public may have been a factor raising prices of Treasury bills and thus keeping yields lower than they would otherwise have been.

In the most recent cyclical peaks of short-term interest rates, in the spring of 1980 and in the summer of 1981, the prime rate rose to unprecedented heights of 20 percent and above. After imposition of consumer credit controls in March 1980 and other measures to restrict demand for credit, rates began to fall. The fall was extremely rapid; by early May 1980, the prime rate was down to 17 percent. Even yields on long-term securities fell, suggesting that perhaps inflation expectations were falling. By summer, the prime rate was in the 11 to 13 percent range.

The sharp peaks in the prime rate, the CD rate, the commercial paper rate, and the Federal funds rate are normally characteristic of peaks in general business activity. Short-term rates fall as demand for credit falls when business enters a recession. Then later, as recovery begins, a new rise in short-term interest rates occurs.

This time, however, short-term interest rates rose again, above the levels shown in Figures 9–1(a) and 9–1(b). Only in the summer of 1982, after a second recession in the last half of 1981 and during 1982, did interest rates fall in the summer of 1982 in what appeared to be a more significant decline. By early 1983 it was clear that inflation had moderated, creating a basis for some decline in long-term interest rates and (as some borrowers shifted to long-term borrowing) a fall in short-term interest rates.

## SIGNIFICANCE OF THE MONEY MARKET FOR THE CONTROL OF ECONOMIC ACTIVITY

The development and growth of the money market is especially significant for the control of economic activity for several reasons. (1) The money market is, as indicated earlier, the first point of impact of monetary policy actions. (2) Money market changes are frequently used as indicators of the impact of monetary policy and as guides for further actions. (3) The growth of the money market means a growth of substitutes for money; funds can be held in the form of money market instruments instead of money.

The significance of the third point requires some further elaboration. The development of instruments such as Treasury bills, commercial paper, and negotiable certificates of deposit tends to increase transactions velocity of money; that is, money is used to buy these instruments and is received by sellers or issuers. It also probably tends to permit an increase in the income velocity of money, that is, the turnover of money in income payments.[47] For example, an increase in commercial paper probably permits financing of purchases of goods and services that might not otherwise be sold. As Richard Selden has suggested, "to the extent that growth in aggregate spending is financed by rising velocity of money, the volume of demand deposits need not— indeed, *should* not—expand. In this manner, therefore, the growth of commercial paper in recent years, along with Treasury bills and other liquid assets, has tended to limit growth of bank deposits and earning assets."[48] If velocity rises, money supply need not rise as rapidly to finance a given rate of growth of the economy; hence a rise in velocity *may* cause the central bank to be more restrictive than otherwise in permitting increases in the money supply.

---

[47] There is no convenient measure of transactions velocity of money, payments/money supply, as there is no convenient measure of total payments. Bank debits (checks drawn on bank demand deposits and withdrawals from such deposits) may be used as a proxy for payments. A convenient measure of income velocity is GNP/money supply, shown in Figure 6–1.

[48] Richard T. Selden, *Trends and Cycles in the Commercial Paper Market*, Occasional Paper 85 (New York: National Bureau of Economic Research, 1963), pp. 88–89.

The general upward trend in velocity of money since World War II may be explained by two factors: (1) the increased efficiency in payment mechanisms that tend to reduce the amount of transactions balances of money needed for a given volume of payments and (2) the gradual transfer of money balances held by business firms, and some balances held by households, into money substitutes such as time deposits, commercial paper, Treasury bills, and others. It seems reasonable to conclude that the second factor was induced in large part by the rise in interest rates. The rise in interest rates reduced the quantity of money demanded. Increasing safety of money substitutes may also have been a factor. This increasing safety is evidenced by the small number of defaults, except for commercial paper in 1970, and is supported by the existence and effectiveness of deposit insurance.

Total spending is the product of money supply times the velocity of money—$MV$ in the well-known equation of exchange, $MV = PT$.[49] ($PT$ is the sum of all transactions, at the price for each transaction, and if only *income transactions* are counted, GNP may be used as $PT$.) If velocity increases at 3 percent in a given year, while an increase in spending of 7 percent is desired, the needed increase in the money stock is approximately 4 percent. Thus changes in velocity are very significant for any attempt to fine-tune the rate of growth of economic activity through monetary policy. The trend in velocity of money gradually declined from the time of the Civil War until 1945; at that point, the direction reversed dramatically. The upward trend in velocity since that time had to be taken into account by those who believed in the effectiveness of monetary policy and a stable relationship of velocity to money supply.[50] What is even more disturbing is the fact that the rate of increase in velocity has not been constant. If the rate of increase in velocity is not stable or does not have a stable relationship to the rate of increase in the money stock, no simple rule for increasing the money stock can be relied upon.

Monetary policy is examined in detail in Chapter 16. At this point it is sufficient to establish the importance of velocity of money and the role of the growth of the money market and money market instruments in affecting velocity.

Finally, short-term interest rates have some impact on long-term rates. In many instances, a rise in short-term rates is accompanied by *some* rise in long-term rates. However, in some years—for example, 1972—short-term interest rates rose sharply with no apparent upward effect on long-term rates. A forecast of the behavior of long-term rates is important because they affect investment spending, stock market prices, consumer spending (probably via stock market prices), and total business activity. Unfortunately, at this point caution is a virtue, and we shall find that even after our

[49] George Garvy and Martin R. Blyn, in one of the few direct research studies in this area, *The Velocity of Money* (Federal Reserve Bank of New York, 1969), conclude that because of possible developments in the more rapid transfer of payments, "judgments about the outlook for velocity are difficult to make" (p. 92).

[50] Richard T. Selden, "The Postwar Rise in the Velocity of Money: A Sectoral Analysis," *Journal of Finance*, December 1961, provided a detailed analysis of the rise, and Milton Friedman and Anna J. Schwartz, *A Monetary History of the United States, 1867–1960* (Princeton, N.J.: Princeton University Press, 1963), devoted a rather long section to speculation on its causes; see pp. 673–675.

survey of interest rate theory in Chapters 12 through 14 we must admit that forecasts of long-term rates are hazardous.

# SUMMARY

The money market refers to the market for short-term loans and investments, both the primary market in which short-term promissory notes and other instruments originate and the secondary market in which many of them are traded. Some short-term promissory notes do not have a secondary market: those arising from business loans made at the prime rate or at higher rates, dealer loans to government securities dealers, and loans to banks by the Fed. Many short-term instruments, however, are traded in the secondary money market: negotiable CDs, Treasury bills, bankers acceptances, Federal funds, repurchase agreements, Eurodollars, short-term government agency securities, and commercial paper. Except for commercial paper, which does not have a very broad secondary market, all these are generally liabilities of banks or of the central bank. Thus risk of default is minimal, and yield differences must presumably result chiefly from factors other than risk of default.

Although, as indicated later, long-term interest rates are probably more important in determining the general level of rates, the money market is significant as the market in which the Fed generally intervenes to implement monetary policy decisions. As the initial point in the transmission of effects of such actions, the money market is carefully watched by economists and financiers.

Major changes in the money market in recent years, such as the introduction of negotiable CDs and the growth in the volume of commercial paper and "repos," have caused shifts in important segments of the market. "Immediately available funds" in the form of Federal funds and RPs have recently become especially important in this respect. An understanding of these factors is essential for effective monetary policy; otherwise we may be in danger, as Henry Wallich commented long ago, of finding that the monetary authority, "instead of controlling the heat . . . had merely been diddling the thermometer."[51]

## Questions for Discussion

**1.** Suggest some reason for the more volatile behavior of short-term interest rates than long-term rates [shown in Figures 9–1(a) and 9–1(b)].

**2.** Show why the money market is important in providing almost instant liquidity for short-term financial assets. What problems might arise if such liquidity could not be provided? Explain why the money market is important as the locus of the open market operations of the central bank. What do central banks do in countries that do not have well-developed, efficient money markets?

**3.** Compare two lists, one of borrowers and one of lenders, in the money market.

---

[51] Henry C. Wallich, "The Fed at the Crossroads," *Morgan Guaranty Survey*, October 1971, p. 10.

Comment on the importance of banks, the central bank, and the government in the money market and on the relative unimportance of the consumer and business sectors of the economy.

**4.** What were the reasons for the first issue of Treasury bills in the United States? Explain why, since 1929, they have become so important in government borrowing.

**5.** What is the importance of government-sponsored agencies to agriculture and housing? Does this constitute a subsidy to these sectors of the economy? Explain.

**6.** Do you foresee growth in "finance bills" in the coming years? Why or why not? Compare your forecast of growth in the volume of finance bills with your forecast for negotiable CDs, and explain. The volume of commercial paper outstanding increased greatly in the 1960s. Give some reasons for this, and discuss the possibility for growing importance of this market in the future.

**7.** How do Eurodollars complicate both the functioning of the money market and the use of open market operations as a tool of monetary policy? Do they also create some questions and uncertainties concerning the balance of payments? If so, how?

**8.** Do you think that a "prime rate" is useful? Why or why not? Is it possible, or likely, that the prime rate may disappear, leaving commercial loan rates without any well-publicized basic rate? Why or why not?

**9.** Distinguish between a forward market and a futures market.

**10.** Assume that your business firm owns a T-bill that will mature in 2 months. You know that you will want to reinvest the proceeds at that time, and you would like to earn today's favorable yield when you do reinvest. How can the futures market enable you to do this?

## Selected References

An interesting and lively discussion of the money market, with a very thoughtful analysis of prospective future developments, is to be found in Wesley Lindow, *Inside the Money Market* (New York: Random House, 1972). An equally lively discussion of the 1970 money market crisis is to be found in Adam Smith, *Supermoney* (New York: Random House, 1972), Chapter 2.

Two booklets, one entitled *Money Market Instruments*, issued by the Federal Reserve Bank of Cleveland, 3rd ed. (1970), and the other entitled *Instruments of the Money Market*, issued by the Federal Reserve Bank of Richmond, 5th ed. (1981), are very useful. The Cleveland booklet is more detailed, with a number of useful references to writings on money market theory and practice.

On the prime rate, see "Floating the Prime Rate," Federal Reserve Bank of Richmond, *Monthly Review*, August 1972, pp. 10–14; Dwight B. Drane and William L. White, "Who Benefits from a Floating Prime Rate?" *Harvard Business Review*, January–February 1972, pp. 121–129; Albert M. Wojnilower and Richard E. Speagle, "The Prime Rate Part I," Federal Reserve Bank of New York, *Monthly Review*, April 1962, pp. 54–59, and "Part II," May 1962, pp. 70–73; and Randall C. Merris, "The Prime Rate," Federal Reserve Bank of Chicago, *Economic Perspectives*, July–August 1977, pp. 17–20.

The development of the Federal funds market is discussed in detail in Parker B. Willis, *The Federal Funds Market—Its Origin and Development*, 3rd ed. (Federal Reserve Bank of Boston,

1968). See also Dorothy M. Nichols, *Trading in Federal Funds—Findings of a Three-Year Survey* (Washington D.C.: Board of Governors of the Federal Reserve System, 1965).

On the Eurodollar market and questions of its significance, see Alexander K. Swoboda, *The Euro-Dollar Market: An Interpretation*, Essays in International Finance, No. 64 (Princeton, N.J.: Princeton University Press, 1968). For an exchange of views on monetary expansions via the Eurodollar market, see Milton Friedman, "The Euro-Dollar Market: Some First Principles," *Morgan Guaranty Survey*, October 1969, pp. 4–14, reprinted in Federal Reserve Bank of St. Louis, *Review*, July 1971; and Fred H. Klopstock, "Money Creation in the Euro-Dollar Market—A Note on Professor Friedman's Views," Federal Reserve Bank of New York, *Monthly Review*, January 1970. See also Fred H. Klopstock, *The Eurodollar Market: Some Unresolved Issues*, Essays in International Finance, No. 65 (Princeton, N.J.: Princeton University Press, 1968); and Jane S. Little, "The Euro-Dollar Market: Its Nature and Impact," Federal Reserve Bank of Boston, *New England Economic Review*, May–June 1969, pp. 2–31.

In spring 1981, a *Journal of Futures Markets* began publication at the Columbia University School of Business. For a conveniently available discussion of the use of the Treasury bill futures market for hedging, see Donald L. Koch, Delores W. Steinhauser, and Pamela Whigham, "Financial Futures as a Risk Management Tool for Banks and S&Ls," Federal Reserve Bank of Atlanta, *Economic Review*, September 1982, pp. 4–14.

For many details concerning the money market in the early 1980s, see Paul Meek, *U.S. Monetary Policy and Financial Markets* (New York: Federal Reserve Bank of New York, 1982), Chapter 5, "The Money Market."

The Eurodollar market has been surveyed in an extensive literature, both theoretical and empirical. For a brief, general overview, see Charles N. Henning, William Pigott, and Robert Haney Scott, *International Financial Management* (New York: McGraw-Hill, 1978), Chapter 10, and references cited at the end of that chapter. For a more advanced analysis, see Carl H. Stem, John H. Makin, and Dennis E. Logue, *Eurocurrencies and the International Monetary System* (Washington, D.C.: American Enterprise Institute for Public Policy Research, 1976). Another recent analysis is that of Gunter Dufey and Ian H. Giddy, *The International Money Market* (Englewood Cliffs, N.J.: Prentice-Hall, 1978). John Hewson and Eisuke Sakakibara, *The Eurocurrency Markets and Their Implications: A "New" View of International Monetary Problems and Monetary Reform* (Lexington, Mass.: Heath, Lexington Books, 1975) gives a provocative analysis, but one should also read the review of this book by John H. Makin in the *Journal of Economic Literature*, December 1976, pp. 1330–1333.

An interesting book containing much description of how participants in the money market act is Marcia Stigum, *The Money Market: Myth, Reality, and Practice* (Homewood, Ill.: Dow Jones-Irwin, 1978). The book also contains a rather useful glossary of money market and bond market terms.

In the last decade, banks have increasingly engaged in "off-balance sheet banking"—examples are the issue of "standby letters of credit" and sales of loans. (Outstanding standby letters of credit were about $12 billion in 1975 and $175 billion in 1985.) Off-balance sheet liabilities do not require reserves, and sale of loans reduces the amount of capital required and usually the amount of reserves required. These activities are part of banks' increasing emphasis on *services* rather than on credit through loans held as assets. See G. D. Koppenhaver, "Standby Letters of Credit," Federal Reserve Bank of Chicago, *Economic Perspectives*, July–August 1987, pp. 28–38; and Chris James, "Off-Balance Sheet Banking," Federal Reserve Bank of San Francisco, *Weekly Letter*, September 17, 1987.

# CAPITAL MARKETS
# FOR DEBT SECURITIES

Major types of long-term assets include real capital assets, corporate bonds, federal government bonds, state and local government bonds (termed "municipals"), mortgages, and equity securities (stocks). The first five are treated in this chapter. Because of its complexity, the market for equities is discussed separately in Chapter 11.

Individuals purchase all these types of assets, but for some of the financial assets, they hold only relatively small shares of total securities outstanding.[1] For example, in the mortgage market, it is estimated that individuals hold about 10 percent of mortgages outstanding but less than 10 percent of the corporate bonds outstanding. On the other hand, they hold over 30 percent of the state and local government securities outstanding. These figures include holdings of individuals as beneficiaries of trusts managed by trust departments of banks because statistics sel-

---

[1] Data in this and the following paragraphs are drawn largely from Salomon Brothers, *Prospects for Financial Markets* (formerly *Supply and Demand for Credit*), various years.

dom indicate these separately. Thus the share held by individuals *per se* is quite small; this is also true of purchases of new issues. The market for debt securities is largely institutional. Hence the policies of financial institutions are very important in determining all allocations of funds and relative interest rates. In contrast, it is estimated that individuals still hold nearly two-thirds of all outstanding equity securities (stocks).

Each type of financial institution has general characteristics that help to determine the capital markets in which it will participate, and each institution has financial policies that further direct its investment purchases and sales.

Major participants in the mortgage market are the savings and loan associations, the commercial banks, federal agencies, life insurance companies, and mutual savings banks. Other less important participants include the finance companies, mortgage companies, real estate investment trusts, and state and local government retirement funds.

The corporate bond market is somewhat more diverse: significant institutional participants include life insurance companies, state and local government retirement funds, and private pension funds. Less important participants include mutual savings banks, property and casualty insurance companies, mutual funds, commercial banks, and foundations and endowments. Foreign investors also participate in this market, whereas they are insignificant in the mortgage market.

The only major institutional participants in the municipal bond market are the commercial banks and the property and casualty insurance companies; minor participants are life insurance companies, state and local retirement funds, and mutual savings banks. Business corporations also buy small amounts of these securities.

All institutions buy federal government securities. If holdings by U.S. government agencies and trust funds (such as the Social Security trust fund) and the Federal Reserve System are excluded, the remaining privately held debt is about 71 percent of total federal debt. Of this 71 percent, about 12 percent was held by foreigners (who have been important buyers in recent years), about 11 percent by state and local governments, about 10 percent by commercial banks, and about 7 percent by individuals, leaving about 31 percent held by a variety of institutions other than commercial banks. Commercial banks buy chiefly the securities with 10 years or less to maturity.

Of the $400 billion of federal agency debt outstanding at the end of 1982, approximately $75 billion was issued by the farm credit institutions, about $314 billion was issued or guaranteed by the housing credit institutions, and the rest was issued by miscellaneous agencies. Again, almost all institutions buy some of these government agency securities; savings and loan associations, commercial banks, state and local governments, state and local government employee retirement funds, mutual savings banks, life insurance companies, pension funds, and property and casualty insurance companies were all significant purchasers.

To understand the factors affecting particular capital markets, we analyze each of these separately. Before doing that, however, we examine the nature and efficiency of capital markets generally and the role of the long-term rate of interest vis-à-vis the short-term rates found in the money market.

# NATURE, ROLE, AND EFFICIENCY
# OF CAPITAL MARKETS

Capital markets are markets in which lenders and investors provide long-term funds in exchange for financial assets offered by borrowers or holders. We follow tradition in giving attention primarily to financial capital markets, but we must emphasize that the "market" for real capital assets is more fundamental. Returns on financial assets rest on the fact that these are claims on real capital assets; the rate of return on real capital assets is fundamental because it provides the basis for most of the private demand for funds, other than the demand for mortgage funds.[2]

Capital markets are those in which long-term financial assets are bought and sold, and the usual dividing line is that long-term assets have an original maturity of more than one year. On occasion, however, short-term securities may have a more restricted meaning.[3]

## Primary and Secondary Markets

Capital markets and the "money market" involve both a market for new issues (a primary market) and a secondary market for trading in outstanding issues. Secondary markets serve to provide liquidity for financial assets: if there were no secondary markets, anyone who purchased a security would generally have to hold it until maturity. If secondary markets were small and inefficient, holders might be able to sell securities after purchasing them, but perhaps only at significant losses. In this chapter, therefore, attention is devoted primarily to the secondary markets.

Capital markets originate as new issue markets; then as a considerable volume of issues comes into existence, trading in outstanding issues begins. Capital markets in which trading in secondary issues is rather "thin" exist in many countries. Markets in many countries have not yet developed the volume of trading that makes it possible to regard long-term financial assets as liquid because they cannot, in those countries, be sold *quickly without significant loss*. Markets in which this is possible are said to have *breadth* when orders to buy or sell come from many different groups, *depth* when there are both buy and sell orders below and above the current market price, and *resiliency* when new orders come into the market in volume when prices fluctuate. Markets with these characteristics provide liquidity for assets that otherwise would not be liquid; investors are induced to hold these assets because risk is reduced or minimized, and borrowers easily obtain funds.

---

[2] In addition to demand based on expected productive use of capital, there is of course some consumer demand for loans for immediate consumption and government demand based on factors other than expected yields from capital assets. Nevertheless, the major part of demand arises from the fact that a return or yield is expected from real capital assets, and funds are needed to acquire such assets.

[3] For example, short-term capital gains were for many years defined in the income tax law as gains obtained in holding securities not more than six months. This was increased so that gains on securities held less than one year were counted as short-term gains. The Tax Reform Act of 1986 made *all* capital gains taxable at the same rates as other income.

## Efficiency of Financial Markets

An *efficient* market not only provides liquidity but also functions to allocate resources to the most productive uses at the least possible cost. Approximately equal rates of return should be obtained on investments that are comparable in risk. One test is to compare rates of return on new issues with rates of return on the same (or similar) issues that have been outstanding. By this test, several studies indicated that, both for stocks and for bonds, any difference in yields between new issues and "seasoned" securities with the same investment characteristics tended to disappear relatively quickly.[4]

The costs of issuing new securities, "flotation costs," have tended to decline over a long period of time, indicating that capital markets are becoming more efficient in terms of lower costs.[5] Again, in making comparisons, care must be taken to compare costs for similar issues. Trading costs such as brokers' commissions and dealers' price spreads do not show the same secular decline as do flotation costs, and there may be elements of monopolistic profit in these fees. A "third market" in stocks traded on the New York Stock Exchange developed among large institutions because of lack of bidding by brokers for large transactions.[6] Many steps have been taken in recent years both to increase the safety of investors' funds and to stimulate greater competition. It is not yet clear what the result of these actions has been, and the fact that small investors were selling more securities than they were buying suggested that they may have feared a lack of safety or the presence of monopolistic elements or both.

Allocational efficiency in a market such as that for stocks affects both the flow of new funds and the retention of earnings. If stocks must be sold at relatively low prices, flow of funds into such industries is discouraged. Similarly, if prices of stocks fall, stockholders will eventually refuse to permit retention of earnings; if stockholders do not receive dividends, they must be compensated by the expectation that earnings will be high enough to permit higher dividends in the future and/or that earnings will be high enough to cause the price of the stock to rise, so that instead of dividends or in addition to dividends the investors in that stock obtain capital gains.

Although efficiency of capital markets may be improved, it is generally agreed that capital markets in the United States are relatively efficient. One major challenge to this agreement is discussed in Chapter 11. This challenge concerns the valuation of stocks during a period of inflation *relative* to the valuation of debt securities.

[4] Irwin Friend and J. R. Longstreet, "Price Experience and Return on New Stock Issues," in *Investment Banking and the New Issues Market* (New York: World Publishing, 1967), Chapter 8; Joseph W. Conard, *The Behavior of Interest Rates* (New York: Columbia University Press, 1966), pp. 117–118; and Irwin Friend, "The Economic Consequences of the Stock Market," *American Economic Review*, Papers and Proceedings, May 1972, pp. 212–219. See also William J. Baumol, *The Stock Market and Economic Efficiency* (New York: Fordham University Press, 1965).

[5] Morris Mendelson, "Underwriting Compensation," in *Investment Banking and New Issues Market*, Chapter 7.

[6] See Murray E. Polakoff and Arnold W. Sametz, "The Third Market—The Nature of Competition for Listed Securities Traded Off-Board," *The Antitrust Bulletin*, January–April 1966. The evidence of monopolistic elements is not firm. For some of the issues involved, see Murray C. Polakoff et al., *Financial Institutions and Markets* (Boston: Houghton Mifflin, 1970), pp. 590–606.

Long-term assets may be divided into real capital assets and seven categories of financial assets. Each category of long-term financial assets has a market with somewhat unique characteristics. These categories are government long-term securities (bonds and notes); long-term securities of the government-sponsored agencies, usually referred to as agency securities; securities of state and local government units, referred to as municipal bonds or "municipals"; corporate bonds; mortgages; stocks; and the recently developed Eurobonds. Before examining each asset and market, we note the special importance of some representative long-term interest rates.

## Rates of Interest in the Capital Markets

The theory of the determination of interest rates developed in Chapter 12 is based on the premise that, although there are many long-term interest rates and many short-term rates, fundamental long-term rates are determined by supply of and demand for long-term loanable funds. Insofar as demand for loanable funds varies in response to changing interest rates, it varies chiefly because business firms find it more or less profitable to borrow funds for real investment purposes.[7]

Various short-term interest rates discussed in Chapter 9 fluctuate above and below long-term rates, as shown in Figure 10–1. Theories that attempt to explain the relations between short and long rates are discussed in Chapter 13.

In economic theory courses, "the" interest rate is often referred to as an important variable. In reality, there are many groups of long-term interest rates in addition to the short-term rates already discussed in Chapter 9.

First, there are rates of return (profit, in layman's language) on real capital assets. These are fundamental interest rates that must exist (implicitly or explicitly) in any society. They exist because capital is productive—funds borrowed now and invested in factories and machinery produce more than could be produced without the factories and machinery. Even in a socialist economy, interest rates exist in this sense implicitly.

Second, there are rates of return on stocks that constitute evidence of ownership of physical (real) capital assets.

Third, there are interest rates, or yield rates, on corporate bonds, on government bonds, and on government agency securities.

Fourth, there are interest rates on "municipal" securities issued by state and local government units.

Finally, there are mortgage interest rates.

Reference is usually made to separate markets for stocks, corporate bonds, government bonds and government agency securities, municipal securities, and mortgages. Each of the foregoing is really a market in which there is a whole family of

---

[7] Government demand for borrowing is not influenced very much by interest rates, since government must borrow enough to meet any deficit. Consumer borrowing does vary, but it too is not heavily influenced by changes in interest rates unless they are extreme. Thus business borrowing is more sensitive to interest rates than is government or consumer borrowing.

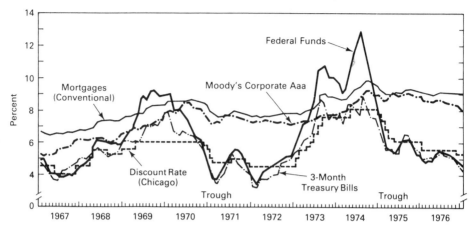

FIGURE 10–1
Selected Long-Term and Short-Term Interest Rates, 1967–1976*

*Market rates are monthly averages of daily figures.

SOURCE: Federal Reserve Bank of Chicago, *Economic Perspectives,* January–February 1977, p. 25.

rates—rates for various grades of quality of corporate bonds, rates for various maturities of government bonds, and so on. Before developing the theory of the determination of interest rates, we examine each of these markets.

Any capital asset—any asset held for a period of time rather than being consumed immediately—normally has a value or price. This price is determined by expected returns, including return of principal and interest (or dividends or profits), but, since the returns are expected in the future, they must be discounted at some appropriate interest rate. Future income is worth less than the same amount of present income because the present income can be invested and obtain earnings in the interim period.[8]

## REAL CAPITAL ASSETS

Real capital assets (plant, machinery, equipment, etc.) yield rates of return that constitute the fundamental determinant of demand for loanable funds for investment, whereas the major determinant of the supply of loanable funds is saving. These rates of return may be represented by an average rate, the rate of profit for the average firm. This rate must be high enough to induce wealth owners to hold such assets at their current prices; if wealth owners wish to hold more such assets, prices of the assets will

---

[8] Thus we need not assume that people prefer present goods over future goods. Some do, some do not. Some people even save for the purpose, in part, of being able to leave an estate to their heirs. Interest is paid, primarily, not to induce people to save, but because of expected returns on capital assets (because of their productivity).

rise; if they wish to hold less, prices will fall. The demand for these assets by wealth owners will depend on their portfolio choices among the various types of assets they can hold, including money, short-term government securities, long-term government securities, corporate bonds, and real capital assets.

The problem in analyzing the rate of return on real capital assets is, as noted, that measurement of this rate is difficult because of the diversity both in types of real capital assets and in the ways of measuring rates of return on such assets. Different accounting methods, especially for such things as depreciation, result in quite different estimates of rates of return.

Presumably, the values of real capital assets owned by business firms are reflected in some manner in the values of the equities (stocks) that constitute claims on such assets, after creditors' claims are satisfied.

If corporations and other business firms are to undertake new projects (investment), an after-tax rate of return on such projects must at least be greater than the cost of capital. Funds for such investment must often be borrowed. In a period of inflation, expected after-tax return increases if business managers expect that they will be able to raise the prices they charge. An alternative is to compare current earnings with *real* interest rates, on the assumption that earnings may be expected to rise enough to compensate for inflation. (This assumes that the average business firm can raise prices by the average rate of inflation; this may not be exactly correct, but it may be a good first approximation.) The cost of capital can thus be measured approximately by subtracting from nominal corporate bond yields an "expected" inflation rate. Measuring cost of capital in a period of inflation has always been complicated by the facts that (1) the "expected" inflation rate is not observable and thus cannot easily be measured correctly and (2) there is also a premium in the nominal rate of inflation that compensates investors for the uncertainty of the inflation; if people are uncertain as to what the inflation rate will be, there is risk that it may be greater than their estimate.

If the value of equities falls, the fall must presumably be caused either by a decline in expected earnings or a rise in the cost of capital. A decline in expected earnings could occur if the productivity of capital is less, for example, if factories and machinery are obsolete. If expected earnings are measured on the assumption that productivity of capital did not change, the estimates may be too high if productivity of capital has declined.

To put it another way, the price of a financial asset was defined in Chapter 1 as being equal to expected income from that asset discounted by (divided by) the cost of capital. If prices of stocks (one type of financial asset) are relatively low, it may be either because expected earnings are low or because the cost of capital is high.

Measurement of expected income and of the cost of capital (the real interest rate) are both difficult. Hence, explanations of long-run trends in stock market prices are topics on which there is significant disagreement among economists and among those who take a "fundamental" approach to stock market prices. (Some analysts try to explain changes in stock market prices by "technical" analysis that does not involve the more fundamental concepts of expected earnings and cost of capital.) Because yield rates on real capital assets and values of stocks in the equities market are intertwined, we return to the question of explaining changes in yields on real capital assets when we discuss the stock market in Chapter 11.[9]

## THE CORPORATE BOND MARKET[10]

Yields on corporate bonds are higher than yields on government securities, presumably because there is some risk of default on corporate securities. This risk may be negligible in the case of the best grades of corporate bonds, but its existence means that yields are at least slightly higher. Figure 10–1 shows relationships among corporate bond yields, mortgage yields, and selected short-term interest rates. Note that short-term interest rates fall sharply in recessions, whereas corporate bond yields may change very little.

Note in Figure 10–1 that short-term interest rates continued to fall after the trough of the 1973–1975 recession had been reached in spring 1975. Figure 10–2 shows long-term and short-term interest rates from 1976 through 1979. Note the sharp rise in short-term interest rates in that period of economic expansion, rising from below the level of long-term rates to substantially above it.

Figure 10–3 shows the paths of long-term and short-term interest rates in a period of inflation followed by two recessions—one in the first half of 1980 and the second from mid-1981 to the end of 1982. Long-term interest rates gradually rose as the rate of inflation increased, while short-term interest rates reached very high levels. As it became evident by 1982 that inflation had moderated, short-term interest rates fell, as shown in Figures 9–1(a) and 9–1(b) in Chapter 9. Long-term interest rates remained relatively high, reflecting fears that inflation could be a continuing problem in the long run.

By 1986, with inflation below 2 percent at an annual rate (down from an annual rate of over 10 percent in 1980), both long-term and short-term interest rates had fallen sharply, as shown in Figure 10–4.

Unlike the government, which must market new debt issues whenever refunding is necessary and whenever expenditures exceed revenues and cash balances cannot be further reduced, corporations take the initiative in financing decisions. New plant and equipment purchases are planned with consideration of financing costs, and corporations may defer some investment plans if financing costs seem likely to be too high.

[9] For more detail on the measurement problems involved in estimating expected earnings and cost of capital, see the following studies: James Tobin and William Brainard, "Asset Markets and the Cost of Capital," in *Economic Progress, Private Values, and Public Policy: Essays in Honor of William Fellner* (Amsterdam: North-Holland, 1977); William Brainard, J. Shoven, and L. Weiss, "The Financial Valuation of the Return to Capital," *Brookings Papers on Economic Activity*, No. 2, 1980; and Patrick J. Corcoran and Leonard G. Sahling, "The Cost of Capital: How High Is It?" Federal Reserve Bank of New York, *Quarterly Review*, Summer 1982, pp. 23–31.

[10] For further details and more analysis of a number of points covered in this section, see Burton Zwick, "The Market for Corporate Bonds," Federal Reserve Bank of New York, *Quarterly Review*, Autumn 1977, pp. 27–36.

**FIGURE 10–2**
**Long-Term and Short-Term Interest Rates, 1974–1979**

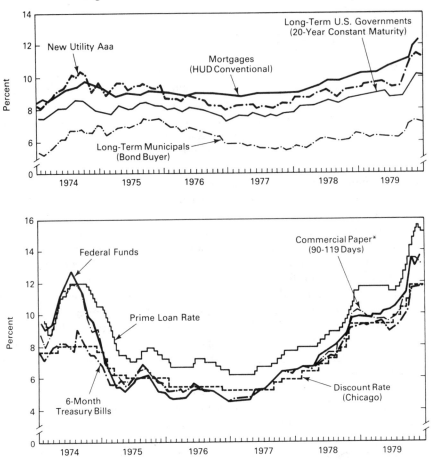

*Beginning November 1979, 90-day maturity

SOURCE: Federal Reserve Bank of Chicago, *Economic Perspectives,* January–February 1980, p. 25.

Although the corporate bond market is largely for the obligations of profit-making corporations, mention should be made of bonds issued to provide funds for building schools, hospitals, and churches. The interest to be paid on such bonds is usually covered by anticipated revenues, which can usually be projected with some assurance. These bonds have a good record, therefore, and are sold in the same manner as are lesser known corporate bonds.[11]

---

[11] These are termed "church bonds" by one author; see Roland I. Robinson, *Money and Capital Markets* (New York: McGraw-Hill, 1964), p. 207.

## FIGURE 10–3
### Representative Long-Term and Short-Term Interest Rates, 1978–1982

Long-term interest rates declined from recent highs . . .

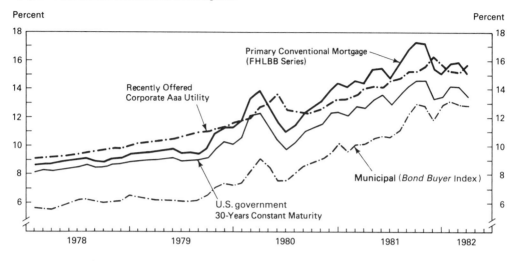

. . . with short-term rates following a similar but more pronounced pattern

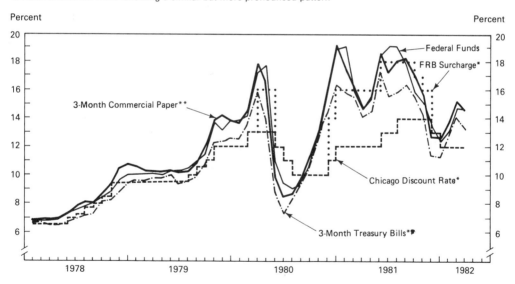

\*Last day of the month.
\*\*Bond equivalent yields.

SOURCE: Federal Reserve Bank of Chicago, *Economic Perspectives*, Midyear 1982, p. 26.

## FIGURE 10–4
### Yields on Selected Securities, 1985–1986
### (averages of daily rates)

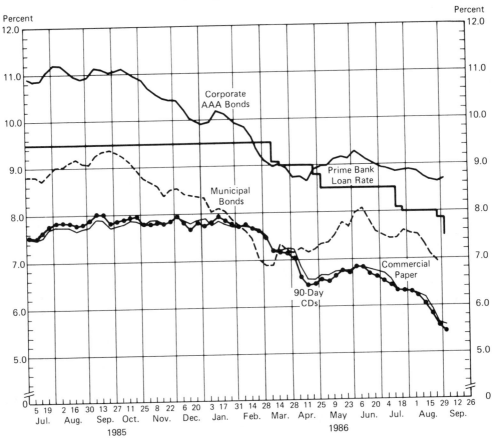

Latest data plotted are averages of rates available for the week ending September 5, 1986.

Corporations borrow by issuing bonds when they do not generate sufficient funds internally to meet their needs. In years when needs are low (in recession years), corporations in fact have sometimes used a part of internally generated funds to pay back a part of external debt. Hence there are substantial fluctuations in corporate bond issues. Because the supply of bonds fluctuates significantly, yields fluctuate rather widely. Because the major purchasers of corporate bonds are life insurance companies, pension funds, state and local government retirement funds, and individuals and nonprofit organizations, if these groups do not purchase more bonds in years of high business activity, bond prices inevitably fall, and yields rise.

**FIGURE 10–4 (cont.)**
**Selected Interest Rates**
**(averages of daily rates)**

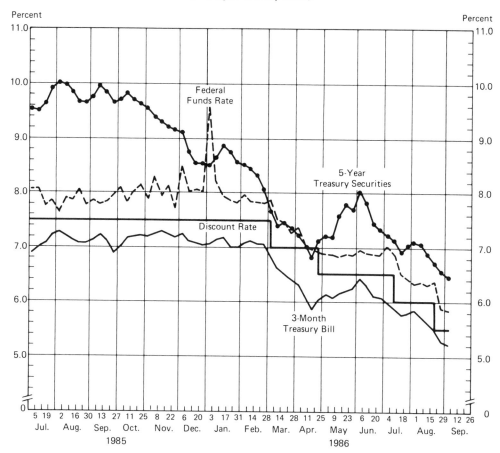

Latest data plotted are averages of rates available for the week ending September 5, 1986.

SOURCE: Federal Reserve Bank of St. Louis, *U.S. Financial Data,* September 4, 1986, pp. 6 and 7.

## Bond Prices and Yields

Corporate bonds are issued in denominations ranging from $100 to $10,000 or more, with $1,000 being the most common face value. They may be unsecured (debentures) or secured by mortgages (mortgage bonds), rolling stock (equipment obligations), or marketable securities (collateral trust bonds). Debentures are not actually unsecured, but are backed by the general credit of the issuing corporation and are issued, generally, by corporations with excellent credit ratings. Historically, secured issues generally have had more defaults than unsecured issues.[12] Some bonds contain promises to pay the principal, but not the interest, if earnings are insufficient; these are termed "income" or "adjustment" bonds. There are also "assumed" bonds, assumed by a company acquiring another company in a merger, and "guaranteed" bonds, usually guaranteed by a company acquiring another company in a merger. Maturities usually vary from 10 to 30 years. Most corporate bonds contain a call provision, permitting redemption after certain dates but before maturity; corporations may set aside sinking funds to provide for retirement of bonds; and bonds may have provisions for retirement of a portion of an issue each year (serial bonds). Mention should also be made of convertible bonds, which can be converted under certain conditions into other securities, usually common stock.

Prices of bonds of the highest quality—for example, those rated as Aaa by Moody's Investor Service—are highest, and therefore the yields the lowest; yields for lower grades of quality are higher, although differences may vary from time to time. The rates usually quoted and shown on charts are those for "seasoned" bonds—those that have been outstanding for some time. Yields on new issues are slightly different, as investors may not at first appraise them in the same way as they do later, when time for evaluation has occurred.

## Fluctuations in the Volume of Bond Issues

As indicated in Chapter 7, business demand for funds increases as business activity rises. At first, much of the demand may be for short-term funds, needed to increase inventories as rising sales reduce stocks of goods on hand. As a business recovery period progresses, however, business firms turn to long-term borrowing; recovery of confidence leads to planning for more capital investment, and the need for long-term funds becomes evident. Of course, there are firms, such as utilities, that must borrow at all times, because they must continue long-term investment to provide facilities for new customers as population and household formation increase.

It is significant that the amount of corporate bonds increased in the period 1960–1975 as interest rates rose. In that period capital expenditures of corporations increased, whereas the amount of internally generated funds rose very little after 1966. The growing need for external funds caused a large volume of new issues of corporate bonds at high yields; the share of corporate bonds outstanding rose, whereas the share of long-term Treasury issues, the share of mortgages, and the share of state and local government securities all declined.

A key factor was the decline in retained earnings in a period of growing need for funds to meet planned capital investment. The increased supply of bonds drove yields on Moody's Aaa corporate bonds to a peak of over 8 percent yield in 1970, from a level of about 4 percent in the early 1960s. Bond buyers benefited from the higher yields,

---

[12] W. Braddock Hickman, *Corporate Bond Quality and Investor Experience* (Princeton, N.J.: Princeton University Press for the National Bureau of Economic Research, 1958), pp. 431–465; see also Thomas R. Atkinson, *Trends in Corporate Bond Quality* (New York: National Bureau of Economic Research, 1967).

and the share of interest in national income, as compared with wages, rent, and profit, increased somewhat.[13] The rise in bond yields did not deter corporations from issuing bonds, and the share of bonds in the capital market continued to rise. The share of mortgages, municipal bonds, and long-term Treasury issues, on the other hand, declined as issuers were discouraged and the demand for such securities seemed to lessen. For mortgages, this occurred despite a rise in yields on FHA mortgages in the secondary market equally as great as the rise in corporate bond yields.

Two factors encouraged firms to finance spending by issuing bonds rather than stock: (1) interest on bonds is deductible before income is determined for tax purposes, whereas dividends are not, and (2) the *real* cost of debt financing declines in a period of inflation because, once debt is incurred, interest payments are usually fixed, whereas investors may expect (or hope) that dividends will be increased. On the other hand, the increased use of debt, with fixed obligations to pay interest and to repay principal, means an increase in the possibility of bankruptcy if earnings decline. Avoiding possible bankruptcy meant lawyers', accountants', and other fees and the devotion of managerial time to the task.

The steady rise in the ratio of debt to total assets of business firms is evident throughout the 1960s and much of the 1970s if physical assets are valued at historical costs. However, if they are valued at replacement costs, the ratio of debt to total assets began to decline in the mid-1970s, as inflation raised the replacement value of physical assets.

Short-term fluctuations in volume of bond issues are related to changes in business conditions. As business activity rises, inventories must be increased. Increases in inventory are usually financed by short-term borrowing. It may seem odd that such borrowing occurs just when short-term interest rates are reaching their peaks, and indeed may be above long-term rates, but it must be remembered that at such times both long-term and short-term rates are relatively high. If any later decline in rates is expected, it is better to borrow short-term than to borrow long-term at high rates.

## Who Are the Final Purchasers of Corporate Bonds?

As indicated earlier, the final purchasers of corporate bonds are chiefly life insurance companies, state and local government employee retirement funds, private pension funds, and foreigners. The end of one "bull" market in stocks in the late 1960s stimulated individuals and pension funds to shift some of their assets from stocks to bonds. As inflation continued and became more severe, however, individuals began to invest more in short-term assets (such as money market mutual funds and

---

[13] From 1965 to 1970, net interest increased from 3.2 to 4.2 percent of national income; in the same period, corporate profits before taxes declined from 13.8 to 9.5 percent of national income, and the decline would have been greater had the inventory valuation adjustment been included in the profit figures. In this period, interest received rose 81 percent while total national income rose by 41 percent.

money market certificates described in Chapters 4 and 9) and in "real" assets such as gold and houses. Several times, short-term rates rose above long-term rates. Individuals were also induced to invest more heavily in municipal securities because the income from such securities is exempt from income tax. Since the investment income of pension funds is not subject to income tax, pension funds need not be concerned about tax differences. When capital gains on stocks became infrequent, pension funds shifted part of their assets to corporate bonds. However, with the very rapid growth of pension funds, the increased investment in bonds did not increase the percentage share of their funds invested in bonds, and the private pension funds still held large percentages of their total assets in stocks. At the end of 1982, it was estimated that private pension funds held 66 percent of their assets in stocks and only 18 percent in bonds.

## New Issues of Corporate Bonds—Underwriting and Direct Placement

Corporations have two alternatives in the issue of bonds: public sale with the assistance of investment banks or direct placement with one or a small number of institutions. In a public offering, a syndicate of investment bankers (one of them usually acting as manager) undertakes the marketing of the issue; arrangements vary from "best efforts" agreements to complete underwriting, in which sale of the securities is guaranteed by the investment banks that hold any securities that they are unable to sell to the public. In a private or direct placement, the corporation may be aided by an investment bank, but an agreement is made directly with one or a small number of financial institutions for purchase of the securities, and the provisions of the agreement are tailored, by negotiation, to the desires of the two parties.

Growing concern over liquidity on the part of bond buyers in 1969 and early 1970 probably contributed to the shift away from privately or directly placed bonds to marketable bonds (directly placed issues are less marketable because they may contain special provisions, and in any event their marketability has not been tested because they were privately placed). Until the decline in stock market prices in late 1969, inflation may also have been a factor inducing institutions to purchase stocks rather than privately placed issues of bonds.

Another factor in the shift away from private placement was the relatively smaller share of bonds purchased by life insurance companies, for they have been the major purchasers of privately placed issues.

## The Secondary Market for Corporate Bonds

Corporate bonds are negotiable instruments; some are in bearer coupon form so that they may easily be transferred. Corporate bonds are traded on the organized exchanges, although the volume of trading is small compared with that in stocks. Corporate bonds are also traded in the over-the-counter market; volume of trading is small compared with that in government securities. The major purchasers of corporate bonds are life insurance companies, state and local governments—which purchase them because states often require their retirement funds to be invested partly in bonds—and private pension funds. As most bonds are bought by institutional investors, there is less need for sale for liquidity purposes than if bonds were largely owned by individuals. Commercial banks buy few corporate bonds because the increased risk and less liquidity, as compared with government securities, makes them unattractive, especially considering the transactions costs necessary because of the need for analysis of quality.

Because most bonds are now purchased by institutional investors, the secondary market is rather "thin." Institutions that purchase corporate bonds seldom need liquidity, except perhaps in a crisis, and hence need not often sell many bonds. Since institutions, having bought them, are not likely to sell high-quality bonds, the market for these is especially thin.

Because of the nature of corporate bonds, however, the secondary market could probably handle larger volume if necessary. The bid-and-ask spreads of dealers are not large, as they probably would be if a dealer were in a position to take advantage of a shortage of buyers or sellers. The relatively small corporate bond market could probably expand in size without difficulty. Thus lack of liquidity of corporate bonds is generally not likely to be a serious problem.

## Financial Innovation in the Corporate Bond Market

In the 1970s and early 1980s, financial innovation was widespread in the financial markets. New types of financial assets were offered, interest rates changed dramatically, and new rules for selling and redeeming financial assets were inaugurated.

### "Zero-Coupon" Bonds

At this point we discuss one innovation in the government and corporate securities markets—certificates with no interest specified, sold at prices much below future redemption prices. The entire yield on such securities is in the form of capital gain. We also discuss the increasing sale of "high-yield" corporate bonds.

Because "zero-coupon" (no interest coupon) bonds were expected to be subject to income tax on the rise in value from sale price to maturity price, and were sold primarily to retirement accounts and other funds that generated tax-deferred income (income deferred until accounts were withdrawn or until retirement), no income tax law questions were anticipated.

When the same form of securities was offered in the corporate bond market, however, income tax authorities saw the issue of corporate bonds at low prices, with no interest income, and the entire return to be received in the form of the rise in price from initial sale to maturity, as an attempt to reduce taxes by paying capital gains taxes rather than ordinary income tax (capital gains tax rates were much lower until 1987). It was thought by some that, in fact, zero-coupon bonds might easily be marketable in some countries (e.g., Japan) that had no capital gains tax or a very low capital gains tax rate. This innovation proved to be distasteful to tax authorities, and rules were modified or interpreted in such a way that the income was taxed at regular rates. Thus the advantage of the new form of corporate bonds was removed.[14]

There are other aspects of original issue discount bonds (including zero-coupon bonds) that create advantages or disadvantages for borrowers and/or for investors; for example, reinvestment risk is less (since there are no interest coupons to be reinvested, investors need not worry about possibly having to reinvest interest payments received and finding that rates are lower). Investors also are protected against call of the bonds by the corporation (calling in the bonds for redemption) and the risk of reinvestment of such funds, since corporations are not likely to call original issue deep discount bonds. The complications involved are discussed in more detail in Chapter 14.

It should be understood that the basic reasons for the use of these types of securities are the high interest rates and the volatility in interest rates associated with a period of inflation, combined with the nature of the tax laws. If long-term interest rates fall, even slowly, and if they become less volatile, the incentives for issuing special types of bonds are reduced.

Most special types of bonds (original issue discount bonds, convertible bonds, variable-rate bonds, bonds on which the principal value is linked to the value of a specified quantity of some commodity, and so on) have advantages to investors but disadvantages to borrowers. Unless the advantage to the investors increases because of high or volatile interest rates or other conditions, there is little reason for a borrowing corporation to incur the disadvantage to attract investors who receive only a small advantage.

### High-Yield Bonds ("Junk Bonds")

An interesting development in the 1970s and 1980s was the issue of a relatively large volume (over $100 billion from 1981 to 1986) of high-yield bonds. Reasons for issue of such bonds included the difficulty of borrowing funds in periods of "credit crunches," low prices of stocks until after 1982 (and hence high cost of obtaining equity capital), financial deregulation, and increased competition.

High-yield bonds (that is, bonds with high yields relative to other bonds) have relatively low ratings by the rating agencies, and on the average a significant percent of defaults. One study indicated that most of the major investment houses that have

---

[14] Technically, a bond purchased at a discount in the *secondary* market is treated differently; the rise in price as the bond approaches and reaches maturity is treated as a capital gain. Original issue discount bonds had been issued in the past by companies with low credit ratings or sometimes by companies with higher credit ratings when the bonds were privately placed. These bonds carried, usually, some interest coupon, so that return to investors was partly interest and partly rise in price; but in that case, investors had to prorate the discount on a straight-line basis and treat the prorated amounts as current income (not capital gain). The question for interpretation was, "Would the same treatment apply to bonds with *zero* coupons?" For more details on this and other aspects of discount bonds, see Andrew Silver, "Original Issue Deep Discount Bonds," Federal Reserve Bank of New York, *Quarterly Review*, Winter 1981–1982, pp. 18–28.

sponsored issues of high-yield bonds have seen from 2 percent to 17 percent of the total volume default at some point.[15]

Reasons for buying high-yield bonds probably include the desire to obtain high yields comparable to those obtainable on some other investments, the relatively low yields (including capital gains) in the stock market until it began to rise in 1982, and the fact that many companies issuing high-yield bonds were well-known companies. The events after 1973 created major problems for certain industries (e.g., energy and steel); the high inflation rate made some industries less competitive in the export field; and the great volatility in interest rates probably affected interest rate expectations.

## THE EUROBOND MARKET

A new market has developed in the past two decades for what are termed Eurobonds. Eurobonds may be most easily defined as bonds denominated in a currency other than that of the country or countries in which most of the bonds are initially sold. Most Eurobonds are sold in Europe, in one or more countries, and most of them are denominated in U.S. dollars. Eurobonds are usually underwritten by an international syndicate of investment banking houses and are sold simultaneously in several countries. They may be distinguished from foreign bonds, which are bonds issued by a foreign firm but denominated in the currency of the country in which the bonds are issued. Thus, a U.S. subsidiary in France might issue bonds in Italy in lire; these are foreign bonds. Or it might issue bonds denominated in dollars or marks and market the bonds in Italy and perhaps several other countries in Europe (other than Germany). These are Eurobonds.

Most Eurobonds are publicly marketed, rather than privately placed, and most have maturities of 10 to 15 years. Convertible Eurobonds are not very common, but most are callable (or were when issued in years for which data are available). A few Eurobond issues have been denominated in several currencies, one part of the issue being denominated in each currency. A few issues have had currency options—holders can ask for payment of interest and principal in one of several currencies. Some have been denominated in the European unit of account (EUA). The EUA was defined as a weight of gold, the weight being that contained at the time, by definition, in the U.S. dollar. Payment on these bonds was to be made in one of a number of currencies. The aim of these provisions was to eliminate the risk of holders receiving payment in currencies that had been devalued. In the case of bonds denominated in EUA, if a currency in the list were devalued, a bondholder who asked for redemption in that currency would receive a greater amount, corresponding to the current value of the EUA in that currency. In 1970, on one issue floated in the European currency

---

[15] *The Wall Street Journal*, September 29, 1986, p. 17. In this study, total volume of an issue was assigned to the lead manager of that issue, private placements were not counted, and issues in default at one time are not necessarily currently in default. For broader coverage of high-yield (low-grade) bonds, see Jan Loeys, "Low-Grade Bonds: A Growing Source of Corporate Funding," Federal Reserve Bank of Philadelphia, *Business Review*, November–December 1986, pp. 3–12.

unit, holders could choose payment in any one of the Common Market currencies. A holder of EUA bonds could gain if his or her home currency were devalued, as the holder could ask for repayment in a currency not devalued. A holder of European currency unit bonds could gain if his or her home currency were devalued, and also if any of the five major Common Market currencies (German marks, Dutch guilders, Italian lire, or French or Belgian francs) were revalued upward. Obviously, these various provisions have been designed to reduce risk of fluctuations in bond value.

## Origin and Development of the Eurobond Market

The Interest Equalization Tax (IET), proposed in 1963 and enacted in 1964 retroactive to July 1963, increased the cost for U.S. residents of buying foreign bonds. This encouraged foreign borrowers, including foreign subsidiaries of U.S. firms, to issue bonds elsewhere; but, because the U.S. dollar was still regarded as very sound currency, unlikely to be devalued, bonds were frequently denominated in dollars. The voluntary foreign credit restraint program and mandatory controls introduced in 1963 further encouraged borrowing in foreign countries.

Eurobond issues were also encouraged by their freedom from the withholding of income taxes on interest to bondholders, which would generally occur on bond issues sold in the United States.

Although Eurobond issues are publicly marketed rather than directly placed, the actual process is a mixture of the two methods. A group of managers of a bond marketing syndicate arranges to buy the issue from the issuing corporation. Then the underwriting group sells to an international selling group of houses, and they in turn sell to dealers, at successively smaller discounts. The bonds are then sold by dealers through direct contact with buyers; the public is not invited to buy bonds.

Although there is no central collection of data on Eurobond issues, several agencies make estimates of the volume. It appears that by 1970 sales of new issues of Eurobonds totaled about $3 billion. By 1979, such sales exceeded $3 billion *per quarter*. There is apparently also a fairly sizable volume of secondary market trading in Eurobonds.

## Present Status and Future of the Eurobond Market

The freedom from government control that has been characteristic of the Eurobond market is very appealing to issuers of bonds. Continued growth of a secondary market and the expertise and knowledge of the underwriters and distributing houses in this market may very well maintain the Eurobond market even though the IET, the original major cause of its development, was eliminated in 1974.

Probably about one-third of the total Eurobond issues have been issued by foreign subsidiaries of U.S. corporations. They were thus able to borrow funds they probably could not have obtained in the United States in the period of controls on foreign investment and lending. These firms may in many cases continue to find it convenient to obtain funds in the countries in which they operate.

Flexibility in currencies of denomination and repayment may be an advantage since greater market flexibility has been introduced into exchange rates. A gradual lessening of the role of the dollar as the "key" currency might also contribute to a desire for flexibility in currency designation.

With gradual relaxation of controls on foreign investment by the United States and by some other countries, the Eurobond market may contribute somewhat to reduction of international differences in interest rates among the major industrialized countries. As long as capital market controls continue to be important in European capital markets, the Eurobond market offers an alternative that, at least thus far, is subject to few controls.

From the standpoint of the U.S. capital markets, perhaps the major significance of the Eurobond market has been that it made it possible for foreign subsidiaries of U.S. firms to obtain funds in a period when balance-of-payments controls on foreign investment were deemed necessary by the U.S. government. Absence of this source of demand for funds from the U.S. capital markets in this period must surely have moderated somewhat the rise in interest rates, but there is no research thus far indicating the possible magnitude of moderation.

For Eurobond securities denominated in Deutsche marks or in yen, another factor is significant. When there is concern about the value of the U.S. dollar, as during the Iranian crisis of 1979–1980, the demand for bonds denominated in Deutsche marks or yen rises. Some such bonds were selling nearly at par, even though the coupon rate in some cases was less than 8 percent.

Convertible bonds offered a double advantage (or disadvantage): they could rise in price if the value of the currency in which they were denominated rose, and they could rise in price if the value of stocks into which they were convertible rose. Of course, they could also fall in the reverse cases.[16]

The late 1970s was a nervous time in currency markets because of concern over the value of the dollar, formerly regarded as a haven of stability. Clearly, the long-run future of the Eurobond market is linked to stability of the dollar, the increasing importance of the Deutsche mark as an international currency, and the potential importance of the yen.

## THE LONG-TERM GOVERNMENT SECURITIES MARKET

Government debt is still a very important part of the total of long-term securities. Because of their high degree of liquidity, government securities play an important role in portfolios of investors, particularly banks; in times of uncertainty, when desire for liquidity increases, they may be of great significance because of their convertibility

---

[16] See, for example, "A Rush for Bargains in Eurodollar Bonds," *Business Week*, December 10, 1979, pp. 102–107.

into money to meet necessary payments. Some economists have emphasized the role of government debt in providing "ultimate" liquidity for the economy, that is, financial assets that would be liquid even if private institutions failed and could not redeem their debts (financial assets).[17] The key role of such liquidity is evident from a consideration of what might happen if numerous corporations and banks failed, as they did in the early 1930s, and people attempted to hold the remaining liquid assets, such as currency, thus reducing spending and causing a depression.

## The Government Debt in Perspective

Government debt in the United States and in many other countries has increased greatly in wartime. In the period of World War I, government debt rose from a very small amount to more than $25 billion; in the period of World War II, it rose from about $50 billion to nearly $300 billion; in the period of involvement in the Vietnam conflict, it rose from a little over $300 billion to considerably more than $400 billion. By 1986 it exceeded $2 trillion. However, in relation to nominal GNP (national income), *domestic* federal government debt declined from 1955 to 1980, and even by 1986, it was only about 50 percent of nominal GNP, whereas in 1955 it had been over 60 percent. In the first half of the 1980s, both federal debt and private nonfinancial domestic debt (i.e., excluding debt of financial institutions) rose, not only in amounts, but as percentages of nominal GNP.

Debt must in the long run be repaid from income, but this does not tell us what ratios of debt to income are appropriate. The rise in private debt is certainly more worrisome than is the rise in government debt, since the federal government *can* raise taxes (increase its income) if necessary. One example of concern is the ratio of consumer debt to disposable personal income (roughly, income after taxes). This ratio reached a postwar peak in the mid-1980s, nearly 60 percent, compared to about 30 percent in 1955.

In the 1980s there has been much discussion of government budget deficits, which have been large. Two points should be clarified. First, in the mid-1980s, the ratio of domestic federal government debt to nominal GNP was about 50 percent, compared to 60 percent in 1955, so that *relatively*, government debt held domestically is not high.[18] Second, talk of domestic government debt creating a burden for our children is not realistic: if higher taxes are necessary to repay some of the government debt, then at the same time, it must be recognized, those who hold government securities will receive payments. Thus any "burden" rests on *some* individuals; others receive payments as debt is reduced. (It should be noted that foreign debt (debt

---

[17] See, for example, Hyman P. Minsky, "Can 'It' Happen Again?" in Deane Carson, ed., *Banking and Monetary Studies* (Homewood, Ill.: Richard D. Irwin, 1963), and "Longer Waves in Financial Relations: Financial Factors in the More Severe Depressions," *American Economic Review*, Papers and Proceedings, May 1964, pp. 324–335.

[18] It may be argued that federal budget deficits should be reduced so that, with less government borrowing, the relatively low rate of saving can better provide for domestic investment, and dependence on inflows of foreign capital will be reduced. See, for example, Paul A. Volcker, "The Rapid Growth of Debt in the United States," *Federal Reserve Bank of Kansas City, Economic Review*, May 1986, pp. 3–12.

owed to residents—including governments—of foreign countries) *is* a burden; its repayment reduces income, which is paid to the foreign countries. Thus large *foreign* debt relative to income (a situation faced by Mexico and other countries) *does* create a burden. In this way, the United States *has* incurred a burden in the 1980s.)

## Marketable Government Debt

Nearly three-fourths of the government debt is marketable. Nonmarketable debt includes foreign issues, savings bonds, and some other issues. Of the marketable government debt, about one-fourth consists of Treasury bills, discussed in Chapter 9, over half is notes, and one-seventh consists of bonds.

Commercial banks need to hold large amounts of government securities for liquidity purposes, and deposit-type institutions also must keep significant amounts, though less in percentages of their portfolios because their liabilities are not as volatile as those of commercial banks. Insurance companies (especially nonlife insurance companies), state and local governments, and the federal government trust funds must also hold substantial amounts, and individuals may be expected to be holders. Thus any judgment of appropriate size of national debt rests partly on the need for liquid assets to be held by various institutions and individuals; partly, it rests on considerations related to the size of interest payments on such debt as a part of total government expenditures. As the economy grows and as financial institutions grow, the need for additional government securities for liquidity purposes increases.[19] It should be noted that under some conditions, such as those existing in the early 1970s, when the volume of long-term government securities was relatively small and the market for them relatively inactive, the liquidity of such securities was reduced. However, they can always be used as security for loans from the Federal Reserve System to meet liquidity crises such as that in May 1970.

## The Dealer Market

What is significant about the government debt is not so much its size as the fact that there is an extremely well-organized, efficient market that assures the liquidity of these securities. The center of this market is a group of dealers, including some who specialize in trading in government securities, departments of investment houses, and departments of about a dozen commercial banks. Telephone and teletype connections make possible instant communication, and absolute reliance on verbal agreements makes possible very rapid trading. Although many other financial institutions make markets in government securities for their customers—that is, they are ready and

---

[19] Procedure in projecting an appropriate amount of government debt may be to (1) project nominal GNP, (2) project total primary debt instruments, either on the basis of the past ratio of debt assets to nominal GNP of about 1.8 to 1 or with some adjustment of that ratio, or (3) determine an appropriate ratio of government debt instruments as liquid assets in portfolios of individuals and institutions. If the expected rate of growth of government debt indicates a figure higher or lower than the projected appropriate value, liquidity may in the future be too great, or insufficient.

willing to buy or sell given amounts—the dealers at the core of the market are those with whom the Federal Reserve Bank of New York trades, in carrying out open market operations recommended by the Federal Open Market Committee.[20] Dealers may apply to the bank for inclusion in the group, and the bank will decide on the basis of their reputation, financial situation, and apparent readiness, willingness, and ability to make a market in government securities.

Unlike brokers, who place orders and receive commissions, dealers buy and sell for themselves, maintaining inventories of various issues of government securities.[21] Thus they must be able to purchase these in large amounts and must often hold large amounts ready for sale. To do this they must borrow, as the amount of capital necessary would otherwise be too great.[22] If dealers did not have access to adequate financing, they would not be ready to take positions, and hence liquidity of government securities would suffer. If dealers were not ready to buy, a sudden item of news, announcement of government policy change, or economic forecast might cause sellers to become more vigorous and prices to drop sharply. Of course, over a period of time, prices of long-term government securities may and do decline, as market interest rates rise and securities issued when rates were lower become less attractive. But sharp declines in short periods would be detrimental to liquidity. These have occasionally occurred, but efforts to maintain an efficient, broad dealer market have limited such occasions to a relatively small number.

Thus the basic reason for the dealer market in government securities is to maintain a high degree of liquidity because of the fact that government securities are largely held by financial institutions and other holders for liquidity purposes. An auction market, such as that on the stock exchanges, might at times lead to sharp price fluctuations, whereas in a dealer market, dealers can absorb demand by selling from their own inventories when demand is increasing and can buy for their own inventories when sellers are anxious to sell.

Dealers participate both in the primary market and in the secondary market for government securities. In the primary market, they subscribe to new issues and then resell them to the public, thus in effect underwriting large parts of the new issues. In exchange refundings, dealers buy large amounts of rights, and they are helpful in distributing securities in advance refundings. In cash refunding they are less active, as the Treasury aims to sell bonds directly for cash to private investors.

In the secondary market, dealers began early in the twentieth century to serve commercial banks, which were required to buy large amounts of government securi-

---

[20] At the end of 1986, there were 40 dealers in this group, including 3 Japanese firms and 6 others that were foreign owned.

[21] The dealers generally deal in all maturities of government securities, although some of them restrict themselves to trading in certain maturities. They trade in short-term government securities as well as in bonds and notes, although at this point our concern is with the latter. For further details, see Ira O. Scott, Jr., *Government Securities Market* (New York: McGraw-Hill, 1965).

[22] The volume of trading in government securities by these dealers (including both short-term and long-term securities) may be as high as $2 billion or more a day. The reader may compare this, for example, with a 50-million-share day, at an average price of perhaps $30 per share, on the New York Stock Exchange—a trading volume of $1.5 billion.

ties because at that time national bank notes had to be secured by government bonds. When these dealers demonstrated efficiency during World War I, most trading in government bonds shifted from the stock exchange to the dealers. Dealers make a market by quoting, in fractions of one-thirty-second of a point, firm prices at which they will buy or sell; $100 (100 points) represents par value. Dealers vary their inventories with fluctuations in interest rates because high rates make inventories expensive to carry (carrying is largely financed by borrowing). Moreover, rising rates mean falling bond prices, and dealers therefore suffer capital losses on bonds held at such times. In periods of widely fluctuating interest rates, dealers' inventories may be low, and it may be difficult to execute large sales of bonds. Deterioration in the market for bonds at such times could be so great as to undermine liquidity; those who need to sell bonds to pay maturing liabilities might find themselves unable to pay. Such a liquidity crisis could degenerate into a sharp decline in business activity, and, therefore, measures are taken to avoid such a situation.

## New Issues of Government Securities

New issues of government securities are sold with the same concern for the effect on liquidity. When the government wishes to market a new issue, announcements are made by the Treasury through the Federal Reserve System, which acts as fiscal agent for the government. Decision must be made whether the new offering is to be for cash or in exchange for outstanding securities.[23] Because debt issues mature in time, refunding issues are needed simply to maintain a given level of debt. If debt must increase because tax and other revenues are insufficient to meet spending, additional issues must be arranged.

One technique used in certain periods was that of "advance refunding." New, long-term securities were offered to holders of outstanding issues that would mature some time in the future, in exchange. Yields on the new securities were slightly higher than both the yield to maturity on the outstanding issue and the current yields on other comparable government securities available in the market. The spread between the yield on the new issue and the current market rate for securities of comparable maturity has been, at least sometimes, about ¼ percent, thus providing a real incentive for investors to accept the exchange offering. Obviously, however, as pointed out by Ira Scott, terms of a refunding could vary depending on the Treasury's desires—to provide great incentive for exchange or little incentive.[24]

Through this technique the Treasury lengthens the time to maturity of the debt because the new issue will mature later than the outstanding issue for which it is

---

[23] An exchange refunding can be used instead of a cash refunding. Holders may exchange for the new issue or redeem in cash; they may obtain cash directly or sell their "rights" to subscribe to the new issue to investors who want to subscribe. Holders may be offered either a new bond or a note, so that, if they do not wish to buy a new long-term issue, they will be able to buy the intermediate-term note (which may have a maturity of from 3 to 10 years). If the amount of "attrition" (securities turned in for cash) becomes great, as it may if interest rates are rising, so that investors hope to buy the new securities later at lower prices, cash refundings and cash sales may be used.

[24] Scott, *Government Securities Markets*, p. 43.

exchanged. The mere passage of time shortens the maturity of outstanding securities, and, unless longer-term securities are sold, the gradual shortening of average maturity may mean that a great part of the debt must be refinanced each year, putting a burden on the market. In the early 1960s, aggressive use of advance refunding offset the decline in average maturity that had occurred previously. As indicated, it has generally been difficult to do this in recent years because of the interest rate ceiling on government bonds and the fact that yields have generally been above this ceiling. In 1971 the Treasury was authorized to issue $10 billion in bonds without regard to the interest rate ceiling to enable the Treasury to issue long-term bonds and maintain the length of time to maturity of at least a very small portion of the debt. This amount was later increased several times, and was $110 billion in the early 1980s.

The government usually does not wish to issue securities at much of a discount from par. In fact, a new issue is usually sold at par or slightly above par; the price often rises soon afterward, giving a "free ride" to purchasers of the new issue. Of course, at a later date, the securities may fall below par in price because, if interest rates rise, bond prices fall.

The Federal Reserve System, as fiscal agent for the Treasury, handles the issuing of the securities. The Federal Reserve is also concerned, however, that its activities in the government securities market may cause difficulties in selling the new issue, thus damaging the liquidity of the government securities market. For a number of years the Federal Reserve System followed what was termed a "bills-only" policy; it was argued that, by buying and selling only Treasury bills in its open market operations, the Federal Reserve System would have less effect on prices and yields on intermediate-term and long-term government securities. Although the "bills-only" policy was abandoned in 1961, most open market purchases and sales are still in Treasury bills.

Obviously, debt management actions by the Treasury, in issuing securities of certain types and maturities, are closely related to open market operations by the Federal Reserve System, in buying and selling government securities. Appropriate policy coordination, discussed in Part Five, could influence yields on government securities of various maturities if such an effect is possible.

Auction of long-term government securities was tried in the 1930s, but results were not very satisfactory. In 1963, the auction technique was tried again, this time with competitive bidding by underwriter groups. The issues were allocated to the highest bidder for resale to the public. The first time, in January, the issue was quickly sold and went to a premium in price; the second time, in a less receptive market, the underwriters had some difficulty in disposing of the securities. Because, as stated, the government is concerned when new issues of government securities are difficult to sell or quickly go to a discount from par, the auction technique was not used again for some time.[25]

---

[25] *The Wall Street Journal*, December 29, 1972, p. 2; Salomon Brothers, *Comments on Credit*, December 29, 1972, pp. 1–2.

In late 1972, the Treasury announced 6¾ percent, 20-year bonds for sale under a different ("Dutch") auction technique, in which bonds were awarded to all accepted bidders at the lowest accepted bid price. It was suggested that pension funds, personal trusts, savings banks, and other institutions, which are not accustomed to bidding for Treasury bills as commercial banks are, might bid for bonds if they could expect to be awarded the right to purchase at the same price as other bidders, as long as their bids were within the range of accepted bids.[26] Immediate results did not indicate that this procedure was successful in attracting institutions other than commercial banks and investors outside the New York area. Almost all bidders were from the New York area; there were relatively few noncompetitive bids (only $72 million out of $625 million), and all bids of 99½ or more were accepted, so that the bonds were sold to yield 6.795 percent. They sold at several thirty-seconds below 99½ the first day.[27]

One argument for the Dutch auction technique is that it may result in a larger number of bidders and thus higher prices and lower yields generally (even if only slightly). Whether this is true—whether there are more bidders because they know they will not have to pay more than other bidders—is not certain. Hence the Dutch auction technique was used for a time and then was not used. It is plausible that if a bidder thinks that he or she may have to pay a higher price than other bidders, some will be discouraged from bidding, but it is not certain that such bidders are significantly influenced by the small differences in prices (and yields) when bids are each accepted at the bid price (in contrast to the Dutch auction technique, in which all bids accepted are accepted at the average price bid by those bidders).

The auction process works as follows. Bidders for both notes and bonds usually submit either noncompetitive bids up to $1 million or competitive bids that may be in larger amounts. Competitive bids are expressed in yields specified to two decimal points, for example, 7.31 percent. If the coupon rate were 7¼ percent, such a bond would sell slightly below par; if the yield bid were 7.25 percent, the 7¼ percent coupon bond would sell at par. The coupon rate is established by the Treasury after an issue has been allotted to bidders—noncompetitive bidders first and then competitive bidders beginning with the lowest yield bid, until the desired amount has been allotted. As previously noted, price auctions in the secondary market are expressed in points (a point being $1) and in thirty-seconds of a point. Accrued interest since the last semiannual coupon interest date is added to the price.

Introduction of electronic quotation systems has caused the dealer market to evolve into almost an integrated auction.[28] Electronic billboards show bid and offer quotations, subject to change of course, as market conditions change rapidly. On large bids, changes in bids may now be only one-sixty-fourth of a point. Costs of searching

---

[26] For more details about sales of Treasury securities in the 1960s, see "Managing the Debt of the 60s," Federal Reserve Bank of San Francisco, *Monthly Review*, January 1969, pp. 3–10.

[27] See Aubrey G. Lanston & Co., Inc., weekly letter, January 8, 1973.

[28] For extensive detail, see Kenneth D. Garbade, "Electronic Quotation Systems and the Market for Government Securities," Federal Reserve Bank of New York, *Quarterly Review*, Summer 1978, pp. 13–20.

for the best bids diminish as all dealers are quickly aware of bid and offer prices. Electronic purchase and sale execution systems also have been introduced. Thus technological development of the electronics industry has transformed the dealer market into an auction market even though there is no central place for display of prices and execution of orders, as there is, for example, on the New York Stock Exchange. Such a place is no longer needed for the dealer market in government securities to function as an auction market.

Under a program initiated in the summer of 1986, investors who buy Treasury notes and bonds receive statements of account instead of engraved certificates. The statement provides information on an investor's entire portfolio of government securities; earlier, this system had been adopted for Treasury bills. Investors can obtain information, if they wish, from any Federal Reserve Bank (12 of them) or any Federal Reserve Bank branch (25 of them); they can also purchase Treasury bills, notes, or bonds, or shift such securities from one account to another, through any of the above. Investors can arrange for direct (electronic) deposit of principal, interest, or refund payments to designated checking accounts or savings accounts at specified financial institutions. This eliminates the possibility of theft of certificates from the mail and provides immediate access to funds received. The new system for purchases, sales, and transfers of Treasury securities has been termed "Treasury direct."[29]

Records for financial institutions dealing in government securities and for private investors who choose to hold their government securities in the book-entry accounts of financial institutions (entries on the books of the Federal Reserve System) are maintained in a system termed "trades."

Thus an electronic transfer system is now extended to government securities as well as to deposit of Social Security checks, private pension benefits checks if desired by recipients, and payroll checks if firms and employees desire this.

## TIGRs and CATs

Investment and brokerage houses in the early 1980s were issuing some certificates, for purchase by investors, that indicate claims for the income (and, in a few cases, some of the principal) of government securities due some time in the future. The investor pays an amount that, compounded to the specified date, yields a specified rate. Attractiveness of these certificates depends on (1) the low cash outlay needed for a high future return, especially if the date is far in the future, (2) the safety of certificates backed by Treasury securities, (3) a specified rate of return, with no concern about the need to reinvest interest, possibly at lower rates—no payment is received until the specified date, and (4) in most cases, the fact that investors may sell the certificates back to the issuers.

These certificates are not an attempt to gain a tax advantage, as was the case with some zero-coupon corporate bonds and some coupon strippers—in those cases, it was hoped that the income, being the difference between the purchase price and the

---

[29] For further details, see *Dallasfed Roundup*, Federal Reserve Bank of Dallas, June 1986, pp. 1, 3.

maturity price of the bond, would be taxed at capital gains rates rather than at the higher regular income tax rates. The certificates accrue income, and the income is subject to tax. Hence the certificates are purchased chiefly for IRAs and other funds on which tax is deferred. (IRAs are individual retirement accounts, to which individuals who do not contribute to another pension fund may contribute up to $2,000 a year, tax on the principal and interest being deferred until the individual begins to receive income from the account—this cannot be done before age 59½ and must be begun at age 70½). The government securities used as backing for the certificates are effectively removed from the market. To the extent that sales of such certificates grow, the outstanding marketable government debt is reduced somewhat; presumably this would tend to cause bond prices to be slightly higher (and yields lower). Also, yields on the certificates are a little lower than are yields on comparable government securities. Why buy them? Individuals may buy them because they can buy $1,000 or $2,000 in certificates, whereas minimum amounts for long-term government bonds are $5,000.

Merrill Lynch termed its certificates Treasury Investment Growth Receipts (hence, TIGRs or tigers); Salomon Brothers termed some issues Certificates of Accrual on Treasury Securities (hence, CATs).[30] These instruments represent additional examples of financial innovation stimulated by changing conditions in financial markets in the late 1970s and 1980s. They also reflect the impetus to saving provided by the Economic Recovery Tax Act of 1981, which provided for reducing tax rates and authorized broad use of the individual retirement accounts (IRAs) already mentioned. Tax reform legislation in 1986 reduced the number of persons eligible to invest in IRAs. In view of the well-known difficulties facing Social Security in the 1980s and probably again after the year 2000, and the possibility that *increases* in Social Security benefits *may* be delayed or reduced, private saving for retirement in *some* form is likely to increase. From a social viewpoint, this is beneficial, since Social Security contributions are *not* saving, as currently handled. The contributions go into the trust fund and are almost immediately paid out in benefits, so that they are simply transfers from employers and workers to Social Security beneficiaries. It is, of course, possible that beneficiaries may save some of the benefits received, but such saving may be small in view of the relatively small size of average monthly benefits.

# THE MARKET FOR GOVERNMENT
# AGENCY SECURITIES

Federal government agencies, discussed in Chapter 5, have sold debt issues since 1919, but the volume of such issues was not very large until the late 1960s.[31] Now the outstanding volume of federal agency securities is about one-fifth that of government

---

[30] *Business Week*, September 13, 1982, p. 97.

[31] For further detail on this and other points discussed in this section, see Lois Banks, "The Market for Agency Securities," Federal Reserve Bank of New York, *Quarterly Review*, Spring 1978, pp. 7–19.

securities and one-third that of corporate bonds. Income on agency securities is subject to federal income tax, and income from any of them is subject to state and local income taxes if such taxes exist. Income on Federal Home Loan Bank securities and on the securities of farm credit agencies, discussed in the following paragraphs, is not subject to state and local income taxation.

A small part of this agency securities market consists of the market for debt of agencies that are part of the federal government. These agencies include the Export-Import Bank (EXIM), the Farmers' Home Administration (FHA), the General Services Administration (GSA), the Government National Mortgage Association (GNMA, or Ginnie Mae), the Postal Service (PS), and the Tennessee Valley Authority (TVA). A separate agency is the Washington Metropolitan Area Transit Authority (WMATA). Most of these agencies formerly issued their own debt securities, but in 1973, the Federal Financing Bank (FFB) was created, and they now borrow from it, and it in turn borrows from the Treasury. Of course, there are debt issues of these agencies still outstanding. The FFB issued one debt issue of its own, but it was found that it could borrow more cheaply through the Treasury. Eventually the outstanding issues of these federal agencies may mature and disappear.

The role of the FFB has been criticized by some because agencies such as those mentioned may borrow from it and the FFB may, in turn, borrow from the Treasury. Thus such agencies obtain the benefit of borrowing at interest rates lower than those paid by other institutions, yet some are not subjected to review of their appropriations and expenditures by Congress, in the budget process.

Such off-budget borrowing should be added to Treasury borrowing in determining the total amount of federal government borrowing, but this is not done in the "unified" budget. Thus the deficit (or surplus) indicated in the budget is not accurate. There are, of course, several other reasons why the deficit or surplus figures do not accurately reflect the impact of federal government borrowing on the credit markets.[32]

The major part of the agency securities market is that for debt issues marketed by agencies sponsored and originally owned by the government, but now *privately* owned. These are termed federally sponsored agencies and include the Banks for Cooperatives (BCs or COOPs), Federal Intermediate Credit Banks (FICBs), and Federal Land Banks (FLBs), which extend farm credit. There are also issues referred to as Federal Farm Credit Bank issues, which are joint obligations of the BCs, the FICBs, and the FLBs.

The sponsored agencies also include the Federal Home Loan Banks (FHLBs), the Federal Home Loan Mortgage Corporation (FHLMC, or Freddie Mac), and the Federal National Mortgage Association (FNMA, or Fannie Mae), which make loans to assist the housing market. The federal government still exercises some control over these agencies and approves the terms, size, and timing of their debt issues. Some

[32] For a discussion of some of these, see Brian Horrigan and Aris Protopapadakis, "Federal Deficits: A Faulty Gauge of Government's Impact on Financial Markets," Federal Reserve Bank of Philadelphia, *Business Review*, March–April 1982, pp. 3–16. Other reasons include the rise in interest rates during inflation: even if a government spent no more on goods and services and had the same tax revenues, its interest payments on the public debt would rise and it would have to borrow to pay the additional interest.

agencies, such as FNMA, are regulated by a government department (in this case, the Department of Housing and Urban Development, or HUD). Some are regulated by special boards; the Federal Home Loan Bank Board, whose three members are appointed by the president, regulates the FHLBs, and the Federal Farm Credit Board, whose members are also presidential appointees, regulates the farm credit agencies.

All the housing agencies and the FICBs operate through financial intermediates. They lend to or purchase mortgages from other financial institutions, which in turn provide housing or farm credit. FLBs and BCs lend directly to farmers.

Obligations of the sponsored agencies do not carry government guarantees, but the interest rates on them are nearly as low as rates on comparable government securities, and the lack of government guarantee does not seem to affect adversely the marketability of the securities.

In some cases debt issues were issued by these agencies rather than by the Treasury simply to reduce Treasury borrowing at times when further Treasury issues would have been difficult to market or impossible because of debt limitation. A number of the issues are exempted from state and local income taxes on the interest paid.

New issues are marketed either through a network of securities dealers and banks or through underwriting syndicates. A fiscal agent makes arrangements for an issue, and the selling group is expected to place the securities with "true investors." One indication of the success of such placement is favorable price behavior in the secondary market—presumably if an issue is not placed with true investors, it may be quickly resold and price decline may result.

Agencies tend to market long-term issues in greater volume when interest rates are below their peaks. Coupon rates on new agency issues are above coupon rates on comparable Treasury issues, but below coupon rates on comparable corporate bonds.

Major purchasers of agency issues are commercial banks and savings institutions; state and local governments (including their retirement funds) are also significant buyers. Many agency securities are purchased by "other" investors, which may include trust departments of banks, individuals, foreign investors, nonprofit organizations, and nonbank securities dealers. The Federal Reserve System began buying agency securities in the secondary market in 1971, as part of its open market operations.

The secondary market is similar to that for government securities, and many dealers who make markets for government securities also make markets for agency securities.

About 10 percent of outstanding agency securities are held by U.S. government accounts and Federal Reserve Banks, about 20 percent by savings and loan associations, and another 20 percent by commercial banks. Small percentages are held by each of a variety of other financial institutions, and the rest by unidentified holders (presumably individuals).

The agency securities market is closely related to the government securities market. Generally, yields on agency securities are higher than are those on government securities but lower than those on Aaa corporate utility bonds. Spreads tend to widen when more agency securities are issued and also in periods of "tight money," because investors seem to prefer more liquid securities when money is "tight." "Deep discount" government bonds (selling at large discounts from par because they carry low coupon rates but interest rates have risen) may have had lower yields than agency securities because capital gains on such bonds, if held to maturity, were taxed at lower rates than interest income.

The farm agencies seem to have a secure place in the credit system, providing credit that supplements that available from such institutions as commercial banks and insurance companies. However, they had difficulties in the mid-1980s; the rising value of the dollar in 1981–1985 was a factor hindering U.S. farm (and other) exports. They seemed likely to need government aid, just as such aid was provided for the Federal Savings and Loan Insurance Corporation (FSLIC).

The housing agencies are more controversial. The question is whether the agencies can borrow in the securities market and lend enough funds to (or buy enough mortgages from) institutions that finance housing so that declines in housing can be prevented from being as severe as in the past. Some institutions that finance housing can also buy corporate bonds and may even do so with funds borrowed from a housing agency. Moreover, issues of agency securities tend to push interest rates higher, thus increasing the flow of funds out of institutions that finance housing. These questions are considered more fully in the section of this chapter on the mortgage market. FNMA is specifically criticized because some would like it to sell mortgages regularly instead of chiefly buying them, thus improving the mortgage market as well as providing a source of funds, and others would like it to focus, in part at least, on buying mortgages on properties in central city areas.

EXIM, the FNMA, and the TVA are all likely to expand their operations and their borrowing, but they secure their funds from the FFB and indirectly from the Treasury. FHLBs are likely to continue to borrow rather heavily when money is "tight." The future of FNMA is not so clear: if it sold more mortgages, its borrowing might fluctuate somewhat like that of the FHLBs.

## THE MUNICIPAL BOND MARKET

Municipal bonds are issued by about 25,000 out of about 80,000 state and local government units in the United States. They are available in varying maturities, are often issued in serial form to mature so much each year for a period of years, and the interest income on them is exempt from federal income tax. The after-tax income on these securities is higher for some investors than is the yield on alternative investments.

### "Municipals" and Their Purchasers

About three-fifths of municipal bonds are what are termed "full faith and credit" or general obligation securities, based on the taxing authority of the government unit. State and local government units frequently have rather small limits, in their constitutions and elsewhere, on the amount of these bonds that they may issue. For this reason and because of the increase in specific services, "revenue bonds" have been issued; payment of interest and principal is based on revenue to be received from sale of water, highway and bridge tolls, and so forth. These securities are likely to carry higher yields than are "full faith and credit" bonds.

Commercial banks and high-income individuals are now the major holders of municipal bonds because they are interested in the tax exemption and the intermediate-term maturities, because the banks frequently underwrite general obligation issues and some types of revenue issues, and because banks are frequently required to hold such bonds as collateral security for deposit of local government funds.

Issues of municipal bonds are underwritten by numerous firms, many underwriting issues of government units in their own areas. Bonds are frequently purchased by individual investors in the area as well. Underwriting bids for issues may be submitted by dealers and banks in the area, and bids are quite competitive for intermediate-sized and large-sized issues.

The presumption has been that municipal bonds are issued for public purposes—this is the basis for the exemption of income on them from tax. When state and local "industrial development" bonds were issued to finance low-interest loans to business firms to construct industrial facilities, the Revenue Adjustment Act of 1968 was passed by Congress to restrict this practice. In the 1970s, states and local government units began to sell bonds to finance housing. Presumably the intent was to finance low-income housing that would not have been built by private industry. However, local government units began to sell bonds to provide funds for mortgage lending when interest rates rose to high levels; the backing for such bonds became the revenue to be derived from mortgage interest and amortization payments. Congressional Budget Office economists objected that the federal government was losing revenue because the bonds were tax-exempt and that sale of such bonds drove all interest rates higher. In 1980 Congress restricted the use of tax-exempt bonds to finance single-family housing.

Two issues are involved: (1) Should housing be subsidized at the expense of other types of investment? (2) Should both the federal government (through GNMA, etc.) and the state and local governments subsidize housing? Is encouragement of housing a policy objective for the federal government, or for both the federal government and the state and local governments? The federal government has more than 70 programs to aid housing; should state and local governments also provide such aid? These and similar questions are raised later, in Chapter 15, in which we discuss the policy objectives of monetary, fiscal, and other government actions.

## "Thinness" of the Market

The same firms that underwrite issues maintain secondary markets for them. Investors are usually able to sell securities when desired, but the market is hardly very deep or resilient, as municipal bond issues are small and varied, many dealers are small, and the number of dealers able and willing to handle a given issue is small.

The continued need of state and local government units to borrow to finance capital expenditures and the limited groups of investors interested in buying these securities has led to some concern about the viability of this market in the future.

The tax-exempt feature has limited purchases of municipal bonds almost entirely to commercial banks, high-income individuals, and property and casualty insurance companies. Individuals who had a marginal income tax rate of 50 percent (then the maximum) would find municipal bond rates attractive as long as they were somewhat more than half the yields on Treasury securities. Banks and property and casualty insurance companies have somewhat lower tax rates and, hence, need slightly higher yields to be attracted to municipal bonds. (If the marginal tax rate is 45 percent, then if Treasury securities yield 12 percent, municipal securities must yield above 6.6 percent to be attractive.) The yield ratio (the ratio of yields on municipals to yields on Treasuries) must be higher than 1 minus the marginal tax rate.

Banks began in the 1970s to look more to leasing arrangements than to purchase of municipal bonds to shelter income from taxes, and property and casualty insurance companies have had underwriting losses that reduce their need for tax shelter. Some individuals, in recent years, have found IRAs and All Savers Certificates attractive as a means of deferring or eliminating taxes.

In the late 1970s and early 1980s, when short-term interest rates were relatively high, the demand for short-term municipals was fairly heavy. Tax-exempt money market funds wanted them; banks (which prefer short-term securities in any event) bought fairly heavily. Hence yield ratios for municipal securities with one year or less to maturity remained between .56 and .60 relative to yields on government securities in the early 1980s.

The market for long-term municipals was very different. In that market, for 30-year securities, ratios ranged between .8 and .9. One reason for this was the greater credit risk in municipals, exemplified in fiscal problems of state and local governments (which generally worsened, although New York City had resolved its fiscal problems). Long-term borrowing by state and local governments doubled from the early 1970s to the early 1980s, at a time when the demand for municipal securities was declining.

The result has been that the benefit of lower interest rates (lower than Treasury rates, that is) for state and local governments had become small, and the loss of revenue to the Treasury was still substantial.

Naturally, suggestions for change have been made. Some suggest that state and local governments offer taxable bonds; this would probably have to be optional, since, if it were required, constitutional questions of separation of powers could arise. The federal government could reimburse the state and local governments for the higher interest cost on taxable bonds. This would remove some of the supply of tax-exempt bonds from the market.

Another alternative would be to increase the amount of short-term borrowing. But this would expose state and local governments to risks of not being able to roll over these borrowings when necessary, at least not at moderate interest rates. A major problem is that tax-exempt bonds have increasingly been used to finance public power projects and public housing projects—activities that were formerly chiefly private. Such securities are usually revenue bonds, not general obligation bonds.

Hence, one possibility would be to restrict the amount of revenue bonds that could be issued. Congress used this method in denying tax exemptions for industrial revenue bonds in 1968 and single-family mortgage bonds in 1980. Another possibility would be to limit the amount of tax-exempt bonds that any state or local government could issue. A third possibility would be to eliminate tax exemptions for revenue bonds (but not for general obligation bonds). General obligation bonds are now only about one-third of total municipal bonds issued. However, some revenue bonds have even been used to finance schools; in some cases, schools may be owned by a special agency and leased to school boards.[33] Probably some general obligation bonds would be issued for such purposes if tax exemption were denied for revenue bonds.

As long as no change occurs, state and local governments are paying very high interest rates because the supply of municipals exceeds the demand by individuals and institutions in high tax brackets; at the same time, the federal government is losing a substantial amount of revenue because of the tax exemption.

### Zero-Coupon Municipal Bonds and Certificates

Tax reform legislation of 1986 made capital gains on zero-coupon municipal securities *currently* taxable, unless the securities are held in accounts such as IRAs (and it limited the number of people permitted to invest in IRAs).

Zero-coupon *municipal* bonds, therefore, became more common, since income on them is not taxed. To create zero-coupon municipals, investment houses "strip" coupons from the bonds and sell each coupon as a zero-coupon bond, in the same manner in which this has been done for government bonds (see the section earlier in this chapter on TIGRs and CATs). For municipal bonds, Salomon Brothers call the resulting bonds and certificates M-CATs (Municipal Certificates of Accrual on Tax-Exempt Securities); other firms have other names. All zero-coupon bonds and certificates are, of course, subject to changes in value as bond prices change and, hence, are not suitable for investment by those who desire to obtain regular income. They may, however, have been desirable for so-called "Clifford trusts" (trust accounts established to provide funds in future years for children's education or similar purposes). Tax reform legislation of 1986 effectively eliminated Clifford trusts invested in zero-coupon government securities, but probably has created demand for zero-coupon municipal bonds and certificates. Investors, however, will presumably wish to buy such securities only if the bonds are protected against call, since early call would disrupt plans for obtaining funds at later dates.

---

[33] A more detailed discussion of the problem and of these alternatives may be found in David C. Beek, "Rethinking Tax-Exempt Financing for State and Local Governments," Federal Reserve Bank of New York, *Quarterly Review*, Autumn 1982, pp. 20–40. For an analysis in the mid-1970s, see Rodney Johnson, "A Fresh Look at the Municipal Bond Market," Federal Reserve Bank of Philadelphia, *Business Review*, July–August 1976, pp. 11–22.

# THE MORTGAGE MARKET

The mortgage market is the largest debt segment of the capital markets. Moreover, real estate is a very large part of total real wealth; thus, although mortgage debt may be a high ratio of the value of properties recently purchased (whether new or old), it is a fairly small fraction of the total value of all real property.

A significant fact about mortgages as financial instruments is that those who purchase them tend to place more weight on the value of the real estate mortgaged than on the ability of the debtors to repay the mortgage debt. Whether they actually place more weight on the value of the collateral—and frequently they are urged to examine the debt repayment ability of the debtors—they certainly give this factor relatively more weight than in other segments of the capital markets. In the case of all types of bonds and stocks, relatively more weight is certainly given to the income-generating ability of borrowers.

## Determination of Mortgage Rates and Fees

Down payments and maturities tend to be critical factors in mortgages. Especially in residential mortgages, individuals usually have difficulty in making large down payments, and the maturity is also critical because maturity determines the amount of repayment of principal and interest required each period. Fifty years ago, most mortgages were written to mature on a certain date, without amortization, but were usually renewed; the spread of the amortized mortgage loan has changed this situation. Loans may be made for periods shorter than those for which they are amortized, the loans being renegotiated before maturity, perhaps giving an opportunity to change the interest rate.

Another factor is the cost of making and servicing mortgage loans, which is fairly high. The cost of making mortgage loans is partly reflected in mortgage loan fees charged for "closing" mortgage loans. These are often substantial, although part of the total paid represents taxes of various types and fees charged by government offices. Cost of servicing is high because mortgage payments are made so frequently (usually monthly) and because it must be ascertained whether taxes and insurance premiums are being paid—otherwise value of the collateral may decline.

Mortgage interest rates themselves have had two significant characteristics in comparison with other capital market yields: (1) they generally tend to be less volatile, and (2) their movements have tended to lag behind those of other rates. The less degree of volatility in yields on conventional and FHA-insured mortgages, in comparison with Aaa corporate bond yields, is clearly shown in Figure 10–2, showing the long general rise in these interest rates in the 1960s and the drop in 1970. Mortgage rates are also typically higher than the other yields in the capital markets, but, because costs of servicing mortgages are difficult to estimate, it is not clear whether rates are higher if this differential is removed. The cost of servicing single-family home mortgage loans has been estimated at about ½ percent per year, and, if this is so, mortgage loans may have earned slightly higher yields than high-quality bond investments in many cases.

As Figure 10–2 shows, the pattern changed somewhat in recent years. Mortgage rates appeared to be almost as volatile as Aaa corporate bond yields, and the lag of mortgage rates behind corporate bond rates at turning points seemed largely to have disappeared. All were greatly affected by the double-digit inflation that peaked in 1974 and again in 1980, at an even higher level.

## Primary and Secondary Mortgage Markets

Individuals were at one time the principal mortgage lenders, but three groups of institutions now are the chief suppliers of mortgage money: savings and loan associations and mutual savings banks, commercial banks, and life insurance companies. A fourth group of institutions, mortgage companies, do not themselves hold large amounts of mortgage loans; instead, they make a number of mortgage loans and then arrange with another institution (usually a life insurance company) to purchase a block of mortgages. Advance commitments for such purchases assure the mortgage companies of liquidity and contribute to the lag of changes in interest rates and mortgage terms.

Building usually involves construction loans, often made by commercial banks. Thus there is an interconnection between the market for short-term loans and the mortgage loan market. Another interconnection appears when mortgage companies, and sometimes life insurance companies, "warehouse" mortgages with commercial banks—transfer them to the banks for a short period of time to permit the mortgage company to make arrangements for placing them with a final holder or because a life insurance company temporarily holds more mortgages than it wishes to or is able to hold in its portfolio.

Since the advent of FHA-insured and VA-guaranteed mortgages in the 1930s, the primary and secondary markets for mortgages have been divided between "conventional" mortgages and the insured or guaranteed mortgages. Ceilings on interest rates that could be charged on insured or guaranteed mortgages tended to dry up the market for these types of mortgages when credit became tight and interest rates high. Institutions have also differed in their policies in purchasing mortgages: mutual savings banks have sometimes held more than half their total residential mortgage loans in insured and guaranteed loans, and commercial banks have held as much as one-third, whereas life insurance companies have usually held a much smaller fraction of their mortgage portfolios in such mortgages, and savings and loan associations an even smaller fraction. The reason for the very small fraction of insured and guaranteed mortgages in the portfolios of savings and loan associations is that these are generally local institutions that make most of their mortgage loans in areas in which they themselves have some familiarity with the properties. The frequently higher yield on conventional mortgages and the lesser amount of "red tape" make savings and loan associations prefer conventional mortgages generally.

The growth of mortgage banks or mortgage companies as institutions probably is closely related to the growth of insured and guaranteed mortgages. Long ago, mortgage brokers and bankers did function in arranging mortgage credit. But the growth in the volume of insured and guaranteed mortgages and the fact that these could be purchased with some assurance of quality by institutions such as life insurance companies that had no offices in an area (for this purpose—although they may have had sales personnel and agents who collected premiums) led to growth of mortgage companies. The mortgage companies sought commitments from the life insurance companies and other institutions and assisted in arranging for construction loans from commercial banks, which could make construction loans with more assurance if they knew that the sale of the completed houses could be financed.

## New Institutions in the Secondary Mortgage Market

The small size and varying amount, quality, and characteristics of mortgage loans inhibited the development of a secondary market for mortgages. To encourage such development and to provide liquidity for mortgages so that institutions that hold them would have a degree of liquidity in that part of their asset portfolios, the government has established a number of agencies. The Federal National Mortgage Association (FNMA) was established in 1938, but served for a considerable time merely to acquire mortgages. It was reorganized in 1954, with the intention that one part of it, at least, would engage in both purchases and sales in an effort to create a significant secondary market. In 1968, the functions of holding and liquidating loans previously purchased were given to a new agency, the Government National Mortgage Association (GNMA). This agency has also subsidized and underwritten many of the programs developed by the Department of Housing and Urban Development for low-income and other special housing.[34] FNMA was converted into a privately owned agency under 1968 legislation; it borrows by issuing short-term and intermediate-term securities; thus incurring higher costs when interest rates rise, while its return on assets in the form of mortgages remains relatively constant. Of course, GNMA is most needed to purchase mortgages when interest rates are high; at the same time, this is the time when its costs are high. FNMA now acquires mortgages by an auction procedure, in which FNMA offers a commitment to buy new mortgages from private institutions; the institutions need not sell to FNMA, but may, if interest rates fall and the prices of mortgages rise, sell them elsewhere.

---

[34] Under what is called the Tandem Plan, Ginnie Mae buys mortgages from holders such as savings and loan associations at prices higher than private investors are willing to pay and sells the mortgages to Fannie Mae at the going market price. In effect, Ginnie Mae was helping to pay the discount charges on mortgages in a market in which yields were high and/or rising and in which therefore mortgages sold at discount. Otherwise, either home buyers or sellers would have had to absorb the entire discount, thus in effect reducing the prices at which sellers could sell homes or increasing the cost of buying homes (mortgage costs).

Because FNMA was heavily engaged in buying mortgages from mortgage companies, Congress created in 1970 the Federal Home Loan Mortgage Company (FHLMC) to sell securities to the public and to buy (and then sell) mortgages, primarily buying from savings and loan associations. Incidentally, FHLMC helps to standardize documents, appraisals, and other features of mortgages to make them more easily salable.

A related agency is the MGIC Mortgage Corporation (MGIC, or Maggie Mae), a private company that began business in the spring of 1972 to establish a secondary market for mortgages it insures. It also sells securities to the public to obtain funds for this purpose.

Thus four agencies are now engaged in creating a secondary market for mortgages. Originally this market was entirely for insured and guaranteed mortgages, but FNMA, FHLMC, and MGIC buy conventional mortgages (FNMA and FHLMC buy both types). The result is that the mortgage market is in a better position than it has ever been to compete for funds when credit is tight and interest rates high. The institutional structure of the mortgage market has become quite complex, as shown in Figure 10–5, but the credit crunches of 1966 and especially that of 1969 did not affect the mortgage market as adversely as they might have in the absence of these arrangements for liquidity for mortgages.[35]

## The Development of Mortgage-Backed Securities

The most significant development in the 1970s in this field was the partial integration of the mortgage market into the traditional capital market through the development of mortgage-backed securities. This occurred as bonds were sold, at first by FNMA and later by other institutions; the bonds were backed by government-insured mortgages. Then GNMA, later FHLMC, and still later private mortgage-originating institutions developed "pass throughs"—securities that would "pass through" payments of interest and principal on a pool of underlying mortgages. GNMA and FHLMC guaranteed payments of interest and principal on the securities they sponsored.[36] Traditionally, commercial banks, savings and loan associations, and mutual savings banks "originated" mortgages (made mortgage loans) and serviced them, usually holding the mortgage loans themselves. Mortgage companies originated and serviced mortgage loans and packaged the mortgages for sale to insurance companies, but this was of relatively small significance in the financial system as a whole.

---

[35] For an entertaining account of the activities of Fannie Mae, Ginnie Mae, and Freddie Mae, see Gurney Breckenfeld, "Nobody Pours It Like Fannie Mae," *Fortune*, June 1972, pp. 86–89, 136–147. The increased flow of loanable funds to housing may, when demand exceeds supply at current interest rates, result in inability to obtain funds on the part of small businesses, consumers, privately financed mortgage borrowing, and state and local governments.

[36] For extensive detail on these securities and their marketing, see Charles M. Sivesind, "Mortgage-Backed Securities: The Revolution in Real Estate Finance," Federal Reserve Bank of New York, *Quarterly Review*, Autumn 1979, pp. 1–10.

## FIGURE 10–5
### Structure of the Residential Mortgage Market

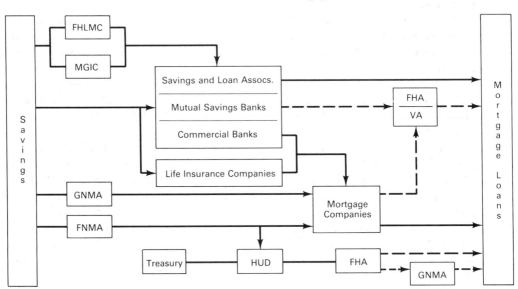

SOURCE: Federal Reserve Bank of Richmond, *Monthly Review,* September 1972.

Now, with the development of bonds and pass-throughs backed by mortgages, long-term investors could buy securities backed by mortgages.[37]

FHLMC developed participation certificates (PCs) representing ownership in pools of conventional mortgages bought by FHLMC, and later it issued guaranteed mortgage certificates (GMCs), on which interest is paid semiannually and principal repayments annually. Timely payments are guaranteed by FHLMC. The GMC is thus in effect a bond backed by a pool of conventional mortgages.

Private mortgage lenders also began to issue both mortgage-backed bonds and pass-through securities. This advice makes it possible for thrift institutions to obtain funds in the capital market to supplement savings account funds or to replace them when disintermediation occurs.

Finally, mortgage-backed revenue bonds were issued by state and local government units to finance housing. Use of tax-exempt bonds to finance housing was criticized by some, and at the time of writing it was uncertain as to what limitations might be placed on this activity.

Private institutions have also sold publicly issued pass-throughs (PIPs) without any government guarantee; Bank of America was first to do this, followed by savings and loan associations.

[37] The process of issuing securities backed by "pools" of other assets (e.g., mortgages or other loans) has come to be termed "securitization." For more details and some implications of this process, see Christine Pavel, "Securitization," Federal Reserve Bank of Chicago, *Economic Perspectives*, July–August 1986, pp. 16–31.

A special problem in this new market for mortgage-backed securities is that of forward (future) delivery and commitment. Institutions that originate mortgage loans make commitments to lend funds to builders and home buyers who are not obligated to borrow the funds (since the building situation may change). Costs of checking collateral and creditworthiness are significant. While completed mortgage loans are being accumulated for sale to investors or as collateral for mortgage-backed securities, interest rates may rise (or fall). There is risk in making commitments at specified interest rates. Banks and thrift institutions can make either firm or standby (optional) commitments to deliver mortgages. FNMA holds biweekly auctions to determine "strike" prices (prices at which delivery will be made). FNMA accepts commitments from bidders offering the highest yields. Of course, if low bids (high yields) are offered, bidders offering standby commitments will not deliver unless interest rates rise.

For other pass-through securities, dealers make commitments to buy or sell certificates with designated rates, for delivery one to six months or more in the future. Dealers may hedge their commitments. For government-guaranteed securities, the dealing is exempt from Securities and Exchange Commission (SEC) regulation, and unfortunately there have been some failures. It is possible that some regulation of this forward contract market may be desirable, as risks of fluctuating interest rates and the small margins of cash required in this dealing create leverage risks.

The practice of "stripping" government securities has also occurred with respect to mortgage-backed securities, separating the interest payments from principal repayments. The Federal National Mortgage association (FNMA), for example, has sold stripped mortgage-backed securities that it held. Instead of making interest coupons and principal amounts into separate securities, as is usual for government and municipal securities, interest payments are moved so that some securities receive much more interest than others. This means that the resulting securities sell at different prices—at premiums for those scheduled to receive more interest, and at discounts for those scheduled to receive less. Risk because of early repayment of underlying mortgages is thus reduced, as is risk of lengthening of the term of repayment. Some investors apparently find this attractive. Since investors who hold both certificates receiving higher interest and certificates receiving a lower rate of interest *can* recombine the interest and principal amounts, thus holding certificates on which the original rate of interest is earned, the average price of the stripped securities should not fall below the original certificates' price level.[38]

Stripped mortgage-backed securities thus constitute one more example of innovations developed as financial markets have been to some extent deregulated and as new techniques have evolved.

Nevertheless, the development of new forms of securities, new types of contracts, and new markets has made profound changes in housing finance. In a period of inflation, with rising interest rates and rising values of homes, a high level of housing activity has been maintained—a level probably impossible if banks and thrift institu-

[38] *The Wall Street Journal*, October 24, 1986, p. 34.

tions had had to finance it from savings flows into those institutions. Of course, mortgage yields have been high at times—70 basis points above grade A corporate bonds in the late 1970s.[39] Competition by mortgage borrowers may also have been in part responsible for a relatively low level of business borrowing for investment purposes. Since the growth of population in the age group that typically is active in buying homes will be significant in the 1980s, if the private market for mortgage-backed securities continues to expand, it might be possible for government activity in this field to be somewhat reduced. The private market development makes one other contribution to mortgage finance—it provides long-term funds, from purchasers of passthroughs and similar securities, instead of short-term savings funds, for financing what is, certainly, long-term real investment (housing). The matching of long-term real investment with (in part) long-term capital funds is surely desirable.

The revolution in housing finance in the 1970s makes it likely that housing will be in a better position to compete for funds since inflation is now reduced and interest rates are lower. Housing starts began to revive in late 1982, and the deregulation of interest rates on time deposits makes it unlikely that housing will again suffer the same lack of availability of funds as in the periods of *high* market interest rates but *low* rates on deposits that existed in the 1970s and early 1980s.

## SUMMARY

Return on capital assets, both "real" and financial, is simply the increase in value of any asset held for a period of time, including capital gain or loss plus interest or other income. Expressed as a rate per period and excluding capital gains or losses arising from price fluctuations, this increase is the rate of return.

The *fundamental* rate of interest is the rate of return on real capital assets. James Tobin has emphasized what he termed the "supply price" of capital, or the rate of return that just induces those who hold real capital assets to hold the existing stock of such assets at their current prices. This rate of return is a key factor determining the amount of investment and thus constitutes a major determinant of the rate of economic growth. But since it is an *expected* rate of return, it is difficult to observe and measure. Indeed, it may be that at times, in the words of J. M. Keynes, "decisions to do something positive . . . can only be taken as a result of animal spirits . . . and not as the outcome of a weighted average of quantitative benefits multiplied by quantitative probabilities." This passage from Keynes reflects the uncertainty of forecasting the amount of investment likely to be undertaken, especially when managers of business firms are quite uncertain about future economic conditions.

Other rates are generally lower than this rate because of less risk involved in holding various financial assets. Yields in the corporate bond market are especially significant because they represent in general the marginal cost of long-term funds for corporations, except for those that resort to new issues of stock.

---

[39] "The Revolution in Home Finance," *Morgan Guaranty Survey,* November 1979, pp. 9–15.

The Eurobond market basically developed because various measures prevented foreign companies, including foreign subsidiaries of U.S. firms, from borrowing in the United States to the extent desired. The market has now developed a size and status that may enable it to continue to be of significance even without such controls on capital movements. By meeting some of the demand for funds, the existence of this market may have moderated to some extent the rise in interest rates that occurred after 1965. Essentially, the advantage of the Eurobond market is that it is an *unregulated* market, whereas the corporate bond market in the United States is regulated by the Securities and Exchange Commission (SEC).

The market for long-term government securities is quite important because government securities provide much of the "ultimate liquidity" that is important whenever the possibility of substantial defaults on other obligations occur. As the long-term portion of the debt has been reduced, the importance of this market has also lessened somewhat, but other problems, including those of refunding large amounts of federal debt each year, have arisen.

Government agency securities have been growing rapidly in volume since 1965, and they now constitute a significant part of the capital market. They are likely to continue to grow and may become a source of liquidity comparable to Treasury securities.

The municipal bond market has limited demand because its special feature, tax exemption, appeals to a limited group of investors. This may give rise to a problem of financing construction activities of state and local government as growth of such activities continues.

The mortgage market, especially the secondary mortgage market, has been aided and significantly improved by establishment and activities of government agencies and agencies initiated as such but later becoming private agencies. The development of new forms of mortgage-backed securities in the 1970s, combined with other activities of the housing agencies, made it likely that although declines in housing during recessions will occur, recovery in housing will be facilitated after interest rates are lowered enough that mortgage borrowers feel they can pay such rates.

In conclusion, capital markets provide liquidity for financial assets, thus making investors more willing to hold them. Improvements in information, functioning, and efficiency in capital markets improve this liquidity and hence facilitate the flow of funds into investment. Fluctuations in rates in various segments of the capital markets tend to shift funds from one segment to another and may adversely or favorably affect particular types of activity for which funds are needed.

## Questions for Discussion

**1.** Develop a diagram showing the major connections between financial institutions and particular sectors of the capital markets for debt securities; show individuals also, where they are very important.

**2.** Why is the quick disappearance of differences between yields on new issues and those on comparable "seasoned" securities one indication of a relatively efficient capital market?

**3.** Discuss possible reasons for differences between the rate of return or yield on real capital assets and equities and that on corporate bonds; between that on corporate bonds and that on long-term government bonds; between government bonds and short-term government securities; and between short-term government securities and money (zero in the past). Where would the yield on "near-monies" (deposits and similar accounts in deposit-type financial institutions) fall in this model?

**4.** Forecast the future growth of the Eurobond market (rapid growth, moderate growth, no growth, or decline), and explain your forecast in terms of characteristics of that market and changes anticipated in factors that affect the market. Discuss the probable effects that development of the Eurobond market has had on interest rates in the U.S. bond market and in Europe.

**5.** Why is there a dealer market in government securities, rather than an auction market like that for stocks on the New York Stock Exchange?

**6.** Why did net new issues of government agency securities increase so rapidly in 1973? Is this characteristic of a year of rapid growth in business activity, or were other factors significant?

**7.** Why did the Federal Reserve System begin buying government agency securities in 1971?

**8.** Why was the spread between yields on seasoned corporate bonds and yields on U.S. government bonds so much wider in the early 1970s than in the 1960s?

**9.** Why did the spread between yields on U.S. government securities and yields on municipals narrow during many recent years?

**10.** Discuss the role played by the various recently established government agencies in the mortgage market. What beneficial results has this activity had? Has it had any detrimental effects? If so, what and how?

## Selected References

A series of articles in the *Quarterly Review* published by the Federal Reserve Bank of New York provides useful information concerning developments in various parts of the capital markets: Burton Zwick, "The Market for Corporate Bonds," Autumn 1977, pp. 27–36; Christopher J. McCurdy, "The Dealer Market for United States Government Securities," Winter 1977–1978, pp. 35–47; Kenneth D. Garbade, "Electronic Quotation Systems and the Market for Government Securities," Summer 1978, pp. 13–20; Lois Banks, "The Market for Agency Securities," Spring 1978, pp. 7–19; and Charles M. Sivesind, "Mortgage-Backed Securities: The Revolution in Real Estate Finance," Autumn 1979, pp. 1–9.

Trends in the bond market and price and yield data are conveniently presented in the weekly *Bond Market Roundup* and the *Quarterly Bond Market Review*, both published by Salomon Brothers. These are supplemented by an annual review. The Federal Reserve Bank of New York's *Quarterly Review* contains a section reporting and analyzing developments in the capital markets.

Problems facing the municipal bond market in the early 1980s, and possible actions to improve the functioning of this market, are reviewed in David C. Beek, "Rethinking Tax-Exempt

Financing for State and Local Governments," Federal Reserve Bank of New York, *Quarterly Review*, Autumn 1982, pp. 30–40.

For a detailed discussion of advantages and disadvantages of original issue deep discount bonds (of this the extreme is "zero-coupon" bonds), see Andrew Silver, "Original Issue Deep Discount Bonds," Federal Reserve Bank of New York, *Quarterly Review*, Winter 1981–1982, pp. 18–28.

On origins and general nature of the Eurobond market, see Gunter Dufey, *The Eurobond Market: Function and Future* (Seattle: Graduate School of Business Administration, University of Washington, 1969). Recent information is scattered, but *World Financial Markets*, issued monthly by Morgan Guaranty Trust Company, is useful, and such articles as Stanislas M. Yassukovich, "The Secondary Market in Eurobonds," *Euromoney*, June 1970, pp. 8–10, and "Eurobonds—Uneasy Peace in '71," *Euromoney*, March 1971, pp. 18–20, are informative. The Eurobond market as a force for capital market integration is examined in Morris Mendelson, "The Eurobond and Capital Market Integration," *Journal of Finance*, March 1972, pp. 110–126.

A review of some studies of mortgage finance and housing may be found in Neil G. Berkman, "Mortgage Finance and the Housing Cycle," Federal Reserve Bank of Boston, *New England Economic Review*, September–October 1979, pp. 54–76.

Alfred Broaddus, "Financial Innovation in the United States—Background, Current Status and Prospects," Federal Reserve Bank of Richmond, *Economic Review*, January/February 1985, pp. 2–22, calls attention to the following significant trends in the capital markets: increase in the amount of floating-rate bonds and in the volume of zero-coupon bonds; increase in the amount of adjustable rate mortgages (ARMs); development of an active market for securities backed by pools of mortgages; and growth of trading in interest rate futures for mortgage-backed securities issued by the Government National Mortgage Association (GNMAs), U.S. Treasury bonds, bills, and notes, domestic bank CDs, and Eurodollars.

"Securitization" of loans, which began in the secondary mortgage market, is now important for banks. Banks are now "securitizing" auto finance loans and credit card receivables. For a brief review of possible future trends, see Barbara Bennett, "Where Are Banks Going?" Federal Reserve Bank of San Francisco, *Weekly Letter*, September 25, 1987.

# THE MARKET FOR EQUITIES

Equities (stocks) differ from debt securities (bonds and others) in several respects: (1) Equities represent ownership rather than creditor claims. Creditor claims by bond-holders and others have priority; in cases of financial difficulties and bankruptcies, although creditors often suffer some losses, owners almost always suffer greater losses. (2) Equities normally have no maturity date; they may be outstanding as long as the company continues to operate. (3) Hence, the secondary market for stocks—transferring ownership from one party to another—is large. The volume of stocks outstanding is great relative to the volume of new issues in any given year, and most trading is in issues already outstanding rather than in new issues.

Equities are traded on exchanges and in the over-the-counter market. No attempt is made in this chapter to cover details of operation of these markets. Nor is any attempt made to develop methods for analyzing factors determining or affecting selection of individual equities for investment portfolios. These are topics covered in courses on investments.

Our concern in this chapter is the general relationship of the market for equities to the other financial markets. The basis for payment of interest by business firms is that capital (factories, machinery, and inventory) is productive. By borrowing funds and paying interest, business managers can buy equipment and build factories to produce more (and better) products than could be produced without the use of such capital. Owners of business firms can thus earn enough to repay loans, pay the interest, and retain enough profit to provide a yield enough higher than the yield on the borrowed funds to cover the extra risk of ownership.

Thus we believe that a theory of interest should begin with a theory of the rate of return on real capital assets. Stocks represent real capital assets because they represent ownership of such assets. Only if earnings of business firms are high enough to repay loans and pay interest and still leave an adequate return for the risk involved in investing in real capital assets can business firms pay interest.

Although we recognize the validity of Alfred Marshall's principle that demand and supply are like the blades of scissors—both are needed for cutting—we think that generally *variations* in the demand for borrowed funds are more likely to cause changes in interest rates than are changes in the supply of funds for loans or investments. This is reinforced by the *consumption function principle* that individuals save a relatively regular percentage of their income, in a given culture, and usually vary this proportion in the short run only by a relatively small percentage.

Thus yields on real capital assets (and hence on stocks) depend primarily on the productivity of real capital assets, and interest rates vary primarily because of demand for borrowing, which in turn is fundamentally dependent on expected yields on real capital assets.

The values of real capital assets should depend on the prospective net earnings of business firms (after payment of wage, salary, interest, and other costs). If earnings rise, the values of real capital assets that help in producing earnings should also rise. Since equities represent net ownership of real capital assets, equities also should rise in value if earnings rise. The value of equities should approximately equal the net value of the underlying assets.[1] Thus in a period in which wages, interest, and profits all rise, values of stocks should rise unless for some reason profits rise less than wages, interest, and any other share in national income.

Since stocks involve more risk than bonds and other financial assets held by creditors of firms, it is expected that rates of return are normally higher on stocks than on bonds and other securities representing debt. Thus we are surprised when evidence from the 1970s indicates that the total return to stockholders (dividends plus capital gain from price increases of stocks) was much lower than return on bonds and

---

[1] This would imply a ratio of 1 : 1 for Tobin's "q" if net value of assets is considered to be equal to replacement cost. In an efficient market, replacement cost of assets should be approximately equal to the discounted present value of their expected earnings—why pay to replace assets having a discounted present value of expected earnings less than their replacement cost? (Some firms producing poor-quality products or products not in demand by consumers may not be justified in replacing assets that wear out or are destroyed, but firms may be justified in acquiring assets to produce better products or products in greater demand.)

some other financial assets. For roughly 40 years, extensive studies had shown that yields on stocks (counting both dividends and increase in stock prices, and assuming the reinvestment of dividends) had been approximately 4 percent *higher* than yields on bonds. Unless there is a convincing explanation for the poor performance of the stock market in the 1970s, fundamental theory of finance must be in error.

We therefore devote much space in this chapter to the fundamental basis for valuation of equities, the long-run trend of stock prices, the interconnections between stock prices (and hence their yields) and the yields on bonds and other financial assets, and the possible reasons for poor performance of the stock market during the 1970s.

We also give some attention, at the end of the chapter, to the efficiency of the market for equities and to some problems of that market as an integral part of financial markets as a whole.

Aside from efficiency, another aspect of the equities market may give rise to concern. Heavy activity in this market can result in a rapid increase in *transactions* velocity of money. This may lead to an increase in the *income* velocity of money, although the manner in which this occurs must be explained.[2] The stock market is often cited as a barometer of business, and in fact stock market prices are one of the 12 leading indicators designated by the National Bureau of Economic Research as consistently rising in business upswings, falling in recessions, and changing direction of movement *prior* to a change in direction for business activity generally.

Whether this should be interpreted to mean that a stock market decline is a *cause* of a business recession—whether, for example, the stock market crash of 1929 was an important causal factor related to the depression—is still debated. Perhaps the most common conclusion is that because the economy was vulnerable to unfavorable influences, the effect of the crash was much greater than it might otherwise have been. It caused a greater decline, once a decline had begun.

Let us first consider the nature of the market for equities, commonly referred to as "the stock market." This term covers a range of markets, including the New York Stock Exchange (NYSE), the American Stock Exchange (ASE), a number of regional exchanges, and the over-the-counter market. Several thousand equity securities are listed on the organized exchanges, about half of them on the NYSE. Several thousand more corporations have more than 300 shareholders each, a level that leads the Securities and Exchange Commission to regard them as potentially being traded over the counter. Stock of companies with less than that number of shareholders is likely to be sold so infrequently that no regular market can be maintained for it. In the following discussion, the general term "the stock market" is used to apply to all secondary trading in equities. Although some reference is made to the well-known Dow Jones Industrial Average as an index of stock prices, no attempt is made to give a detailed analysis of stock price averages and their relative merits as indicators. These details would require much more space than can be devoted to this subject. Neverthe-

---

[2] As indicated in Chapter 6, transactions velocity means the rate of turnover of money in *all* transactions, while income velocity is the rate of turnover when only *income* (GNP) transactions are counted. Income transactions are only about 4 percent of total transactions.

less, a basic framework of analysis of the determinants of stock market prices and a foundation for analysis of the role of stock prices in affecting spending is essential.

## EQUITIES AS CLAIMS ON REAL CAPITAL ASSETS

Equities represent residual claims to the values of assets of business firms after claims of creditors have been satisfied. Claims of creditors are almost always fixed in money terms. Thus a rise in either earnings or capital gains (increase in prices as inflation occurs) should be reflected in stock market prices. Unfortunately, values of assets of business firms are difficult to estimate. Even replacement costs or current costs may not represent the values of those assets, since they may be expected to be less (or more) in the future. Value should be based on expected earnings. Thus, even if replacement costs have risen, if there is reason to believe that earnings may fall, values of assets of business firms should be reduced. Of course, in an efficient market for capital goods, prices offered for new capital goods to build and equip new factories should not exceed their values in terms of discounted future earnings—but can we be sure that the market for capital goods is efficient?

If the price of Chevrolets rises, shouldn't the value of factories and equipment used to build Chevrolets rise? The plausible answer is yes—*if* profits as well as wages and other costs continue to rise proportionately, *if* government does not tax business firms disproportionately heavily, and *if* price and wage controls are not imposed or, if they are imposed, if they do not bear more heavily on prices and profits than on wages. Fear of a squeeze on profits, either because of taxes or government price controls, may diminish the values of capital goods.

When values of equities are low, it is difficult for business firms to raise capital through new equity issues. A number of firms, finding that profitability of additional investment is of doubtful probability, may be tempted to buy up shares of their own stock instead of investing in additional real capital assets. When values of equities are rising, it is easier to raise new capital through equity issues, and the rising values of real capital assets, reflected in the values of equities, tend to induce business firms to increase investment.

As is indicated subsequently, the market for equities is, of course, a market for claims on *future* earnings or dividends. As such, it is subject to more uncertainty than are most capital markets, as earnings are more uncertain than bond repayment or refunding, and, potentially at least, the earnings discounted may be far in the future. Hence it is not likely that a simple formula can be derived to explain stock prices; this is demonstrated later in this chapter. The short-run movements in equity values are likely to exhibit volatility and to respond to many factors that may be quite indirectly related to prospective earnings. Nevertheless, the importance of investment as a determinant of both full employment and economic growth is great, and the level of values of equities is an important factor affecting investment in the long run. For this reason, much more attention is given to long-run values of equities than to short-run fluctuations or cyclical variations.

# THE STOCK MARKET

Four important differences exist between stocks and debt securities and the markets where they are traded. First, corporate stocks are in effect perpetual securities, with no maturity date. They continue to exist unless a firm goes out of business; when firms merge into other firms, stockholders in the merged firm are usually offered shares in the resulting firm, on some basis determined by relative valuations. Second, in large part because of the first difference, most of the trading is in the secondary market; relatively small amounts of new issues of stock are sold, especially in relation to the total volume of stock outstanding. This is even more true than it appears to be, because many new issues of companies that were privately owned and "go public" represent simply sale to the public of ownership equity already accumulated by the private owners. Third, trading in the secondary market is divided into two major segments, the over-the-counter market and the organized exchanges, whereas trading in bonds and mortgages is chiefly over the counter. The organized exchanges are widely publicized and attract interest and often purchases by a large segment of the public. Fourth, whereas bonds and mortgages usually have fixed interest rates and maturity values, so that their yields are affected by price changes occurring during their life, common stocks have no fixed yields.[3] Thus changes in prices of common stocks may result from either changes in yields (dividends or dividends plus capital gains) *or* changes in interest (discount) rates, the former usually being the more important.[4]

## The Fundamental Approach to Valuation of Stocks[5]

These four differences constitute the keys to the fundamental approach to valuation of stocks. Since bonds and mortgages have maturity values, the formula for their value on a one-period basis is

$$PV + PV \cdot i = Y + F$$

$$PV = \frac{Y + F}{1 + i}$$

[3] Preferred stocks occupy a special position, as they have a specified fixed yield that must be paid before common stock dividends can be declared. The volume of preferred stock is relatively very small, but brief comment on their valuation is made later.

[4] It is useful to keep in mind that, as the terms are used here, interest is simply the increase in value from the present moment to a future specified date, whereas discount is the decrease in value from that date to the present moment. Thus in the formula $PV \cdot i = Y$ (present value times the interest rate equals income), $i$ is the interest rate; in the rearranged formula, $PV = Y/i$, $i$ is the discount rate.

[5] The first systematic attempt to derive principles for valuation of common stocks is probably John B. Williams, *The Theory of Investment Value* (Cambridge, Mass.: Harvard University Press, 1938), although the basic idea was expressed at least as early as Edgar L. Smith, *Common Stocks as Long-Term Investments* (New York: Macmillan, 1924). The analysis was supported and extended by Nicholas Molodovsky in such writings as "Stock Values and Stock Prices," *Financial Analysts Journal*, May/June 1960. An interesting nontechnical review is Daniel Seligman, "Why the Stock Market Acts That Way," *Fortune*, November 1966, pp. 154–157, 234–238.

In contrast, the formula for the value of a stock is basically

$$PV = \frac{Y}{i}$$

In these formulas $PV$ means present value, $Y$ is the expected income, $i$ is the rate of discount if one is looking at the discounting of a future value to the present, and $F$ is the final maturity value.

Because stocks have no final maturity, only the yield need be considered in the basic formula. However, as soon as one views the yield over a number of periods instead of one period, the time horizon of investors becomes relevant. If, for example, investors look ahead only three years, although there is no final maturity value, there is a price at which the investors hope or expect to sell the stocks at the end of three years.[6] As this is an *expected* price, $F_e$, rather than a fixed price, it may vary substantially with investors' expectations. And, because income, $Y$, in the case of stocks is also quite variable, there is significant basis for wide fluctuations in values of stocks.[7] Predictably, therefore, stock prices fluctuate much more than do bond prices.

What determines expected prices of stocks at the ends of investors' time horizons? Basically, we must return to the preceding formula. Present value *at that time* will be equal to expected income divided by the discount rate,

$$F_e = \frac{Y_3}{i}$$

where $Y_3$ is all income (both dividends and retained earnings) expected to continue in the future.[8] Thus, if a higher level of earnings were expected to continue, the value at that date would be that level of earnings discounted by the appropriate interest rate.

[6] In this case, the formula becomes

$$PV = \frac{Y_1}{1 + i} + \frac{Y_2}{(1 + i)^2} + \frac{Y_e}{(1 + i)^3} + \frac{F_e}{(1 + i)^3}$$

where $Y_1$, $Y_2$, and $Y_3$ are expected earnings in each of the years to which the investor looks forward and $F_3$ is the final expected price of the stock at that time.

[7] The position taken in this section is that values of common stocks depend on both expected dividends and expected capital gains. This view is perhaps still somewhat controversial, although the definition offered by Benjamin Graham, David L. Dodd, and Sidney Cottle, *Security Analysis*, 4th ed. (New York: McGraw-Hill, 1962) included both. Writers such as Myron J. Gordon, *The Investment, Financing and Valuation of the Corporation* (Homewood, Ill.: Richard D. Irwin, 1962), especially Chapter 5, preferred to include only dividends. On the other hand, Franco Modigliani and Merton Miller went so far as to state that whether earnings are paid out in dividends or held as retained earnings "is a mere detail"; see "The Cost of Capital, Corporation Finance, and the Theory of Investment," *American Economic Review*, June 1958, pp. 261–297. Empirical evidence that retained earnings have been important was supplied by several studies, including Irwin Friend and Marshall Puckett, "Dividends and Stock Prices," *American Economic Review*, September 1964, pp. 656–682, in which comparisons were made between prices for stocks of companies in "nongrowth industries" such as foods and steel and in "growth industries" such as electronics and chemicals.

[8] Problems of fluctuating interest or dividend or retained earnings yield rates are ignored here for simplicity.

This has led to the use, for present values of stocks at any time, of the expression "times earnings." If a discount rate of 5 percent were used for earnings, the present value of the stock would be 20 times earnings.[9]

What determines the appropriate rate of interest or discount? On a bond or a mortgage, a coupon rate or interest rate is specified, but the yield may differ from the coupon rate. If more attractive opportunities for investment in similar securities become available, investors are likely to sell bonds, reducing the price but raising the yield for new investors. On the other hand, if a bond looks more attractive, investors are likely to buy bonds, raising their prices and reducing their yields for new investors. Similarly for stocks, the rate of yield may vary *if* other opportunities for investment, similar in quality, are found in the market. To the extent that stocks are similar to bonds, providing a relatively fixed income in the form of a steady dividend comparable to the steady rate of interest on bonds, the yield on stocks may be compared directly with yields on bonds. Since bondholders have priority over stockholders in claims on earnings, but no claim on earnings above a specified interest rate, the risk of *variation* in returns on stocks is greater. Yields that may be obtained may be much higher or much lower than those on bonds. To the extent that investors have an aversion to risk, yields they desire on stocks will be higher than on bonds. The presence in the stock market of both very well-informed investors, including large institutions and, at times at least, of large numbers of less well-informed investors, may create problems of information flow.

To recapitulate briefly, the fundamental approach to valuation of stocks tells us that stock values depend on (1) the expected earnings over whatever time horizon is foreseen by investors, (2) the expected price at the end of that time horizon (which is based on a continuation of yields current at that time, in the absence of any reason to expect further change), and (3) the appropriate rate of discount, based on other opportunities for yield available in other capital markets, with appropriate adjustment for differences in risk.

## Valuation of Stocks When Inflation Occurs

The theory of valuation of stocks when inflation occurs was not very well understood, even in recent years. It was generally expected by some that stocks would be a hedge against inflation; that is, that stock prices would rise by about as much as prices generally rose, because earnings (profits) of corporations would rise about as much as other incomes. Some economists warned from time to time that there was evidence in the record that stock prices were not a very good hedge against inflation during *short* periods, because stock prices seemed to be adversely affected when

---

[9] The "times earnings" ratio is simply $1/i$—if $i$ is 5 percent, the times earnings ratio is $1/.05$, or 20. A stock is then said to be selling at 20 times earnings. The earnings referred to may be the current year's earnings or earnings for a year just ended, or they may be expected earnings over some time period.

inflation occurred or accelerated. But fundamental theory was not examined very carefully.

The period 1968–1982 (more than a decade) was in general one of inflation—more in some years, less in others, but in general a rising *trend* in the inflation rate, culminating in double-digit inflation at the beginning of the 1980s. During this period, general stock market averages had approximately *no* net rise at all; the stock market rose in some years and fell in others. By 1982 the *real* value of stocks (stock prices adjusted for inflation) had fallen by approximately one-half. This result, quite the opposite of the widely held view that stock prices would rise and stocks would be good hedges against inflation, stimulated much research and many different opinions.[10]

Some concluded that the decline in *real* stock prices was because of a decline in real earnings, if properly measured; others concluded that it was the result of other errors, most specifically a failure to recognize that, although the discount rate applied to expected bond returns must rise because the maturity value and in most cases the interest rate on bonds are fixed, the same rule need not apply to stocks. If earnings are expected to rise, the need for a higher discount rate is offset by the expected rise in earnings. Interestingly, both those who believed that inflation hurt corporate profits and those who believed that investors made an error in discounting expected profits agreed that if inflation were reduced, stock prices should rise. However, those who believed that inflation hurt corporate earnings also believed that if inflation returned after its slowdown in 1980–1982, stock prices would fall again.[11]

Stock prices are, of course, of interest to investment analysts. But stock prices are also significant for the economy because (1) as indicated, stock prices have been a major leading indicator of business activity, (2) a rise or fall in stock prices may stimulate (or reduce) consumer spending because those who own stocks have capital gains (increased wealth) when stock prices rise (and losses when they fall), and (3) a rise in stock prices should stimulate (and a fall in stock prices should discourage) investment spending—if firms are valued higher because investors expect higher earnings, added investment is likely to be worthwhile if investors are correct, and companies obtain more dollars per share of new stock issued, and thus more funds per such share, for investment.[12]

---

[10] Specific studies are cited in later footnotes, but a very useful general summary is found in Douglas K. Pearce, "The Impact of Inflation on Stock Prices," Federal Reserve Bank of Kansas City, *Economic Review*, March 1982, pp. 3–18.

[11] In the summer of 1982, stock prices began a rapid rise; the Dow Jones Industrial Average was 875 at the beginning of 1982 and 1046 at the end of that year. Some economists had been predicting such a rise (although not necessarily its timing) but were warning that a *sustained* rise would occur only if the inflation rate remained relatively low. For this latter view, see Richard W. Kopcke, "The Continuing Decline in Corporate Profitability and Stock Prices," Federal Reserve Bank of Boston, *New England Economic Review*, July–August 1982, pp. 5–17.

[12] James Tobin has regarded the ratio of the market value of a firm to the replacement cost of its capital stock (a ratio he designated as "q") as the primary determinant of investment spending. See James Tobin, "A General Equilibrium Approach to Monetary Theory," *Journal of Money, Credit and Banking*, February 1969, pp. 15–29.

On the basis of the fundamental theory of stock prices already discussed, since stock prices are determined by expected earnings discounted at some interest rate, changes in stock prices must depend on expected earnings and the discount rate. The formula may be expressed either as $P = Y_e/i$ or as $P = x$ times $Y_e$, where $P$ is stock prices, $Y_e$ is either current or expected earnings, $i$ is the discount rate, and $x$ is 1/the discount rate; $x$ is termed the *times earnings* rate. A times earnings rate of 14 or 15 was common in the early 1960s, but by 1980, this rate was about 7.

### Why Did the Stock Market Perform Poorly During Inflation?

Within this analytical framework, possible explanations for the poor performance of the stock market in the 1970s include (1) higher taxes on higher nominal before-tax earnings may have reduced after-tax earnings; (2) earnings, or "sustainable" earnings, may have been adversely affected, perhaps without this being evident, because accounting methods overstated profits and because of other factors; (3) investors may have recognized such overstatement of profits but may not have recognized that inflation reduces the *real* amount of corporate debt—if prices and profits rise, bond issues can be paid off at par if they mature, and stockholders gain by any rise in earnings or capital gains on fixed assets because debt is fixed in nominal amounts; (4) higher energy costs and other factors may have reduced the productivity of capital; (5) even if earnings rose, a still greater rise may have been desired because of (a) attractiveness of other assets, such as houses and gold, or (b) greater perceived risk in stocks; and (6) an incorrect discount rate may have been applied to current earnings, for example, investors may have treated stocks as risky bonds, discounting them at a rate somewhat above the current nominal bond rate, not recognizing that bonds *must* be discounted at higher rates when inflation occurs because their maturity values are fixed, whereas stock prices need not be if earnings rise.

The term "sustainable earnings" was used in the preceding paragraph because it may not be possible to sustain current earnings; it may be clear that some losses may occur.[13] The argument that an incorrect discount rate may have been used was presented in an article by Modigliani and Cohn, which generated further discussion.[14]

---

[13] Richard W. Kopcke, "The Continuing Decline in Corporate Profitability and Stock Prices," Federal Reserve Bank of Boston, *New England Economic Review*, July–August 1982, pp. 5–17, argued that as long as inflation continued, maturing debt would have to be replaced by new debt at higher cost. He also suggested that, although firms may gain from debt during inflation, they also lose on debt securities that they own in their own pension funds.

[14] Franco Modigliani and Richard Cohn, "Inflation, Rational Valuation, and the Market," *Financial Analysts Journal*, March–April 1979, pp. 24–44. The hypothesis advanced by Modigliani and Cohn was distasteful to many financial economists because it suggested that investors were *not* promptly and intelligently using inflation in valuing stocks as they would do in an efficient market. For this reason, Modigliani himself hesitated in first considering the hypothesis. The concept of an efficient market is discussed in more detail later in this chapter.

Let us examine the possible explanations and see whether we can discard any that are incorrect or only minor; the others remain as possible hypotheses.

### Taxes

The evidence seems to indicate that the role of taxes was small. If taxes were a major factor, then after-tax earnings should have been *more* adversely affected than before-tax earnings. This does not seem to have been true; both declined, but the extent of decline did not differ much.[15]

### Accounting Methods and Profits

That present accounting methods overstate profits in a period of inflation has been recognized for some time. Replacement costs of capital assets rise in inflation, with other prices; yet depreciation charges, no matter how calculated, cannot total over a period of years more than the historical cost of the assets. Thus depreciation charges, added up, are much less than the replacement cost of the assets. Earnings after depreciation are not properly income unless total depreciation on assets equals their replacement cost.[16] The same argument applies for inventories—inventory carried on the books at cost is sold at higher prices later (if there is inflation), but they must also be replaced by new inventory at higher cost. Hence the "inventory profit" is illusory.[17]

It is thus clear that accounting methods used in calculating earnings overstate earnings during inflation, and investors could cause a decline in stock prices if they recognized the need of adjusting reported earnings for overstatement. But at the same time, if investors *also* recognized the need to adjust for the gain from inflation because debt of business firms, once incurred, is fixed, while profits can rise, much of the

---

[15] See the article by Pearce, cited earlier, and also Nicholas J. Gonedes, "Evidence on the 'Tax Effects' of Inflation Under Historical Cost Accounting Methods," *Journal of Business*, April 1981, pp. 227–270.

[16] Hicks' classic definition of income is as follows: income is what can be spent during a period and leave an individual or a business firm as well off at the end of the period as at the beginning. (See John R. Hicks, *Value and Capital*, 2nd ed., London, Oxford University Press, 1946, p. 172.) An individual can spend during a month salary received during the month and still be as well off as at the beginning of the month. But a business firm *cannot* spend funds needed to replace capital assets and still be as well off, because if the capital assets are not replaced, the firm cannot produce as much as previously. For those receiving them, incidentally, capital gains on stocks or similar assets *can* be regarded as income; the individual could sell shares of stock equal to the capital gain and still be as well off as before, as long as the stock prices did not fall.

[17] In national income accounting, it has been recognized for some time that an "inventory valuation adjustment" and a "capital consumption allowance" adjustment must be made to make these corrections. Beginning in 1980, large firms were required by Financial Accounting Standards Board (FASB) Statement 33 to report figures necessary to make such adjustments, either in replacement cost values or in inflation figures that could be used. On the basis of experience with this information, they *might* in the future be required to present adjusted financial statements, if inflation continued.

overstatement would be offset. Hence a crucial question is whether investors recognize the gain on debt—and we simply don't know.

### Decline in Productivity of Capital

One reason we don't know is that we must still consider the other possible reasons for the poor performance of the stock market during inflation. One is that higher energy costs and other factors may have reduced the productivity of capital. Perhaps some factories are obsolete, perhaps some airplanes use too much fuel, and so on. This reduced productivity may be heavily reflected in expected earnings.[18] High interest rates, real or nominal, may be a cause for poor performance of the stock market; earnings must be discounted at real rates even if they need not be discounted at nominal rates, and real rates were high in the late 1970s and early 1980s.

### Rise in Desired Rate of Return

There is also the possibility that investors may have desired a higher rate of return than that obtained. They might desire a higher rate either (1) because of attractiveness of return on other assets such as houses and gold or (2) because of greater *perceived* risk in stocks.[19] But in the early 1980s, both houses and gold ceased to rise in price at the rates prevailing in the 1970s, and it became uncertain whether large capital gains would be obtained on either asset in the near future. Nominal yields on alternative financial assets were higher, but for some time, *real* yields on such assets were *negative* for government securities.[20] Yields on short-term assets such as money market mutual funds and money market accounts were high enough at certain times that real rates were positive, but short-term interest rates declined as the recession of 1981–1982 continued. If investors desired the high return obtainable on houses when house prices rose sharply, and if investment in houses was further stimulated by tax benefits (deductibility of mortgage interest payments and $125,000 of capital gains, without tax, for those selling houses they had lived in, after these owners reached age 55), the attractiveness was much reduced in the 1980s because, as the rate of inflation fell, house prices did not rise rapidly as had occurred in the late 1970s.

[18] The possibility that lower productivity of capital may have affected stock prices is emphasized by Patrick J. Corcoran and Leonard G. Sahling, "The Cost of Capital: How High Is It?" Federal Reserve Bank of New York, *Quarterly Review*, Summer 1982, pp. 23–31. See also M. N. Baily, "Productivity and the Services of Capital and Labor" *Brookings Papers on Economic Activity*, No. 1, 1981.

[19] On the attractiveness of houses as an investment, see Patric H. Hendershott and Sheng Cheng Hu, "Inflation and Extraordinary Returns on Owner-Occupied Housing: Some Implications for Capital Allocation and Productivity Growth," *Journal of Macroeconomics*, Spring 1981, pp. 177–203; and Lawrence H. Summers, "Inflation, the Stock Market, and Owner-Occupied Housing," *American Economic Review*, May 1981, pp. 429–434. On increased perceived risk in stocks, see Burton G. Malkiel, "The Capital Formation Problems in the United States," *Journal of Finance*, May 1979, pp. 291–306; and William Fellner, "Corporate Asset-Liability Decisions in View of the Low Market Value of Equity," in *Contemporary Economic Problems, 1980* (Washington, D.C.: American Enterprise Institute, 1980).

[20] See R. B. Ibbotson and R. A. Sinquefield, *Stocks, Bonds, Bills, and Inflation: Historical Returns, 1926–1978*, Financial Analysts Foundation, 1979.

### Error in Desired Rate of Return

Finally, there is the possibility suggested by Modigliani and Cohn: investors may have used a wrong (improperly high) discount rate in discounting earnings. A high discount rate could also have been used (perhaps appropriately) if investors perceived greater risk in stocks.

Modigliani and Cohn pointed out that the nominal rate of interest is used to discount expected income on bonds because that income is fixed—it could be less, if there were default, but it cannot be more, from issue time to maturity time. Of course, it can be more if the bonds fall in price and are then purchased in the market; the price will then rise to par value at maturity, in the absence of default. But a nominal rate of interest is not appropriate to use for discounting expected income on stocks, because that income *can* rise. In fact, if corporate earnings rose at approximately the same rate as did other earnings (wages, interest, and so on) during a period of inflation, the discount rate appropriate for use in discounting expected earnings would be the "real" rate of interest (the nominal rate minus the current or expected inflation rate) plus, of course, the premium appropriate for stocks because they are more risky assets than bonds. Modigliani and Cohn agreed that this risk premium could increase in a period of inflation, but found that the decline in the "real" value of stocks (adjusted for inflation) correlated so well with the rise in the rate of inflation that it seemed probable that investors were using the nominal rate of interest to discount expected earnings. If so, this was an error, and if investors realized that this was an error, stock prices would rise sharply; also, if the rate of inflation declined, stock prices would rise sharply, because in that case, the nominal rate of interest also would fall, so that even if it were used to discount expected earnings, it would be lower. The sharp rise in stock prices from mid-1982 to mid-1987 could have been evidence that they were correct, although stock prices could have risen for other reasons.

### Conclusion

In reviewing the hypotheses, we can conclude that taxes were not a major factor and that attractiveness of such assets as houses and gold could have been a significant factor only at certain times. Remaining plausible reasons for the poor performance of the stock market during inflation are (1) investors may adjust reported earnings downward for inadequate depreciation and illusory inventory profits, but may not recognize the gain from debt; (2) investors may have used too high a discount rate, either because they perceived greater risk in stocks (Malkiel and others) or because they made an error (Modigliani and Cohn); and (3) the decline in the productivity of capital may have reduced future possible earnings. It seems fair to conclude that inflation hurt stock prices (1) primarily by causing investors to require a higher rate of return to invest in stocks—perhaps because they perceived greater risk in stocks, perhaps because they mistakenly discounted expected earnings at too high a rate—and (2) perhaps because (at least temporarily) there were very attractive rates of return on certain *real* assets. It may also have hurt stock prices because a decline in productivity of capital reduced possible future earnings and because investors ignored the gain on debt obtained during inflation.[21] It does not seem that adjustments to earnings to reflect effects of inflation can account for the poor performance of stocks unless investors made a negative adjustment and ignored a positive one.[22]

All in all, the results cast doubt on the efficient market hypothesis for the market for *one type* of financial asset (stocks) *vis-à-vis others* and for *one* time period (a period of worsening inflation).[23]

## Future Stock Prices

Even if it were shown that it is irrational, on the basis of discounting *current* earnings, for the stock market to have been no higher in 1980 than it was in 1970, there may still be questions about its future in the 1980s. Valuation of stocks is based on *expected* earnings. Are earnings likely to continue to rise and thus justify a continued rise in stock prices once they have caught up with rational levels?

A good "layman's" discussion of this question appeared in late summer 1979.[24] The author argued that prospects for profits are dimmed somewhat by five major factors. (1) Although corporate income taxes have not adversely affected the average company,[25] they *have* adversely affected companies with relatively little debt, for those with little debt cannot deduct much interest cost from profits subject to tax. (2) The unfunded liabilities of corporate pension funds are large and might reduce corporate earnings by about 7½ percent, as a very rough estimate. (3) Certain large expenditures, estimated by Murray Weidenbaum to be perhaps 10 percent of total capital

---

[21] The idea that debtors gain and creditors lose during inflation is an old one. One study often cited is Reuben A. Kessel, "Inflation-Caused Wealth Redistribution," *American Economic Review*, March 1956, pp. 128–141. Firms with large amounts of debt gain because increases in prices and hence in earnings accrue to stockholders, while bondholders obtain a fixed maturity value. Firms with financial assets lose if the financial assets have fixed maturity or redemption values, although if funds can be invested in assets on which interest rates rise with the inflation, this may not be true. Finally, fixed assets provide an (admittedly rough) hedge against inflation, as their prices rise with inflation. A study by Kenneth R. French, Richard S. Rubak, and G. William Schwert, "Effects of Nominal Contracting on Stock Returns," National Bureau of Economic Research Conference on Inflation and Financial Markets, May 15 and 16, 1981, indicated that firms do not gain from debt when only effects of *unanticipated* inflation are considered; this differs from Kessel's study based on data for earlier time periods.

[22] This conclusion is reached in Phillip Cagan, *Do Stock Prices Reflect the Adjustment of Earnings for Inflation?* Monograph Series in Finance and Economics, Monograph 1982–2, Salomon Brothers Center for the Study of Financial Institutions, Graduate School of Business Administration, New York University, 1982.

[23] Cagan (footnote 22) concludes that "stock prices appear to have reflected . . . inflation adjustments in general quite inadequately. The adjustments are partially offsetting and so do not explain the decline in real value of stocks. But the incomplete adjustments reinforce the doubts about the complete efficiency of this market under inflationary conditions" (from the preface).

[24] A. F. Ehrbar, "Unraveling the Mysteries of Corporate Profits," *Fortune*, August 27, 1979, pp. 90–96.

[25] This is true because corporate income taxes tax what they should not tax—a rise in income that simply parallels inflation—and do not tax what they should—increased income paid out to bondholders as increased interest.

spending, do not generate increased earnings because they are regulatory costs imposed by government. (4) There is a political problem in pricing: even if managers know how much increase in prices is needed to maintain profit margins during inflation, can they politically increase prices that much without risking price controls by government? (5) Much higher energy prices have made capital less productive relative to labor and have thus caused a declining capital/output ratio and hence declining productivity per worker-hour—which reduces the basic rate of profit, as already noted.

Perhaps, in the light of the foregoing adverse factors, the rise in stock prices in the 1980s may not be quite as great as some have suggested. But a significant rise occurred as the rate of inflation declined from 1980 to 1983, and by 1986 stock prices were approximately triple their level when the rise began in the summer of 1982 (as measured by the Dow Jones average).

## Holding Period Yields and Risk-Premium Curves

Since 1964 the capital asset pricing model has been made familiar to students of finance. In this model, choices of capital assets are a function of risk and return; the rate of return rises as risk rises. Buyers of securities try to get higher return with minimum risk, and sellers of securities try to pay lower returns with the inherent risk. Basic to the capital asset pricing model is the concept of holding period yield: how much capital assets yield over specified holding periods. Yield rates cannot properly be specified unless the holding period is defined.[26] In the capital asset pricing model, stocks are valued so that returns for specified time periods (holding periods) equal the risk-free interest rate plus an appropriate premium for risk. A number of empirical tests have been made for the stock market and tend to show that *within* the stock market, valuation is rational in view of risk.

To supplement the tests involving stock portfolios and their yields in comparison with the yields on a (nearly) risk-free asset, some economists have attempted to develop a risk premium curve (RPC) in which return rises as risk increases, on various assets—Treasury bills, bank CDs, commercial paper, bonds, and stocks would be among those included. Because they entail the greatest degree of risk, stocks should obtain the highest yields. That is, the RPC should be positive, meaning that both yield and risk should rise so that commercial paper yields would be higher than Treasury bill yields, bond yields higher than commercial paper yields, and stock yields higher than bond yields.[27]

Data show that the RPC for 1910–1919 was negative and that a negative RPC reappeared in the 1964–1973 period as returns on debt instruments rose with inflation

---

[26] "Holding period yield" means the yield for a specified period of time during which stocks are held. The yield includes both dividends and capital (price) gains or losses over the specified period.

[27] See Robert M. Soldofsky and Roger L. Miller, "Risk-Premium Curves for Different Classes of Long-Term Securities, 1950–66," *Journal of Finance*, June 1969, pp. 429–445; and Robert M. Soldofsky and Dale F. Max, *Holding Period Yields and Risk-Premium Curves for Long-Term Marketable Securities: 1910–1976*, New York University, Monograph Series in Finance and Economics, Monograph 1978–2.

and holding period yields on stocks fell. As the authors state, the negative slope is "inconsistent with very long-run expectations on positive and normative grounds." *Lower* yields on *riskier* assets are hardly what is to be expected in the long run!

Thus it would not be surprising to see a long-term rise in stock prices, so that dividends plus capital gains would again provide yields consistent with the higher risk in owning stocks. The 1970s may in the long run appear to be an abnormal period in the money and capital markets.

## Interconnections Between the Bond Market and the Stock Market

To trace more precisely the influence of bond yields on valuation of stocks, let us focus attention on a group of stocks most similar to bonds in nature: utility stocks. Such stocks have rather regular yields because of regulation, and their earnings do not generally rise and fall rapidly, as may occur for the stocks of industrial companies. These stocks are as closely comparable to bonds as any we can examine. Thus, if yields on bonds rise sharply, those who invest in utility stocks might be tempted to switch to bonds; if bond yields fall sharply, those who invest in bonds might be tempted to switch to utility stocks. Thus there may be a rather direct impact of changes in bond yields on the prices of utility stocks. Because purchase and sale of other stocks also may be influenced, there may be some (but probably less) effect on their prices, and the effect may lag somewhat.

Thus the effect of changes in bond yields on stock valuations may appear to result from a change in the appropriate rate of discount used. This may be true, but careful analysis is needed. Utility stocks are bought partly for current dividends; they are also bought because dividends rise, sometimes because a utility is growing, and sometimes, when there is inflation, because utilities are permitted to charge higher rates to consumers because they need to earn higher rates on higher "fair values" of their properties.[28]

Since bond yields may be rising at a given time, while even under these assumptions stock dividend yields may not rise for a year, there is some reason to prefer higher bond yields currently, for those heavily dependent on current income from investment. But, *if* higher earnings and dividends on utility stocks are confidently expected, there is no need for an inflation premium in the discount rate for those earnings or dividends. If there are fears that regulatory commissions may delay rate increases and that other factors may hold down future earnings, the switch to bonds may be justified. But it occurs because of either lower expected earnings for utility stocks or greater risk because higher earnings may not materialize. If lower earnings are expected, they should be discounted at the regular rate (the fundamental interest

---

[28] For example, suppose that I purchase a share of a utility stock for $15 and that the current dividend rate is $1.50 (10 percent dividend yield on the current price). If dividends are permitted to rise by 10 cents a year (approximately 6.7 percent a year, substantially less than the inflation rate in the late 1970s), in five years I will be receiving a dividend of $2 on my investment of $15, or a dividend yield of 13.3 percent.

rate based on productivity of capital plus the appropriate risk premium). If there is more risk of variability in those earnings, they may be discounted logically at a higher rate, but the rate is higher because of a greater risk premium, not because of any "inflation premium." We repeat: the fundamental long-term interest or discount rate is based on the productivity of capital; a risk premium is appropriate for the risk inherent in the particular security being purchased; and an inflation premium is appropriate *if* the security being purchased is one that has a fixed maturity value, so that its value cannot rise with inflation, and a fixed rate of specified interest, so that yield rate can rise only if price falls.

## The Role of "Technical" Factors

Changes in stock prices, especially short-term changes, depend on technical factors as well as on the fundamental factors that determine long-run levels of stock prices. Because our attention in this book is on the role of capital markets in the economy rather than on the speculative fluctuations in day-to-day prices that are part of the subject of investments courses, only brief comments are made.[29]

Technical factors include the important position of institutions (especially pension funds and mutual funds, and also trusts managed by trust departments of banks) in stock market trading, the effect of trends in stock market prices in influencing stock price expectations, and the short-run impact of orders to buy at specified prices and investors' desires to sell when significant profits have been made.

The growing role of institutions in stock market trading has tended to make stock prices more volatile. Individuals have often been selling more stocks than they have purchased, and, although individuals still hold the majority of the total value of all stocks, individuals are not the dominant factor in buying and in the near future may not be the dominant factor in market movements. Because institutions tend to trade in larger blocks than do most individuals (sales of blocks of 10,000 or more shares are sometimes regarded as an indication of institutional trading), a simultaneous decision by a number of institutions to buy or sell particular stocks can quickly cause sharp fluctuations in their prices.

Finally, investors frequently think in terms of buying securities when their prices fall to specified levels, on the ground that at those levels there is sufficient likelihood of rise in prices to justify purchase. Investors may leave specific limit purchase orders with brokers, or they may simply have price limits in mind. Similarly, investors who have accumulated significant profits may, unless deterred by

---

[29] As John Maynard Keynes remarked long ago, "it is not sensible to pay 25 for an investment of which you believe the prospective yield to justify a value of 30, if you also believe that the market will value it at 20 three months hence" (*General Theory of Employment, Interest, and Money*, p. 155). Hence investors (or speculator-investors) must concern themselves with the developments likely to affect the views of other investors; individuals investing in the stock market must concern themselves with the groups of stocks likely to be bid up in price by other investors, as otherwise a particular stock, even though it has a potential long-run value much higher than its present price, may not be bid up for a considerable period of time. Institutions can afford to wait longer periods of time than can most individuals, but even they tend to engage in "parallel buying."

potential capital gains taxes, sell when profits reach a point at which the likelihood of further increases in the prices of the stocks is relatively low. These facts aid in predicting the amplitude of short-term fluctuations in stock prices.

Because earnings of companies vary greatly, rates of growth of earnings vary, and because investors' expectations of earnings may vary even more, no single price-earnings or "times-earnings" ratio can be applied to *present* earnings to obtain the present value of a given stock. Times-earnings ratios vary from 3 or 4 to more than 100. Is it possible, however, to apply a times-earnings ratio, under specified conditions, to the *average* of stocks traded on an exchange or a particular average of certain stocks, such as the Dow Jones average? Because earnings vary much more than interest rates on bonds do, there is obviously much more risk of price fluctuation and hence, possibly, of capital loss in investing in most stocks than in investing in bonds. The theory of effect of risk differentials on values is explored more thoroughly in Chapter 14, but at this point, it may be noted simply that, because of the greater risk, total yields on stocks, including capital gains, must usually be greater than yields on bonds. Hence times-earnings ratios for stocks, if based solely on past earnings, might be expected to be lower than such ratios for bonds. Times-earnings ratios on stocks are *not* based solely on past earnings, however; as described earlier, they are based on expected earnings for a period equal to the time horizon of the average investor, discounted at an appropriate rate. If earnings are expected to grow, the times-earnings ratio applied to present earnings must be higher. Based on postwar experience, this ratio has been about 18 times earnings in periods when investor confidence was relatively high, and about 12 to 14 times earnings for the Dow Jones average when investor confidence was relatively low. In the absence of reasons for different ratios, these might be expected to prevail. Thus, if confidence reaches a high level, as it is likely to do at peak levels of business activity, a times-earnings ratio of 18 may be appropriate. When confidence is relatively low—either because it is believed that profit squeeze may threaten profits or that high interest rates resulting from inflation may cause a high rate of discount of expected earnings, or both—a times-earnings ratio of 12 to 14 may be appropriate.

## The Random Walk Hypothesis

Many financial economists argue that *past* stock market price trends have no effect on future stock prices; prices are assumed to be random fluctuations from past levels—the "random walk" hypothesis. On the other hand, market traders have numerous guides or rules that they believe can be used to predict future trends and patterns in stock prices on the basis of past trends. Rules such as that based on appearance of what are termed "head and shoulders" patterns and many others are believed to signal specific shifts in trends in stock prices. As these are in any event short-run changes, and as the issue between "random walk" theorists and "technicians" is by no means settled, we leave it at this point. Those who speculate in the stock market must make their own judgments about the validity of these rules.

The theoretical basis of the random walk hypothesis rests on two assumptions.[30] First, it is assumed that investors make "rational expectations"—they use all the current information that they think is worthwhile and relevant in forming their expectations. Forecasts may differ, but they are not irrational. Rational expectations imply that investors try to acquire information as long as the improvement in their forecasts is enough to equal the cost of getting the additional information. Rational expectations means that investors' forecasts are based on all the available information that they think is relevant and worth acquiring. Second, it is assumed that additional information, if it becomes available, is *quickly* reflected in changes in stock prices. Thus, if it is expected that business activity will rise in the near future and that corporate profits will therefore rise, investors will buy stocks, driving their prices up to a level justified by the expected rise in profits.

The random walk hypothesis implies that stock prices are independent of past changes in stock prices—thus simple extrapolation of trends cannot be used for prediction of stock prices. One test of the random walk hypothesis is whether or not greater profits can be made by some trading rule than by simply buying and holding a stock. The random walk hypothesis does not require rejection of traditional methods of valuing stocks, such as that used in a preceding section in this chapter. It does suggest, however, that investors try to forecast developments that may tend to cause stock prices to rise or fall, so that by the time the developments occur, their effects may already have been felt on stock prices. This explains why stock prices are a "leading indicator" for business conditions.

The random walk hypothesis has been widely accepted by financial economists. It is not nearly so widely accepted among brokers and stock market advisers, many of whom believe that some methods are available for forecasting stock prices by the use of data on past stock prices.[31]

The random walk hypothesis does *not* suggest that investors cannot make money in the stock market, nor does it suggest that stock prices are not related to other economic changes. It *does* suggest that it is *difficult* to make *more* profits by trading than can be gained by buying and holding a group of stocks with specified risk levels (often measured by beta coefficients, or coefficients between returns on a stock and on an assumed portfolio of all the stocks in the market or on enough stocks to be generally representative of the market). It is difficult to beat the S&P 500 stock average!

The random walk hypothesis also suggests that rules based on past movements of stock prices are not likely to be helpful in forecasting future stock prices. No doubt, however, investors (at least some of them) will continue to try to use such rules in the hope that some may be useful.

---

[30] This discussion draws heavily on Neil G. Berkman, "A Primer on Random Walks in the Stock Market," Federal Reserve Bank of Boston, *New England Economic Review*, September–October 1978, pp. 32–50. This article cites a number of the studies made to test the random walk hypothesis.

[31] It is interesting to note that some proponents of the random walk hypothesis have had second thoughts about its complete validity. See J. Michael Murphy and William F. Sharpe, "Second Thoughts About the 'Efficient Market,'" *Fortune*, February 26, 1979, pp. 105–107.

Finally, the random walk hypothesis does not basically affect the argument of Modigliani discussed previously. If investors generally make the mistake of discounting current earnings (profits) at the nominal interest rate rather than the *real* interest rate, it is not necessarily true that they are making other mistakes in the valuation of stocks. Granted, it is somewhat puzzling why they might make a mistake *only* in this one respect, but it is also puzzling why the 1970s were one of very few periods in which bond yields exceeded stock yields. This suggested that a substantial rise in stock prices might cause a more normal yield pattern to reappear in the 1980s and 1990s.

## Institutional Trading and the Stock Market

The share of institutional trading in stock market activity has steadily increased in recent years. In 1961, institutions accounted for only one-third of all trading on the New York Stock Exchange. By 1971, institutions accounted for over 60 percent and individuals for only 40 percent. Commercial banks alone accounted for nearly 40 percent of trading; commercial bank trust departments are important in this respect because they manage noninsured pension funds and also trust funds. The New York Stock Exchange anticipates that the share of banks in trading will grow.

The growing role of institutions in stock market trading led to an extensive study of such trading by the Securities and Exchange Commission (SEC). The study, made on the basis of sampling during 1968 and 1969, found that, although mutual fund trading was price aggressive (buying more when prices rose and selling more when prices fell), bank trading was neutral—banks just as frequently sold when prices were rising and bought when prices were falling.[32] It may be that banks have become more interested in "performance" since 1969 and now tend to contribute more to price changes. One investigation of "parallel trading" indicated that, although it could have been the result of change, when it did occur, prices were positively related to it in the current month, and negatively related to it in the next month. Thus no firm evidence was found to support the need for restriction on trading activity of institutions.[33] Nevertheless, the rapid increase in block trading (trading of 10,000 or more shares in one trade), from 3 percent of trading volume in 1965 to nearly 18 percent of total trading volume in 1971, indicates their potential impact on prices of particular stocks.[34]

Personal trust departments of commercial banks in 1971 held $224 billion in common stocks, as compared with $51 billion for mutual funds, $17 billion for life insurance companies, and $14 billion for property and casualty insurance compa-

[32] *Institutional Investor Study Report of the Securities and Exchange Commission*, Vol. 4.

[33] Alan Kraus and Hans R. Stoll, "Parallel Trading by Institutional Investors," *Journal of Financial and Quantitative Analysis*, December 1972, pp. 2107–2138.

[34] Gertrude Mazza, "Growing Role of Institutional Investors on Wall Street," Federal Reserve Bank of Philadelphia, *Business Review*, August 1972, pp. 9–12. Statistical data were obtained from the SEC *Statistical Bulletin*.

nies.[35] These figures reflect a rapid rise in common stocks held in bank-managed pension funds (one-third increase in a single year, 1971) and a shift of assets in personal trust from bonds to stocks.[36] Trust departments of commercial banks were thus the largest single institutional holder of common stocks, holding in 1971 over 20 percent of the market value of all stocks outstanding. Because other institutions held about 8 percent, total institutional holdings were nearly one-third; individuals held about two-thirds, in contrast to over 70 percent in 1965.

Investment and brokerage houses have become concerned about the absence of many individual investors from the stock market since the market decline of 1969–1970. The low level of stock prices in 1973, relative to current earnings of corporations, and the fact that the stock market was little if any higher in 1980 than in 1970 led to a number of suggestions of measures to induce individuals, particularly small investors, to participate in the market. These suggestions range from changes in brokerage commission fees to suggestions for more favorable treatment for capital gains, including the suggestions that individuals be permitted to charge off against current income, for income tax purposes, as much as $5,000 a year of losses, instead of the current amount of $3,000 a year. The suggestion has also been made that the first $100,000 of capital gains for any individual, during his or her lifetime, not be taxed. Capital gains on houses, under certain conditions, are not taxed, up to $125,000 for owner-occupied houses that are sold.

Suggestions such as those just presented are opposed by persons who desire heavier taxation of capital gains. Tax reform legislation of 1986 eliminated the distinction between long-term and short-term capital gains and provided for taxation of capital gains at the same rates as other income.[37]

## Options Markets

Contracts are agreed upon to buy (or sell) something. They may also be agreed upon to buy (or sell) something at a future date, at a price specified when the contract is made. These are futures contracts, or forward contracts.[38] One market for futures contracts, the Treasury bill futures market, was discussed in Chapter 9.

Contracts may also be made to give someone an *option* to buy (or sell) something on (or before) a specified date, at an agreed price, the *striking price*. Thus forward

---

[35] Board of Governors of the Federal Reserve System, Federal Deposit Corporation, and Office of the Comptroller of the Currency, *Trust Assets of Insured Commercial Banks* (1970 and 1971).

[36] Edna E. Ehrlich, "The Functions and Investment Policies of Personal Trust Departments: Part II," Federal Reserve Bank of New York, *Monthly Review*, January 1973, pp. 12–19.

[37] Some countries do not tax capital gains because a large part of capital gains simply offsets inflation, in the long run. Capital gains for those holding capital assets are thus similar to indexing for inflation of wages and other incomes.

[38] In markets for foreign exchange, the usual term is forward contracts or forward exchange. In futures markets for commodities or financial assets, unlike foreign exchange markets, delivery of the assets is often not intended; the contract to buy is sold before time for actual delivery.

markets, futures markets, and options markets all exist.[39] In options markets, the buyer is given the option to buy (or the seller is given the option to sell); the buyer may buy if desired, but need not do so (a *call* option). Similarly, in such contracts, sellers may be given options to sell; they may sell if they desire, but need not do so; these are termed *put* options. In a call option, the *writer* of the option contract agrees to sell to the buyer; in a put option, the writer agrees to buy the asset if the seller exercises his or her option to sell. In options markets, delivery of the assets is very seldom intended, as we shall see.

Especially for institutional investors, stock index options as a means of hedging against losses have become popular, especially when volatility of the stock market has increased. Popular stock index options changed or initiated in 1986 were the S&P 500 index option offered on the Chicago Board Option Exchange (CBOE) and the index option based on 75 stocks widely held by institutional investors, offered on the American Stock Exchange (AMEX). The CBOE stock index option became a European-style option in April 1986—a contract cannot be exercised before a specified date. The AMEX initiated a European-style stock index option in October 1986. Let's examine the functioning of forward, futures, and options markets in more detail, to understand how they are useful to those who wish to hedge and to speculate. Hedgers wish to protect against losses that they may incur when prices change; speculators hope to gain from price changes. One purpose of forward markets, futures markets, and options markets is to make it possible for those who wish to reduce their risk to do so. An importer purchasing goods to be paid for in a foreign currency may avoid the risk of a sharp rise in the foreign exchange rate by agreeing to buy forward exchange at, perhaps, a rate slightly above the current rate. The importer need not pay for the exchange until the agreed future date and may not have the funds to make payment until that date. An owner of a financial asset may make a futures contract to sell it, thus limiting the extent of possible loss if the price of the asset falls (because interest rates rise).[40] Options contracts may be used in the same way to limit risk.

We should also note that forward, futures, and options markets also make it possible for speculators to buy foreign exchange, other financial assets, or options to buy financial assets, with the hope of profiting if the price rises. In the forward market, until recently, speculation was somewhat limited because many of the buyers and sellers of forward exchange were importers and exporters trying to hedge against risk, and they bought and sold from and to banks, which in turn bought and sold equal amounts because they generally did not wish to take speculative risks.[41]

The reason for increased use of all these markets is the increased volatility of exchange rates and interest rates. Volatility in interest rates leads to volatility in prices

---

[39] Delivery of foreign exchange at the agreed time is the general practice in the foreign exchange markets. The intention is, for example, for an importer to buy forward exchange, accept delivery, and use the foreign exchange received to pay for an import that he or she knew required payment at a certain time.

[40] Futures markets have, of course, existed for a long time, for commodities such as wheat, corn, and so on. Because this is a book on financial markets, we do not discuss commodities futures.

[41] Banks often, in the past, discouraged individuals from speculating, if it seemed that that was the intended purpose. But recently other markets for forward exchange have developed.

of financial assets unless those prices are fixed in value (as demand deposits and savings accounts are, for example; they do not fall in value unless a bank fails, and they rise in value only by the interest). With increased volatility of exchange rates and interest rates, risk has increased. Therefore, markets for hedging against risk have become more widely used, and new markets have developed.[42] Of course, such markets also make it possible for speculators to try to make gains from changing prices.

In futures markets, contracts must be carried out; a buyer of a futures contract must pay at the agreed price on the specified date. Delivery, however, need not occur. A buyer of a futures contract may sell (perhaps to the party from whom he or she bought) before delivery date, and no delivery need occur. In options markets, neither payment (except for the price of the option) nor delivery need occur. The buyer of a call to purchase an asset need not buy it.

Options of this kind have value if prices of the assets rise. The purchaser of a call option gains if the price of the asset (a stock, a Treasury bond, a Treasury bill, a GNMA certificate, or a negotiable bank certificate of deposit) rises. Since such gain is possible, the writer (seller) of the call option is paid for selling the option—whether the option is ever exercised or not. A right to do something at a specific price is valuable. In the stock market, a call option may, for example, be written to buy a stock, currently selling at $20 a share, at $30 a share. The price of the option may be $10. If the price of the stock rises, the value (price) of the option rises. Of course, if the price of the stock falls, the value of the option may fall to zero.[43]

Options are not issued by corporations, and they are seldom written by individuals, although they may be.[44] Most options are traded on exchanges and are written by the exchanges in standardized forms. For this reason delivery of stock seldom occurs; if the price of the stock rises sufficiently, the option rises in value, and the purchaser of a call option can gain by selling the option to the exchange.

An option gives only the *right* to buy at a specified price; if the purchaser of the option actually bought the stock, he or she would have to pay the current market price, but with the option can pay the option price. In Figure 11–1, an option to buy a stock at $30 might be purchased for, say, $10 when the price of the stock is $20. If the price of the stock rises to $30, the value of the option increases somewhat if it is expected that the price of the stock will rise further. Since there is probably some limit to potential rise in the price of the stock, the option to buy at $30 continues to rise in value, but more slowly than does the price of the stock. An option to buy at $30 could never be worth more than $30—why pay more than $30 for an option to buy at $30 when the stock can currently be bought at $30?

---

[42] A very readable and clear discussion of futures markets and options markets is Bluford H. Putnam, "Financial Options: Passing the Risky Buck," Chase Manhattan Bank, *Economic Observer*, September–October 1981, pp. 3–6.

[43] An American call option can be exercised at any time during a specified period; with a European call option, the purchase can be made only on the expiration date.

[44] If individuals who own stocks write options for others to buy them, they are said to have written covered calls; if they do not own the stocks but plan to buy them to deliver if a buyer exercises the option to buy, they are said to have sold options short.

**FIGURE 11–1**
**Market Values of Options and Stocks**

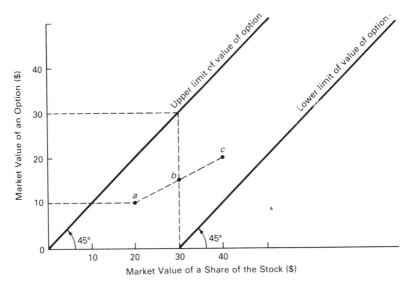

Thus the price of the stock sets an upper limit to the value of the option, as shown in Figure 11–1. A lower limit is set by two facts: (1) when the price of the stock is less than $30, the value of the option cannot be less than zero; (2) if the price of the stock rises above $30, the option must have some value—if the price is $40, the option to buy at $30 would be worth at least $10, perhaps more (if it is believed that the price of the stock will rise). Thus the value of an option may rise from point *a* (at which it was $10, we assumed, and the price of the stock was $20) to point *b* (about $15) and perhaps to point *c* if the expiration date has not yet been reached.

At point *a*, the price of the stock is below the striking price—in a price range sometimes termed "out of the money." At point *b*, it is at the striking price; this is sometimes termed "on the money." And at point *c*, it is above the striking price, in a range sometimes referred to as "in the money." Note that for the buyer of the call option to make a profit, the price of the stock must rise above $40, since the buyer must pay $30 for the stock and has already paid $10 for the option. This "premium" for the option—the amount by which the cost of the option exceeds the lower limit— is greatest when the stock is "on the money."

A put contract is one that gives a buyer a right to *sell* a certain quantity of an asset at a specified striking price at any time before the expiration date. Buyers of put options gain when prices of stock (or other assets) fall; writers of the contracts lose.

On futures exchanges, assets are "marked to market," that is, they are valued each day at closing prices (determined by the exchanges, and not always precisely the price of the last trade). Those who have gained are paid by those who have lost. Of course, in the long run, this makes no difference; long-run gain or loss is determined by the long-run result. But in the interim, there may be a cash flow problem for losers.

On options markets, the only cash drain is the price paid for the options. No more need be paid; the buyer of the option may not exercise his or her right to buy the stock. Cash flow drain is thus more limited than on a futures market. Option writers, of course, have greater risks; a stock might rise in price to $50, after an option writer sold an option to buy at $30. Hence option writers might have to deposit more collateral (cash) with the exchange. Since buyers of call options benefit from limited less potential (all they can lose is the cost of the option), they pay small premiums in buying call contracts, for this benefit. Different tax treatment of gains and losses on futures and options creates other differences, but these are beyond the purposes of our discussion here.[45]

Writers of calls and puts make money when asset prices are stable; they risk loss when prices change sharply.

Stock markets have had options trading for years, but its importance has increased with the increasing volatility of stock prices in recent years. Trading in options on other financial assets was initiated and increased. By 1982, the Chicago Board Options Exchange had begun trading in $100,000 GNMA certificates and in Treasury bonds, on options. On the American Stock Exchange, trading began in options on Treasury notes. The Chicago Board of Trade had introduced trading in options, not on Treasury securities themselves, but on futures contracts for Treasury securities.

Options offer those who wish to reduce risk in buying and selling certain financial assets an opportunity to do so. In effect, "risk insurance" can be obtained for the risk of changes in prices in direction and in variance (volatility). It can also be obtained for cash flows resulting from these changes. At the same time, options offer speculators opportunity to gain or lose.[46]

In the long run, options markets have implications for the economy. Both unanticipated inflation and unanticipated changes in interest rates (and hence in financial asset prices) can be hedged to some extent in these markets. Thus if variability in monetary or fiscal policies causes variability in prices, interest rates, and real output (real GNP), the importance of such shocks may be reduced.

Options markets are also important because they have implications for the valuation of firms on whose stocks options are written. If bonds are sold by firms to finance new projects, and if the projects are profitable, the value of the firms' assets should rise, so that bondholders may be paid off as bonds mature, and stockholders' equity may have increased. If projects are not successful, of course, properties may be sold, and there may be defaults on bonds. Buying stocks of growing (expanding) firms is like buying options on those firms' assets. Stocks can themselves be viewed as a type

---

[45] There has also been some question about what agency has the responsibility for regulating option trading. It appears that the Commodity Futures Trading Commission (CFTC), established in 1975, will regulate options on commodity futures exchanges and boards of trade; the SEC will regulate options traded on stock exchanges and options exchanges. See Randall Pozdena, "Options Fever," *Federal Reserve Bank of San Francisco, Weekly Letter*, October 31, 1982.

[46] Volatility of prices causes hedgers to want to reduce risk of price changes; it also causes speculators to want to speculate.

of option. Options on stocks can be viewed as bases for estimating risks involved in options on the assets. The option market can be viewed as a basis for constructing a model for the valuation of business firms.[47]

Markets develop as needs are perceived. Volatility of interest rates in the 1970s and early 1980s made more investors want to hedge their interest rate (financial asset price) risks. Financial markets change as needs perceived by investors and borrowers change. We anticipate further changes in financial markets.

## Program Trading (Computerized Trading)

With the widespread use of computers, program trading (computerized trading) began to be important in the stock market. Program trading refers to buy and sell orders in large amounts, in most cases, generated by computer programs. Orders may be for options to buy or sell certain stocks or on stock market indexes (to buy or sell a multiple of the index), or to buy or sell futures contracts for stock market indexes. Program trades may be used for hedging, for speculation, or for gaining arbitrage profits. Arbitrage profits can be gained when prices of index futures deviate from the prices of the underlying stocks by more than the "cost to carry" (the cost of borrowing short-term money minus any dividends received during the period). If futures prices are higher than prices of the stocks by more than the "cost to carry," a person can get an arbitrage profit by selling futures and buying the underlying stocks.

Clearly, program trading cannot be done by most individuals—it would take perhaps $25 million to arbitrage the S&P 500 stocks. Hence program trading is chiefly done by the managers of large mutual funds. Since futures expire on four specific dates in each year, program trading can cause great volatility in the stock market on such days, as futures mature.

Prices are affected on such dates by program trading—the evidence of this being that changes in prices occur and that such changes are usually reversed on the next trading date.

Opinions vary as to whether effects of program trading are desirable or undesirable.[48] Some argue that arbitrage and speculation are good because they tend to increase the efficiency of the market. Others are impressed by the large ups and downs of stock market averages on the futures expiration dates—the obvious volatility of the market on such days. To those who buy and sell stocks for long-run gain, such volatility should not make much difference. If stocks yield more than bonds, as they did (including both dividends and capital gains) in most long periods from 1926 to 1968, a portfolio of carefully selected stocks should provide a better long-run yield

---

[47] See Fischer Black and Myron Scholes, "The Valuation of Option Contracts and a Test of Market Efficiency," *Journal of Finance*, May 1972, pp. 399–417; "The Pricing of Options and Corporate Liabilities," *Journal of Political Economy*, May–June 1973, pp. 637–654; and "From Theory to a New Financial Product," *Journal of Finance*, May 1974, pp. 399–412. See also Kenneth D. Garbade, *Securities Markets* (New York: McGraw-Hill, 1982), pp. 388–393.

[48] A very readable discussion is Daniel Seligman, "Don't Fret About Program Trading," *Fortune*, October 13, 1986, pp. 87–92.

than a portfolio of most other financial assets. Except for the period 1968–1982, stocks offered good return, if carefully selected, or if the portfolio was large enough to obtain the same return as the S&P 500 or another index. The dramatic rise in the stock market from 1982 to 1986 brought stock prices close to being in line with the long-term rising trend, and a portfolio of carefully selected bonds and/or mortgages yielded only slightly more than a portfolio of the same size that consisted of stocks that rose (or fell) in line with the S&P 500 average.

# EXPLAINING AND PREDICTING STOCK MARKET PRICES

The theory of valuation of stocks discussed earlier in this chapter is a long-run theory. In effect, it explains the factors that determine the general level to which stock prices should move over a period of time. Many would like to have a theory or model that could predict stock prices for shorter time periods and that could more precisely predict their movements over these periods. In view of the random walk hypothesis and the general view that it is supported by the results of many studies, development of such a model is difficult. The random walk hypothesis says that stock price movements follow a random walk—they cannot be predicted from past prices. Hence it is likely to be impossible to develop a model that predicts small variations in stock prices.

## Medium-Term Stock Market Price Forecasting

In one study, an equation based on earnings and a rate of discount as the major variables determining stock market prices yielded moderately satisfactory results in terms of intermediate-term trends, but the coefficient of correlation was only .26.[49] Stock market prices were much more variable than the predicted values based on the equation. A much better correlation (.47) was obtained when the money supply was added as a variable in the regression equation. Why? Here we have an interesting puzzle. Some have argued that individuals attempt to maintain constant proportions among holdings of various types of assets; hence, when the money supply is increased, individuals attempt to reduce money holdings by acquiring stocks, bonds, and other assets.[50] But this argument ignores the effect of yields on assets and assumes that *fixed* proportions of holdings are desired. Some have argued that changes in the stock of money affect interest rates and thus affect stock prices, but why should the addition of the money supply to a regression in which an interest rate is already included improve predictive ability? A third suggestion is that the regression ignored the risk premium, because it is difficult to measure, and that, although this may be legitimate during some periods when the risk premium remains constant, it is not useful when risk

[49] Stephen F. LeRoy, "Explaining Stock Prices," Federal Reserve Bank of Kansas City, *Monthly Review*, March 1972, pp. 10–19. The index of stock prices used in the study was Standard & Poor's index of 500 common stocks; the corporate bond yield was measured by Moody's Aaa corporation bond yield.

[50] Beryl W. Sprinkel, *Money and Stock Prices* (Homewood, Ill.: Richard D. Irwin, 1964).

premiums change. High interest rates may cause risk premiums to change. High interest rates may cause the risk premium to increase because tight money increases the *variability* of corporate profits. Although this explanation has not been verified by conclusive tests, it seems plausible; even if it is correct, however, much remains to be done to provide a complete explanation of stock prices.

If Modigliani is correct that over fairly long periods (as much as a decade or more) stocks may not be valued rationally, then it would seem that development of a model predicting stock market prices in a period of inflation, especially one of a changing rate of inflation, would be difficult indeed. Hence we do not include any model applied to the 1970s.

## Short-Term Stock Market Price Forecasting

In recent years, the effort to improve short-term and medium-term predictions of the general levels of stock market prices focused on the role of money in influencing stock prices. Remember that we are not here concerned with prediction of prices of *individual* stocks, which involves specialized analysis of industries and firms.

The monetary approach was given some impetus by Beryl Sprinkel's book. Sprinkel compared the level of an index of stock prices with a moving average of rates of change in the money supply and compared turning points in each with turning points in the general business cycle. He concluded that changes in rates of monetary growth preceded upper turning points in business cycles by about 4 months, on the average, while stock prices preceded them by about 4 months; with respect to troughs, the similar leads were 15 months and 2 months.

Some have argued that changes in stock market prices may precede changes in the money supply if the stock market is an efficient market. In an efficient market, well-informed traders adjust prices to all known facts and to predictions based on such facts, when prediction is possible. Unexpected changes in the money supply, as in other variables, would immediately be reflected in stock prices as traders incorporated the new information into their price bids and offers. One adherent of the "efficient market" theory found a weak relationship between stock yields and rates of change in the money supply.[51] The hypothesis was that stock yields are related to forecasted changes in the money supply. Perhaps public understanding is sufficient that, given knowledge of the process by which money is created, the public can forecast changes in the money supply. Some concluded that studies finding a close relationship between stock prices and changes in the money supply are simply measuring the effects of common trends and cycles in both variables.

If this type of analysis is correct, it is very difficult to predict short-term movements in stock market prices. If the stock market is an efficient market, then stock market prices should be based on evaluations of all available information at a given

---

[51] Richard V. L. Cooper, "Efficient Capital Markets and the Quantity Theory of Money," *Journal of Finance*, June 1974, pp. 887–908.

time and should adjust quickly to any new, or surprise, information that becomes available. Thus much doubt is cast on any formula for predicting short-term changes in stock market prices.[52]

## Long-Term Trend Projections for Stock Prices

In the long run the level of stock prices depends largely on what happens to profits as a share in national income. If profits are a "normal" percentage of national income, whether inflation continues or not, in the long run earnings will rise as nominal GNP rises. If risk of fluctuations in profits is deemed great, the rate of discount to be applied may be higher than when less risk is anticipated, but if a period of relatively rapid growth in GNP continues, fears will tend to subside. Fears in the mid-1970s were twofold: (1) that profits might not be at "normal" levels in relation to GNP, partly because of controls on profits and partly because union labor power could cause wages to rise more rapidly than prices, and (2) that controls designed to curb inflation might prevent prices from rising as rapidly as wages and thus squeeze profits.

What must be emphasized is that fundamental determinants of the long-run level of stock market prices are (1) the rate of increase in nominal GNP and (2) the share of profits in nominal GNP. For long-run investors, this understanding is quite relevant, although short-run speculators may not find it very helpful in assisting them to select those stocks that may, in a short period, rise most rapidly in price.

In conclusion, no attempt has been made to describe or analyze the mechanics of trading in stocks, either on the organized exchanges or on the over-the-counter market. This is part of the subject of courses in investments. But an attempt has been made to show what factors are likely to influence average stock market prices in the long run. The reason for this is that, in an analysis of financial markets and the economy, the level of stock market prices is significant both for the flow of funds into financial and real investment and for effects the level of stock prices may have on other spending.

A continued flow of funds into stocks is vital to attract capital into equity investment, which in turn is an important determinant of economic growth. It is also vital, perhaps over a longer period, to retain funds already invested. Investors will not be satisfied to leave retained earnings in the hands of corporations unless such retained earnings are reflected in capital gains and dividends.

Second, stocks and real estate (and occasionally inventories of certain goods) are the chief assets held by consumers that fluctuate significantly in value, usually with a rising trend in a growing economy. Thus, if net worth affects spending, as some recent theories hypothesize, a rise in net worth from rising prices of stocks and real estate may be a second significant determinant of economic growth. The third major

---

[52] This is the conclusion of Robert D. Auerbach, "Money and Stock Prices," Federal Reserve Bank of Kansas City, *Monthly Review*, September–October 1976, pp. 3–11.

determinant, or group of determinants, of economic growth—productivity and the factors that affect it, such as education, innovations, and application of knowledge to production (improved technology)—should not be overlooked, but cannot be given much attention in this book.

## EFFICIENCY OF THE STOCK MARKET

If profits are the key rate of return, and if the stock market functions to allocate funds to more profitable firms, as well as to provide some liquidity for equity financial assets (stocks), the efficiency of the stock market is a matter of some concern. As pointed out at the beginning of the chapter, efficiency may be judged by two criteria: (1) Does the market efficiently allocate funds to the most profitable uses? and (2) Does the market have low costs of transactions?

Indirect tests of allocational efficiency have been made by attempting to determine whether the stock market responds quickly to new information. The studies supporting the "random walk" hypothesis—that past stock prices do not provide significant basis for predicting future price movements—have been interpreted by some as indicating that the market does respond quickly to new information. Tests have also been made comparing prices of stocks on which new information became available (e.g., earnings announcements) with prices of those on which such information did not become available; these tests have indicated that such information is quickly reflected in stock prices.[53] A third type of indirect test has been studies to determine whether insiders (specialists trading on the exchanges, corporate officers and directors, and so on), have above-average trading profitability. The evidence is in doubt: If a small group has monopolistic trading advantages, does this mean that the market is inefficient or simply that these groups are able to profit in the short period before the market adjusts to the new information?

More direct tests have attempted to determine whether or not risks perceived by investors correspond fairly closely to actual risks, on the presumption that investors have an aversion to risk. Studies have shown that the risk as measured by relative variability of return seems to be about the same for considerable periods of time, at least if groups of stocks are used for the test. Tests have also been made to determine whether or not return varies with risk of variability in return, which for stocks includes both dividends and capital gains or losses. The fact that over long periods of time returns on stocks were about 9 percent compared with about 5 percent on bonds is some evidence that return varies with risk, but for stocks alone, the answer to the question is not so clear. A hump-shaped relationship has usually been found, but the location of the hump varies with the measures. That is, up to a certain point, return varies directly with risk; beyond that point, it varies indirectly. The location of the point depends on the use of arithmetic or geometric averages of returns.

---

[53] Eugene Fama, "Efficient Capital Markets: A Review of Theory and Empirical Work," *Journal of Finance*, Papers and Proceedings, May 1970, pp. 383–417.

Other studies indicate that new issues of stocks have not been particularly good investments over long periods. If it is assumed that new issues are somewhat more risky than seasoned issues and therefore should have higher returns, then the evidence indicates that higher returns are a short-run thing.

Sometimes it is presumed that the return on a single stock should in general remain in the same relationship (higher or lower) to the return on all stocks. It is also sometimes presumed that the trend in return on single stocks should rise directly as risk is greater, risk being measured by variation in return compared with variation in the return on all stocks. If these presumptions are made, results of tests indicate that the performance of the stock market has been better since World War II than it was before that, in meeting these conditions.

One study indicated that mutual funds performed very little better than did the average investor, when the ratios of subsequent earnings to initial prices were compared, and when ratios of trends in subsequent earnings and prices were compared.[54]

The authors of another study concluded that security analysts' forecasts were little better than past earnings growth in predicting future earnings. However, only five firms participated in the study, and the predictions were made for earnings growth over five years; perhaps a larger number of participants or a shorter period of forecasting would have given different results.[55]

A complete review of evidence from studies cannot be provided, but perhaps this is enough to indicate the basis for the general conclusion reached: evidence from studies indicates that the stock market is *not* very efficient as an allocator of resources, and this is confirmed by hindsight evaluation of unwarranted price changes. Moreover, there is extensive evidence of misrepresentation and manipulation.[56] However, performance of the stock market has been better since World War II than before the war. The conclusions should not lead the reader to believe that the stock market is unnecessary. An allocational mechanism is certainly needed, and perhaps (except for manipulation) the stock market does about as well as can be expected, given the uncertainties of future earnings. The question that should be considered is whether significant improvements can be made.

One attempt at improvement has been regulatory action to make commission charges for buying and selling stocks on the New York and American stock exchanges competitive rather than fixed. Presumably the public would benefit from lower transactions costs (commissions). Commissions on large transactions (over $300,000) first were made negotiable; then in April 1974 competition was required for small transactions. Whether or not the changes in brokerage pricing practices will constitute a significant improvement in the efficiency of the market remains to be seen in the results of long-run studies.

[54] Irwin Friend, "The Economic Consequences of the Stock Market," *American Economic Review*, Papers and Proceedings, May 1972, p. 218.

[55] John G. Cragg and Burton G. Malkiel, "The Consensus and Accuracy of Some Predictions of the Growth of Corporate Earnings," *Journal of Finance*, March 1968, pp. 67–84.

[56] Irwin Friend and E. S. Herman, "The SEC Through a Glass Darkly," *Journal of Business*, October 1964, pp. 382–405.

## SUMMARY

Fundamentally, stocks are valued in the same way as bonds or any other capital asset is—on the basis of the discounted present value of expected returns. The problems in correctly valuing stocks are much greater, however, especially when inflation occurs. Measures of profits are never accurate because of the many factors determining profits, in contrast to the specified interest yields to be obtained from bonds. When inflation occurs, accuracy of profit measures is diminished by accounting problems arising from valuing assets at historical cost rather than at current cost or replacement value. Because of this, illusory inventory profits appear, and depreciation charges are less than they should be if reported profits are to reflect net income after replacing capital. The need for adjustments to correct for these two factors has been recognized for some time. But it was not generally recognized that there is also need to adjust for the fact that stockholders are residual claimants to the values of business firms, whereas claims of bondholders and other creditors are usually fixed in dollar amounts. If profits rise, the *share* of creditors' claims on the values of firms must fall, and the *share* of stockholders' claims must rise. Of course, profits are reduced to some extent by payments of higher interest rates on new debt. But, as long as there is older debt outstanding, its *relative* claim is reduced.[57] Since this has not been generally recognized, many have concluded that the relatively low stock market prices of the later 1970s were the result of the fact that reported profits were overstated and hence that, when profits were adjusted for this overstatement, they were enough lower to possibly justify the relatively low level of stock prices. Recognition of the rising relative share of stockholders as claimants to the values of firms, and of the incorrectness of discounting current profits (or earnings) by an interest rate containing an inflation premium, may be considered sooner or later; "eventually rationality should win."

When investors become nervous about values of assets that are expressed in monetary terms, because they see inflation eroding the value of money, they tend to turn to physical assets: land, houses, gold, art works, and so on. The soaring price of gold (over $800 an ounce early in 1980) is another illustration of this fear that monetary assets and also real assets located in given places may lose their value. Stocks are claims on physical assets, and unless a country goes through a revolution in which such claims are obliterated or price controls are imposed in such a manner that profits do not share proportionately in the rise in nominal incomes, stock values should rise as wages, interest, and profits rise. Stocks represent physical assets, in contrast to bonds, bank deposits, and other claims that are monetary in nature.

Based on the assumption of rational expectations and the assumption that additional information is rapidly reflected in stock prices, the stock market should be an efficient market in the sense that current prices should reflect the information available to investors and the forecasts they have made on the basis of this information. In

---

[57] Another way of stating this may be helpful: the managers of the business firm can either pay back debt at less than its maturity amount (less because, with inflation, interest rates have risen and bond prices have fallen) or they can wait and pay the debt at maturity—but then, if the economy has been growing either nominally or in real terms, they will in all likelihood have larger profits with which to pay the fixed amount of debt.

such a market stock prices follow a random walk, and stock prices cannot be forecast by methods that use past stock prices for prediction. But this does not mean that stock price *levels* cannot be forecast on the basis of a rational valuation of stocks—How much rise in earnings can be expected, after adjusting for illusory inventory profits, inadequate depreciation, and the reduced relative claim of creditors? And at what interest rate (the basic rate determined by productivity of capital plus an appropriate risk premium) should those expected profits be discounted?

In contrast to comments frequently made in the financial press, the stock market is probably not a very efficient market in terms of the second test, the level of transactions costs. But, as a wit might remark, "It's the only market we have." Efforts to reform the market to improve its efficiency in allocation or to minimize transactions costs should not create conditions that cause investors to lose confidence in the market; otherwise the continued gradual rise in stock prices, in line with the expected or hoped for rise in GNP, cannot occur and, as a result investors may be reluctant to invest in stocks and the liquidity provided by the stock market may be diminished.

## Questions for Discussion

**1.** If stock values are based on discounting expected future earnings, how can Levitz Furniture stock reasonably sell (as it did for a time) at 100 times current earnings?

**2.** If long-term interest rates on corporate bonds average 7 percent or more instead of 5 percent, what effect would this probably have on the price of stocks?

**3.** Is it possible for a company to earn $1 per share one year, and $3 per share the next year, without significant changes in sales or operating costs? If so, how?

**4.** Make your own calculation of the possible Dow Jones Industrial Average in 1990, based upon a growth of the economy of 6 percent a year in nominal GNP (3 percent a year in real growth and 3 percent a year in inflation), profits at a "normal" ratio to GNP, profits on stocks included in the DJIA at a "normal" ratio to profits in all corporations, and a "reasonable" multiple of the DJIA to earnings on stocks in the DJIA. Explain how you selected a "normal" ratio of profits in all corporations and a "reasonable" multiple of the DJIA to earnings on stocks in the DJIA.

**5.** Why should the stock of money be an important determinant of stock prices?

**6.** Why did inflation in the 1970s seem to be a factor causing stock market prices to fall? What about the belief, generally accepted in the past, that stocks are a hedge against inflation?

**7.** Much evidence has been presented recently to indicate that few investors can do better, in the long run, than the Dow Jones index or the S&P index of 500 stocks. What can be inferred from such evidence, if it is valid?

**8.** Does the increasing dominance of institutions in *trading* on the stock market (not in volume of stock owned) seem likely to be harmful? Why or why not?

**9.** Read the final chapter of *Supermoney* (see Selected References) and evaluate "Adam Smith's" comment that "Something else is going on."

**10.** Explain (by some hypothesis) why stock market prices were far below predicted levels in the spring of 1970. How would you test your hypothesis?

## Selected References

John Kenneth Galbraith, *The Great Crash: 1929* (Boston: Houghton Mifflin, 1954), gives a very entertaining account of the crash and its impact upon the economy.

The generally accepted theory of the determination of stock prices is set forth in a relatively rigorous manner in Stephen F. LeRoy, "The Determination of Stock Prices," unpublished Ph.D. dissertation, University of Pennsylvania. A more easily accessible discussion by the same author is "Explaining Stock Prices," Federal Reserve Bank of Kansas City, *Monthly Review*, 1972, pp. 10–19.

Everyone should read the irreverent but very relevant books by "Adam Smith," *The Money Game* (New York: Random House, 1967), and *Supermoney* (New York: Random House, 1972); the first of these was referred to by Paul Samuelson as "a modern classic."

The now rather extensive literature on the efficiency of the stock market is reviewed briefly by Irwin Friend, "The Economic Consequences of the Stock Market," *American Economic Review*, Papers and Proceedings, May 1972, pp. 212–219. The references cited by Friend and the studies to which he refers provide a lengthy list, but somewhat inconclusive results. A subsequent review by the same author may be found in "Economic Foundations of Stock Market Regulations," *Journal of Contemporary Business*, Summer 1976, pp. 1–27. Despite Friend's favorable conclusion, there are still those who look less favorably on regulation and question whether its benefits are greater than its costs. One test for bonds is a comparison of the efficiency of the U.S. bond market with that of the Eurobond market; there is no comparable test for stocks.

Two stimulating discussions are found in James H. Lorie and Mary T. Hamilton, *The Stock Market: Theories and Evidence* (Homewood, Ill.: Dow Jones-Irwin, 1973), and Burton G. Malkiel, *A Random Walk Down Wall Street* (New York: W. W. Norton, 1973).

The provocative article by Modigliani and Cohn should be required reading for all serious students of business economics and finance. See Franco Modigliani and Richard A. Cohn, "Inflation, Rational Valuation and the Market," *Financial Analysts Journal*, March–April 1979, pp. 3–23.

For a less technical article that reaches the same general conclusion for a different reason, see Burton Malkiel, "Common Stocks—The Best Inflation Hedge for the 1980s," *Forbes*, February 18, 1980, pp. 119–128; for a more extended discussion, see *The Inflation-Beater's Investment Guide*, by the same author (New York: W. W. Norton, 1980).

In addition to Modigliani and Malkiel, other writers have pointed out that "valuation myopia" is nothing new for the stock market: in 1947–1953 stocks were far undervalued by any rational criteria, and in 1967–1972 they were overvalued. See, for example, Peter L. Bernstein and Peter Carman, "Valuation Myopia in the Stock Market," *Harvard Business Review*, September–October 1979, pp. 6–12.

A good summary of the explanations for the poor performance of the stock market in the 1970s is Douglas K. Pearce, "The Impact of Inflation on Stock Prices," Federal Reserve Bank of Kansas City, *Economic Review*, March 1982, pp. 3–18.

Some recent tests of "efficiency" of the stock market suggest that, at least part of the time, even "rational" individuals may overreact to new information and thus cause unreasonably great volatility in the stock market. For a brief summary, see Tom Klitgaard, "Are Markets Really Efficient?" Federal Reserve Bank of San Francisco, *Weekly Letter*, September 30, 1983.

For a very readable discussion of program (computerized) trading and its impact on the stock market, see Daniel Seligman, "Don't Fret About Program Trading," *Fortune*, October 13, 1986, pp. 87–92. Program trading can be used for hedging, speculation, or to obtain arbitrage profits.

# THE DETERMINATION OF THE LEVEL OF INTEREST RATES

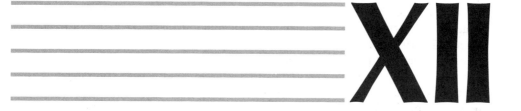

Institutions and markets dealing with loanable funds have been discussed in Chapters 3 through 11. We now focus our attention on the "price" of borrowing those funds, expressed as an interest rate. In Chapters 12–14 we explore briefly theories of the determination of interest rates at various levels of income and prices. Because rates differ on the myriad different securities at any time, we also discuss reasons for interest rate differentials.

Chapter 12 contains a discussion of the basic economic theory of interest rate determination and some analysis involving uses of this theory. In Chapter 13, special emphasis is placed on the theory of the "term-to-maturity" structure of rates, that is, the theory explaining why interest rates on long-term securities differ from those on short-term securities. Finally, in Chapter 14, other factors such as risk, callability, taxability, and so forth that cause interest rate differentials are discussed.

The study of interest rates and security prices is important because of the role that they play in the allocation of economic and financial resources and thus the importance that they have for the nation's standard of living over time. This chapter begins with definitions of interest rates as expressed in yields on securities. Following this is a brief outline of the classical and neoclassical views of interest and interest rates. One of the most important neoclassical models, that of Irving Fisher, is discussed in the appendix.

In the next section, two major approaches to interest rate theory are presented. These are (1) two forms of asset choice theory—the liquidity preference theory and Tobin's alternative multiple asset choice theory— and (2) the loanable funds theory. Then we examine the role that price expectations are thought to play in the behavior of interest rates. We include a section on interest rate behavior in the short run, in the long run, and among different countries and an explanation of this behavior in terms of loanable funds theory.

# DEFINITIONS AND RELATIONSHIPS
## OF YIELDS AND PRICES

Under a contract, the issuer of a bond offers to pay an investor a fixed amount of interest. This amount is expressed as a percentage of the bond's par value. For example, if it is a $1,000 bond and the issuer pays $60 per year, the rate of interest (coupon rate) is 6 percent. The issuer also agrees to redeem the bond at par value at maturity.

As long as the market price of the bond equals its par value, the coupon rate equals the security's *yield*. But changing supply and demand for bonds bring about changes in market prices, and bonds may (1) sell at a premium, in which case market price is greater than par value and the effective yield is less than the coupon rate or (2) sell at a discount, in which case the market price is less than the par value and the effective yield is greater than the coupon rate. The redemption value, the ultimate obligation of the issuer of the bond, does not change, but the return (yield) to investors who buy the bond changes if the bond price differs from par value.

Bond prices and bond yields vary inversely. If a bond's market price rises, its yield declines; if the price declines, its yield rises. This inverse relationship was described in Chapter 1. We observe this relationship in the market for debt instruments whenever supply of or demand for these securities changes. A period of falling bond prices occurs when the demand for bonds falls off or when the supply of bonds increases. Bond yields rise under these circumstances.

The formula

$$PV = \frac{R}{i}$$

is the formula for the present value of a bond with equal annual interest payments of R dollars to be made forever—a perpetual bond or a consol, that is, a bond with no maturity date.[1] Here, $i$ is the "yield" or the "rate of discount." The inverse relationship between $PV$ and $i$ is obvious in the formula. The formula is definitional; that is, for a given present value of \$1,000 and a given annual interest payment of \$50, the rate of discount $i$ must be .05, or 5 percent; the relation described in the formula defines the rate of discount, $i = R/PV$. Given any two of the three variables, the value of the third is fixed by definition—by the formula.

The formula for the present value of a bond of $n$ periods to maturity with coupons payable at the end of each period is

$$PV = \frac{R_1}{(1 + i)} + \frac{R_2}{(1 + i)^2} + \cdots + \frac{R_n}{(1 + i)^n} + \frac{F}{(1 + i)^n}$$

In this formula, $PV$ represents present value, $R$ is the amount of interest paid periodically, $F$ is the face value to be redeemed at maturity, $n$ is the number of periods until maturity, and $i$ is the rate of interest.

Consider a two-year bond with face value of \$1,000 and a coupon yield of 3 percent so the $R$ is \$30; then,

$$\$1,000 = \frac{\$30}{(1 + .03)} + \frac{\$30}{(1 + .03)^2} + \frac{\$1,000}{(1 + .03)^2}$$

Now assume that an increase in the demand for loans occurs, so that comparable bonds yield 4 percent. What price would one be willing to pay for this bond to realize a 4 percent return? That is, what would $PV$ be if $i$ were 4 percent?

$$PV = \frac{\$30}{(1.04)} + \frac{\$30}{(1.04)^2} + \frac{\$1,000}{(1.04)^2}$$

$$= \$28.85 + \$27.74 + \$924.56$$

$$= \$981.15$$

If interest payments are made semiannually, \$15 appears in the numerator, and the denominator changes as shown for $n$ semiannual periods.[2]

$$PV = \frac{\$15}{1 + i/2} + \frac{\$15}{(1 + i/2)^2} + \cdots + \frac{\$15}{(1 + i/2)^{2n}} + \frac{\$1,000}{(1 + i/2)^{2n}}$$

---

[1] The term "consol" is derived from the word consolidated. It refers to the consolidation of a number of outstanding British securities after World War I into perpetual bonds.

[2] For quarterly interest payments $R = 30/4 = 7.5$ and in the denominator $i$ would be divided by 4 as well. If interest payments are "compounded" continuously over time, the formula becomes $A = PVe^{ni}$, where $e$ is the mathematical constant $2.7182818+$ and $A$ is the amount to which $PV$ will grow in $n$ years at rate of interest $i$.

**TABLE 12–1**
**Present Values (*PV*) of Coupon Bonds 3 Percent Coupon,**
***R* = \$3.00 Face Value, *F* = \$100.00**

| Yield to Maturity Percentage, i | Years and Months to Maturity, n | | |
|---|---|---|---|
| | 9 Years, 10 Months | 9 Years, 11 Months | 10 Years, 0 Months |
| 2.90 | 100.85 | 100.85 | 100.86 |
| 2.95 | 100.42 | 100.43 | 100.43 |
| 3.00 | 100.00 | 100.00 | 100.00 |
| 3.05 | 99.58 | 99.57 | 99.57 |

NOTE: If the face value of a bond were \$1,000 instead of \$100, one would simply move the decimal point on *PV* to the right one digit.

Readily available bond tables provide information on the variables in the equation so that the analyst does not have to perform the computations on each occasion. Also, hand calculators are now programmed to provide the answers at the touch of a button. There are five variables:

$F$ = face value to be repaid at maturity

$PV$ = present value

$i$ = the rate of interest (discount) or yield to maturity

$R$ = the periodic payment that indicates the value of a coupon, usually expressed as a percentage of face value

$n$ = the number of periods

If we know any four of these, the fifth can be found from the formula.

A section taken from a bond table is shown in Table 12–1. A \$100 face value bond ($F$ = \$100.00) with a 3 percent coupon ($R$ = \$3.00) that sells for 100.86 and has 10 years to run to maturity will yield 2.90 percent; $PV$ = 100.86, $n$ = 10 years, $i$ = 2.90 percent. By knowing $PV$ from the cells of the table, one can determine the yield to maturity in the left-hand column. Similarly, if we know the yield to maturity, we can find the appropriate current price of the bond. Other tables not shown give $PV$ and $i$ when the bond carries a 3.25 percent coupon, a 3.50 percent coupon, and so forth.

An approximate method for determining the yield to maturity is found in the simple formula[3]

$$i = \frac{\text{annual interest} \pm \text{average annual appreciation or depreciation}}{\text{average investment}}$$

[3] This formula is taken from William C. Freund, *Investment Fundamentals* (New York: American Bankers Association, 1966), p. 44.

If an investor pays $800 for a $1,000 bond paying 5 percent each year and maturing in 20 years, then

$$i \cong \frac{\$50 + \$10}{(\$800 + \$1,000)/2} = \frac{60}{900} = 6.57\%$$

the approximate average *yield to maturity*. The *current* or market yield on this security is $50/$800 = 6.2 percent, but this calculation does not take into account the return to be realized because of the appreciation in value of this security as it approaches maturity or par value.

# THE CLASSICAL AND NEOCLASSICAL THEORIES OF THE DETERMINATION OF INTEREST RATES

## The Classical Theory

Adam Smith, a classical economist, stressed the role of parsimony (saving) in fostering economic growth. In 1776 Smith wrote that

> Capitals are increased by parsimony, and diminished by prodigality and misconduct. Whatever a person saves from his revenue he adds to his capital, and either employs it himself in maintaining an additional number of productive hands, or enables some other person to do so, by lending it to him for interest, that is, for a share of the profits. As the capital of an individual can be increased only by what he saves from his annual revenue or his annual gains, so the capital of a society, which is the same with that of all the individuals who compose it, can be increased only in the same manner.[4]

These sentiments carry through the writings of economists to this very day, although not without qualification. If one has an income, by abstaining from consumption—that is, by saving—one can purchase productive resources so that one's income in subsequent periods is increased. In this manner, standards of living rise.

For society to accumulate real wealth and capital, capital goods must be produced, and resources devoted to production of capital goods cannot at the same time be devoted to production of consumer services. Thus, people must save, or refrain from consumption, if society's stock of wealth is to expand.

Along with thrift, there must be productivity. Eugen von Böhm-Bawerk stressed the concept of the "period of production" and "roundaboutness" in the production process.[5] As an example, he suggested that one might imagine himself or herself living alone in a cabin by a lake, perhaps as Henry Thoreau once lived near Walden Pond. One could walk to the lake for water whenever it was needed. Or one

---

[4] Adam Smith, *The Wealth of Nations* (New York: Modern Library, 1937), p. 321.
[5] Eugen von Böhm-Bawerk, *Capital and Interest* (1922), trans. G. D. Huncke, South Holland, Illinois, 1959.

could devote time and effort to construct a bucket so as to reduce the number of trips necessary for obtaining water. Or one could spend even greater time and effort and construct a trough from a spring, running it past the cabin door so that water would be readily available whenever it was desired. Thus, acquiring water for consumption can be done directly or in a roundabout way. Roundaboutness in obtaining the water leads to a far greater amount of water available for consumption with a given amount of effort than the direct method of obtaining water. Thus, increasing roundaboutness in production of goods by using capital goods leads to greater productivity, increased output per worker-hour, and higher living standards.

To the extent that, in a given country, those who save tend to save a constant percentage of their income over the long run, although with minor short-term fluctuations, saving (thrift) is determined by income, which usually changes slowly. Thus, although both thrift and productivity determine interest rates, productivity tends to have a greater role in causing *changes* in interest rates. If saving is relatively fixed in amount in the short run, short-run changes in interest rates must be largely due to changes in productivity (or expected productivity) and to resulting changes in the interest rates that borrowers are willing to pay. At this point, we ignore the effects of inflation.

We can regard consumer borrowing as simply borrowing the saving of other consumers and, hence, treat net consumer saving (gross consumer saving minus consumer borrowing) as the usual major source of the supply of saving.[6] We know that governments (as least national or federal governments) seldom save; they borrow whatever they need to meet deficits, regardless of the interest rate. Business borrowers are the chief source of demand for funds. Business borrowers must expect that productivity of capital will provide a higher rate of return than the rate of interest they pay for borrowed funds; otherwise, they will not rationally borrow. Thus business borrowing is the key factor in *changes* in interest rates, still ignoring the effect of inflation.

## The Neoclassical Theory

The neoclassical theory differs from classical theory in that it incorporates major amendments developed by later economists. These economists stressed freedom of choice on the part of those who save or dissave, given the interest rate that measures the reward. Individuals are thought to have a "time preference" for a consumption pattern over time. Some may choose not to save but to dissave and perhaps go to school, travel, and so on. They may wish to consume today, realizing, of course, that their future income will be lower because of the interest that they must pay. Others may wish to save. People in business may have investment opportunities that are productive in the sense that they yield increased real output in the future. The yield from investment allows them to pay interest out of future earnings. Thus, consumers

---

[6] A nation may also receive funds from foreign countries, thus adding some foreign saving to domestic saving.

sometimes supply saving and sometimes demand (borrow) saving. Businesspeople also supply saving and demand (borrow) saving. Competition in the market for saving and for capital goods and consumer goods sets an equilibrium price on saving (interest yield) at which the amount of saving supplied equals the amount demanded. Thus, the neoclassical economist views the interest rate as the price that rations the available supply of saving to borrowers and that induces suppliers of saving to enter the market. They also recognize that the volume of saving depends not only on the interest rate but also on the income of society. The neoclassical position does not provide an answer to ethical questions on the virtue of saving or thrift, stressing instead the desirability of freedom of consumer choice, not only to choose among alternative goods, but also to choose a time path of consumption by saving or not saving as one may desire.

In neoclassical economic theory, prices are determined by demand and supply. Goods have value only if there is a demand for them, but, given a demand, costs help determine the supply at relative prices, and demand and supply together determine price. Because productivity of real capital assets is the basis for demand for investment funds, the fundamental "real" rate of interest is the rate of return on real capital assets. This "real" rate of interest is reflected in the "money" rate of interest charged on loanable funds.

## ALTERNATIVE APPROACHES TO THE DETERMINATION OF THE RATE OF INTEREST

Two broad approaches to the theory of the determination of the general level of interest rates are discussed. In the liquidity preference theory, the rate of interest is determined by demand for and supply of money. Money is the one perfectly liquid asset that people may prefer to hold. Thus, liquidity preference theory can also be called demand for money theory. In Tobin's alternative form of this approach, attention is focused on choice between real capital assets and several types of financial assets instead of on choice between money and other financial assets. In the loanable funds approach to interest rate theory, the rate of interest is determined by demand for and supply of loanable funds.

The liquidity preference approach is a stock model requiring explanations of motives for holding cash balances and relating these to the stock (supply) of money existing at a given time. In Tobin's model, motives for holding various financial and real assets are also related to stocks of such assets. Loanable funds theory, on the other hand, is stated in a *flow* form in which demand is the amount people would borrow, and supply is the amount that people would lend during a period at different interest rates.

In the economy as viewed here, individuals and institutions can do any one or a combination of three things: spend, lend, or hold money balances (barter is ignored). These activities are conducted in markets for goods and services, loanable funds, and money. At equilibrium in each market, demand for goods and services equals the supply of goods and services, amounts that lenders wish to lend equal amounts that borrowers wish to obtain, and quantity of money demanded equals the supply of money.

An asset choice model (or a multiple asset choice model) and a loanable funds model are two alternative frameworks for a theory of interest.

## The Liquidity Preference Approach

The liquidity preference theoretical structure developed out of the writings of John Maynard Keynes in the 1930s as an integral part of his macroeconomic model of income determination. Readers of this text have already surveyed the Keynesian model of income determination in their introductory economics course; to examine it in detail here would be repetitious. It is appropriate, however, to mention briefly a few of the salient features of the model to note the connecting links between the various approaches to the study of interest.

Essentially, Keynes asked, as others before him had done, "Why do people bother to hold money—to keep money on hand?" As money is the most "liquid" of all assets, the question can be phrased, "Why do people desire liquidity?"—hence the reference to a "liquidity preference" function. His answer was that they hold money for transactions purposes, for precautionary purposes, and for speculative purposes. The amount held for transactions varies with the level of economic activity. The larger the volume of trade as measured, say, by GNP, the larger the quantity of money demanded to carry out this trade. The amount held for precautionary purposes is more or less constant and is not significantly related to other macroeconomic variables. The amount held for speculative purposes is inversely related to the level of interest rates.[7] If interest rates are high, people attempt to reduce the level of their idle cash balances and buy interest-earning bonds. They also expect that interest rates may fall, meaning that the price of bonds may rise and they might realize a capital gain. Thus, at high interest rates people buy bonds and economize on their cash balances, running them down to very low levels. If interest rates are low, people prefer to hold cash rather than interest-earning bonds; that is, they prefer having the liquidity of money rather than the interest return on the bonds, and they may expect bond prices to fall, as well, if and when interest rates rise. Thus the interest return on a bond is the opportunity cost of holding money—it is the cost of liquidity. If people hold money instead of interest-earning bonds, they give up the interest return, and this represents an implicit cost to them.

The transactions demand for money is now thought to be sensitive to interest rates as well as to the level of economic activity as measured by income. This addendum to Keynesian theory was developed by Tobin and Baumol.[8] They noted that, as

---

[7] Subsequent development of theory elaborated on these motives, and in some analyses the precautionary and speculative motives are interrelated.

[8] See James Tobin, "The Interest-Elasticity of the Transactions Demand for Cash," *Review of Economics and Statistics*, August 1956, pp. 241–247; and W. J. Baumol, "The Transactions Demand for Cash: An Inventory Theoretic Approach," *Quarterly Journal of Economics*, November 1952, pp. 545–556.

**FIGURE 12–1**
**The Liquidity Preference Theory of Interest**

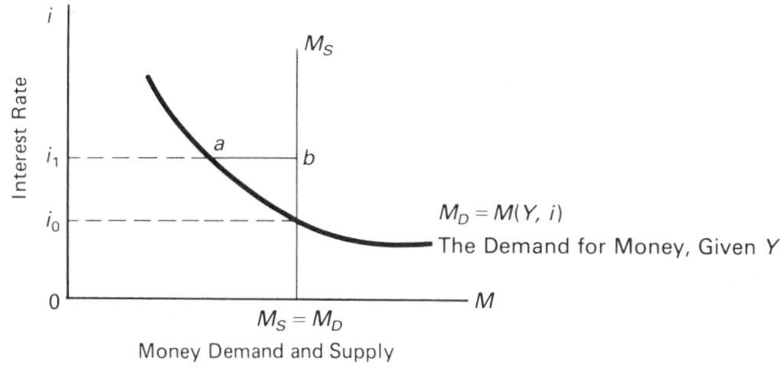

income rises and interest rates rise, people begin to "economize" on their transactions balances; that is, they allow their transactions balances to fall, in relation to income. Individuals who usually carry an average balance of $1,000 in a checking account when savings accounts pay only 3 percent may let their average checking balance fall to $500 and increase their savings account balance by $500 when yields on savings accounts rise to 5 percent. There is not a great deal of income difference in this example, but corporate treasurers with $1 million in a demand deposit will find it profitable to put these funds into a time deposit account over the weekend. The higher the rate of interest, the greater the profit incentive to "manage" the checking account balance on a day-to-day basis. Thus, the transactions demand for money is held to be sensitive to interest rate levels.

By combining the parts of the puzzle, we can write $M_d = M(Y, i)$, which is called either a liquidity preference function or a demand-for-money function. The equation reads that the quantity of money demanded, $M$, is related to income, $Y$, and the rate of interest, $i$. The relationship between changes in money and changes in income, $\Delta M/\Delta Y$, is believed to be positive, and the relationship between changes in interest and changes in money, $\Delta M/\Delta i$, is believed to be negative. The money supply in this model is assumed to be given, $M_s$. Thus, for a given level of income, the demand for money and the supply of money determine $i_0$, as shown in Figure 12–1. At any rate higher than $i_0$, for example, $i_1$, the demand for money is less than the supply of money, and people try to reduce their holdings of money. They try to do this by buying securities, driving up the price of securities and driving down the interest rate to $i_0$.

This, of course, is only part of the Keynesian model. The level of $Y$ depends on the rate of investment spending, consumption spending, government spending, and net exports. Consumption and investment spending are related to $i$; therefore, $i$ and $Y$ are interdependent in the complete Keynesian model, as they are in the neoclassical framework. But here we have introduced the money supply as a partial determinant of the rate of interest. As the money supply rises, interest rates fall, and vice versa.[9]

[9] In Hicksian *IS-LM* diagrams used in most macroeconomic texts, if the *IS* curve is positively sloped, an increase in $M$, which shifts the *LM* curve to the right, will lead to an *increase* in $Y$ and in $i$ as well.

Because $Y$ and $i$ are interdependent, we cannot have a complete theory of the determination of $i$ without explaining the determination of $Y$ as well, a project beyond the purpose of this book. But we can view the analysis as a *partial* equilibrium model and simply say that, for a *given* $Y$ and a *given* supply of money, $i$ is determined.

Milton Friedman and other monetarists have criticized the sloping money demand curve shown in Figure 12–1; Friedman argued that the quantity of money demanded is relatively insensitive to interest rate changes. Friedman believed that the quantity of money demanded shifts as economic conditions change, a smaller quantity of money being demanded as optimism increases concerning the size and safety of return (yields) on other assets. Of course, the quantity of money that people *want* to hold at various interest rates is difficult to determine. For example, a quantity of money demanded that is less than the money supply, as at $i_1$ in Figure 12–1, simply indicates that at that rate of interest people *would wish* to lend or invest more money; such actions cause the interest rate to fall to the level $i_0$. How much money people *would wish* to hold at different interest rates is difficult to estimate.

Of course, whether demand for money is sensitive to changes in the interest rate depends on the measure being used for money. Friedman used M2 in his major studies, and M2 includes time deposits, on which interest is paid. Had he used M1, on which no interest was generally paid, at least explicitly, he might have found more elasticity—when interest rates rise, it is plausible to think that people may try to hold less money (M1) and more in savings accounts and other places where interest is obtained.

## An Alternative Version of the Liquidity Preference Approach

James Tobin has emphasized the importance of investment in real capital assets and of borrowing funds to be used in making such investment. Tobin argued that the most important "interest" rate is the rate of return on real capital assets.[10] Unless this rate of return that borrowers can earn on real assets is high enough, business borrowers will not be willing to pay high interest rates to borrow money to finance such investment. Business investment depends on expected rates of return on real investments; that is, it depends on the productivity of capital. Government borrows whatever it needs to borrow to meet its needs for spending, but business borrowing changes as expected earnings are reevaluated. This causes changes in total borrowing.[11]

In focusing attention on demand for money, Keynes argued that an increase in demand for money would be reflected in the bond market as a decrease in demand for securities. Similarly, a decrease in the demand for money is expressed as an increase in

[10] James Tobin, "Money, Capital, and Other Stores of Value," *American Economic Review*, Papers and Proceedings, May 1961, pp. 26–37.

[11] In this view, the hundreds of articles about whether investment demand is interest elastic or not were almost pointless. The key fact is that investment demand *shifts* as expected returns on real capital assets change because of innovations, improved or deteriorating political conditions, and other factors.

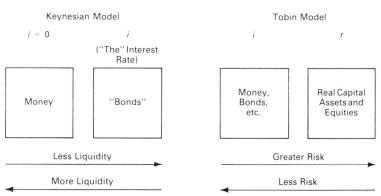

FIGURE 12–2
**Keynesian and Tobin Models for Interest Rate Determination**

demand for securities. Thus, in this part of the Keynesian model, attention is focused on two groups of assets: (1) money, generally treated as currency plus demand deposits, and (2) all other financial assets, sometimes termed "bonds" for convenience.

Tobin, on the other hand, focusing on the rate of return on real capital assets, argued that, if only two groups of assets are used in a model, one group should include real capital assets and equities, which represent ownership of such assets, whereas the other group should include all other financial assets (including money). The difference between Keynes' liquidity preference view and Tobin's view can be seen in Figure 12–2.

Note that emphasis in the Keynesian model is on interest as an inducement for people to buy bonds or other securities and acquire assets that are less liquid than money. The emphasis in Tobin's model is on the return on real capital assets that induces people to accept the greater risk involved and invest in real assets or equities.[12] In the Keynesian model, it is assumed that the interest rate on bonds is equal to the rate of return on real capital assets.

It is easy to infer from the Keynesian model that (1) a zero or very low interest rate on money is fundamental, (2) short-term interest rates must be above that level to induce people to hold short-term securities, and (3) long-term interest rates must bear some relationship to short-term rates, usually being higher. Tobin, however, argued that any inference that short-term rates are fundamental is backward—the fundamental rate of interest is what can be earned on real capital assets (often referred to as the rate of profit), because that rate determines what business firms are willing to pay in interest for long-term borrowing.

---

[12] Money, bonds, and other financial assets (except equities) are shown in the Tobin model as if there were a rate of interest paid on them. Although it is difficult to think of interest being paid on paper money and coins, interest is paid on demand deposits in many countries. Thus in effect interest is or may be paid on much of the money supply. Payment of interest on checking accounts (NOW accounts and others) has been widely offered in the United States since the early 1980s.

Tobin carried this analysis one step further by suggesting that a two-asset model may be inadequate for proper analysis. A model is intended to include the essential or most important factors without trying to include all elements found in nature—if it did that, it would be too cumbersome. But there is no magic in a two-asset model. Tobin has suggested that a model containing perhaps five assets may be useful for analysis of causes of differences in interest rates. Such a model is shown in Figure 12–3.

An important consequence of using such a model is that shifts in demand for various assets *need not involve demand for money*. If expected returns on real capital assets rise, there may be a shift in demand from bonds to stocks. If people think that long-term interest rates may rise, there may be a shift in demand from government bonds to Treasury bills, as people hold Treasury bills and wait for the expected rise in long-term interest rates. Such a rise in interest rates may be forecast if people expect a continued rise in borrowing of funds and/or if they expect a tightening of credit by the Federal Reserve.

Obviously, shifts in demand for various assets depend in part on the degree to which such assets are good substitutes for each other. If two groups of assets (such as government bonds and Treasury bills) were *perfect* substitutes, shifts would be caused immediately by any changes expected in yields.

To emphasize the difference between his view and that of those using the Keynesian model, Tobin gave an extreme example. He pointed out that a reduction in government debt would, in the Keynesian model, mean a smaller supply of government securities. If demand for government securities did not change, this would mean higher prices for and lower yields on government securities. Lower yields on government securities, and then on corporate bonds, would mean lower costs of borrowing funds for investment in real capital assets and, therefore, would probably lead to expansion in the economy. On the other hand, in Tobin's two-asset model, reducing government debt would reduce the size of one component of the total of relatively safe and liquid assets held by the public. With a smaller amount of government debt in its

**FIGURE 12–3**
**A Five-Asset Model for Interest Rate Determination**

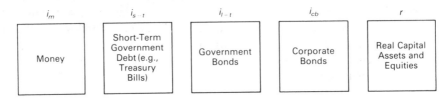

$i_m$ = average rate of interest on money
$i_{s-t}$ = a representative short-term interest rate
$i_{l-t}$ = a representative long-term rate without risk of default
$i_{cb}$ = the yield rate on corporate bonds
$r$ = the rate of return on real capital assets and equities

hands, the public *might* decide to invest less than it did before in risky real capital assets. Less real investment would lead to a recession rather than to expansion in the economy. This is, of course, an extreme example, but it illustrates Tobin's main point: holders of financial and real assets attempt to balance safety and liquidity against greater return.

Four points in Tobin's argument have merit. (1) The most significant rate of return is that on real capital assets, essentially based on productivity. (2) Degree of risk may be a better criterion than degree of liquidity to distinguish among groups of financial and real assets. Risk means the possible variation in the rate of return—the fact that the rate of return may be high *or* low, for many reasons. (3) A portfolio choice model with, perhaps, five assets may be more useful than a two-asset model, especially if major shifts can and do occur in demand for other types of financial and real assets, *without necessarily affecting the demand for money.* (4) Any inference from the liquidity preference model that a zero or low interest rate on money is fundamental is erroneous—the long-term yield or rate of return on real capital assets is fundamental, and other rates are generally lower (although occasionally higher) for various reasons.

It may be useful to work through an example to provide a bit more clarity for Tobin's multiasset model. Assume that people generally receive utility from holding assets. If assets consist of money $(M)$, bonds $(B)$, stocks $(S)$, and tangible assets $(T)$, then an individual's utility function may be written $U = U(M, B, S, T)$. This simply says that utility depends upon the amounts of money, bonds, stocks, and tangibles that an individual holds. An individual's wealth position is the value of these assets (ignoring, for present purposes, the wealth implied in earning power from sale of labor services). Thus, wealth becomes $W = P_M M + P_B B + P_S S + P_T T$, where the $P$s refer to the respective prices and the variables refer to the number of units of each type of asset held. The sum of the items gives wealth, $W$, the amount that could be consumed at once if all assets were sold. Wealth is the sum of the present purchasing power one holds command over. Of course, the price of money is simply a dollar, but the prices of bonds, stocks, and tangible assets are all market prices per unit of each. One should remember, too, that as the price of an asset rises, its effective yield falls if there is no change in the revenues it produces. Price and yield are inversely related.

Given the utility function for wealth and the definition of wealth it is possible to calculate necessary conditions for maximization of utility.[13] Let us begin with this equation:

$$\frac{MU_M}{P_M} = \frac{MU_B}{P_B} = \frac{MU_S}{P_S} = \frac{MU_T}{P_T}$$

---

[13] The Lagrangian multiplier method is used to do this. Assume $U = U(M, B, S, T)$ and that $W = P_M M + P_B B + P_S S + P_T T$. Let prices of assets be given. Form a new function using a nonzero constant, $\lambda$. Multiply $\lambda$ by the equation as follows: $\lambda(W - P_M M - P_B B - P_S S - P_T T)$. Notice that the sum of items in the parentheses is zero. Now simply add this term to the utility function to form a new function

$$L(M, B, S, T) = U(M, B, S, T) + \lambda(W - P_M M - P_B B - P_S S - P_T T)$$

This equation says that the ratio of the marginal utility of money to its price will be equal to the ratio of the marginal utility of bonds to their price, which will equal . . . and so on, for each asset held by an individual if the individual is maximizing his or her satisfaction. This equilibrium position follows from this theory of asset choice.

Assume that a helicopter drops money and now people hold more money. If the marginal utility of money falls when people have more of it, the ratio $MU_M/P_M$ will fall, so that now

$$\frac{MU_M}{P_M} < \frac{MU_B}{P_B} = \frac{MU_S}{P_S} = \frac{MU_T}{P_T}$$

This inequality means that the individuals are less satisfied with the portfolios of money, bonds, stocks, and tangible assets than they could be. By giving up money they lose some utility but by using money to buy bonds and other assets, they gain back more utility than they lose. So they shift from money to other assets, as indicted:

This drives up the prices of the other assets and higher prices mean that $MU_B/P_B$ and the other ratios fall, since prices are in the denominators of the ratios. These ratios continue to fall until the inequality in the equation is removed and market equilibrium is restored. A rising price of a bond, of course, implies a falling yield or interest rate; therefore, an increase in the money supply leads to lower interest rates. This result is consistent with macroeconomic theory.

To see Tobin's contribution more clearly, we may use a different example. Let us assume we start from equilibrium and let the government debt increase—that U.S.

---

Taking partial derivatives of $L$ with respect to each of the four variables gives

$$\frac{\partial L}{\partial M} = \frac{\partial U}{\partial M} - \lambda P_M$$

$$\frac{\partial L}{\partial B} = \frac{\partial U}{\partial B} - \lambda P_B$$

$$\frac{\partial L}{\partial S} = \frac{\partial U}{\partial B} - \lambda P_S$$

$$\frac{\partial L}{\partial T} = \frac{\partial U}{\partial T} - \lambda P_T$$

By setting each of these four partial derivatives equal to zero, and recognizing that $\partial U/\partial M$ is the marginal utility of money, $\partial U/\partial B$ is the marginal utility of bonds, and so forth, one can establish that

$$\frac{MU_M}{P_M} = \frac{MU_B}{P_B} = \frac{MU_S}{P_S} = \frac{MU_T}{P_T}$$

This is a set of necessary conditions for the maximizing of utility from wealth holdings.

Treasury bonds are dropped from a helicopter. People will find they are holding more bonds than they want, relative to other assets. Now an inequality is introduced

$$\frac{MU_M}{P_M} > \frac{MU_B}{P_B} < \frac{MU_S}{P_S} = \frac{MU_T}{P_T}$$

Therefore, people will attempt to trade bonds for other assets, as indicated:

$$M \quad B \quad S \quad T$$

In this case, since the price of money cannot change, all that happens as bond-holders sell off bonds for money is that the price of bonds falls and the yield on bonds rises. But if they trade bonds for stocks, the price of stocks *may* rise, and so may the prices of tangible assets if bonds are sold and tangible assets are purchased. The rise in the price of stocks implies a *lower* yield on stocks for those buying the stocks after the price has risen. However, if stock prices rise, the ratio $MU_S/P_S$ falls and becomes *less* than the ratio $MU_M/P_M$. Because of this disequilibrium some people may sell stocks to acquire money. Thus, on the one hand, some pressures come into play that would lower the yield on stocks and, on the other, there are pressures that come into play that would raise the yield on stocks. Therefore, interest rates on bonds will surely fall while yields on stocks *may* or *may not* fall.

Another way to view it is to consider the six price ratios that can exist among the four types of assets:

$$(1) \quad (2) \quad (3) \quad (4) \quad (5) \qquad (6)$$

$$\frac{P_B}{P_M} \quad \frac{P_B}{P_S} \quad \frac{P_B}{P_T} \quad \frac{P_S}{P_M} \quad \frac{P_T}{P_M} \quad \text{and} \quad \frac{P_S}{P_T}$$

The first three ratios show the price of bonds in the numerator. With a larger supply of bonds their prices will fall relative to the other assets, so these ratios will decline. But what will happen to the fourth and fifth ratios? The price of money is a dollar and cannot change, but the money prices of stocks and of tangible assets may *either rise or fall*. Neither do we know how the sixth ratio will change. The way these ratios change will depend in general upon asset holders' tastes.

One would normally think that an increase in borrowing by the Treasury, with Treasury issue of more debt, would lead to a stock market decline. But if $P_S/P_M$ should rise, as it might, more debt *might* lead to *rising* stock prices and *lower* yields on stocks. This possibly occurred in 1982–1987.

One final example. Assume that the Treasury issues a large volume of Treasury bills. T-bill prices will fall and yields rise. But T-bills are close substitutes for money. Therefore, people may try to hold less money and more stocks. This pushes stock prices *up* and yields *down*. Higher stock prices should lead to increased investment spending. Thus, the increased volume of Treasury short-term debt outstanding *may* actually exert an expansionary influence on economic activity. This result of Tobin's analysis would not exist in the Keynesian world of only two assets, money and "bonds."

Both the liquidity preference model and the Tobin model focus on demand for available *stocks* of certain types of assets. The loanable funds model, described in the following section, is a *flow* model. In it, we examine flows of funds into and out of financial markets, from lenders to ultimate borrowers.

## The Loanable Funds Approach

This approach is preferred by financial analysts because institutional elements can be handled more easily under it and because it is more amenable as a basis for forecasting. So far as can be determined, the liquidity preference and loanable funds approaches are internally consistent with each other.

The loanable funds approach is surely the simplest and easiest to understand. The rate of interest is determined by the supply of and demand for loanable funds, where these funds are flows into the market for securities representing loans and investments. Rather than analyzing why people hold the money they do *at any time*, as we do in the liquidity preference approach, the loanable funds approach asks why people lend or borrow for *periods of time*. In the loanable funds approach, it is assumed that there is a downward-sloping demand curve for funds and an upward-sloping supply curve for funds, as in Figure 12–4.

Analyzing the supply curve first, we note that the supply of loanable funds is derived from three principal sources. First, funds are supplied by saving out of income. When interest rates rise, most savers lend more.

Second, the supply of loanable funds is increased whenever the money supply is increased, that is, whenever $\Delta M$ is positive. As described in Chapter 5, the money

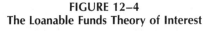

**FIGURE 12–4**
**The Loanable Funds Theory of Interest**

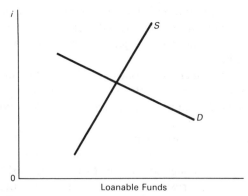

FIGURE 12–5
The Loanable Funds Theory of Interest

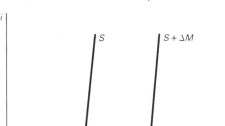

supply is increased through a complicated process. Money is created through central bank action to change the size of the monetary base, and the money multiplier indicates how much the money supply increases with each dollar of increase in the monetary base. This process thus eventually leads to an increase in the money supply, part of the supply of loanable funds, as noted in Figure 12–5 where $S$ is the supply of saving and $\Delta M$ is the increase in the money supply. It is assumed that changes in the money supply are independent of the rate of interest and, therefore, that the $S$ curve is simply shifted rightward by an amount, $\Delta M$, representing the increase in $M$.

Third, the supply of loanable funds may be increased when individuals attempt to dishoard money and decreased when individuals attempt to hoard. If, for example, the interest rate should rise, we note from Figure 12–1 showing liquidity preference that the quantity of money demanded would be less than the quantity supplied. Individuals would attempt to hold less money and would probably offer to buy bonds or other financial assets. Dishoarding would add to the supply of loanable funds. Thus, in Figure 12–5, to the total supply of funds would be added the amount of funds that would be dishoarded if interest rates were higher, as in Figure 12–6. The distance $ab$ in Figure 12–6 represents the distance $ab$ in Figure 12–1. In case the interest rate should fall to $i_2$ in Figure 12–6, individuals would wish to hoard money and would sell bonds or other financial assets to add to their stock of money. Hoarding, represented by the distance $cd$, would reduce the volume of loanable funds. This hoarding and dishoarding behavior is depicted in the curve labeled $S + \Delta M + D$ and $S + \Delta M - H$, where $S$ stands for saving, $\Delta M$ stands for the increase in the money supply, $D$ stands for dishoarding (or negative hoarding), and $H$ stands for hoarding. This curve represents the total supply of loanable funds.

The demand for loanable funds is the result, first, of business demand to finance its capital and liquidity requirements. The long-term capital requirements are described by the investment opportunity curve of the neoclassical model. The lower the money rate of interest, the larger the volume of funds demanded; hence in Figure

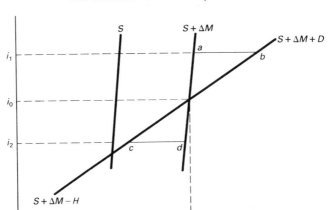

**FIGURE 12–6**
**The Loanable Funds Theory of Interest**

12–4 the demand curve slopes down and to the right. However, total demand for loanable funds also is meant to reflect demand by the federal government for funds as it seeks to finance its deficits by issuing bonds or other securities, and demand by state and local governments, which they express by issuing bonds to finance projects. Thus the total demand for funds is made up of business demand, federal government demand, and state and local government demand, labeled *B*, *G*, and *SG* in Figure 12–7. Foreign demand is ignored here, and consumer demand is hidden because saving refers to *net* saving of the consumer sector (gross saving minus borrowing) plus gross business saving and government saving.[14]

It is widely held that the line indicating federal government demand, *G*, should be vertical. That is, unlike business demand, which is greater at lower interest rates, the quantity of funds borrowed by the federal government is insensitive to interest rates. State and local government demand is sensitive to interest rates; indeed, state and local regulations sometimes prohibit borrowing at interest rates above, say, 6 percent. When the market interest rate on bonds exceeds this level, some local governments may be preempted from effectively demanding any funds at all. Thus total demand for funds may shift leftward at levels above the 6 percent legal maximum for certain state and local governments.

Figure 12–7 shows components of the demand and supply for funds that are nearly always considered by market analysts. However, the student should realize that many unmentioned factors affect these supply and demand schedules. For example, if new banks, savings and loan institutions, or finance companies are established, this may affect the supply of loanable funds. If international trade barriers are lowered,

---

[14] Gross personal saving could be included in the supply of loanable funds and consumer borrowing in the demand for loanable funds if desired.

FIGURE 12–7
**The Loanable Funds Theory of Interest—Components of Supply and Demand**

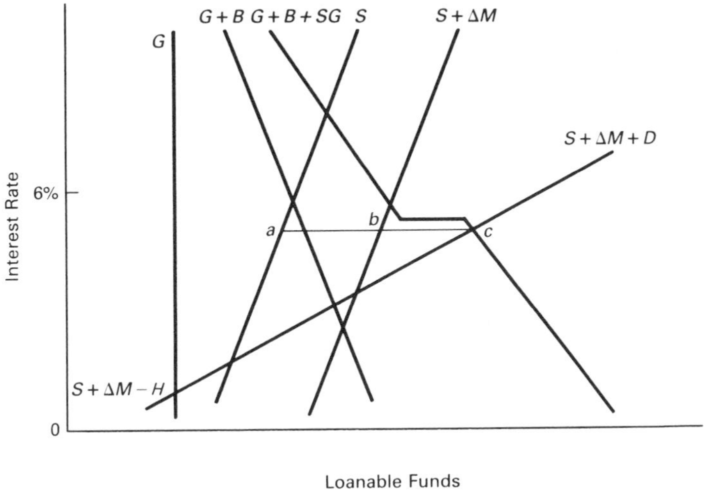

Loanable Funds

businesses may increase their demand for funds (the demand curve may shift to the right) to take advantage of their newly found opportunities. Thus, these demand and supply curves are best thought of as abstract analytical frameworks useful to market observers as a frame of reference in which one can couch the many varied factors that affect the rate of interest and the volume of funds flowing into the market for loans.

The equilibrium point in Figure 12–7 (point $c$) is only a temporary equilibrium point. For at the point, there is dishoarding (in the amount of $bc$). If increase in the money supply should cease next period, the supply curve would shift to the left. Furthermore, dishoarding in the current period would not be expected to continue in future periods. The current rate of increase in the money supply and the dishoarding that is taking place mean that the current supply of funds is increasing and current levels of interest rates are lower. Thus, we would expect investment and income to rise in the near future, leading to (1) a rightward shift in the $G + B$ curve as businesses expand and borrow and (2) a leftward shift in the $G$ curve because higher income means higher tax receipts and a smaller budget deficit (less federal government borrowing), provided, of course, that government spending does not increase to offset this effect.

One defect of the loanable funds theory is that it shows only a partial or temporary equilibrium point. A final equilibrium point is not shown, because it depends on shifts in income, which are ignored in loanable funds theory as normally presented. The demand for and supply of loanable funds do not indicate what shifts in income will be. Hence the final equilibrium level of the interest rate, after all the interactions have been worked out, may be lower or higher than the point usually shown in a diagram—loanable funds theory does not by itself indicate the final equilibrium level of the rate of interest but, rather, shows the current status of the financial market.

Thus care must be used in interpreting financial market developments, using the supply and demand for funds framework. These supply and demand curves are *not* independent of each other, as is assumed for typical supply and demand curves for commodities. Factors influencing the supply of funds may eventually affect the demand for funds, and care must be exercised in interpreting the longer-run effects of an initial shift in either supply or demand.

In concluding, it is perhaps well to note again that one may use either gross or net figures in the loanable funds approach, as long as internal consistency is maintained. For example, consumer dissaving (borrowing) is subtracted from gross consumer saving to arrive at net consumer saving as the supply of funds from consumer saving. Alternatively, gross consumer saving could be used in the supply of saving curve, and consumer dissaving could be part of the demand for saving curve. The same is true of business saving. One may look at gross business saving (depreciation plus retained earnings) and gross demand for funds, or one may subtract depreciation and retained earnings from gross business demand for funds to arrive at net business demand for funds.

## Liquidity Preference Versus Loanable Funds Theory

Earlier we indicated that use of the liquidity preference theory versus use of the loanable funds theory might be a matter of convenience. A theory in which the interest rate is determined by the supply of money and the willingness to hold money and one in which the interest rate is determined by willingness to lend or invest and desire to borrow should lead to the same results. In a money economy, if demand for goods and services equals supply of goods and services, then either equality of the supply of and the demand for loanable funds or of the supply of and demand for money may determine the interest rate.

The loanable funds theory was developed primarily by the monetary economist Dennis Robertson.[15] His analysis was a dynamic one involving changes over periods of time, whereas the later Keynesian theory was a comparative static theory, concerned with the equilibrium positions of demand for and supply of money and, in additional development, with equilibrium positions for investment/saving (*IS*) and liquidity preference/money supply (*LM*).

Why do some consider the loanable funds theory to be a better theory than liquidity preference theory? First, the liquidity preference theory of interest can be criticized as a "bootstrap" theory; if the interest rate is determined mainly by what investors *expect* interest rates to be, one must then ask, why do expectations change? Answers are possible, but the theory is not one that is entirely satisfactory.[16]

---

[15] See D. H. Robertson, "Saving and Hoarding," *Economic Journal*, September 1933, pp. 399–413, and "Industrial Fluctuation and the Natural Rate of Interest," *Economic Journal*, December 1934, pp. 650–656. A somewhat similar theory was developed by the Swedish economist Bertil Ohlin, "Some Notes on the Stockholm Theory of Savings and Investment," *Economic Journal*, 1937.

[16] See J. R. Hicks, "IS-LM: An Explanation," *Journal of Post-Keynesian Economics*, Winter 1980–1981, pp. 139–154.

Second, the liquidity preference theory does not explicitly recognize the role of productivity of capital—according to some, the most significant determinant of the rate of interest. Basically, interest is paid because capital is productive enough to warrant payment of interest and to provide profit after repayment of a loan and payment of interest. Saving (a supply of funds) is of course also essential.

Third, it may be that people tend to think in terms of how much of their income they wish to *lend* or *invest*, not in terms of how much they wish to *hold* in money balances. If so, there is justification in this for using the loanable funds approach.

Fourth, the argument has recently been made that (1) the loanable funds theory is a dynamic theory, as opposed to the comparative static approach of the liquidity preference theory; (2) the loanable funds approach is more general; and (3) it does not depend on intervention in financial markets by speculators who hold money balances because they expect security prices to fall (interest rates to rise). Liquidity preference theory leaves the interest rate dependent on expectations of speculators, but the reasons for their expectations concerning securities prices (interest rates) are not explained.[17]

Finally, is interest a reward for *not* doing something (not consuming or not hoarding)? Why isn't interest the reward for *doing* something—lending or investing?[18]

Of course, in general equilibrium theory, all prices (including interest rates) are interdependently determined. Whether the interest rate is determined by the market for lending and borrowing (the loanable funds theory) or by the "market" for the existing stock of money (the liquidity preference theory) is a matter of convenience. Since lending is both not spending and not hoarding (not choosing to hold money rather than using funds to make loans or investments), it makes sense to use a loanable funds framework as long as one is using partial equilibrium analysis.

One further point: in liquidity preference theory, an important element is what has been called the "speculative" demand for money—holding (or not holding) money because of expected gains or losses due to fluctuations in prices of securities. But this has the defect of all expectations theories: it does not explain what determines the expectations. As Coddington pointed out, Robertson's explanation was that productivity and thrift determine the interest rate that should exist.[19]

---

[17] This argument is developed at length and with sophistication by Meir Kohn, "A Loanable Funds Theory of Unemployment and Monetary Disequilibrium," *American Economic Review*, December 1981, pp. 859–879. Kohn recognizes that the liquidity preference theory is a "pure bootstrap" theory only when the LM curve is horizontal; otherwise it contains elements of a productivity-thrift theory.

[18] Dennis Robertson made this point as long ago as 1940: to paraphrase his argument, if a person has a choice of two prizes for winning, and is asked why he or she got a prize, should the reply be "for not choosing the other prize" or "for not losing"? Or shouldn't it simply be "for winning"? Dennis H. Robertson, "Mr. Keynes and the Theory of Interest," *Essays in Monetary Theory* (London: Staples, 1940), pp. 16–17. The concept that interest is the reward for not spending on consumption is sometimes thought of as a "classical" theory; Keynes argued that interest is the reward for not hoarding money. The loanable funds theory states that interest is the reward for lending (or investing), which is *simultaneously* not consuming *and* not hoarding.

[19] Alan Coddington, "Hicks's Contribution to Keynesian Economics," *Journal of Economic Literature*, September 1979, pp. 970–988, esp. pp. 980–981. According to Coddington, Robertson argued that liquidity preference theory "far from determining the rate of interest, actually leaves its determination dangling in mid-air" (p. 980).

## PRICE EXPECTATIONS AND THE RATE OF INTEREST

In the theoretical explanation of determination of the level of interest rates outlined, no explicit account was taken of the influence of price level changes (inflation or deflation) on the level of interest rates. It is clear that price level changes affect the real return that lenders receive from their loans and that borrowers must pay for their loans. If a contract is made under which a lender receives a return on a $100 loan of $8 at the end of one year, the nominal interest rate, $i$, is 8 percent. However, if on the date of maturity of the loan, the price level is found to have risen by 5 percent, then the real rate of earnings on the loan, $r$, would be only 3 percent. The borrower repays the lender with dollars that are less valuable in terms of purchasing power than the ones he or she borrowed a year earlier. In equation terms, we may write

$$i = r + \dot{p}/p$$

where $\dot{p}$ stands for $dp/dt$, or the derivative of the price level with respect to time, and $p$ is the price level, so that $\dot{p}/p$ is the percentage rate of change in the price level.[20]

---

[20] If prices increase from 100 to 110 in one year, then $dp/dt$ is approximately $\Delta p/\Delta t = 10/1 = 10$. If the original price level, $p$, were 100, then $10/100 = .10$, or 10 percent, the rate of increase in $p$ expressed in percentage terms so as to be consistent with the mode of expression for $i$ and $r$. If $\Delta p/\Delta t = 30$ when the original $p$ was 200, then the percentage rate of increase of $p$ would be only 15 percent. A more exact formulation of the equation for discrete changes in $i$, $r$, and $p$ would be

$$(1 + i) = (1 + r)\left(1 + \frac{\dot{p}}{p}\right)$$

or

$$1 + i = 1 + r + \frac{\dot{p}}{p} + r\left(\frac{\dot{p}}{p}\right)$$

or

$$i = r + \frac{\dot{p}}{p} + r\left(\frac{\dot{p}}{p}\right)$$

The last term on the right-hand side is the interaction term and is usually very small so that it is ignored in most discussions. If, for example, $i = 26$ percent, $r = 20$ percent, and $\dot{p}/p = 5$ percent, then

$$(1.26) = (1.20)(1.05) = 1 + .20 + .05 + .01$$

Omitting the interaction term would have made $i = 25$ percent instead of 26 percent. Thus, the error in omitting the term becomes significant if $r$ or $\dot{p}/p$ or both are large. In the case of continuous functions rather than the discrete changes, the interaction terms drop out altogether. To illustrate, assume $i =$ nominal rate of interest, $r =$ real rate of interest, $p =$ price level, $V_n =$ nominal value of an asset, $V_r =$ real value of an asset, and

$$V_n = pV_r$$

## The "Fisher Effect"

Irving Fisher used this formula as a basis for what is known as the "Fisher effect."[21] He argued that uniform expectations on the part of borrowers and lenders about future rates of inflation would affect the current nominal rate of interest. If borrowers believe that 5 percent inflation will occur during the year, they willingly pay this premium to borrow their funds, and if lenders believe that 5 percent inflation will occur, they require a 5 percent premium to induce them to lend their funds. Thus,

$$i = r + (\dot{p}/p)^e$$

where the right-hand term no longer describes the *results* of *past* inflation but rather the *expected future* rate of inflation as indicated by the superscript $e$. If one believes that current expectations about future inflation rates are formed by the past history of inflation in a country, then one can construct a proxy for measuring $(\dot{p}/p)^e$. With a time series of data for the proxy and a series of observations on $i$, estimates of the real rate of return, $r$, can be calculated by simply subtracting $(\dot{p}/p)^e$ from $i$. If, on the other hand, one assumes that $r$ is relatively constant, then variation in inflation rate expectations would be the prime determinant of variations in $i$. From early 1930 to the mid-1960s, economists in the United States had little interest in the problem of inflation. But, in the late 1960s and in the 1970s, inflation proved to be a problem. Numerous studies have been made that have focused attention on the "Fisher effect."

---

$$i = \text{the percentage change in } V_n = \frac{1}{V_n}\left(\frac{dV_n}{dt}\right)$$

$$r = \text{the percentage change in } V_r = \frac{1}{V_r}\left(\frac{dV_r}{dt}\right)$$

Solving for $i$, find

$$i = \frac{1}{pV_r}\frac{d(pV_r)}{dt} = \frac{1}{pV_r}\left(p\,\frac{dV_r}{dt} + V_r\,\frac{dp}{dt}\right)$$

$$= \frac{1}{V_r}\frac{dV_r}{dt} + \frac{1}{p}\frac{dp}{dt}$$

and, therefore,

$$i = r + \frac{\dot{p}}{p}$$

for an infinitesimal unit of time.

[21] Irving Fisher, *The Theory of Interest* (New York: Macmillan, 1930), reprinted by Augustus M. Kelley, New York, 1961.

The equation appears to be valid, but, upon closer examination, use of it in economic forecasting could be fraught with pitfalls. We cannot examine these in depth, but we can briefly suggest their nature.

First, when prices fell rapidly, as in 1930–1932, recent price experience would have led to expectations of deflation, and if the real rate were constant, then, according to the formula, the nominal rate might have been negative, but it was not, and indeed it cannot be, negative, for lenders would simply retain cash holdings rather than lend at negative rates.

Second, a period of recent past experience without inflation could be upset by an outbreak of hostilities so that current expectations of future inflation would fail to be formed on the basis of past experience alone. Hence, the proxy variable for expected future inflation might fail regularly to predict significant turning points in expectations.

Third, in Fisher's view the real rate of return, $r$, is probably constant over time since it results from the productivity of capital. But what if the real rate does vary over time? If we assume that nominal yields reflect expectations of inflation so that the implied real rate is the nominal rate less the expected inflation rate, the implied real rate has been highly variable. One study of the past 75 years implied that "real rates have ranged from as low as minus 13 percent to over a positive 15 percent. Over this entire interval the average implicit real long-term rate of interest was 1.55 percent."[22] Neither the great magnitude of variation nor the low average value of the implied real rate is easily believable. Thus, although the real rate may not have remained constant as Fisher argued, it surely did not vary as greatly as the implied rate suggests.

Fourth, it is questionable whether "expectations of inflation" can ever be measured in a scientific way. By scientific, of course, we mean capable of being confirmed or refuted by reference to experience. If, for example, we asked everyone to declare his or her expectations, and if we observed the true $i$ in the marketplace and the true $r$ by looking at the technology of production and markets for commodities, and if the difference between $i$ and $r$ did *not* equal our observed $(\dot{p}/p)^e$, then we might presume that our measures were wrong—that we had *not* actually observed the true expected rate of price change. One can record a verbal expression of them, but one cannot *observe* people's opinions, and if their actions belie their words, the recorder of opinion may take the *actions* as evidence of *what the true opinion must have been.*

After interest rates rise, financial analysts often simply rationalize this rise by reporting that investors are now expecting an increase in the rate of inflation. That is, rather than explain the rise in rates as having been caused by expected inflation, they explain changing expectations by inferring how expectations must have changed from the rise in rates. To use expected inflation as part of a theory to predict future changes in interest rates, one must be able to observe changes in expected inflation and test to see if these changes do lead to the theoretically predicted changes in rates. Until this happens, expectations can only be a rationalization rather than a causal force in explaining changes in interest rates.

[22] Brian J. Fabbri, "How Inflation Affects Interest Rates," Salomon Brothers, December 1977, p. 6.

The nature of the fundamental problem in dealing with the "expected inflation" approach to explaining nominal interest rates can be uncovered by reference to two articles published by research departments in two Federal Reserve Banks. One article by an outstanding economist, John H. Wood, contains an interesting review of the equation's origin and early uses.[23] One part of the article discusses measuring expected inflation by assuming that $r$ is constant and letting

$$(\dot{p}/p)^e = i - r$$

It should be obvious that if the equation is used to measure expected inflation, it can never be used also to explain or predict movements in $i$, which is its original purpose, simply because $i$ itself was already used to measure expected inflation.

In the second article, which shows great technical skill, proxy variables are used as estimates for $(\dot{p}/p)^e$ and the equation $r = i - (\dot{p}/p)^e$ is then used to estimate $r$.[24] Again it should be obvious that the equation cannot then be used to explain $i$, since $i$ was already used to measure $r$. To the author's knowledge, all research has either focused on these two implicit forms of the equation or has simply used the assumption that $r$ is constant.[25]

Thus, the equation showing the "Fisher effect" may be challenged because (1) it may not work at all in periods of deflation, (2) proxies for expectations are unreliable, (3) the assumption of a constant real rate may be false, and (4) direct observation of changing expectations, while tempting, may give us untestable theory in a scientific sense.

It is tautologically true, for all investors who purchase a contract for which the unit of account (the dollar, say) is variable in real value, that their realized rate of return will differ from the nominal rate:

$$r \equiv i - \dot{p}/p$$

where $r$ is their ex post "realized" rate of return. But to proceed from this and attempt to explain $i$, and variation in $i$, through observation of $(\dot{p}/p)^e$, is quite another matter. Finally, to predict future $i$—the purpose of a theory of interest rate determination— one must observe not only *changes* in $(\dot{p}/p)^e$ but also changes in $r$.

Most economists would agree that the assertion "$i$ will rise by the rate of inflation" is empirically true in the long run (readers should notice that the term "expected rate" of inflation does not appear in this sentence). But few would say that short-run fluctuations in $i$ are explained by recent changes in the rate of inflation. Short-run fluctuations are best explained by examining the variety of forces of supply

[23] John H. Wood, "Interest Rates and Inflation," Federal Reserve Bank of Chicago, *Economic Perspectives*, May–June 1981, pp. 3–12.

[24] W. W. Brown and G. J. Santoni, "Unreal Estimates of the Real Rate of Interest," Federal Reserve Bank of St. Louis, *Review*, January 1981, pp. 18–26.

[25] One article that focuses on the effect of expected inflation on interest rates and reviews the literature is Herbert Taylor, "Interest Rates: How Much Does Expected Inflation Matter?" Federal Reserve Bank of Philadelphia, *Business Review*, July–August 1982, pp. 3–12.

and demand for loanable funds in the context of the theory of interest rate level determination.

## Inflation in the Loanable Funds Model

We can use supply and demand for loanable funds to analyze the impact of inflation on financial markets. Assume that inflation is fully anticipated by both borrowers and lenders. Then an expected proportional rise in *all* prices of $\dot{p}$ will mean that businesspersons will expect a return on their investment equal to $i = r + \dot{p}/p$. Thus, the demand for funds will shift upward by precisely $\dot{p}/p$ as shown by the demand curve of Figure 12–8 shifting from $D$ to $D'$. Without anticipated inflation $i = r$ and demand curve $D$ obtains; with inflation $i' = r + \dot{p}/p$ and the demand curve becomes $D'$ as borrowers are willing to pay the inflation premium. Similarly, lenders, anticipating inflation, will supply less to the market, and their changed willingness to supply will cause the supply curve to shift to the left from $S$ to $S'$. Lenders "require" a higher nominal yield to induce them to part with their funds. Thus, demand and supply curves both shift up by the full amount of the uniformly anticipated inflation rate. This characterizes the "Fisher effect" in graphical form. The nominal interest rate has risen by the full amount of anticipated inflation, and the quantity of loanable funds remains unchanged at $Q$. Therefore, the real rate of interest remains at $r$, even though $i$ has risen.

**FIGURE 12–8**
**Inflation and the Loanable Funds Theory of Interest**

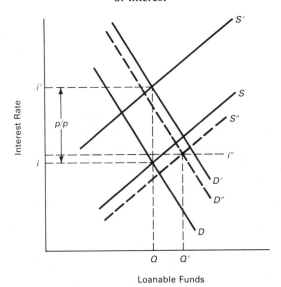

Loanable Funds

However, this scenario of the actual effects of inflation differs significantly from reasonable alternatives proposed by other economists.[26] In the figure there is a dashed demand curve labeled $D''$ that has shifted to the right, but not so far rightward as $D'$. First, federal deficit spending that creates federal demand for funds is not responsive to inflation. Indeed, if prices rise, taxes may increase, and the deficit might actually be less if no offsetting increases in spending occur. Second, when the nominal interest rate rises above legal maximum rates paid by some state and local governments, their demand for funds is restrained. Thus, the demand curve may shift only to $D''$.

The supply curve may shift, not to the left as in the Fisher theory, but to the right as described by the dashed curve labeled $S''$ in the figure. First, wealth holders will try to reduce their balances of money when they anticipate inflation. This *dishoarding* increases the supply of funds; that is, it shifts the supply curve to the right. Second, anticipated inflation lowers consumer confidence in their ability to consume in the future. They feel that prices and taxes will rise while their income will not rise by as much; at least they are uncertain. Therefore, consumers will reduce their expenditures and save *more*. Third, institutions that collect funds on a steady basis, such as life insurance companies, supply these funds to the market and do *not* reduce their willingness to lend because of anticipated inflation, so the supply of funds for many investors does not move left. Thus, it would appear that the $S$ curve may move right to $S''$ in the short run.

The actual result of inflation is likely to be one in which $S''$ and $D''$ curves determine a rate of interest $i''$ and a quantity of funds $Q''$. With $\dot{p}/p$ inflation, this means that the real interest rate falls and the amount of funds traded in the market increases. In a sense one could say that in the short run there is "incomplete adjustment" to the inflation. Only in the very long run would the "Fisher effect" occur fully.

# INTEREST RATE THEORY AT WORK

In the following two chapters we elaborate on some of the more important factors affecting the rate of interest on any particular security. In concluding this chapter we wish to indicate briefly how the theory developed so far provides the market analyst with a general appreciation of why interest rates rise or fall in the short run, in the long run, and among different regions or countries.

## Interest Rate Levels in the Short Run

On a day-to-day basis, short-term interest rates fluctuate in response to temporary and erratic forces affecting supply and demand for short-term funds. For example, the Federal Reserve float may fall unexpectedly and leave banks deficient in

---

[26] See an excellent review of these issues by William D. Jackson, "Federal Deficits, Inflation, and Monetary Growth: Can They Predict Interest Rates?" Federal Reserve Bank of Richmond, *Economic Review*, September–October 1976, pp. 13–25, and the many references cited therein.

reserves. The Federal funds rate rises as a consequence. Cash may flow into circulation, and again there is upward pressure on rates. The demand for funds may increase if an announced Treasury security offering is larger than expected—again short-term rates may rise.

When supply and demand forces change as described, the Fed enters the market through open market purchases of government securities to help offset the rise in rates. Fed officials usually allow the rate to rise, but not by as much as it would have risen without intervention by the open market trading desk. Sometimes the Fed maintains an "even keel" for several days before and after a refinancing operation by the Treasury to ensure that the government securities market will not become "disorderly" and that the Treasury's issue will be well received.

Over a period of several months, however, longer-lasting forces interact to set the level of rates. These forces are related principally to changes in economic activity and the rate of inflation. In a period of economic expansion, demand for funds on the part of business and private individuals tends to increase—the demand curve shifts to the right. This occurs as business firms expand their operations and borrow funds for inventories and working capital. For a time, expansionary monetary policy may contribute to an increase in the supply of funds through the saving that follows. On the other hand, government demand for funds may decline as tax receipts rise, reducing previous deficit levels in the federal budget. Thus the supply of funds shifts rightward, but the demand may also shift rightward, so that interest rates may not change perceptibly at this stage of the cycle in business activity.

However, as capacity utilization of fixed plant and equipment is approached, business firms begin to review and revise upward their heavy investment and construction requirements. The demand for large amounts of long-term funds is likely to begin to rise dramatically, pushing interest rates to higher levels, especially if monetary authorities begin applying brakes to the expansion by reducing the rate of growth in the money supply. The velocity of money increases at higher interest rate levels because of dishoarding. As full capacity is approached and money income continues to rise, prices also begin to rise. Insofar as inflation occurs, nominal interest rates rise further. Thus, a booming economy is characterized by high and rising interest rates as the demand for funds exceeds the supply.

We might characterize the analysis of nominal interest rate levels by listing three types of effects: (1) liquidity effects, (2) income effects, and (3) inflationary effects. As the Fed increases the money supply, the liquidity position of the community improves. The initial effect of this increased liquidity is to push bond prices up and yields down. But more money and lower rates stimulate economic activity and increase income. This increase in income tends to offset the initial decline in yields and subsequently raise them (the income effect). If the economy is operating at or near capacity, the higher income is nominal and reflected heavily in inflation. Inflation pushes nominal interest rates up further (the inflationary effect).

In a downturn of the economy, the situation is reversed. Being uncertain of the economic outlook, consumers may increase the rate at which they save out of disposable income. As output is cut back and unemployment develops, this conservative consumption behavior on the part of the public is accentuated. The supply of funds derived from saving increases, and the demand for durable goods falls. At the same time, there is reduction in the demand for funds, as business firms begin programs of retrenchment (or reduce the rate at which they were expanding in the recent past). As income falls, this reduction in demand is accompanied by a reduction in saving and therefore in the supply of funds. With reduction in the supply of funds, interest rates do not fall as far as they might otherwise. But eventually, the leftward shift in demand overcomes the leftward shift in supply, especially if monetary authorities begin to increase the supply through expansionary policies. Thus interest rates fall. The fall may lead to increased hoarding of money and a decline in the velocity of money, which also occurs as spending is reduced.

## Interest Rate Levels in the Long Run

Over somewhat longer periods of time, monetary factors are less important than are those stemming from thrift and productivity. Interest rate levels may show long-term trends when the influence of short-run monetary factors is eliminated. For example, in countries that are developing their economies and are in the process of industrialization, demand for capital goods means high interest rates. These high rates attract foreign capital. This was true of the United States, which was a net importer of capital up until the 1930s. British funds were supplied to build much of the railway network in the United States in the late 1800s. These funds were attracted by the relatively high rate of interest to be earned.

When an economy matures and standards of living rise, the domestic supply of saving also usually rises, causing an increase in the supply of funds. Thus, interest rates tend to fall to more moderate levels if inflation is held under control.

## International Comparisons of Interest Rates

A considerable amount of the difference in interest rates among countries can be explained by the different rates of inflation they experience. Several countries in South America seem to be able to live with almost steady rates of inflation of 10 or 20 percent per year. This makes nominal interest rates much higher in these countries than the rates for comparable securities in other countries with lower rates of inflation.

"Real" factors also affect interest rates. In some societies positive attitudes toward thrift are strongly entrenched, leading to relatively high saving rates, which add to the supply of funds. In others, people live from day to day with little in their culture that makes thrift a virtue. These differences explain differences in the supply of saving and thus in interest rates. Japan has been a prime example of a country in which, for various reasons, people have maintained a relatively high rate of saving.

The natural resource bases of countries and the rates at which they are exploited *help* determine demand for funds and interest rates in particular countries. However, demand for funds may be strong in countries that have relatively meager natural resources—again, Japan is an example.

Finally, the political process that leads in one direction toward a welfare state or in the other direction toward less government activity also affects demand for funds on the part of government. The greater the degree of government activity in providing additional services, the greater its borrowing is likely to be because unpopular tax increases are not likely to keep up with increases in government expenditures.

## SUMMARY

Classical economists stressed the combination of productivity and thrift as the two principal determinants of interest rates. Neoclassical economists, while retaining the recognition of the importance of productivity and thrift, emphasized the desire for a certain pattern of consumption and saving over time. Thus, borrowing to increase current consumption (rather than to add to the stock of machinery, for example, as emphasized by classical thought) is also a determinant of demand for funds and, therefore, of the level of interest rates.

A brief description of the liquidity preference approach indicates the way in which demand for money and supply of money affect interest rates. If the money supply increases, the interest rate is expected to fall, other things being equal. However, if the money supply continues to increase, this will lead to increased economic activity and eventually to inflation and higher interest rates.

Tobin has offered an alternative approach, focusing on the rate of return on real capital assets, based on productivity and thrift, as the fundamental rate of interest, with other rates varying from it chiefly because they are rates of return on assets involving less risk.

The loanable funds theory of interest rate determination is the theory most often used by financial market analysts. The supply of funds is composed of (1) net saving, (2) changes in the supply of money, and (3) dishoarding. Demand for funds comes mainly from business and government, including state and local governments.

Price level changes affect the "real" rate of interest realized from an investment. Expected price level changes may also affect the willingness of borrowers and lenders to act, but a theory of interest based on expected inflation rates has several pitfalls.

In the short run, temporary and erratic factors affect interest rates. In the long run, productivity of capital and inflation are the major factors affecting nominal interest rates.

### Appendix: The Fisherian Time-Preference Model

In neoclassical economic theory the pricing system allocates scarce resources among alternative uses. All prices are interrelated, and all are relative, indicating the rate at which one commodity will exchange for another at a point in time. An interest rate is a unique form of price—it indicates the rate at which a commodity can be exchanged for itself at *two* points in time. If I give you 10 bushels of wheat today and you return 11 bushels to me one year from today, the real rate of interest is 10 percent. There-

**FIGURE 12A–1**
**Time-Preference Curves for Two Periods**

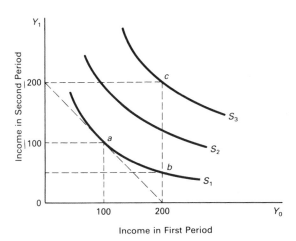

Income in First Period

fore, interest rates serve to determine the time pattern of resource allocation. Individuals have preferences with a time dimension. Students may dissave now in anticipation of a higher income when they begin their careers and earn income out of which they can repay their indebtedness. Middle-aged people may save today in anticipation of an income decline when they enter retirement. In these cases, the individuals prefer to even out the time flow of their consumption. Furthermore, people may wish to borrow now to bring out productive investment.

To describe in a general way the forces giving rise to saving behavior, economists use "indifference curves." These are shown in Figure 12A–1, which is called Irving Fisher's two-period diagram.[27] An individual is assumed to have a time horizon of two periods. Income of the initial period, $Y_0$, is measured on the horizontal axis, and income of the subsequent period, $Y_1$, is measured on the vertical axis. The three indifference curves represent three levels of satisfaction that an individual may acquire from consumption during the two periods. If a person consumes 100 each period, the person will reach the same level of satisfaction (be on the same indifference curve) as would have been reached had he or she consumed 200 this period and only 50 next period (points $a$ and $b$). But the individual would reach a higher level of satisfaction if he or she could consume 200 each period (point $c$). There is, at any point on an indifference curve, a slope of the curve. At point $a$ the slope of the curve $S_1$ is equal to the slope of the tangent to the curve (dashed line). The slope is defined to be $Y_1/Y_0$, and at $a$ this is $-1$.

The slope of the indifference curve is called the marginal rate of time preference. At $a$, the individual is just willing to exchange a dollar's worth of this period's consumption for a dollar's consumption next period. However, if the individual is at

[27] See Fisher, *The Theory of Interest* (New York: Macmillan, 1930).

point *b* the curve is flatter. If we measured $Y_1/Y_0$ it would be, perhaps, $-\frac{1}{4}$. This indicates that the individual's present consumption of 200 is high relative to next period's consumption and that he or she would be happy to give up $4 of this year's consumption if he or she could only have another dollar's consumption next period.

Assume that the individual is at point *a*, where $Y_0$ and $Y_1$ both equal 100. Assume also that the interest rate is zero. Then the dashed line represents the variety of ways in which the individual can consume his or her income of 200. The individual could consume all of it this period and none next period, or he or she could consume equal amounts each period, or all next period and none this period. Indeed, any point on the dashed line represents a possible pair of consumption amounts. We could call it the consumption possibility curve. At *a* the individual is on his or her highest indifference curve.

Now assume that the individual faces a positive interest rate. The consumption possibilities will now be different. They are reflected in the straight solid line in Figure 12A–2.

The slope of the solid line is $-(1 + i)$, where *i* is the market rate of interest. If $i = 20$ percent, the slope is $-1.20$. The horizontal intercept is $183.33, indicating that, if the individual borrowed $83.33 today, he or she could repay this amount along with $16.67 interest a year from today, by using his or her next period's income of $100. The intercept of the vertical axis is $220, indicating that the individual might save all his or her $100 and regain it with $20 interest and receive next period's $100 income as well. Thus, with a positive interest rate the individual's possibilities have changed and he or she can now reach a higher indifference curve at point *b* by lending some of this period's income and receiving his or her income and the repaid principal,

**FIGURE 12A–2**
**Current Saving and Lending**

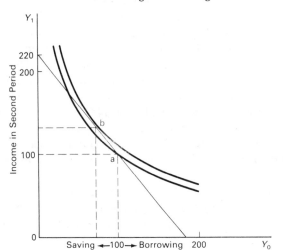

along with earned interest, in the next period. A positive interest rate has induced the individual to save and lend, as noted in the diagram.

Another individual might have a preference map with a tangency point somewhere along the possibility curve below and to the right of point $a$, and that person would be a borrower. In the economy as a whole, all the lenders would supply saving to the economy, and all the borrowers would compete for this saving. The market rate of interest would be determined by competition among those who supply saving and those who demand loanable funds. In equilibrium the rate set in the market would be such that for each and every individual his or her marginal rate of time preference would equal $-(1 + r)$; that is, the slope of his or her indifference curve would equal the slope of the possibility curve. Every borrower and lender would be better off (in the sense of being on a higher indifference curve and realizing a higher level of satisfaction) when a market for saving and dissaving could be freely entered than they would be if such a market were denied existence.

To illustrate these propositions in greater detail, assume that there are two individuals in an economy, each with a two-period time-preference function as suggested by Figures 12A–3(a) and 12A–3(b). In Figure 12A–3(a), individual $A$'s income is given at point $X$—that is, the individual has income this period, but unlike the case of Figures 12A–1 and 12A–2 he or she has none next period. Individual $B$ has income next period but none this period. Using the Edgeworth box diagram technique, rotate individual $B$'s axes by $180°$ and superimpose the $X$s. This appears in Figure 12A–4.

The indifference curves of $A$ and $B$ have points of tangency that, if connected, form what is called a contract line; that is, the set of all points for which $A$'s marginal rate of time preference equals $B$'s marginal rate of time preference. The size of the box represents total income of the two individuals in the two periods. At point $a$ the marginal rate of time preference is the same for both $A$ and B and also equals the slope

**FIGURE 12A–3**
**Time-Preference Curves for Two Persons**

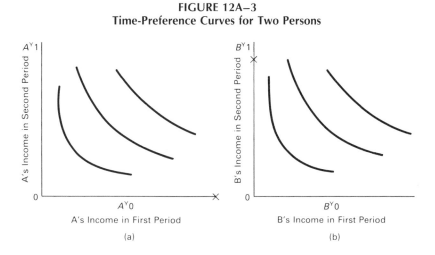

### FIGURE 12A–4
### The Two-Person Market for Borrowing and Lending

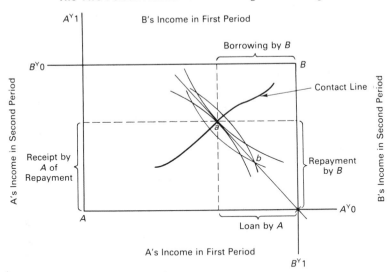

of the line from the $X$ point representing the original incomes of the two individuals to point $a$. The slope of this line equals $-(1 + i)$. Individual $A$ lends to $B$ the amount of current income as noted. This reduces $B$'s next period income by an amount noted by "repayment of loan," and it increases $A$'s second-period income by this amount as well.

If the amount of the loan were represented by point $b$, for example, at this point $A$'s marginal rate of time preference (the slope of his indifference curve) would be less (flatter) than would be $B$'s marginal rate of time preference. This indicates that at this rate of interest $B$ would be on a higher indifference curve if he or she could borrow more from $A$ and also that $A$ would be on a higher curve if he or she could lend to $B$. Both $A$ and $B$ are better off if they move toward point $a$.

We can avoid thinking of $A$ and $B$ as particular individuals, but rather as representative groups of borrowers and lenders, who meet in the marketplace and supply and demand funds. This competitive interaction determines the market rate of interest at any point in time. Thus, the interest rate, which is a market clearing price for loanable funds, is determined, like other prices, by forces of supply and demand.

From Figures 12A–1 and 12A–2, we can see how a supply curve of loanable funds can be generated. A supply curve shows the interest rate on the vertical axis and the quantity of funds supplied on the horizontal axis. This appears in Figure 12A–5.

In Figure 12A–1, at point $a$ the individual supplies no funds when interest rates are zero. This point is reflected in point $a$, in Figure 12A–5. From Figure 12A–2 we find the lender willing to move to point $b$; this is reflected as point $b$, in Figure 12A–5, which shows a positive amount of saving at a positive interest rate of 20 percent. (In

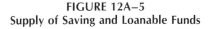

**FIGURE 12A-5**
**Supply of Saving and Loanable Funds**

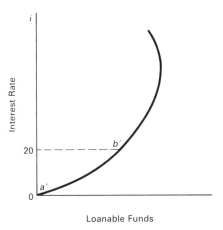

this frame of reference we are making the simplified assumption that saving is the only source of supply of loanable funds.)

The supply curve as shown *may* bend backward to the left at high rates of interest, indicating that the volume of saving *may* fall rather than increase if interest rates reach very high levels. This, of course, is an "individual" supply curve. The aggregate market supply of savings curve would be derived simply by adding together the amounts that would be supplied at various rates of interest by all the individuals in the economy.

The demand for loanable funds on the part of borrowers can also be derived in a similar way to that used to derive the supply curve. However, the demand for loanable funds is affected not only by the desires of different individuals to even out their income streams, but also, and more important, the demand for loanable funds arises because there exist real investment opportunities that provide a yield in the form of increases in income in the future.

Assume, for example, that the individual whose time-preference curves we are studying believes that by purchasing a $10 machine with a life of one year he or she can earn 100 percent return. That is, in a year's time the individual will realize an addition to profits of $10 beyond the $10 that he or she pays in costs for the machine. The machine earns $20 so that at the end of the year the individual receives back $10 principal on his or her investment and an additional $10 in "real" interest. This "real" interest rate is often called the "internal" rate of return. Now assume that a second machine, when employed along with the first, will yield a return of 50 percent. Finally, let a third machine yield a return of 20 percent. Thus, on the individual's two-period diagram, note the line from the X origin sloping up to the left in Figure 12A-6. The lower part of the curve shows the 100 percent rate on the first $10

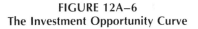

FIGURE 12A–6
The Investment Opportunity Curve

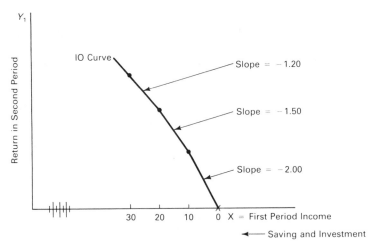

machine, then the next segment of the curve shows the 50 percent return on the second $10 machine, and so forth.

The curve in Figure 12A–6 is called an investment opportunity *IO* curve. Assume that the curve is smooth for simplicity, and superimpose it on the individual's map of indifference curves as in Figure 12A–7.

In the absence of investment opportunities this individual could move along the line from $X$ to point $a$ and reach a higher indifference curve than he or she would be on at point $X$. The individual could do this by saving part of his or her income and lending it at the interest rate of 20 percent. This line represents a set of possible options open for dividing his or her income between the two periods. With the *IO* curve the individual now expands his or her opportunities. The individual can move along the *IO* curve to point $b$ and reach a higher indifference curve because the investments will give him or her some income in period 1. But, if the market rate of interest is still 20 percent, the individual may invest in the three machines a total of $30, but then borrow $20 at the going interest rate of 20 percent and move down along the new straight line to reach point $c$, a point on the highest indifference curve to him or her. Thus, the individual may invest (save) and borrow at the same time to raise his or her current consumption above what it would be at point $b$. Most individuals both invest and borrow simultaneously. The individual could, for example, put up $10 of his or her own money and borrow the other $20 to make the $30 investment. This is essentially what homeowners do with their "down payments."

With investment opportunities, the possibility of increasing future income arises. Economic growth, in the sense of raising the income and consumption levels of the people, follows from investment. From the diagram it is clear that lower interest rates lead to higher rates of investment spending and to higher income next period. Of

FIGURE 12A–7
Individual Saving and Investment

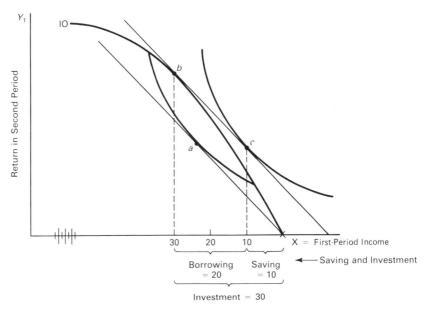

course, new technology leads to investment opportunity and is undoubtedly the root source of economic growth. But investment made feasible by low interest rates is the proximate source of higher living standards.

Thus, the neoclassical economic description of the saving-investment process rests upon certain assumptions: (1) that people have time preferences from which appropriate indifference curves may be derived; (2) that there exists a technology such that investment will provide a positive return (that is, a higher real income in the future than would be possible without it); (3) that a competitive, free market exists where borrowers and lenders can meet; and (4) that competitive forces will drive the rate of exchange between present and future income (the interest rate) to an equilibrium position where $-(1 + i)$ equals the marginal rate of time preference for each individual and also equals the marginal rate of return on all the current investment opportunities. At this equilibrium the market clears. The analysis turns on the concepts of "thrift" and "productivity." If government imposes ceilings on interest rates or other constraints on the freedom of individuals to engage in borrowing and lending and saving and investing, then the competitive equilibrium cannot be attained and welfare (utility) will generally be lower than otherwise.[28]

[28] An individual's wealth and utility do not always move in the same direction when interest rates change. See Robert Haney Scott, "A Paradox in the Relation of Wealth to Utility," *Nebraska Journal of Economics and Business*, Autumn 1979, pp. 65–71.

## Questions for Discussion

**1.** Using the approximate method described in the text, estimate the yield to maturity if an investor pays $900 for a $1,000 bond that pays 6 percent interest and matures in ten years. Now assume that the individual pays $1,200 for the same bond and estimate the yield to maturity.

**2.** The "roundaboutness" of the production process leads to efficiency in production. Imagine that you wanted to make a single pair of eyeglasses and speculate on how much roundaboutness you would have to engage in.

**3.** In what sense is the interest rate a "price"?

**4.** Draw a money demand curve like that in Figure 12–1 and draw two money supply schedules showing an increase in the money supply. Interpret the market process by which the increase in the money supply leads to a fall in interest rates.

**5.** List the principal components of the supply of loanable funds and of the demand for loanable funds.

**6.** Explain why the supply and demand curves for loanable funds are not independent of one another.

**7.** What is the relation between the nominal interest rate and the expected rate of inflation?

**8.** What are some of the difficulties with the "expected rate of inflation" theory?

**9.** From the appendix, draw a time-preference function showing *A* as a borrower. Note how the current market interest rate that he or she faces is shown in the diagram. Would *A* borrow more or less if the interest rate were higher?

**10.** Redraw Figure 12A–7 for yourself and explain how most of us are *both* borrowers and lenders and why.

## Selected References

Most macroeconomic texts contain a thorough treatment of the theory of interest rate determination at an elementary or intermediate level. In addition, most of the texts cited at the end of Chapter 1 provide coverage.

At a more advanced level of analysis, see the discussion of interest rate theory by the late Joseph W. Conard, *Introduction to the Theory of Interest* (Berkeley: University of California Press, 1959).

The classic work of Irving Fisher, first published in 1930, still merits the attention of student and scholar alike. Fisher's *Theory of Interest* was reprinted by Augustus M. Kelley, New York, in 1955 and 1961.

For a concise discussion of various factors (including expectations) affecting the level of interest rates, see articles by Robert Eisner, W. E. Gibson, Thomas J. Sargent, W. P. Yohe, and D. S. Karnosky, in W. E. Gibson and George G. Kaufman, eds., *Monetary Economics: Readings on Current Issues* (New York: McGraw-Hill, 1971), Part 4. Also see W. E. Gibson, "Interest Rates and Inflationary Expectations," *American Economic Review*, December 1972, pp. 854–865, in which the author uses forecasts of price level changes collected by Joseph Livingston, a financial columnist, as a measure of expected rates of inflation, to help explain variations in nominal interest rates.

It is clear that interest rates have been higher and more volatile since 1967 than they were before that year, at lest until 1982. G. J. Santoni and Courtenay C. Stone, "What Really Happened to Interest Rates? A Longer-Run Analysis," Federal Reserve Bank of St. Louis, *Review*, November 1981, pp. 3–14, present evidence that the major cause for this behavior of interest rates was a higher and more variable rate of growth in the money supply.

Stephen G. Cecchetti, "High Real Interest Rates: Can They Be Explained?" Federal Reserve Bank of Kansas City, *Economic Review*, September–October 1986, pp. 31–41, attempts to provide evidence that *real* interest rates were high in the first half of the 1980s and that the major reasons were (1) tight money from 1980–1982; (2) increased profitability of investment, causing increased borrowing, from late 1982 through the end of 1983; and (3) a decline in the rate of saving during 1984 and 1985.

# INTEREST RATE DIFFERENTIALS: THE TERM STRUCTURE OF INTEREST RATES

In earlier chapters we frequently referred to "the" interest rate or the "level" of interest rates as if there were only one rate or only one representative average of rates. In Chapter 12 we expanded our horizon to examine choice among a variety of interest rates on assets that lie along a liquidity or risk spectrum from money to real assets. It is now time to examine a different dimension that gives rise to interest rate differentials—the *maturity spectrum*. Thus, in this chapter we relate differences in yield to maturity on securities to differences in length of time to maturity. In the following chapter we examine other factors giving rise to yield differences, but for now we hold other factors constant and assume that in all respects except term to maturity the securities are homogeneous; they are alike with respect to credit risk, tax status, call provisions, and so on.

# THE YIELD CURVE: A "PICTURE" OF THE TERM STRUCTURE AT A SPECIFIC TIME

We begin describing the term structure of interest rates by constructing a so-called "yield curve." We first select a certain class of securities, for example, U.S. Treasury securities. These are presumed to be default-free, the risk of default at maturity being negligible. We may also exclude U.S. Treasury issues that have special tax provisions attached. Thus, we have a set of securities that is as homogeneous as we can find. We observe *on a particular day* (1) the yield to maturity and (2) the length of time to maturity of these securities.

By measuring yield to maturity on the vertical axis and time to maturity on the horizontal axis, a set of points can be plotted as in Figure 13–1. The points shown are hypothetical, for illustrative purposes only. Each "x" represents a particular Treasury issue, with the time until its maturity indicated on the horizontal axis and its yield to maturity (or to earliest call date if it is selling at a price above par) indicated on the vertical axes. The curve is drawn as of a specific date, say, March 20, 1990. The shape of the curve will be slightly different on successive days.

Yield curves are often drawn on the basis of data on U.S. Treasury obligations because these obligations are more homogeneous than, say, corporate securities or municipals, and the data are more readily available. Other yield curves are occasionally plotted by analysts especially interested in a particular market, although it is recognized that, because these securities are less homogeneous than government securities, factors other than term to maturity probably affect the yield curves. For example, the *Annual Review of the Bond Market*, by Salomon Brothers, often includes yield curves for federal agency, corporate, and municipal securities.[1]

## The Observed Behavior of the Term Structure

At various times yield curves have different shapes. In January the yield curve might assume its usual upward slope as in Figure 13–1. A month later, the curve could be nearly horizontal (termed a "flat" curve). Six months later it could be downward sloping instead of positively sloped. The purpose of developing a theory of the term structure of interest rates is to explain the shape of the yield curve and outline the reasons for changes in the shape over time. Figure 13–2(a) shows a set of yield curves, in various years from 1974 to 1986.

These curves illustrate some of the variety of patterns that have occurred at various times. The yield curves for February 15, 1977 and for July 25, 1986 are somewhat more "typical" than the others. In recent decades, short-term rates have frequently been lower than long-term rates. Humped curves, such as that for August

---

[1] There are many problems associated with fitting the "curve" to the observations. Most often the analyst simply makes a freehand drawing. But this may be inadequate for sophisticated statistical tests; therefore, other methods have been suggested. See Martin E. Ecols and Jan Walter Elliott, "A Quantitative Yield Curve Model of Estimating the Term Structure of Interest Rates," *Journal of Financial and Quantitative Analysis*, March 1976, pp. 87–114.

**FIGURE 13–1**
**The Yield Curve**

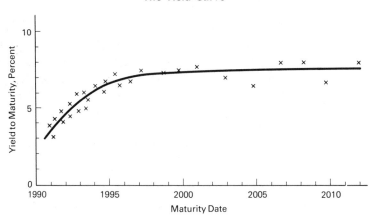

**FIGURE 13–2(a)**
**Yields on U.S. Government Securities**

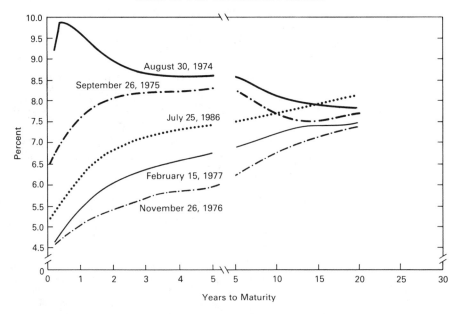

30, 1974, with peaks in the short-term maturity range, are found fairly often but less frequently than those with a positive slope in the short-term and intermediate-term maturities. The upward-sloping curves prevail mostly during periods of moderate economic growth and periods of recession. Flat and downward-sloping curves, perhaps with humps, are usually observed during periods of vigorous economic expansion and near peaks of business activity, or during periods of a *declining* rate of inflation, as in the early 1980s.

At some point in periods of vigorous expansion, the Federal Reserve is likely to pursue restrictive monetary policies. Therefore, flat and downward-sloping yield curves are also observed in periods when the Federal Reserve assumes a restrictive monetary policy posture, because restrictive policies usually require pushing short-term interest rates to high levels. The effect of restrictive policies is illustrated clearly in Figure 13–2(b). In 1979 inflation grew worse and the Federal Reserve kept tightening and tightening bank credit until by March 1980 yields on 6-month bills reached nearly 17 percent. By May of 1980, however, these yields had fallen to 8 percent while long-term yields remained at 10 percent. Thus yield curves in 1985, with only slowly rising business activity and with inflation at a relatively low level, were positively sloped again, as shown in Figure 13–2(c), but their level by the end of 1985 was much lower than it had been in the late 1970s.

## FIGURE 13–2(b)
### Yields on U.S. Government Securities

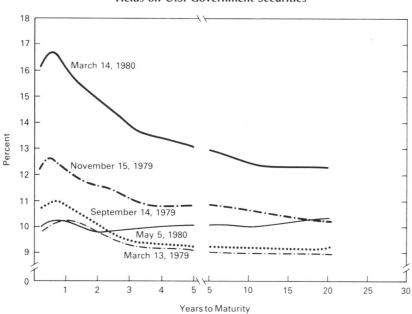

SOURCE: Federal Reserve Bank of St. Louis.

**FIGURE 13–2(c)**
**Yield Curves for Selected U.S. Treasury Securities**

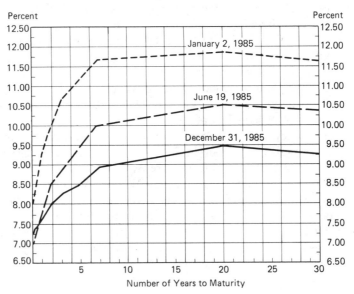

SOURCE: Federal Reserve Bank of New York, *Quarterly Review*, Spring 1986, p. 41.

A comparison of yield curves suggests that, as interest rates in general fluctuate up and down, short-term rates rise and fall relative to longer-term rates. Treasury bill rates, for example, fluctuate with greater amplitude than do bond yields. On the other hand, *prices* of long-term bonds are far more volatile than prices of short-term issues, *given the same percentage change in the yield*, and other things equal. This is a result of the mathematics of interest rates and security prices. Consider an example of a $1,000 consol and a $1,000 one-year security, each having a coupon rate of 5 percent and an initial market price equal to par value. Assume that the market yield on each rises from 5 to 6 percent, a 20 percent increase. The price of the consol declines from $1,000 to $833.33 ($PV = R/i$, or $833.33 = $50/.06$). The price of the one-year security declines from $1,000 to $990.55

$$PV = \frac{R + F}{(1 + .06)}$$

or

$$\$990.55 = \frac{\$1,050}{1 + .06}$$

Clearly, the consol's price falls far more than the price of the one-year security. If yields were to *fall* instead of rise, say, from 5 percent to 4 percent, the consol's price would rise by a greater amount than would the price of the short-term security.

Alternatively, if the price of the consol fell by a given amount, say, $100 (from $1,000 to $900), there would be only a slight increase in yield to maturity. A $100 decline in the price of a one-year security would imply a very large increase in its yield.

Time to maturity is, therefore, a major factor affecting the volatility of a security's price. In general, volatility increases with maturity, although the incremental increases in volatility accompanying the lengthening of time to maturity by one more year become less and less as maturity lengthens.

The volatility of the price of a bond is also affected by the coupon rate. The lower the coupon rate, the greater the price volatility. In the formula

$$PV = \frac{R}{1+i} + \frac{R}{(1+i)^2} + \cdots$$

the $R$s in the numerator affect the response of $PV$ to a percentage change in $i$. The smaller the $R$s, the greater the change in $PV$.[2]

## Business Fluctuations and the Term Structure

During periods of economic expansion, interest rates generally rise and yield curves typically change from upward-sloping curves to flat curves; late in an expansion, the curve tends to become downward sloping or humped. This process is reversed when inflationary pressures subside. Short-term rates fall and the yield curves flatten and then resume their positive slope. This is illustrated in Figure 13–2(a) covering the period from August 1974 to February 1977. More generally, as market rates fluctuate over time, yield curves tend to oscillate in a range between a top and a bottom curve, as shown in Figure 13–3.

The range indicated in that figure as the "normal" range is the range within which the representative long-term rate usually fluctuates during the period under observation. This range may, of course, change with long-run trends in the underlying factors determining interest rates. During the depression of the 1930s and during World War II, interest rates were much lower than in subsequent decades. Thus what

---

[2] For a detailed description of the relation between yields and prices, see Burton G. Malkiel, *The Term Structure of Interest Rates* (Princeton, N.J.: Princeton University Press, 1966), pp. 54–56. Also see a discussion of Malkiel's theorems in Paul F. Smith, *Economics of Financial Institutions and Markets* (Homewood, Ill.: Richard D. Irwin, 1971), pp. 173–175; and Michael H. Hopewell and George G. Kaufman, "Bond Price Volatility and Term to Maturity: A Generalized Respecification," *American Economic Review*, September 1973, pp. 749–753.

**FIGURE 13–3**
**The Normal Range for Yield Curves**

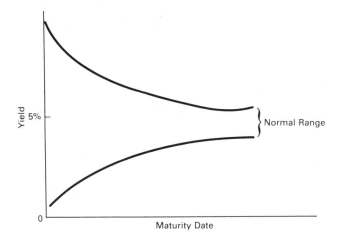

is considered "normal" today is different from "normal" in those earlier years and perhaps from levels that will prevail in the future.[3]

Either or both theories of the term structure discussed in the following section may be used to explain the observable behavior of the yield curve—that is, to explain (1) why the short rate varies with greater amplitude than the long rate (this is not merely a matter of mathematics), (2) why sometimes the yield curve has humps, and (3) why there is a tendency for upward-sloping curves to rise rather steeply, whereas downward-sloping curves typically fall with a bit more gentle slope.

## THE THEORY OF THE TERM STRUCTURE OF INTEREST RATES

We have chosen to focus our discussion on two major theoretical approaches used to explain the term structure of interest rates: we refer to these as the "segmented markets" approach and the "expectations" approach. Sometimes economists attempt to synthesize various elements of the two approaches, but it is useful at the outset to dichotomize them to examine their differing characteristics. Occasionally a third

---

[3] This empirical description of yield curves should not be confused with the theory discussed in the section on expected changes in long-term rates. The theory is based on the proposition that market participants have a general idea of what constitutes a "normal" level of long-term rates, so that, if rates are significantly above that level, investors expect them to fall, whereas if they are significantly below that level, investors expect them to rise. Theories incorporating this hypothesis are found in Frank DeLeeuw, "A Model of Financial Behavior," in J. Duesenberry, G. Fromm, L. Klein, and E. Kuh, eds., *Brookings Quarterly Econometric Model of the United States Economy* (Chicago: Rand McNally, 1965); and in Franco Modigliani and Richard Sutch's article, cited in footnote 4, this chapter.

approach, the "liquidity premium" approach, is mentioned, but it is most frequently viewed not so much as a separate approach but more as an addendum to either the expectations approach or the segmented markets approach.[4]

## The Segmented Markets Approach

Under the segmented markets approach, the approach almost universally used by financial analysts, securities in different maturity ranges are considered to be imperfect substitutes. An increase in the supply of securities in one maturity range will lead to a decline in prices (rise in yields) of those securities. An increase in demand will lead to an increase in their prices. That is, we simply apply the usual supply and demand analysis we use in discussing determination of prices of commodities. Of course, "segmented" does not mean totally separate or independent. Indeed, all analysts recognize that the various markets for securities of different types may be highly interdependent. Three-month bills are very good substitutes for 6-month bills, and 6-month bills are good substitutes for 9-month bills. Also, 19-year bonds are good substitutes for 20-year bonds. But 3-month bills are not good substitutes for 20-year bonds. Thus, the more distant different securities are from each other in the maturity range, the less substitutable they are for each other.

There is a tendency for firms to match the maturity of their assets with the maturity of their liabilities. Commercial banks have short-term liabilities; hence, for liquidity purposes, they hold large amounts of short-term assets. Insurance companies, on the other hand, have liabilities that extend into the distant future, and they hold large amounts of long-term securities to be sure that the revenues that they need will be available when the time arrives. Businesses with large inventories borrow short term to finance them, perhaps by pledging accounts receivable against commercial bank loans. Manufacturing firms constructing plants with an expected life of 20 years may sell 20-year bonds to finance the construction. This tendency to match assets with liabilities is tantamount to "hedging" on a bet to avoid the risk of sizable loss.

Lenders purchasing a short-term security know that its price will not change greatly while they hold it; that is, there is little risk of being forced to assume a capital loss in case they might wish to sell the security prior to maturity. Thus, short-term securities minimize the risk of capital loss. However, lenders who purchase a long-term security have greater certainty of a steady income flow over the extended period than do those who make repeated purchases of short-term securities over the years. Thus, long-term securities minimize the possibility of income variation. Persons

---

[4] There are several different views on this topic. For example, L. G. Telser, "A Critique of Some Recent Empirical Research on the Explanation of the Term Structure of Interest Rates," *Journal of Political Economy*, Supplement, August 1967, pp. 546–561, discussed the expectations theory and the liquidity preference theory as alternatives and did not even mention the segmentation theory. Franco Modigliani and Richard Sutch, "Debt Management and the Term Structure of Interest Rates: An Empirical Analysis of Recent Experience," *Journal of Political Economy*, Supplement, August 1967, pp. 569–589, described their "preferred habitat" theory as an "adaptation of the expectational theory," while Reuben A. Kessel ("Comment" in the same journal issue, p. 592) regarded it as "another name for what the late Professor Conard referred to as market segmentation."

wishing to avoid capital loss will buy short-term securities, and those wishing to avoid income variation will buy long-term securities.

Furthermore, short-term securities are more "liquid" than are long-term securities. They are "closer" to money because they are (1) more readily marketable and (2) subject to less price variation because they are closer to maturity. Hence it is generally assumed that lenders will be willing to pay a premium price for short-term over long-term securities, thereby pushing the yield on short terms below those of long terms. *This "liquidity premium" exists because lenders have a positive preference for liquidity, other things being equal.*[5]

Besides these institutional preferences for certain maturity ranges because of liquidity and risk preferences, there also exist certain legal restrictions that make securities of different maturities poor substitutes for each other. Formerly, some state-chartered commercial banks were allowed to count certain short-term securities as part of their legally required reserves, but long-term securities were not eligible for this purpose. A variety of other legal restrictions affect the demand for securities on the part of savings banks, insurance companies, and the managements of pension funds.

To summarize, the segmented markets approach treats securities of different maturities as related, but with unique characteristics. Short-term securities have liquidity and provide certainty of capital value, even for very short periods. Long-term securities have certainty of income flow. Legal restraints on investment activity also affect demand in the various maturity ranges. Therefore, different buyers have preferences for different maturities so that yields respond to changes in conditions of supply and demand in the different maturity ranges.

To see how the segmented markets approach works, let us refer to Figure 13–4. In this figure the yield curve may be divided into four maturity ranges for illustrative purposes: within 1 year, 1 to 5 years, 5 to 10 years, and over 10 years to maturity. The lines of segmentation are chosen arbitrarily to suit the analyst's needs.

This type of segmentation is routine in economic analysis. For example, an agricultural economist may wish to study the supply and demand for food. More likely, however, the food category will be broken arbitrarily into various segments. Basic categories include meat, grain, vegetables, and fruit. There are many types of fruit, one of which is citrus fruit. The market for citrus fruit may be divided into oranges, grapefruit, and lemons. Finally, the agricultural economist may wish to narrow the inquiry to the market for oranges, which is simply a market that is segmented from other markets. All supply and demand analyses require segmentation. But when the market is segmented in this way, it is *not* separated. The analyst will observe that the demand for oranges depends upon the price of oranges and *also* upon the price of grapefruit because grapefruit is recognized to be a close substitute for oranges.

---

[5] The pervasive existence of a liquidity premium on short-term securities implies that the yield curve should generally be positively sloped—but this is not to suggest that negatively sloped curves would never appear, and indeed they do appear from time to time. For empirical evidence of the liquid premium, see Kessel's monograph, cited in footnote 11 in this chapter.

**FIGURE 13–4**
**A Change in the Yield Curve**

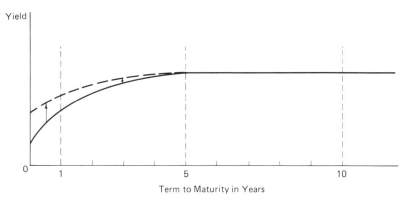

Term to Maturity in Years

The analogy is straightforward. First, we have chosen to look at a special category of securities—those issued by the U.S. Treasury—to draw yield curves. Some of these securities are money market securities, and some are capital market securities.

In Figure 13–5 there are two graphs of supply and demand. One is for securities within 1 year to maturity. The other is for securities with maturity in the range of 1 to 5 years. Assume that the U.S. Treasury decides to sell an increased volume of T-bills. The supply of securities in the within-1-year segment of the market will increase. The increase is shown as a shift to the right from initial position $S_0$ to subsequent position $S_1$. This increased supply of short-term securities leads to a decline in price. The decline in price implies a concomitant increase in yield on securities in this range. The increased yield is shown in Figure 13–4.

**FIGURE 13–5**
**Effects of Changes in Supply and Demand**
**for Different Maturities**

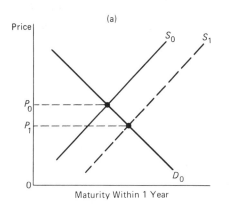 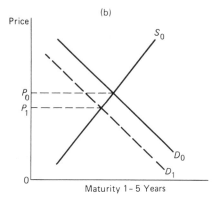

But does this mean no change in the market for securities in the 1- to 5-year maturity range? Not at all, because the securities in the two ranges are substitutes for each other. The new lower price of the within-1-year securities will make those securities attractive. Some investors will switch out of the market for 1- to 5-year securities to buy the higher-yielding (lower-priced) securities in the within-1-year segment. That is, there will be a reduction in demand for securities in the 1- to 5-year segment of the market. This reduction is shown by a leftward shift in the demand curve from the initial demand $D_0$ to the subsequent demand $D_1$. The prices of these securities decline from initial position $P_0$ to the lower level $P_1$. Again, the lower price is reflected in a higher yield, and in Figure 13–4 the higher yield in the 1- to 5-year maturity range is shown.

Because of substitutability of securities along the maturity spectrum, the yield curve is pushed up in the short end of the market but shows little or no response in the long end. The yield curve changes its shape toward a flatter position.

Think of the supply and demand graphs in Figure 13–5 as graphs for oranges on the left and grapefruit on the right. Assume a bumper crop of oranges and an increase in supply. This lowers the price of oranges. Because they are good substitutes for grapefruit, the demand for grapefruit falls and so does the price of grapefruit. From your microeconomics course, you may recall the concept of cross-price elasticity of demand. Here it is positive, indicating substitute goods.

Similar considerations apply if the Treasury were to issue a big block of 20-year bonds. Long-term yields would rise. So would intermediate-term yields. But yields on securities in the within-1-year range would be little affected, and the yield curve would assume a steeper positive slope in the short maturity segments.

Thus, to apply a segmented markets approach to the analysis of the term structure of interest rates is simply to apply the usual supply and demand approach that is a mainstay of all applied economic analysis.

## The Pure Expectations Approach

In this approach to the explanation of the term structure, expectations alone determine the structure of yields. Expectations concerning future interest rates determine the demand for securities, which in turn determines their yields, but relative supplies of securities do not affect their yields.

### Assumptions and Inferences

The pure expectations theory of the term structure is based upon a number of simplifying assumptions.

1. That a large enough number of financial investors (or a smaller number who are well financed) hold uniform expectations about future values of short-term interest rates.
2. That no transactions costs exist, so that investors may enter and leave the market frequently without cost.

3. That no market imperfections inhibit interest rates from moving to their competitive level.
4. That investors wish to maximize their holding period yield; that is, they wish to obtain the maximum income (profit) available over a given period of time.

In a world in which these assumptions hold, the long-term rate will equal the average of short-term rates expected to prevail over the long-term period. To maximize holding-period yield, an investor may invest in, say, either a 2-year security or two 1-year securities, reinvesting at the end of each year. If a 2-year security gives a higher return at the end of the 2 years than the same amount invested in two successive 1-year securities, then, to maximize his or her income, the investor will purchase the 2-year security. But, if higher income will result from two successive 1-year investments, then this is the investment that he or she will make to maximize the return over the 2-year investment period.

For example, if an investor can purchase a current 1-year security for a 3 percent return, and then a second 1-year security for a 5 percent return, over the two years the investor will earn approximately 4 percent (the two-year average of 3 percent and 5 percent).

If $R_1$ is the current market rate of interest on a 1-year security, $R_2$ is the current market rate on a 2-year security, and $r_1$ is the market rate on a 1-year security that is expected to prevail one year from today, then in our example, $R_1 = 3$ percent, $r_1 = 5$ percent, and

$$R_2 = \frac{(R_1 + r_1)}{2} = \frac{(3 + 5)}{2} = 4\%$$

This is the same as

$$(1 + R_2) = \frac{(1 + R_1) + (1 + r_1)}{2}$$

or

$$1.04 = \frac{(1.03) + (1.05)}{2}$$

From these formulas it is clear that, if a 2-year bond is selling at a price to yield greater than 4 percent, the lender will choose it. But if the 2-year security is selling to yield less than 4 percent, the lender will choose to invest in the current 1-year security and reinvest at the end of the year in another 1-year security to obtain a 4 percent yield over the 2 years.

The crucial element in the decision about which investment to make is the value of the 1-year rate that investors *expect* to exist 1 year from today. If they hold this expectation with certainty (whether they prove to be right in the future or not), they

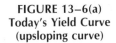

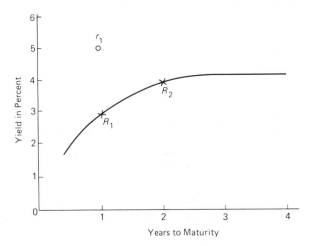

FIGURE 13–6(a)
Today's Yield Curve
(upsloping curve)

will invest in a way that will bring the maturity pattern of rates into line with their expectations.

The slope of the yield curve is said to *reflect* expectations held by investors about what the yield on a 1-year security will be 1 year from today. We show this in Figure 13–6(a), in which today's yield curve is upward sloping, and in which yields on 1-year and 2-year securities today are 3 and 4 percent, shown with x's and labeled $R_1$ and $R_2$. If these $R$ values are placed in the formula $R_2 = (R_1 + r_1)/2$ and if the formula is

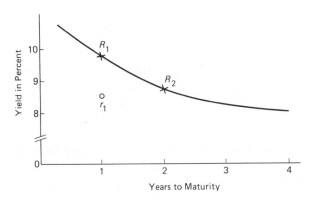

FIGURE 13–6(b)
Today's Yield Curve
(downsloping curve)

solved for $r_1$, $r_1$ turns out to be 5 percent. This value is shown in Figure 13–6(a) and is designated by a small zero to distinguish it from the observations of today's yields.

The $r_1$ in the graph is, presumably, the 1-year yield that investors expect to prevail next year. It is called the *implied forward rate;* that is, current spot yields $R_1$ and $R_2$ *imply* that investors expect $r_1$ to be the 1-year yield *next year.* In this case, $r_1$ is simply calculated from the formula by inserting the current values of $R_1$ and $R_2$. In this example the yield curve is upward sloping, and the implied forward rate is *greater* than the current rate $R_1$ and also *greater* than the current rate $R_2$.

Thus, when the yield curve slopes upward, some economists say that this *implies* that investors expect 1-year yields to rise over the coming year. Indeed, from the calculation they could even say that investors expect 1-year yields to rise to a level *above* the current 2-year yield. Not only are short-term yields expected to rise, but they are expected to rise by a considerable amount. A belief in rising short-term yields is *implied* by the current upward-sloping yield curve.

A belief that yields will fall is implied when the current yield curve is downward sloping. This is shown in Figure 13–6(b). Here the spot rate on a 1-year security is 10 percent, and on a 2-year security it is 9 percent. Using these rates as values of $R_1$ and $R_2$ in the formula $R_2 = (R_1 + r_1)/2$ and solving for $r_1$ gives a value of 8 percent for $r_1$. When today's yield curve is downward sloping, the implied forward rate is below the spot rates. Investors are presumed to believe not only that yields will fall over the coming year, but also that 1-year yields will fall to levels below the current yields on 2-year securities.[6]

In our examples we used the arithmetic mean of two short-term rates to find the long-term rate; however, the geometric mean is the correct one to use. Thus,

$$(1 + R_2) = [(1 + R_1)(1 + r)]^{1/2}$$

The exponent $^{1/2}$ means that we take the square root of the product of the two rates, which is the correct procedure.

### Explaining Humped Yield Curves

The pure expectations approach is somewhat more cumbersome when it is used to explain the humped yield curve. If investors expect future short-term rates to rise *temporarily,* but to fall in a subsequent period, then a hump might arise in the yield curve. Thus, expectations of both rising and falling short-term yields must exist simultaneously to explain the hump. Even more complex sets of expectations could, according to the theory, give rise to yield curves with multiple humps—but such curves seldom if ever appear.

---

[6] There is a limit to the steepness of the negative slope of the curve, which is set by the opportunity for pure arbitrage. Assume, for example, that the 1-year rate is 4 percent and that the 2-year rate is only 2 percent. Then one could borrow $1 million at 2 percent and invest it at 4 percent and at the end of 1 year have sufficient funds to repay at the end of 2 years—keeping as profit whatever one could earn from investing the $1 million for the second year.

### Formal Statement of the Theory

To generalize and formalize the theory, it is necessary to introduce additional notation to set the time dimension of investment. We attach prescripts $t, t + 1, t + 2$, and so on to the variables $R$ and $r$ to indicate the *dates* on which the variables are observed or are expected to be observed. Let $_tR_1, _tR_2, \ldots$, and so on, represent the current yields on securities of $1, 2, \ldots$, periods to maturity existing at a moment in time, $t$, and let $_{t+1}r_1, _{t+1}r_2, \ldots$, represent the yields on securities of $1, 2, \ldots$, periods to maturity that are expected to prevail in the future at time $t + 1$. Capital $R$s represent *current* or spot rates and the lowercase $r$s represent *forward* rates, the rates expected to prevail in the future at time $t + 1$. The prescript to the $R$ tells us at what point in time we are observing current rates, the subscript tells the length of time to maturity of the security being observed. Because $r$ represents forward rates, the prescript indicates the future date on which we expect to observe (estimate) the forward rate; the subscript, as in the case of $R$, represents the length of time to maturity. Thus, if $t =$ January 1, 1989 and the rate on 1-year bills on that date is 5 percent, then $_tR_1 = 5$ percent, or $.05$; and, if on this same date, $t$, the forward rate, which is the rate that will exist on the future date $t + 1$ (or January 1, 1990), on a 1-year security is 6 percent, then $_{t+1}r_1 = .06$.[7]

This notation is complex, but it becomes less confusing as we interpret the formula. Making the simplifying assumption that all coupon payments are accumulated and paid out upon maturity, then in the case of a 2-period holding period,

$$(1 + _tR_2) = [(1 + _tR_1)(1 + _{t+1}r_1)]^{1/2}$$

This formula says that the yield on a 2-year security will equal the geometric mean of the current (spot) rate on a 1-year security and the forward 1-year rate. As in our earlier example, if the spot 1-year rate is 3 percent ($_tR_1 = .03$) and the 1-year-forward 1-year rate is 5 percent ($_{t+1}r_1 = .05$), then the spot 2-year rate may be found from $\sqrt{(1.03)(1.05)} = 1.039+$, or $_tR_2 =$ approximately $.0399$.

As an investor, one has two choices: One may purchase a 2-year bond that yields 3.9 percent; alternatively, one may purchase a 1-year bond that yields 3 percent and reinvest the proceeds at the end of 1 year at the forward rate of 5 percent so as to obtain an overall yield of 3.99 percent. Thus, if one plans to hold bonds for a period of 2 years (the holding period) and if one wishes to maximize the holding period yield, then either course of action will give the same yield. If the current 2-year rate happened to be above 3.99 percent, the investor would buy the 2-year securities, and other investors would also buy them until the prices rose and the yield fell into line with the 3.99 percent. That is, anytime that the rates in question were out of line with the formula, investors with sufficiently large sums to invest would bid for securities in a way that would return them to balance.

---

[7] The notation follows that suggested by David Meiselman, *The Term Structure of Interest Rates* (Englewood Cliffs, N.J.: Prentice-Hall, 1962).

Use of the simple arithmetic average of two percentages, 3 and 5, in our first example gave an average of 4 percent. The geometric mean was only slightly different, 3.99 percent. This difference seems small, but it is significant; in many cases, the difference would not be small. It is important to remember that we used a simple arithmetic average of percentages only to present an intuitively understandable example. In real-life situations, one *must* use the geometric mean to obtain correct results.

The examples we have provided thus far have used rates for only two periods: today's rates and rates expected to prevail one year from today. The formula can easily be extended several periods into the future. An investor may consider purchasing a 10-year bond at today's current yield, $_tR_{10}$, or a 1-year security with current yield $_tR_1$, knowing the expected 1-year yields for each of the following 9 years, $_{t+1}r_1, _{t+2}r_1, \ldots$ $_{t+9}r_1$. On the basis of these actual and expected values, an investor may choose either to buy the 10-year security or to make 10 successive annual investments in 1-year securities.

The relevant formula, for $N$ periods into the future, is

$$(1 + _tR_N) = [(1 + _tR_1)(1 + _{t+1}r_1)(1 + _{t+2}r_1) \ldots (1 + _{t+N-1}r_1)]^{1/N}$$

Thus, the current or spot yield on a bond of $N$ years to maturity is equal to the $N$th root of the product of the current 1-year rate and all of the remaining forward 1-year rates (the geometric mean).

Let us glance at a matrix (Table 13–1) of symbols for spot and forward rates. The first column, labeled "Today's Spot Rates," is a column of $R$s. One may call a broker, or look in a newspaper, to find today's yields on government securities and fill in the values of these $R$s. These are given to us by the market. The $R$s are known. The other columns represent unknown rates at dates in the future. For example, the second column headed by "$t + 1$" indicates the set of rates that will be observed *next period* on securities with 1, 2, 3, . . . $N$ periods to maturity. Similarly, the column

#### TABLE 13–1
#### A Matrix of Spot and Forward Rates

| Maturity | Today's Spot Rates $t$ | Implied Forward Rates Implicit in the Structure of Today's Spot Rates | | | |
|---|---|---|---|---|---|
| | | $t + 1$ | $t + 2$ | $t + 3$ | $t + N - 1$ |
| 1 period | $_tR_1$ | $_{t+1}r_1$ | $_{t+2}r_1$ | $_{t+3}r_1$ $\cdots$ | $_{t+N-1}r_1$ |
| 2 periods | $_tR_2$ | $_{t+1}r_2$ | $_{t+2}r_2$ | $_{t+3}r_2$ $\cdots$ | $_{t+N-1}r_2$ |
| 3 periods | $_tR_3$ | $_{t+1}r_3$ | $_{t+2}r_3$ | $_{t+3}r_3$ $\cdots$ | $_{t+N-1}r_3$ |
| 4 periods | $_tR_4$ | $_{t+1}r_4$ | $_{t+2}r_4$ | $_{t+3}r_4$ $\cdots$ | $_{t+N-1}r_4$ |
| . | . | . | . | . | . |
| . | . | . | . | . | . |
| . | . | . | . | . | . |
| $n$ periods | $_tR_n$ | $_{t+1}r_n$ | $_{t+2}r_n$ | $\cdots$ | $_{t+N-1}r_n$ |

headed "$t + 2$" represents the set of rates that will turn out to be the set of spot rates 2 periods from now.

Items in the matrix appear in the formula expressing the expectations approach to the term structure. For example, the 2-period spot rate $_tR_2$, in the first column, equals the geometric average of the first two items in the top *row*, $_tR_1$ and $_{t+1}r_1$. Similarly, $_tR_3$ is the geometric average of the first three items in the top *row*. Going down to the bottom of the first column, to $_tR_n$, we find that this is the geometric average of all the items in the top row, according to the theory.

But an investor need not choose only between, say, a 10-year bond and ten 1-year securities; the range of choice is much wider. He or she may choose to buy a 9-year bond, hold it until maturity, and then buy a 1-year security to complete a 10-year holding period. Or, an investor may purchase 5 successive 2-year securities, or 2 successive 5-year securities, or any of a variety of patterns. The general formula fits all patterns that he or she may consider. For example, the yield on a 10-year security, $_tR_{10}$, is equal to the geometric average of the current yield on a 9-year security, $_tR_9$, and the yield expected to prevail on a 1-year security purchased 9 years from today, $_{t+9}r_1$. This formula may be written in general terms by substituting $(1 + _tR_{N-1})$ for the first $_{N-1}$ terms within the brackets in the preceding equation so that the formula becomes

$$(1 + _tR_n) = [(1 + _tR_{n-1})^{n-1}(1 + _{t+n-1}r_1)]^{1/N}$$

If $N = 10$, this formula reads as follows: the current 10-year bond yield will equal the geometric mean of the current 9-year bond yield carried to the ninth power and the forward 1-year rate expected to prevail 9 years from today.

Thus, according to pure expectations theory, today's long-term rate is determined by the geometric mean of the successive forward 1-period rates, and one may purchase 10 successive 1-period securities or a 9-period security and a 1-period security, or any combination of maturities for a 10-year period and realize the same earned income over the entire period. Indeed, the formula is constructed so that an investor wishing to hold a security for, say, 2 periods can purchase a 10-year bond and sell it at the end of the second period and realize the same *holding-period* yield as if he or she purchased a 2-year security at the outset. Any combination of purchases is satisfactory if the equation holds true.

Another view of the theory is gained by turning the formula around. By transformation of terms, place the forward yield on the left-hand side of the equation. For an example, return to our 2-period equation:

$$(1 + _tR_2) = [(1 + _tR_1)(1 + _{t+1}r_1)]^{1/2}$$

square both sides to get

$$(1 + _tR_2)^2 = (1 + _tR_1)(1 + _{t+1}r_1)$$

divide by $(1 + {}_tR_1)$

$$\frac{(1 + {}_tR_2)^2}{(1 + {}_tR_1)} = 1 + {}_{t+1}r_1$$

or

$${}_{t+1}r_1 = \frac{(1 + {}_tR_2)^2}{(1 + {}_tR_1)} - 1$$

In general notation for $N$ periods, the formula becomes

$${}_{t+N-1}r_1 = \frac{(1 + {}_tR_N)^N}{(1 + {}_tR_{N-1})^{N-1}} - 1$$

On the right-hand side of the formula, we have only the current interest rates that we observe in today's marketplace. By using these we can "estimate" all forward rates; that is, currently observable rates *imply* what forward rates are expected to be.[8]

If we let $N$ in the formula be 10, and if ${}_tR_n$ is 8 percent, then the numerator in the fraction on the right side is $(1.08)$ to the tenth power, or 2.159. In the denominator a value of ${}_tR_{N-1}$ of 7.9 percent is $(1.079)$ to the ninth power, or 1.982. Dividing denominator into numerator and subtracting 1 gives a value for ${}_{t+N-1}r_1$ of 8.93 percent. Presumably, according to the pure expectations approach, this implies that investors expect the 1-year yield on securities 9 years from today to be 8.93 percent.

In this implicit form, the theory uses the currently observable yield structure to explain current expectations of forward rates; the theory does *not* use expected rates to explain the current level of long-term rates, as it appeared to do in the early formula. We began to explain term structure, and expectations were to be an explanation, but in this implicit form of the equation, we find that we are explaining expectations rather than the term structure. The expectations approach began by saying that long-term rates are determined by expectations, but in this form expectations are determined by long-term rates. To say that, given a yield curve, expected rates can be predicted does not explain the yield curve.[9]

A theory should enable analysts to predict changes, for example, to explain how a future rate would change in response to a change in an *expected* future rate. Most analysts do not use the theory for this purpose; most of them use the implicit form of the equation to show what the market is predicting for future interest rates. This

---

[8] In this form the equation can easily become a tautology; $r$ is the forward rate that people must expect if the current term structure gives us the $R$s.

[9] In spite of the problems just discussed, many authors praise the expectations approach because "it tells you what the market is predicting about future short-term interest rates just by looking at the slope of the yield curve." See Frederic S. Mishkin, *The Economics of Money, Banking, and Financial Markets* (Boston: Little, Brown, 1986), p. 147.

assumes the theory is correct, but we do not know whether the theory is correct because we cannot observe *expected* future rates.

Note also that nothing is said in expectations theory about supply of securities. Expectations theory is a theory of the term structure of interest rates being determined by *demand* for securities; changes in supply of securities have no influence.

## Liquidity Premium

A "liquidity premium" or "liquidity preference" adjustment can be attached to either the segmented markets or the expectations approach. If there is a general preference for "liquidity," the demand for securities based on expectations alone can be supplemented by an additional demand for the *shorter-term* maturities because of their greater liquidity. This liquidity premium suggests that lenders will bid more strongly for short-term securities, driving their price up and their yield down; thus, positively sloped yield curves should be more prevalent than negatively sloped yield curves, which fits the casual observation of yield curves. Throughout history, yield curves have been more often positively sloped than they have been negatively sloped. Under the expectations approach, one might suppose that roughly half the time investors expect future short-term rates to rise and that half the time they would expect future short-term rates to fall. Thus, roughly half the time the yield curve would be positively sloped and half the time negatively sloped. Because yield curves are positively sloped more frequently than they are negatively sloped, adding the "liquidity premium" to account for this improves the explanatory power of the theory.[10]

Reuben A. Kessel studied both the evidence and theory of the term structure and found that addition of a liquidity premium to the expectations theory greatly enhanced its explanatory power. He argued that the short-term forward rate should be viewed not merely as an expected rate, but as an expected rate minus a premium for liquidity because short and long maturities are not perfect substitutes for one another. He found that expectations inferred from short-term portions of yield curves were biased upward, in comparison with the actual rates found in yield curves for succeeding periods. If bias were caused merely by error, why shouldn't the error be random—sometimes above and sometimes below actual future yields? Kessel stated, therefore,

---

[10] Downward-sloping yield curves seemed to prevail during the early 1900s. This would appear at first glance to cast doubt on the liquidity premium hypothesis. However, during this period commercial banks operated under national banking laws that required them to hold certain long-term government securities as reserves against note issues. At the same time, the national debt was falling, and such bonds were being retired from circulation. In a sense, these bonds provided liquidity to banks, and the short supply of them meant higher prices and lower yields. Thus, the yield curve could have been merely reflecting this liquidity factor. See R. H. Scott, "A 'Liquidity' Factor Contributing to Those Downward Sloping Yield Curves, 1900–1916," *Review of Economics and Statistics*, August 1963, pp. 328–329; also see Jean M. Gray, "New Evidence on the Term Structure of Interest Rates, 1884–1900," *Journal of Finance*, Vol. 28, June 1973, pp. 635–646.

The joining of liquidity preferences to expectations explains the lack of symmetry in the movement of short- and long-term rates over the cycle. It explains why short-term rates do not exceed long-term rates at peaks by as much as they fall below long-term rates at troughs; why yield curves are positively sloped during most of the cycle; and why yield curves, when short-term rates are unusually high, never seem to be negatively sloped throughout their full length, but show humps near the short end.[11]

The yield curves of Figure 13–7 suggest the effects that Kessel refers to in this quotation.[12] The top curve is a hypothetical market yield curve; it is the result of adding the other two curves. Note that the bottom curve refers to the value of the liquidity premium that investors require if they are to be induced to purchase a security; this premium is generally greater (at least to a certain point) as maturity is longer. The middle curve indicates the structure of rates that would prevail, given only investors' expectations about forward yields. The top curve, showing the actual market yields, is (as stated) the result of the addition of the liquidity premium to the expected yield. In this view, the hump in the curve is explained not by expectations but by a liquidity premium.

Academic economists use the expectations approach often, but nonacademic financial analysts nearly always use the segmented markets approach. One reason why the theorists and practitioners differ so widely is the difficulty in observing "expectations."[13] Unless one can observe *changes* in expectations from period to period, one can never use *observed* changes in expectations to predict changes in the yield curve. And the purpose of any theory is to provide a framework useful in predicting future events.

Use of the expectations approach rests on the assumption that securities in a certain group (such as government securities) are homogeneous or nearly so.[14] The segmented markets approach does not regard them as homogeneous. A liquidity premium resulting in higher prices (lower yields) for short-term securities may be included with either approach. As Figure 13–7 suggests, existence of a liquidity premium does not necessarily imply that yield curves must always be upward sloping; it simply implies that short-term rates will be lower (and prices of short-term securities higher) than they *otherwise would be.*

---

[11] Reuben A. Kessel, *The Cyclical Behavior of the Term Structure of Interest Rates*, Occasional Paper 91 (New York: National Bureau of Economic Research, 1965), p. 88.

[12] This figure is adapted from ibid.

[13] Hamburger and Latta compared methods of estimating "expected interest rates." See their article, "The Term Structure of Interest Rates: Some Additional Evidence," *Journal of Money, Credit, and Banking*, February 1969, pp. 71–83, and a reply by Richard Sutch and Franco Modigliani in the same issue, pp. 112–120.

[14] Homogeneity has been accepted by many economists who have studied yield curves. However, some studies do not support this assumption. One study indicated that, in tests using a disaggregated structural model including 10 categories of investors, short-term and intermediate-term government securities cannot be regarded as perfect or nearly perfect substitutes for long-term government securities, and that a change in the supply of Treasury securities has an impact on the yield curve. See V. Vance Roley, "The Determinants of the Treasury Security Yield Curve," *Journal of Finance*, December 1981, pp. 1103–1126.

FIGURE 13–7
How Liquidity Premium Affects Yields

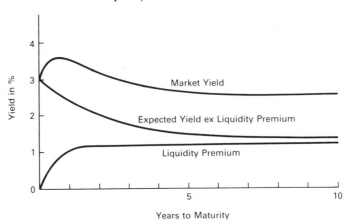

Years to Maturity

## Expected Changes in Long-Term Rates

The "pure" expectations approach is chiefly concerned with expectations about future short-term rates, but many observers suggest that expected changes in *long-term* rates have a very significant effect on term structure.

If, for example, interest rates are judged to be "high" by normal (historical) standards, why are short-term rates above long-term rates, as the evidence clearly shows they are at some times? [See Figures 13–2(a), 13–2(b), and 13–2(c).] An answer is that (1) lenders may at such times buy long-term securities in the belief that yields will soon fall back to their normal level (prices of long-term securities will rise), and they may avoid short-term issues, and (2) borrowers may wish to borrow short, so they issue short-term securities rather than long-term securities because they believe that long-term yields will soon fall back to their normal range. Why borrow long term in such a situation?

If long-term yields are high, borrowers who normally would issue 20-year bonds will "wait" until the long-term yields return to their normal range. To finance their current programs, however, they are willing to pay high yields on short-term issues, believing that they can "fund" their debt at a later time at lower interest rates. The attitude of lenders reinforces that of borrowers. Hence the yield curve will be downward sloping because of a large demand for short-term funds and a slack supply and because of a large supply of long-term funds and slack demand.

In a period when interest rates are low by historical standards, the pressures on the yield curve are just the opposite. Lenders believe that interest rates will soon rise (prices of securities will fall), so they avoid buying long-term securities. Instead, they buy short-term securities, and this drives short-term yields down relative to long-term yields. Again, borrowers reinforce this by selling as much long-term debt as they can while yields are believed to be below their "normal" range.

Thus it is argued that the cyclical pattern of interest rates reflects the normal response of profit-maximizing lenders and borrowers who have experienced the oscillation of yields in the past. In a booming economy, borrowers supply large amounts of short-term securities to the market, but in an economy during a recession they may supply more long-term securities. Thus changes in supply and demand occur over a business cycle—changes that lead to the type of oscillation in the yield curve that we regularly observe.

Warren L. Smith expressed many of these considerations succinctly:

> let us consider a situation in which the consensus of expectations on the part of borrowers and lenders is that interest rates are going to rise in the near future . . . lenders would have a tendency to eschew long-term securities, because they would expect to suffer capital losses on investments in such securities when interest rates rose and because they would feel that it was preferable to hold back and wait until prices of longer-term securities fell before investing in them. Investors with this kind of expectations would tend to shift their flow of funds toward shorter-term loans and securities. . . . Borrowers, on the other hand, would tend to make a reverse shift. To the extent that they felt that interest rates were going to rise, they would feel that the present was an auspicious time to borrow at long-term in order to take maximum advantage of the existing relatively low rates. As a consequence of the shift of supply from the long- to short-term market and the shift of demand from the short- to the long-term market, the long-term rate would tend to rise relative to the short-term rate, thus producing an upward-sloping yield curve. Under circumstances in which interest rates were expected to fall, precisely the opposite kinds of shifts would tend to occur. Supply would shift from the short- to the long-term market and demand from the long- to the short-term market, thus producing a rise in the short-term rate relative to the long-term rate and a downward-sloping yield curve.[15]

Warren Smith's explicit introduction of capital gains and losses necessitates further comment on the concept of "holding-period yield." Suppose that the short-term rate is currently 2 percent and is expected to rise to 4 percent in the next period, and to 6 percent in the following period. In the first period, the long-term rate would be approximately 3 percent, if the assumption of perfect substitutability held true. But, if perfect substitutability exists, why should anyone accept 2 percent on short-term securities when he or she can obtain 3 percent on long-term securities? The answer is that, if expectations are correct (or are believed to be correct) and the short-term rate does rise to 4 percent and then to 6 percent, the long-term rate will rise in the second period, and *holders* of long-term securities will suffer a capital loss if they sell the securities. Their total yield (coupon yield minus capital loss) on a 2-year security over a 1-year holding period may be approximately the same as that obtained by the holder of 1-year securities. The yield over a 2-year holding period will be a 3 percent coupon rate (or yield to maturity at the time of purchase) minus a capital loss, the amount of which would depend on the term to maturity. If the security were a

---

[15] Warren L. Smith, *Debt Management in the United States*, Study Paper 19, materials prepared in connection with the study of employment, growth, and price levels for the Joint Economic Committee, 86th Cong., 2nd sess., January 28, 1960, p. 82.

2-year security, there would be no capital loss over the 2-year holding period, but on any longer-term security, there would be a capital loss, increasing with the length of maturity of the security. On a 10-year bond, the capital loss would be slightly more than 8 percent. This fact suggests that, although securities with only small differences in length of maturity may be close substitutes, there is doubt about the substitutability of securities with great differences in maturity for any holders who may have to sell before maturity.

## SOME EMPIRICAL EVIDENCE ON THE THEORY OF THE TERM STRUCTURE

David Meiselman attempted to shore up the expectations theory by drawing certain implications from the expectations approach and testing these implications.[16] He proposed an "error-learning" model; that is, he suggested that, if investors made errors when they forecast the forward 1-year rate, they would revise their next forecast of the 1-year rate by some proportion of the previous error. To test this theory, he ran statistical estimates of a formula of the general form[17]

$$\Delta r = a + b(R - r)$$

On the left we have the change in expected future short-term rates, and this is thought to be related to the difference between the actual rate today, $R$, and the rate that was expected to prevail today, $r$. This difference $(R - r)$ represents the error in expectations, and $\Delta r$ represents the revision of expectations. Investors are presumed to revise their expectations when they "learn" they have erred. Therefore, it is called an error-learning model.

Professor Meiselman's equations had good fit to the data, and this was widely heralded as an indirect confirmation of the expectations theory. What was tested, of course, was whether *presumed* expected rates, revised on the basis of errors, could explain changes in the pattern of rates. Because expectations were not observed, the expectations theory was not tested directly.

---

[16] Meiselman, *The Term Structure of Interest Rates.*

[17] The formula he actually used looked like this:

$$_{t+N}r_{1,t} - {}_{t+N}r_{1,t-1} = a + b({}_tR_1 - {}_tr_{1,t-1})$$

In this equation we have introduced a second subscript attached to $r$. This subscript designates the date on which the expected forward rate is assumed to have been anticipated. Thus, if today is January 1, 1984, then $t - 1$ is January 1, 1983. If $N$ is 3, then $_{t+N}r_{1,t-1}$ is the rate on a one-year security that, as of January 1, 1984, was expected to prevail on January 1, 1987. The left-hand side of the equation shows the difference between the expected 1-year rate, expected to prevail at time $t + N$, and the one-year rate that a year earlier had been expected to prevail at this time $(t + N)$. Thus, the left-hand side of the equation depicts the revision of the forecast of the forward 1-year rate. The right-hand side of the equation shows the difference between the actual 1-year rate today and the 1-year rate that a year earlier had been expected to prevail today. Thus the right-hand side depicts the error in forecasting the current 1-year rate.

## Surveys of Interest Rate Expectations

Others have tried to test expectations directly by sending questionnaires to market participants. Malkiel and Kane selected a sample of 119 banks, 16 life insurance companies and 65 nonfinancial corporations. They received responses from 57 percent of the firms.[18] They asked for predictions of forward rates, among other questions. Without a detailed examination of their study—which merits the attention of the serious student—we wish to note their conclusions:

> Our various findings each support a single conclusion: that the demands for various maturities of debt are not infinitely elastic at going rates and, therefore, that changes in the relative supplies of different maturities . . . can alter the term structure. That expectations are not uniform but nevertheless influence investors' appraisals of market opportunities suggests that in order to induce investors to hold more of any maturity, it is necessary to accept a rise in the associated rate.[19]

The Goldsmith-Nagan "Bond and Money Market Letter," published in Washington, D.C., contains information about forthcoming Treasury needs and other matters affecting the market outlook. For several years it has also conducted a survey of the forward rates expected by a group of individuals who work with and advise banks, investment houses, and at times about the interest rate outlook.[20] The group varies slightly in size from report to report but runs in the neighborhood of 30 persons, most of whom participate in each group forecast. The forecasts are made each quarter, and the averages of forecasts of the participants are printed in the "Letter." Forecasts are for yields on securities 2 and 5 months in the future. The securities are Treasury bills, notes, bonds, Aaa utility bonds, the discount rate, and so forth.

It might appear that surveys of expectations would be good measures of market expectations that could be used to test the expectations theory of the term structure. Unfortunately, there is a fundamental problem with such an approach. Assume, as in the earlier example, that 1- and 2-year interest rates today were 3.0 and 3.9 percent, respectively. These market rates imply that the "market" expects the 1-year rate to be about 5 percent a year from today (4.8 percent to be more precise). Now assume that a sample of opinions by market experts is obtained, and the average forecast is that a year from today the 1-year rate will be 4 percent. Could one then say that the expectations theory is in error? The answer is no, because an excuse for the difference between the 5 percent "market" predicted and the 4 percent the sample of individuals predicted would be attributed to the failure to have a comprehensive sample. But even if a sample of opinions covered every individual in the country, would the theory be rejected? Still the answer is no, because one would always be able to presume that the sample of opinions collected simply did not represent "true" opinion. Opinions defy scientific measurement, although they are often interesting to read about.

---

[18] Edward J. Kane and Burton G. Malkiel, "The Term Structure of Interest Rates: An Analysis of a Survey of Interest-Rate Expectations," *Review of Economics and Statistics*, August 1967, pp. 343–355.

[19] Ibid., p. 354.

[20] See the issue of October 4, 1979 for the first survey.

The opinions reported by Goldsmith-Nagan were compared with the "market's" opinion by Adrian Throop.[21] The comparison was not reported upon directly; that is, the reader of Throop's article was not told directly about the extent of differences between the forecast implicit in the current spot rate structure (the "market's" forecast) and the forecast made by the group of experts. Instead, the two forecasts were compared with the actual rates that came to pass. The questions addressed were, Which of the two forecasts turned out to be the most accurate? And how does their accuracy compare with a naive forecast?

Naive forecasts take several forms. One is a forecast that simply says that interest rates will be just the same in 6 months as they are today, that is, the forecast is one of no change. Another form of naive forecast is that the past change will be repeated. If rates rose 1 percent last month, then they will rise 1 percent again this month. A naive forecast is simply one that can be made mechanically and without any analysis.

The root mean squared error (RMSE) is a form of average. It is found by taking the difference between the forecasted rate and the actual rate that occurred—this is the error in the forecast. This value is squared. All the errors observed over the sample period are squared, and then added together, and then averaged by dividing by the number of observations. The result is the mean or average of the squared errors. The square root of this average is then calculated to find the RMSE.

| FORECAST | RMSE |
|----------|------|
| Naive (no change) | 1.25 |
| Market (implied) | 1.24 |
| Goldsmith-Nagan | 1.10 |
| Autoregressive | .94 |

The findings relating to forecasts of interest rates on Treasury bills were that the naive forecast of no change was in error by $\pm 1.25$ percentage points, on average. Sometimes it was off by more than this amount, and at times by less than this amount. On average, if today's rate is 10 percent, it would typically turn out to be either 1.25 percent more or 1.25 percent less than 10 percent. The error in the forecast implied by the current term structure was 1.24 percent, and this finding is consistent with many tests that have discovered that, if the implied forward rate is taken as the "market's" forecast, then the market is incapable of forecasting accurately. That is, the "market's" forecasts are wrong in the sense that they are no better than one could do by predicting no change in rates.

The experts surveyed by Goldsmith-Nagan do marginally better. Their error is only $\pm 1.10$ percent. Since the experts' forecasts are slightly better than the "market's" forecasts, this implies that the experts' and market's forecasts were different.

---

[21] Adrian Throop, "Interest Rate Forecasts and Market Efficiency," Federal Reserve Bank of San Francisco, *Economic Review*, Spring 1981, pp. 29–43.

Should we conclude that the sample of market expectations solicited from the experts was a poor sample and a poor measure of market expectations? Or, should we conclude that interest rates do not depend upon market expectations and that interest rates are not really explained by market expectations as the theory suggests? There is no way for us to decide which conclusion to draw from this analysis.

The autoregressive structure, for which the RMSE was only .94 percent, is a type of naive forecast. Past patterns of interest rate changes are forecast into the future. Using this type of mechanized forecast, one can outperform even the experts in the accuracy of predictions if the results found by Throop hold in the future.

A means of "observing" expectations about future Treasury bill rates has developed since the Chicago-based International Money Market (IMM) and the Commodity Exchange, Incorporated (COMEX) in New York, and other exchanges now offer futures markets in selected U.S. Treasury bills.[22] Investors can arrange a contract today to buy bills at a fixed price several months in the future. Speculators are active in the futures market—selling future securities if they believe that when the day arrives they can buy them at a lower price and deliver them to their customer and make some profit in the process. Thus, an "expected future price" is presumably an element in the behavior of speculators in this market. Several attempts have been made to compare this "expected future price" with the expected price (or yield) implied by the term structure of interest rates. One sophisticated study concluded "that futures rates are significantly different from the associated [implied from the term structure] forward rates."[23] However, others found little difference in the two estimates of expected future rates and little reason to expect to find differences.

One reason that we might expect to find differences was pointed out by Sir John Hicks. He argued that the current futures price of a security in today's market would have to be lower than the price that the speculator really believes will prevail in the future because the speculator is assuming some risk, and he or she must be compensated for this risk-assuming action. To compensate for this risk it follows that today's futures price will be lower than what is really expected to prevail when the contract becomes due. In terms of yield, this means that today's futures yield will be higher than the yield that speculators really believe will exist at the future date. But it is nearly impossible to discover such differences within the current state of statistical art.

There have been many tests of the impact of changes in supplies of Treasury securities on the level of yields and on the difference between short- and long-term yields. These tests, of course, were designed to see whether supply changes affect

[22] Practical use is already being made of this market in making interest rate forecasts; see C. Richard Cross, William C. Dale, and David Meiselman, "T-Bill Futures and the Term Structure of Interest Rates," *Monetary Perspective*, Vol. 1, No. 10, May 28, 1976, Bache Halsey Stuart, Inc., New York, New York.

[23] Richard W. Lang and Robert H. Rasche, "A Comparison of Yields on Futures Contracts and Implied Forward Rates," Federal Reserve Bank of St. Louis, *Review*, December 1978, pp. 21–30. Also see Louis H. Ederington, "The Hedging Performance of the New Futures Market," *Journal of Finance*, March 1978, pp. 157–170. This article contains a good list of references on theoretical and practical aspects of hedging.

yields, as suggested by the segmented markets approach. Because, under the expectations approach, changes in supply are presumed to have no effect, any evidence of some effect would tend to refute the expectations approach and support the segmented markets approach.

The controversy over the theory of the term structure provides an interesting example of a conflict in scientific theory. Practitioners seem to prefer the segmented markets approach; academics often prefer the abstract elegance of the expectations approach. The two approaches lead to divergent policy conclusions: the one suggests that monetary authorities can affect the yield curve by varying the volume of securities in the various maturity ranges; the other suggests that attempts to do so will surely fail. Testing for empirical verification of the two theories is fraught with difficulties—those relating to the selection of variables affecting supply and demand and those relating to the measurement (observation) of elusive expectations. As mentioned in the previous chapter with regard to expected rates of inflation, the use of expectations as a variable may be nonscientific because, if expectations as revealed fail to support the theory, an investigator may be led to reject his or her sample of expectations rather than to reject the theory itself. Theories with this characteristic are called nonoperational—the assumptions of the theory are such as to make it impossible to refute by empirical methods. Thus, persons who use the expectations hypothesis frequently end up with a rationalization of the current term structure rather than with an explanation. They argue that the currently observable term structure implies what expectations of future short-term yields must be—the very opposite of arguing that expectations determine the current term structure of rates.[24]

What is needed is a theory of the determination of expectations. To say that forward rates determine the yield curve is to beg the question, "How are these expectations determined?" If they are determined by supply and demand, then we are right back to the segmented markets approach. If they are determined by investors' appraisals of the current level of interest rates in relation to what they believe to be the "normal" or "typical" level of long-term rates, then further empirical study should be undertaken to discover how these beliefs come to be held.

### The Accuracy of the Market's Forecasts

Proponents of the pure expectations approach correctly point out that the theory itself cannot be rejected just because the implied forecasts of market investors turn out to be wrong a significantly large part of the time. All the theory implies is that investors hold those expectations at the time the yield curve is drawn. Is this an adequate defense of the theory?

To consider this question let us draw some implications about the accuracy of market forecasts calculated from the expectations equations. First, over time interest

[24] John T. Emery and Robert H. Scott, "Evidence on Expected Yields Implied from the Term Structure and the Futures Market," *Business Economics*, Vol. 14, May 1979, pp. 22–27. See also Bradford Cornell and Marc R. Reingnam, "Forward and Futures Prices," *Journal of Finance*, December 1981, pp. 1035–1046.

rates rise and fall as the result of macroeconomic conditions. When interest rates rise over time, it is usually the case that both long and short rates rise. When they fall, both fall. Second, when the level of rates rises generally, short-term rates rise more than long-term rates and the yield curve often becomes downward sloping. When rates fall, short-term rates often fall more than long-term rates and the yield curve becomes positively sloped. To see this in an abstract example, let us glance at Figure 13–8.

Assume that we begin in an initial period when the yield curve is horizontal. The yield curve is labeled 0. Assume that rates rise generally in subsequent periods 1 and 2. The yield curves of periods 1 and 2 assume steeper downward slopes as interest rates rise in the two subsequent periods. Consider now period 1 when the 1-period rate is $_tR_1$ and the 2-period rate is $_tR_2$ as shown. Using these rates to calculate the implied forward 1-period rate, $_{t+1}r_1$, gives the lower rate as shown. The downward slope implies that investors expect short-term rates to fall. But, if rates rise generally during the time from period 1 to period 2, the *actual* 1-period rate in period 2 will be $_{t+1}R_1$. It will not be $_{t+1}r_1$. The *actual* rate would be higher, whereas the presumed expected rate would be lower. The market's forecast of the *direction* of movement in rates turns out to be incorrect. The market was forecasting a decline, and an increase occurred instead.

Using the same reasoning but starting with the top downward-sloping yield curve labeled 2, and moving downward to curves 1 and 0, gives the opposite conclusion. The market's forecast of a decline in short-term yields next period turns out to be in the correct direction, as a decline actually takes place.

**FIGURE 13–8**

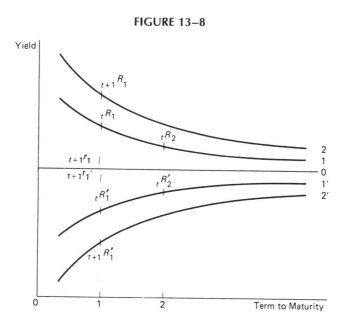

Starting from the horizontal yield curve again and assuming that yields fall to 1′ and 2′ in subsequent periods, the reasoning implies that when yield curve 1 exists, the market's forecast is for higher short-term rates next period. But when period 2 arrives, the actual yield turns out to be lower, not higher, and the direction of the forecast was incorrect. As the yield curve returns to its horizontal level, the market's forecast will be in the correct direction.

Thus, as the level of yields departs from the horizontal, forecasts will be in the wrong direction. And as yields return to the horizontal level, forecasts will be in the right direction. Forecasts will be in the wrong direction half of the time, and in the right direction half of the time.

Consider yield curve 1 again. According to the theory, market investors expect short-term yields to fall. But why would they expect yields to fall if experience has shown that half of the time yields fall and half of the time they rise? The rational expectation to hold would be that yields will not change from their current structure and level.

Statistical evidence indicated that one could not reject the hypothesis that the market's forecast of the direction of change in yields is wrong 50 percent of the time.[25]

# THE THEORY OF THE TERM STRUCTURE AND ECONOMIC POLICY

Economists paid relatively little attention to the term structure of interest rates prior to the 1930s. They were concerned principally with the level of rates and the relation of this level to other economic variables. In recent years, the literature on the term structure has ballooned. This strong attention to a rather narrow, detailed subject grew out of a series of events, perhaps beginning with the writings of Keynes in the 1930s. Keynes did not believe that monetary policy could be very strong medicine to cure a depression but that long-term interest rates should be kept low so as to encourage investment spending as much as possible. His principal concern was with long-term interest rates and long-term investment. When World War II began, the entire structure of interest rates was still low in the wake of the Great Depression. The Federal Reserve System "pegged" the market for U.S. government securities at the prevailing yields. (In World War I, the Treasury had issued successive issues of securities, each at a slightly higher yield, so the market for securities dried up as everyone began to wait for the next issue. The Treasury did not want to see this

---

[25] Robert Haney Scott, "Interpreting Intertemporal Movements in Interest Rate Levels in the Light of the Expectation Approach to the Term Structure of Interest Rates," Working Paper No. 38, Center for the Study of Banking and Financial Markets, Graduate School of Business Administration, University of Washington, Seattle, 1986. See also Michael T. Belongia, "Predicting Interest Rates: A Comparison of Professional and Market-Based Forecasts," *Federal Reserve Bank of St. Louis, Review*, March 1987, pp. 9–15. Belongia compared actual changes in interest rates with rates based on expected future rates and with rates forecast by professional economists. Of 90 predictions of the *direction of change* by forecasters, the direction of change was correctly predicted 42 percent of the time. Of 40 predictions derived from the futures market, predictions were correct in nearly 55 percent of the cases.

situation repeated.) To "peg" the yield curve, the Federal Reserve simply bought any securities not bought by the private sector, at prices that maintained yields at fixed levels. In doing this, large volumes of reserves were added to the assets of commercial banks, and because loans were restricted principally to firms with legal priorities for activities related to war production, the banks' excess reserves were used to purchase government securities.

But the yield curve was positively sloped, with very short-term Treasury bills yielding three-eighths of 1 percent and long-term bonds yielding 2½ percent. As the war continued, many portfolio managers recognized that long-term securities were just as "liquid" as short-term securities because of the (unannounced but finally recognizable) Fed purchasing policy. This meant that they did not buy low-yielding short-term securities, and the Federal Reserve's portfolio of short-term issues began to expand by large amounts.

Soon after the war came to an end, the Federal Reserve allowed the short-term rate to rise, but it retained the peg on long-term securities. There was much talk of a postwar recession, which never came about, but the Fed believed that low long-term rates were appropriate in a setting in which the war economy was winding down. After a slight recession in 1948–1949, the economy began to boom again, and in June 1950, the war in Korea broke out. At this point, Federal Reserve officials decided that a measure of restrictive policy might be desirable, and they discussed with Treasury officials their plan to allow long-term rates to rise. But Treasury officials had enjoyed a ready market for their issues at a very low interest rate. They were reluctant to give up this privileged position. In March 1951, the Treasury and Federal Reserve announced their *Accord*. President Truman had been asked to resolve the controversy, and he finally ruled in favor of the Federal Reserve. Thus, long-term interest rates were freed from the peg and began to rise.

In 1953, an ad hoc subcommittee of the Federal Open Market Committee reported on a study of the government securities market. It recommended that open market operations be confined to the market for Treasury bills, except that trading in long-term securities would take place to prevent or subdue any "disorderly conditions" that might develop among long-term issues. The bills market, it was argued, had depth, breadth, and resiliency and was, therefore, the appropriate market to use to adjust member bank reserve positions. The Federal Open Market Committee adopted a resolution that became known as the "bills-only" policy.

When academic economists learned of this policy, some of them questioned its wisdom, and a considerable debate broke out. If, they argued, lower long-term interest rates were desirable, would bill purchases, adding to bank reserves, lead to lower long-term interest rates? Would they not simply lower bill rates, and only after considerable lag would trading along the maturity spectrum bring down the long-term rates? Would it be a better policy if long-term rates were attacked directly by Fed purchases in the long-term range of maturities? If so, this would be more consistent with Keynesian theory.

The debate continued for several years. It was not until 1961 that the Fed abandoned the "bills-only" policy to engage in "operation twist." At that time, the economy was operating at less than full employment, and it was considered desirable to lower long-term rates if possible, through expansionary monetary policy. But, it was also believed that the U.S. balance of payments required *higher* short-term interest rates because, if domestic short-term rates fell too far below foreign short-term rates, U.S. citizens would use dollars to buy foreign money and foreign short-term securities. Thus, the United States would "lose" dollars, adding to our balance-of-payments difficulties. The Fed wanted (1) to lower long-term rates but (2) to avoid lowering short-term rates, which would tend to result from buying short-term securities to expand the money supply. Thus, it abandoned the "bills-only" policy and purchased some long-term government securities. In practice, the Fed still operates on a "bills-usually" policy, operating in the long-term market only on special occasions.

Thus, the Fed had pegged the rate structure during World War II and was forced to continue the peg long after it was desirable to do so. In reaction, it responded by not only refusing to peg the structure, but also by not trading long-term securities at all. But, if long-term interest rates were important for economic stabilization, should it not operate in the long-term market? What is the relation between the long- and short-term markets?

The segmented markets theory suggested that changing relative supplies of long- and short-term securities outstanding, as might be done by Federal Reserve open market operations or by Treasury debt management, would affect the shape of the yield curve and could help achieve overall economic objectives. The expectations theory of the yield curve, on the other hand, suggests that changes in relative supplies have no perceptible effect on the yield curve and therefore that neither the Treasury nor the Federal Reserve should bother to take any action in an attempt to affect it. The controversy will continue until more convincing evidence in support of one of the two theories is provided.

It may be noted that the general model of portfolio choice developed by Tobin and described in the previous chapter is inconsistent with the expectations approach to the term structure of interest rates. Suppose something causes investors to prefer other financial assets rather than bills, and bills are sold while money and/or stocks and bonds are acquired, as indicated:

Money    Bills    Bonds    Stocks

If the Treasury finances a deficit by selling large amounts of T-bills, people will initially have more T-bills and may attempt to sell them, and buy bonds or stocks, or perhaps simply hold money. Prices of T-bills would fall and their yields would rise. But it is quite possible that bidding for bonds and stocks would push bond and stock prices up and yields down. Thus, deficits financed by sales of bills *could* lead to a combination of higher short-term rates and lower long-term yields. The yield curve might have been twisted by this single policy. The twist, as described, would be the result of a change in the outstanding supply of securities in a given maturity range.

According to the expectations approach, expected future interest rates determine bond yields, not changes in the relative supplies of assets. Thus, the two approaches are contradictory.

In the tight money period after October 6, 1979, the yield curve was downward sloping almost continuously until November 1982. Of course, a downward-sloping yield curve implies that the market expected short-term interest rates to fall in the future. But they did not fall until late in 1982. Repeatedly, predictions of a fall were wrong, and the period turned out to be one in which forecasters of future interest rates were notoriously in error. In the fall of 1981, the press was full of speculation about why interest rates did not fall because, by then, two years after a tight money control regime was initiated (as discussed further in Chapter 16), the rate of inflation had fallen drastically. This combination of high interest rates and downward-sloping yield curves raised important issues. The theory discussed in Chapter 12 holds that the nominal interest rate will equal the real interest rate plus the expected rate of inflation, or

$$i = r + (\dot{p}/p)^e$$

and the expectations theory of this chapter implies that the market's expectations about future short-term rates are found in the current term structure,

$$_{t+1}r_1 = \frac{(1 + {}_tR_2)^2}{(1 + {}_tR_1)} - 1$$

The actual rate of inflation began to decline in 1980. But $i$ did not fall. It was argued, therefore, that *expected* inflation as represented by the right-hand term in the first equation, had not come down, although the actual rate of inflation had. In other words, interpreters of market conditions, including Paul A. Volcker, chairman of the Board of Governors of the Federal Reserve System, blamed the continuation of high interest rates on the unwillingness of the "market" to "believe" that the Fed was determined to break the back of inflation. The conclusion was that $i$ remained high because $(\dot{p}/p)^e$ remained high.

But, *at the same time,* the yield curve had a steep downward slope. This slope implied that the "market" believed that interest rates would soon fall! If the market believed that interest rates would fall, it must also have believed that inflation would subside, according to the first equation. Thus, simultaneously, one theory of interest rate levels implied that market expectations were that the inflation would continue and interest rates would remain high, while the theory of the term structure of interest rates implied that market expectations were that interest rates would soon fall (and presumably inflation would subside). The two theories implied exactly opposite market beliefs about the outlook for inflation in this instance. There's an old saying that summarizes the study of logic: you can't have it both ways.

Supply and demand theory and the segmented markets approach can easily explain the financial conditions of this period. The Federal Reserve was restricting the growth of money. It used open market operations to do so. It either sold Treasury bills or bought fewer than it otherwise would have purchased. This reduced the growth of bank reserves. Banks were suppliers of short-term credit to businesses. And recessionary influences kept tax collections low, so the Treasury demanded (borrowed) more funds than before. The combination of increased demand for funds on the part of the Treasury, the reduced supply of funds on the part of the Fed, and the reduced supply available from banks all pushed interest rates up, and short-term interest rates up more than long term. The mystery of expectations and their various influences need not be introduced into this explanation of events. Perhaps it is just as well, because expectations are difficult if not impossible to measure, while quantities of debt supplied and demanded are operationally meaningful variables.

## USES OF YIELD CURVES IN FINANCIAL ANALYSIS

Financial analysts frequently draw a variety of yield curves as they keep track of movements of interest rates on a daily basis. They observe the yields on individual securities over time, and they also compare yields on similar securities. With the yield curve, they can readily compare the yields of securities that differ in respect to maturity.

The first and most obvious reason to plot yield curves is to find an individual security that has a higher yield than other similar securities. If a single plotted point clearly lies above other points, then the analyst must decide whether it is leading the way to higher yields generally or whether its yield is simply out of line with others and will shortly fall into line again. In the latter case, the security represents a "good buy" in comparison with other similar outstanding securities.

A second reason to examine yield curves is to find a place in the time dimension of outstanding securities that looks like a good place to float a new issue. U.S. Treasury officials look at yield curves, and they observe not only the yields but also the volume of outstanding securities in each maturity range. A combination of volume and yield indicates in which maturity range the market will most likely accept (digest) a new issue. Business firms offering a new issue for the market have the same interest in yield curves.

A third motive for drawing yield curves is to lay the ground for analyzing whether or not it would be profitable to "play the pattern of rates" or "ride the curve." Assume, for example, that short-term rates are low and that the curve rises from left to right, but that it levels off at a point about three years to maturity. If the analyst wishes to invest a sum for about 6 months and believes the yield curve is going to remain about this same shape for 6 months, he or she will buy that security situated at 3 years, at the corner of the decline. Then the analyst will allow time to pass and "ride" down over the corner, selling the security in 6 months time. The analyst will have earned more interest than he or she would have if a 6-month-to-maturity issue had been purchased at the outset *and* will also have realized a capital gain that comes about when the price of the security rises concomitant with the decline in yield. Thus the chance for higher rates of return is increased if humps in the curve, or corners in the curve, are evident and are expected to remain.

Let us be more specific about this. Assume that you are an investor and that you want to invest your money for 1 year. At the end of 1 year, you may expect to have to pay a debt, so that 1 year is your time horizon for investment. Assume that you look at today's spot market and find a 1-year note yielding 6 percent, and a 2-year note yielding 7 percent.[26] You can get 6 percent from buying the 1-year note. But what will you get if you buy the 2-year note and sell it at the end of 1 year? This depends on the price that you expect to get from the 2-year note at year's end. At that time it will be a 1-year note. So, you need to forecast what 1-year notes will be yielding a year from now. If, 1 year from now, the yield on a 1-year note has dropped from 6 percent to 5 percent, and the price of the note has increased accordingly, your yield from holding a 2-year security for 1 year will turn out to be 8.85 percent instead of only 7 percent; the extra 1.85 percent is the result of appreciation in price. On the other hand, your yield from holding the 2-year security for 1 year will be only 4.29 percent if prices of 1-year notes fall so that the one-year yield rises to 10 percent a year from now. "In fact, the 2-year note will provide a 7 percent total return over a 1-year period only if 1-year rates are 7 percent one year hence."[27]

It is obvious that the next question is, "What do you suppose 1-year yields will be a year from now?" Say that we know that today's 1-year and 2-year yields are 6 and 7 percent, respectively, as assumed earlier. Now say that we expect *the same* yield structure to exist a year from today. That is, assume we expect the 7 percent 2-year note to yield 6 percent 1 year from today, in line with today's 6 percent yield. Then, if you buy the 2-year note, realize a 7 percent return for the first year, and also realize the appreciation in note price when you sell it in a year's time, you find that the total return made up of both yield and appreciation in value becomes 7.92 percent.

In these examples, for every percentage point decline in yield on a 1-year security, the total return will increase by approximately 92 basis points (.92 percentage points).

But, of course, it all works in the opposite direction, too. Assume that today's 1-year yield is 8 percent and that the 2-year yield is 7 percent, so that the yield curve is downward sloping. In this case, buying the 2-year note with the 7 percent yield and keeping it for a year means that you will receive 7 percent, but when you sell the note it will have fallen in value. So your loss from the decline in value will mean your total return will be only about 6.08 percent instead of 7 percent.

Notice that in the example we have looked at the total return from a 1-year investment in buying a 2-year note as the yield *plus* the appreciation (or minus the depreciation) in capital value that takes place as the year passes. If the yield curve is

---

[26] This example is taken from a study by Martin L. Leibowitz, vice president and manager of the Bond Portfolio Analysis Group, "The Rolling Yield: A New Approach to Yield Curve Analysis," Salomon Brothers, 1977. Also see his subsequent publications by Salomon Brothers, One New York Plaza, N.Y., N.Y., 10004.

[27] Ibid., p. 3.

upward sloping from left to right, then you can buy the longer-term security and "ride the yield" down the slope from 2-year maturity to 1-year maturity to get a return made up of yield and capital appreciation. But, if the yield curve is downward sloping, obviously riding *up* the yield curve will give you a depreciation in capital value that must be subtracted from the stated yield to give a total return that is lower than the stated yield.

The next obvious concern to market analysts, of course, is to recognize that the yield curve will probably not have the same shape a year from today as it has today. Thus, to make estimates of 1-year total return on a 2-year note requires that the analyst specify what the 1-year yield is going to be a year from today. The analyst must articulate the reasons for believing that the yield curve will remain the same, become flatter, or become steeper than it now is. The potential gains from trying to ride down the yield curve can easily be erased by a simple shift in the yield curve's position—in this case it is erased if the entire yield curve shifts up or if only short-term yields shift up.

An investment analyst, therefore, finds that advice to bond portfolio managers requires an understanding of the intricacies of yield curve relations if the analyst is to perform effectively.

On some occasions an investor may be deciding between a 2-year security and a 1-year security. The investor may not have thought about what the 1-year rate will be a year from today. So he asks his financial agent to calculate the implied expected future yield. Assume, as in the earlier example, that the 1-year rate is 3.0 percent and that the 2-year rate is 3.9 percent. He would ask what is the implied 1-year rate expected a year later, and be told that it is 5 percent. Then he can consider whether or not 5 percent is sensible from his own viewpoint. If it is clearly too high, then he chooses the 2-year yield at 3.9 percent. If the 5 percent seems low to him, he would choose the 1-year security and plan to roll it over for a second year at the expected 5 percent rate, or higher. In other words, *he uses the calculation of the implied forward rate as a way of informing himself of the value that the future short-term yield must assume if his decision to buy short-term securities is to turn out to be the correct decision.* He does *not* use the calculation as a forecast. Rather, he uses it merely to discern the decision rules related to his own, independently arrived at, forecasts. Financial analysts say that requests for such calculations are rare, but do come in from time to time.

## SUMMARY

This entire chapter was concerned with one principal factor giving rise to interest rate differences, namely, the difference in term to maturity. The chapter began with description of the construction of yield curves and examples of a variety of yield curves and their behavior over time. Yield curves are usually positively sloped; down-ward-sloping curves do occur frequently, usually at or near peaks of business activity.

Two theories can be used to explain the shape of the yield curve. These theories are the "pure expectations" approach and the "segmented markets" approach. According to the expectations theory, the long-term interest rate equals the geometric average of the several short-term rates expected to prevail during the period to maturity of the long-term security. According to the segmented markets theory, securities are imperfect substitutes for one another. Some investors such as commercial banks seek protection from risk of capital loss; they prefer to invest in short-term securities. Other investors such as life insurance companies and pension funds seek certainty of income and thus favor long-term instruments. In this view, the term structure of rates reflects the different sets of supply and demand conditions in the money and capital markets for securities of different maturities.

These two major theories have different implications for government policies. The expectations approach suggests that attempts to alter the yield structure by changing the relative supplies of securities of different maturities is doomed to failure. The segmented markets theory holds that the yield curve can be twisted by actions of government. More attention is paid to this issue in Chapter 17.

Many economists are likely to take a more eclectic view of the term structure of interest rates and *combine* the various theories. Thus, a "liquidity premium" can be grafted onto the expectations hypothesis to allow for a general preference for liquidity by lenders. This permits uncertainty of future rates and the risk of capital loss to be explicitly introduced into the model. In addition, the eclectic approach would incorporate an important element from the segmented market theory: the risk of instability in interest income. Some investors do prefer long-term securities to reduce this type of risk. One eclectic theory that combines many of these elements was set forth by Modigliani and Sutch; it is referred to as the "preferred habitat" theory. In this view, expectations largely explain the term structure, but risk premiums must also be taken into account. Different market participants have different maturity preferences; risk aversion will lead them to remain in their preferred habitat unless other maturities offer an expected rate premium sufficient to induce them to move out of the preferred maturity.[28]

Some possible uses of the yield curve in economic policy and by financial analysts are to aid in identifying securities with higher yields than those on many similar securities, to find the maturity of a new issue most likely to be "digested" easily by the market, and to analyze whether or not it is likely to be profitable to "ride the yield curve" in buying and selling securities.

## Questions for Discussion

**1.** Does "segmented markets" mean "separated markets"? Explain your answer.

**2.** Distinguish between risk of capital loss and risk of income variability. On which type of security (long or short term) is each type of risk greater?

---

[28] F. Modigliani and R. C. Sutch, "Innovation in Interest Rate Policy," *American Economic Review,* 1966, Papers and Proceedings, pp. 178–197, and "Debt Management and the Term Structure of Interest Rates: An Empirical Analysis of Recent Experience," *Journal of Political Economy,* 1967, pp. 569–589; F. Modigliani and R. J. Schiller, "Inflation, Rational Expectations and the Term Structure of Interest Rates," *Economica,* Vol. 40, 1973, pp. 12–43. For an empirical study following the lines of the Modigliani-Schiller study, see Rose McElhattan, "The Term Structure of Interest Rates and Inflation Uncertainty," Federal Reserve Bank of San Francisco, *Economic Review,* December 1975, pp. 27–35.

**3.** Define the term "liquidity" as it is used in reference to securities. What is a "liquidity premium"?

**4.** List the four simplifying assumptions made under the pure expectations theory of the term structure.

**5.** Under the pure expectations theory, what determines the long-term interest rate? Give a numerical example using a simple average.

**6.** If long-term yields are thought to be above their normal range, what will be the shape of the yield curve? Why?

**7.** Briefly discuss some of the difficulties in measuring or observing expectations.

**8.** What was the Treasury–Federal Reserve *Accord* announced in March 1951?

**9.** Explain the "bills-only" policy of the Fed and its abandonment in pursuing "operation twist."

**10.** Explain how it may be profitable to "play the pattern of rates" or "ride the yield curve."

## Suggested References

For a formal, classic description of the expectations theory with a liquidity premium, see Sir John Hicks, *Value and Capital,* 2nd ed. (Oxford: Clarendon Press, 1946), esp. Chapter 11.

Burton G. Malkiel's book, cited in footnote 2, contains an excellent theory presentation and a broad review of most research efforts devoted to term structure prior to 1966. Another fine description of term structure theory and evidence, tied to macroeconomic theory, is found in Jacob B. Michaelsen, *The Term Structure of Interest Rates: Financial Intermediaries and Debt Management* (New York: Intext Educational Publishers, 1973).

For a discussion of yield curve analysis from the point of view of the financial analyst, see studies by Martin L. Liebowitz, "The Rolling Yield," Parts 1, 2, and 3, Salomon Brothers, 1977.

Reviews of empirical research and policy implications may be found in Robert J. Shiller, John Y. Campbell, and Kermit L. Schoenholtz, "Forward Rates and Future Policy: Interpreting the Term Structure of Interest Rates," *Brookings Papers on Economic Activity,* Vol. 1, 1983, pp. 173–217; and Campbell and Shiller, "A Simple Account of the Behavior of Long-Term Interest Rates," *American Economic Review,* May 1984, pp. 44–48.

V. Vance Roley, "The Determinants of the Treasury Security Yield Curve," *Journal of Finance,* December 1981, pp. 1103–1126, found that various Treasury securities (of different maturities) did not seem to be close substitutes and that a change in the supply of Treasury securities has an impact on the yield curve.

# INTEREST RATE DIFFERENTIALS: FACTORS OTHER THAN MATURITY

## XIV

In Chapter 13 we examined the relationship between yield and term to maturity of debt securities, with emphasis on government securities to avoid insofar as possible the influence on yield of factors *other than* term to maturity. It was assumed that these securities were homogeneous in all other major respects. In this chapter we relax that assumption and consider the influence on yields of other important factors, including (1) risk of default, (2) callability, (3) tax status, and (4) marketability. We also examine certain other characteristics generally of less importance, such as transaction costs, "seasoning," and so on. In addition we examine the nature of interest rate differentials on other specialized types of financial assets such as preferred stock and convertible bonds, and on mortgages, business loans, and savings deposits.

We begin with a discussion of bond yields, and later discuss interest rates (or yields) on other financial assets except common stocks. Yields on common stocks include both dividends and price gains or losses, and were discussed at length in Chapter 11.

## OBSERVED DIFFERENCES IN YIELDS

An elementary principle of scientific method that applies in economics as well as in physics and other "hard" sciences is that "no two things differ in but one respect alone." If we observe that yields on two securities differ, we are led by this principle to examine the securities more carefully to find other differences that might help explain our original observation. At one time a casual examination of some widely reported long-term interest rates showed 7.40 percent on long-term Treasury issues, 6.00 percent on state and local Baa-rated bonds, 8.00 percent on Aaa-rated corporate bonds, 8.60 percent on Baa-rated corporate bonds, 8.75 percent on new mortgage loans with average maturity of 25 years, and so forth. Selected short-term rates at that time were 4.50 percent on prime commercial paper, 4.50 percent on prime acceptances, and 4.30 percent on 3-month Treasury bills.

The difference between the yield on state and local bonds and on Baa-rated corporate bonds, the difference between prime commercial paper and Treasury bill yields, and all the other yield differences tend to vary over time as business activity fluctuates. A large part of the explanation of these observed differences in yields can be found in certain general attributes of securities, to which we now turn.

## REASONS FOR DIFFERENCES IN YIELDS ON SEASONED SECURITIES

Our primary emphasis in this section is on bond yields, and we examine the effects of differences in risk, in call provisions, in taxability, and in marketability on such yields. Many comments, especially those on risk differences, apply equally to differences in yields on other financial assets. We are concerned primarily with "seasoned" securities, namely, those that have been on the market long enough for their yields to reach a "normal" level (recognizing that yields on securities when first issued may be somewhat higher or lower than this normal level).

### Risk and Uncertainty

The term "risk" refers, in general, to the fact that the outcome of an action may vary. If the rate of return on a security is *certain*, there is no risk, whether the rate is high or low. Often, risk is said to exist when the outcome of an action may vary from what is expected. If you toss a coin 100 times, for example, you may expect to get 50 heads and 50 tails, but it could be 60 : 40, or 40 : 60, or some other ratio. Gambling is risky. You might even get 90 heads and 10 tails or 10 heads and 90 tails. The range of outcomes is a measure of the risk involved. One measure of the range of outcomes is the *standard deviation*. The mean or average outcome is referred to as the "expected" outcome.

In purchasing bonds, there are several types of risk, each associated with the chance that the yield actually received may vary from that based on the interest rate indicated on the bond. The most important of these is "risk of default." Three other forms of risk that are also important to prospective investors are described briefly, and somewhat more extensive consideration is then given to risk of default.

## Types of Risk Other than Default Risk

First, there is the risk associated with unanticipated inflation. The borrowing contract requires that a debtor repay a loan with certain nominal units of money, but inflation erodes the purchasing power of money, and debtors find that the real burden of the repayment is reduced. One of the principal reasons that unanticipated inflation in even moderate degree is held to be undesirable is that it leads to a redistribution of wealth away from creditors in favor of debtors.[1]

Second, a risk of capital loss arises if an investor decides to sell securities before they mature. As yields vary, market prices of securities also vary, and sales of securities prior to maturity may result in gain or loss. This type of risk is an important factor in considering the term structure of interest rates, because short-term securities carry less risk of capital loss than do long-term securities (see Chapter 13).

A third risk was also discussed in our analysis of the term structure of interest rates—the risk of variability of income, sometimes called the reinvestment risk. An investor may wish to realize a steady income flow from his or her financial investments. An investor who buys real capital assets or equities incurs the risk of variability in income. Even if the investor buys a short-term security rather than a long-term bond, income may vary over the longer period. To obtain a steady or uniform income stream over 20 years, one might purchase a new 20-year bond with a 5 percent coupon yield even though 5-year bonds were selling at 6 percent yield. The choice of the lower yield is made because one does not wish to risk the possibility that at the end of 5 years the rate of return on the 5-year bonds might be only 4 percent, which would mean a 33 percent drop in income.

These kinds of risk and the relative strength of investors' desires to avoid them affect choices among the variety of types of security purchased.

## Risk of Default

To default is to fail to meet the terms of an agreement. To default on a bond is to fail to pay the interest when due or to fail to pay the full amount of the principal at maturity. It does not mean that the creditor receives nothing, although this is sometimes the case. Occasionally, the only loss to the creditor is a *delay* in receipt of payment. It is clear, therefore, that there are varying degrees of loss in defaults. U.S. Treasury securities are held to be default-free because the Treasury and the Federal Reserve System have the combined power to create whatever amounts of money are

---

[1] In spite of the importance of the subject, relatively little work has been done to evaluate the harm done by inflation versus the benefits of inflation. For one summary, see Edward Foster, *Costs and Benefits of Inflation*, Studies in Monetary Economics, No. 1 (Minneapolis, Minn.: Federal Reserve Bank of Minneapolis, 1972). But also see John A. Tatom, "The Welfare Cost of Inflation," Federal Reserve Bank of St. Louis, *Review*, November 1976, pp. 9–22, and the references cited therein.

TABLE 14–1
Investors' Services Rating Classifications

| Moody's | General Description | Standard & Poor's |
|---------|-------------------|-------------------|
| Aaa | Highest quality | AAA |
| Aa | High quality | AA |
| A | Upper-medium grade | A |
| Baa | Medium grade | BBB |
| Ba | Lower-medium grade | BB |
| B | Speculative | B |
| Caa | Poor standing (may be in default) | CCC, CC |
| Ca | Often in default | C for income bonds |
| C | Lowest grade (in default) | DDD, D |

required to pay interest and principal when due. Thus, the difference between the yield on a Treasury security and that on a private security with identical provisions is often used as a measure of default risk.

Two agencies in the United States that provide services to investors by examining various securities offered for sale and rating them according to the risk of default are Moody's Investors Service and Standard & Poor's. The highest-grade bonds are rated triple A. Although the risk of default on these securities is presumed to be negligible, they nevertheless carry a higher yield than that prevailing on default-free U.S. government bonds. The classifications used by the two rating services are described roughly in Table 14–1.

Studies made of the default experience of securities with the various ratings seem to support the conclusion that analysts working for the rating services do have the ability to discriminate among risk elements of different securities.[2]

Lest the reader misinterpret this statement, we must clarify one important but subtle point. Assume that, out of 100 securities, experience shows that only one of them was in default during its life. Then the probability of default is one in a hundred. This does not necessarily mean that a given security in this group has a one out of 100, or 1 percent, probability of default, because the 100 securities are not completely identical. If we knew the precise probability of default of each of the 100 securities, we could place each in the appropriate risk class, but reality forces us to group securities into heterogeneous classes according to a handful of general characteristics. For an analogy, consider fire insurance on homes. One home in 1,000 in a certain community may suffer fire damage in a given year, and the insurance company may establish your fire insurance premium on the basis of this suggested rate of loss, but a given home, because of the owner's excellent care with respect to fire protection, may be less likely to burn than the typical house in the group. Because it is impossible to reach the ideal situation in which each security would be in an exactly appropriate risk class, the best we can do is to establish broad risk categories. Thus, probability of default applies to a

---

[2] W. Braddock Hickman, *Corporate Bond Quality and Investor Experience* (New York: National Bureau of Economic Research, 1958).

group of securities and not to individual securities within that group, and an analyst must look beyond the general risk class if he or she wishes to evaluate the merits of a particular security. The logic of probability refers to frequency within a group or class of events, not to a single event, although the term is often misused in everyday conversation. We know that it is probable that there will be more fires in one city than in another, but that does not help us to know whether John Doe's house is likely to burn.

### Certainty, Risk, and Uncertainty

The concept of probability allows one to draw useful distinctions among certainty, risk, and uncertainty. If the probability that an event will occur is 1.00, then we say that this event is certain to occur. If we *believe* that this event will occur, then we behave as if, in this particular case, we lived in a world of certainty. On the other hand, past experience with classes of events and our knowledge based upon this experience allow us to attach probabilities between zero and one to the frequency of occurrence of an event. Given this probability, we can measure the extent of "risk"; we are uncertain of the precise outcome, but we are reasonably certain of the probability of the outcome. When we do not know the probability that an event will occur, we say we are uncertain of the outcome.[3] Thus, a "risk" situation differs from an "uncertain" situation; in the former the probabilities are known or believed to be of a certain level, whereas in the latter neither the probabilities are known nor can they be estimated with any degree of confidence.

Investors, aware of the possibility that a borrower may default, presumably estimate subjective probabilities of the possibility that default may occur, to judge the riskiness of an investment. These subjective probabilities are presumed to exist in the mind of the investor; they may be based upon highly objective data collected as a result of intensive study of a certain class of investments, or they may be the result of an investor's emotional response to a class of investments. They are called subjective probabilities because there is no way of knowing with precision how they were reached.[4] Undoubtedly the rating services contribute to the formation of such subjective probabilities by the very act of rating bonds.

While the investor is assumed to have arrived at a subjective evaluation of the probability of default (risk), it is also assumed that he or she has formulated certain preferences concerning income from investment and risk. It is generally assumed that most investors are "risk averse"; that is, if faced with two choices of assets with the same expected yield and identical in all other respects, they will choose the one with the lower risk of default.[5] This implies that those borrowers who offer a security with

---

[3] Extensive development of these concepts may be found in Frank H. Knight, *Risk, Uncertainty, and Profit* (New York: Houghton Mifflin, 1921).

[4] Just as in the case of "expectations" as a variable in a model, "subjective probabilities" present the researcher with difficult if not impossible measurement problems. There is some question as to whether the concept of a subjective probability is operational, that is, whether it is refutable by experiment.

[5] It is recognized, of course, that some people may receive psychic satisfaction from choosing a risky situation, as gamblers often do. An investor with such preferences would choose the more risky security even though it had the same expected yield as the less risky security.

a lower risk of default can also offer a lower yield. Similarly, if they offer a security with a high risk of default, they must offer a high rate of return to induce investors to purchase the security. Such "high-yield" securities were discussed briefly in Chapter 10. Investors, then, balance risk against rate of return to fit their preferences and maximize their satisfaction from investments.

To achieve the desired balance between risk and return, an investor almost never places all of his or her eggs in one basket; that is, an investor almost never invests in only *one* asset. Instead, he or she develops a diversified portfolio. On the one hand, the investor may concentrate large proportions of financial assets in Baa bonds and reach an optimum balance of risk and return; on the other hand, the investor may keep some funds in a relatively risk-free savings account and invest in a highly speculative stock at the same time and again reach an optimum balance between risk and return. The reason for diversifying a portfolio is to reduce the risk of default. To diversify means not only that the investor buys different securities in a given risk class and different securities in different risk classes, but also that the investor chooses securities whose returns have a low correlation with each other over time. Some firms prosper during economic booms; others prosper in recessions (producers of recap tires, for example). To diversify, one would not have a portfolio filled only with securities, all of which move up and down with gross national product, even though they may be in different risk classes. One reason for *international* investment is that one country may have rising business activity while another is in a recession.

The demand for funds is also affected by risk. Borrowers of funds who supply securities to the market are well aware that the risk on their securities affects the rate of interest that they must be willing to pay. If this rate of interest is high, a business firm may decide that the potential return from the project that the firm is considering is insufficient to warrant undertaking it. When a few borrowers at the margin reduce their demands for funds, the rate of interest may fall somewhat. In equilibrium, rates of interest on securities in each risk class are just sufficient to clear the market. Investors supply funds and absorb risks of default, and borrowers demand funds and offer securities with risks such that the rate of return on each class of risky security will just be sufficient to clear the market. Preferences of lenders and borrowers are satisfied at going market yields.

Given the attitudes of the investing public toward absorption of risk and the risks in investment projects that borrowers wish to undertake, the yield on risk assets will rise to an equilibrium position somewhat above the yield on assets that have no risk of default. The difference between these two yields is called the *risk premium*. The larger the risk premium, the larger the flow of funds into risky undertakings, as suppliers of funds shift from less risky assets to more risky assets, to take advantage of the higher return offered. Similarly, the lower the risk premium, the smaller the flow of funds into risky projects. On the demand side, the higher the premium, the less the quantity of funds demanded; the lower the premium, the larger the quantity of funds demanded.

## A Formal Explanation of the Trade-off Between Risk and Return

Portfolio decision theory is an integral part of courses in financial management.[6] It is sufficient for our purposes to note the importance of risk in determining relative supplies of funds that flow to various financial markets. Obviously, relative supplies of funds are determined by investor preferences and attitudes toward accepting risk. If investors are, for the most part, risk averse, then a premium must be paid to them to overcome their aversion to risk. The premium is paid in the form of a higher yield (return) on the security or real asset. Thus, there is said to be a trade-off between risk and return.

The trade-off can be shown in a graph, as in Figure 14–1. First, let us focus our attention on the three curves labeled $U = 10$, 20, and 30, where $U$ stands for "utility" or "satisfaction" and reflects investor attitudes and desires. Points $b$ and $c$ are both on the same curve labeled $U = 20$. Point $b$ shows the expected return as measured on the vertical axis to be $r_1$ or 10 percent, whereas at point $c$ the expected return is 12.5 percent. Thus the expected return is higher at point $c$, but so is the risk associated with point $c$, for the point is farther to the right, and we are measuring risk on the horizontal axis as the standard deviation of the expected return. The standard deviation is simply a measure of the amount of dispersion of actual returns around expected levels.

A movement from point $b$ to point $a$ implies greater risk with the same expected rate of return of 10 percent. This situation is less desirable from the investor's point of view than is point $b$, and therefore $U$ is only 10 if the investor is at point $a$ whereas it is 20 at point $b$. Thus, a movement from point $b$ to point $c$ can be thought of as two movements, first, a movement to $a$ that means losing satisfaction from assuming more risk and, then, a second movement up to point $c$ giving greater return to compensate for the investor's aversion to risk taking. The additional 2.5 percent return at $c$ can be thought of as the risk premium that must be paid to this investor to induce him or her to accept the added implicit risk. The investor is willing to make a trade-off between risk and return provided the terms are satisfactory.

Notice that the utility or indifference curves become steeper as they rise from *left* to right. This means that for a given increase in risk, the added returns in the form of expected yield must be larger and larger because the investor doesn't like risk, and his or her dislike of risk becomes greater as risk becomes greater.

---

[6] A large volume of readings in the theory of portfolio choice has developed in recent years. Basic among these are Harry M. Markowitz, *Portfolio Selection: Efficient Diversification of Investments* (New York: John Wiley, 1959); William F. Sharpe, "Capital Asset Prices: A Theory of Market Equilibrium Under Conditions of Risk," *Journal of Finance*, Vol. 19, September 1964, pp. 425–442; John Lintner, "Security Prices, Risk, and Maximal Gains from Diversification," *Journal of Finance*, Vol. 20, December 1965, pp. 587–615; and Eugene F. Fama, "Risk, Return and Equilibrium: Some Clarifying Comments," *Journal of Finance*, Vol. 23, March 1968, pp. 29–40. Some empirical evidence may be found in Robert M. Soldofsky and Roger L. Miller, "Risk-Premium Curves for Different Classes of Long-Term Securities, 1950–66," *Journal of Finance*, Vol. 24, June 1969, pp. 429–445.

**FIGURE 14–1**
**The Trade-off Between Risk and Return**

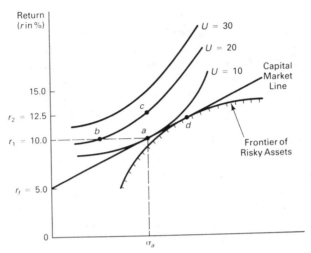

σ (standard deviation of returns, a measure of risk)

Now let us look at the curve labeled the "frontier of risky assets." This curve is constructed from the various packages of risks and returns that are attached to the securities that borrowers have issued or are contemplating issuing. This curve indicates the "best" combinations of risk and yield (i.e., the highest returns with given degrees of risk) available to investors.

On the vertical axis the risk-free rate of return is labeled $r_f$ and is shown to be 5 percent. In the case of default risk, this could be the return on a U.S. Treasury bond.

The line drawn from $r_f$ to point $d$ on the frontier of risky assets line is just tangent to the frontier. The line from $r_f$ to $d$ is extended and labeled the "capital market line." Moving along the capital market line, we find that the investor's utility is 10 at point $a$. This is the highest utility level that the investor can achieve, given the risk-free interest rate that the market offers and the yields on the set of risky assets found in the market. But, how can the investor achieve this level of utility if point $a$ lies outside the frontier of risky assets? There is no asset that will give the expected return of 10 percent with a degree of risk $\sigma_a$ as indicated at point $a$, so what can the investor do? The answer is that the investor can invest a portion of his or her portfolio in default-free securities and another portion in assets represented at point $d$. By balancing these proportions, the investor can (under the assumptions of the model) create a package of assets that will yield the same rate of return as that on assets with risk and return represented by point $a$.[7] Part of the investor's securities have

---

[7] Our presentation of this model is a bare outline only. Students of financial markets should read further in textbooks in financial management to understand the model's attributes, strengths, and limitations. The authors wish to thank their colleague Alan Hess for assistance on this section.

**FIGURE 14–2**
**Changing Risk Premiums**

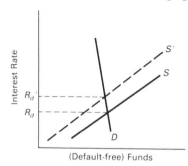
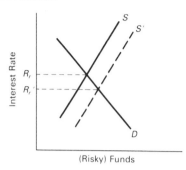

no risk, but low yield. Another part of the portfolio has significant risk but higher yield.

The results of our analysis can be summarized in the context of supply and demand for funds. In Figure 14–2, the market for default-free funds and the market for risky funds are shown. The solid lines represent the initial demand and supply for funds, and their intersection point depicts the original equilibrium rates of interest at which funds are being traded in the two markets. The difference between $R_r$, representing the yield on risky funds, and $R_d$, representing the yield on default-free funds, represents the risk premium $(R_r - R_d)$. Assume, for example, that there occurs an exogenous reduction in risk because, let us say, of a general improvement in the business outlook. This leads to an increase in the supply of funds flowing into the market for risky assets, as shown by the dashed supply curve; there has been a shift in the supply curve, rightward. For simplicity, we ignore possible accompanying shifts in the demand curve. The likely source of this increased supply of funds is found in the market for default-free assets. In this market, the supply curve shifts to the left. In this way, shifting supplies of funds flowing to the two markets narrow the risk premium to $(R_r - R_d')$.[8]

---

[8] Several studies have attempted to determine whether the risk premium is approximately the same as the loss suffered. W. Braddock Hickman, in *Corporate Bond Liquidity*, found that, for bonds he studied, realized yields were the same as promised yields because capital gains on called bonds and favorable conditions at the end of the period he studied offset losses from defaults. He also found that realized rates were higher for low-grade than for high-grade bonds. Higher losses were more than offset by higher yields. Other studies, such as Harold G. Fraine and Robert H. Mills, "Effects of Defaults and Credit Deterioration on Yields of Corporate Bonds," *Journal of Finance*, September 1961, pp. 423–434, used somewhat different measures and found that premiums in yields were greater than losses. Lawrence Fisher, "Determinants of Risk Premiums on Corporate Bonds," *Journal of Political Economy*, June 1959, pp. 217–239, found that earnings variability, length of time a company was solvent and creditors suffered no loss, and certain other factors explained much but not all of the risk premium.

## Cyclical Behavior of the Risk Premium

Risk premiums vary over the business cycle, as might be expected; they rise and fall inversely with the level of business activity. As economic conditions improve, yields begin to rise, and risk premiums decline as the difference in yield between default-free and risky securities narrows. But, when business activity slows down and interest rates fall, the yields on default-free securities fall relative to those on risky securities, and the premium increases. This, at least, is the general pattern one would expect to prevail because bankruptcy rates are lower in an expansion and higher in a depression. However, the period from 1965 to 1970, generally held to be a period of expansion, was characterized by increased premiums for risk. On the one hand, this could have been the result of the inability of the Treasury to issue long-term securities because of the 4¼ percent ceiling set by Congress on the rate that could be paid on bonds. This meant that the supply of long-term U.S. government securities could not be increased and that their yields were also held down because demand for them continued to be relatively strong. The supply of corporate bonds, on the other hand, increased at a rapid pace, and their yields rose. Thus the differential between the rates on U.S. Treasury issues and on corporate issues may have widened because of supply changes and not necessarily because of increased risk differences.[9] On the other hand, a variety of troubles faced the nation during this period: the Vietnam conflict escalation, balance-of-payments problems, racial strife, and so on. All of these could generate apprehension on the part of lenders about the riskiness of financial assets.

## Risk and the Term Structure

Three variables can be shown on two axes by plotting a set of curves, each one of the set representing yields at a different level of the third variable. Thus, in Figure 14–3 yield is plotted on the vertical axis, time to maturity on the horizontal axis, and a set of yield curves is shown, each depicting yield on a different risk class of securities at any given time.

Intuitively one might expect that the *gap* between the yield on risky securities and that on default-free securities would be narrow when both have but a short time to run to maturity. If the firm has survived for years, as maturity approaches, the likelihood of default wanes. Empirically, this seems to be true for high-grade securities. However, especially in recession periods, the yield curve may be downward sloping for low-grade securities, even though government securities and high-grade corporate securities have upward-sloping yield curves. Low-grade securities that are close to maturity may have high yields (low prices). This is presumably the result of fear that the firms will be unable to redeem the outstanding securities at maturity, principally because of difficulties in obtaining refinancing privileges. R. E. Johnson refers to this as the problem of "crisis at maturity."[10]

---

[9] For further discussion, see Murray E. Polakoff et al., *Financial Institutions and Markets* (Boston: Houghton Mifflin, 1970) pp. 453–454.

[10] R. E. Johnson, "Term Structures of Corporate Bond Yields as a Function of Risk Default," *Journal of Finance*, May 1967, pp. 318–321.

**FIGURE 14–3**
**Yield Curves for Different Categories**
**of Securities**

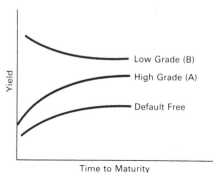

Low Grade (B)

High Grade (A)

Default Free

Time to Maturity

A financial analyst, if considering recommending a particular security for a private portfolio, may wish to examine the term structure of rates on other securities of that class for purposes of comparing current yields to see whether the issue in question is a "good buy" relative to other issues. What appears at first glance to be a high yield for a short maturity may merely reflect the overall tendency for yields to be high on that particular high-risk class of securities.

## Callability

If interest rates change, borrowers may wish to pay the principal of a loan before maturity. Clauses may be inserted in the agreements to permit this or to provide a penalty for doing so. In the case of mortgages, the usual clause (if any) provides a penalty for prepayment. Yield differentials on mortgages may be related to such penalty clauses; borrowers may accept penalty clauses if the interest rate to be paid is somewhat lower than would otherwise be required. For bonds, the usual clause is one permitting the corporation (borrower) to "call" the bond, paying the principal prior to maturity.

### Call Provisions in Corporate Bonds

Corporate bonds usually carry call provisions that provide for possible retirement of the bonds at a variety of times over their life.[11] Just as in the case of mortgages, borrowers wish to be able to pay off other loans if interest rates fall. Lenders, on the other hand, hope to tie borrowers to long-term commitments at high rates of interest. Thus, lenders desire protection against calls, and bonds with call

---

[11] For example, a corporate bond may be callable according to its terms at $1,080 (for a $1,000 bond) at any time during the first year it is outstanding, for $1,070 during the second year, for $1,060 during third year, and so forth. The interest coupon on this bond might be 8 percent. Had there been no call provision, the bond might have been salable at par with a 7 percent coupon. Thus, the premium for the call provision would be 1 percent in this example.

provisions must carry a higher interest rate than must similar bonds without them. However, because corporate bonds without call provisions are rare, it is difficult to test this presumption. Some bonds have an immediate call provision; others have a deferred call provision. In one study, bonds with an immediate call provision had a premium of over ¼ percent in a period of high interest rates (1966–1968), but no noticeable premium in a period of moderate interest rates (1963–1965). This supports the presumption that the value of the call provision for firms that issue bonds exists chiefly in periods when interest rates are high and therefore are expected to fall.[12]

### Call Provisions in Government Securities

The U.S. Treasury also attaches call provisions to some of its securities. For example, the issue of 5/5/94-89 is callable on May 15, 1989. Its coupon rate is 4⅛ percent. In the case of corporate bonds, the purpose of a call provision is to make it possible to call the bonds and replace them with new bonds as interest rates fall. In the case of U.S. Treasury issues, the purpose is somewhat different. As noted in Chapter 8, the Treasury is forced to borrow whenever the budget deficit requires that new funds be raised and cannot postpone projects and borrowing, as corporations can to some extent. The Treasury has less flexibility. However, it can adjust the maturity structure of its debt, within limits. Therefore, when the Treasury attaches a call provision to its debt, its main purpose may be to enable it to decide *when* to refund a debt issue. If the budget deficit is large and the demand for funds by the Treasury is likewise large, the Treasury will often let a call date go by, not wishing to add to its funding at that time. However, if the budget is balanced, is in surplus, or has a small deficit, and a call date arrives, Treasury officials may feel it is a good time for refunding. Of course, interest charges that must be paid by the Treasury are also relevant to a refunding decision. But, because the Treasury must respond if deficits occur, considerations concerning call provisions differ somewhat from those faced by corporations.

## Taxability

Tax laws cause differences in yields on otherwise similar securities. Of particular importance in this regard are the tax on capital gains, estate taxes, and the income tax exemption on municipal securities.

### Capital Gains Taxation

The law has until recently provided that long-term capital gains are generally taxable at half the rate applicable to short-term capital gains, with a maximum rate of 28 percent. A long-term capital gain arose when one bought a security, held it for at least one year, and then sold it for a price higher than that paid for it. The difference

---

[12] Frank C. Jen and James E. Wert, "The Deferred Call Provision and Corporate Bond Yields," *Journal of Financial and Quantitative Analysis*, June 1968, pp. 157–169.

between the purchase price and the selling price is the amount of capital gain, which was taxed at lower rates than other income. Tax reform in 1986 eliminated the distinction between long-term and short-term capital gains and raised the maximum capital gains tax rate to 33 percent beginning in 1988.

To see how yield differentials can arise because of a capital gains tax provision, consider the following example. Assume that 10 years ago the government sold a $1,000 20-year bond with a 3 percent coupon. If the current yield on 10-year securities is 6 percent, the present value of this outstanding 3 percent coupon issue would be in the neighborhood of $770. Now assume that the government sells a new 10-year bond with a 6 percent coupon. Thus, we have outstanding at the same time two U.S. Treasury securities, each default-free and with 10 years to run to maturity. But the older bond will sell for more than $770 and carry a lower yield to maturity than will the new 6 percent security. The older security is referred to as a "deep discount" bond, the term being a reference to its discounted price. The buyer of this bond could hold it to maturity and realize a capital gain of nearly $230. But this "income" was taxable at the capital gains rate.[13] Thus, individuals in tax brackets higher than the tax rate on capital gains realized a greater after-tax income if they had bought deep discount bonds than if they had bought new 6 percent bonds. All of the 6 percent was taxable as income, but only part of the roughly 6 percent yield to maturity of old bonds was taxed as income; the remainder was taxed as capital gain. This tax advantage would lead investors to prefer deep discount bonds; bidding for them would, to some extent, push their prices up and their yields down. Thus in the marketplace, with two similar bonds side by side, the deep discount bond usually carries a lower yield to maturity than does the bond with the higher coupon.

### Estate Taxes and "Flower Bonds"

Estate taxes are another reason for yield differentials on bonds. The federal government has sometimes attached a provision to a bond permitting it to be used to pay estate taxes levied on the estate of the bondholder at his or her death. If this bond (called a "flower bond") is selling at par value of $1,000, there is no advantage to the bondholder's estate and his or her beneficiaries. But, if the bond is selling at, say, $800, then at death the Treasury accepts the bond in lieu of $1,000 of tax liability, and the after-tax inheritance is clearly higher than it otherwise would be. Thus bonds with estate tax eligibility that are selling at a discount have an inheritance element that causes them to be preferred by some investors. Yields on such securities are lower than are those found on other comparable securities that do not carry the estate tax eligibility provision.[14]

---

[13] The actual rate of tax paid was much less than 20 percent, partly because 20 percent was the maximum tax and partly because no tax is paid on capital gains unless they are realized. It has been estimated that only about one-fifth of the gains that accrue each year are realized by some investors.

[14] For example, on February 18, 1977, the estate tax eligible bond of 2/15/80 sold to yield 6 percent before taxes whereas the noneligible bond of 8/15/79 sold to yield 6.23 percent. Of course, differences in maturity and coupon also affect the differential, but the rates noted are suggestive of the premium paid for estate tax eligible bonds.

Since most "flower bonds" were issued some time ago, when coupon rates on bonds were much lower than in recent years, they have all fallen in price and hence there is a substantial gain if and when an owner of such bonds dies. However, because of the investor preference, the discount on such bonds is not as great as might be expected in view of their coupon rates as compared with coupon rates on bonds recently issued.

Prior to the Tax Reform Act of 1976, these bonds had an additional tax advantage feature. The typical investor who sold a bond for $1,000 after paying $800 for it would have had to pay a capital gains tax on the $200 increase in value. Flower bonds were exempt from this tax. But the tax law that took effect on January 1, 1977 treated all capital gains the same, so that an estate would be liable for the capital gains tax. Furthermore, the law extended the holding period required for capital gains to one year, beginning in 1978. This, too, reduced the attractiveness of flower bonds.

Although reduced somewhat in attractiveness, the amount these securities outstanding still provides an element of tax advantage to certain investors and would be expected to sell at a premium for that reason.

### Municipal Securities—Tax-Exempt Income

Exemption of interest income on bonds from income taxes has been provided in several cases, including exemption of interest income on U.S. government bonds from state income tax in some states and, in the past, partial exemption of interest income on certain federal government bonds. Today, however, the important exemption of interest income on bonds from income taxation is that for interest income on certain state and local securities called "municipals."[15]

Interest income on municipals was taxed before the Civil War, but later such taxation was declared unconstitutional. The Sixteenth Amendment to the Constitution permits the federal government to tax income "from whatever source derived," but Congress passed a law exempting income on municipals from federal government income taxation. The constitutional issue has not been tested; states seem to like the law, bondholders seem to like it, and it does not seem to deprive anyone of his or her rights and privileges. There has been little reason for a test.[16]

However, this tax exemption feature has come under the spotlight of public concern in recent years. This is partly because of public knowledge that certain individuals with millions of dollars of income each year have found a variety of

---

[15] Tax reform of 1986 resulted in issue of *taxable* municipal bonds for "nonessential" projects such as parking garages. Yields on such bonds are relatively high and some have desirable features for investors, such as call protection. See *Fortune*, October 27, 1986, p. 133.

[16] It should be noted that municipal obligations are subject to federal estate, gift, and capital gains taxes. The exemption from income taxation is derived from a series of Supreme Court decisions, reaching back as far as *McCulloch* v. *Maryland* (1824), in which it was held that a state could not tax bank notes issued by a bank established by the federal government because "the power to tax is the power to destroy." Gradually, through court decisions, both the immunity of state and local bond interest from federal government taxation and the immunity of interest on federal government obligations from taxation by state and local governments have become well established.

loopholes so that they "pay no taxes" on their income. In some cases, part of their income is derived from holdings of municipal bonds.

What is the real economic impact of this tax exemption? It is in effect a subsidy, partly a subsidy paid by the federal government to the state and local governments, and partly a subsidy to bondholders. The situation may be clarified by an example.

Suppose that individual *A* was in a 50 percent income tax bracket and had income consisting entirely of interest and dividends on securities. Now suppose that the yield on U.S. government bonds is 6 percent and that the yield on similar municipal bonds is 3 percent. It is clear that *A*'s after-tax income is the same whether he or she buys only U.S. bonds and pays taxes on the interest at 50 percent or buys only municipal bonds and pays no taxes, except that in the latter case it is easier to fill out the tax form. Of course, the example is oversimplified; if the yield spread were less than 50 percent, which it usually is, then the taxpayer who owns "municipals" pays somewhat more taxes than otherwise. If the yield spread were only 30 percent, then someone in the 30 percent tax bracket would be just indifferent as to whether he or she held tax-exempt municipals or U.S. government bonds. But to say that the taxpayer *escapes* taxation is patently false. What is ostensibly a tax loophole is usually largely "closed" by the market, as yields on municipal bonds fall below those of other comparable securities. The state governments, on the other hand, may have construction projects to undertake and issue bonds to finance them. Without the tax exemption provision, states would have to pay 6 percent (probably somewhat more because of other factors). Thus the property taxes out of which debt repayment is provided would have to be increased; with the tax exemption, these property taxes are lower. In essence, then, the principal real economic impact is simply to shift some of the tax burden of the interest cost on state construction projects from the shoulders of the state taxpayers and onto the shoulders of federal income taxpayers, including those who accept the lower income from municipal bonds instead of paying taxes on income from government bonds.

The spread between yields on municipals and other securities is not estimated to be large enough to result in the total elimination of all tax advantage to the individual investor. Indeed, the marginal investor is at a point of indifference, but all other investors have presumably found that some tax savings can be realized through the tax exemption privilege. Just how much tax saving can be realized depends on many factors other than the privilege itself. Investors in different tax brackets have different tax-savings potential. The higher the tax bracket, the greater the potential saving. In one study, it was estimated that the average top-bracket private investor might receive a net after-tax yield on corporate securities (with 5 percent gross yield before tax) of only 1.5 percent, whereas these same individuals could realize a net after-tax yield of 3.6 percent on municipals; corporations would receive only 2.6 percent from buying corporate bonds but 3.6 percent from municipals, and so forth.

The spread between yields on municipals and on other securities tends to narrow in periods of tight money; that is, the yield on municipals rises relative to the yields on other securities as the economy moves on the upswing. One author attributed this phenomenon to the large role sometimes played by commercial banks in the market for municipals.[17] In periods of rising interest rates, banks are pressed to unload bonds from their portfolios to meet increased customer demand for loans. This has the general effect of pushing prices of bonds down and yields up, relative to yields on other securities. In any case, the narrowing of spreads does mean that, in the business upswing, that portion of the differential going to states as a subsidy falls and that portion going to individuals or corporate investors as a tax exemption rises.[18]

Some economists argue that the existence of a subsidy in the form of exemption of interest income from taxation may wrongly encourage financing of projects that can be financed by bonds, thus shifting the allocation of resources from what it might have been if the subsidy had not existed. For this reason they may favor elimination of the subsidy. Because the tax exemption provision enables some investors to escape from some part of their tax liability, others favor its elimination. Direct subsidy by the federal government to state and local governments would probably be a less costly way to achieve the same goal.[19] However, some groups will undoubtedly continue to voice strong support of the status quo for a variety of reasons.

Bonds issued by state and local governments are divided into two major classes: *general obligation* bonds, backed by the "full faith and credit" of the issuing governmental authority, and *revenue* bonds—bonds on which interest and principal is repaid from specific taxes or tariffs levied on users of public facilities. For example, tolls collected from a toll bridge are often used to repay bondholders. Under provisions of the Glass-Steagall Act of 1933, commercial banks were prevented from underwriting revenue bonds, although they are active participants in the general obligation market. However, in 1968 the Housing and Urban Development Act permitted banks to underwrite revenue bonds when proceeds from bond sales were to be used to finance housing and university dormitory projects. In addition, whenever the issue is backed by the full faith and credit of the government entity, the Comptroller of the Currency may rule that it is eligible even if it is principally a revenue-type bond. As much as 40 percent of revenue bond issues have been eligible.[20]

## Marketability

The terms "liquidity" and "marketability" are often used interchangeably. They describe financial instruments that may be converted into cash with certainty and without delay. More precisely defined, however, liquidity is a broader term; it

[17] Sidney Homer, "Factors Determining Municipal Bond Yields," U.S. Congress, Joint Economic Committee, *State and Local Public Facility Needs and Financing*, Washington, D.C., December 1966, Vol. 2, p. 270; summarized in Polakoff et al., *Financial Institutions and Markets*, pp. 334–335.

[18] James C. Van Horne, *Financial Market Rates and Flows* (Englewood Cliffs, N.J.: Prentice-Hall, 1978), esp. p. 195.

[19] Roland I. Robinson, *The Postwar Market for State and Local Government Securities* (New York: National Bureau of Economic Research, 1960), p. 159. One recent study found that tax-exempt securities issued in 1969 will probably cost the federal government about $2.6 billion in lost revenues over the life of the bonds, whereas state and local governments will save only $1.9 billion because of lower interest rates on the bonds. Of course, these figures are based on estimates of the taxes not paid by holders of municipal bonds (which depend on their tax brackets). See Richard Armstrong, *Fortune*, December 1972, p. 89.

[20] Timothy Q. Cook, "Determinants of Individual Tax-Exempt Bond Yields: A Survey of the Evidence," *Economic Review*, Federal Reserve Bank of Richmond, May–June 1982, pp. 14–39.

covers marketable assets but also those that are very close to maturity or may be redeemed by the holder prior to maturity. Thus, a business or consumer loan that matures in a few days or weeks is considered liquid whether it is marketable or not. Similarly, a U.S. government savings bond, because it can be redeemed at the owner's option, after an initial period, is a liquid asset after that period although it is not marketable. Marketability implies that a *third party* is willing and able to buy the financial instrument. With these distinctions in mind, we turn to this aspect of liquidity.

A security that is readily marketable will tend to sell at a higher price (lower yield) than will a comparable security that is less marketable. By "marketability" we mean that a significant amount of the security can be sold relatively quickly and without large price concessions. A portfolio manager can usually sell a small amount quickly at "market price," but one who wishes to unload a large amount of, say, bonds, may have to sell at a price below the one currently quoted. Of course, small amounts may be sold each day at market price, and a large holding may eventually be liquidated in this manner. But this means that the entire holding is not sold quickly. Thus, marketability has two dimensions: one is the time required to effect the sale; the other is the spread between the current market price and the realized price at time of sale. Marketability, therefore, must be measured in relative, not absolute, terms. Financial assets have different degrees of marketability that derive in part from the features of the instruments themselves and in part from the market where the sale is to be made. In general, financial instruments require the following characteristics to make them readily marketable: they must be relatively homogeneous, appeal to a wide variety of buyers, and be easily transferable without undue cost or delay. For their part, the markets must have depth, breadth, and resiliency, as discussed in Chapter 10.

Most corporate and government securities are actively traded in secondary markets. Large sales can be consummated and large blocks trade at close to the bid price in many maturity ranges. This in turn enhances their initial sale in the primary markets. However, this is less true in long-term markets; they are "thin" compared with those for short-term credits. The salability of corporate and municipal securities is also affected by changes in the credit ratings assigned to them by Moody's and Standard & Poor's. An unexpected downgrading in rating can reduce the marketability of outstanding issues and add to the problems of selling new ones. For example, the municipal market took several years to recover from the fall-out from New York City's financial troubles in the early 1970s. Likewise, the market for securities of the Washington Public Power Supply System (WPPSS) may be negatively affected for some time by the default by WPPSS in 1983. Since the State of Washington Supreme Court said that utility districts that were members of WPPSS *need not* pay, because plants were not completed and therefore generated no power, this default may have repercussions on many municipal bond issues in the state of Washington. Previously, defaults had occurred only when borrowers *could not* pay.

Registered municipal bonds (bonds registered in the names of particular holders) are generally less marketable than are those in bearer form. Many buyers avoid them because of the costs and time involved in deregistering them for subsequent sale.

Because they are not "good delivery" bonds, registered municipals trade less actively and at lower prices (higher yields) than do bearer bonds. For this reason buyers who plan to hold to maturity may be attracted to registered issues because of their higher yield. This also reduces trading in such securities.

The secondary market for mortgages is not as well developed as is that for most corporate and government obligations. This is especially true for so-called conventional mortgages as compared with, say, FHA mortgages that are underwritten by the U.S. government. In recent years, however, a number of federal credit agencies have been established to provide a secondary market for both types of mortgages, as discussed in Chapter 10. Mortgage rates may be lower because of these programs.

Finally, the size of a particular issue is important. A small issue of securities is not widely held, and there are not many market participants who hold large amounts of such an issue. Therefore, the general lack of knowledge about the issue makes its marketing more costly.[21] This cost will be reflected in a higher yield. Small amounts of an issue can be traded at the going market price, but large amounts often must be negotiated. Mutual funds and other investors have found that, if they hold a large amount of one security, they drive the price down by virtue of their own selling activity when they attempt to unload onto the market. Such securities lack a high degree of marketability—the market is said to be "thin" as opposed to "broad."

Thus, marketability is a general term for a wide variety of characteristics of securities reflecting the ease with which they can be bought and sold. It is expected that readily marketable securities will sell for lower yields (higher prices) than will other securities that are similar in all other respects; degrees of marketability give rise to varying yield differentials.

## THE YIELD SPREAD BETWEEN SEASONED AND NEW ISSUE BONDS

A seasoned issue, one that has been outstanding for some period of time, seems to be more acceptable to investors than does a new issue of comparable risk, maturity, and call provisions. Yields on newly issued corporate bonds, for example, have usually exceeded those on seasoned issues. From 1951 to 1971, the yield spread averaged about 35 basis points (.35 percent). In addition, the size of the spread has typically widened during periods of rising rates and narrowed when rates declined. In the early 1970s there were exceptions to this behavior, but the period 1970–1981 was unusual for interest rates, because of the generally accelerating inflation.

Since yields on comparable securities should be equalized by market forces, how can one account for the spread and for changes in its size?[22]

---

[21] Lawrence Fisher used the market value of publicly traded bonds of a corporation as a proxy for marketability in the study cited in footnote 8.

[22] The following discussion draws substantially upon John D. Rea, "The Yield Spread Between Newly Issued and Seasoned Corporate Bonds," Federal Reserve Bank of Kansas City, *Monthly Review*, June 1974, pp. 3–9. Rea cites evidence from a study by Joseph W. Conard and Mark W. Frankena, "The Yield Spread Between New and Seasoned Bonds, 1952–63," in *Essays on Interest Rates*, Vol. 1, ed. Jack M. Guttentag and Phillip Cagan (New York: National Bureau of Economic Research, distributed by Columbia University Press, 1969), pp. 153–159.

Recent studies suggest that much of the yield spread, perhaps 60 percent, is attributable to differences in coupon rates on seasoned and new issues. Because of these differences, the two types of securities have different degrees of call protection and after-tax yields. Thus, the securities are not comparable, and yields should be expected to differ. The remainder of the spread is perhaps due to market imperfections associated with risk in underwriting new issues or with portfolio practices of large institutional lenders.

Bonds that have a high degree of call protection tend to have lower yields than do those with less protection. Buyers are willing to forgo some yield on securities that are less likely to be called. For bonds with the same call *provisions*, for example, both callable and at the same price, the risk of call is greater the higher the coupon rate. Because interest rates trended upward from 1960 to 1980 and because bonds are usually issued at or near par, new issues have carried higher coupon rates than have seasoned issues. Not surprisingly, we find that yields are usually higher on new issues.

Coupon differences also explain cyclical changes in the yield spread. When interest rates rise, new issue coupon rates rise relative to the fixed coupon rates on outstanding issues. This reduces the risk that seasoned securities will be called before the new issues. The yield spread widens further as investors come to expect a subsequent decline in interest rates to levels at which refinancing would be likely. When interest rates do decline, the yield spread narrows as coupon rates on new issues are lowered. In some years, negative yield spreads have appeared for several months in a row as seasoned bonds became the high-coupon issues. If interest rates were to trend lower in the years ahead, we would expect a narrowing of the spread, reflecting the change in call protection status of old and new bonds.

Changes in the trend of rates also have tax implications for the yield spread. When rates have been rising for many years, most seasoned bonds sell at a discount to make them competitive with new ones. Because of the large capital gains component in their return, and its favorable tax treatment in the past vis-à-vis interest income, seasoned bonds tended to carry somewhat lower yields than did new issues.

In summary, the spread between yields on new and on outstanding issues may be due primarily to differences in coupon rates. Higher coupon rates on new issues give them less call protection and a lower after-tax return than provided by seasoned issues. New issues are expected, therefore, to carry higher market rates. When coupon rate differences are eliminated, by comparing seasoned bonds with new issues having the same coupon rates, the average spread during 1951–1971 narrowed from about 35 basis points to around 14 basis points. Some market analysts attribute much of this remaining spread to market imperfections.[23]

One such impediment has to do with the marketing of new corporate bonds. Unless privately placed, new issues are bought initially by underwriters who make their profit by selling at a higher price than they paid. While these bonds are being offered to the public, underwriters run the risk of decline in market price. To reduce this risk, they often underprice the bonds to sell them quickly. This creates excess demand for the new issue, which cannot be eliminated by a rise in price, since the price is fixed by the underwriter. The excess demand spills over into the market for

[23] Rea, "Yield Spread," p. 5.

seasoned issues, which pushes prices up and yields down. In this view, risk aversion accounts for some of the spread remaining after coupon rate differences have been allowed for. Since this risk is greater when rates are rising (prices declining), the yield spread varies directly with the level of rates.

A second market impediment that may explain some of the spread relates to portfolio practices of institutional lenders such as life insurance companies and pension funds. These institutions buy corporate bonds primarily for income. They usually hold to maturity and seldom switch between securities to improve yield from the portfolio unless major rate differences appear. An important reason, besides inertia, for this market behavior is that these institutions are permitted to carry bonds on their books at amortized cost rather than market price. Capital losses are shown, therefore, *only* if the securities are sold. Because of aversion to reporting losses, seasoned bonds become locked into the institutions' portfolios when interest rates are rising. Thus, an important group of investors is prevented from switching out of seasoned and into new bonds. Yield spreads are maintained or tend to widen as rates rise, and portfolios become increasingly "loss constrained."

There is, however, some doubt about the importance of the lock-in effect in explaining rate behavior. First, a large share of outstanding corporate bonds is held by individuals. These investors appear willing to transfer funds between markets and may be less constrained by capital losses than the large institutional lenders. Second, as Rea has pointed out, the size of the spread that triggers switching between seasoned and new issues is apparently quite small.[24] Third, to the extent that underwriter risk accounts for some of the spread, less remains to be explained by reference to portfolio practices. Finally, much of the spread may stem from the fact that the seasoned yield series used in studies of 1951–1964 data is based upon the *asked* yield, whereas the new issue yield is the *bid* yield. Perhaps much of the spread can be attributed to transactions costs.[25]

Thus, new and seasoned issues may sell at different yields for a variety of reasons. For securities that are alike with respect to risk, maturity, and call provisions, differences in coupon rates appear to be the most important factor. As interest rates have trended upward since the 1950s, seasoned issues have had greater call protection in most periods than have new issues. The preferred tax treatment of capital gains also makes outstanding bonds more attractive to some buyers and helps to account for the yield spread. Though perhaps less important, market imperfections in the form of risk-averting behavior seem to have played a part in maintaining higher rates on newly issued bonds during much of this period.

## INTEREST RATE (YIELD) DIFFERENTIALS ON OTHER FINANCIAL ASSETS

In our analysis thus far, we have discussed both general and somewhat more specific characteristics giving rise to differentials in yields on securities. Our focus has been on notes and bonds, securities containing contractually fixed obligations as opposed to

[24] Ibid., p. 8.
[25] Conard and Frankena, "Yield Spread on Corporate Bonds," p. 161.

instruments of ownership represented in the market by shares of common stock. We have not attempted a comprehensive examination of the many diverse types of clauses that can appear in loan agreements. This diversity is limited only by the imagination of the parties to such contracts. However, two general types of contracts that overlap fixed-rate obligations and ownership securities are quite common. These are preferred stock and convertible bonds. Convertible bonds have characteristics that make them partly like bonds and partly like stocks, and differentials in yields are often observed because of these provisions. The other major types of financial assets—mortgages, loans, and savings deposits—are discussed briefly because many of the factors causing differences in bond yields also cause differences in yields on these financial assets.

## Common and Preferred Stocks

Common and preferred stocks differ from bonds in several significant ways: (1) stocks may pay dividends, which may or may not be declared, whereas bonds pay interest, which *must* be paid or default occurs and bondholders may sue; (2) stocks have no maturity, unless a company goes out of business, and normally continue to be outstanding, whereas bonds have definite dates at which they must be redeemed at face value; and (3) because stocks have no maturity and no face redemption value, they may rise (or fall) in value almost indefinitely.

Dividends on common stock may be measured as a percentage of current market price of the stocks—a current market *dividend yield* rate. This current dividend yield was for a long time greater than the yield on most bonds. The usual explanation was that common stocks are riskier because profits vary much more than bond interest. Bond interest must be paid even if a firm has losses in a particular year. In many recent periods, dividend yields on common stocks have been lower than yields on most bonds. A "negative yield gap" appeared. One reason for this is that dividend yields are only part of the total yield on stocks. Like bonds, stocks may rise (or fall) in price, and the capital gain (or loss) is part of total yield. But, unlike bonds, stocks may in the long run rise in price almost indefinitely; hence capital gain is usually, in the long run, a very significant part of yield, along with dividends.[26]

Many economists therefore measure historical yields on stocks as the rate of return, including both dividends and any price appreciation. This gives a *total rate of return* on stocks. For a considerable period after World War II, this rate approximated 9 percent per year, whereas average bond yields on high-grade bonds approximated 5 percent per year.

Bond yields are not likely to be greater than a "normal" real rate plus a premium approximately equivalent to the rate of inflation. This is because bond prices must approach par at maturity; if they rise above par, they must fall. Hence bonds cannot in general be a hedge against inflation. But stock may rise in price indefinitely, as the values of the assets on which they constitute claims rise, with inflation and with economic growth. Thus stocks *may* be a hedge against inflation. They may not be, of course; 1968–1982 was one period in which they were *not* an inflation hedge. But

---

[26] This is because stocks represent ownership of real capital assets, and as long as productivity of those assets, and hence earnings, are increasing, stock prices can, in the long run, rise.

many studies indicate that stocks are likely in the very long run to be an inflation hedge, as earnings rise both in real terms and in nominal terms. If this were not so, dividend yields on stocks, having been less than yields on bonds, could not provide the higher yield that is presumably necessary to induce investment in stocks, the more risky asset.

Preferred stock is somewhat of a hybrid between common stock and bonds. The term "preferred" means that, if dividends are declared, holders of preferred stock take precedence over holders of common stock; holders of preferred stock receive the full stipulated dividend before holders of common stock receive any dividends. A preferred stock carries an "interest rate" in the form of a specified number of dollars and cents per share. Thus, if earnings of $3 a share on total capital are realized, and management decides to declare these, or part of them, in dividends, holders of 6 percent preferred (par value, $100) will receive $6 per share, and common stockholders will receive nothing if there are equal amounts of preferred and common stock. As there is usually more common stock than preferred stock, common stockholders would usually receive something, but less than $6 a share. If earnings are $12 a share, holders of preferred stock receive only $6, whereas common stockholders would receive more than $12 a share, unless, as occasionally is true, the preferred stock is "participating" preferred. This is rare; much more common is a provision for "cumulative" preferred stock; cumulative preferred stockholders receive all their specified return before common stockholders receive any dividends, even if this means that common stockholders wait for years without any dividends.

Because declaration of dividends is a discretionary act of management, preferred stockholders not only may not receive dividends if there are no earnings or insufficient earnings; they cannot receive dividends if these are not declared. They have no contractual claim on the firm's assets, as bondholders have. In such a situation bonds would be in default and bondholders could bring suit.

Thus one might expect that the effective yield on preferred stock would have to be higher than the yield on bonds of the same quality if the company were successful in inducing people to purchase the preferred stock. In general, this has been true. However, there are certain tax provisions that, as always, affect the "after-tax" yield. Only 20 percent of the dividends received by corporations that hold preferred stock or common stock of other corporations is subject to the income (profits) tax; the remaining 80 percent is tax exempt. Thus *corporate* holders find that preferred stock has some tax advantage over bonds, as an investment. As corporations, including nonbank financial institutions, hold more preferred stock, this leads to bidding up of prices and a corresponding lowering of yields.[27]

Additionally, the corporate issuer of a bond can deduct interest payments from the firm's income for tax purposes. But payments to preferred shareholders are not deductible. Therefore, there is less incentive for corporations to issue preferred stock than bonds, and the supply of new preferred shares has not been large in recent years.

---

[27] Common stock would have the same tax advantage, but we do not consider common stock at this point because risk is greater and common stock would be less likely to be held as a liquid investment. Before the tax law of 1986, only 15 percent was subject to tax.

This restricted supply also leads to higher prices and lower yields. Thus there exists no large differential in yields between those on preferred shares and those on bonds, under present institutional arrangements, and, in fact, since the mid-1960s, preferred stocks have sometimes yielded less than have high-grade bonds.

## Convertible Bonds

Some corporate bonds (and some preferred stocks) carry provisions that allow the holder to exchange them for the common stock of the company on prearranged terms. Because of this conversion privilege, these bonds have characteristics of both bonds and stocks. Since the purchaser of a convertible bond may share in any potential appreciation in value accorded to the company's stock by exercising his or her conversion rights, this investment resembles a stock purchase. On the other hand, if the company's profit position falters and this results in a decline in the price of outstanding shares of stock, the value embodied in the fixed obligation in the bond is retained by the investor. The convertible bond, therefore, has little downside risk of loss, while it is capable of realizing gains.[28] For these reasons, the price of a convertible bond carries a premium over the prices of other bonds of similar quality, as buyers bid for the right to take advantage of any appreciation in share values while retaining the protection afforded the bondholder. Yields on convertible bonds are below those on other similar bonds.

Several other reasons for a yield differential between convertible and nonconvertible bonds have been suggested by market analysts. First, the option to convert to common stock usually has a fixed duration. Presumably, the longer the life of the option, the more valuable it is. Second, clauses in the bond's "fine print" may provide for restraint on the firm's ability to dilute its stock by issuing more stock. The stronger the antidilution clauses, the more valuable the bond. Third, it is frequently the case that margin requirements on the purchase of convertible bonds are lower than are those on stock. It is, therefore, less difficult for speculators to finance the purchase of convertible bonds than to finance the purchase of stock, but the extent to which this is true depends upon margin requirements set by the Board of Governors of the Federal Reserve System. Fourth, the transactions costs connected with the trading of bonds are usually less than those incurred in trading a like amount of common stocks.

It is clear that in evaluating the desirability of investing in a convertible bond, many factors must be considered.[29] It is sufficient to note here that the conversion feature in general is an attractive attribute and leads to a premium price. Convertible bonds have a *bond value* floor price, although this is not constant; if a company incurs losses, it may not even be able to pay interest on its bonds. Convertible bonds also

---

[28] Of course, the market price of a bond can fall, as it will when interest rates rise; however, a convertible bond with the same timing, coupon rate, and so on, as a nonconvertible bond will fall in price no farther than its counterpart. In this sense a "floor" to the fall in value is retained by convertible bonds.

[29] For a detailed statistical examination of the premium for the conversion privilege, see R. L. Wil, Jr., J. E. Segall, and David Green, Jr., "Premiums on Convertible Bonds," *Journal of Finance*, June 1968, pp. 445–463, and comments and a reply by P. D. Cretien, Jr., D. T. Duvel, and G. A. Mumey, *Journal of Finance*, September 1970, pp. 917–933.

have a *conversion value*, the value of the bonds if converted into stock at the current market price of the stock. It is common for convertible bonds to sell at premiums over both values; the convertible bond is worth as much as the stock into which it is convertible, and a little more because of the fact that it is less likely to decline sharply in value, as there is some protection because of the bond value floor price. If the premium of the market price over the bond value is large, there is usually only a small premium in the market price over the conversion value, and vice versa. This is because, when the premium of market price over bond value is great, it is usually because the price of the stock is high; investors may feel that it cannot go much higher, and therefore the premium of market price of the convertible bond over its conversion value is small. If the premium of market price over conversion value is large, it is usually because the price of the stock is rising, and conversion would enable the former bondholder to benefit from further rise in the price of the stock.

Firms issuing convertible securities must weigh these factors, for, although the conversion feature may enable the firm to obtain funds at lower interest costs, there are costs to the firm in other ways. In particular, conversion to common stock, if profitable, dilutes the stock, and presumably this tends to hold the price of the stock to a lower level than it otherwise might reach.

## Mortgages

Interest rates on mortgages are generally higher than are rates on high-quality corporate bonds. Mortgage rate levels are, of course, affected by many of the factors already discussed in this chapter.

Risk on a conventional mortgage, negotiated between a bank or savings and loan association and a homeowner, is greater than is that on a comparable loan that has been insured by the FHA. Banks frequently require a larger down payment, perhaps 30 percent of the purchase price, in the case of a conventional mortgage loan, whereas insured and guaranteed loans, in some cases in the past, were made with no down payment (there was even at one time a "no-no-down payment," in which some of the transactions costs were absorbed by lenders). The different treatment of down payments tends to absorb the risk differential so that interest rates as quoted to the public may appear the same. High down payments are like stringent collateral requirements, the value of the home under mortgage is the value of the "collateral" pledged in case of default. Moreover, the smaller the loan outstanding against this collateral, the lower the risk assumed by the lender.

Tax laws also have a significant effect on the demand for mortgage money and its supply. The Congress has often expressed a desire to see citizens well housed; hence it allows a homeowner to deduct from his or her income the amount of interest payments before computing his or her income tax liability. This is a form of subsidy to the homeowner that pushes mortgage rates higher than they might otherwise be and induces lenders to supply more funds to the mortgage market rather than to other sectors.

Mortgages are not as readily marketable as bonds and many stocks. Again, to support the marketability of mortgages, the government formed FNMA, GNMA, and other agencies discussed earlier. It is difficult to know precisely what effect these programs have on mortgage yields. When these agencies tap the bond market, this tends initially to lower mortgage rates but to push business loan and bond rates up. Perhaps these higher bond rates simply induce funds to flow back out of the mortgage market to other sectors. However, the marketability of mortgages is enhanced, and there is probably some *net* lowering of mortgage yields.

Mortgages require considerably more servicing than do business loans, and, although some services are paid for directly through fees, others may be paid for in somewhat higher rates charged on mortgages. Services include negotiating the mortgage, certifying the deed, collecting mortgage payments, and in some cases paying insurance premiums and property taxes. Servicing costs are sometimes estimated at about ½ percent per year, and mortgage rates are sometimes shown with this (estimated) deduction from the quoted contract rate, which includes an amount sufficient to offset servicing costs. Sometimes service fees are paid directly to local institutions (such as mortgage banks or mortgage companies) by a life insurance company that does not wish to service loans it holds.

Mortgage rates tend to be less volatile than bond rates because lenders tend to increase or reduce rates by ½ percent or ¼ percent at a given time. The differential between mortgage rates over bond rates tends to be greatest when bond rates are relatively low, as mortgage lenders seem to be slow to lower their rates. They also seem to be somewhat reluctant (or fearful?) to raise them in periods of very high interest rates, and in these periods the differential may become quite small, as was shown in Figure 10–2.

## Loans and Savings Deposits

A number of factors already discussed, particularly risk and transactions costs, explain differences in loan yields or interest rates. Interest on savings deposits differs for other reasons, discussed in part in Chapter 4, where it was pointed out that commercial banks appear to be able to pay lower interest than savings and loan associations, perhaps because of convenience of "one-stop" banking. In this section we examine two factors somewhat peculiar to loans—compensating balances and collateral requirements—that cause differences in interest rates charged; we also comment briefly on geographic factors affecting both loan rates and savings deposit rates.

### Compensating Balances

Commercial banks often arrange agreements with borrowers to prevent deposit accounts from falling below a certain level. That is, borrowers must keep on deposit a "compensating balance" of a certain sum as one condition for obtaining loans. This was described in Chapter 3, where it was noted that the effective interest rate is higher than the quoted rate when compensating balances are required because the borrower does not have full discretionary use of the funds. Size of compensating balances varies considerably—usually 10 to 20 percent of the original loan amount. Thus, effective yields vary directly with the compensating balances required, and nominal interest charges vary inversely with compensating balances.

The added cost to borrowers, however, depends on how much balance they *would have* maintained in the absence of the compensating balance requirement. When a business firm borrows, it frequently increases its sales, and with a larger volume of sales, it needs larger working balances. As a matter of fact, it might be possible for banks to reduce compensating balance requirements somewhat, to charge borrowers slightly higher nominal rates of interest, and for both to benefit. This is because required reserves (on which earnings are zero) would be smaller with smaller compensating balances.[30]

Although compensating balance requirements increase effective interest rates, banks generally view them as a means of cementing bank-customer relationships and thus inducing customers to obtain future loans from the same bank and to use other bank services. An understanding about a compensating balance usually follows from a long-standing bank-customer relationship. A large business firm usually maintains a line of credit with its bank (or banks), enabling it to borrow whenever additional funds are needed, up to the limit of the line of credit, in exchange for agreement to keep a compensating balance. An individual not maintaining a compensating balance would pay a fee for establishing a line of credit; the fee is waived in exchange for the compensating balance.

Over business cycles, the size of compensating balances tends to vary. As monetary conditions become tight, banks require larger compensating balances in lieu of increasing nominal interest rates on loans. This applies principally to customers eligible for the prime rate, or a fixed rate above the prime rate, agreed upon in establishing lines of credit. In this way, commercial banks can introduce yield flexibility while keeping nominal rates fixed. In recent years some major banks introduced a "flexible" or "floating" prime rate, as noted in Chapter 9. With flexibility in setting the prime rate, it may be that variability in compensating balance requirements will no longer be necessary.[31]

---

[30] For further detail on some of these points, see Jack M. Guttentag and Richard G. Davis, "Compensating Balances," *Essays in Money and Credit,* Federal Reserve Bank of New York, 1964, pp. 57–61.

[31] Under pressure from the government's Committee on Interest and Dividends in 1973, some banks suspended their "floating" prime rates because the rates would have risen under the formulas used. Later the government acquiesced in a rise in the prime rate, but suggested what became termed a "dual prime rate"—increases in the prime rate should be delayed and should be small, but, if made, rates charged on loans to small business firms and consumers and on mortgage loans should not be increased unless absolutely necessary. See Federal Reserve Bank of San Francisco, *Business & Financial Letter,* March 2, 1973. Some banks later returned to use of floating prime rates, but did not always follow their formulas precisely. See Randall C. Merriss, "The Prime Rate," Federal Reserve Bank of Chicago, *Business Conditions,* April 1975, pp. 3–12.

### Collateral Requirements

It is clear that, if a lender takes possession of a borrower's stocks or bonds, or acquires liens on the borrower's real property, the lender assumes less risk of loss from default by the borrower than he or she otherwise would. Thus, borrowers with collateral to pledge can usually obtain additional funds at a lower cost than otherwise. (If you have wealth, it is easier to borrow.) Indeed, in many instances such collateral is a necessary requirement to obtain funds at all from the lender.

The "quality" of the collateral pledged is also often a factor that affects the yield. If warehouse receipts on inventories are pledged, the bank requires that such inventories be insured against fire and theft, and so on. The size of a down payment on a piece of property also may affect the lender's willingness to lend at a lower interest rate. The larger the down payment, the smaller will be the amount of the loan relative to the market value of the property and, therefore, the greater the assurance that the lender will be repaid from the sale of the property should the borrower default.

If a borrower owns a savings account, he or she may wish to withdraw cash from the account to pay for, say, a new automobile. The banker may suggest that the borrower pledge his or her savings account as collateral and borrow the funds to purchase the car. The interest rate charged on such a loan would be very low compared with that charged if the car were mortgaged by the bank. But it would be higher than the rate earned by the savings account, perhaps 2 percent higher. Thus, if the borrower earned 4 percent on a savings account and paid 6 percent for a loan, his or her net interest charges would be only 2 percent. However, by pledging his or her savings account, the borrower would relinquish the liquidity it had provided—the ability to withdraw funds from the savings account would be restricted. Thus, what appears to be a low 6 percent loan has its implicit costs, and these may make the "true" interest rate paid equal to 9 or 10 percent, or more, which is normally charged on automobile loans.

There are almost as many different kinds of collateral requirements as there are loans, and rates charged reflect this variety.

## GEOGRAPHICAL DIFFERENCES

Some noticeable differences in yields have persisted in different geographical regions of the United States. Interest rates in the East are usually lower than those in the West and Southwest. These differentials are most pronounced in the mortgage market, and they are reflected in rates paid on savings deposits, inasmuch as these deposits provide the principal source of mortgage money for home building. Just why these rate differentials persist is not well understood. Of course, the mortgage market is principally a local market, and rates must be negotiated between lenders and borrowers. The market lacks the degree of perfection that the national securities markets have.

There are also geographic differences resulting from market participation by countries that have different interest rate policies (e.g., Japan, in which interest rates are generally low and rates on savings deposits are extremely low).

One may speculate that as means of communication improve and flexibility in portfolio management on the part of savings institutions becomes greater, these regional differences will be reduced or eradicated.

# TRANSACTIONS COSTS

Some types of loans cost more to originate or manage than others. For example, loans that call for installment payments over an extended period have higher handling costs than do single-payment loans. Loans to finance consumer durables and housing are important examples. Mortgage loans also entail preparation of documents and appraisal of property that adds to costs. And in some cases special accounts are set up to ensure that the borrower makes tax, property insurance, and mortgage payments on schedule. Other costs include payments for title search and title insurance, change of ownership, recording fees, and escrow charges. Most of these, however, are not part of the lender's costs and are not included in the mortgage rate. Nevertheless, they are transaction costs and are paid by the purchaser of the property.

Some loan transactions require extensive legal work and often a detailed appraisal of the borrower's business situation and the collateral behind the loan. Finally, some loans become overdue. The lender incurs collection costs and, if the loan is uncollectible, the expense of liquidating assets pledged as collateral and charging off the loan against reserves or earnings.

For most types of loans operating costs are not closely related to the size of the loan. It costs little more, for example, to make a $500,000 loan to finance the purchase of an apartment building than one for $50,000 to buy a house. The average cost declines, therefore, as the loan increases in amount; small loans are often more costly, per dollar of loan, than are larger ones.

The services and facilities that lending institutions provide to extend credit add to operating costs and overhead. Some of the necessary charges are covered by fees, but part of the total expense is included in the rate of interest charged the borrower. Thus, transactions costs differ from one type of loan to another, and these differentials are reflected in the pattern of rates observed in the market.

Transactions costs also affect prices and yields of marketable securities. In the primary markets underwriting expenses may be paid separately by the issuer or included in the spread between bid and ask prices. In secondary markets brokerage fees, though listed separately, are included in the net price paid or received by settlement date. Where trading is through dealers in over-the-counter markets, transactions costs are part of the quoted prices. No brokerage fees or commissions are paid to the dealer making the market.

In the case of equities, common and preferred stocks are usually traded in "round lots." For actively traded securities, a round lot is 100 shares of stock. Trades in less than 100 shares are "odd-lot" transactions. For low-priced stocks there is normally a ⅛-point odd-lot charge; a charge of ¼ point is made for transactions in higher-priced stocks. These charges are included in the net price to compensate the odd-lot dealer who breaks the 100 share units into a smaller number of shares. Such charges reduce the effective return to investors and suggest that transactions be confined, if possible, to round lots.

Financial institutions pay different rates on different types of deposit accounts. Higher rates are usually paid on longer-term certificates than on short-term certificates and on passbook accounts. At present, explicit interest on demand deposits is not allowed. One reason for the differential on different types of time and savings accounts is that shorter-term accounts have a higher turnover rate and, therefore, higher handling costs. In the case of commercial bank demand deposits, an implicit rate of interest is paid to the extent that the costs of issuing and processing checks are not covered by fees for such services. Although the prohibition of payment of explicit interest on demand deposits remains in effect, 1980 legislation legalized automatic transfer services under which demand deposits may be kept at zero and funds may be transferred automatically from time deposits to meet checks as they are written. Also, effective January 1, 1981, NOW accounts (time deposit accounts on which checks may be written) were authorized in all states. Thus the prohibition of payment of interest on demand deposits has little significance for individuals. Business firms, of course, and *some* individuals continue to hold demand deposit (checking) accounts on which they receive no explicit interest.

## SUMMARY

Several factors other than term to maturity, the subject of the preceding chapter, affect the yield on securities: (1) *risk* and the risk premium that borrowers pay to lenders—presumably, the greater the risk of default, the higher the yield; (2) *callability*—call provisions on securities make them more desirable for issuers, but less attractive to investors, and hence securities with call provisions presumably sell for lower prices and higher yields than do those without call provisions; (3) *tax status*— the reduced tax on long-term capital gains, estate tax provisions, and the income tax exemption for interest income on municipal bonds all affect yields; and (4) *marketability* is a general term reflecting various attributes of a security that make it more or less marketable—presumably, the greater the marketability and the smaller the transactions costs, the lower the yield.

Causes of differences between yields on *new* and on *seasoned* issues are related to call provisions, tax provisions, "lock-in" effects, and marketing conditions.

The total yield on common stocks includes both the dividend yield and capital gain (or loss). Yields on stocks are presumed to be higher than are yields on bonds because of the greater risk in investing in stocks, and, even if dividend yields are below bond yields, capital gains on stocks may in the long run provide a hedge against inflation and the higher yield on stocks needed to induce investors to hold stocks, which are assets entailing more risk than bonds.

Two hybrid forms of securities are preferred stocks and convertible bonds. In general, preferred stocks are less attractive than are bonds issued by the same companies because preferred stocks do not contain fixed obligations to pay interest. Convertible bonds, on the other hand, are more attractive to investors than are ordinary bonds, because convertibles may appreciate in value if converted to stock that is rising in price.

Differentials in interest rates on mortgages result from such factors as servicing costs, whereas differences in rates on loans and on saving deposits result from compensating balance and collateral requirements and from geographical location.

## Questions for Discussion

**1.** What are the four kinds of risk that should concern students of financial markets?

**2.** Define the term "risk premium."

**3.** Explain the importance of a call provision to the buyer of a security.

**4.** Why *might* a deep discount bond be expected to sell at a price giving a lower yield to maturity than a bond selling at par?

**5.** Present three economic effects of the income tax exemption on interest from municipal bonds. Do the rich escape taxation when they buy these tax-exempt securities? Explain your answer.

**6.** What are compensating balances, how do they alter the "effective" interest rate on a loan, and what other purposes do they serve?

**7.** What category of investors might be especially likely to buy preferred stock? Why?

**8.** What factors increase marketability of securities? How would you test whether greater marketability is accompanied by lower yields?

**9.** Why may yields on new issues be quite high at certain times, in comparison with yields on similar "seasoned" bonds?

**10.** List some of the factors that may increase the attractiveness of convertible bonds, especially at certain times.

## Selected References

A statistical study by Roy C. Fair and Burton G. Malkiel examined yield differentials that result from the relationship between the supplies of bonds outstanding and the anticipated level of new offerings. See "The Determination of Yield Differentials Between Debt Instruments of the Same Maturity," *Journal of Money, Credit, and Banking,* November 1971, pp. 733–749.

An analysis that integrates the effects of differences in tax treatment, call provisions, and default risk into the traditional yield-to-maturity formula is set forth in Timothy Q. Cook, "Some Factors Affecting Long-Term Yield Spreads in Recent Years," Federal Reserve Bank of Richmond, *Monthly Review,* September 1973, pp. 2–14.

For more details on loan rates, see *Essays in Money and Credit,* Federal Reserve Bank of New York, 1964, especially "The Prime Rate," by Albert M. Wojnilower and Richard E. Speagle, pp. 47–56; "Compensating Balances," by Jack M. Guttentag and Richard G. Davis, pp. 57–61; and "Term Lending by New York City Banks," by George Budzeika, pp. 67–71.

James C. Van Horne, *Financial Market Rates and Flows* (Englewood Cliffs, N.J.: Prentice-Hall, 1978) gives a thorough analysis of the effects of default risk, callability, and taxes on interest rates (see Chapters 6, 7, and 8).

On automobile manufacturers' low-rate financing of loans to buy autos, see "The Market Share Fight over Auto Loans," *Fortune*, October 27, 1986, p. 93. Competition between banks and finance company subsidiaries of the automobile companies is strong, and the latter are a potentially important factor in other lending.

On Japanese competition in interest rates, see Gary Hector, "The Japanese Want to Be Your Bankers," *Fortune*, October 27, 1986, pp. 96–104.

# ECONOMIC GOALS
# AND POLICIES

XV

We now turn our attention to policies of the Federal Reserve System and the Treasury and to the role that these agencies play in financial markets. Chapters 15, 16, and 17 constitute Part Five. In Chapter 15 we examine the nation's major economic goals and policies used to attain these goals, and we consider some arguments in support of different policy prescriptions. In Chapter 16 we outline the transmission mechanism by which monetary policy affects output, employment, and prices. We then discuss various strategies that the Fed might follow in conducting its open market operations and some implications of different strategies for financial markets. We conclude the chapter with a section on policies and techniques used by the Fed in recent years. In Chapter 17 we discuss some of the ways in which Treasury operations impinge on financial and economic variables. Mostly, our attention is on the government budget, the composition of the federal debt, and the interrelationship among monetary, fiscal, and debt management policies, which are of vital concern to financial managers and financial analysts.

# GOVERNMENT AND THE ECONOMY—THE 1930s TO THE 1980s

The state of the economy, as such, is not a fundamental issue referred to in the Constitution because for the most part our founding fathers believed in free enterprise as expounded by Adam Smith. In a *laissez-faire* economy the government stays out of commerce and industry. The growth of government activity affecting the economy has been substantial, however, since the Great Depression of the 1930s. Many actions taken have reflected the need that was felt for government action to increase employment, to prevent bank and business failures, and to provide special assistance for certain groups (Social Security at first for older people, then also for illness—Medicare—and also for disability, and then after 1965 a variety of programs such as food stamps, school lunches, and many others). These expanded many times more rapidly than did the growth of the economy as a whole.

In the 1930s, the economic legislation was largely regulatory legislation—the Banking Acts of 1933 and 1935, which restricted the powers of banks, established deposit insurance (the FDIC, which was initiated by those laws), the securities legislation to reduce risk in the securities markets, and others that have been mentioned in earlier chapters.

Although legislation providing for the interstate highway program was passed in the 1950s, the major part of recent social legislation came after the mid-1960s—in what was sometimes termed President Johnson's "Great Society" program. This legislation resulted in a more active role for government in providing economic programs for particular groups and also a substantial increase in the federal debt as budget deficits became an annual occurrence after 1965, with the single exception of 1969.

The major thrust of the Reagan administration program, beginning in 1981, was to reverse a number of these trends. The major components of the Reagan economic program were (1) slowing the rate of growth of government spending, (2) reducing tax burdens, (3) introducing regulatory reform involving some degree of deregulation of various lines of business, and (4) providing support for control by the Fed of the growth of the money supply, to slow the rate of inflation. In earlier chapters we have noted the rather remarkable progress made in slowing the rate of inflation, the legislation that provided some degree of deregulation for the financial services industry, and the laws that enacted tax cuts. Progress in reducing the rate of growth of government spending was slow, however, and a recession (brief) in 1980 and another (longer) in 1981 and 1982 reduced revenues and increased some spending, resulting in increasing deficits, both current and projected.

## ECONOMIC GOALS

In the Employment Act of 1946, Congress for the first time stated the specific responsibility of the federal government to promote the nation's economic welfare. This law required an economic report by the President early each year, established a three-person Council of Economic Advisers to provide economic advice, and provided for establishment of a Joint Economic Committee of Congress to hold hearings on economic conditions and problems. The relatively brief economic report of the President has been published every year with a more detailed report by the Council of Economic Advisers, in the *Economic Report of the President*. It has become traditional for an economic forecast for the year to be included in this report.

Although the Employment Act of 1946 did not refer specifically to inflation control, promotion of economic growth, or achievement of an appropriate position in the balance of payments (the record of all international transactions of the country), these goals came to be regularly discussed in the *Economic Report of the President*. In some years useful analytical tools were developed or used in these reports: a basis for selecting an unemployment rate of 4 percent of the labor force as an "interim goal" in the early 1960s; a method of projecting growth of real GNP based on growth of the labor force and on productivity—originally of labor, but in later analyses on productivity of capital also; "Okun's law" relating the gap between "potential" GNP (what real GNP would be at high or full employment) and the actual GNP to the unemployment rate; and Phillips curves (relating unemployment rates to inflation rates in a trade-off of some increase in inflation in exchange for some reduction in unemployment).

Wide discussion of economic growth, as distinct from reduction in unemployment, came at the time of the election of President Kennedy. Reduction in unemployment provides a cyclical increase in output; the increase in output is limited to what is possible with high or full employment. Economic growth, however, means a rise in the long-term rate of increase in potential GNP. In President Kennedy's term, there was much discussion among economists as to whether the then current rate of increase of nearly 4 percent a year could be raised to 5 percent. (In the 1960s, Japan was achieving a growth rate of about 11 percent a year.)

A major milestone in legislation concerning economic goals was passage in 1978 of the Humphrey-Hawkins Full Employment and Balanced Growth Act, which established national economic priorities and objectives. One of these extends the Employment Act and declares that individuals should have the right to full opportunity for useful paid employment. Another stated objective is "reasonable price stability." The act also calls for increased private and public capital formation to provide growth in productivity. It calls for a steady reduction in the extent of government intervention and for increased reliance on the private sector to meet its objectives. It sets a balanced budget as a goal of national policy. Finally, it recognizes that we should maintain a strong position in the world economy and that we should pursue goals to that end.

But the Humphrey-Hawkins Act did not stop short with the articulation of goals—it directed the President to establish, and the Congress to consider, means or avenues to reach these goals. It also specified procedures for the President, the Congress, and the Federal Reserve to use to improve the coordination and development of economic policies designed to attain the goals and objectives. For example, the act required that the administration set annual numerical goals for key indicators over a five-year period.[1]

The goals of high employment (low unemployment) and price stability (a low rate, or perhaps no positive rate, of inflation), both specified in the Humphrey-Hawkins Act, are certainly not the only economic goals that are sought. For example, (1) an "adequate" national defense, as well as a strong position in the world economy, is a major goal (although there is dispute about what is "adequate"); (2) economic freedom, with the reduction or elimination of burdensome government regulation, is argued by some to be essential for increased economic activity; (3) a "better" environment, especially cleaner air and water, is desired by many; (4) "equitable" distribution of income and wealth may be a desired goal, although there is disagreement about what is "equitable"; (5) an increase in homeownership has been favored by many, on the grounds that homeowners are "better citizens" and are more interested in their communities. Other goals could be added, for example, avoidance of defaults on loans by borrowing countries, that might result in bank failures that were so great a problem in the early 1930s, and may again be a problem in the 1980s.

If they are to be achieved, some of these goals involve specific legislation, for example, requirements limiting the extent of permissible pollution of air or water and so on. But progress toward most of these goals could be achieved through macroeconomic policies that have direct impacts on the financial markets and indirect impacts on income and output. For example, homeownership has been encouraged by the establishment of government-sponsored institutions that created secondary markets for mortgage loans, insured such mortgage loans, and gave tax reductions to homeowners.

The major macroeconomic policies that are used to aid in achieving desired goals are (1) monetary policy (control of growth of the money supply and/or control of credit); (2) fiscal policy (policy concerning increase or reduction in taxes, in government spending, and government borrowing); (3) debt management policy, which determines the forms and maturities of securities issued for government borrowing; and (4) incomes policies, which directly regulate changes in prices, wages, interest rates, or dividends.

In the remainder of this chapter, we discuss some problems in defining and achieving various goals, outline the nature of the macroeconomic policies just listed, and summarize the current state of economic discussion of macroeconomic policy. Major topics of discussion include the "Keynesian" view stressing fiscal (taxation and government spending) policy, the monetarist view stressing the importance of monetary policy, and the revival in the 1980s of "supply-side" economics stressing the importance of incentives to stimulate increased productive activity.

---

[1] For further description of the provisions of the Humphrey-Hawkins Act, see the *Economic Report of the President, 1979*, pp. 106–110.

# SOME PROBLEMS IN DEFINING AND ACHIEVING ECONOMIC GOALS

There are problems in defining as well as in achieving economic goals such as those just discussed. What is "full employment"? How much unemployment can exist in a situation that is still recognized as essentially one of "full employment"? How should unemployment be measured? How should inflation be measured? Is one price index, such as the consumer price index (CPI), a better or worse measure than another index, such as the GNP deflator, which measures the change in prices of everything included in GNP? What is the difference between an increase in output and income resulting from reduction in unemployment and such an increase resulting from a rise in the rate of economic growth? How is this difference measured? What measure should be used to indicate whether the balance of payments is in an appropriate or equilibrium status? Such problems in defining goals must be addressed before measures to achieve the goals can be clearly specified.

There are then problems in attempting to achieve the goals. If an attempt to achieve a reduction in unemployment results in more inflation, is the action desirable? How important is general price stability? Is "some" inflation acceptable, and if so, how much? What is needed to achieve more rapid economic growth? What balance-of-payments situation is consistent with other economic goals? Is an excess of imports of goods over exports of goods harmful, even if it is matched by an excess of exports of services over imports of services? Is an outflow of gold or other assets used in international payments harmful? How much outflow? Is an increase in dollar liabilities owed to foreigners (dollar deposits held by foreigners) harmful? Does it make a difference whether the foreigners are individuals, business firms, or governments? In the rest of this section, we intend to clarify the choices that must be faced.

## Full Employment, Inflation, and the Phillips Curve

Full employment is an ambiguous concept. Virtually no one interprets the term literally and seeks an unemployment rate of zero percent. Some degree of "frictional" unemployment is considered inevitable, and even desirable, in a dynamic economy where factors of production are free to respond to changing conditions in the product and factor markets. When unemployment, which had exceeded 7 percent of the labor force in the 1957–1958 recession, nearly reached that level again in the 1960–1961 recession, concern over this problem resulted in the selection in 1962 of an interim target of 4 percent as a goal of policy.[2]

---

[2] The labor force is defined as persons 16 years of age or over who are employed or are looking for work. Unemployment as a percentage of the labor force may rise if people lose jobs and also if new entrants or reentrants into the labor force cannot find work. The rate of unemployment has not been below the target of 4 percent since 1950 except in the Korean war period; on selection of the target, see *Economic Report of the President, 1962*, pp. 44 ff. Recently there has been discussion of the need for greater equality of incomes instead of, or in addition to, high employment and rapid growth. For some reasons why the goal of

During the 1970s the rate of unemployment rose; in the latter half of the 1970s there were years in which unemployment rates reached 6, 7, and 8 percent. Observing these rates, Congress, in the Full Employment and Balanced Growth Act of 1978 (the Humphrey-Hawkins Act), established a target for 1983 of a rate of unemployment of 4 percent for workers ages 16 years and over and 3 percent for workers ages 20 and over. (Incidentally, the unemployment rate in early 1983 was over 10 percent.)

Inflation was also increasing rapidly. In 1978 the rate of increase in the consumer price index was 9 percent; by the first quarter of 1980, the annual rate of increase was over 15 percent. (Incidentally, the rate of increase in 1982 was 3.9 percent; the goal for 1983, specified in the act, was 3 percent.)

The authors of the Humphrey-Hawkins Act apparently believed that it would not be possible to reach goals such as 4 percent unemployment and 3 percent inflation in a brief period of time; hence they set the target year five years ahead.

If these two goals are inherently in conflict, it may be necessary to abandon one goal, at least temporarily, to reach the other. Do these goals conflict? Do efforts to reduce unemployment cause a rise in the rate of inflation, and vice versa?

Prior to the mid-1950s, there was little empirical evidence concerning the relationship between unemployment and inflation. Serious inflation had seldom occurred in the United States except during and immediately following periods of mobilization for war. The inflation that did result was attributed to excessive aggregate demand and was expected only if and when unemployment was no longer a matter of concern. As a consequence, the likelihood of peacetime inflation was largely ignored and economists directed their attention to the prevention or elimination of high unemployment. Toward the end of the 1950s, however, the emergence of inflation at a time of slack demand when the economy was experiencing slow growth of output and rising unemployment led to new analyses of inflation and the relationship between inflation and the rate of unemployment.

### The Phillips Curve

In 1958, a study of the British economy by A. W. Phillips offered evidence that the rate of increase in money wages and the rate of unemployment are inversely related.[3] Similar studies of the U.S. economy relating wage or price changes to the rate of unemployment, though far from conclusive, seemed to confirm this finding.

---

greater equality of income is not emphasized in this chapter, see Sanford Rose, "The Truth About Income Inequality in the U.S.," *Fortune*, December 1972, pp. 90–93, 158–172. A very perceptive note on additional complications in measuring inequality of incomes may be found in the letter to the editors by our colleague, Dean A. Worcester, *Fortune*, March 1973, pp. 65, 68. He points out that much of observed inequality in incomes is due to differences in *age*.

[3] A. W. Phillips, "The Relationship Between Unemployment and the Rate of Change of Money Wage Rates in the United Kingdom, 1861–1957," *Economica*, Vol. 25, November 1958, pp. 283–299. See also P. A. Samuelson and R. M. Solow, "Analytical Aspects of Anti-Inflation Policy," *American Economic Review*, Vol. 50, May 1960, pp. 177–194, reprinted in W. L. Smith and R. L. Teigen, eds., *Readings in Money, National Income and Stabilization Policy*, 2nd ed. (Homewood, Ill.: Richard D. Irwin, 1970).

**FIGURE 15–1**
**Phillips Curve**

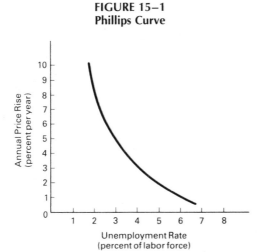

This relationship, referred to as a Phillips curve, is shown in Figure 15–1, which relates various rates of inflation to hypothetical rates of unemployment.

If such a Phillips curve is found to exist over a considerable period of time, then it is indicated that there is an economically feasible menu of rates that are compatible. Policymakers may not be able to achieve desired targets for unemployment and inflation simultaneously. A low rate of inflation may not be compatible with a low rate of unemployment.

If a relationship such as that shown in Figure 15–1 is typical and stable over time, it may be necessary to set a target for "full employment" that is compatible with a rate of inflation that is acceptable to the public.

There are several possible explanations of this inverse relationship between inflation and unemployment: the power of labor unions to push up money wages when unemployment is low; the emergence of bottlenecks in product markets; excess demand for labor, which bids up wage rates; and so on. Expressed differently, the downward-sloping character of the curve may be attributed to the presence of market imperfections, including elements of cost-push inflation. That is, if all markets were perfect and inflation was due solely to excessive demand for goods and services, the Phillips curve would be vertical at approximately full employment of labor; if cost-push were the only source of inflation, the curve would be horizontal at a rate of inflation corresponding to the difference between the annual rate of increase in money wages and productivity. In the latter case, the administration of prices by business or the power of labor unions to set wage rates independent of the rate of unemployment would rationalize the inflation during periods of recession.

### Criticisms of the Phillips Curve Analysis

A number of economists have serious reservations concerning the validity and usefulness of the Phillips curve. One criticism is that the relationship is far too volatile to be useful as a policy tool. A given Phillips curve implies a particular set of expectations concerning inflation: the higher the anticipated rate of inflation, the higher the curve lies, because workers will demand higher wages at any rate of unemployment. Now if expectations change, the curve shifts and the trade-off values are different. Only if expectations change slowly would the Phillips curve be a useful guide for stabilization policy.

A second, and related, criticism is that if the authorities try to secure a different pair of trade-off values from the "expected" combination shown on the curve, the entire curve will break down until expectations are reestablished. Many observers who oppose the use of the Phillips curve for policy purposes argue that except for very-short-run periods the trade-off is an illusion. In the longer run, when people come to anticipate the actual rate of inflation, the rate of unemployment will settle at the "natural" rate, whatever the rate of inflation. In other words, the long-run Phillips curve will be a vertical line at a rate of unemployment determined by the real demand and supply for labor. In this view, an increase in aggregate demand may *temporarily* reduce the unemployment rate below the "natural" rate by increasing both the demand and supply of labor. However, when workers become aware of the decrease in the real wage, they demand higher money wages, which reduces the quantity of labor demanded; unemployment increases, returning to the natural rate. Accordingly, we cannot "buy" full employment, except perhaps temporarily, with a given rate of inflation. Only by accelerating the rate of inflation over time can unemployment be maintained below the natural rate. This is not to say that these critics of the Phillips curve regard a high rate of unemployment as desirable. They would, however, seek to reduce unemployment by means other than expansionary monetary or fiscal policy, such as repeal of minimum wage laws, elimination of monopolistic practices of business and labor, and other measures designed to improve the mobility and skills of labor. Nonetheless, although many economists would favor such measures to shift the Phillips curve downward and to the left, and so reduce the cost of high employment, they continue to view the problem of goals as one of trade-offs. To accept the concept of a "natural" rate of unemployment goes against the grain of those who believe that economic policy *should* be used to achieve full employment and that monetary and fiscal measures are more likely to be effective than sole reliance upon reducing market imperfections, desirable though that may be.

### Empirical Evidence on the Phillips Curve

Since Phillips' study appeared, many other economists have sought further evidence on the relation for different time periods and different countries.[4] In recent years it appears that the curve as shown in Figure 15–1 has not been stable. In 1970, average unemployment was 4.9 percent, and the consumer price index rose by 5.9 percent from 1969 to 1970. Clearly such a pair of values would lie above and to the right of the curve in Figure 15–1. George L. Perry estimated two short-run curves: one for the mid-1950s and one for the period 1967–1970. These were flatter and above

---

[4] See G. L. Perry, "Changing Labor Markets and Inflation," *Brookings Papers on Economic Activity*, No. 3, 1970, pp. 411–441, and Charles L. Schultze, "Has the Phillips Curve Shifted? Some Additional Evidence," *Brookings Papers on Economic Activity*, No. 2, 1971.

## FIGURE 15–2
## The Shifting Phillips Curve

Inflation and Unemployment

(annual data)

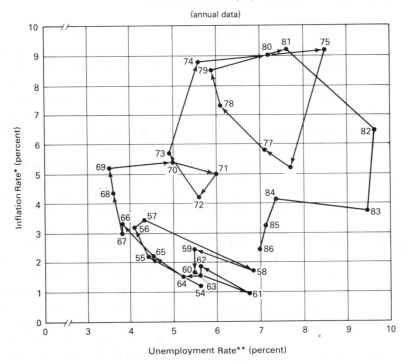

\* Percentage change in the GNP implicit price deflator.
\*\* Percent of civilian labor force.

SOURCE: Economic Report of the President, 1986, except for 1986, which is estimated by the authors.

the one shown. He argues that part of the reason for this shift is the changing composition of the U.S. labor force. A larger proportion of women and youths, two groups with typically high rates of unemployment, are now in the labor force. Thus, the average rate is higher than formerly.

Eckstein and Brinner have also reported that the Phillips curve has shifted rightward.[5] They argue that, as the rate of inflation increases, the Phillips curve will shift upward year by year. This is because inflation leads to expectations of more inflation, all of which feeds the inflation itself. Thus, the rate of inflation remains high even in the face of relatively large unemployment, and the Phillips curve is then said to have shifted upward.

In Figure 15–2 there is ample evidence of a shifting Phillips curve. Average rates of unemployment for the year and the percentage change in the inflation rate as

[5] Otto Eckstein and Roger Brinner, "The Inflation Process in the United States," Joint Economic Committee of Congress, February 22, 1972.

measured by the GNP deflator for the year are plotted for the period 1961–1986. The figure seems to show a clockwise spiral moving upward to the right.[6] From 1961 to 1969, as the level of unemployment declined from around 7 percent to a level below 4 percent, the rate of inflation gradually rose to the 5 percent level. This seemed to verify the Phillips curve and the concept of a trade-off between inflation and unemployment. But then in 1970 the data moved away from the tentative curve. That year we had both more inflation and more unemployment. It was then that the word "stagflation" was coined—stagflation is growing unemployment combined with inflation.

Economists who accept the quantity theory of money explain stagflation somewhat as follows. The public's demand for *real* money balances is assumed to be relatively stable; if there is more real output, people want to hold more money—in fact, they need to hold more money to buy the additional output. If the nominal money supply is increased more than real output is increased, people *try* to get rid of the excess supply of money by spending it or lending (investing) it. As this occurs, such a general increase in spending causes a rise in the general price level. Especially as "full employment" is approached, the price level begins to rise. For a time, there may be both rising prices and lower rates of unemployment. But as people begin to anticipate increases in money supply and increases in prices, price increases tend to outweigh increases in output. If, then, for any reason, demand for goods and services slows its increase, inventories become excessive, orders for goods to replace them are canceled, and output falls. So does employment, but prices continue to rise. Stagflation is the result.[7]

Many economists worried that it might take years to slow down inflation and that the cost in unemployment and lost output might be tremendous. But the German hyperinflation of 1923 provides one example of how even an extreme inflation can be controlled relatively quickly. In that inflation, money supply was increasing 1,300 percent a *month*, prices were rising at an annual rate of 300,000 percent, the interest rate on bank loans was over 7,300 percent a year, and a postage stamp cost 200 billion marks. The government attempted to control this inflation in autumn 1923. A new director of the central bank was appointed, a new currency was issued, each mark being equal in value to 1 trillion of the old paper marks, and a fixed upper limit on the amount of the new currency that could be issued was established (no more of the old paper currency was issued). The central bank was in effect also directed to issue no more paper money for the government.[8]

Within a few weeks, the rate of inflation dropped rapidly. And, in contrast to the fear expressed by many economists that there would be a tremendous fall in real

---

[6] An excellent discussion of the theory and evidence relating to the Phillips curve, and a diagram similar to Figure 15–2, may be found in Thomas A. Gittings, "The Inflation-Unemployment Trade-off," Federal Reserve Bank of Chicago, *Economic Perspectives*, September–October 1979, pp. 3–9.

[7] For a somewhat more detailed, but still brief, discussion, see Robert L. Hetzel, "The Quantity Theory Tradition and the Role of Monetary Policy," Federal Reserve Bank of Richmond, *Economic Review*, May–June 1981, pp. 19–26.

[8] Thomas M. Humphrey, "Eliminating Runaway Inflation: Lessons from the German Hyperinflation," Federal Reserve Bank of Richmond, *Economic Review*, July–August 1980, pp. 3–7.

GNP, the decline in real GNP was only approximately 10 percent. Apparently the public believed that the government was indeed determined to stop further increases in the money supply and thus stop inflation. The public therefore ceased to expect (and to ask for or initiate) wage and price increases.

Although the United States did not take such stern measures as Germany had in 1922–1923 (partly because the problem of inflation was much less serious), the evidence indicates that inflation can be controlled in a relatively short time. A policy focusing on control of the money supply was adopted by the Fed in late 1979, and by 1983, the rate of inflation as measured by the consumer price index was only 3.9 percent. In the first half of the 1980s, inflation fell to such a low rate that it was not a significant problem.

## Price Stability

It is evident from the foregoing paragraphs that price stability is not a simple concept, since a choice must be made among several indexes designed to measure price changes. The consumer price index is intended to measure changes in prices of a fixed "basket" of goods and services purchased by a certain group—urban wage earners in the past and all urban consumers more recently. Although revised in 1978, further revisions seemed necessary, especially because rapidly rising costs of houses and mortgage interest rates seemed to overstate the rise in consumer prices. Part of those costs reflected an investment in a house, which increased in value; rental costs did not rise as rapidly. Beginning January 1983, the CPI incorporated a rental equivalence measure.

There is also a producer price index, formerly known as the wholesale price index. This index has fluctuated much more widely than the CPI; prices of given products seem to rise sharply, then increased output is generated, and prices level off. It is sometimes suggested that producer price increases forecast subsequent increases in consumer prices, but this is not nearly always the case.

There is also the GNP implicit price deflator. It differs from the CPI in two major ways: it measures, or attempts to measure, prices of all goods and services included in GNP, not simply those purchased by urban consumers; and it measures the change in prices for what is purchased, not for a fixed basket of goods and services. The CPI answers the question, "How much more *would* consumers have paid if they had bought the same basket of goods and services as they bought in the base year?" The GNP deflator answers the question, "How much higher were prices for what was bought this year than for what was bought last year?" (In technical terms, the CPI is known as a Laspeyres-type index, the GNP deflator as a Paasche-type index.)

Which index more accurately measures inflation? The CPI has been criticized in the past for overstating inflation, since not all improvements in goods were taken into account, although some were. Thus a price increase might reflect improvement in a product as well as (or instead of) pure price increase. It has also been criticized because it uses prices for a fixed basket of goods, whereas consumers may shift, for example, from purchase of expensive products to cheaper products. Again, the CPI would overstate price increases unless the question asked is, "How much more *would* they have to pay for the same goods they bought in the base year?" But how is one to assume that a particular base year represented a desirable basket of goods? Perhaps a shift in consumption from high-priced butter to lower-priced margarine would be better for health. Finally, if the cost of staying one day in a hospital rises, but people who have appendix operations stay only three days on the average instead of five, have hospital costs increased as much as the index (based on cost per day) indicates?

Most economists would be willing to regard 1 or 2, or perhaps 3 percent inflation as tantamount to price stability, partly because of error inherent in the indexes and partly because if inflation is slight, it is not likely to cause significant dislocations. Any actions taken to avoid (or hedge against) harmful effects of inflation involve some cost. If one buys gold as a hedge (instead of investing in business), storage and insurance costs are involved. Hence people are likely to try to hedge only if inflation exceeds 2 or 3 percent.

So far we have simply assumed that a stable price level is desirable, but a case can be made for gently rising or falling prices as a long-run goal. One argument for gradually rising prices is that a slight degree of inflation helps to create an aura of prosperity and promote economic expansion and growth by rewarding the more venturesome, risk-taking elements of society.[9] On the other hand, declining prices (with stable or more slowly falling money wages) provide a method of sharing the gains of productivity broadly and benefit some segments of society that would otherwise suffer from reduced real income. However, neither a rising nor falling price level has found favor with most economists and policymakers. First, there are no safeguards to guarantee that gently rising (declining) prices will not become cumulative and lead to runaway inflation (deflation). Second, our pricing mechanism is not sufficiently flexible, at least in the downward direction, to make such a goal institutionally feasible. It is doubtful that business or labor would welcome a regime of, say, falling prices and stable wages. As a consequence of these limitations, the consensus appears to be that the safest and most acceptable long-run goal is a stable price level, or one rising at a very modest rate, part of which may simply be the result of the statistical bias of the price indexes.

## Economic Growth

One way for a nation to realize increases in output over time is to maintain full employment of its resources, including labor. To the extent that unemployment obtains, policies that restore full employment will provide a fairly rapid, one-shot increase in the production of goods and services, a process that closes the gap between the current and the potential levels of GNP. Once a full-employment level is reached, output can increase at the rate of growth provided by a growing labor force and improvements in the nation's productivity. In this process, further increments in real

---

[9] See Summer H. Slichter, "On the Side of Inflation," *Harvard Business Review*, Vol. 35, May–June 1957, pp. 15 ff.; and for a reply to his position, see Neil H. Jacoby, "The Threat of Inflation," in the same journal, September–October 1957, pp. 15 ff.

**FIGURE 15–3**
**Potential GNP, Actual GNP, and the "Gap"**

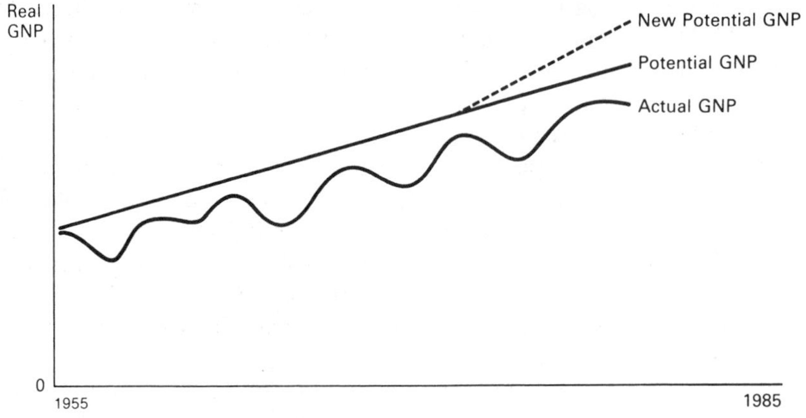

output may only be realized by raising the economy's *capacity* to produce. Economists usually reserve the concept "economic growth" to refer to the latter process and measure growth in terms of the percentage increase in potential output or output per capita. In common parlance, however, the term is broadly used to include growth in actual *or* potential output, depending upon the particular context in which it is used.

### Distinguishing Between Attaining "Full Employment" and Achieving More Rapid Long-Run Economic Growth

The difference between achievement of "full employment" and achievement of a more rapid rate of economic growth is illustrated in Figure 15–3. In simple terms, the line designated as "potential GNP" can best be understood as, at some point, being the real GNP in a year in which "full employment" was achieved; the rise in real GNP is determined by the rise in the labor force, which increases output if full employment continues, and the rise in productivity (output per worker-hour), which also increases output and which depends on a number of factors (education and training of workers, amount of capital used by workers, experience of workers, technological improvements in capital used, and so on). The line designated as "actual GNP" indicates the path of real GNP, rising as business activity increases and falling in recessions. The "gap" indicates a loss of potential output and can be related to the extent of unemployment (as GNP falls, unemployment increases).[10]

In contrast to a policy aimed at full employment, which would only raise output to the potential level, a growth policy would aim at raising the long-term potential growth of GNP, as indicated by the dashed line for new potential GNP. At the time of

---

[10] This relationship is known as Okun's law, because Arthur Okun, when chairman of the Council of Economic Advisers, developed the first formula for relating unemployment to the GNP gap.

the election of President Kennedy, when the president used the phrase, "Let's get America moving again," there was much discussion as to whether it would be feasible to increase the growth rate, which was then nearly 4 percent a year for potential GNP, to 5 percent a year. Over the long run this would have created a tremendous rise in the standard of living.

For many years, Japan's rate of increase in real GNP exceeded 10 percent per year, in contrast to 3 or 4 percent for the United States. Some other countries in Asia have had very rapid growth. Japan has a very high rate of saving, more than double the rate in the United States, but it is difficult to say that this is a major factor in Japan's rapid growth. Certainly it is not the only factor.

### Policies of the Reagan Administration

The Reagan administration believed that an increased rate of capital formation was essential for the 1980s. Reasons included (1) the sharp drop in additional capital per worker added in the 1970s (from almost the same amount in the late 1960s to about one-third of that amount in the late 1970s); (2) the evidence that of six major countries (France, Germany, Italy, Japan, the United Kingdom, and the United States), the United States ranked lowest in net fixed investment as a percentage of GNP (only 6.6 percent per year during the 1970s for the United States compared with 19.5 percent for Japan); and (3) evidence that, for the same six countries, net fixed investment as a percent of GNP was very closely related to increase in productivity in manufacturing (rate of increase in output per hour). The last piece of evidence meant that countries with a higher productivity had more net fixed investment as a percentage of their GNPs, in about the same relationship (where productivity growth was three times as high, net fixed investment was three times as high a percent of GNP). The evidence from a number of countries, not from one country alone, indicates that the relationship was probably not the result of "catchup" (as might have been the case if Japan alone, for example, had had large increases in productivity and a high rate of net fixed investment as a percentage of GNP).[11]

Decline in the rate of increase in productivity was a major economic change in the United States in the 1970s. From 1948 to 1964, the average increase in productivity in the private sector was 3.1 percent per year; in 1967–1973, it was only 2.3 percent per year; and in 1973–1981 it was only .8 percent per year.[12] There is much disagreement about the causes of this decline in productivity. Higher energy costs, regulatory changes, less spending for research and development, fewer technical innovations, and other factors could be causes, as well as inadequate net fixed investment. But some of these could not be influenced by government policies, and hence need be given less consideration when growth policies are discussed.

With the decline in the rate of capital accumulation, there was a decline in the rate of private saving as a percent of GNP—from over 7 percent in the 1950s to 6.5 percent in the second half of the 1970s, and to less than 6 percent in 1981. In the

---

[11] *Economic Report of the President*, February 1983, pp. 77–82.

[12] Ibid., p. 83.

decade of the 1960s, one of generally high economic growth, the rate of private saving was 7.9 percent of GNP.[13] Many economists believe that levels of taxes, inflation, and interest rates have encouraged consumption and discouraged saving. During the 1960s, the real return on saving, as measured by the interest rate on 3-month Treasury bills (a market interest rate) minus the rate of inflation as measured by the CPI was 1.7 percent; for savers in the 30 percent tax bracket, the after-tax return was .5 percent. But in the 1970s, the average inflation rate was 7.1 percent and the average interest rate only 6.3 percent. Thus the *real* rate of return was *minus* .8 percent (approximately), and the after-tax real rate of return for persons in the 30 percent tax bracket was *minus* 2.7 percent.[14] Why save? We might add that for many lower-income savers, real rates of return were even further below zero because of interest rate ceilings on savings held in banks and related institutions.

One further point: tax rates remained high in this period on corporate investment, but the tax system benefited those who invested in housing. Mortgage interest was deductible before calculation of taxable income (and still is), and people aged 55 or older could sell homes under certain conditions with no tax on capital gain if it were $125,000 or less. Capital was diverted from investment in business fixed investment to investment in housing. Although housing is a form of capital investment and construction of houses employs workers, houses are producers of services rather than goods, although home building leads to purchases (and hence to production) of such goods as appliances. As house prices rose (and rather sharply in the later 1970s), the market value of capital as measured by equity values, relative to its reproduction cost, fell from over 1 in 1970 to about .67 in 1980. Housing benefited, stock market prices suffered! As indicated in Chapter 11, it is not clear what factors were most significant in causing this change in relationship.

A major objective of the Reagan administration was to reduce personal and corporate taxes, to encourage work, saving, and investment. Another objective was to reduce capital gains taxes (which often tax gains chiefly attributable to inflation) and to index the personal income tax system to inflation so that both those who obtain capital gains and those whose incomes rise simply because of inflation would be protected from higher taxes. Of course, not all capital gains are correlated with inflation, but a high percentage are. Indexation, beginning in 1985, also forces the government to raise tax rates if it desires more revenue from taxes (beyond the rise which occurs as incomes rise in a recovery from recession). Without indexation, government obtains more revenue when inflation occurs, as people are shifted to higher tax brackets as their incomes rise to offset inflation.

### The Aim: More Rapid Long-Run Growth

Reduced taxes were not expected to result in an immediate increase in investment. In fact, with the rate of use of capacity below 70 percent during the recession of 1981–1982, it could hardly have been expected that much new investment would

---

[13] Ibid., p. 85. Private saving is measured as saving after the allowance for depreciation and other capital consumption, and with a capital consumption adjustment to allow for changing prices.

[14] Ibid., p. 87.

occur soon. The sectors leading business recovery were (1) additions to inventory as sales rose and inventory ratios appeared to be too low; (2) increased consumer spending for automobiles and, later, for other goods and services; and (3) housing (for which there was demand, but demand which could not become effective with very high interest rates). Because of increases for defense spending and because it was difficult to reduce the rate of growth of other government spending, increase in government spending also contributed to economic recovery.

The actions of the early 1980s were aimed at laying foundations for long-run economic growth, not for immediate economic expansion. It was recognized that the unemployment rate might fall slowly; not until early 1983 was it down to a little over 10 percent, from nearly 11 percent at the peak; but by 1986, it was below 7 percent.

The key objective of this part of the Reagan program was the shifting of some income from consumption to investment. Policies to provide incentives for saving, incentives for investment, and some reduction in grants aimed purely at providing funds generally used for consumption were aimed at long-run economic growth. It is in fact possible that the short-run decline in output associated with the recession of 1981–1982 could have been (or perhaps even was) foreseen by some. In any event, slightly less current consumption and more saving and investment were the goals.

Kotlikoff has pointed out that incentives that may induce more saving do not differentiate between old capital (existing factories, machinery, and equipment) and new capital, whereas investment incentives favor new investment over old. Since equally productive new and old capital should sell at the same prices, old capital values are likely to be hurt (relative to other values) by investment incentives. Also, since much of the total claims on capital (bonds, stocks, and so on) are held by older people, these people are likely to be somewhat adversely affected by investment incentives.[15] Since many of the elderly tend to consume and may produce relatively little, consumption is likely to be reduced as their income is reduced if grants are reduced and their wealth is reduced by tax changes that adversely affect the value of "old" capital. The reduced value of capital represents an implicit tax on *existing* capital (wealth). If an explicit tax were levied instead of an implicit tax, the government deficit would be much less. The budget deficit was largely a result of the manner in which taxes were changed.

### The View Opposing Rapid Economic Growth

Some take the view that more rapid economic growth may lead to more rapid depletion of natural resources, that it may increase pollution, and that income levels in some countries may already be high enough to meet most desires. This view, common a few years ago, now has less influence. Of course, some resources will be depleted at some future date—but if so, does it matter much if that date is 100 years from now or 200 years from now? At that time, substitutes must be found for such resources. Moreover, the recessions in 1973–1975, 1980, and again in 1981–1982 led to concern for increased output and income. There is also growing recognition that in many of

[15] Laurence J. Kotlikoff, "National Savings and Economic Policy: The Efficacy of Investment vs. Savings Incentives," *American Economic Review*, May 1983, pp. 82–87.

the less developed countries (LDCs) poverty, infant mortality, short life span for the average person, and high incidence of disease tend to stimulate the desire for economic growth. The process of economic growth through industrialization, which led to rising incomes from levels that had hardly risen at all since medieval times, has only been operative for about two centuries. Even if we discount the economists' traditional view that wants are limitless, President Kennedy's statement that "a rising tide raises all boats" can be applied on a worldwide basis as well as in the United States. The best hope for rising incomes in LDCs is rising *world* income, accompanied by loans and investments from rich countries to finance part of the development process. It is difficult to envision some of the poorest LDCs saving enough to make rapid progress in development without external borrowing—and the United States itself financed development of the West (including railroads and other infrastructure) as late as the 1880s.

### Conclusion: The Causes of Rapid Economic Growth Need More Study

Some agree that decisions to save or consume (involved in policies to affect the rate of growth) should be left to individuals. Others recognize that government affects individual choices in attempting to stimulate a recovery from a recession and that there is little to divide this from an attempt to increase the rate of growth. They focus attention on the means of achieving more rapid economic growth and ask questions about the reasons for rapid economic growth in some countries such as Japan, Korea, and others, chiefly on the Asian side of the Pacific Rim.

What is required to achieve rapid growth? Resources? Japan, Korea, Singapore, and Hong Kong have very few natural resources. Some countries that have discovered resources such as oil have encountered economic difficulties: Iran and Mexico are examples. The study of the causes of economic growth has not reached many generally accepted conclusions.

### Balance-of-Payments Equilibrium

Another important goal is equilibrium in the balance of payments. The balance of payments has two parts: (1) the current account, showing imports and exports of goods and services, plus gifts and transfers, and (2) the capital account, showing flows of capital and gold or other items used to balance the accounts. Deficits in the current account reflect excesses of imports over exports; deficits in the capital account reflect investment being made in foreign countries. Current account deficits reduce income; capital account deficits normally add to income in the future, as capital invested in foreign countries earns interest, dividends, and/or profits.

In recent years, the United States has had a large deficit on current accounts. At the same time it has had a surplus on capital account, as foreign countries have made financial and real investments in the United States.

Beginning in 1980, the U.S. dollar began to rise in value relative to currencies of other major industrial countries; by early 1985, it had risen about 70 percent. In contrast, the dollar rose very little relative to currencies of "newly industrialized countries" (NICs) such as Taiwan and Singapore. It rose only moderately relative to the currency of another NIC, South Korea.

In a period of fixed exchange rates, such as existed from 1946 to 1973, there would have been a flow of reserve assets (such as gold) from other countries to the United States. With the advent of "floating" exchange rates in 1973, the demand for dollars caused the dollar to rise. As the dollar rose in value, imports into the United States were cheaper, causing a larger current account deficit. Exports, being higher priced, were reduced.

In 1985–1986, the dollar fell in value relative to a number of currencies. Although late in 1986 it was still about 20 percent higher than it had been in 1980, the decline in the dollar should reduce imports and stimulate exports, in time. Economists recognize a "J-curve," indicating that exports don't rise immediately, because it takes time to generate new export sales after prices (dollars in terms of other currencies) have fallen. Since the dollar was slow to fall relative to currencies of some NICs, imports from those countries might be expected to continue to increase for a time, even after other imports fall and U.S. exports begin to increase.[16]

# MACROECONOMIC POLICIES

The types of policy available to the federal government to help achieve the economic objectives just outlined are often referred to as "stabilization policies." They are (1) monetary policy, (2) fiscal policy, (3) debt management policy, and (4) an incomes policy. These macroeconomic policies, which affect total spending and are in a sense financial in nature, are generally regarded as the major economic policies used to achieve the goals discussed previously. Some policies such as policies to promote labor mobility and to increase labor skills and programs to enhance the general level of education may be important, but their discussion in any detail is beyond the scope of this book. At this point we provide brief introductions to those policy tools that are discussed in detail in the following chapters.

## Monetary Policy

Broadly construed, monetary policy refers to those actions of the Federal Reserve that affect the behavior of the monetary aggregates (e.g., monetary base, the money supply, bank credit), interest rates, and the overall liquidity of the economy. Accordingly, a policy of monetary restraint would entail a slower rate of growth of the monetary aggregates and *tend* to raise interest rates and lower the liquidity of the economy as compared with a policy of monetary ease. This does not mean that, whenever interest rates are high or rising, monetary policy is restrictive in an *absolute* sense or that it alone is responsible for the degree of credit restraint. Clearly the demand for funds, as well as the supply, affects the level of interest rates, and Federal

---

[16] Brazil and Mexico are often also mentioned as NICs, but in view of their economic problems and especially their very large foreign debts, they are not mentioned in the foregoing discussion.

Reserve policy is but one of several influences on credit conditions. When interest rates are rising over a period of weeks or months, as during a typical period of economic expansion, we attribute this development to a *relative* excess of demand over supply of funds at lower rates. Presumably, the Fed could moderate the rise in rates or even lower them, temporarily at least, if it increased the monetary base and money supply at a fast enough rate. Whether or not it could *maintain* lower rates over a longer period of time is a moot point—it would depend on the relative changes in the demand for and supply of loanable funds.

Conversely, low or declining interest rates, which occur during an economic downturn, cannot be said to be *caused* by Federal Reserve policy alone. A decline in the demand for funds *relative* to the supply of funds is the proximate cause of the observed decline in rates. These points are worthy of emphasis because all too often monetary policy is blamed or applauded for developments in financial markets through a failure to appreciate the meaning of Alfred Marshall's analogy that it takes *both* blades of the scissors of demand and supply to cut.

Our definition of monetary policy encompasses control over both money and credit. (That is, it covers both control over M1, M2, etc., and control over loans and other credit.) Controls may be divided into those that regulate the *volume* of money and credit (quantitative or general controls) and those that restrict the *users* of credit (qualitative or selective controls). The two groups are shown in Table 15–1. Each was discussed briefly in Chapter 5 following the section on the monetary base and multiplier. They have also been referred to on numerous occasions in other chapters, and it suffices here to make a few summary comments about their relative use and importance in monetary control.

The most important single control available to the Federal Reserve is open market operations. They have several advantages over the other measures, which explains why most observers identify monetary control with purchases and sales of government securities. First, as compared with the discount rate, open market operations are far more powerful, more flexible, and more precise in effect. With a portfolio of over $175 billion of securities at the end of 1986, and the ability to create monetary liabilities, the Fed can exert an enormous influence on bank reserves. Moreover, it can do so flexibly and at its own initiative. By comparison, the discount mechanism is a weak tool in that changes in the discount rate may or may not induce desired changes in bank borrowing, excess reserves, and deposits. Also, compared with changes in

**TABLE 15–1**
**Monetary and Credit Controls**

| *Quantitative (General)* | *Qualitative (Selective)* |
|---|---|
| 1. Open market operations | 1. Interest rate ceilings (Regulation Q) |
| 2. Changes in reserve requirements | 2. Margin requirements (Regulations T, U, and G) |
| 3. Discount mechanism | 3. Consumer credit controls (Regulation W) |
| | 4. Mortgage credit (Regulation X) |
| | 5. Moral suasion ("jawboning") |

reserve requirements, open market operations are again more flexible, more easily reversed, and perhaps more acceptable to banks and other depository institutions.

In short, the Federal Reserve can initiate changes in policy through purchases or sales of government securities, the quantitative effects on bank reserves can be estimated with reasonable precision, the operations can be adjusted or reversed easily and quickly, and financial institutions are less apt to blame the Federal Reserve for the instability in their reserve position in the case of a restrictive policy if it results more from open market sales than from an increase in reserve requirements.[17] Against these important advantages it should be observed that open market operations may have some disadvantage in that their impact is not as immediate and uniform on all banks as the impact of the other quantitative controls: the initial effect of open market purchases and sales is on banks in the major financial centers, and it takes time for these developments to be transmitted to the rest of the country.[18] Although the length of the lag is not known, it is now presumably less than in former years because of the increasing integration of financial markets and the development of new techniques for mobilizing reserves and deposits, for example, Federal funds, certificates of deposit, and repurchase agreements.

### Fiscal Policy

Fiscal policy refers to federal government actions determining the size and composition of the budget, that is, expenditures and receipts. As usually understood, the term "fiscal policy" excludes state and local government budgets because these agencies have neither the responsibility for maintaining national prosperity nor the power to use their budgetary processes for that purpose. A large part of federal government spending is for currently produced goods and services; the remainder represents mostly transfer payments to individuals and grants-in-aid to state and local governments. Receipts, on the other hand, consist mainly of personal and business taxes; contributions for social insurance make up most of the balance. As we shall see in Chapter 17, there are some reasons for arguing that the budget need not always be balanced and that a balanced budget at full employment *may* be the best objective.

A deficit results whenever receipts are less than expenditures. When a cash flow deficit occurs, the shortfall of receipts must be supplemented by drawing down cash or borrowing funds by issuing securities. Because of the need to maintain working cash balances, the deficit is financed almost entirely by borrowing from the public, the commercial banks, or, and only rarely, from the Federal Reserve System. A surplus budget, of course, means that receipts are currently in excess of expenditures. When this occurs, the federal government may increase its cash balances or reduce its outstanding debt. Again, the budget imbalance is normally reflected in a change in outstanding Treasury securities.

---

[17] For a fuller exposition of these points, see Thomas Mayer, *Monetary Policy in the United States* (New York: Random House, 1968), pp. 52–55.

[18] See Ira O. Scott, Jr., "The Regional Impact of Monetary Policy," *Quarterly Journal of Economics,* May 1955, pp. 269–284.

Fiscal policy, like monetary policy, affects the levels of employment, output, and prices by raising or lowering the level of money spending. But unlike monetary policy, which works via changes in monetary aggregates or interest rates, fiscal policy affects economic activity mainly by altering the level of disposable income available to the private sector. Changes in government expenditures produce initial changes in total spending because they are part of aggregate demand; they produce secondary changes in total spending to the extent that consumer spending changes are in response to changes in disposable income; that is, there are "multiplier" effects. Changes in tax rates, on the other hand, have chiefly the secondary effect; they change disposable income but have weaker multiplier effects on total spending and income than do changes in expenditures, dollar for dollar. However, whether a deficit or surplus budget is the result of changes in expenditures or tax rates, economists are generally agreed that, *at a given level of GNP*, deficit budgets are more expansionary than are surplus budgets. This means also that the larger the deficit (the smaller the surplus), relative to GNP, the greater the fiscal stimulus. How a deficit budget is financed is a significant element in determining the impact that the deficit has on both the level of spending and interest rates.

The types of taxes and composition of federal government spending are also important. First, the distribution of income is apt to be different, depending upon the types of taxes used to raise revenue. Second, different tax structures, which affect private spending, and different expenditure programs will influence the composition of output and hence the allocation of resources. Fiscal policy, therefore, has effects on both the level and the composition of national output.

## Debt Management Policy

Debt management refers to those actions of the Treasury and Federal Reserve System that affect the *composition* of the federal debt held by the public. The Treasury is responsible for issuing securities to raise funds when deficits are incurred, to meet seasonal requirements even though the annual budget is in balance, and to refinance maturing securities. On the other hand, if tax proceeds exceed expenditures, surplus funds are available to retire outstanding Treasury obligations. The decision to include the Federal Reserve's actions in the definition of debt management stems from the fact that the open market purchase or sale of government securities, in addition to its monetary effects, changes the *composition* of the public's holdings of these securities. The monetary authority, therefore, has a part in the debt management policies of government.

To the extent that the structure of interest rates or the liquidity of the economy can be changed through debt management operations, stabilization of the economy might be enhanced by policies that would raise spending during recessions and restrict it when aggregate demand was generating inflationary pressures. Whether the government *should* manage the debt with this objective in mind or whether in this event such a policy would be likely to have significant effects on economic activity is subject to much debate. The question will be considered in Chapter 17.

## "Incomes" Policies

Although it is widely agreed that monetary and fiscal policies constitute the main weapons in our arsenal of anti-inflation controls, some economists would supplement these conventional measures with "incomes policies." As usually understood, this concept includes government programs "aimed at securing restraint in labor demands regarding pay and in business decisions regarding prices."[19] Such programs might, for example, take the form of a zero-increase wage-price freeze or a 5½ percent wage increase guideline and profit margin ceilings. Whatever the precise form, incomes policies are intended to reduce inflationary pressure emanating from the cost or supply side of the market.

Proponents of incomes policies allege that cost-push inflation cannot be dealt with satisfactorily through restrictive monetary and fiscal policies. In this view, policies that restrain aggregate demand, though perhaps effective in reducing inflation, do so only by raising unemployment to intolerable levels. Because, the argument continues, this type of inflation derives from the monopoly power of unions to secure excessive wage payments and of business to "pass through" these increased unit costs by raising prices, incomes policies are the appropriate instruments to cope with this exercise of market power.

Incomes policies might also prove an effective means of dealing with the problem of inflationary expectations as it relates to the wage-price spiral. If wage demands are based upon expected rates of inflation, as well as on the rate of unemployment, then price increases will induce wage increases, which in turn exert subsequent upward pressure on prices, and so forth, generating a spiral of inflation. Part of the rationale for incomes policies is that a program that temporarily freezes prices and wages or establishes percentage guidelines reduces the likelihood that inflationary expectations will be self-fulfilling.

The case against incomes policies is pressed by those who argue that such policies (1) interfere with the market mechanism and misallocate resources and/or (2) are an ineffective means of combating inflation. Critics charge that, to the extent that such controls work, they do so by preventing the market from clearing at equilibrium prices: resources will not flow into their highest and best use, and such inefficiency reduces economic welfare. Moreover, those who hold that inflation is due solely to excessive demand, rather than to cost-push factors, deny that incomes policies can prevent or combat inflation. In their view, government is the real culprit, which, instead of controlling monetary factors or the budget, seeks to blame labor or business for its own failure to control aggregate demand.

Which view of the inflationary process is correct? Have incomes policies been effective in curtailing inflation? Will incomes policies become a permanent part of our anti-inflation program? Unfortunately, there is no clear-cut consensus on these or related questions. Most observers would probably agree that, at times, inflationary

---

[19] Thomas M. Humphrey, "The Economics of Incomes Policies," Federal Reserve Bank of Richmond, *Monthly Review*, October 1972, p. 3.

pressures emanate from the supply side; but whether such developments can be *sustained* at a critical rate in the absence of excess demand is subject to much debate. As to the question of effectiveness, there is no way to "prove" empirically that incomes policies have, or have not, worked. The critical and unanswerable question is, "What would have happened if wage and price controls had not been imposed?"

Even though the evidence on effectiveness is inconclusive, many observers believe that *some* types of incomes policies will be employed from time to time in the foreseeable future. In a world in which the goals of high employment, price stability, and economic freedom are difficult to reconcile, it seems likely that incomes policies will be adopted in some cases, even though they may be only temporarily effective.

## MONETARISM AND FISCALISM ("KEYNESIANISM")

Traditional economic theory before the 1930s had generally held that if a recession occurred, the economy would automatically return to "full-employment" equilibrium. Consistent with this, it was generally argued that government should do nothing in a recession except to avoid actions or restrictions that might delay recovery.

Monetarist theory used the equation of exchange ($MV = PT$ or $MV = PY$) as a basis. The equation of exchange is not a theory, but a fact—spending *must* equal the value of what is bought. The *theory* argued that since velocity of money was relatively stable and that increases in $T$ or $Y$ (total transactions or total output) could be only moderate once full employment was reached, any increase in money supply ($M$) would result *primarily* in increases in the price level ($P$). Thus increases in money supply, intended to stimulate economic activity, would tend to cause inflation.

The worldwide depression of the 1930s and the promulgation of Keynesian theory in England and in the United States caused a revolution in economic thought. The persistence of widespread unemployment in the United States (25 percent of the labor force in 1933 and over 14 percent as late as 1940) led many economists to believe that action should be taken to achieve higher employment.

### The "Keynesian Revolution"

Keynes' concept of the consumption function (that consumption depended on income) led to the view that consumers were passive and unlikely to increase their spending unless their income rose. Second, in Keynes' view, an increase in the money supply must necessarily reduce interest rates to stimulate investment spending, and this might not occur if the demand for money were interest-elastic. In fact, Keynes suggested that there might be, at very low levels of interest, a "liquidity trap," in which additional money would simply be held rather than invested. In Keynes' view also, investment depended primarily on interest rates and might increase only slightly unless interest rates fell considerably. Federal government deficit spending on a large scale was the Keynesian alternative to secular stagnation, and by 1940 many economists and policymakers had accepted this idea. Those who favored a larger role for government also supported the idea of using taxes and government spending for social purposes.

The war that begun in 1939 in Europe and America's subsequent involvement pushed our economy to full employment; the depression was over and control of inflation became the prime concern. The problem of controlling inflation was magnified because Federal Reserve policy had been dedicated to pegging the market price of government securities at par for at least the duration of the war. Low and stable interest rates became the primary objective: low rates to minimize the Treasury's borrowing costs, stable rates to facilitate the sale of securities to the public.

The depression and the war years convinced most observers that monetary policy was relatively impotent against depression and was likely to produce undesirable side effects if used forcefully against inflation. Economic literature reflected this view of the world, and research efforts were focused on various elements of Keynes' basic theory: consumption-income relationships and budget multiplier models replaced work on money and its velocity, the stock-in-trade of macroeconomic researchers in earlier times.

With the advent of the Kennedy-Johnson administrations and the stewardship of Walter W. Heller as chairman of the Council of Economic Advisers, the "new economics," as neo-Keynesian theory was dubbed, became the conventional wisdom. The long period of business expansion beginning in 1961 and reinforced by the "magnificent tax cut" of 1964 ushered in a new period of prosperity without significant inflation until after 1965. Along with it came the new language of "full-employment surplus" (the government budget was likely to have a surplus when there was "full employment"), "fiscal dividends" (this meant that funds would be available from the excess government revenues), and "fine-tuning" (fiscal policy could be used to "fine-tune" the level of the economy). If not household words, these and others became part of the jargon of the financial press and the business community. The Keynesian revolution had changed economic thinking.

## The Monetarist Counterrevolution

But in the background there were signs of change, changing events and changing ideas. In the world of affairs, the rate of inflation began to increase in 1965; in the world of ideas, the reemergence of the quantity theory of money, dressed in modern garb by the new monetarists, raised serious questions for the new orthodoxy. On the one hand, the acceleration of inflation, in spite of fiscal restraint, and the failure of Keynesian economists to forecast the degree of inflation that occurred in the late 1970s, led many observers to search for new answers. Second, the articulation of an alternative theory of money, prices, and interest rates advanced by monetarists received increasing attention. New studies offered a different, perhaps better, way of looking at government policies and their relationships to aggregate demand, prices, and financial markets.[20]

[20] David I. Fand, "A Monetarist Model of the Monetary Process," *Journal of Finance*, May 1970, pp. 275–289; and Leonall C. Andersen and Keith M. Carlson, "A Monetary Model for Economic Stabilization," Federal Reserve Bank of St. Louis, *Review*, April 1970, pp. 7–21.

Since the mid-1960s, a strong vocal minority within the economics fraternity has achieved increasing acceptance by appealing to those who had become disenchanted with continual deficit spending and inflation and to those who always believed that monetary influences were of utmost importance. "The central issue that is debated these days in connection with macroeconomics is the doctrine of monetarism."[21] Monetarism must be recognized as an important alternative to Keynesianism, which had been largely unchallenged since the Great Depression.

A modern Keynesian's lack of confidence in monetary policy has three major bases. First, he or she believes that changes in the quantity of money are the *result* as well as a *cause* of changes in business conditions; changes in income and spending induce changes in money, as credit is granted and demand deposits increase. In technical terms, money is to some extent an "endogenous" variable. It follows that the policy of the monetary authority is only one of many factors determining the short-run behavior of money. Second, a Keynesian views securities rather than goods and services as close substitutes for money and argues that, *if* a change in the money stock *does* affect spending, it does so *indirectly* by changing credit conditions and interest rates. It is *not* expected that new money will be spent *directly* on consumer goods, at least not on a large scale. Finally, the Keynesian believes that a change in the money supply, although it has some impact on interest rates, may not, say, lower market rates of interest significantly or lead to significantly increased spending even if rates do fall.

Fiscal policy, on the other hand, has direct effects on income whether the deficits, say, are financed by new money created by the banking system or by the sale of securities to the public, that is, the "activation of idle balances." In the former case the multiplier effects will be larger, but either method will be expansionary. Today's Keynesians agree with the monetarists that money matters and that control over money (and credit) is necessary. The difference between them is one of degree.

Monetarists reject most of the preceding analysis concerning money and the relative roles of monetary and fiscal policies. For them, the money supply can be, or is, a crucial variable, and its control is vital. Money in this view is controllable by the Federal Reserve; it is an "exogenous" variable. It is also a close substitute for real goods and services as well as for financial assets. *If, then, the money stock is increased, it will spill over into the market for consumers' and producers' goods as well as the market for securities and real estate.*[22] In this way the quantity of money has strong direct effects on private expenditure, not merely weak indirect effects via changes in the money and capital markets (and interest rates).

Because the public's desire to hold money is not highly sensitive to changes in the market rate of interest, hoarding and dishoarding do not occur on a significant scale. Thus, there will be no "activation of idle balances" to finance government deficits but, rather, a "crowding out" of private expenditures when government

---

[21] Paul Samuelson, "The Role of Money in National Economic Policy," *Controlling Monetary Aggregates*, Federal Reserve Bank of Boston, 1969, pp. 152–174.

[22] Some suggest, for example, that open market purchases tend to lower interest rates and that this tends to raise stock market prices, thus increasing consumer wealth (through capital gains).

borrowing drives up the cost of credit.[23] In short, the rate of interest is considered much more important in the decision to borrow and spend than in the decision to hold money or securities. Accordingly, the impact of fiscal policy hinges on the sources of finance. If no new money is forthcoming to finance, say, a budget deficit, the pure fiscal effect on the level of total spending, which Keynesians feel is strong, is expected by monetarists to be relatively minor.

Inflation, which helped to give modern quantity theorists a new lease on life, is judged by them to be mainly a monetary phenomenon. The pronouncement that "at all times and in all places" inflation is associated with a rapid increase in the money supply leaves little doubt as to that point. Demand-pull, not cost-push, factors are the source of inflation. To control inflation, control money; some would say that nothing more or less is required; most would say that nothing else will do. Many monetarists, following Milton Friedman, believe that the technique for monetary control is relatively simple, in principle. In this view the Federal Reserve should expand the money supply at a fixed rate of growth per year regardless of the state of economic activity. A monetary rule would replace the use of discretionary policy, the approach used since the inception of the Federal Reserve. The percentage rate of growth would depend upon the definition of the money stock used, the expected long-run demand for money, and the expected long-run growth rate of real output. For these monetarists such a program would seem far more likely to promote prosperity without inflation than would any system of fine-tuning.[24] Some monetarists, however, do not necessarily favor a fixed rule for monetary growth. They believe that the Fed should focus on control of growth of the money supply, but not necessarily at a fixed percent per year. Clearly, if velocity varies, they are right—5 percent increase in money supply minus 5 percent decrease in velocity would result in zero increase in aggregate demand—not a desirable outcome if growth or a rising economy is desired.

## Recent Research: Methods and Findings

Two main lines of research by monetarists have been used to present and support their position. One group of studies, exemplified by the pioneering work of Friedman, Schwartz, and Cagan, has examined the cyclical and secular relationship between the quantity of money and output, prices, and employment in the United States for as far back as 1867. Much of this work was done under the auspices of the National Bureau of Economic Research and led to the monumental study, *A Monetary History of the United States, 1867–1960*, by Milton Friedman and Anna Schwartz. Friedman's tentative conclusions were that

> Changes in the quantity of money have important and broadly predictable economic effects. Long-period changes in the quantity of money relative to output determine the

---

[23] Roger W. Spencer and William P. Yohe, "The 'Crowding Out' of Private Expenditures by Fiscal Policy Actions," Federal Reserve Bank of St. Louis, *Review*, October 1970, pp. 12–24. See also Keith M. Carlson and Roger W. Spencer, "Crowding Out and Its Critics," Federal Reserve Bank of St. Louis, *Review*, December 1975, pp. 2–17.

[24] For an excellent summary of the rules versus authorities debate and the problem of lags, see Mayer, *Monetary Policy in the United States*, pp. 178–190, 200–210.

secular behavior of prices. Substantial expansions in the quantity of money over short periods have been a proximate source of the accompanying inflation in prices. Substantial contractions in the quantity of money over short periods have been a major factor in producing severe economic contractions, and cyclical variations in the quantity of money may well be an important element in the ordinary mild business cycle.[25]

The conclusions are offered as "qualified" and "limited," and Friedman stresses the importance of interpreting the results obtained as representing average behavior, not applicable to every episode in our monetary history. He is also quick to point out that many factors other than the quantity of money are significant, perhaps dominant, especially in the case of long-run movements in real output, which depend on technological improvement and population growth. However, the finding of Friedman and Schwartz that in *every one* of the six major depressions during the past century—*and at no other time*—the money supply declined significantly and began to decline prior to the downturn in general economic activity is impressive evidence of the importance of money.[26] They stressed, moreover, that the change in the money supply in these cases resulted from what might be termed exogenous factors and could not be interpreted as feedback effects.

What then has been proved? Certainly that there is an important historical tie between money and economic behavior. But as Tobin and others have observed, it is one thing to demonstrate that "money matters" and quite another to conclude from this that "money is all that matters."[27]

The second approach has been vigorously pursued by monetarists at the Federal Reserve Bank of St. Louis. It consists of using correlation analysis to test the explanatory power of monetary and fiscal variables. By relating changes in gross national product to changes in money (or the monetary base) and various measures or components of the budget, the St. Louis economists sought to measure the relative importance of monetary and fiscal actions in explaining the variations in economic activity. They concluded from their equations that the response of GNP to fiscal actions relative to monetary actions were not (1) larger, (2) more predictable, or (3) faster. *In fact, the St. Louis studies find "no measurable net fiscal influence on total spending in the test period," from 1952 to mid-1968.*[28] By implication, monetary actions explain more (nearly all) of the variance in GNP and are more powerful than fiscal actions.

Critics argued that the St. Louis equations were spurious and incorrectly specified. Some contended that the equations were not derived from any specific structural theoretical model and therefore had no theoretical content. They were a weak substi-

---

[25] Milton Friedman, "The Monetary Studies of the National Bureau," *The National Bureau Enters Its 45th Year, 44th Annual Report*, 1964, pp. 7–25.

[26] Milton Friedman and Anna J. Schwartz, "Money and Business Cycles," *Review of Economics and Statistics*, February 1963, Supplement, p. 34.

[27] James Tobin, "The Monetary Interpretation of History," *American Economic Review*, June 1965, pp. 646–685.

[28] The St. Louis study used changes in the high-employment expenditures and receipts as measures of fiscal influence. Leonall C. Andersen and Jerry L. Jordan, "Monetary and Fiscal Actions: A Test of Their Relative Importance in Economic Stabilization," *Federal Reserve Bank of St. Louis, Review*, November 1968, pp. 11–24.

tute for the specification of important behavioral relationships amenable to empirical verification. A clearly superior approach, it was argued, would be the specification and testing of a complete model of the economy.[29]

Second, even if the equations used were legitimate, some reviewers alleged that the proxy variables chosen to represent monetary actions were endogenous rather than exogenous. In other words, the questions of feedback and possible reverse causation weaken or destroy the meaningfulness of the high correlation coefficients obtained by the equations. Close association does not prove causation.[30]

Although the controversy continues, it seems to be taking a turn toward synthesis. With high inflation rates, Keynesians have been more willing to support the proposition that money growth rates have been too rapid. Monetarists seem more willing to agree that other things than money "matter," even if they are considered to be of less importance. In 1977, Franco Modigliani characterized the current status of the debate and argued that, looking carefully at the theory, there is no real difference between monetarists and Keynesians. There may be differences in approach in the case of a particular topic, but no fundamental difference. He argued that the only real difference between the two groups is found in the empirical assessment of the evidence. Milton Friedman agreed with this appraisal.[31]

But, while the issue is empirical, there remained a controversial point. Modigliani believed that we know enough about policy impacts to use actively both contracyclical monetary and fiscal policies. Friedman, on the other hand, did not believe that he or anyone else knows enough about policy impacts to do the right thing at the right time. Furthermore, even if he or someone else did know enough, any person in a position to push the policy buttons would have to face political realities—realities that could impair the effective implementation of policy. Thus, he argued against attempts at active implementation of monetary and fiscal stabilization policies, as a practical matter.

## SUPPLY-SIDE ECONOMICS

Both Keynesian and monetarist theory focus on aggregate demand. Keynesians view the spending by sectors—consumers, business firms, government, and net exports—as important, while monetarists focus attention on money—money is what is spent, and if money supply is restricted, spending is also limited.

[29] James Tobin, "The Role of Money in National Economic Policy," *Controlling Monetary Aggregates*, Federal Reserve Bank of Boston, 1969, p. 23. Large, multiple-equation models of the economy were pioneered by Lawrence R. Klein of the Wharton School of Michigan, the Brookings-Social Science Research Council group, and a group of economists from the Massachusetts Institute of Technology who worked with the staff of the Federal Reserve Board of Governors. Many other models also exist today.

[30] Frank DeLeeuw and John Kalchbrenner, "Monetary and Fiscal Actions: A Test of Their Relative Importance in Economic Stabilization—Comment," Federal Reserve Bank of St. Louis, *Review*, April 1969, pp. 6–11. Also, see Henry A. Latané, "A Note on Monetary Policy, Interest Rates and Income Velocity," *Southern Economic Journal*, January 1970, pp. 328–330.

[31] See the article by Franco Modigliani and discussion by Milton Friedman, "The Monetarist Controversy," Federal Reserve Bank of San Francisco, *Economic Review, Supplement*, Spring 1977.

Yet aggregate supply is important—number of workers employed, average hours of work, and capital used in production. Training and education of workers are also important, as is a policy of management that leads to increased output.

## Historical Origins of Supply-Side Economics

In a way, supply-side economics is much older than the economics of demand. The title of Adam Smith's book in 1776 was *An Inquiry into the Nature and Causes of the Wealth of Nations*. The word "wealth" would now be replaced by "real GNP," perhaps, but the fundamental analysis of what causes a rise in real output and income, especially in the long run, is just as basic (perhaps more so) than the theory of demand analyzed in Keynesian and monetarist theories.

The French economist J. B. Say, 150 years ago, wrote about what became known as Say's law: supply creates its own demand. It is certainly true that if people work (let us say in a new business) and create goods or services, the income of the workers, those who lent money to start the business, and the owners who receive profits would be sufficient to buy the products or services produced. Hence, *general* overproduction cannot occur; of course, the firm could produce things that consumers would not buy, but that would be simply an error. However, Say's law does not allow for change in the demand for money, in a monetary economy; if demand for money increases, some workers, lenders, and entrepreneurs may buy less and attempt to hold more money. Of course, they can't, unless the money supply is increased by the central bank, but their attempt to hold more money reduces the velocity of circulation of money.

There is no question but that supply-side economics is important. Why people work more or more hours, what tends to create more capital and improved capital goods, means of obtaining better educated and better trained workers, and the study of management methods (both for firms and for the economy) that will lead to increased output per worker-hour are vital.

There is also no question but that programs for increasing demand can easily create a danger of serious inflation. The discussion between monetarists and "Keynesians" has been, as we have seen, chiefly a discussion of whether more government (or other) spending would be effective in increasing demand or whether an increase in the money supply would be more effective. If the demand for money is very elastic, an increase in the money supply is much less effective. If the demand for money is quite *inelastic*, an increase in the money supply is quite effective, and caution is necessary to be sure that such an increase is not too rapid; otherwise, serious inflation may be the result.

## Recent Discussion of Supply-Side Economics

Supply-side economics, as discussed, was not much concerned with the short run. It was generally assumed that significant increases in capital, training and education of workers, application of inventions, and so on could occur only in a medium or long run.

With the election of the Reagan administration in 1980, there were economists, both within and outside the administration, who argued that supply-side measures could have effects in the short run. Some assumed that tax rates may have been so high as to reduce output and that a reduction in taxes, especially marginal tax rates, would not only produce more effort but would also increase revenue for the government. Obviously, if marginal tax rates were 100 percent, the government would get little if any revenue—who would work more if all additional income were taken away in taxes? It is also obvious that if tax rates were zero, the government would get no tax revenue. But whether the U.S. economy has been at a point at which reduction in tax rates would produce more work *and* more government tax revenue, and especially whether this would occur in the short run, required careful analysis.[32]

There *is* some evidence in careful economic studies that reduction in high marginal tax rates tends to produce some increase in work and output. There is also some evidence that tax reductions may cause *some* increase in saving.[33] Moreover, there is some evidence that tax reductions for business firms lead to some increase in investment.[34]

The economic program proposed by President Reagan was based on proposals to reduce marginal tax rates, reduce the rate of increase in federal government spending (especially that for domestic transfer programs), initiate some deregulation of various industries to remove regulatory restraints that hindered expansion, and restrain the growth of the money supply to reduce the rate of inflation and to reduce interest rates. By 1983, progress had been made on all these except reducing the rate of increase in federal government spending, on which relatively little progress was made (partly because of rapid increases in defense spending). Government budget deficits projected for the years through 1988 remained large—partly because relatively slow economic growth had occurred until 1983 and cautious projections were deemed to be more appropriate.[35] On the other hand, by 1987 it was clear that the economy was in the longest peacetime expansion in real growth since World War II, the unemployment rate remained relatively low (about 6 percent), and inflation was very low.

---

[32] Concerning early supply-side economics, see Robert E. Keleher, "Historical Origins of Supply-Side Economics," Federal Reserve Bank of Atlanta, *Economic Review*, January 1982, pp. 12–19. On more recent analysis, see Richard H. Fink, *Supply-Side Economics: A Critical Appraisal* (Frederick, Md.: University Publications of America, 1983). Some economists have been very critical of recent supply-side economics proposals. One of the strongest critics, James Tobin, argues that tax cuts and budget cuts of the early 1980s transfer income and wealth from poor to rich, because tax cuts increase after-tax income for the rich more than for the poor and budget cuts in many cases restrict social programs aimed at helping the poor. See Tobin's section in the book edited by Fink or Tobin's brief discussion, "Supply-Side Economics: What Is It? Will It Work?" *Economic Outlook USA*, Summer 1981, pp. 51–53.

[33] For a general review, see Robert E. Keleher, "Supply-Side Tax Policy: Reviewing the Evidence," Federal Reserve Bank of Atlanta, *Economic Review*, April 1981, pp. 16–21.

[34] Otto Eckstein, testimony submitted to the Joint Economic Committee of Congress, April 10 and May 21, 1980. Many large econometric models are based on demand equations, with few supply equations. Some models show more effects of tax cuts than suggested by Eckstein.

[35] James R. Barth, "The Reagan Program for Economic Recovery: Economic Rationale (A Primer on Supply-Side Economics)," Federal Reserve Bank of Atlanta, *Economic Review*, September 1981, pp. 4–14.

Not monetarism, Keynesianism, or the ideas recently discussed that might be labeled as supply-side economics makes much contribution to the analysis of reasons for the slowdown in productivity in the U.S. economy that has occurred since the late 1960s. Because the slowdown began much before the oil crisis of 1973, that crisis cannot be assigned the entire blame. Japan's success in increasing productivity in manufacturing by nearly 30 percent in the years 1977 to 1981, compared with a U.S. increase of only 4.5 percent, is cause for further careful analysis of the factors that have contributed to Japanese increases in productivity.[36] Supply-side economics cannot yet sufficiently explain what measures might best increase productivity in the U.S. economy. The merit of supply-side economics is that it focuses attention on the right questions: What caused the slowdown in productivity in the 1970s? What measures might stimulate increased productivity? Can the United States attain a more rapid rate of growth? Should it if it can?

## SUMMARY

Most economists and policymakers agree that the government should use monetary and fiscal policies to achieve high employment, price stability, economic growth, and balance-of-payments equilibrium. There is less agreement on how these goals should be defined and on whether they are compatible. The relationship between the rate of unemployment and the rate of inflation (the Phillips curve) and its implications for economic policy is one such area of controversy.

Although monetary and fiscal policies are widely regarded as the most important anti-inflation controls, some would supplement these measures with incomes policies to combat inflation, which they believe is largely caused by an upward cost-push on wages and prices. Others point to the many failures of incomes policies and suggest that disruption of the market mechanism by such policies is likely to result in a wrong allocation of resources as well as development of gray and black markets. Incomes policies may be necessary in wartime when many goods and services are not produced in sufficient amounts to meet consumer demand, but they have not proved to be very helpful in other circumstances.

Since the early 1950s, there has been extensive debate between monetarists and fiscalists about the effectiveness of monetary versus fiscal policy. Fiscalists have argued that changes in government spending and tax rates can help significantly in recovery from recessions and in progress toward "full employment." Monetarists have argued that effects of such changes are relatively weak, unless accompanied by an expansion of the money supply, and that increase in the money supply is the major factor in an increase in real as well as nominal income, although they warn that rapid expansion of the money supply is likely to lead to inflation.

With the election of the Reagan administration in 1980 and its announced

---

[36] Donald L. Koch, "Regaining the U.S. Competitive Edge: The Shared Destiny," *Federal Reserve Bank of Atlanta, Economic Review,* October 1982, pp. 4–12. Several leading economic researchers in this field leave a large part of the slowdown in productivity unexplained in their studies.

policies of slowing both inflation and the rate of increase in government spending, there was much discussion of "supply-side" economics. Supply-side economics, with its emphasis on the causes of increased real income (work and increased productivity), had been given less attention until the combination of inflation and a slowdown in productivity in the 1970s, plus loss of major foreign and domestic markets to foreign competition, made it appropriate again to focus attention on aggregate supply and its determinants. Unfortunately, research on such determinants has not always been conclusive, and even when significant increases in output may be expected to result from certain policies, the short-term effect may be small. As suggested by one well-known economist, "the central concern of supply-side economics—that more attention needs to be paid to the capability of the economy for delivering gains in real incomes and output—is now very much in order."[37] Concern may well be justified even if continuing economic recovery brings some improvement in employment and productivity.

## Questions for Discussion

**1.** Explain what is meant when one says that the Phillips curve represents a "trade-off."

**2.** How would expectations of inflation affect the position of the Phillips curve?

**3.** List the factors generally recognized as contributing significantly in economic growth.

**4.** Use examples to distinguish between "general" and "selective" controls exercised by the Federal Reserve System in the interest of economic stabilization.

**5.** What are the arguments in favor of and against imposition of a national incomes policy?

**6.** Briefly state the nature of the monetarist-fiscalist controversy.

**7.** What is the difference between the goal of high employment and the goal of rapid economic growth?

**8.** What are Milton Friedman's major arguments supporting his claim that changes in the quantity of money have a special importance in policy actions?

**9.** Explain Say's law and indicate its relationship to "supply-side economics."

**10.** How was supply-side economics related to the programs suggested by the Reagan administration?

## Selected References

In addition to the Samuelson-Solow article referred to in the text, a helpful reference regarding the Phillips curve in Thomas M. Humphrey, "Changing Views of the Phillips Curve," Federal Reserve Bank of Richmond, *Monthly Review*, July 1973, pp. 1–13.

---

[37] Paul W. McCracken, book review of *Supply Side Economics: A Critical Appraisal*, edited by Richard H. Fink, *The Wall Street Journal*, January 28, 1983, p. 26.

The student may find it illuminating to compare the views of three past chairmen of the Council of Economic Advisers on the monetary-fiscal "mix." See Walter W. Heller, *New Dimensions of Political Economy* (New York: W. W. Norton, 1966), Chapter 2; Arthur M. Okun, "Rules and Roles for Fiscal and Monetary Policy," *Issues in Fiscal and Monetary Policy: The Eclectic Economist Views the Controversy*, ed. James J. Diamond (Chicago: DePaul University Press, 1971), pp. 51–74; and Herbert Stein, "Where Stands the New Fiscal Policy?" *Journal of Money, Credit and Banking*, August 1969, pp. 463–473.

Monetarist models of inflation are analyzed in Thomas M. Humphrey, "A Monetarist Model of the Inflationary Process," Federal Reserve Bank of Richmond, *Economic Review*, November–December 1975, pp. 13–23; and Thomas M. Humphrey, "A Monetarist Model of World Inflation and the Balance of Payments," Federal Reserve Bank of Richmond, *Economic Review*, November–December 1976, pp. 13–22.

On the status of the monetarist controversy, see Franco Modigliani, "The Monetarist Controversy" and discussion by Milton Friedman, Federal Reserve Bank of San Francisco, *Economic Review, Supplement*, Spring 1977.

Formation of inflation expectations is a key element in the transmission of effects of monetary policy changes to inflation; for a recent study, see David H. Resler, "The Formation of Inflation Expectations," Federal Reserve Bank of St. Louis, *Review*, April 1980, pp. 2–12.

It is now generally agreed that changes in monetary policy affect *nominal* GNP, but do they affect *real* GNP, and if so, how much? One recent study of this question is Keith M. Carlson, "Money, Inflation, and Economic Growth: Some Updated Reduced Form Results and Their Implications," Federal Reserve Bank of St. Louis, *Review*, April 1980, pp. 13–19.

For a brief review of some problems facing supply-side economic proposals and its potential usefulness, see Aris Protopapadakis, "Supply-Side Economics: What Chance for Success?" Federal Reserve Bank of Philadelphia, *Business Review*, May–June 1981, pp. 11–23.

# FEDERAL RESERVE POLICY
# AND THE FINANCIAL MARKETS

Our interest in Federal Reserve policy extends beyond the fact that what the Fed does strongly influences the course of economic activity. We are also interested in the Federal Reserve because in the conduct of its policies it participates directly in financial markets and produces important effects on monetary variables and credit conditions. Earlier we observed that the most important monetary policy tool, open market operations, impinges initially on commercial bank reserves and on the prices and yields of U.S. government securities. But the effects of policy are not limited to bank reserves and the market for government securities. They spread rapidly to other money and capital markets and, with a lag, to the markets for goods and services and thence to income, employment, and prices. However, thus far we have said little about *how* monetary changes are transmitted to other markets and sectors of the economy.

In the first section of this chapter we outline the transmission mechanism and indicate the channels through which monetary policy operates. Next, we look at the implementation process of monetary policy and discuss several alternative strategies that the Fed could employ in its open market operations. The central issue in the selection of a potential strategy is the question of targets or guides: the variables that the Fed should seek to control to achieve its economic objectives. We examine some implications that different strategies have for the behavior of interest rates and the money supply.

## MONETARY POLICY'S TRANSMISSION MECHANISMS

The current status of monetary theory is such that it is not entirely clear how a change in monetary policy works its way through the financial and real sectors of the economy. Although economists agree that the initial impact is mainly on bank reserves, some emphasize subsequent changes in bank credit and interest rates and the influence that they have on aggregate demand via spending for investment goods and consumer durables. Other analysts stress the importance of changes in the money supply and argue that these changes may directly affect spending for goods and services as well as indirectly through the prices and yields of financial assets. The disagreement is not so much over *which* variables enter the transmission process but over their *relative* importance in the linkage sequences.

However, most theories can be accommodated by viewing the transmission process as working through the following elements: (1) portfolio adjustments, (2) wealth effects, and (3) credit availability effects. Most theories interpret the process as working principally through portfolio adjustments, as spending units react to changes in the relative prices and yields of financial and real assets that are induced by a change in monetary policy. As a result of these adjustments, the level of spending and income is altered; subsequent multiplier-accelerator effects reinforce the initial changes in spending; and all these factors produce feedback on financial variables, including the money supply and interest rates.

### Portfolio Adjustments

To trace the effects of a monetary change, let us assume that the portfolios of commercial banks, other depository financial institutions, and the public are initially in equilibrium: portfolios are optimal with respect to size and composition of assets. Assume further that the Fed wishes to increase total spending to reduce the rate of unemployment and that to do so it buys Treasury bills from a government securities dealer. The immediate effect is an increase in demand deposits and reserves of commercial banks and probably of other institutions. The purchase also tends to raise prices and lower yields on Treasury bills. The following adjustments take place as depository institutions and the public react to the change in reserves and to the new bill yields.

Commercial banks and other institutions may repay borrowings from the Fed or add temporarily to their excess reserves. Thus, free reserves—excess reserves minus institutional borrowing from the Fed—initially rise, and the Federal funds rate declines. More important, the increase in excess reserves subsequently induces banks and other institutions to expand their loans and investments. This is accompanied by a reduction in the rates charged to borrowers and the yields on securities. The decline in bill yields makes other money market instruments more attractive and induces substitution into these assets, which raises their prices and lowers their yields— money market rates all tend to decline. Within a short time, the process of substitution of higher- for lower-yielding securities and loans would be expected to spread to longer-term markets as lenders and borrowers adjust their portfolios of financial assets and liabilities. Corporate bond yields, as well as those on long-term Treasury issues, on municipal securities, and on mortgages, decline, reflecting the general easing of credit conditions in both the money and capital markets.[1] It should be recognized, of course, that long-term yields are affected much more by expectations of inflation than are short-term yields, so that if action of the Fed causes expectations of a rise in the rate of inflation, a decline in long-term yields may not occur.

These interest rate effects tend to increase investment expenditures by business firms, spending by state and local government, and outlays by consumers for durable goods. Thus the main channel through which portfolio adjustments affect economic activity is the interest rate–investment channel. Figure 16–1 shows major effects.

With an expansion in bank credit, bank deposits rise. The public holds more deposits both as a direct result of the open market purchases by the Fed and as a result of the creation of deposits by banks. As new deposits begin to be held by consumers as well as by business firms (which constitute the major initial borrowers), consumers begin to adjust their asset portfolios. They may transfer funds from checking accounts to time deposits in commercial banks, to mutual savings banks, or to savings and loan accounts. As a result, additional loans may be made and the velocity of money tends to rise. If these latter institutions create checkable accounts for borrowers, M1 rises, also.

After a period of time, perhaps several months, following the initial monetary action, interest rates stop declining and begin to rise as the economic expansion exerts increasing pressure on financial markets. Just when this occurs depends upon the magnitude of the initial monetary stimulus and upon the response of borrowers and lenders in the money and capital markets to the changes in income and spending. But at some point rates rise. Further impetus to the upward movement is provided if commodity price increases build a premium for expected inflation into interest rates.

To summarize, monetary policy actions impinge initially on reserves of deposit-type institutions and on the market for government securities. Changes in other financial markets occur as a result of changes in relative prices and yields. These, in turn, induce further changes in the prices of existing goods and services. The increased relative profitability of consumer and producer goods opens up a gap between actual and desired stocks of real goods, which raises output and employment. Subse-

---

[1] A very helpful publication, which may be useful in classes, is Paul Meek, *U.S. Monetary Policy and Financial Markets* (New York: Federal Bank of New York, 1982).

**FIGURE 16–1**
**Transmission of Monetary Policy I**

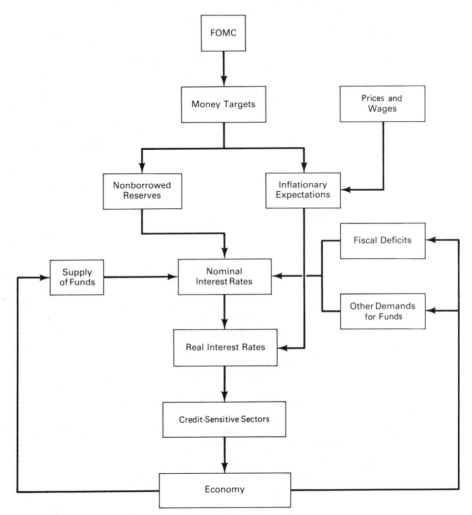

SOURCE: Paul Meek, *U.S. Monetary Policy and Financial Markets* (New York: Federal Reserve Bank of New York, 1982), p. 29.

quently, prices of commodities increase as production is expanded; the rise in economic activity reverses the decline in market rates of interest, which rise toward new equilibrium levels. The process continues until output, prices, and interest rates reestablish equilibrium in the portfolios of market participants—until prices and quantities of financial and real assets again satisfy the preferences of asset holders.

## Wealth Effects

Many economists, while interpreting this process in terms of portfolio adjustments, suggest that monetary policy *also* operates through a "wealth effect"—through a change in the *size* as well as the composition of assets. Thus, changes in wealth are expected to alter spending-saving decisions with consequent effects on output, employment, and prices. In economists' jargon, an increase, say, in the public's wealth will produce an upward shift in the consumption function. Similarly, a decline in wealth will lower consumer spending. Figure 16–2 shows the effects on consumer spending, construction, and business investment in equipment.

The wealth effect is induced by a change in interest rates resulting from Federal Reserve open market operations. When, for example, the Fed buys government securities, market rates tend to decline, and the prices of securities rise. As noted, these changes spill over into the markets for other securities and real assets. Thus, an expansionary monetary policy, the argument runs, lowers a broad range of capitalization rates by which investors value expected income; this is reflected in higher market values of stocks, bonds, real estate, and other forms of wealth. The predicted effect is an increase in consumer spending because of this increase in wealth, and thus an increase in aggregate demand, which induces higher levels of output, employment, and prices.[2] For example, in the Federal Reserve–MIT–Penn model of the economy, a major portion of the effect of monetary policy on economic activity derives from the effect of policy on the stock market. Moreover, in this model the introduction of the stock market–wealth effect link significantly speeds up the response of changes in nominal GNP to changes in monetary measures. It reduces the lag in effect of policy from three years (the lag without the wealth effect) to five to six quarters.[3]

Some have questioned this line of reasoning by pointing out that, although wealth holders experience an immediate increase in the market value of their assets when capitalization rates decline, the lower level of yields may require more saving in the future to maintain the same level of income. In short, although the wealth holder's present need for saving is reduced, his or her future requirements may be increased by the decline in yields, and the longer-run effect on spending may be uncertain.[4] However, most economists have come to accept the hypothesis that current consumption is a function of "life-cycle" or "permanent" income and the implication of that hypothesis that increases in net worth, including capital gains, cause an increase in consumption spending. It should be noted that this is classified as a wealth effect rather than an income effect because capital gains are not treated as income in national income

[2] See Warren L. Smith, "On Some Current Issues in Monetary Economics: An Interpretation," *Journal of Economic Literature*, September 1970, pp. 768–769.

[3] See Franco Modigliani, "Monetary Policy and Consumption: Linkages via Interest Rates and Wealth Effects in the FMP Model," *Consumer Spending and Monetary Policy: The Linkages*, Federal Reserve Bank of Boston, June 1971, pp. 9–58.

[4] Henry C. Wallich raises this point in his discussion of Warren L. Smith's "A Neo-Keynesian View of Monetary Policy," *Controlling Monetary Aggregates*, Federal Reserve Bank of Boston, 1969, pp. 130–131.

**FIGURE 16–2**
**Transmission of Monetary Policy II**

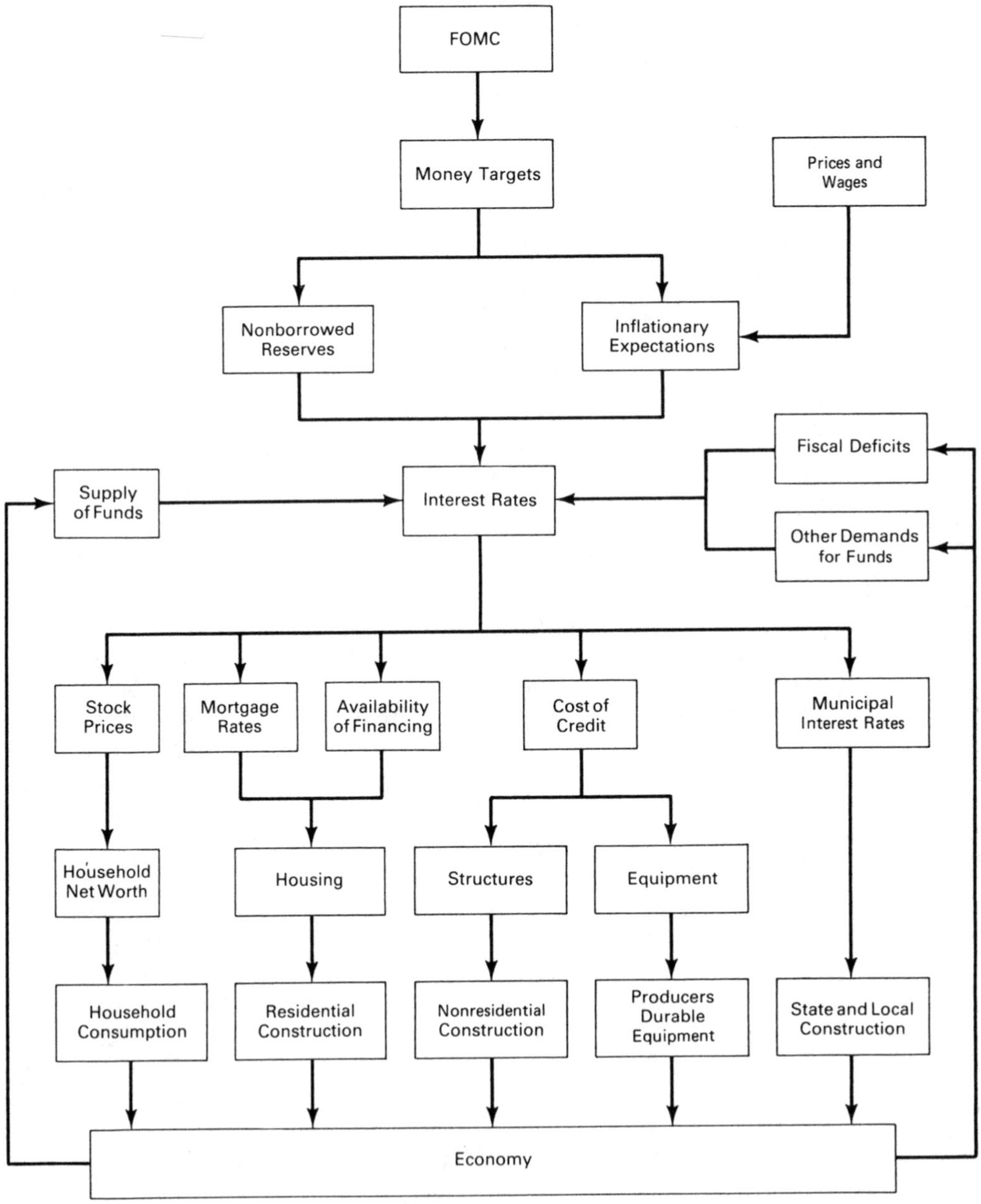

SOURCE: Paul Meek, *U.S. Monetary Policy and Financial Markets* (New York: Federal Reserve Bank of New York, 1982), p. 164.

accounting, in which income is defined as the revenue *earned* in a period as a result of the production of goods and services during that period.

## The Availability of Credit

If all markets were perfect and prices and yields adjusted rapidly to changes in supply and demand, the full effects of monetary policy would be transmitted promptly through changes in relative prices. However, many financial markets are characterized by imperfections and institutional factors that do not allow prices to equate supply and demand. For a period of time, prices may fail to clear the market, and an excess of demand or supply must be accommodated by nonprice factors— there are changes in the "availability" rather than in the price of credit.[5] The most important examples of how monetary policy works through changes in the availability of credit are found in the markets for bank loans, mortgages, and savings deposits. Although changes in the availability of credit may signal a shift toward monetary ease or restraint, the following discussion is limited to the effects that might be expected to occur during a period of restrictive monetary policy.

It has been observed in earlier chapters that commercial bankers employ certain devices such as compensating balance requirements, standards of creditworthiness, or the pledging of collateral as part of loan agreements. If these nonprice elements are used to restrict loan demand, the volume of credit outstanding may be restrained without immediate or appreciable changes in rates of interest. In this regard it is often charged that credit rationing discriminates against small businesses, in that these firms, having virtually no access to capital markets, are heavily dependent upon bank loans. If, the argument runs, the lending capacity of banks is restricted by monetary policy, bankers continue to lend to their regular (presumably larger) customers and curtail their loans to smaller, less creditworthy borrowers. On the other hand, there is some evidence that small firms obtain some additional bank credit indirectly during such times in the form of trade credit extended by the larger firms, which continue to receive bank financing. In this way small business firms may be able to carry additional inventories and accounts receivable financed by the larger firms rather than directly by commercial banks. In this view, credit restraint impinges on business firms in general rather than solely on small business. But in either case a program of monetary ease or restraint may be effective even though loan rates are slow to adjust to equilibrium levels.

For somewhat different reasons, the mortgage market and the construction industry may also be affected by changes in Fed policy that work through changes in the availability of credit. Legal restrictions on interest rates charged to mortgage borrowers or paid to savers may reduce the flow of funds into new mortgages and

---

[5] An analysis of the arguments that changes in the availability of credit may be an effective aspect of monetary control is provided in Thomas Mayer, *Monetary Policy in the United States* (New York: Random House, 1968), pp. 126–137.

hence restrict construction spending, as during the "credit crunches" of 1966, 1969, 1974, and 1979–1980, with the result that monetary restraint impinges severely on these markets as compared with other markets in which prices are flexible and competitive.

Similarly, state and local governments may reduce their borrowing and their spending during periods of monetary restraint, not only because the cost of credit is high and rising, but also because of restrictions on the rate of interest they are allowed to pay for borrowed funds. Such restrictions result from ceiling rates established by bond referenda, statutory law, or state constitutional provisions. They effectively preclude borrowing when market rates rise above the rates permitted, as occurred during the credit crunches referred to earlier. For essentially the same reason, the federal government has often been denied access to the *long-term* capital market because of the 4¼ percent limitation on the rate it may offer investors on securities having a maturity in excess of 10 years. When yields on corporate securities, municipals, and mortgages rise sharply, the U.S. Treasury finds it necessary to restrict its new issues to the shorter-term markets, unless it is specially authorized to issue bonds at higher yields.

Thus, the availability of credit effects are especially important because of the selected impact that they seem to have on various sectors of the economy. Although the evidence is by no means conclusive, it appears that a policy of monetary restraint imposes a special burden upon small business, state and local governments, and the mortgage market and construction industry.[6] Although some of the restrictiveness is due simply to the fact that the cost of credit is higher during such periods, part of the restraint results from certain nonprice elements, including legal restrictions imposed by government regulations and laws, business practices in oligopolistic markets (bank lending practices), and information costs that delay interest rate adjustments.

Nonetheless, most of these restrictions on the flow of credit are temporary, and, when interest rates do subsequently rise and perform their function as a rationing device, the only *lasting* impact of monetary restraint results from the changes in market rates and prices.

## The Problem of Time Lags

One of the most important problems inherent in programs aimed at maintaining high employment without an undesirably high rate of inflation is that of time lags. Briefly stated, the problem is that it takes time for policymakers to recognize that economic conditions have improved or worsened (the recognition lag), to take correc-

---

[6] A survey of econometric studies on the impact of monetary policy is found in Michael J. Hamburger, "The Impact of Monetary Variables: A Survey of Recent Econometric Literature," *Essays in Domestic and International Finance*, Federal Reserve Bank of New York, 1969, pp. 37–49, reprinted in W. L. Smith and R. L. Teigen, eds., *Readings in Money, National Income and Stabilization Policy*, 2nd ed. (Homewood, Ill.: Richard D. Irwin, 1970), See also Mayer, *Monetary Policy in the United States*, pp. 164–174.

**FIGURE 16–3**
**Lags in Monetary and Fiscal Policies**

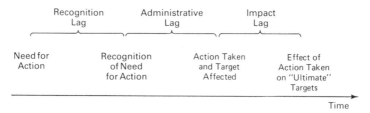

tive steps to restore the desired level of economic activity (the administrative lag), and time for these measures to have effects on the levels of the "ultimate" targets: output, employment, and prices (the impact lags). These time lags are shown in Figure 16–3.[7]

If the lags were always short in duration or highly regular in timing, they could either be ignored or, in the latter case, incorporated into the policymaking process. In these circumstances, lags would not interfere significantly with macroeconomic policies. Long and variable lags, on the other hand, increase the risk that policies designed to achieve our economic goals may in fact destabilize the economy by accentuating fluctuations in spending and income emanating from the private sector. The problem of lags is especially troublesome for "discretionary" as opposed to "automatic" policy, because the former institutes changes in policy only after the need for action has become evident, rather than automatically when economic conditions themselves change. Although estimates differ as to the average length and variability of these three lags, the consensus seems to be that (1) the recognition lag is the same for monetary and fiscal policies, (2) the administrative lag is longer for fiscal policy, and (3) the impact lag is longer for monetary policy.

### Recognition and Administrative Lags

The recognition lag results from the fact that the monetary authority is unable to predict turning points in the level of economic activity with precision. Thus, it must collect and interpret data to confirm that economic conditions have changed. This may require several weeks, even months, because there are many economic series, and often these data give conflicting information about the direction of the economy.

Once the monetary authority has ascertained that policy should be changed, the necessary steps can be taken very quickly because the decision-making power is concentrated in the hands of the 12 members of the Federal Open Market Committee, a meeting of which can be convened on short notice.

---

[7] The recognition and administrative lags are sometimes referred to as an "inside" lag and the impact lag as an "outside" lag. The impact lag is both *initial* and *cumulative* (the effect as measured by *final* response of GNP, etc.). See Mary Susan Rosenbaum, "Lags in the Effect of Monetary Policy," Federal Reserve Bank of Atlanta, *Economic Review*, November 1985, pp. 20–33.

### Lags in the Impact of Monetary Policy

The crucial question for monetary policy concerns the impact lag—the time it takes for policy actions to affect final spending decisions. Much of the disagreement over the length and variability of this lag relates to the choice among the variables used to measure effects of monetary policy, for example, bank reserves, money supply, bank credit, or interest rates. When, for example, can it be assumed that a change in monetary policy has taken place—when reserves have changed, or the rate of growth in M1, or in credit conditions and interest rates?

Some disagreement also centers on how to measure the appropriate changes in whichever policy variable is selected and in the real variables that are the objectives of policy. Richard G. Davis noted that it makes a great deal of difference how this is done:

> If, for example, the rate of change in the money supply is replaced by deviations in the level of the money supply from its long-run trend, the average lag between monetary peaks so measured and peaks in general business apparently shrinks from the sixteen months previously cited to a mere five months. Alternatively, it can be plausibly argued that the appropriate measure is the lag between the rate of change in the money supply and the *rate of change* rather than the level of some measure of business activity such as gross national product (GNP) or industrial production. When peaks and troughs for money and business are compared on this basis, the lead of money over business appears to be quite short.[8]

Although most estimates of the average length of the impact lags are in the neighborhood of 6 to 9 months, the empirical evidence is sketchy. More important for monetary policy, the question of the variability of lags remains unresolved as well. Some hold that lags are both long and variable; they therefore favor a monetary rule such as that proposed by some monetarists. Others find shorter and less variable lags in their studies of the transmission mechanism, leading them to support the continuation of discretionary monetary control. In between are those who assert that although the impact lag is relatively stable, it is longer than the standard estimates suggest.

To summarize, monetary policy is intended to raise or lower the level of spending by the private sector, and it operates through (1) portfolio adjustments, (2) wealth effects, and (3) credit availability effects. Most economists agree that monetary policy influences are transmitted primarily through portfolio adjustments that occur as a result of a change in the Federal Reserve's holdings of government securities. Wealth holders, including commercial banks, are induced, by changes in the money supply and the yield on financial assets, to alter their relative holdings of various types of financial and real assets. Thus the prices of existing real assets rise when the money

---

[8] Richard G. Davis, "The Role of the Money Supply in Business Cycles," Federal Reserve Bank of New York, *Monthly Review*, April 1968, p. 71 (italics in original). The reference to the 16-month lag is to Milton Friedman's estimate. See "The Lag Effect in Monetary Policy," *Journal of Policital Economy*, October 1961, p. 456. More recently Friedman seemed to have revised his estimate to 6 to 9 months. See Milton Friedman, "How Much Monetary Growth?" Morgan Guaranty Trust Company, *The Morgan Guaranty Survey*, February 1973, pp. 5–10.

supply is increased, and this, in turn, induces an increase in newly produced goods and services, with subsequent effects on the level of employment and on prices in general. At the same time, these changes in economic activity have feedback effects on the financial system, so that financial and real variables interact, moving the economy toward a new equilibrium position. Financial yields affect the components of aggregate demand through the three channels already discussed.

## The Stability or Predictability of Velocity of Money

Whether an increase in money supply leads to an increase in spending depends on the behavior of *income* velocity of money (GNP/$M$). For many years after World War II (from 1945 to the beginning of the 1980s), it was generally assumed that income velocity of money was *predictable*—velocity of M1 increased about 3 percent a year, on the average. Since spending ($MV$) must equal the value of what is bought ($PT$), a 5 percent rise in money supply in a given year, added to a 3 percent increase in velocity, would mean an 8 percent increase in total spending and, therefore, would cause a rise of about 8 percent in *nominal* GNP. Depending on the situation, much of the rise might be in prices ($P$) or, under other conditions, in $T$ (real GNP).

However, in 1982 and again in 1985–1986, the rate of growth of income velocity of M1 not only slowed down, velocity of M1 actually *declined*.[9] Thus in 1985, for example, a 5 percent increase in M1 combined with the 6 percent decline in velocity would have led to about a 1 percent *fall* in nominal GNP. Clearly, a 5 percent increase in M1 would not have been enough in that year. A moderate increase in M1 would have led to a decline in prices, real output, or both.

Money (at least, M1) is presumably held for spending; hence, it has been presumed that more money leads to more spending for items comprising GNP. It is not generally recognized that the distinction between the *transactions* velocity of money (total transactions/M1) and the *income* velocity of money (GNP/$M$) is important. But only about 4 percent of all spending is for items comprising GNP; the remaining 96 percent is for purchases of stocks, bonds, and other financial assets; for lending and repayment of loans; for purchase of old houses and used automobiles; and for gifts and other transactions.[10]

Income velocity of money may be quite different from transactions velocity of money, and rates of changes of the two may be quite different. At times, a large part of an increase in money supply may be used in financial transactions, and may not lead to increases in real GNP or prices, except perhaps stock prices. But it is unlikely that increased financial or other non-GNP transactions is a major reason for increased

[9] "Monetary Policy and Open Market Operations in 1985," Federal Reserve Bank of New York, *Quarterly Review*, Spring 1986, pp. 34–53, esp. p. 37. See also Diane F. Siegel, "The Relationship of Money and Income: The Breakdowns in the 70s and 80s," Federal Reserve Bank of Chicago, *Economic Perspectives*, July–August 1986, pp. 3–15.

[10] Richard W. Kopcke, "Bank Funding Strategy and the Money Stock," Federal Reserve Bank of Boston, *New England Economic Review*, January–February 1985, pp. 4–14, esp. pp. 5–6.

*holding* of M1. Some financial transactions occur because people wish to manage money more efficiently and hold less M1, and many financial transactions do not require the use of checking accounts, for example, people who have a cash management account at a broker can use it to buy stocks. We can explain part of the rise in transactions velocity of money by the increase in financial transactions, but it is difficult to explain total increase in M1 by a need for M1 for financial transactions.[11]

Since velocity of money is not always predictable, ultimate targets of monetary policy (prices, output, and employment) change for reasons other than the changes in money supply, and the timing of the impact of monetary policy varies at different times, monetary policy is not yet entirely a scientifically predictable activity. It is somewhat of an art and not entirely a science. It is somewhat like trying to shoot at a moving target with a weapon that fires with varying rapidity. Just as interest rates in the money market were not a satisfactory target in the 1960s and 1970s, M1 is not a satisfactory target in the 1980s.

Some simple changes have been proposed to improve the results of monetary policy actions. For example, some economists argue that M1 should be redefined, to eliminate some types of checkable accounts that are less often used for spending. Would velocity of money, thus redefined, be greater? Maybe, but it is doubtful. For example, NOW accounts are less used for spending than other checkable deposits; should NOW accounts be excluded from a redefined M1? Most NOW accounts are held by individuals; a large part of demand deposits is held by business firms. But many transfers of deposit funds by business firms are not for purchase of items comprising GNP—often, they are for "intermediate" purchases, such as an automobile company buying steel from a steel firm. Such purchases are not spending for "final" output (GNP).[12] Redefining money is not likely to solve the problems created by the falling velocity of M1 in the mid-1980s.

## THE IMPLEMENTATION OF MONETARY POLICY

Economists widely agree that monetary policy works through the transmission mechanism described in the preceding section. There is less agreement as to the relative importance of money, credit, and interest rates in this process. There are, therefore, differences of opinion over *how* the Federal Reserve should manipulate its policy instruments so as to achieve the desired movement in output, employment, and prices. This is the implementation problem of monetary policy.

Our discussion of the implementation of monetary policy was begun in Chapter 5, in which we presented a simple framework within which the Fed influenced the behavior of the money supply by altering the so-called "monetary base." This framework was used for expository purposes: it was intended to show how the money

---

[11] John Wenninger and Lawrence J. Redecki, "Financial Transactions and the Demand for M1," Federal Reserve Bank of New York, *Quarterly Review*, Summer 1986, pp. 24–29.

[12] For more details, see Brian Motley, "Should Money Be Redefined?" Federal Reserve Bank of San Francisco, *Weekly Letter*, September 5, 1986.

supply is determined by the portfolio decisions of commercial banks, the public, the Treasury, and the Fed. It also served as an introduction to the policy instruments used by the Federal Reserve.

The monetary base–money supply specification is *one* approach that the Federal Reserve could use in implementing its policy. Indeed, many economists, especially those who take a monetarist view of the transmission mechanism, argue that such a procedure is more likely than most to satisfy our economic objectives. However, a large number of strategies could be used, and it is useful to consider a few of them, including, of course, approaches used by the Fed in recent years. In this section we indicate the need for policy guides, and we examine various policy strategies available to the Federal Reserve. Then, we look at the implications that different policies have for the financial markets; we review recent open market policies; and we conclude with a brief section on how monetary policy is carried out.

## The Need for Monetary Policy Guides

The way in which monetary policy changes are transmitted to the rest of the economy is imperfectly understood: there are variable lags in the effect of policy; changes in income and employment are related to nonmonetary factors; there is continual interaction between real and financial variables. What all this means to the Fed is that it often cannot be sure whether its current policy is expansionary or restrictive—and therefore appropriate in terms of its objectives—by simply observing *current* changes in, say, GNP, prices, or the rate of unemployment. These ultimate target variables are too remote from the impact of open market operations to serve as reliable guides to policy; their movements may mislead the monetary authority instead of providing it with useful information about the current thrust of policy.

The Fed needs a guide, a variable located somewhere in the transmission mechanism, that will provide this information. The "ideal" guide to policy is an important linkage variable that changes only in response to actions by the Federal Reserve; that is, it is not influenced by other factors, including changes in the ultimate target variables. In other words, the ideal guide would be unaffected by "feedback" from the real sector of the economy. If, for example, the money supply met these requirements, the Fed could manipulate its open market operations with a view to changing the money supply and hence the level, say, of GNP with confidence that the money supply would reflect only the impact of its policy actions. The money supply would serve as both the guide and the target of policy.

Unfortunately, the money supply does not fully meet these requirements, nor for that matter does any other variable in the transmission process. Those variables that are closely related to GNP, such as the money supply, interest rates, and bank credit, are importantly affected by other factors, including changes in GNP (through changes in the demand for money and credit). This makes it difficult for the monetary authority to distinguish between the effects of its policies (money supply factors) and the effects of other influences (money demand factors). If the guide is used as the day-to-day operating target, then the short-run influence of these other, nonpolicy factors causes it to transmit misleading information about the day-to-day effects that policy actions are having on the intermediate-term behavior of the indicator.

Thus the Fed needs two guides to provide it with two pieces of information: (1) an "indicator" to provide information about the current thrust of the entire financial sector, including Federal Reserve actions, on future movements in the ultimate target variables, and (2) an "operating target" to tell the Fed whether or not its policy actions are the probable cause of the current changes in monetary and credit conditions.[13] For example, the Fed needs to know whether current monetary conditions are becoming more expansionary, remaining unchanged, or becoming more restrictive. They also need to know whether these developments are the results of their actions or of other influences, such as changing demand for credit. This latter information allows the Fed to judge the appropriateness of its current policy position.

The indicator variables link the operating targets with the ultimate target variables. The most widely used indicators are the money supply, bank credit, long-term interest rates or some variant of these. The operating targets are variables that the Fed can readily control through day-to-day open market operations, for example, money market interest rates, bank reserves, and so on. Because economists disagree over the information content of alternative variables, there are several possible strategies, including (1) a "money supply" strategy, so called because the money supply is the variable that is alleged to determine GNP, (2) an "interest rate" strategy, and (3) a "bank credit" strategy.

Each strategy is based upon a different hypothesis about the way in which open market operations are related to the ultimate targets—about the transmission mechanism. They all imply that the relationships between variables are sufficiently stable so that the monetary authority can determine with reasonable accuracy the effects of its policy actions. How can the policymaker choose among them? Which strategy should be followed? The choice between them is an empirical question—which will best predict the actual results? Let us consider the kind of information necessary to predict these effects by looking at what is required if the policy action is to be successful.[14]

1. The Fed must be able to *control* the operating target on a near-term basis.
2. A change in the operating target must be followed by a *predictable* change in the indicator over a somewhat longer period of time.
3. A change in the indicator must have a *predictable* influence on the ultimate target.

In much of the following discussion of these criteria, we restrict our attention to strategies in which a reserve aggregate serves as the operating target and a monetary

---

[13] In some discussions, what we call the "target" and what we call the "indicator" are both referred to as targets. The difference lies in the speed of impact; Fed purchases of Treasury bills have an impact on Treasury bill yields and prices immediately, whereas change in the money supply may occur somewhat later. Thus, items such as the monetary base, bank reserves, and certain interest rates (such as the Treasury bill rate and the Fed funds rate) are affected more quickly than are other targets. The *ultimate* "targets," of course, are GNP, prices, and employment, but these are affected much later.

[14] A discussion of the criteria listed and of interest rate and money supply strategies is found in Albert E. Burger, "The Implementation Problem of Monetary Policy," *Federal Reserve Bank of St. Louis, Review*, March 1971, pp. 20–30.

aggregate is the indicator. We do so because most of the problems of monetary control can be illustrated by reference to reserve and monetary aggregates and the relationships between them. Moreover, much of the empirical work concerned with implementing policy has been undertaken within this framework. Later in the chapter we relate this analysis to the procedures used by the Federal Reserve in recent years.

## The Problem of Controlling the Monetary Aggregate

Let us suppose that the Fed has decided upon the desired rate of growth in, say, the M1 money supply. Assume further that it views the monetary control process in terms of the monetary base–money supply hypothesis outlined earlier. What sources of difficulty are there in such a procedure?

The main difficulty is in predicting the effects that a given change in the monetary base may have on the money multiplier, $m$. We recall that

$$m = \frac{1 + k}{r(1 + t + g) + k}$$

is the definition of multiplier used in Chapter 5.[15] In essence, the problem is that a change in the base may induce subsequent adjustments in the portfolios of the banks and the public that, by changing the value of the money multiplier, partially offset the effects of the change in the monetary base on the money supply.

If, for example, the Fed buys government securities to increase the growth rate of the monetary base, interest rates on these securities tend to decline. If the fall in rates induces commercial banks to hold additional excess reserves rather than to increase their loans and security holdings, the money multiplier declines as the ratio of reserves to deposits, $r$, rises. In the same way, if the decline in market rates induces the public to raise its time deposit/checkable deposit ratio, $t$, the multiplier declines. In both cases, the decline in the multiplier offsets some of the expansionary effect of the larger base. These changes in the multiplier are referred to as "feedback" effects; they occur because the multiplier is a function of the base; that is, $m = f(B)$. The problem for monetary control is that the magnitudes of these effects, which depend upon the interest sensitivity of the demand for excess reserves and time deposits, are difficult to predict. It may also be true that a rise in the base induces a shift by the public toward larger currency and time deposit holdings because of rising income. If so, the multiplier will decline. However, these effects due to changes in income and economic activity occur somewhat slowly and for that reason do not interfere unduly with *short-run* monetary control.

Similarly, a restrictive monetary policy means a slower rate of growth in the base. But open market sales of securities by the Fed tend to raise market interest

---

[15] Remember that $k$ is the ratio of currency to private checkable deposits, $t$ is the ratio of time deposits to private checkable deposits, $g$ is the ratio of government deposits to private checkable deposits, and $r$ is the average reserve ratio *actually* maintained by institutions having checkable deposits.

rates; this rise may induce banks to reduce their holdings of excess reserves. Also, the public may decide to increase its holdings of market instruments and reduce its time deposits. In these cases, where $r$ and $t$ decline, the money multiplier rises. Thus a major issue in the money supply control procedure is the interest elasticity of the uses of the base. How predictable are the interest rate effects on the distribution of the base among, say, demand deposits, time deposits, and excess reserves?

Considerable empirical research has been aimed at measuring the interest elasticity of the money supply. Much of this work was undertaken in the process of constructing large-scale econometric models of the U.S. economy. These studies differ in a number of significant ways, including the specification of demand functions for excess reserves, currency, and deposits, the time period from which the data are taken, the extent of disaggregation of data, and so forth. For these and other reasons, the studies reach somewhat different conclusions. There is a wide range of estimates of interest elasticity, which are difficult to reconcile. However, one review of these studies concludes that "the available evidence suggests quite conclusively that the short-run feedbacks through interest rate changes, which would be generated by policy changes in reserve aggregates, are very weak and should cause little, if any, difficulty for the implementation of policy actions aimed at controlling the money stock through the control of a reserve aggregate."[16]

Changes in Treasury deposits at commercial banks also affect the money multiplier. The $g$-ratio, where $g$ = government deposits/private checkable deposits, rises and falls, reflecting changes in Treasury receipts relative to expenditures and Treasury decisions concerning the proportion of its balances it wishes to hold at commercial banks rather than at Federal Reserve Banks. If, say, tax payments by the public or loan proceeds from the sale of government securities are credited to the Treasury's Tax and Loan accounts at commercial banks, the money multiplier declines. This means that the money supply may be subject to rather abrupt short-run changes that the Fed must try to anticipate if it is to achieve a target rate of growth in M1.

The second problem in monetary control relates to changes in the size of the monetary base itself. Without doubt the Fed can control the behavior of the base over a period of several months, but shorter-run control is made difficult because of unexpected changes in such items as float, borrowings from the Fed, U.S. Treasury deposits at Federal Reserve Banks, and adjustments because of changes in reserve requirements. In some cases, the changes result from random developments; at other times, cyclical or seasonal changes occur, such as in the case of float or U.S. Treasury deposits, which do not conform with previous experience. Errors in sampling or reporting of data, or simply information lags, cause the actual rate of growth to deviate from the desired rate. The significance of this is that the Fed is unable to predict these changes in operating factors on a daily, weekly, or perhaps monthly basis. Instead, they must aim for control over a longer period and thus accept wider swings in the money supply than desired. However, the evidence is quite clear that

---

[16] Robert H. Rasche, "A Review of Empirical Studies of the Money Supply Mechanism," Federal Reserve Bank of St. Louis, *Review*, July 1972, pp. 11–19; see p. 19.

the quarter-to-quarter changes in the base—those important for control over economic activity—can be controlled through open market operations if the Federal Reserve wishes to do so.

A third problem is the accurate measurement of the money stock itself. Weekly and monthly money growth figures are subject to statistical errors in estimating the money stock, distortions in the seasonal adjustment factors applied to these estimates, and "transitory variations" that make these figures unreliable. Although annual statistics are free of many of these errors and distortions, they too must be revised as more accurate estimates become available. At times, the changes that show up on the Fed's annual revision are considerable.

Some institutions do not report to the Fed every week; since they report less frequently, their share in the money supply must be estimated for short-run decisions. The DIDMCA, discussed in Chapter 3, gave the Fed the power to raise actual reserves for all of these institutions above the required level (or to lower them below the required level), assuming that all are affected. Again, some are affected much more quickly than others.

A final problem is that money is spent for used cars and houses, for gifts and transfer payments, for purchases of financial assets (stocks, bonds, and so on), and for intermediate purchases (an automobile company buying steel from a steel company, for example). Expenditures for GNP are only about *4 percent* of total spending of money. How can we believe that the velocity of money (the relationship of money, which is used for all types of spending, to GNP, which is spending for final goods and services produced this year) is constant? Careful research of monetarists convinced many that *income* velocity of money (GNP/M1) was predictable during the period 1945–1982, although *short-term* predictions could not be accurate.

### Selection and Control of the Operating Target

Until October 1979, the Fed funds rate was the primary target. It was recognized that changes in reserves had an almost immediate impact on the Fed funds rate, and the operating procedure was to try to affect the Fed funds rate so as to affect reserves, as shown in Figure 16–4. Of course, if banks' reserves are below requirements, they must attempt to obtain more reserves (or to reduce deposits). But this is not the usual situation.[17] What banks primarily respond to is the difference between the Fed funds rate (and other rates for marginal borrowed funds) and the rate at which they can lend or invest funds. They are profit-maximizing firms, just as other business firms are. An interest rate target seemed to be sensible; banks would respond to changes in the rate. So what it was believed the Fed should do was to choose a Fed funds rate that would be consistent with banks making just enough loans and investments to result in a money supply of the desired amount. It proved to be very difficult

---

[17] Even if it were the case, banks can borrow Fed funds. For a clear, simple discussion that makes it clear that the usual textbook description is not entirely accurate, see Robert D. Laurent, "Lagged Reserve Accounting and the Fed's New Operating Procedure," Federal Reserve Bank of Chicago, *Economic Perspectives*, Midyear 1982, pp. 32–55.

### FIGURE 16–4
### Operating Procedure Before October 1979

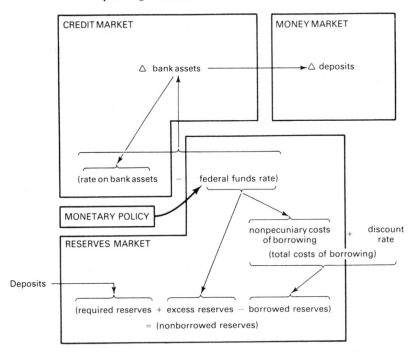

SOURCE: Federal Reserve Bank of Chicago, *Economic Perspectives,* Midyear 1982, p. 40.

to determine what interest rate (Fed funds rate) was consistent with this result. Hence a basic change in procedures occurred in October 1979, as discussed later in this chapter.

For a time in the 1970s, the Fed experimented with a target designated as reserves behind private deposits (RPDs). RPDs are total reserves minus the reserves required for government and interbank reserves.

A number of economists have urged that the Fed adopt the monetary base (reserves plus currency) as a target. One question, on which evidence is not conclusive, is whether the "multiplier" between RPDs and the money supply is any more stable than that between the monetary base and the money supply (the multiplier we discussed in Chapter 5). One study that tested for stability of the multiplier relationships found no "basis for conjecture that there has been a more stable relationship between the money stock and RPDs than between the net source base and money."[18]

In any event, the RPD experiment did not prove very useful, and inflation continued to become a more serious problem toward the end of the 1970s.

[18] Albert E. Burger, "Money Stock Control," Federal Reserve Bank of St. Louis, *Review,* October 1972, pp. 10–18. The complete version of the paper is published in *Controlling Monetary Aggregates II: The Implementation,* Federal Reserve Bank of Boston, September 1972, pp. 35–55.

To control inflation, the Fed shifted in October 1979 from use of the Fed funds rate to nonborrowed reserves as a target and gave special attention to the money supply (especially M1) as an indicator. In autumn 1982, it shifted again, to a *borrowed* reserves target; it also deemphasized M1 as an indicator. In early 1984 there was apparently another shift, further reducing emphasis on M1 as an indicator. In one analysis, results showed that the Fed funds rate became less volatile after autumn 1982, but remained more volatile than it had been before October 1979; these results were interpreted to mean that the money market probably perceived Fed procedure to have shifted to a borrowed reserves target in the autumn of 1982—if the Fed used an interest rate target, interest rates would be significantly less volatile. Results also indicated that "surprises" in money supply announcements were not expected to be offset in the near future, indicating less emphasis on M1 as an indicator for Fed policy. Finally, results indicated that response of money market interest rates to announcements of changes in real economic activity and prices were somewhat more significant after autumn 1982, suggesting that the money market was more concerned about these variables and less concerned about changes in money supply, especially in M1. All these results are consistent with a shift to borrowed reserves as a target in early 1984 and less emphasis on M1 as an indicator after autumn 1982. Thus both targets and procedures of the Fed seem to have shifted as financial deregulation, less inflation, continued economic growth (although at varying rates in different years), and the increased complexity of items comprising the money supply made such changes in policies and procedures necessary.[19]

## Choice of the Indicator or Intermediate Target

Whether the Fed uses the Fed funds rate, the monetary base, total reserves, unborrowed reserves (total reserves minus those borrowed from the Fed), "free reserves,"[20] or some other target, it is important to choose also an indicator that may not

[19] See V. Vance Roley, "Market Perceptions of U.S. Monetary Policy Since 1982," Federal Reserve Bank of Kansas City, *Economic Review*, May 1986, pp. 27–40. Roley classified policy periods as autumn 1977 to autumn 1979 (Fed funds target, lagged reserve requirements), autumn 1979 to autumn 1982 (nonborrowed reserves target, lagged reserve requirements), autumn 1982 to February 1984 (borrowed reserves target, lagged reserve requirements), and the period after February 1984 (borrowed reserves target, contemporaneous reserve requirements). In the most recent period, the Fed funds rate did not show a significant response to money announcement "surprises." With respect to interest rates, if the target is *borrowed* reserves, the Fed funds rate may be expected to be more volatile than if the target is the Fed funds rate (since in the latter case, the Fed tries to stabilize the rate). If the target is *nonborrowed* reserves, the Fed funds rate may be expected to be *quite* volatile, since it is not a target and if institutions need more reserves, they are likely to borrow them in the Fed funds market, causing volatility in the Fed funds rate. When the target is borrowed reserves, *non*borrowed reserves may be increased to accommodate demand for reserves (caused, e.g., by increased demand for bank deposits). For a chronological account that includes other policy changes and some of the developments that caused them, see Robert L. Hetzel, "Monetary Policy in the Early 1980s," Federal Reserve Bank of Richmond, *Economic Review*, March–April 1986, pp. 20–32.

[20] Free reserves are excess reserves minus borrowed reserves (borrowed, that is, from the Fed). Free reserves were used as a target for many years until it became apparent that a decline in free reserves did not mean that banks needed more reserves; instead, it often meant that banks were lending (and creating money) so rapidly that they were reducing their free reserves. A former chairman of the Fed finally told Congress that he wished they had never focused so much attention on free reserves.

be available as quickly in statistics as reserves, but has a demonstrated effect on the economy. This target could be one measure of the money supply (probably either M1 or M2) or some measure of credit, or perhaps both could be watched as indicators.[21] Monetarists would argue that money supply should be the target, but they would reject the attempt to "fine-tune" the money supply and suggest instead that the Fed aim at a steady, moderate growth in the money supply.

There are empirical problems in evaluation of change in the indicator. M1 may not grow at the same rate as M2; with recent financial innovations, it may be difficult to know whether an increase in M1 is really an increase in transactions balances (money used for spending) or an increase in "money market accounts" or some other new form of financial asset not frequently used for payments. Remember, the basis for measuring M1 is to include everything that is commonly used for spending for goods and services, on the ground that control of what is used for spending tends to control spending.

If interest rates were used as an indicator, similar problems would arise. The Fed funds rate may fall when other money market interest rates rise; short-term interest rates may rise when long-term rates do not rise; and so on.

Money supply, credit, and interest rates are affected by factors other than Fed policy actions. Demand for money is important, as well as money supply. Demand for borrowing affects interest rates as well as credit. Those who favor interest rates as indicators argue that they are very important as determinants of spending. This is essentially the nonmonetarist (sometimes termed Keynesian) position discussed in Chapter 15. Those who argue for some measure of the money supply as an indicator allege that the velocity of money is sufficiently stable that moderate growth in the money supply will lead to similar growth in spending and output. This is the monetarist position. Monetarists further point out that when output cannot be increased, increased spending simply leads to inflation. Many economists agree that if the money supply is increased at a rapid rate, inflation will occur. But there is disagreement as to results from less rapid rates, since it is clear that more money available for spending can affect both the quantity of goods and services purchased (and hence output) and prices.

Nonmonetarists often argue that if spending by private sectors is insufficient, the government should spend—spending to create jobs, as was suggested in early 1983. Monetarists respond that such spending was not effective in the past—the unemployment rate was still over 14 percent in 1940, after years of effort to create jobs.[22] Instead, they argue, the Fed should have increased the money supply so that business firms and consumers would spend; they note that the money supply had been reduced by roughly one-third between 1929 and 1933. Business and consumer spend-

---

[21] Benjamin Friedman has argued that the Fed should have two targets—money supply and the amount of outstanding credit—because money at best determines *demand*, but many of the current problems arise from supply-side disturbances—higher costs of energy, reduced increases in productivity, and so on. See his "Time to Reexamine the Monetary Targets Framework," *Federal Reserve Bank of Boston, New England Economic Review*, March–April 1982, pp. 15–23.

[22] *Economic Report of the President*, January 1952, p. 177.

ing would lead to more jobs, not "make-work" jobs. Nonmonetarists counter that increasing the money supply might have been just "pushing on a string"—the public might have just held the additional money. There *is* some evidence that banks did this in the 1930s—they held excess reserves of about $7 billion in 1940, indicating that they were not lending or investing as much as possible. But there is little evidence that this was true for the public in general. Monetarists conclude that what finally brought economic recovery in the 1940s was the spending and hiring for World War II. Although much was government spending, the funds were paid to firms that then hired war workers and purchased materials, thus generating purchasing power for the public.

Evidence from studies by monetarists finally convinced many that the money supply is an important causal variable and that (contrary to the Keynesian view) velocity of money is stable or predictable enough in many long-run periods to rely on changes in money supply to result in predictable changes in GNP.[23]

## Money Market Conditions Strategy

Thus far, we have restricted our attention to strategies in which reserve aggregates serve as the operating target and money, credit, or long-term interest rates are the indicators. However, money market conditions may also provide the basis for open market operations, either in conjunction with these aggregates or in an independent strategy. Indeed, during the 1950s, 1960s, and most of the 1970s, money market conditions played several roles in Federal Reserve policy.

The particular strategy used by the Fed in its open market operations may have important implications for the financial markets. It seems likely, in the short run at least, that interest rates will fluctuate somewhat more under a money supply or bank credit strategy than under those aimed at money market conditions or interest rates. This follows from the fact that the Fed cannot simultaneously control both money and interest rates. Thus, if the Fed aims at a week-to-week or month-to-month growth rate in the stock of money, it must allow changes in the demand for money to be reflected in interest rate movements. On the other hand, the Fed may be able to maintain relatively stable interest rates in the short run if it is willing to allow whatever changes in the money supply are required to equate supply and demand for money at those rates.

Figure 16–5 is used to illustrate this short-run trade-off between changes in interest rates and changes in the money stock.[24] We use the term "money stock" to denote the quantity of money determined by the interaction of the demand and supply *schedules* (functions or curves) for money. The demand schedule for money, *D*, is assumed to depend upon both the rate of interest and the level of income. The supply

---

[23] The degree of stability or predictability of velocity for the 1960s and 1970s was shown in Chapter 6.

[24] See Albert E. Burger and Neil A. Stevens, "Monetary Expansion and Federal Reserve Open Market Committee Operating Strategy in 1971," Federal Reserve Bank of St. Louis, *Review*, March 1972, pp. 11–31, esp. pp. 16–19.

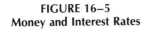

**FIGURE 16–5**
**Money and Interest Rates**

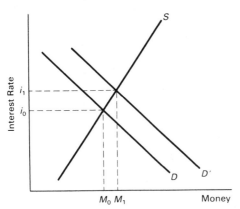

curve for money, $S$, depends upon both the rate of interest and the monetary base (or reserves). The initial equilibrium rate of interest is $i_0$ and the money stock is $M_0$.

Let there be an increase in the demand for money, as might occur during a period of economic expansion. The demand schedule shifts right to $D'$, and the interest rate rises toward the new equilibrium rate, $i_1$. The money stock rises to $M_1$ as the rise in the interest rate induces the banks to reduce their holdings of excess reserves and expand their loans. Under a money supply strategy the Fed would permit the rate of interest to rise. If the accompanying increase in the money stock were deemed excessive, the Fed could reduce the monetary base (bank reserves), with the result that the interest rate would rise above $i_1$. In Figure 16–5 this would be shown by a shift to the left in the money supply curve. But, if the money stock increase were relatively small and consistent with current policy objectives, the base would not need to be reduced; the result would be as shown.

But suppose now that the Fed aims at stable money markets or stable long-term interest rates rather than stable monetary growth. In this case, illustrated in Figure 16–6, the rise in the interest rate to $i_1$ requires an increase in the monetary base—a shift in the supply curve to $S'$—to restore the initial target rate of interest, $i_0$. The money stock increases in this case to $M_2$. As our illustration shows, the Fed is unable to control both the money stock *and* the rate of interest, where changes in the latter are demand induced. Of course, the situation is quite different if the initial rise in interest rates resulted from a reduction in the monetary base, perhaps because of unexpected reductions in float or member bank borrowings. In this instance the rise in interest rates would be supply induced and would be accompanied by a reduction in the money stock. Under *either* a money supply or an interest rate strategy, the Fed would increase the monetary base to lower interest rates *or* to increase the money stock to the equilibrium position.

Thus far, we have assumed that the Fed can stabilize interest rates, if it wishes to do so, through appropriate open market operations. This seems a reasonable assumption for the short run. But, in the long run, the monetary instability that such

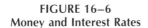

FIGURE 16–6
Money and Interest Rates

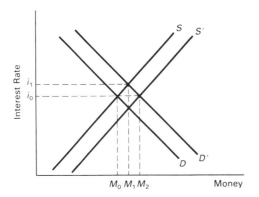

a policy would produce might cause large swings in income; the demand for money would therefore also change, with the result that interest rates might be highly unstable. In short, monetary policy aimed at stable money market conditions or stable longer-term interest rates might in the longer run be self-defeating. The longer-run behavior of interest rates, wide swings or relative stability, depends in part on how successful monetary and fiscal policies turn out to be in maintaining high levels of income and employment without significant rates of inflation. In this regard, the jury is still out on the important empirical question, "How can economic stability be achieved and maintained?"

In the meantime, the Fed faces a dilemma: Should it try to control the growth of money or temporarily offset demand-induced changes in interest rates?[25] There are arguments for both courses of action. Abrupt changes in interest rates and money market conditions are apt to interfere with Treasury financing operations because of the uncertainty they create in the marketplace. More important, volatile interest rates and security prices may impair the liquidity position of commercial banks; they also disrupt the plans of other borrowers and lenders of loanable funds. High market rates occasionally lead to "credit crunches," as in 1966, 1969, 1974, and 1980, with severe impact on the stock market, housing, and expenditures of state and local governments.

On the other hand, many economists believe that the social benefits of stable money market conditions or interest rates are negligible compared with the costs of such policy. Moreover, they believe that the Treasury's financing problems and "credit crunches," for example, are the product of rigidities in the financial structure, such as interest rate ceilings on long-term government securities, ceilings on rates paid on time and savings deposits at financial institutions, fixed-rate mortgages, and so on. In this view, these problems should be resolved by eliminating these restrictions or altering the institutional framework in other ways that introduce more flexibility.

[25] See David P. Eastburn, "The Future Role of Interest Rates in Open Market Policy," *Federal Reserve Bank of Philadelphia, Business Review,* January 1973, pp. 3–7.

More important, those who stress the importance of control over monetary aggregates believe that this is the primary responsibility of the Fed and that credit markets should be allowed to ration the available supply without interference from the central bank.

Recently, a number of economists have proposed an eclectic approach as a rule of thumb of monetary policy. According to this analysis, if the monetary authority's primary concern is to stabilize the economy, the choice between controlling money or interest rates depends upon the *source* of economic instability. Governor Wallich of the Federal Reserve has offered the following prescription: "When there are disturbances on the side of the real sector, monetary policy should focus on the (monetary) aggregates and allow interest rates to move up or down to counter the disturbance. Conversely, when there are disturbances on the monetary side, monetary policy should focus on interest rates to avoid transmitting these disturbances to the real sector."[26] Here, "disturbances" in the real sector refers to changes in saving or in investment spending; monetary "disturbances" are those deriving from changes in the supply of or demand for money.

The logic of this prescription can be illustrated by the following examples. Suppose that an economic downturn occurs because of a reduction in investment spending for plant and equipment. Interest rates, will, other things being equal, tend to decline. In this circumstance appropriate monetary policy calls for allowing interest rates to decline while maintaining the target rate of growth in money. If the recession is severe, an increase in the money stock may be needed to push interest rates even lower to stimulate interest-sensitive expenditures so as to promote an economic recovery.

But suppose instead that the source of instability is a sudden increase in the public's demand for money. If the money stock is set at a given level by the Federal Reserve, interest rates will tend to rise. The increase in interest rates will dampen investment spending, which in turn will reduce income and other spending, resulting in a general slowdown in economic activity. In this situation, the monetary authority should match the initial increase in the demand for money with an increase in the money stock so as to prevent interest rates from rising.

More broadly, if recession or inflation are apt to result from changes in saving or in investment demand, interest rates should be allowed to fluctuate while the money stock is stabilized. If recession or inflation are likely because of changes in the monetary sector, interest rates should be stabilized and the money stock should be increased or lowered as necessary in the particular circumstances.

It should be noted that this prescription may be inconsistent with the maintenance of orderly conditions in the financial markets. If inflationary pressures emanate

---

[26] Henry C. Wallich, "Some Technical Aspects of Monetary Policy," Remarks to the Institutional Investor Institute, May 6, 1976, p. 8 (also quoted in Federal Reserve Bank of San Francisco, *Business & Financial Letter*, October 8, 1976). See also Richard G. Davis, "Implementing Open Market Policy with Monetary Aggregates," Federal Reserve Bank of New York, *Monthly Review*, July 1973, pp. 170–182, and William Poole, "Interest Rate Stability as a Monetary Goal," Federal Reserve Bank of Boston, *New England Economic Review*, May–June 1976, pp. 30–37.

from the real sector, high and/or rising interest rates may become a matter of great concern to market participants and to the monetary authority.

It is, of course, difficult to determine with certainty whether a disturbance originates in the real or the monetary sector. In our dynamic world, forces for change are continually interacting and their economic effects occur with variable lags. How then can the monetary authority decide whether to focus on interest rates or on money? William Poole, whose analysis has contributed much to this approach to monetary policy, observes that "the odds favor interpreting upward (downward) pressures on interest rates as a sign of expanding (contracting) economic activity. In the absence of clearly identifiable causes of interest rate changes, in my opinion money growth should not be accelerated (decelerated) when interest rates are rising (falling)."[27] The implication is that, *if* the Fed is to pursue a countercyclical monetary policy, the rate of growth in the money stock should rise during recession and decline during economic upswings. Interest rates should not be prevented from falling during economic slowdowns or restrained from rising during a period of business expansion.

# FEDERAL RESERVE STRATEGIES SINCE 1965

During the period since the mid-1960s, Federal Reserve open market strategy has incorporated several sets of guides, including money market conditions, the level and structure of interest rates, and monetary and credit aggregates. The relative importance of these guides has changed over the years, reflecting changes in the economy, in financial markets, and in monetary theory. In general, there has been a shift in emphasis from money market conditions to the behavior of the monetary aggregates. This change in policy has been one of degree, and money market conditions (and interest rates) remain important areas of concern. Most economists have welcomed this development; they believe that the shift toward monetary aggregates has been long overdue. It is, of course, recognized that efforts to control the rate of growth of money may at times conflict with the maintenance of orderly financial markets and stable interest rates. Indeed, this conflict often presents the dilemma posed earlier in this chapter: Should the Fed seek to control money or interest rates?

Since the early 1970s, the Federal Reserve has also taken a number of steps to improve the efficiency of its operations and to communicate more clearly its objectives and policies to the financial community, to Congress, and to the public. In this section we outline some of the major changes that have taken place with respect to open market policy.

## The Shift Toward Monetary and Credit Aggregates

The shift in emphasis from interest rates and money market conditions to the money and credit aggregates began in 1966. Early in that year the Fed modified its open market procedure by using the so-called "proviso clause" in the directive issued

---

[27] Poole, "Interest Rate Stability," p. 37.

by the Federal Open Market Committee (FOMC) to the manager of the System Open Market Account (SOMA).[28] Under this new procedure open market operations were to be conducted with a view toward maintaining certain specified conditions in the money market *provided, however,* that the behavior of bank credit was deemed appropriate under the circumstances. By this device, the FOMC, for the first time, made a monetary aggregate—bank credit—a goal of policy along with money market conditions. However, the Committee focused mainly on money market conditions during the late 1960s and did not adopt explicit goals for bank credit or for any measure of the money supply.

In early 1970, the Federal Open Market Committee of the Federal Reserve System issued new instructions concerning open market operations that said

> it is the policy of the Federal Open Market Committee to foster financial conditions conducive to orderly reduction in the rate of inflation, while encouraging the resumption of sustainable economic growth and the attainment of reasonable equilibrium in the country's balance of payments.
>
> To implement this policy, the Committee desires to see moderate growth in money and bank credit over the months ahead. System open market operations until the next meeting of the Committee shall be conducted with a view to maintaining money market conditions consistent with that objective.[29]

This was the first time the Committee explicitly focused on the behavior of the money stock and bank credit. The reason for this policy change was that it had become increasingly evident during the late 1960s that money and credit were not under sufficient control. Their annual rates of growth were often excessive, and there were wide swings in growth rates of both series on a monthly and quarterly basis. No doubt the growing acceptance of the monetarist view was an important element too in the decisions to stress *money* as well as credit and to keep an eye on both aggregates rather than primarily on money market conditions.[30]

## Reporting Targets

Beginning with the *Policy Record* for the January 1974 FOMC meeting, the numerical target ranges for the short-run targets have been reported regularly.[31] At that meeting the Committee concluded that

> growth in $M_1$ and $M_2$ over the January–February period at annual rates within ranges of tolerances of 3–6 percent and 6–9 percent, respectively, would be consistent with its

[28] The FOMC directives and the role of the manager of SOMA are discussed in the last sections just before the summary at the end of this chapter.

[29] "Record of Policy Actions of the Federal Open Market Committee," *Federal Reserve Bulletin,* June 1970, p. 512.

[30] See Andrew F. Brimmer, "The Political Economy of Money: Evolution and Impact of Monetarism in the Federal Reserve System," Paper delivered at the Eighty-Fourth Annual Meeting of the American Economic Association, New Orleans, Louisiana, December 27, 1971, pp. 344–352.

[31] Since July 1976, the *Policy Record* covering a particular FOMC meeting has been published in the *Federal Reserve Bulletin* about a month after the meeting.

longer-run objectives for the monetary aggregates. . . . would be likely to involve RPD growth during the January–February period at an annual rate within a 4¾ to 7¾ percent range of tolerance, and . . . the weekly average Federal funds rate might be permitted to vary in an orderly fashion from as low as 8¾ percent to as high as 10 percent, if necessary, in the course of operations.[32]

This approach to short-run targeting distinguishes between short-run and longer-run targets for the monetary aggregates. It also specifies a range of tolerance for the Federal funds rate that becomes in effect an operating target.

The persistence of serious inflation and the deepening of the recession in late 1974 led to widespread concern about the state of the economy and the conduct of monetary policy. Reflecting this concern the Congress passed House Concurrent Resolution 133 in March 1975. Though not a binding prescription, the resolution requested the Board of Governors and the FOMC to

> Maintain long-run growth of the monetary and credit aggregates commensurate with the economy's long-run potential to increase production, so as to promote effectively the goals of maximum employment, stable prices, and moderate long-term interest rates.[33]

The resolution also called for the Board of Governors to consult with Congress quarterly as to its "objectives and plans with respect to the ranges of growth or diminution of monetary and credit aggregates in the upcoming twelve months."[34]

In response to this resolution, and later to the requirements of the Federal Reserve Reform Act of 1977, the chairman of the Federal Reserve Board has met quarterly with the Congress since May 1975. At each meeting he has reported on the state of the economy and has disclosed the longer-run targets for the monetary and credit aggregates. Under the Full Employment and Balanced Growth Act of 1978 (the Humphrey-Hawkins Act), the Board of Governors must report in writing to the Congress by February 20 and July 20 of each year on the Fed's "objectives and plans" for the aggregates for that calendar year and (July report) for the year ahead.[35]

For example, in the report of July 20, 1982, tentative ranges of monetary and credit targets for 1983 (fourth quarter 1982 to fourth quarter 1983) were stated as follows: M1, 2½ to 5½ percent; M2, 6 to 9 percent; M3, 6½ to 9½ percent; and commercial bank credit, 6 to 9 percent. All these targets were unchanged. It was stated further that "because the monetary aggregates in 1982 will likely be close to the upper ends of their ranges, or perhaps even somewhat above them, the preliminary 1983 targets are fully consistent with a reduction in the actual growth of money in 1983."[36]

---

[32] "Record of Policy Actions of the Federal Open Market Committee," *Federal Reserve Bulletin*, April 1974, pp. 279–280.

[33] U.S. Congress, Senate Committee on Banking, Housing and Urban Affairs, *First Meeting on the Conduct of Monetary Policy*, 94th Congress, 1st sess., April 29 and 30 and May 1, 1975, p. 3.

[34] Ibid.

[35] The chairman's statement at each congressional meeting and the longer-run targets are reported in "Statements to Congress," *Federal Reserve Bulletin*.

[36] *Report to Congress on Monetary Policy*, Federal Reserve Board, July 20, 1982, pp. 1, 2.

At the same time, in testimony before the Joint Economic Committee of Congress, Chairman Volcker indicated that the FOMC would tolerate "growth somewhat above the target ranges . . . for a time in circumstances in which it appeared that precautionary or liquidity motivations, during a period of economic uncertainty and turbulence, were leading to stronger than anticipated demands for money."[37] In other words, in a situation of some uncertainty because recession seemed to be continuing, and in which some money balances were probably being held for precautionary or liquidity motivations rather than for spending, more rapid growth of the money supply might be tolerated temporarily.

## The Situation That Caused a Major Change in Strategy

OPEC prices for oil rose sharply in 1979, but many other developments also indicated serious economic problems: inflation was reaching a rate of nearly 9 percent a year, productivity was declining rather than increasing, the rate of personal saving (saving as a percentage of disposable personal income) declined sharply, and in other countries serious concern about the value of the dollar (in view of the inflation) was creating anxiety. After some temporary actions in late 1978 to stabilize the dollar, it had remained reasonably stable, but with inflation constantly rising, the concern over the value of the dollar could not be ignored. A currency that is widely used for international payments, held as an international reserve asset, and held as an asset that under normal conditions is one likely to be stable in value, cannot be regarded as being useful for these purposes if rising inflation indicates its purchasing power to be declining.

In summer 1979, Paul Volcker, until then president of the Federal Reserve Bank of New York, was appointed chairman of the Board of Governors of the Federal Reserve System. Internationally, the reaction was favorable; it was widely believed that he would make a serious attempt to control inflation. Nevertheless, no major changes were announced immediately.

On October 6, 1979, however, it was announced that the FOMC had voted to shift from an interest rate targeting procedure to a reserves targeting procedure, with the aim of achieving levels of bank reserves consistent with the goals of money supply as measured by M1 and M2. The appendix to this chapter gives details of the strategy, as reported in a monthly review of one of the Federal Reserve banks somewhat later.[38] It was recognized that this strategy might very well result in increased volatility in interest rates, and indeed this was a result.

---

[37] Statement by Paul A. Volcker before the Joint Economic Committee, November 24, 1982, in *Federal Reserve Bulletin*, December 1982, p. 747. For a view by a private economist that temporary rapid expansion of the money supply was not inflationary, see Bluford H. Putnam, "This Money Bulge Isn't Inflationary," *The Wall Street Journal*, April 27, 1983, p. 26.

[38] The reasoning behind this choice was explained in detail in *New Monetary Control Procedures*, 2 vols., Board of Governors of the Federal Reserve System, February 1981.

## Elements of the New Strategy After October 1979

Total reserves consist of (1) vault cash held by financial institutions that have checkable deposits plus (2) deposits that they hold, directly or indirectly, in Federal Reserve Banks. Deposits held at the Fed are in part created when financial institutions borrow at the discount window, and a larger part results from Fed purchases of assets, chiefly government securities, through open market operations.

A diagram may be helpful in visualizing the differences between the new operating procedure and the old procedure, which was diagrammed in Figure 16–4. The new procedure is illustrated in Figure 16–7. Instead of interest rate targeting, as in the old procedures, the specific target was nonborrowed reserves. This was chosen, in preference to total reserves, because borrowing at the discount window is carried out at the initiative of the financial institutions. The desired levels of nonborrowed reserves are those that will be consistent with desired levels of the money supply.

**FIGURE 16–7**
**Operating Procedure After October 1979**

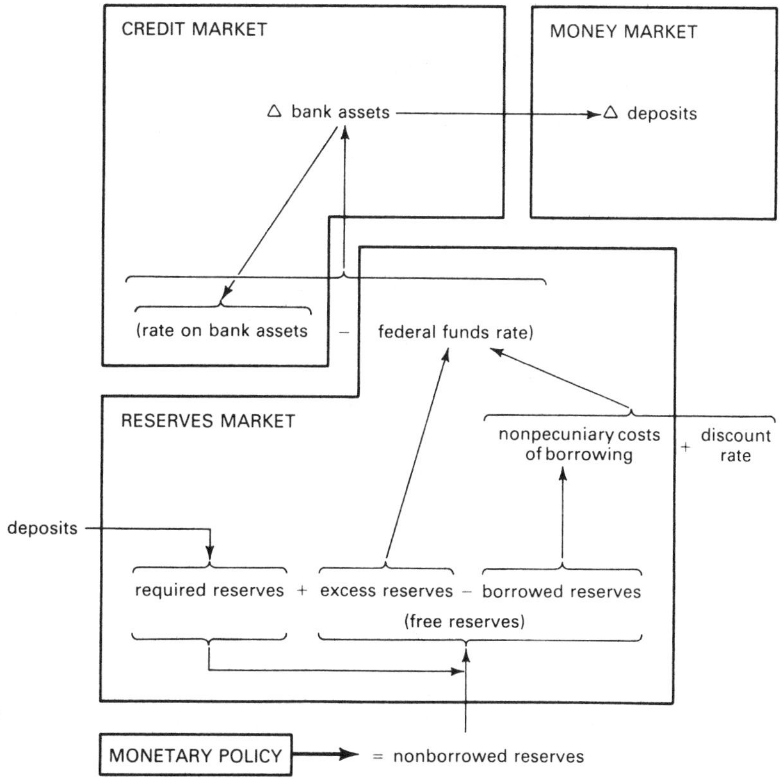

SOURCE: Federal Reserve Bank of Chicago, *Economic Perspectives*, Midyear 1982, p. 43.

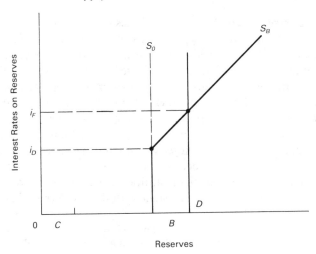

**FIGURE 16–8**
**Supply and Demand for Reserves**

A more technical analysis may be helpful in explaining the ways in which various elements shown in Figure 16–8 affect the change in money supply. In Figure 16–8, demand and supply curves for bank reserves are shown. The quantity of reserves is measured on the horizontal axis, while the interest rate on Federal funds, $i_F$, and the discount rate, $i_D$, are both measured on the vertical axis. These demand and supply curves have some unique characteristics that make them different from the usual curves drawn in economics texts.[39] First, the demand curve shown is vertical; depository institutions must have a certain volume of reserves to meet reserve requirements. Under lagged reserve accounting, the required amount of reserves is set by deposit levels two weeks earlier, as noted in Chapter 3. Banks thus have a required amount of reserves to meet, regardless of the interest rate. The real-world curve would probably have a slight negative slope because, if the Fed funds interest rate were low, banks might hold more excess reserves. The vertical demand curve is an approximation.

### The Supply of Reserves

The supply curve for reserves consists of three parts. Let $C$ stand for the amount of reserves in the form of currency in depository institution vaults. Let $O$ stand for reserves supplied through Fed open market operations. The total in vault

---

[39] The frame of reference used here was suggested by John P. Judd and John L. Scadding, "Short-Run Monetary Control Under Reserve Accounting Rules," Federal Reserve Bank of San Francisco, *Economic Review, Supplement,* Summer 1980. See also Paul L. Kasriel and Randall C. Merris, "Reserve Targeting and Discount Policy," Federal Reserve Bank of Chicago, *Economic Perspectives,* Fall 1982, pp. 15–25. For a similar analysis, see Gordon H. Sellon, Jr., and Diane Siebert, "The Discount Rate: Experience Under Reserve Targeting," Federal Reserve Bank of Kansas City, September–October 1982, pp. 3–18; and Robert D. Laurent, "Lagged Reserve Accounting and the Fed's New Operating Procedure," Federal Reserve Bank of Chicago, *Economic Perspectives,* Midyear 1982, pp. 32–55.

FIGURE 16–9
Effect of an Increased Supply of Nonborrowed Reserves

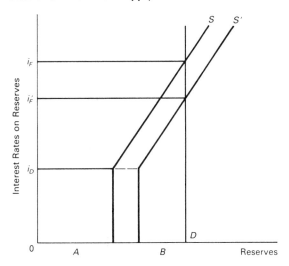

cash and in deposits at the Fed is nonborrowed reserves: $N = C + O$. The remaining reserves, $B$, are borrowings from the Fed through its discount window.

The supply of nonborrowed reserves is determined principally by open market operations; hence, this part of the supply curve is also vertical, and is labeled $S_O$.

When the interest rate on Fed funds, $i_F$, rises above the discount rate, $I_D$, depository institutions borrow more from the Fed.[40] It is well documented that there is a positive relation between two variables: (1) the difference between the Fed funds rate and the discount rate, $i_F - i_D$, and (2) borrowing from the Fed, $B$.[41] The positively sloped part of the supply curve, labeled $S_B$, represents borrowing from the Fed as $i_F$ rises above $i_D$. It is a supply curve in the sense that it represents the willingness of the authorities in control of discount window lending to supply reserves. Of course, it could also be viewed as demand for reserves on the part of depository institutions.

Thus, the supply curve for reserves consists principally of amounts supplied through open market operations and amounts supplied through the discount window, recognizing that reserves are supplied through the discount window in response to requests.[42]

In Figure 16–9, the entire supply curve is shifted to the right, from $S$ to $S'$, as a result of open market operations that provide more reserves. Nonborrowed reserves

[40] Some borrowing at the discount window is not interest sensitive and may occur even at high discount rates. Some depository institutions need added reserves at certain times and do not have access to Fed funds or other national market borrowing, at least not at all times.

[41] See Federal Reserve Bank of St. Louis, *U.S. Financial Data*, December 10, 1982, p. 1.

[42] The Fed has rules regulating borrowing from the discount window and discourages repeated or extensive borrowing. Banks may have some "reluctance" to borrow. Moreover, there are necessary forms and procedures that impose nonpecuniary costs (time and effort), as shown in Figure 16–7.

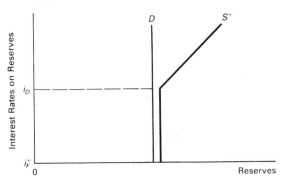

FIGURE 16–10
Effects of a Supply of Nonborrowed Reserves Greater than Demand

increase and the interest rate on Fed funds falls to $i_F'$. Borrowed reserves fall as the difference between $i_F$ and $i_D$ is reduced. Depository institutions that have more reserves supply them to the Fed funds market, and rates fall. This makes borrowing from the Fed less attractive.

What happens if the supply of nonborrowed reserves, $S$, shifts rightward to the position $S''$, where it lies to the right of the demand curve? This is shown in Figure 16–10. Under this condition, $i_F$ may fall precipitously, perhaps nearly to zero. Depository institutions have more nonborrowed reserves than they need to meet requirements and hence offer Fed funds at sharply lower rates. In April 1979, for example, the rate fell from double-digit levels to 2 percent in one day.

Sharp fluctuations in the Fed funds rate often occur on certain days, the last day of the reserve accounting week. If many banks need to borrow Fed funds, the rate rises sharply; if many banks have a supply to sell, it falls sharply. Financial market watchers realize that there is a special situation on that day of the week.

### The Demand for Reserves

If the Fed funds rate is above the discount rate, some interest-sensitive borrowing occurs at the discount window; if the discount rate is reduced, the Fed funds rate (and, hence, other money market rates) tend to fall, although there may be no more borrowing at the discount window. If the discount rate were a penalty rate, say, ½ percent above the Fed funds rate, there would be no interest-sensitive discount window borrowing. The Fed funds rate could be very unstable; it could fall nearly to zero if there were ample funds, or it could rise sharply if there were a need for funds (of course, if it rose much, it would rise above the discount rate, and the discount rate would no longer be a penalty rate). Encouraging some interest-sensitive borrowing by keeping the discount rate below the Fed funds rate tends to lead to greater stability in the Fed funds rate.

If the discount rate is below the Fed funds rate, or is reduced so that it is below that rate, there is more interest-sensitive borrowing at the discount window and, hence, less demand for Fed funds, and the Fed fund rate (and other market rates) is likely to fall. This explains why it may be necessary for the Fed to reduce the discount rate to reduce money market interest rates. For many years, the discount rate has generally followed other rates. But in 1981, it became clear that reduction in the discount rate would be helpful if it were desired that other rates should fall.

### Increased Interest Rate Volatility

The diagrams help to explain the dramatic increase in interest rate volatility after October 6, 1979, as shown in Figure 16–11. The Fed cannot simultaneously control *both* reserves *and* money market interest rates. If reserves are increased, interest rates are likely to fall, assuming no change in demand for borrowing. If borrowing increases, they may rise, but in either case, they cannot be controlled simultaneously with control of changes in reserves. Thus, in the period when the Fed used the Fed funds rate as a target, rate changes would elicit a response from the open market desk, and the volume of open market operations would be changed to prevent an undesired change in the Fed funds rate. But when nonborrowed reserves were the target, interest rates were volatile.[43]

## Some Problems

As might have been expected, some problems were encountered and some questions arose as the new strategy was followed. Here we discuss (1) the technical problems arising from the way in which reserve requirements have been determined, (2) the short-run volatility of the money supply, (3) questions about possible use of *real* interest rates as a target (since a nominal rate such as the Fed funds rate had proved unsatisfactory), (4) exchange rates as possible indicators (in view of the volatility of measures of the money supply and the fact that institutional changes caused changes in items included in such measures), and (5) an evaluation of the success of the new strategy.

### Desirability of Contemporaneous Reserve Accounting

Before 1968, banks had been required to meet reserve requirements contemporaneously: reserves for a week had to equal the required percentage of deposits for that week. Bank reserves and deposits, of course, continually change as funds are deposited and withdrawn, reserves are increased and decreased, and changes in types of deposits result in changes in percentages of reserves required. Because neither the

---

[43] For an analysis of the problem of volatility of interest rates, see Neil G. Berkman, "Open Market Operations Under the New Monetary Policy," Federal Reserve Bank of Boston, *New England Economic Review*, March–April 1981, pp. 5–20; Paul L. Kasriel, "Interest Rate Volatility in 1980," Federal Reserve Bank of Chicago, *Economic Perspectives*, January–February 1981, pp. 8–11; and Paul Evans, "Why Have Interest Rates Been So Volatile?" Federal Reserve Bank of San Francisco, *Economic Review*, Summer 1981, pp. 7–20.

**FIGURE 16–11**
**Daily Percentage Changes in Selected Interest Rates**

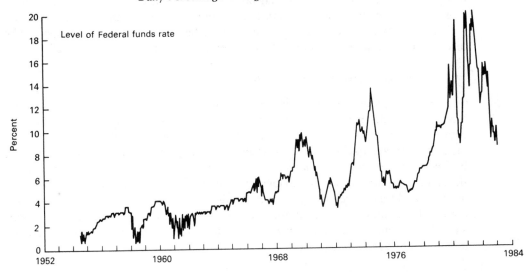

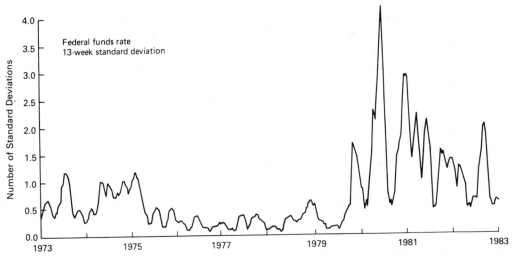

SOURCE: George W. Cloos, "The Midwest and the Recession," Federal Reserve Bank of Chicago, *Economic Perspectives*, January–February 1981, p. 11.

average deposits for a week nor the average amount of required reserves could be known with any degree of certainty until toward the end of the week (in fact, precise amounts were not known until after the close of the last day), it was, for a bank, "like trying to hit a moving target (its required reserves) with a shaky rifle (its actual reserves)."[44] Therefore, in 1968, lagged reserve accounting (LRA) replaced contemporaneous reserve accounting (CRA). Under LRA, required reserves depended on deposits in the second preceding week, and thus the total amount of required reserves, for each bank and for the banking system as a whole, was known in advance. Actual reserves could vary, but the target was stable.

However, this meant that the Fed had to provide enough reserves to meet known requirements, either through open market operations or through the discount window. Banks *as a whole* could not obtain more reserves very easily, and their attempt to do so resulted in wide fluctuations in interest rates. (If they held T-bills, they could sell them, but this would push the prices of T-bills down and the yield rates up.) The Fed thus could, for the most part, change the proportions of borrowed versus nonborrowed reserves.

This situation meant that Fed actions could affect the money supply, but with a lag. If the Fed (for example) made open market sales, banks would bid up the Fed funds rate, trying to obtain more reserves. As the Fed funds rate rose, some banks would be induced to borrow at the discount window. As funds became most costly, banks would be induced to raise interest rates on loans and quite likely on CDs also. These actions slowed the growth of the money supply, but there was a lag—it took time.

With LRA, a rise in M1 cannot cause a rise in required reserves for the *current* week, but it does cause such a rise two weeks later. Hence there is *delayed* pressure by banks to obtain additional reserves. As they try to obtain reserves, the Fed funds rate and other interest rates rise. The rise in interest rates limits loans and in other ways slows the growth of the money supply, but it takes time. Meanwhile, the rise in M1 has occurred, and it may take some time before M1 is back on the desired track.

The Board of Governors of the Federal Reserve System finally announced that it would reintroduce CRA, but with some changes to avoid some difficulties. The accounting period would be two weeks instead of one, so that deposits on the last day would be one-fourteenth of the total to be averaged instead of one-seventh. CRA would apply only to transactions deposits (after all, the main indicator is M1, transactions deposits). Also there would be a two-day lag: reserves periods would end on Wednesdays, but deposits periods would end on the preceding Mondays.

These changes would permit adoption of *total* reserves as the target instead of nonborrowed reserves, but even if this occurs, we must wait for a time to see results. Banks would have the option, under CRA, of changing deposits totals *and* reserves. Their demand for reserves need not be vertical, as shown in preceding diagrams, but would be downward sloping, in all probability, as shown in Figure 16–12. It seems

---

[44] Brian Motley, "Contemporaneous Reserve Accounting," Federal Reserve Bank of San Francisco, *Weekly Letter*, August 6, 1982, p. 1.

### FIGURE 16–12
#### Demand for and Supply of Reserves Under Contemporaneous Reserve Accounting

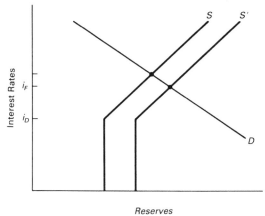

likely that the money multiplier relationship between total reserves and money may be more stable than that between nonborrowed reserves and money, since borrowings at the discount are volatile but a small part of total reserves.

Under CRA, reserve management for financial institutions is more difficult. Perhaps banks will simply hold more excess reserves to be sure that they have enough, or in some cases borrow more freely at the discount window. There is also a short-run problem, expected to disappear after the mid-1980s: reserve requirements having been phased in, they will be the same for most transactions deposits, so that it will be easier to predict required reserves. Finally, under CRA, required reserves rise immediately with the creation of deposits; hence, there is immediate upward pressure on the Fed funds rate. The Fed must, therefore, allow this rate (and hence other money market rates) to fluctuate.

We do not yet know whether depository institutions will try to change deposit totals or simply try to borrow reserves, if needed. If the Fed tries to control *total* reserves, borrowing at the discount window does not increase reserves for all depository institutions. Some might, therefore, have to reduce loans or shift from deposits to CDs (which would reduce required reserves). We do not know what behavior will be until CRA has been tested for a number of years. If depository institutions *do* try to change deposit totals and thus change the amount of required reserves, the supply of reserves *could* shift without causing a large rise or fall in the Fed funds interest rate. This is shown in Figure 16–12. Also, the discount rate could be above the Fed funds rate, as shown in Figure 16–13, and, because of increased demand for Fed funds as the Fed funds rate declined, the fall in the Fed funds might not be precipitous, as it often was in the early 1980s.[45]

---

[45] On increased volatility of interest rates in the early 1980s, see Carl E. Walsh, "The Federal Reserve's Operating Procedures and Interest Rate Fluctuations," Federal Reserve Bank of Kansas City, *Economic Review*, May 1982, pp. 8–18.

FIGURE 16–13
The Effect of a "Penalty" Discount Rate

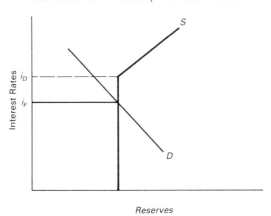

Reserves

Perhaps the discount rate could be a penalty rate, as was intended in the Fed's early years—a lender of last resort charges a high rate. This might impose hardship on some banks, especially small institutions that have seasonal borrowing needs and do not have reasonably reliable access to national markets such as the Fed funds market.[46] One study (not many have been published) showed that when the Fed funds rate was lower than the discount rate, total borrowing at the discount window fell, but the percentage of seasonal borrowing (under the special seasonal borrowing privilege available since 1973) increased.[47]

### Short-Run Volatility of the Money Supply

In the short run, M1 has been very volatile under the new strategy. In 1982, for example, when the upper bound of the target range was 5.5 percent for the year, the rate of growth was 10.8 percent for several months, 3.2 percent for several months, 3.5 percent for several months, and then very rapid for the remaining months of the year. As noted, Chairman Volcker had indicated that because of the existence of new forms of deposits in which precautionary and liquidity balances might be held (and these, therefore, were not necessarily transactions balances), and for other reasons, the FOMC might ignore to some extent temporary increases in M1. Velocity of M1 had declined in late 1981 and the first half of 1982, which would be expected in a

---

[46] A penalty discount rate would create problems when reserve requirements are not uniform, since shifts of deposits to banks with high reserve requirements would create problems for those banks. When the 1980 law is fully implemented in the later 1980s, reserve requirements will be more uniform and the problem will be less serious. See John P. Judd and Adrian W. Throop, "Penalty Discount Rate: I" and "Penalty Discount Rate: II," Federal Reserve Bank of San Francisco, *Weekly Letter*, October 30 and November 6, 1981.

[47] John E. Yorke and Charlotte Herman, "Seasonal Borrowing Privilege: Profile of the Tenth Federal Reserve District," Federal Reserve Bank of Kansas City, *Economic Review*, September–October 1982, pp. 19–26.

period of low interest rates—but interest rates had not yet declined significantly. Volcker also noted the sharp increase in NOW accounts in late 1981 and the first quarter of 1982 (NOW accounts are included in M1). This suggested "the importance of a high degree of liquidity to many individuals in allocating their funds."[48] Short-term interest rates were still very high; even as late as September 1982 the Fed funds rate averaged over 10 percent, and Treasury bill rates around 11 percent, depending on maturity. Of course, by December all such rates averaged between 8 and 9 percent. But why had interest rates remained so high so long?

Before considering interest rates, we should comment briefly on another aspect of the money supply data: "Fed watching." Economists have always been interested in monetary policy, and in recent years, as that policy became more important, they paid even more attention; "Fed watching" became a vocation for some. There also developed in the financial markets and among some economists a fascination with money supply figures. The weekly announcements on late Friday afternoons generated special interest and often were followed by money and capital market changes that may have been results of analysis of the money supply figures. Since records of FOMC meetings are not published for about a month after a meeting, these are not available for instant analysis, although a "Shadow Open Market Committee" of economists discusses monetary policy and especially FOMC actions with great interest and often makes forceful comments, supportive or negative. The interest of the money market participants in money supply figures is obvious.[49]

All this interest may be useful, but it is not likely that weekly money supply figures or, indeed, statistics for any economic variable for one week or even one month are very informative. *Trends* must be analyzed, and those who direct monetary policy, along with those who try to understand it, must develop or understand the forecasting process discussed briefly at the end of this chapter.

One study investigated the effect of the weekly money supply announcements on the volatility of short-term interest rates. The Fed had announced money supply figures late in the afternoons on Fridays. The increased volatility is obvious in Figure 16–14. In this writer's model results, about one-third of the increased volatility may have been caused by increased market response to unanticipated changes in money supply.[50] Thus although an increase in volatility could have been expected from the shift to reserve targeting instead of interest rate targeting, unanticipated changes in money supply in the Friday announcements have increased the volatility still further.

---

[48] *Monetary Policy Objectives for 1982*, Midyear Review of the Federal Reserve Board, July 20, 1982, Testimony of Paul A. Volcker, p. 8.

[49] One comment may illustrate the attitude of many who participate in the money market: "Every week is about one ninth of a two-month span. If the money market is your life and livelihood, moving a ninth closer to knowing where you are is important. Sensing trends in the money supply ahead of the competition—and hopefully even ahead of the Fed—isn't just the name of the game, it's the only game in town today." Quoted from "Tracking Fed Policy," *Morgan Guaranty Survey*, September 1975, p. 7.

[50] V. Vance Roley, "Weekly Money Supply Announcements and the Volatility of Short-Term Interest Rates," Federal Reserve Bank of Kansas City, *Economic Review*, April 1982, pp. 3–15.

**FIGURE 16–14**
**Changes in the Three-Month Treasury Bill Yield, 1977–1981**
**(3:30 P.M. to 5:00 P.M. on days of money announcements)**

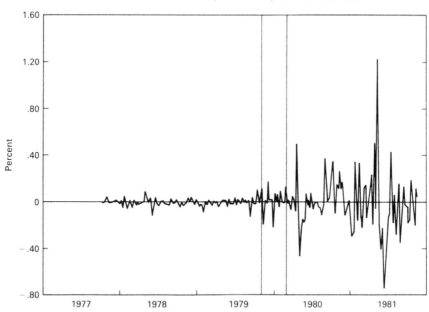

SOURCE: V. Vance Roley, "Weekly Money Supply Announcements and the Volatility of Short-Term Interest Rates," Federal Reserve Bank of Kansas City, *Economic Review*, April 1982, pp. 3–15.

## Importance of Interest Rates—Nominal and Real

Although targeting an interest rate (the Fed funds rate) did not prove satisfactory in trying to control inflation in the 1970s, there has been some discussion of the possibility that the real rate interest might be a possible target, and in any event, it is a variable that should be watched. Unfortunately, the difficulty of measuring real interest rates is very great. To determine the real rate, the expected rate of inflation must be deducted from the nominal rate; but what is the expected rate of inflation? Which price index should be used? Should past rates of inflation be used? For how many years? Weighted in what way? Some articles reported a *negative* real rate of interest; but this seems very unlikely to have existed—except under very unusual conditions, people are not likely to accept a negative real rate of interest when they lend or invest. Fisher suggested long ago that such a rate would be likely only if the only assets held for future consumption were consumer goods that deteriorated over time (food spoiled, clothing became moth-eaten, etc.). Under those conditions, those who lent goods, and received the goods back later, would receive something worth less than what they had loaned. This is not the real world, although it is possible in very rapid inflation for prices to rise faster temporarily than interest rates so that a *temporary* negative real rate of interest exists.

Hence, estimates of real rates of interest that indicate a negative real rate are suspect. But beyond that, most measures have assumed that past inflation, as measured by price indexes, is the proper measure of *expected* inflation. But these indexes differ, and changes in real interest rates can affect them.

This discussion does not intend to argue against efforts to measure expected inflation, but in view of the difficulties mentioned, measures thus far obtained for real rates of interest must be used very cautiously—they may be wrong.[51]

Another question has been raised by some economists who emphasize the importance of rational expectations. They suggest that the expected real rate of interest may be constant. If so, it cannot be affected by monetary policy. If an increase in the money supply causes people to try to reduce the amount of money they hold by spending or by lending or investing, nominal interest rates should fall as they acquire financial assets, as discussed at the beginning of this chapter. But this need not mean that changes in the real money supply cause changes in expected real interest rates. With an increased money supply, people may expect more inflation, thus affecting their expected nominal interest rate, but perhaps not changing the real rate of interest that they expect.

However, there is evidence that real short-term interest rates are not constant, although changes may be temporary.[52] The change in real interest rates does not imply that we know how to measure them precisely. We know that many economic measurements are not precise, but since we measure the same way in each period, if our measures show increases, presumably increases occurred, unless measurement errors occurred in one direction in one period and in the opposite direction in the next period, which is unlikely.

The Fed has little direct effect on long-term interest rates, which depend primarily on (1) productivity of capital and (2) expected inflation rates. Whether it has an indirect effect depends partly on the expectations theory of the term structure of interest rates and partly on whether it affects expected inflation rates. Even if we do not fully accept the expectations theory of the term structure, as we did not in Chapter 13, we can believe that it may affect expected inflation; if short-term interest rates fall, and people believe that the Fed is buying or will monetize government debt, then long-term interest rates may rise as people expect the increased money supply to result in higher inflation later.

Since an attempt to reduce short-term interest rates implies an increase in money supply by the Fed, there is a question as to how much such effort is desirable.

---

[51] W. W. Brown and G. J. Santoni, "Unreal Estimates of the Real Rate of Interest," Federal Reserve Bank of St. Louis, *Review*, January 1981, pp. 18–26. See also Patrick J. Lawler, "Are Real Interest Rates Good Measures of Monetary Policy?" Federal Reserve Bank of Dallas, *Economic Review*, July 1982, pp. 3–12.

[52] R. W. Hafer and Scott E. Hein, "Monetary Policy and Short-Term Real Rates of Interest," Federal Reserve Bank of St. Louis, *Review*, March 1982, pp. 13–19.

But an answer to this question depends on the reliability of the measures of money supply. If they are rising for special reasons (e.g., if M1 is rising because it includes money *not* likely to be used for transactions purposes), further increases in M1 may be acceptable and perhaps desirable. Long-term interest rates should indicate whether inflation is expected to rise; hence, a rise in long-term interest rates would be an indication that the public expects more inflation.[53]

At times, the measures of money supply may be questioned as proper measures of transactions balances (M1) and of liquidity balances (M2 and M3). Such a period occurred in 1982 and 1983. New money market accounts and Super-NOW accounts were authorized for depository institutions, but it was questionable how much of those accounts consisted of funds likely to be used for transactions purposes. If the main incentive for opening such accounts was the higher interest rates obtained, then perhaps the accounts would not be used very often for transactions purposes.

### Exchange Rates as Indicators

It is possible that, if money supply measures are poor indicators, other variables may be useful—although they must be used with great caution. We have already considered the use of interest rates. Exchange rates also may be considered. In the long run, the trend of exchange rates follows purchasing power parity, which depends on inflation and on the competitiveness of a country's exports. If one country has a higher inflation rate than other countries with which it trades in substantial amounts, its exchange rate will fall in the long run. If its goods are less competitive, the rate will fall because exports will fall relative to imports, thus causing a greater demand for foreign currencies.

Any use of trade balances and exchange rates as indicators means that those who determine monetary policy must examine economic conditions in at least some foreign countries, as well as review the situation in the United States.

It should be noted that any increase in expected inflation would chiefly affect the *forward* exchange rates for the dollar. A rise in interest rates in the United States may raise the value of the dollar, as investors in foreign countries seek to invest in the United States. But this is a short-term effect, and it affects primarily the *spot* (current) exchange value of the dollar. So if the spot value rises and the forward value (rate) also rises, one might conclude that perhaps interest rates, rising, are causing the spot rate to rise and that expected inflation, falling, is causing the forward rate to rise. This may well have been the situation in 1981. Obviously use of the exchange rate as an indicator is most helpful when conditions in foreign countries are relatively stable—if they are unstable, we do not know whether the dollar is rising, say, because of changes in the United States or because of changes in other countries.[54]

[53] This analysis is based, with some modifications, on Michael Keran, "How Low Can Interest Rates Be Pushed?" Federal Reserve Bank of San Francisco, *Weekly Letter*, January 28, 1983.

[54] Charles Pigott, "Exchange Rate Indicators," Federal Reserve Bank of San Francisco, *Weekly Letter*, February 11, 1983.

The use of several indicators suggests that it may be quite difficult to construct mathematical or econometric models that can, by themselves, be used as guides for policy. Hence, at times, although econometric models may still be consulted, policy may be more dependent on judgment than at other times.

### Target Achievement—How Successful?

In broad terms, the steady decline in the rate of inflation from 13.3 percent in 1979 to 3.9 percent in 1982 was remarkable when one considers that in 1980 many economists were saying that it would take 5 to 10 years to reduce inflation.

In more specific terms, it is evident that the Fed has had difficulty controlling short-term volatility of the money supply measures. Even over a year, such as 1982, the rate of increase was rapid for the first month or two, very slow for the next six months, and very rapid for the final four months. From the beginning of the year to about August, the target was attained with remarkable success, if one overlooks this volatility. The final four months of rapid increase may have been caused by special factors, such as the maturing of All-Savers certificates, from which funds were in many cases transferred into checking, passbook savings, or NOW accounts, and the authorization for money market accounts (although this was effective only at the very end of the year).

The occurrence of a recession, and especially its length, from mid-1981 to the end of 1982, was surprising to some. Yet if one reflects, it is difficult indeed to reduce money supply and to have the entire effect reflected in price changes. If prices were free to respond immediately, if business firms reduced prices promptly, and if workers moderated their requests for wage increases promptly, this might occur. The major remarkable fact about the recession was its length. The average post–World War II recession lasted only 10 or 11 months before recovery began; this one lasted about 18 months. The other obvious fact was the rise of unemployment to very high levels; but in some respects this may have been the result of increasing rates of labor force participation. Although the male labor force participation rate remained at between 77 and 78 percent between 1975 and 1981, there was an increase in the female participation rate from 46 percent to 52 percent. *Total* employment *as a percentage of the population* declined very little (from 59 to 58 percent) and total *employment* rose nearly 15 million persons in the six-year period. One could view the situation as one in which larger numbers of people desired to work, and the economy could not accommodate this rise. Monetary policy probably played some part in the slowdown in economic activity, but the continued rise in inflation in the late 1970s had to be curtailed, somehow.

## Changes in Strategy in the 1980s

Although the major change in Fed strategy occurred in October 1979, significant changes in other factors also occurred in the 1980s: (1) the decline in the rate of inflation, (2) partial deregulation of financial institutions, (3) a dramatic change in the income velocity of money, and (4) changes in the composition of M1 resulting from introduction of new types of bank deposit accounts.

With decline in the rate of inflation, it was reasonable to expect some change in *demand* for money, and this in turn could require some change in strategy for control of the money supply. Partial deregulation of financial institutions and the accompanying introduction of new forms of deposit accounts, some of them counted in M1 and some in M2, made it reasonable to ask whether the role of M1 had changed. The dramatic change in velocity of money (especially of M1) in 1982 and in 1985–1986 made it reasonable to reduce the emphasis on M1. If income velocity of M1 was not stable or predictable, then changes in M1 could not be used to predict changes in prices and real GNP.

As income velocity of M1 declined in 1982, Federal Reserve strategy shifted from an attempt to control *nonborrowed* reserves to an attempt to control *borrowed* reserves. The Fed began to try to stabilize lending through the discount window. That is, the Fed allowed nonborrowed reserves to change as demand for reserves increased and as the Fed funds rate rose. With changes in nonborrowed reserves, more or less reserves are available; hence, the Fed funds interest rate fluctuates. Fluctuations in that rate are greater than when the Fed used that interest rate as a target, but they are less than when nonborrowed reserves are a target. In the latter case the Fed does not try to offset changes in the Fed funds rate.

The difficulty in interpreting effects of changes in the size of M1—the difficulty of knowing whether increases in M1 were *used for spending*—led to deemphasizing M1 as an indicator. As a result, the Fed watched for changes in price indexes and in the real GNP and its components, as indicators of changes in the demand for money.

Change from lagged reserve requirements to contemporaneous reserve requirements in early 1984 tightened the link between a given week's money supply and the market for reserves in that week. When reserves had to equal a certain percentage of checkable deposits for the *current* week, clearly some financial institutions would probably have to borrow more (and others perhaps could lend more) reserves in the week. When required reserves were a percentage of checkable deposits in a *previous* week, institutions knew in advance how much reserves they needed, and, hence, borrowing to meet sudden last-minute increases in deposits was not necessary.

In effect, changes in strategy in the first half of the 1980s reflected the increased importance of changes in income *velocity* of money, and hence reduced importance of changes in money supply as the *prime* cause of changes in prices and real GNP. They also reflected an attempt by the Fed to *moderate* the volatility of money market interest rates but not an attempt to limit changes in such rates as much as had been the aim before the shift in procedure in October 1979. Although there is merit in the monetarist position that changes in money *supply* cause changes in real GNP and in prices, changes in *demand* for a particular group of financial assets such as M1 may also be important in causing change in prices and GNP. Finally, although the Fed cannot simultaneously control money supply *and* interest rates (if money supply is reduced, interest rates are likely to rise), great volatility in money market interest rates is undesirable.

# HOW MONETARY POLICY IS CARRIED OUT

Open market operations are carried out by the Federal Reserve Bank of New York under the direction of the FOMC. About every four weeks, the FOMC meets in Washington, D.C., to assess the current economic and financial outlook and to decide what changes if any should be made in current policy.

## The FOMC Meeting[55]

Prior to each meeting, FOMC members are kept apprised of current economic and financial developments. The Board of Governors and the Federal Reserve Bank presidents receive a continual flow of reports on business and financial trends and developments. At a meeting, the manager for foreign exchange operations (from the New York Federal Reserve Bank) reports first on international and exchange rate developments, followed by the manager of the open market operations desk. Board staff members summarize forecasts of economic trends and major developments; they assume continuation of trends in money supply approved at the last meeting at which such trends were formally agreed upon.[56] (These meetings are usually the February and July meetings, because in those months, the Fed must report to Congress on its projected trends.) The staff also outlines expected interest rates and credit flows. One member of the staff then outlines options available to the FOMC—what rate of money growth is desired, to promote rising business activity (but not too rapidly rising), moderation of inflation, and appropriate changes in employment and interest rates.

Board staff members have the results of simulations of the economy made with the aid of an econometric model containing more than 100 equations. Some equations relate to consumer spending, others to housing, and so on. These trend projections can be used in decisions concerning open market actions.

Monetarists (meaning economists who place greater emphasis on monetary supply change) believe that consumers, for example, rapidly adjust spending to changes in money supply. They tend to be skeptical about the ability to build large-scale econometric models that can be used to forecast behavior of sectors of the economy and expectations. The staff of the Federal Reserve Bank of St. Louis has used this approach to develop an eight-equation model. Compared with the Board's model, the St. Louis model indicates more rapid effects of monetary growth on production, employment, and prices. Many monetarists would prefer to target on *total* reserves or

---

[55] Members of the FOMC are the 7 members of the Board of Governors of the Federal Reserve System plus 5 presidents from 5 of the 12 Federal Reserve Banks (1 of whom is always the president of the Federal Reserve Bank of New York, while the others rotate). All presidents usually attend, although only 5 vote. Thus 19 persons participate (of whom 12 vote). Senior research staff from the Board and from the Federal Reserve Banks attend as advisers.

[56] The booklet by Paul Meek, *U.S. Monetary Policy and Financial Markets* (New York: Federal Reserve Bank of New York, 1982), provides much detail concerning this and related topics. It is a useful reference to supplement this book.

on the monetary base (as discussed in Chapter 5) rather than on *nonborrowed* reserves or on *borrowed* reserves, as was done in the early 1980s.

FOMC members at a meeting have a "green book" summarizing the Board's staff report and forecast, a "red book" giving summaries from the 12 Federal Reserve Banks (emphasizing regional developments), and a "blue book" giving alternative paths for monetary targets when these are being discussed and voted upon in February and July.

There is then a general discussion (especially in February and July) of money growth targets and the resulting changes in the economy. Policymakers must form their views on the basis of the information available and on the basis of their own judgments as to whether, in view of all relevant factors, a different forecast from that of the staff may be more probable. Then, on the basis of all relevant information, they decide how to vote.

After a vote on money and credit growth targets, the FOMC must formulate a "directive" to the trading desk manager of open market operations in the New York Federal Reserve Bank.

## Directives of the FOMC

Directives of the FOMC include both a brief summary of the important information discussed at the meeting, new or reaffirmed targets for money supply and credit, and often some qualifications that might suggest temporary modifications in the targets. The following is an example of a directive, and it is useful because it explains clearly why the target for M1 would perhaps have to be at least temporarily modified—note the sentence in the next to the last paragraph, stating that the FOMC "would tolerate for some period of time growth somewhat above the target range should unusual precautionary demands for money and liquidity be evident in the light of current economic uncertainties." The full directive is quoted here, to indicate the nature of the information and the orders for actions that are included.[57]

> The information reviewed at this meeting suggests that real GNP changed little in the second quarter, after the appreciable further decline in the first quarter, as business inventory liquidation moderated from an extraordinary rate. In May the nominal value of retail sales continued to pick up, while industrial production declined only a little further and nonfarm payroll employment was essentially unchanged. The unemployment rate edged up 0.1 percentage point to 9.5 percent. Housing starts rose appreciably from a depressed level.
>
> The price index for gross domestic business product appears to have risen at a relatively slow rate in the second quarter. Over the first five months of this year the producer price index for finished goods was virtually stable, and the advance in the index of average hourly earnings remained at a reduced pace. The consumer price index rose sharply in May, after a small net increase over the preceding four months.

[57] Federal Reserve press release, August 27, 1982. The next to the last paragraph was changed to the wording used here after July 15; the other paragraphs are as adopted at the meeting of June 30 to July 1.

The weighted average value of the dollar against major foreign currencies has risen sharply over the past month, reaching its highest level since early 1971, in response to a rise in U.S. interest rates relative to foreign rates as well as to hostilities in the Middle East. The U.S. foreign trade deficit in the first five months of 1982 was at a rate substantially less than in the fourth quarter of last year, as imports declined more than exports.

M1 declined somewhat in May, after its sharp rise in April, while growth of M2 remained substantial. Business demands for credit, especially short-term credit, were exceptionally strong. Short-term market interest rates and bond yields generally have risen since late May, and mortgage interest rates have increased.

The Federal Open Market Committee seeks to foster monetary and financial conditions that will help to reduce inflation, promote a resumption of growth in output on a sustainable basis, and contribute to a sustainable pattern of international transactions. At its meeting in early February, the Committee had agreed that its objectives would be furthered by growth of M1, M2, and M3 and from the fourth quarter of 1981 to the fourth quarter of 1982 within ranges of 2½ to 5½ percent, 6 to 9 percent, and 6½ to 9½ percent, respectively. The associated range for bank credit was 6 to 9 percent. The Committee began a review of these ranges at its meeting on June 30–July 1, and at a meeting on July 15, it reaffirmed the targets for the year set in February. At the same time the Committee agreed that growth in the monetary and credit aggregates around the top of the indicated ranges would be acceptable in the light of the relatively low base period for the M1 target and other factors, and that it would tolerate for some period of time growth somewhat above the target range should unusual precautionary demands for money and liquidity be evident in the light of current economic uncertainties. The Committee also indicated it was tentatively planning to continue the current ranges for 1983, but would review that decision carefully in the light of developments over the remainder of 1982.

In the short run, the Committee seeks behavior of reserve aggregates consistent with growth of M1 and M2 from June to September at annual rates of about 5 percent and about 9 percent, respectively. Somewhat more rapid growth would be acceptable depending on evidence that economic and financial uncertainties are leading to exceptional liquidity demands and changes in financial asset holdings. It was also noted that seasonal uncertainties, together with increased social security payments and the initial impact of the tax cut on cash balances, might lead to a temporary bulge in the monetary aggregates, particularly M1. The Chairman may call for Committee consultation if it appears to the Manager for Domestic Operations that pursuit of the monetary objectives and related reserve paths during the period before the next meeting is likely to be associated with a federal funds rate persistently outside a range of 10 to 15 percent.

Votes for this action: Messrs. Volcker, Solomon, Balles, Gramley, Martin, Partee, Rice, and Keehn. Votes against this action: Messrs. Black, Ford, Mrs. Teeters, and Mr. Wallich. Mr. Keehn voted as alternate for Mrs. Horn.

At the February 1983 meeting, the FOMC raised the target ranges for M1 and M2 because flows of funds into both seemed to reflect in part precautionary and liquidity balances rather than an increase in transactions balances. It also published expected rates of growth in total domestic nonfinancial debt, perhaps a preliminary to use of total debt as an additional target. With the inflation much reduced, increases in money supply are likely to cause more rise in output than in inflation. The FOMC assumed a 3½ to 4 percent increase in real GNP from the fourth quarter 1982 to the fourth quarter 1983, a more rapid growth rate than that assumed by the administration or by the Congressional Budget Office and more rapid than that forecast by many private economists, although day by day more economists were revising their forecasts upward. They had been too optimistic in 1982; it seemed that they were somewhat too pessimistic in early 1983. By January, housing starts, retail sales, industrial production, and other variables were rising, and money supply and stock market prices, both reliable leading indicators, had been rising for many months.

The emphasis on targets other than M1 was justified in part by the fact that velocity of M1 *fell* in 1982; if funds included in M1 were used for spending, velocity would have risen or remained nearly constant. M1 did not seem to be as reliable a measure of transactions balances as it had been.

The higher growth targets for money supply suggested a possible small decline in interest rates, at least for a time, although if recovery proceeded, increased demand for funds would at some point cause some rise in short-term interest rates.

It seemed that the FOMC was treading a very fine line between policies that would increase interest rates and discourage recovery, on the one hand, and policies that would encourage new fears of inflation on the other hand. The FOMC's success could be measured only after the passage of time.[58]

Following the recession of 1981–1982, the U.S. economy achieved the longest peacetime expansion since World War II (the period 1961–1969 was longer, but that included part of the Vietnam war). But some aspects of the economic situation were troublesome: growth of real GNP in 1985 and 1986 was relatively slow; the unemployment rate remained rather high, at about 7 percent of the labor force; a very large foreign trade deficit resulted in increased U.S. debt to foreign countries; a large government budget deficit caused government debt to grow more rapidly than GNP; and there was very rapid growth in private debt.

The growth in government and private debt indicated that the United States was spending more than it was producing. The answer, of course, was to save and invest more, but the United States has one of the lowest rates of saving among major industrial countries (and Japan one of the highest). Unless this occurs, there is the danger that pressure may grow to make monetary policy easier to provide more money for spending.

Monetary policy had achieved a reduction in the rate of inflation from double-digit levels in 1980 to less than 4 percent a year as measured by the consumer price index. The stock market had risen remarkably, from less than 800 (Dow Jones Industrial Average) in early 1982 to between 2,500 and 2,600 in summer 1987. By autumn 1986, there were signs that the foreign trade deficit was beginning to shift from increase to decline. Such a shift would eventually mean an elimination of the drag on the economy that resulted as the dollar rose in value from 1980 to 1985, making U.S. exports more costly and imports cheaper.

---

[58] The desirability of independence of the Fed, including the FOMC, is a question which is perennially raised. For an interesting article comparing degree of independence of some central banks, see King Banaian, Leroy O. Laney, and Thomas D. Willett, "Central Bank Independence: An International Comparison," Federal Reserve Bank of Dallas, *Economic Review*, March 1983, pp. 1–13. This article considered chiefly the relationship of degree of independence to degree of success in limiting the rate of inflation.

The growth of debt in the United States, especially private debt, is nevertheless a serious problem. Consumers and business cannot forever live beyond their means (paying for the excess spending by borrowing). U.S. investment in new factories, equipment, inventories, and housing reached about 6 percent of GNP by 1986, but saving remained about 3 percent of GNP. Looking ahead, there was a possibility of serious difficulty if foreign investing in the United States began to slow down. On the other hand, it could be envisioned as possible that consumers might save more (rather unlikely in view of past stability of the rate of saving as a percentage of income) or real GNP might grow more rapidly—3 percent a year or more instead of the 2½ percent growth in 1985–1986. Rapid growth without a recession for several years could occur. But risks clearly existed.[59]

## The Mechanics of Open Market Operations

The authority of the trading desk manager is indicated in a special directive, usually reviewed annually (but it may be amended at any time). This directive authorizes outright purchases of Treasury and government agency securities, dealing with government securities dealers or with foreign and international (such as the International Monetary Fund, or IMF) accounts.[60] Repurchase agreements are also authorized for periods of up to 15 days. There is a limit on the total change in the Fed's holdings of securities between FOMC meetings. Since, in a generally growing economy, a larger money supply is needed over the long run (for transactions, precautionary, and liquidity purposes), open market sales are much less common than are purchases; the major question is how much to purchase, so that M1 or another target may grow at a desired rate. Since 1951 (the time of the "Accord" between the Fed and the Treasury), the Fed has not been obliged to support prices of government securities in the market. The Treasury must design and price its securities in a manner that will attract private investors, a matter of debt management to be discussed in Chapter 17. Even in a refunding, the trading desk cannot subscribe for more securities than the Fed already holds of the maturing issue. The manager of the trading desk can *reduce* its holdings, if desired, by bidding too low. The manager of the trading desk tries to avoid increasing the volatility of government securities prices, which would benefit or hurt private holders and traders of government securities.

### "Outright Trading," RPs, and MSPs

Most outright trading is in Treasury bills, because that market is very "deep" (many buyers and sellers will buy or sell if rates change even slightly). At one time the Fed had a "bills-only" policy, but now it can trade in other government securities. Bills are bought or sold on the best yield obtainable in relation to the yield curve on that day; when other issues are bought, an effort is made to buy issues that are on or

---

[59] For a layman's language discussion of the dangers ahead, see Sylvia Nasar, "The $2-Trillion Debt Headache," *Fortune*, November 10, 1986, pp. 42–48.

[60] Until 1981, the Fed could buy a maximum of $5 billion of government securities directly from the Treasury; in 1981, it lost that authority.

above the yield curve. Securities may be bought, also, from foreign official accounts, if they sell, and it may sell to such accounts from its own portfolio. The advantage of dealing with foreign accounts is that domestic participants need not necessarily know about it; hence, the Fed can affect reserves without an immediate "announcement effect."

The Fed also deals through repurchase agreements (RPs) and MSPs (matched sale–purchase transactions). These are used when it appears that reserves are needed, say, this week, but that they will not be needed next week. Buying on a one-week, say, RP agreement basis permits an increase in reserves that is *temporary*. For MSPs, the sale is an outright sale of Treasury bills; on the purchase side, the Fed makes a contract to buy that bill for delivery to it at a later date.

The officers in the trading desk room begin a day with meetings with government securities dealers. They also gather information from the securities market. At about 11:15 A.M., a desk officer makes a conference telephone call, reviewing the day's program with one of the Federal Reserve Bank presidents serving on the FOMC and with senior staff members at the Board of Governors. Actions are usually taken shortly thereafter, because by 1:30 P.M., it is generally not possible to have an effect on reserves that same day. Before the conference call with FOMC representatives, a call has been made from the Treasury, to discuss reserve changes and the Treasury's deposit balance at the Fed and to help as a basis for a Treasury decision on whether to move funds from commercial banks to that balance.

After October 1979, the target was the level of nonborrowed reserves until the next FOMC meeting. If nonborrowed reserves were not enough to meet reserve requirements, there was, of course, increased borrowing at the discount window. When the FOMC decided, in autumn 1982, to target borrowed reserves—that is, to stabilize the level of borrowing for short time periods—it had to allow nonborrowed reserves to fluctuate. With such fluctuations, the Fed funds rate also continued to fluctuate, although not as much.

Close touch is maintained with Fed funds brokers (to assess the likelihood of changes in the Fed funds rate) and with "money desks" of major New York banks (to evaluate their reserve positions and Fed funds transactions). Contact is also made with major banks in other cities.

Cash transactions affect reserves the same day. Among cash transactions are purchases from dealers, paid for by direct credit to reserve accounts (for bank dealers) or to deposits in banks for nonbank dealers.

Since both the Fed and the depository institutions (chiefly banks, now, but perhaps others will become more important) operate in a situation of uncertainty, minute-to-minute changes affect them. Yet their major attempt is to attain goals for reserves, and hence for money supply, over longer periods of time.

### "Dynamic" and "Defensive" Actions

The "dynamic" activities of the trading desk have in recent years been aimed at nonborrowed or borrowed reserve targets, and hence at money supply targets, established by the FOMC. After an FOMC meeting, staff members translate the money supply targets into reserve targets. Special factors may influence money growth in particular periods. For example, suppose that tax rates have been increased and it is expected that the Treasury will collect more taxes just prior to April 15. Then M1, which does not include Treasury deposits, will be lower than usual. But growth of M1 might then be more rapid in May. When money growth has been adjusted, the staff must estimate the growth of reserves needed for this growth of money supply. The staff must take into account the expected increase in currency, the types of deposits, and the distribution of deposits among institutions that have different reserve requirements. It must also allow for an estimated amount of excess reserves based on past experience. This gives forecast amounts of total reserves. Deducting amounts of expected borrowing at the discount window, amounts expected for nonborrowed reserves are calculated. Figures can be, and are, readjusted as a week or a month passes by.

If there is a change in the discount rate (made by a Federal Reserve Bank and approved by the Board of Governors, and usually followed by the same change at the other Federal Reserve Banks), banks would tend to borrow more (as already explained) if the discount rate is below the Fed funds rate. At the same time, if the Fed were still maintaining the same target for nonborrowed reserves, more borrowing at the discount window would mean less borrowing of Fed funds, causing the Fed funds rate to fall. The Fed *can* use a change in the discount rate as a means of causing lower (or higher) short-term interest rates, but at times, it prefers to let open market operations maintain borrowed reserves growth until the Fed funds rate falls to the level of the discount rate. In such cases, any effect of a discount rate change in causing other short-term rates to fall is psychological.

In addition to "dynamic" operations, the trading desk conducts "defensive" operations—operations designed to accommodate short-term changes in currency needs (for holidays, for example), in Treasury deposits in banks, and in some of the other factors in the bank reserve equation discussed in Chapter 5. There are some who view day-to-day open market operations as undesirable, and in general, they do not favor "defensive" operations. Why not remove legal reserve requirements and let each bank determine the amount of reserves it needs? If that were done, some argue, the trading desk could simply buy a specific amount of government securities in a year, spread over weeks in some way, and thus cause a smooth growth of the money supply at the desired rate. These "monetarists" feel that a smooth long-run growth of the money supply is desirable, although they realize that banks might (by mistake, perhaps) reduce reserves too far and increase the money supply too much. This proposal is controversial, and the authors of this text are not all agreed on it. The economy and the financial markets are complex, and perhaps some effort to "defend" against errors is useful.

Changes in money supply caused by monetary policy actions affect interest rates, bond and stock prices, and the behavior of consumers and other sectors of the economy as explained in earlier chapters. Actions of these sectors plus government fiscal (taxing and spending) activities affect production, prices, employment, and other important variables. The government must decide fiscal policies and debt management policies (the forms, coupon rates if any, and amounts of various types of the public debt). The amount of the national debt is, of course, determined by government spending and taxing decisions over the years. Therefore, we turn, in the concluding chapter, to government activities in fiscal policy and debt management.

## SUMMARY

Monetary policy works through portfolio adjustments, wealth effects, and credit availability effects. Federal Reserve actions impinge on depository institutions' reserves and on the market for government securities. Changes in reserves and in prices (yields) of government securities have spillover effects in other financial markets and subsequently induce shifts between financial and real assets. Ultimately, these changes are transmitted to aggregate demand and the levels of output, employment, and prices. Changes in the availability of credit result from market imperfections and governmental restrictions on the flow of credit, and although these effects are mostly short-lived, they do have an important and selective impact on various sectors of the economy. It is also recognized that monetary policy is subject to certain lags, whose average length and variability are not precisely known.

Because there are different interpretations of the transmission mechanism, economists are divided over the question of how monetary policy should be implemented. Some argue that a money supply strategy is necessary to achieve the ultimate goals of policy. Others emphasize the role of credit conditions and interest rates in economic affairs and favor these variables as indicators of monetary policy. There is also some difference of opinion over the choice of operating targets. Some favor a reserve aggregate or the monetary base (reserves plus currency), while others prefer the Federal funds rate. Even so, most agree that the Fed should follow a strategy in which *quantifiable* variables link the policy instrument to the ultimate goals. Since October 1979, the Fed has used nonborrowed and then borrowed reserves as its initial target (see the appendix to this chapter). From that time through 1982, the rate of inflation fell sharply. But in a rapidly changing environment, there are still questions about appropriate monetary policy.

Shift to monetary aggregates as targets of monetary policy began in the 1970s, after many years of monetarist research had convinced many that money supply played a very important role in causing shifts in aggregate demand. Beginning in October 1979, reserves received more attention as a target than did interest rates. The ensuing volatility in interest rates, and especially the very high nominal *and real* interest rates in 1981 and 1982, caused many to question whether enough is known about what determines interest rates.[61] Certainly interest rate forecasting was not very accurate. Forecasting of real GNP was also not very accurate; it was too optimistic in 1982, and seemed to be too pessimistic in 1983, as forecasts were revised upward.

---

[61] For an analysis of causes of high *real* interest rates, see Stephen G. Cecchetti, "High Real Interest Rates: Can They Be Explained?" Federal Reserve Bank of Kansas City, *Economic Review*, September–October 1986.

The rapid fall in the inflation rate from 1980 to 1982, whether it was solely the effect of the change in Fed policy or not, served to support the emphasis on controlling the money supply to reduce inflation.

The accompanying recession, however, and its relatively long duration (about 18 months compared with an average of 10 or 11 months for others since Word War II) created higher unemployment and reduced tax revenues (which were also reduced by tax cuts). Steady rise in government spending increased the size of government budget deficits, which seemed to many to be a major problem. We turn to this problem in Chapter 17.

## Appendix: Excerpts from "The New Federal Reserve Technical Procedures for Controlling Money"[62]

**1.** The policy process first involves a decision by the FOMC on the rate of increase in money it wishes to achieve. . . .

**2.** After the objective for money supply growth is set, reserve paths expected to achieve such growth are established for a family of reserve measures. These measures consist of total reserves, the monetary base (essentially total reserves of member banks plus currency in circulation), and nonborrowed reserves. Establishment of the paths involves projecting how much of the targeted money growth is likely to take the form of currency, of deposits at nonmember institutions, and of deposits at member institutions (taking account of differential reserve requirements by size of demand deposits and between the demand and time and savings deposit components of M2). Moreover, estimates are made of reserves likely to be absorbed by expansion in other bank liabilities subject to reserve requirements, such as large CDs, at a pace that appears consistent with money supply objectives and also takes account of tolerable changes in bank credit. . . . [E]stimates are also made of the amount of excess reserves banks are likely to hold.

**3.** The projected mix of currency and demand deposits, given the reserve requirements for deposits and banks' excess reserves, yields an estimate of the increase in total reserves and the monetary base consistent with FOMC monetary targets. The amount of nonborrowed reserves—that is, total reserves less member bank borrowing—is obtained by initially assuming a level of borrowing near that prevailing in the most recent period. . . .

**4.** Initial paths established for the family of reserve measures over, say, a 3-month period are then translated into reserve levels covering shorter periods between meetings. . . .

**5.** Total reserves provide the basis for deposits and thereby are more closely related to the aggregates than nonborrowed reserves. *Thus total reserves represent the principal overall reserve objective.* However, only nonborrowed reserves are directly under control through open market operations, though they can be adjusted in response to changes in bank demand for reserves obtained through borrowing at the discount window. [*emphasis* added]

[62] Federal Reserve Bank of St. Louis, *Review*, March 1980, p. 14.

**6.** Because nonborrowed reserves are more closely under control of the System Account Manager for open market operations (though subject to a small range of error because of the behavior of noncontrolled factors affecting reserves, such as float), he would initially aim at a nonborrowed reserve target (seasonally unadjusted for operating purposes) established for the operating period between meetings. To understand how this would lead to control of total reserves and money supply, suppose that the demand for money ran stronger than was being targeted—as it did in early October of last year. The increased demand for money and also for bank reserves to support the money would in the first instance be accompanied by more intensive efforts on the part of banks to obtain reserves in the federal funds market, thereby tending to bid up the federal funds rate, and by increased borrowing at the Federal Reserve discount window. As a result of the latter, total reserves and the monetary base would for a while run stronger than targeted. Whether total reserves tend to remain above target for any sustained period depends in part on the nature of the bulge in reserve demand—whether or not it was transitory, for example—and in part on the degree to which emerging market conditions reflect or induce adjustments on the part of banks and the public. These responses on the part of banks, for example, could include sales of securities to the public (thereby extinguishing deposits) and changes in lending policies.

**7.** Should total reserves be showing sustained strength, closer control over them could be obtained by lowering the nonborrowed reserve path (to attempt to offset the expansion in member bank borrowing) and/or by raising the discount rate. A rise in the discount rate would, for any given supply of nonborrowed reserves, initially tend to raise market interest rates, thereby working to speed up the adjustment process of the public and banks and encouraging a more prompt move back to the path for total reserves and the monetary base. Thus, whether adjustments are made in the nonborrowed path—the only path that can be controlled directly through open market operations—and/or in the discount rate depends in part on emerging behavior by banks and the public. Under present circumstances, however, both the timing of market response to a rise in money and reserve demand, and the ability to control total reserves in the short run within close tolerance limits are influenced by the two-week lag between bank deposits and required reserves behind these deposits.

**8.** Other intermeeting adjustments can be made to the reserve paths as a family. These may be needed when it becomes clear that the multiplier relationship between reserves and money has varied from expectations. . . . Given the naturally large week-to-week fluctuations in factors affecting the reserve multiplier, deviation from expectations in one direction over a period of several weeks would be needed before it would be clear that a change in trend has taken place.

## Questions for Discussion

**1.** What kinds of portfolio adjustments by commercial banks and the nonbank public would we expect to follow open market purchases of government securities by the Fed?

**2.** How do changes in interest rates affect the public's wealth? How would changes in wealth be expected to affect aggregate demand?

**3.** Indicate several ways in which a restrictive monetary policy works through changes in the availability rather than the cost of credit.

**4.** How do time lags complicate the policymaker's job of controlling the level of economic activity?

**5.** Why are current changes in income, employment, or prices unreliable guides in the daily conduct of monetary policy?

**6.** In what ways might an increase in the reserve base affect the behavior of the money multiplier?

**7.** If the monetary authority aims at stabilizing interest rates, it loses control over the money stock, and vice versa. Explain why this happens.

**8.** Some argue that control over the growth rate of money should not be the sole aim of monetary policy. They believe that money market conditions and interest rates are also important. Why might these be a matter of concern?

**9.** What economic and financial considerations affect the decisions made by the FOMC in setting its monetary targets each month?

**10.** Why do Fed-watchers pay close attention to the behavior of the Federal funds rate? What information about the direction of current policy is provided by, say, weekly or monthly changes in the funds rate?

## Selected References

Several conferences on targets, indicators, and the implementation of monetary policy have produced many important papers and reviews of the conferences discussion. See especially the following:

Board of Governors of the Federal Reserve System, *Open Market Policies and Operating Procedures—Staff Studies*, 1971.

Federal Reserve Bank of Boston, *Controlling Monetary Aggregates*, 1969.

————, *Controlling Monetary Aggregates II: The Implementation*, 1973.

Federal Reserve Bank of New York, *Monetary Aggregates and Monetary Policy*, 1974.

Additional articles on the selection and use of operating guides (targets) in monetary policy are the following:

Henry C. Wallich and Peter M. Keir, "The Role of Operating Guides in U.S. Monetary Policy; A Historical Review," *Federal Reserve Bulletin*, September 1979, pp. 679–691.

John P. Judd and John L. Scadding, "Conducting Effective Monetary Policy: The Role of Operating Instruments," Federal Reserve Bank of San Francisco, *Economic Review*, Fall 1979, pp. 23–37.

Raymond Lombra and Frederick Struble, "Monetary Aggregate Targets and the Volatility of Interest Rates," *Journal of Money, Credit and Banking*, August 1979, pp. 284–300.

Each year for a number of years, an article published in the Federal Reserve Bank of St. Louis *Review* has discussed in detail the FOMC actions in the preceding year; the 1979 article (Richard W. Lang, "The FOMC in 1979: Introducing Reserve Targeting," March 1980, pp. 2–25) is especially interesting because of the significant change in policy in October 1979.

Wide variations in the rate of growth of the money supply during 1980–very slow in the spring but quite rapid in the late summer and early fall—led to renewed discussion of the Fed's ability to hit its money supply targets. An interesting review of the situation and of various relevant problems and views is found in John A. Davenport, "A Testing Time for Monetarism," *Fortune*, October 6, 1980, pp. 42–48. The basic question is whether, in the long run, the Fed can slow the *trend* growth of the money supply, even if this means conflict with other government policies.

Paul Meek, *U.S. Monetary Policy and Financial Markets* (New York: Federal Reserve Bank of New York, 1982), cited in footnotes in this chapter, is an excellent reading for class assignment.

An interesting discussion of problems faced in the mid-1980s because of increasing debt is Sylvia Nasar, "The $2-Trillion Debt Headache," *Fortune*, November 10, 1986, pp. 42–48.

On lags in effects of changes in monetary policy, see Mary Susan Rosenbaum, "Lags in the Effect of Monetary Policy," Federal Reserve Bank of Atlanta, *Economic Review*, November 1985, pp. 20–33.

On recent instability in income velocity of money, see Diane F. Siegel, "The Relationship of Money and Income: The Breakdowns in the 70s and 80s," Federal Reserve Bank of Chicago, *Economic Perspectives*, July–August 1986, pp. 3–15.

Two fine articles describing Fed operating procedures after 1982 are "Monetary Policy and Open Market Operations in 1985," Federal Reserve Bank of New York, *Quarterly Review*, Spring 1986, pp. 34–53; and R. Alton Gilbert, "Operating Procedures for Conducting Monetary Policy," Federal Reserve Bank of St. Louis, *Review*, February 1985, pp. 13–21.

# FISCAL POLICY,
# DEBT MANAGEMENT,
# AND FINANCIAL MARKETS

**XVII**

Earlier, in Chapter 15, we defined fiscal and debt management policies and discussed briefly how they might be used to achieve our economic objectives. The reader may recall that *discretionary* fiscal policy refers to federal government actions that determine the size and composition of the budget—expenditures and tax receipts. Many items in the budget cannot easily be changed, but policy can be used to make *some* changes. A closely related policy, debt management, refers to those actions of the Treasury and the Fed that affect the composition of the debt held by the public. Thus far, we have paid little attention to the implementation of these policies or to the manner in which they impinge on financial markets. The primary purpose of this chapter is to cover these aspects of fiscal and debt management policies.

Broadly construed, fiscal policy includes both *discretionary* changes in taxes and spending by government and those that result *automatically* from changes in levels of income and employment. Discretionary policy actions require legislative or administrative changes in expenditure programs or in taxes. Automatic tax and outlay adjustments, on the other hand, are built into the existing structure of tax receipts and spending. They work without deliberate or discretionary actions by government to dampen swings in economic activity. When levels of income and employment change, tax receipts and certain types of expenditures change automatically. As a result of these so-called "built-in stabilizers," the federal budget moves toward larger deficits during recessions and toward smaller deficits during periods of economic expansion. In principle, deficits might be eliminated and surpluses might exist when the economy reaches full employment. The government's budget position, whether the result of discretionary policy or of automatic stabilizers, determines the amount of borrowing that the Treasury must undertake in the financial markets.

In its debt management operations, the Treasury must decide which types of securities and what maturities and other provisions to use when financing its current budget deficit and in refinancing maturing issues. The state of the economy and the interest cost of the debt are important factors in these decisions. Because of the linkage between financial markets, debt management operations can be expected to have effects on the prices and yields of private securities and other financial assets. These changes in prices and yields may affect portfolio policies of financial institutions and the allocation of resources among various sectors of the economy.

## THE FEDERAL BUDGET

In 1986 federal government purchases of newly produced goods and services amounted to about \$360 billion, about 8½ percent of GNP. This figure does not, however, indicate the overall impact of government spending in the economy and in financial markets. First, there are many other expenditures in addition to purchases of goods and services. The most important of these are welfare and social security benefits, interest outlays, and other types of transfers included in the outlays shown in Table 17–1. These outlays accounted for 59 percent of total outlays. Second, the impact of the government on financial markets is measured more accurately by the total borrowing of government than by expenditure minus receipts.

An appropriate measure of federal borrowing would include funds raised to finance (1) the budget deficit, (2) off-budget agencies and the Federal Financing Bank, and (3) any increase in Treasury cash balances. In fiscal 1985, total borrowing from the public amounted to \$197 billion. Table 17–2 shows these figures. It is important to note also that part of the \$197 billion indicated as "borrowed from the public" was borrowed from the Fed, indirectly. The Treasury sells securities to the public and then the public sells them to the Fed. The net effect is as if the Treasury sold securities to the Fed. Sales of securities to the Fed by the public do not reduce the amount of funds available for private borrowers because the Fed creates *new* money when it acquires government securities. In fact, since the Treasury spends the proceeds, bank reserves and the supply of loanable funds are increased by the Fed's purchase of government debt. The Fed increased in holdings of government securities

**TABLE 17–1**
**U.S. Budget Receipts and Outlays, Estimates for Fiscal 1986***
**(billions of dollars)**

| Receipts | | Outlays | |
|---|---|---|---|
| Individual income taxes | $354 | National defense and | |
| Corporate income taxes | 71 | international affairs | $283 |
| Social insurance taxes | 280 | National resources and | |
| Excise taxes | 35 | environment, energy, | |
| Customs duties | 12 | general science, space | 26 |
| Estate and gift taxes | 6 | Agriculture, commerce, | |
| Miscellaneous | 16 | housing, transportation | 57 |
| | | Community development, | |
| | | education, and social | |
| | | services | 39 |
| | | Health (includes Medicare) | 105 |
| | | Income and Social Security | 318 |
| | | Veterans' benefits and | |
| | | services | 27 |
| | | Administration of justice | 7 |
| | | General government | 6 |
| | | Revenue sharing | 6 |
| | | Net interest on debt | 143 |
| | | Offsetting receipts | −36 |
| Total | $774 | Total | $981 |

* Figures do not add exactly because of rounding.

SOURCE: *Economic Report of the President,* February 1986, p. 341.

**TABLE 17–2**
**Federal Fiscal and Financing Operations, Fiscal 1985**
**(billions of dollars)**

| Type of Account or Operation | 1985 |
|---|---|
| U.S. budget | |
| Receipts | $734 |
| Outlays | 946 |
| Surplus or deficit | −212 |
| Deficit financed by | |
| Borrowing from the public | 197 |
| Cash and monetary assets, | |
| decrease or increase (−) | −11 |
| Other | 4 |
| **Note:** | |
| Treasury operating balance (level, end of period) | 17 |
| Federal Reserve Banks | 4 |
| Tax and Loan accounts | 13 |

SOURCE: *Federal Reserve Bulletin,* December 1986, p. A28.

TABLE 17–3
**Federal Government Receipts and Expenditures (Unified Budget), 1960–1987**
**(billions of dollars)**

| Fiscal Year | Receipts | Expenditures | Surplus or Deficit |
|---|---|---|---|
| 1960 | 92.5 | 92.2 | .3 |
| 1961 | 94.4 | 97.7 | −3.3 |
| 1962 | 99.7 | 106.8 | −7.1 |
| 1963 | 106.6 | 111.3 | −4.8 |
| 1964 | 112.6 | 118.5 | −5.9 |
| 1965 | 116.8 | 118.2 | −1.4 |
| 1966 | 130.8 | 134.5 | −3.7 |
| 1967 | 148.8 | 157.5 | −8.6 |
| 1968 | 153.0 | 178.1 | −25.2 |
| 1969 | 186.9 | 183.6 | 3.2 |
| 1970 | 192.8 | 195.6 | −2.8 |
| 1971 | 187.1 | 210.2 | −23.0 |
| 1972 | 207.3 | 230.7 | −23.4 |
| 1973 | 230.8 | 245.7 | −14.9 |
| 1974 | 263.2 | 269.4 | −6.1 |
| 1975 | 279.1 | 332.3 | −53.2 |
| 1976 | 298.1 | 371.8 | −73.7 |
| Transition quarter | 81.2 | 96.0 | −14.7 |
| 1977 | 355.6 | 409.2 | −53.6 |
| 1978 | 399.6 | 458.7 | −59.2 |
| 1979 | 463.3 | 503.5 | −40.2 |
| 1980 | 517.1 | 590.9 | −73.8 |
| 1981 | 599.3 | 678.2 | −78.9 |
| 1982 | 617.8 | 745.7 | −127.9 |
| 1983 | 600.6 | 808.3 | −207.8 |
| 1984 | 666.5 | 851.8 | −185.3 |
| 1985 | 734.1 | 946.3 | −212.3 |
| 1986 | 777.1 | 979.9 | −202.8 |
| 1987 | 850.4 | 994.0 | −143.6 |

SOURCE: *Economic Report of the President,* various years.

every year since 1957, because a growing economy needs more bank reserves and more money.[1]

A glance at Table 17–3 indicates that since 1960, there have been only two fiscal years in which the federal government has not incurred a deficit. These two surpluses were, moreover, very small. The cumulative effect of these net deficits from 1960 to

[1] Because the Fed can so easily buy government securities, create new money, and thus finance any size of government deficit, it is prohibited from purchasing government securities directly. In effect, Fed purchases of government securities result in an increase in bank reserves and, at the same time, an increase in deposits in banks. Also, with additional reserves, banks may create more money.

1982 has been a steady increase in the outstanding federal government debt by $850 billion. Nevertheless, government debt has declined as a percentage of total debt over the past quarter of a century, and it has also declined as a percentage of GNP. During the period 1968–1982, gross federal debt averaged about 38 percent of GNP. In contrast, by the end of 1986 federal debt of over $2 trillion was 47.6 percent of GNP of $4.2 trillion.

It seems likely that in the years ahead, the federal debt will continue to grow. How much it increases will depend upon a host of economic and political considerations, including the state of the economy, attitudes toward government spending and taxing, and the relative roles of federal versus state and local governments. We do not wish to examine in detail the question of whether this prospect is desirable or not. The issue is a complex one and charged with emotion. Some economists prefer balanced budgets and suggest paying off the existing debt. They argue that there are adverse "distributional effects" when tax revenues are transferred to those who hold the debt. They also allege that interest rates are distorted from what they would be in the absence of the debt.

Many, perhaps most, economists, on the other hand, believe that great concern over a domestically held debt is unwarranted. They argue that not only does economic growth require a growing money supply over time but that a growing federal debt is a useful means of increasing the nation's stock of liquid assets. Moreover, financial institutions need to hold some of their portfolio of assets in default-free securities. In this view, continued growth in the federal debt is desirable.

Finally, it may be noted in Table 17–1 that the budget, as now presented, counts capital and operating expenses without any attempt to separate these categories. In effect, building a federal dam is counted as a current (rather than a capital) expenditure. Yet, economically, current expenditures are consumption while capital expenditures create assets that have long lives, and may yield substantial revenue. When such revenue is received, it is treated, under current procedures, as a reduction in the related category of spending. Many economists believe that the budget should have a capital account as a separate part. Segregation of capital expenditures would call attention to their expected life, and to needs for repair and replacement, such as that now urgent for highways, bridges, and other structures.

Good business managers use capital budgets, so why hesitate to adopt a separate capital budget for government? There are several reasons, but the most compelling stems from the fundamental recognition that government is not a profit-making entity as business is. Therefore, it does not need a capital budget in the way that businesses do. Whenever government spends, it purchases real economic resources and diverts these resources away from their use by the private sector and into use by government. This basic transfer of resources from private use to government use occurs whether the spending is financed through taxes or through borrowing. Thus, total spending is the basic economic factor, and it doesn't matter whether the spending is for labor and other current expenses or for buildings and roads that would be considered capital expenditures.

A noneconomic reason not to have a capital budget is that going into debt to build a building is more acceptable to taxpayers because it would be called debt financing of a capital asset. It would *not* be called a budget deficit. Thus, the budget "deficit" could be reduced easily, simply by renaming it through the introduction of a new set of books. This might wrongly take attention away from the size of government and would be deceptive.

Economists have suggested a number of other changes in the budget: some believe that government assets and liabilities should be adjusted for inflation (which reduces the *real* interest cost of the federal debt), some believe that off-budget loans and guarantees should be included in the budget, and some believe that budget should include long-term forecasts of pension program costs and revenues. Because all these suggestions are being studied but are not actively being considered for adoption, we merely note the nature of some of the suggested changes.

## FISCAL POLICY: AUTOMATIC AND DISCRETIONARY

If there is unemployment, and GNP is below potential GNP, increased government spending may lead to an increase in income and therefore an increase in other spending, and as more people are employed, output may rise. If much government spending is for transfer payments, and if those who receive transfer payments save relatively little, consumer spending may rise but saving and investment may not rise, or may even fall.

As shown in Chapter 7, as a business recovery occurs, spending tends to increase. As demand increases, inventories are depleted, more goods are ordered, and production begins to rise. As the increase in spending continues, business firms begin at some point to feel that an increase in investment is necessary, to provide facilities for more output. The recovery may be stimulated by either consumer, business, or government spending. As output increases, employment increases and unemployment falls. At some point, when output is nearly as high as potential GNP, further increase in spending begins to lead to price increases—inflation. Thus government (and other) spending may be beneficial in a recession, but heavy government spending at relatively high employment may lead to inflation.

Tax cuts may be expansionary, just as government spending may be. Tax cuts leave consumers with more after-tax income, and they may consume more or save and invest more. Business firms' spending may also be greater if after-tax income is greater.

An important question, not discussed very much in the 1960s and 1970s, is whether increased government spending leads to more consumer spending and less saving and investment. To the extent that government spending is composed in large part of transfer payments, and to the extent that those who receive transfer payments spend most of their income for consumption, consumption is stimulated and saving and investment is reduced.

Thus whether increased spending (with increased borrowing) by the government is used to stimulate the economy, or reduced taxes are used for the same purpose, the important question is whether consumer spending should be stimulated or whether saving and investment should be stimulated, as a means of increasing long-run economic growth. This was the question in the early 1980s: the Reagan administration argued that those who work and earn should keep more of their earnings (pay less taxes) and spend or save as they chose. Since the tax cuts of 1981–1983 were proportional, it seemed likely that the result would be increased saving and investment, in the long run, since high-income individuals' taxes would be reduced more, in dollars, than would low-income individuals' taxes. Evidence has not been conclusive.

Thus far, we have discussed "discretionary" fiscal policy. But some tax revenue reduction and some increase in spending is automatic. Let us first consider the automatic changes, before discussing specific discretionary changes.

## Automatic Fiscal Responses

Because the amount of income taxes that an individual or business firm must pay is some percentage of income or profits, it follows that tax receipts rise as national income rises. Furthermore, income tax rates are graduated so that the average tax rate also tends to rise as income rises. In an economy with rising income, therefore, existing tax rates and the rate structure lead automatically to a larger amount of tax collection. If the economy moves downward with falling income and rising unemployment, tax receipts fall, leaving more purchasing power in the hands of consumers than they would have had if tax collections were a constant amount. Swings in income and employment are smaller in amplitude than they would be in the absence of this automatic response of taxes. Therefore, we sometimes call this phenomenon an "automatic stabilizer."

Because business and consumer saving, taxes, and transfer payments vary with swings in economic activity, it is difficult to estimate the net effectiveness of automatic stabilizers. In one study, it was estimated that automatic stabilizers may reduce the size of changes in the level of national income to roughly half what they would be in the absence of automatic stabilizers.[2] However, since stabilizers only *respond* to variation in income, they are never able to *prevent* variation in income. Therefore, to prevent variation in income and to supplement the effects of the automatic stabilizers, discretionary fiscal policy actions may be necessary.

Built-in automatic stabilizers help to keep an economy that is near full employment at this position. But they cut two ways. If an economy is below full employment, automatic stabilizers help *restrain* an expansion that is under way. On these occasions the existence of automatic stabilizers increases the need for discretionary policy actions.

[2] Peter Eilbott, "The Effectiveness of Automatic Stabilizers," *American Economic Review,* June 1966, pp. 433–464.

In a period of inflation, the rise in income tends to push individuals (and possibly firms if tax rates on them are progressive) into higher tax brackets. Therefore, since this tends to increase the share of government revenue in GNP relative to private income, legislation was enacted in 1981 providing for indexing of tax rates to inflation beginning in 1985. However, tax brackets were extensively revised under the Tax Reform Act of 1986. Five brackets, ranging from 11 to 50 percent were replaced with two brackets of 15 percent and 28 percent.[3] The new brackets were phased in to become fully effective in the 1988 tax year. Therefore, the adjustment in tax brackets for inflation, as measured by the consumer price index, begins in 1989. Standard deductions will also be adjusted for inflation. This legislation will prevent the rapid increase in tax revenues and in the government revenue share in income resulting from future inflation.

## Discretionary Fiscal Policy

Tax revenues are affected by the level of economic activity, but they are also affected by the tax rates levied by Congress. Any change in tax rates is a discretionary act of fiscal policy. Furthermore, changes in the types of taxes imposed—income taxes, excise taxes, import duties, and so on—affect the extent of fiscal impact. Some government expenditures are also discretionary, and both increases and reductions in spending are sometimes undertaken overtly for the purpose of economic stabilization.

The efforts of the Reagan administration were directed toward slowing the growth of federal government spending (there was much discussion about budget "cuts," but these were cuts from budget figures for following years, figures that were much higher than current figures). A glance at Table 17–1 indicates three reasons why this was difficult: (1) community development, education, and social services, health, income security (Social Security and related benefit programs), and veterans' benefits and services constituted 50 percent of the budget; (2) defense spending constituted another 29 percent; and (3) interest on the public debt constituted another 14 percent (total 93 percent). Interest payments cannot be reduced, although they fall when interest rates fall. Defense spending was increasing. Thus, unless the "entitlement" programs (Social Security and a large number of others) could be reduced for *future* years, there was little room for other major cuts.

### Tax Changes

Although other countries had used countercyclical fiscal policy for years, it was not until 1964 that President Johnson used a large tax cut to stimulate the economy. There were across-the-board income tax rate cuts and reductions in federal excise taxes. The tax cuts had been proposed much earlier, but it took a long time for Congress to pass the legislation. With this act, Congress *for the first time* approved a

---

[3] For some relatively high-income taxpayers, there is a 33 percent marginal tax rate, but at an income of $100,480, the marginal tax rate falls back to 28 percent.

reduction in taxes for the explicit purpose of stimulating economic activity. The continuation of the expansion that followed the tax cuts seemed to validate the action, although some economists argued that the stimulative effect was of a small order of magnitude and came later than it should.

By 1965, U.S. government spending to support military involvement in Vietnam was rapidly accelerating. Government spending for domestic programs also increased, and inflationary pressures grew. In an attempt to slow the rise in prices, an income tax surcharge was imposed in the middle of 1968. This represented a discretionary attempt to implement counterinflationary fiscal policy. In the wake of this tax increase, however, consumption and income continued to rise, and many analysts felt that the failure to stop the inflation showed that fiscal policy actions were weak in effect. Interpretations of the data vary. Because many factors change simultaneously, it is extremely difficult to isolate the relative importance of a single factor. Perhaps consumption was significantly lower than it would have been if the tax surcharge had not been imposed. That this is probably true can be seen by noting that the ratio of personal consumption to income fell after the tax increase, that the ratio of personal saving to income also fell, and that the ratio of personal taxes to income rose as expected in the wake of the tax surcharge. The tax surcharge affected both saving and consumption; to the extent that consumption was held down by the increase in taxes, it is safe to conclude that the tax *did* help dampen the overheated economy.[4]

The Reagan administration, taking office in early 1981, adopted a different strategy. It generally supported the effort of the Federal Reserve to control inflation by slowing the growth of the money supply, and inflation did decline significantly and relatively rapidly. On taxes, it secured passage by Congress of a three-year tax cut, 5 percent in 1981 and 10 percent each year in 1982 and 1983. These cuts were intended to lay a foundation for a period of more rapid long-run growth by making possible a higher rate of saving. A major concern of the administration was that the share of GNP "devoted to capital formation was below the levels achieved by most other industrialized nations."[5] Gross investment in capital structures and equipment averaged 10.8 percent of GNP during the 1970s, but two-thirds of this was required to replace real capital; only 3 percent was devoted to new capital investment. Japan's percentage of GNP devoted to net fixed investment was three times as high as that of the United States, and France, Germany, Italy, and the United Kingdom all had higher percentages than did the United States.[6]

It was argued that increased investment was needed to reverse, in part, the slowdown in productivity, to offset government policies that in the 1960s and 1970s favored consumption over saving and investment, and to increase returns to individuals on capital investment that, during that period, were relatively low; for example, investors did not gain, over the 1970s decade, from stock price increases, and the dividends that they did receive were, of course, taxed, reducing the after-tax yield.

[4] Murray L. Weidenbaum, "Fiscal Policy for a Period of Transition," Federal Reserve Bank of St. Louis, *Review*, November 1970, pp. 8–13.

[5] *Economic Report of the President*, February 1983, p. 77.

[6] Ibid., p. 81.

A major piece of tax legislation, the Tax Reform Act, was passed by Congress in 1986 (TRA '86). Besides reducing the number of tax brackets from 15 to 5 in 1987 and to 3 in 1988, as mentioned, the act provided for several important changes in tax law designed to encourage saving. The law's provisions balanced the tax cuts with other changes that would increase taxes so that no net increase or decrease in the total tax take would result. That is, in this case they did *not* try to change taxes to impose a net overall fiscal impact on the macroeconomy. But many provisions of the law were designed to affect parts of the economy.

In line with the earlier tax decreases of the Reagan administration, the TRA '86 not only phased in lower personal income tax rates, but also increased standard deductions. This provided individuals with larger take-home paychecks. Tax rates on business profits were also reduced. Higher income and higher after-tax returns on saving should both stimulate saving.

Also, TRA '86 severely restricted the deductibility of interest expenses. The interest paid on the mortgage of a home (and a second home) remains deductible from income for tax purposes, as before. But the interest paid on credit card purchases, car loans, and other consumer credit items is no longer deductible. Consumer spending will be dampened by this provision of the law, and saving will be encouraged as people save to pay off credit card loans and other debts.

The investment tax credit was removed under provisions of the TRA '86. An investment tax credit permits a business firm to deduct a certain percentage of its expenditures on fixed plant and equipment from its tax liability. This amounts to a direct subsidy to the firm, since the effective cost of purchasing equipment is lowered. The purpose of this tax credit, first introduced in 1962, was to stimulate employment and output in capital goods industries. The tax has been rescinded and reintroduced on occasion since then. Most recently the credit was set at 10 percent. If it is announced that the tax credit will be allowed for one year, say, then business firms may wish to purchase capital goods before the tax is removed. In this way the tax has a certain "announcement effect" that the simple change in the effective price of equipment does not reflect. Although it has been considered an effective policy measure, it can be criticized on a variety of other grounds. Business managers find that it is difficult to plan when the tax is an on-again, off-again policy. Besides, the tax distorts the relation between the prices of some equipment and of other factors of production for certain firms. Distortion of relative prices tends to induce a misallocation of resources; thus, this tax credit has some unfortunate side effects. These considerations played an important role in the decision to eliminate the tax credit in 1986. But, given the history of the tax credit, it will doubtless be proposed again in future years.

Accelerated depreciation allowances have also been used as a policy tool. A firm may deduct depreciation expenses from its income for tax purposes. If a piece of equipment has an expected life of, say, 20 years, depreciation takes place over this period. Under accelerated depreciation, the firm may deduct all its depreciation allowances over, say, the first 5 years of the life of the equipment. This means, of course, that, after 5 years have passed, the firm will no longer have this accounting expense, and its tax payments will then be larger than they would have been if depreciation had occurred evenly throughout the full 20-year period. For this reason, it is sometimes said that accelerated depreciation allowances represent an interest-free loan by the government to firms, in the form of delayed tax liabilities. Most firms take advantage of this allowance when they can. The TRA '86 generally retained the accelerated cost recovery system, but with modifications.

As noted earlier, in a period of inflation, under present accounting procedures, charges for depreciation will not total, over the life of factories or equipment, as much as the replacement cost of those assets. Thus some "profits" must be used, together with revenues against which depreciation was charged, to replace assets. Profits available for *new* investment are overstated. Some countries have adopted systems of replacement cost accounting. Of course, the problem becomes more serious when inflation is rapid; with declining inflation in the early 1980s, the problem is less serious.

### Expenditure Changes

Discretionary changes may also be made in the level of government spending for stabilization purposes. President Kennedy asked for and received limited discretionary authority to contribute to expansionary spending for public works—mostly on a matching-funds basis for fire stations, libraries, and so on, purchased or built by state and local governments.

In 1973 a debate with significant political implications spread throughout the United States. It concerned the propriety of President Nixon's decision to cut spending by simply refusing to spend money for certain programs for which Congress had appropriated funds. One might call these discretionary spending cuts. It represents a type of veto power that would effectively thwart congressional mandates even though a majority vote were large enough to override a formal veto. It is a direct challenge to the authority of Congress, and President Nixon was not the first president to use it. Needless to say, it strikes at the heart of the political concept of the separation of power among the three branches of government: legislative, executive, and judicial. On the other hand, Congress has often delegated authority to the executive branch and has written legislation designed to provide flexibility in the implementation of its programs. The issue will doubtless have to be resolved by public opinion and perhaps in the courts in the years to come.

When Congress appropriates funds for a program, its purpose is to provide a socially desirable service. The criteria for a spending decision are generally independent of the level of economic activity, although in the Great Depression of the 1930s it was sometimes argued that spending was desirable in and of itself if it led to increased employment. In general, however, government spending is undertaken for specific projects that Congress believes to be appropriate for government. The level of government spending should primarily be determined by the desirability and cost of those projects rather than by the general level of income and employment.

Taxing, on the other hand, is for the purpose of diverting resources from the private sector to the public sector. If the economy is fully employed, an increase in government spending cannot occur without causing inflation unless some purchasing power is diverted to government. Taxes are used for this purpose. However, if the economy is underemployed, there is less justification for collecting taxes equal to the full amount of expenditures.

In the 1930s, Keynes argued that governments could more easily vary the level of spending than the level of taxing, simply because the latter is politically explosive. He suggested that as a practical matter variation in government spending should be used to ensure full employment. However, in 1962, the Kennedy administration proposed that Congress authorize the president to vary the income tax rate by 5 percent in either direction, to raise the 20 percent tax bracket to 21 percent (1/20 = 5 percent) or lower it to 19 percent, for example. The changed rate was to have been effective for a six-month period and the President would then have had to present to Congress the reasons for his decision. He could then ask Congress to approve an extension of the change for another six months. At the end of this period, the tax rate would return to its original level and remain there with no congressional act required.

The details of the proposal were extensive and need not detain us here, but subsequent administrations have continued to search for ways in which to introduce greater flexibility into taxation, so that variation in tax rates may more readily assist in achieving the objectives of fiscal policy. In 1977, President Carter proposed a tax rebate, and it was necessary for him to seek congressional approval. The "rebate" was proposed in the form of $50 for each person filing a tax return showing less than a specified income. It was believed that additional income, creating additional demand by consumers, would spur a continued recovery at a somewhat more rapid rate. Later, the president dropped this proposal because the economy began to recover at a faster rate. Congress is jealous of its prerogative to set taxes and is reluctant to transfer discretionary power to the executive branch of government.

The Reagan administration's program of tax cuts and tax reform was accompanied by increased expenditure, especially on the part of the defense department. Thus, *both* tax cuts *and* increased expenditure acted as economic stimuli. Nevertheless, the economy suffered a recession in 1981 and 1982 because of the strong determination of the Federal Reserve to wring inflationary pressures out of the economy. In general, the Reagan administration did not attempt to introduce any changes in taxes or changes in government spending *for the purpose of* either stimulating or restraining the economy. But, of course, the spending and taxing activities do have their impacts on the economy in the short run.

## Fiscal Policy Aimed at Increasing Saving and Investment

The tax cuts of the Reagan administration in 1982, 1983, and the TRA '86 were based on different ideas. It was believed that the slow rate of real economic growth, especially in the late 1970s, was caused in part by high taxes, which discouraged work, saving, and investment. Inflation was also encouraging spending and discouraging saving.

The major objective was to reduce tax rates on *marginal* income in the hope that lower tax rates on marginal income would encourage more effort.

Marginal "tax" rates may be very high not only for those in the regular labor force but also for welfare and Social Security beneficiaries. If Social Security benefits are reduced by $1 for every $2 earned above a specified level (as has been the case), then the "tax" on the additional earnings is 50 percent. This far exceeds the maximum rate for high-income individuals of 28 percent. In some cases welfare benefits are reduced enough when earnings are increased (whether from zero or from specified level) that the implicit "tax" rate is 75 percent.

Tax cuts, combined with the fact that *large* reductions in *future* budgets seemed impossible, resulted in large projected deficits for the 1980s. Concern arose that large budget deficits would mean that the federal government would compete with private demand in the credit markets, "crowding out" some private borrowing and pushing interest rates up to some extent.

Thus, in evaluating the potential problem created by large projected deficits for the later years of the 1980s, it is necessary to consider (1) adjustments in budget figures necessary to measure the impact of the deficit on the credit markets, (2) the rise in tax revenue that would occur if recovery from the recession of the early 1980s took place, and (3) the changes in projected deficits if inflation rates changed.

The cyclical component of the deficit in 1983 was estimated to be about half. Thus, recovery could reduce a $200 billion deficit to $100 billion. But the prospect of deficits as large as $300 billion in *later* years was cause for concern; hence "evidence of the willingness of the Administration and the Congress to reduce Federal budget deficits substantially in the second half of the 1980s" was desired.

Congress could not reach agreement on measures to raise taxes or cut spending even though one or the other, or both, were necessary if the deficit was to be reduced. In the 1984 election campaign for the presidency, the Democratic platform emphasized the need for tax increases to eliminate the budget deficit; but President Reagan was reelected. In 1986 the Congress passed the Gramm-Rudman Act, which required automatic across-the-board cuts in spending in many categories if a schedule of year-by-year reductions in the deficit did not occur. The TRA '86 has clouded the schedule of reductions as mandated by Gramm-Rudman.

## The High-Employment Budget: A Guideline for Fiscal Policy

The financial analyst must carefully examine Treasury cash flows to assess the prevailing demand for funds by the Treasury. However, he or she must also understand policy positions to interpret the likely evolution of the budget. The national income accounts budget reflects the macroeconomic impact of tax and expenditure policies. At one point in the development of national income theory, economists believed that a deficit in this budget represented an expansionary fiscal policy, whereas a surplus represented a restrictive fiscal policy. To stabilize the economy, it was argued that a deficit should exist in a recession and a surplus should exist in a boom period, so that over a cycle in business activity the budget should roughly balance. Thus the deficit or surplus was taken as an indicator of the fiscal policy that was actually in effect at any given time.

But it soon became clear that a serious problem arises when the *actual* budget surplus or deficit is used as an indicator for fiscal policy because, as we saw in our discussion of automatic and discretionary impacts, the budget not only affects the level of national income but *is also affected* by changes in the level of national income. If income falls because of a decline in investment, tax receipts fall and the budget may turn to deficit. But the deficit does not reflect the posture of fiscal policy—it does not indicate that fiscal policy is expansive; rather, it indicates only that a recession is under way. Similarly, a budget surplus does not indicate a restrictive fiscal policy if the surplus arose because of an investment boom and an expansion in income and tax revenues.

In comparing the strength of fiscal policy in one recession with that in another, one might find that a $5 billion deficit occurred in both periods and conclude that fiscal stimulus was the same in both. But in one instance the deficit might have been merely the result of the decline in income, whereas in the other a deliberate tax cut may have brought on the deficit. Thus, the size of the actual deficit or surplus is an imperfect measure of the impact of fiscal policy.

To arrive at a better indicator for fiscal policy, the concept of a "high-employment" or "full-employment" budget was developed; in 1962, the Council of Economic Advisers stressed the concept in its *Economic Report*.

The high-employment budget is an estimate of the way the national income accounts budget would appear if the economy were operating at full employment instead of at its actual level. It is a hypothetical budget.

To illustrate the concept in abstract terms, remember that tax revenues are related to income. As income rises, the income tax revenues also rise. If government spending remains unchanged, then a rise in income results in a rise in tax revenues and a decline in the size of the budget deficit (or an increase in the surplus). To appreciate this phenomenon, consider Figure 17–1.

On the vertical axis, the budget surplus or deficit is measured. On the horizontal axis, national income is measured. Two levels of national income are noted. $Y_F$ is the level of income that it is estimated would prevail if the nation's economic resources were fully employed; $Y_A$ is the current actual level of income. (It is assumed that government expenditures are fixed.) The straight line from the origin labeled $t_A$ shows the relationship of tax revenue to income with a given tax structure. The $t_A$ line intersects the horizontal balanced budget line at point *a*. If the economy were operating at full employment so that income equaled $Y_F$, tax revenues would be larger, and the budget would be in surplus by $10 billion, as indicated by point *c*. The surplus is represented by the distance *cd*. Because the full-employment budget would be in surplus, it is argued, there is justification for lowering tax rates so that the dashed tax line $t_F$ would prevail. Accordingly, the current actual budget would be in deficit by an amount indicated by the vertical distance from *a* to *b*. At this new tax rate, the stimulus of a deficit would tend to raise income and employment. If this stimulus were

**FIGURE 17–1**
**Illustration of Use of High-Employment Budget Concept**

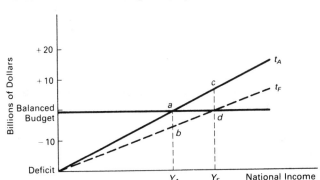

to push income up to $Y_F$, then the budget would be in balance as indicated by point *d*. The distance from *c* to *d* can be used as a measure of "fiscal drag," an indicator of the extent to which current tax rates are *holding back* economic activity. This, then, is the rationale for reducing tax rates and running a deficit in a hypothetical period when employment is less than "full" employment.

Many detailed steps are involved in calculating a high-employment budget, but in general, there are six steps. (1) The potential growth rate of real GNP must be estimated. (2) To this hypothetical growth rate of GNP there is added a measure of the rate of inflation; for example, the current rate may be extrapolated into the future. This gives an estimate of what the full-employment level of *money* income would be. (3) This level of income is allocated among the principal components of income—personal income, corporate profits, and so on—according to the ratios that usually obtain when the economy is operating at full employment. (4) The tax levies that, on the average, apply to each of the components are used to give an estimate of what tax revenues would be under full employment. (5) Current expenditure levels are adjusted, principally by estimating the reduction in unemployment compensation expenditures that would be expected if the high level of income were achieved. (6) The result of the tax revenue estimate and the expenditure estimate, taken together, provide an estimate of the full-employment budget surplus or deficit.

The high-employment budget may, therefore, be used as an indicator of the current and projected status of fiscal policy. In general, if the high-employment budget shows a surplus, this indicates that a certain fiscal drag is imposed on the economy by high tax rates, even though the actual budget is in deficit. A policy to lower taxes would be appropriate. Similarly, if the high-employment budget were in deficit, this could be interpreted as a stimulative fiscal position, even though the actual budget were in surplus. In this sense the high-employment budget is thought to be a better guide to the stimulative or restrictive nature of fiscal policy than is the national income accounts budget.

**FIGURE 17–2**
**Actual and High-Employment Surplus or Deficit, 1956–1980**

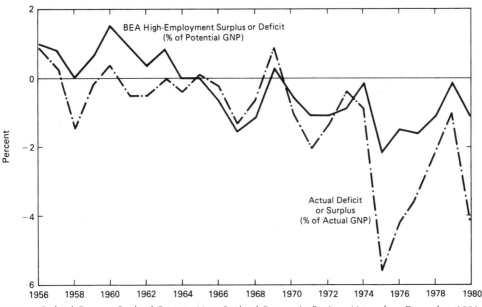

SOURCE: Federal Reserve Bank of Boston, *New England Economic Review*, November–December 1981, p. 12.

During inflation, deficit (or surplus) amounts are not very meaningful compared to deficits of other years if both are stated in current dollars. Hence the budget is often stated and graphed to show high-employment budget surplus or deficit as a percentage of *potential* GNP as shown in Figure 17–2. Actual deficits or surpluses are shown as percentages of *actual* GNP. However, no simple measure of budget surplus or deficit is a really good measure of fiscal policy. Let us examine some of the limitations of the high-employment budget concept.

## Limitations of the High-Employment Budget Concept

Limitations of the high-employment budget concept have become widely recognized.[7] Problems with its use are related to assumptions made in the estimating procedure. For example, the rate of inflation projected may be in error. The estimates

---

[7] Michael J. Prell, "The Full Employment Budget—Its Uses and Limitations," Federal Reserve Bank of Kansas City, *Monthly Review*, April 1973, pp. 3–12; James R. McCabe, "The Full-Employment Budget: A Guide for Fiscal Policy," Federal Reserve Bank of Richmond, *Monthly Review*, May 1972, pp. 2–8; and George Terborgh, "Phantom Budgets and Fiscal Policy," *Morgan Guaranty Survey*, November 1972, pp. 7–10. For a more recent discussion, see Richard W. Kopcke, "Is the Federal Budget Out of Control?" Federal Reserve Bank of Boston, *New England Economic Review*, November–December 1981, pp. 5–15. Kopcke points out that, as one example, inflation can cause higher *effective* taxes on business firms, and thus can hinder economic growth, causing lower tax revenues.

of the share of income realized by the different national income components may also be in error.[8] Corporate profits estimates are especially troublesome in this regard. Of course, in any estimating, assumptions are always questionable.

Estimates of the full-employment budget have been made not only by the Council of Economic Advisers but also by Arthur Okun and Nancy Teeters of The Brookings Institution.[9] Insofar as these sources use different assumptions, the estimates of the surplus or deficit vary and probably represent a source of some confusion to fiscal analysts. However, the concept will surely prevail and does seem to represent some improvement over the previous concept of a "cyclically balanced budget," which suggested that deficits during depressions should be made up by surpluses in times of prosperity so that the size of the national debt would remain more or less constant over the cycle. With the use of the concept of a full-employment balanced budget, the national debt will probably increase in the long run, because deficits will occur at levels below full employment, and surpluses would *only* occur if employment were higher than the rate accepted as "full employment."

Of course, the high-employment budget must not be viewed as the *only* guide to appropriate fiscal policy. One might have thought that, since estimates of this budget showed larger deficits for 1977 and 1978, economists in the Carter administration would have argued for tax increases in early 1977. But they did not do this because a program of tax increases would be expected to dampen further the sluggish recovery. Thus even if the high-employment budget shows a deficit, other factors may dictate a tax cut. The concept of a high-employment budget may be one of several useful guides to those who formulate fiscal policy, but it should not be the only guide.

Because of problems of estimating "high employment" (for example, what level of unemployment constitutes "high employment"), discussion of the high employment budget was less in the 1980s and the concept seemed to have lost much of its usefulness as unemployment remained above 6 percent even in 1986.

## The Congressional Budget Office

Under the provision of the Budget and Impoundment Control Act of 1974, Congress established the Congressional Budget Office (CBO). Its primary function is to assist in coordinating the taxing and spending activity of the federal government.[10] This act also established a procedure for the Senate and House to agree jointly on targets for spending, revenues, and the deficit or surplus. As in the past, appropriations provided for in the president's budget proposals are considered by 12 appropriations subcommittees in each branch of Congress. Tax bills are processed by the House

---

[8] Nancy H. Teeters, "Estimates of the Full-Employment Surplus, 1955–64," *Review of Economics and Statistics*, Vol. 47, August 1965, p. 309.

[9] Arthur M. Okun and Nancy H. Teeters, "The Full-Employment Surplus Revisited," paper delivered at the First Conference of The Brookings Panel on Economic Activity, April 17, 1970, Washington, D.C.

[10] For a brief review of the purposes of the act, see "Congress's New Grip on the Federal Purse," *Morgan Guaranty Survey*, May 1975, pp. 5–11.

Ways and Means Committee and the Finance Committee of the Senate. In the past there has been little coordination between congressional committees responsible for revenues and outlays and no procedure *requiring* an overall consideration of total revenues, expenditures, and the balance. Now the House and Senate budget committees are expected to submit spending and revenue targets and budget estimates to the Congress for a vote of acceptance in the form of a concurrent resolution. The two budget committees are assisted in this task by the CBO.

Under the new procedure, the president submits his proposed budget as usual in January. After deliberation, the Congress is expected to vote a preliminary concurrent resolution in May. Then in September, Congress is expected to vote a final concurrent resolution just prior to the new fiscal year, which now begins October 1 of each calendar year.

The requirement for concurrent resolutions specifying total tax, spending, and deficit (or surplus) targets forces Congress to consider these totals. Modifications in the targets by Congress would receive publicity, which might make Congress hesitant to exceed deficit targets if the public believes that fiscal restraint is necessary to avoid further inflation.

Congress has had difficulty in meeting the budget resolution deadlines and also in passing appropriations bills before the next fiscal year. "Continuing resolutions" to spend the same amounts as in the preceding year have been used to provide money for government spending temporarily when deadlines could not be met.

# FINANCIAL ASPECTS OF DEFICIT BUDGETS

In principle, the federal government could have a balanced budget each year. Expenditures would be matched by tax revenues. However, because of discretionary fiscal actions and the workings of automatic stabilizers, this hardly ever occurs. And a budget surplus is also a rare event in today's economy. For this reason the following discussion of financial aspects of budgets is limited to deficit budgets.

To finance a deficit, the Treasury may (1) draw down its cash balances at commercial banks or at Federal Reserve Banks, (2) sell securities to nonbank investors, (3) sell securities to commercial banks, or (4) sell securities to the Federal Reserve. While in practice these four methods of financing a deficit are not mutually exclusive, each has different implications for financial markets and for the economy. The impact of a given deficit on the level of economic activity depends in large part on how it is financed.

## Drawing Down Cash Balances

If the Treasury draws down its balances at commercial banks to pay its bills, the result is an increase in the public's holdings of deposits at commercial banks. This is true whether the public deposits the government checks directly in a bank, places the funds in a nonbank institution, or uses the money to buy securities in the market. (In the last two examples, deposits at commercial banks, owned by nonbank institutions or by sellers of securities, rise.) If, on the other hand, the Treasury draws down balances held at Federal Reserve Banks, depository institution reserves also increase when the government checks are deposited. Since not all these additional reserves are "required reserves," excess reserves are created that would permit a multiple expansion of bank credit and deposits. This subsequent expansion of loans and deposits is unlikely, however. The Treasury would usually restore its working balances at Federal Reserve Banks by "calling" deposits from its Tax and Loan accounts, reducing reserves. As a result there would be no *net* increase in reserves and no multiple expansion of deposits. More important, the Treasury could not finance large deficits, such as those experienced in recent years, by permanently reducing its cash balances. As a practical matter, the government usually raises most of the needed funds by selling new issues of government securities in the market.

## Selling Securities to Nonbank Investors

Suppose that the Treasury sells securities, for example, Treasury bills, notes, or bonds, to nonbank investors and spends the proceeds. (The term "nonbank investors" includes individuals, nonfinancial business firms, nonbank institutions, and foreign buyers.) The result is that nonbank investors—the public—end up with the same amount of money as before. They also hold additional government securities equal to the deficit. In effect, the government has used the deficit to transfer money from nonbank lenders to recipients of government payments. We would expect this increase in federal debt to push interest rates up to some extent unless offsetting actions were taken by the Federal Reserve.

## Selling Securities to Commercial Banks

It is often claimed that Treasury deficit spending financed by borrowing from commercial banks is inflationary. (The discussion in this section applies to other depository institutions to the extent that they act in the same manner as commercial banks.) In this view, it would be prudent, if a deficit is unavoidable, to make sales of securities only to nonbank investors. This would enable the Treasury to finance the deficit through "real saving" rather than through the creation of new money. The answer is that financing deficits through banks is no more expansionary than through sales of securities to nonbank lenders *unless the Federal Reserve provides the banks with additional reserves.* And, if the banks already have excess reserves and use them to buy government securities, the result is no more expansionary than if banks had instead made loans to private borrowers. Let us examine these observations more closely.

If banks hold excess reserves, they may acquire new Treasury issues, buy private securities, make loans, or simply continue to hold the excess reserves. If they choose to buy Treasury securities, they forgo the opportunity to make private loans or buy, say, bonds. This means that Treasury deposits rise initially, rather than those of private borrowers. Within a short time, however, these deposits are drawn down and are replaced by new deposits held by the recipients of government checks. In this case, bank purchases of Treasury obligations have essentially the same effects as increases in other earning assets and deposits.

If banks are already "loaned up," as many banks have been in recent years, and hold no unneeded excess reserves, the result of Treasury sales of securities to banks is essentially the same as if the Treasury borrows from nonbank investors. Banks may acquire additional government securities only by selling an equivalent amount of other financial assets to the public or by reducing outstanding loans. The public's money balances decline as a result, but they are restored when the Treasury spends the proceeds from the sale of securities. The net effect when banks are fully loaned up is that the public continues to hold the original amount of deposits and additional securities or it has reduced amounts of loans obtained from banks. As in the case of borrowing from nonbank investors, interest rates rise, thus offsetting some of the expansionary effects of the deficit spending by government.

If the Fed provides the reserves necessary to support additional Treasury deposits, bank purchases of government securities have different effects. In this case, banks can acquire Treasury obligations without selling other securities or reducing loans. Bank earning assets rise, as do total deposits. The net effect is an increase in public deposits equal to the size of the deficit. If the Fed provided reserves in excess of those required to support the new Treasury deposits—equal, for example, to the size of the deficit—a multiple expansion of bank credit and deposits would be possible. In this instance, the result would be the same as it would be if the Treasury borrowed funds by selling securities directly to the Fed.

## Selling Securities to the Fed

If the Treasury sold securities to the Fed, the Treasury would receive a credit to its deposit account at Federal Reserve Banks. (After 1981, it cannot do this in *any* amount.) When the government spent the proceeds, public deposits and bank reserves would rise as the Treasury checks are deposited in commercial banks. Since not all the additional reserves are "required," this permits a subsequent multiple expansion of bank credit and deposits. Clearly this means of financing a deficit is the most expansionary of the methods available. It is tantamount to "printing money," and for this reason *direct* sales by the Treasury to the Fed are now prohibited. It is important to reiterate, however, that essentially the same result obtains if the Fed *indirectly* finances the deficit by buying an equivalent amount of securities in the market. In this case, however, there may be less psychological pressure by the Treasury on the Fed to buy the securities.

In summary, several means are available to finance a government deficit. Choice of the methods used is important because the impact on the financial market differs. Borrowing from the public tends to tighten credit conditions, as does borrowing from commercial banks in the absence of accommodating actions by the monetary authority. The most expansionary, and at times inflationary, method of financing a deficit is through "monetization" of the debt by the central bank.[11] This occurs if the Treasury sells securities directly to the Federal Reserve or, which is much more likely, if the Fed buys securities in the market to provide additional bank reserves.

## THE "CROWDING-OUT" EFFECT

Now that we have reviewed alternative ways of financing deficit spending by government, we consider an issue that is widely discussed in financial circles: the "crowding-out" effect. The issue is, "Does government spending displace a nearly equal amount of private spending?" According to one study, "If an increase in Government demand, financed by either taxes or debt issuance to the public, fails to stimulate total economic activity, the private sector is said to have been 'crowded-out' by the government action."[12] But, since economists are mainly concerned about the effects of government deficits and debt financing, only "crowding out" through government borrowing is discussed here.

Some economists have suggested that, although government deficit spending initially raises the level of income, it also pushes up interest rates, which may crowd out private borrowing and spending. In this view, increases in government spending cause private spending to decline or to increase less than it might and thus are apt to cause little net increase in total spending. Accordingly, deficit spending by government is considered by these economists an unreliable means of achieving high levels of income and employment. Let us examine the crowding-out hypothesis in the supply-and-demand-for-funds framework shown in Figure 17–3. In this figure the quantity of funds is on the horizontal axis and the interest rate is on the vertical axis. Assume that the initial equilibrium is the point at which the curves intersect, with $i_0$ and $Q_0$ being the values of the variables. Now assume that the Treasury demands more funds because of its deficit. This shifts the demand curve to the right. The new demand curve is indicated by dashes, and the new equilibrium values are $i_1$ and $Q_1$. Clearly, unless the supply of funds curve is horizontal, the borrowing activities of the Treasury push interest rates somewhat higher than they otherwise would be. But do they "crowd out" other borrowers? If so, to what extent?

These questions can be answered by looking at Figure 17–3. If interest rates had risen to $i_2$, then the total amount of funds supplied would have remained at $Q_0$. Since the Treasury would have obtained the funds it wanted, other borrowers would have been denied an equal amount. This would imply a fixed supply of loanable funds. But, as Figure 17–3 shows, $Q$ rises from $Q_0$ to $Q_1$, indicating that higher interest rates induce a *larger* supply of funds. The demand by the Treasury increases by the amount $Q_2$—$Q_0$. Since $Q_1$—$Q_0$ is added to the supply, only the amount $Q_2$—$Q_1$ is "crowded out" by the Treasury's borrowing. But there is some "crowding out."

---

[11] "Monetization" of government debt occurs when the Fed buys government securities, adding to bank excess reserves, and banks use the excess reserves to create deposits (money).

[12] Keith M. Carlson and Roger W. Spencer, "Crowding Out and Its Critics," *Federal Reserve Bank of St. Louis, Review*, December 1975, pp. 2–17.

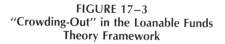

FIGURE 17–3
"Crowding-Out" in the Loanable Funds
Theory Framework

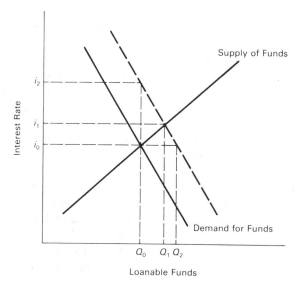

To what extent does Treasury borrowing "crowd out" private borrowers? It depends on the shape of the supply of funds curve. If the supply curve were vertical, interest rates would rise to $i_2$ and private borrowing would be reduced by the full amount of the Treasury's borrowing. On the other hand, if the supply schedule were perfectly flat, $i$ would not rise at all. Private borrowers would not be "crowded out." It is most probable that the supply curve is neither vertical nor horizontal, but somewhere in between. There is *partial* crowding out.

Thus far in this discussion we have ignored the potential role of the Fed in accommodating the Treasury. We have assumed that the supply of funds was given. We know, however, that the Fed can, if it wishes to hold down interest rates, increase the supply of money and hence shift the supply of loanable funds curve to the right. There need be no short-run "crowding out" if the monetary authority provides the additional money necessary to prevent a significant increase in interest rates.

Another rightward shift in the supply-of-funds curve might occur if consumers, in general, and taxpayers, in particular, increase their saving when the Treasury borrows more money. Under certain reasonable assumptions, this is a logical outcome. The result is as if taxpayers increase their saving by an amount sufficient to buy the new debt issued by the government. Then, the supply of funds function would shift rightward sufficiently far so as to leave interest rate levels unchanged even though the demand for funds shifted rightward. There would be no crowding out and no need for the Federal Reserve to accommodate the market by increasing the supply of funds through expansionary monetary policy.

In this view the government's financing decision—whether to tax to pay for spending or whether to borrow the funds—has no overall impact on saving, consumption, or investment, in and of itself. This view stands in sharp contrast with the view of most Wall Street analysts who believe that large federal deficits are responsible for high interest rates—recognizing, of course, that deficits follow either from too much spending, or too little taxing, or both.

What assumptions lead to the logical conclusion that consumers will save additional amounts equal to the added volume of debt? There are two important ones.

First, assume that consumers base their saving decisions on their expected lifetime income. If taxes are lower today, they reason, taxes will have to be higher next year when the government, which has promised to pay off its debt, raises taxes and fulfills its promise. So, if consumers are to have a smooth pattern of consumption over time, they'd better save more now—save the money they realize from a tax cut—so they'll be able to pay higher taxes in the future without cutting future consumption.

But, what if consumers believe that they'll die before the government gets around to raising taxes? The government lives forever, but people don't. Why wouldn't today's consumers ignore higher taxes that will be imposed on future generations? The answer involves the second important assumption, that members of a family care about each other's welfare and will attempt to arrange a steady standard of living from one generation to another. With lower taxes today, people save more and are able to bequeath more to their heirs so their heirs will be able to pay the higher taxes in the future. Assuming that family members are concerned about their children's welfare is equivalent to assuming that families are expected to live forever, just as governments are expected to do. This assumption leads to what has become known as *"Ricardian equivalence."* Since individuals and families have the same infinite time horizon that government has, wealth will not change in the wake of any restructuring of the time pattern of debt and taxes by the government. If wealth doesn't change, neither will consumption. If consumption doesn't change when taxes are cut and current income rises, then saving will rise. And the additional saving that flows into the credit markets will keep interest rates unchanged.[13]

It is very difficult to believe that any average citizen considers his family poorer when a central government borrows money, as if the government's debt were, proportionally, his or hers, or that someone with greater take-home pay as a result of a tax cut does not consider himself better off. But assumptions in theories need not be realistic for theories to yield good predictions. The question is an empirical one.[14] Do increased debt issues by governments lead to increased saving? Of course, when interest rates rise as more federal debt is sold, savers are led to supply a larger *quantity*

---

[13] For an excellent review of these issues, see Michael Dotsey, "Controversy over the Federal Budget Deficit: A Theoretical Perspective," Federal Reserve Bank of Richmond, *Economic Review*, September–October 1985, pp. 3–16. The review contains many useful references and credits Robert J. Barro for reviving interest in Ricardian equivalence, named after David Ricardo (1772–1823).

[14] On this subject, see William Buiter and James Tobin, "Debt Neutrality: A Brief Review of Doctrine and Evidence," in George M. von Furstenberg, ed., *Social Security Versus Private Saving*, (Cambridge, Mass.: Bollinger Publishing Co., 1980), pp. 39–63.

of saving to the market for funds. But do saving flows increase in a manner independent of any response to higher interest yields on saving? Saving out of personal disposable income in the United States has remained remarkably steady in the range of 5 to 6 percent per year in spite of wide swings in the deficit. Thus, casual empirical evidence casts doubt on the Ricardian equivalence proposition. But it may hold over the longer term and cannot be definitively rejected on the basis of the scant empirical evidence that has been analyzed so far. Thus, one might conclude that increased debt issues can be expected to crowd out, at least partially, some private investment spending.

# DEBT MANAGEMENT POLICY

Debt management consists of those actions of the Treasury and the Fed that affect the *composition* of the federal debt held by the public. This definition distinguishes debt management policy from fiscal policy; the latter has to do with government *spending* and *taxes* and the *size* of the budget deficit or surplus. Monetary policy actions are by definition those that change the amount rather than the types of securities bought or sold by the Federal Reserve System in its open market operations. Although these definitions are arbitrary, they help to underscore the interrelation of fiscal, monetary, and debt management policies.

## Debt Management Operations

Treasury and Federal Reserve operations can change the maturity structure of the marketable component of the debt. To isolate the effects of debt management, assume that the total amount of marketable government debt is constant. The Treasury, then, can shorten or lengthen the average time to maturity of the debt by changing the mix of securities sold to the public. To shorten the debt, the Treasury issues bills or notes and buys or retires bonds. To lengthen the debt, the Treasury refunds the debt by replacing maturing bills with longer-term securities.

The Federal Reserve also engages in debt management when it carries out an open market operation that alters the maturity structure of the publicly held debt. If the Fed were, say, to sell $500 million of long-term securities and buy the same amount of short-term securities, the reserves of banks could remain the same but the maturity of the publicly held debt would be lengthened. If the Fed exchanged short-term for long-term government securities, the maturity of the debt held by the public would be shortened.

The *marketable* component of the public debt is important for management. It consists of Treasury bills, notes, and bonds. Nonmarketable issues, those that must be held until maturity or redemption by the Treasury, include savings bonds and notes, foreign issues, and special issues. Table 17–4 shows the types of securities that made up the public debt at the end of June 1986. We see that nearly 73 percent of the total debt was marketable.

**TABLE 17–4**
**U.S. Government Public Debt, June 30, 1986***
**(billions of dollars)**

| Type of Security | Amount | Percentage of Total |
|---|---|---|
| Marketable | | |
| Bills | $ 396.9 | 19.3% |
| Notes | 869.3 | 42.3 |
| Bonds | 232.3 | 11.3 |
| Total marketable | $1,498.2 | 72.9% |
| Nonmarketable | | |
| Savings bonds and notes | $ 82.3 | 4.0% |
| Foreign issues | 5.3 | .3 |
| Government account series | 372.3 | 18.1 |
| State and local government series | 98.2 | 4.8 |
| Total nonmarketable | $ 558.5 | 27.2% |
| Total public debt | $2,056.7 | 100.0% |

* Totals do not add exactly, because of rounding.
SOURCE: *Federal Reserve Bulletin,* December 1986, p. A30.

The Treasury has primary responsibility for managing the debt, and Treasury officials make day-to-day decisions concerning the marketable debt held by the public. They decide on the types and maturities of securities to be issued; the yields on coupon issues; special features such as call provisions, ownership restrictions, and allotments that might attach to these obligations; and so on.

Before turning to questions of the economic impact of the debt and appropriate debt management policy, let us look at the ownership of the debt and its maturity distribution. Table 17–5 shows that 53 percent of the debt was held by private investors, chiefly commercial banks, individuals, and foreigners.

The maturity distribution of the marketable debt is presented in Table 17–6. Clearly, most of the marketable securities are short term. These include bills and those notes and bonds that have been outstanding for a period of time. Some of the notes and bonds were securities whose original maturities may have been intermediate or long term but are now fairly close to maturity. From portfolio managers' point of view, a bond whose original maturity was, say, 10 years is considered a short-term liquid instrument if it is due to mature within 1 or 2 years.

## Economic Impact of Changes in Debt Structure

In one view, changing the maturity structure of the debt may alter the maturity structure of interest rates: lengthening the debt means more long-term debt and less short-term debt. This increased supply of long-term securities should lead to higher

**TABLE 17–5**
**Ownership of Public Debt, June 30, 1986[1]**
**(billions of dollars)**

| Held By | Amount |
|---|---|
| U.S. government agencies and trust funds | $ 374.4 |
| Federal Reserve Banks | 183.8 |
| Private investors | 1,502.7 |
| Commercial banks | 197.2 |
| Money market funds | 22.8 |
| Insurance companies | n.a. |
| Other companies | 59.8 |
| State and local governments | n.a. |
| Individuals | |
| Savings bonds | 83.8 |
| Other securities | 73.4 |
| Foreign and international[2] | 237.9 |
| Other miscellaneous investors[3] | n.a. |
| Total public debt | $2,859.3 |

[1] Totals do not add exactly, because of "n.a." items.

[2] Consists of investments of foreign and international accounts. Excludes noninterest-bearing notes issued to the International Monetary Fund.

[3] Includes savings and loan associations, nonprofit institutions, credit unions, mutual savings banks, corporate pension trust funds, dealers and brokers, certain U.S. government deposit accounts, and U.S. government-sponsored agencies.

SOURCES: Data by type of security, U.S. Treasury Department, *Monthly Statement of the Public Debt of the United States;* data by holder, *Treasury Bulletin.*

long-term interest rates, and the reduced supply of short-term securities should lead to lower short-term interest rates if long-term securities and short-term securities are not perfect substitutes in the eyes of investors. Thus the yield curve should be more positively sloped after a debt-lengthening operation than it was before. There is some evidence that this is the case.[15]

Higher long-term rates dampen the willingness of business managers to engage in long-lived investment, and long-lived investment is below what it otherwise would be. Thus, lengthening the debt should help to restrict a boom in investment and dampen an overheated economy. Lower short-term rates might encourage some forms of investment, specifically investment in inventories. Most economists feel, however, that long-term investment projects are more sensitive to interest rate changes than is

[15] V. Vance Roley, "The Determinants of the Treasury Security Yield Curve," *Journal of Finance,* December 1981, pp. 1103–1136, found effects on Treasury securities yield curves from changes in supplies of Treasury securities. Roley concluded that long-term and short-term Treasury securities may not be regarded as perfect or near-perfect substitutes.

**TABLE 17–6**
**Maturity Distribution and Average Length of Marketable Interest-Bearing Public Debt Securities**
**Held by Private Investors, 1967–1985**
**(millions of dollars)**

| End of Year or Month | Amount Out- standing, Privately Held | Maturity Class | | | | | Average length | |
|---|---|---|---|---|---|---|---|---|
| | | Within 1 Year | 1 to 5 Years | 5 to 10 Years | 10 to 20 Years | 20 Years and Over | Years | Months |
| 1967 | $ 150,321 | $ 56,561 | $ 53,584 | $ 21,057 | $ 6,153 | $12,968 | 5 | 1 |
| 1968 | 159,671 | 66,746 | 52,295 | 21,850 | 6,110 | 12,670 | 4 | 5 |
| 1969 | 156,008 | 69,311 | 50,182 | 18,078 | 6,097 | 12,337 | 4 | 2 |
| 1970 | 157,910 | 76,443 | 57,035 | 8,286 | 7,876 | 8,272 | 3 | 8 |
| 1971 | 161,863 | 74,803 | 58,557 | 14,503 | 6,357 | 7,645 | 3 | 6 |
| 1972 | 165,978 | 79,509 | 57,157 | 16,033 | 6,358 | 6,922 | 3 | 3 |
| 1973 | 167,869 | 84,041 | 54,139 | 16,385 | 8,741 | 4,564 | 3 | 1 |
| 1974 | 164,862 | 87,150 | 50,103 | 14,197 | 9,930 | 3,481 | 2 | 11 |
| 1975 | 210,382 | 115,677 | 65,852 | 15,385 | 8,857 | 4,611 | 2 | 8 |
| 1976 | 279,782 | 151,723 | 89,151 | 24,169 | 8,087 | 6,652 | 2 | 7 |
| 1977 | 326,674 | 161,329 | 113,319 | 33,067 | 8,428 | 10,531 | 2 | 11 |
| 1978 | 356,501 | 163,819 | 132,993 | 33,500 | 11,383 | 14,805 | 3 | 3 |
| 1979 | 380,530 | 181,883 | 127,574 | 32,279 | 18,489 | 20,304 | 3 | 7 |
| 1980 | 463,717 | 220,084 | 156,244 | 38,809 | 25,901 | 22,679 | 3 | 9 |
| 1981 | 549,863 | 256,187 | 182,237 | 48,743 | 32,569 | 30,127 | 4 | 0 |
| 1982 | 682,043 | 314,436 | 221,783 | 75,749 | 33,017 | 37,058 | 3 | 11 |
| 1983 | 862,631 | 379,579 | 294,955 | 99,174 | 40,826 | 48,097 | 4 | 1 |
| 1984 | 1,017,488 | 437,941 | 332,808 | 130,417 | 49,664 | 66,658 | 4 | 6 |
| 1985 | 1,185,675 | 472,661 | 402,766 | 159,383 | 62,853 | 88,012 | 4 | 11 |

SOURCE: *Economic Report of the President, 1986*, p. 349.

inventory investment. Thus, if long-term investments are significantly restricted but inventory investment does not change very much, the net effect of lengthening the maturity structure of the debt would be restrictive.

Another view, consistent with possible interest rate effects, is that the "liquidity" of the public's portfolio can be changed by debt management. Thus, if the Treasury shortens the debt and issues more short-term securities, these securities will, because of their liquidity, be good substitutes for money. Therefore, people will demand less money and lower their cash balances by purchasing goods (and perhaps bonds). This will increase the velocity of money, and the increased spending will be expansionary. The reverse will occur when debt maturity is lengthened.

Thus, by changing the liquidity of the public's portfolio, not only do interest rates change, thereby indirectly changing investment spending, but spending also changes directly, as the desire to hold cash balances is affected. In these ways some economists believe that debt management can significantly affect the overall level of economic activity.

## Effectiveness of Debt Management

Nearly everyone agrees that for stabilization purposes debt management policy is less powerful than either monetary or fiscal policy. However, it is a liquidity policy that can either support or work at cross-purposes with the other policy tools. In general, if a policy direction is called for, it would seem best if all policy tools were coordinated, so as not to thwart each other.

If debt management were completely ineffective as a policy tool, then for stabilization purposes it would not matter whether the Treasury sold long-term or short-term securities. Because short-term interest rates have generally been lower than long-term rates in recent decades, regular issues of weekly bills keeps interest charges low. Why would any pressure to lengthen the debt be warranted? On the other hand, if perverse management of the debt can *interfere* with monetary policy, then it follows that it is a policy tool with noticeable effectiveness and should be handled accordingly. The issue, then, is largely empirical: Just how powerful is debt management policy?

Opinion among economists seems to be divided. Of 125 economists with interest in these issues, some 71 replied to a questionnaire sent out by the House Committee on Banking and Currency.[16] One question was, "Given the goals of the Employment Act, what can debt management do to help their implementation?" Answers of about 55 who commented on this question were summarized by the House committee staff. About 20 percent of those answering, or 11 persons, recommended pursuing debt management policy aggressively, but about 75 percent "would appear to agree that the important contribution debt management can make to economic stability is simply not to interfere with other stabilization policies. This majority consisted of those who stated that debt management has no potential as a stabilization policy yet recommended keeping the age mix of the debt constant, and those who concluded that debt management would be destabilizing if used to minimize carrying costs and recommended that it definitely not be used for this purpose."[17]

Is there any past experience that could give us a hint as to the strength of debt management policy? "Operation Twist" took place in 1961. The Fed bought bonds to help hold yields down in the interest of domestic expansion, while selling bills to push bill yields up to discourage the outflow of funds and mitigate balance of payments problems. Did the program work? Yield differences did not respond significantly, but perhaps this was because the Treasury issued new long-term debt, while at the same time the Federal Reserve was buying long-term debt. Furthermore, it was during this

---

[16] House of Representatives, Subcommittee on Domestic Finance, Committee on Banking and Currency, *Compendium on Monetary Policy Guidelines and Federal Reserve Structure*, December 1978, 90th Cong., 2nd sess.

[17] House of Representatives, *Compendium on Monetary Policy Guidelines*, p. 19. Dudley G. Luckett wrote: "Debt management policy . . . probably has little or no role to play in economic stabilization. Not only is it apparently a weak policy instrument in its own right, but it seems unlikely that it is capable of doing anything different than could be accomplished by a slightly stronger monetary policy." Four sentences later he concluded: "Thus, the role of debt management should be viewed as essentially passive, and coordination should consist simply of holding debt management *interference* with monetary policy to a minimum." (italics added) But, if debt management policy actions are weak, why bother to worry about interference?

period that the market for negotiable certificates of deposit was developed by commercial bankers. Thus, the "experiment" was impure because other forces affected the securities markets at the same time. The question is "What would the pattern of yields have been if the Fed had not purchased those long-term securities?" Controlled experiments are required to answer questions such as this with confidence.

Milton Friedman believes that small changes in maturity structure usually have only a slight effect on the demand for money.[18] He noted, however, that when bond prices were unpegged after the Federal Reserve–Treasury accord of 1951, securities that formerly were effectively demand obligations became long-term securities in fact as well as in name. This was a drastic increase in the "effective maturity" of the debt, and he argued that this loss of liquidity led to an "increase in the demand for money something like 2 or 3 percent."[19]

A more recent study by V. Vance Roley involving a statistical experiment also concluded that the maturity composition of the federal debt does indeed affect Treasury security yields and that federal debt management can possibly be used to help in stabilizing the economy.[20]

In his study of Treasury yield curves, Roley concluded that, using a structural model containing 10 disaggregated categories of investors, the hypothesis that short- and intermediate-term securities and long-term securities are perfect substitutes could be rejected. If correct, this is a major finding: the expectations theory of the term structure of interest rates is based on such perfect substitutability, while the segmented markets theory assumes the opposite. Thus further study of the segmented markets hypothesis, as opposed to the expectations hypothesis, is justified.[21]

It is fair to conclude that debt management, if *aggressively* pursued, *could* become an effective stabilization tool. But other considerations, mostly political, suggest that keeping the debt structure more or less constant and allowing the Fed to carry out monetary policy without interference from perverse debt management policies would represent an appropriate division of responsibilities.

## Holding Interest Cost Down

One of the reasons that the Treasury has not pursued an aggressive countercyclical debt management policy is that it would probably raise the interest cost of the debt. Countercyclical policy calls for the issue of long-term debt during inflation when interest rates are high. In a recession, when interest rates are low, the Treasury would issue short-term debt. From the point of view of minimizing interest charges, this practice is the opposite of the one that a prudent corporate treasurer would use. To

---

[18] Milton Friedman, *A Program for Monetary Stability* (New York: Fordham University Press, 1959), p. 61.

[19] Ibid., pp. 107–108.

[20] See his "Federal Debt Management Policy: A Re-examination of the Issues," Federal Reserve Bank of Kansas City, *Economic Review*, February 1978, pp. 14–23.

[21] Roley, "The Determinants of the Treasury Security Yield Curve," pp. 1103–1126 (see footnote 15).

minimize interest costs, the treasurer would sell long-term debt when interest rates were low and short-term debt when rates were high, so that if interest rates fell, sale of long-term debt could replace short-term debt as the latter matured. Thus a policy of minimizing interest charges on the national debt to reduce the tax burden is inconsistent with debt management policy for stabilization.

In view of the fact that Treasury officials face inconsistent objectives—promoting economic stability on the one hand and minimizing interest cost of the debt on the other—it is little wonder that they sometimes appear erratic in moves to change the maturity of the debt. Furthermore, Congress placed a ceiling of 4¼ percent on the coupon that the Treasury can set on bonds. This clearly reflects a congressional preference for low debt service costs, but its effect has been simply to force the Treasury to use securities other than "bonds" when borrowing.

For some, evaluation of the goal of holding debt service costs to a minimum indicates that in the final analysis this goal should not take precedence over the goal of economic stabilization. The reasons become clear when we consider extreme cases. First, if government wished, the entire debt could be monetized. Interest-bearing debt would be withdrawn and noninterest-bearing money issued in its place. This would bring interest costs to zero, but would surely be accompanied by disastrous inflation, with all its adverse effects on economic stability. Indeed, one can make an even stronger case by noting that the size of the Treasury's operations gives it effective power to corner the market for its own securities. It could probably issue securities, depress the market, buy them back at a discount, and make money on its speculative operations. It clearly has the power to carry out such activities if Congress permits. It does not do so because it does not aim at profit. As with all government activities, the Treasury's debt should be managed from a view toward promoting the general welfare. Economic stability is a primary means to this end.

## Debt Management Techniques

Having discussed the goals of Treasury debt management, let us turn now to certain aspects of debt management techniques.

### Scheduling Issues

Managers prefer to keep things orderly, and Treasury officials are no exception to this rule. Managing a total debt of over $2 trillion is a problem of significant proportions, especially when a major portion of this must be "rolled over" in a year's time. The average length of time to maturity of the total debt was only 7 years and 9 months in mid-1976, and for privately held marketable debt, it was only 2 years and 6 months. This was the all-time low, far below the 1946 average of 9 years. Except for a few temporary periods of debt maturity extension, the average maturity declined slowly but steadily after World War II.

By 1986, after a decade of persistence on the part of the Treasury, the average maturity of the Treasury's outstanding marketable debt had reached 5 years and 6 months—over double its level in 1976.

In the 1960s the Treasury attempted to lengthen the maturity of the debt by a program of "advance refunding," under which the Treasury offered to replace securities due to mature in one or two years with new long-term governments. This program was instituted because, at times, holders of long-term governments, such as life insurance companies, sold them prior to maturity and reinvested the funds in other long-term instruments. Often the government securities were sold to banks or other short-term investors who were not interested in replacing the maturing issue with new long-term Treasury bonds. The Treasury, through an advance refunding operation, sought to refund the bonds before such a change in ownership took place. By offering an attractive refunding package, the Treasury could forestall additional shortening of the debt maturity. But advance refunding had its own complexities and the experiment lasted but a few years.

In view of its management problems, the Treasury has moved more and more in the direction of making debt offerings simple and routine. Every week the Treasury sells at auction about $6 billion of 3- and 6-month bills, and every month about $5.5 billion of 1-year bills and 2-year notes.

To facilitate the lengthening of the debt, Congress gave the Treasury authority to sell some bonds that are exempt from the legal restriction that bonds may not be sold with a coupon rate greater than 4¼ percent. In 1971 Congress permitted a change in the definition of "notes," increasing their maximum maturity to 10 years. Essentially, this change extended to the Treasury the authority to issue 10-year maturities without the restriction of the 4¼ percent ceiling, and over the years Congress has given the Treasury greater leeway to sell securities at yields that exceed 4¼ percent.

While lengthening the debt is a "housekeeping" goal of Treasury management, others have suggested that it might be better to sell securities in appropriate maturities so that the yield curve might become flat. This suggestion has been called "the flattening policy."[22] Proponents of this policy suggest that the usual rising yield curve indicates greater preference for short-term securities by the public. Thus, providing this liquidity might be an appropriate action of government. The government, in this view, would not offer long-term bonds and thus compete with private demand for long-term funds, if long-term interest rates were higher than were those on short-term securities. Problems arise with this approach, as they do any time the government attempts to set a price or a pattern of prices in a world of changing tastes of borrowers and lenders. Nevertheless, the suggestion merits serious consideration.

### Other Techniques

We can only mention a few other issues concerning debt management techniques. The Treasury sometimes auctions its securities, but sometimes offers them on a subscription basis. If it offers a subscription issue, the Fed may feel obligated to

---

[22] This proposal was put forward for consideration by William D. Nordhaus and Henry C. Wallich, "Alternatives for Debt Management," *Issues in Federal Debt Management*, Conference Series No. 10, Federal Reserve Bank of Boston, June 1973, pp. 9–25.

stabilize the market so that the sale will be successful. Such stabilization activity on the part of the Fed is referred to as "maintaining an even keel." Since the auction technique does not require an even-keel policy, it interferes less with the Fed's pursuit of monetary policy than a subscription offering does.

If securities are auctioned, should all awards be made at the same price—the lowest of the accepted bid prices—as in the case of a "Dutch" auction? Whether or not a Dutch auction encourages greater investor participation is a subject of debate.

Should commercial banks be allowed to credit the Treasury's Tax and Loan accounts when they purchase government securities for their own account and that of their customers? This privilege has been curtailed in recent years, and banks have paid for most of their purchases of government securities by having their reserves reduced at Federal Reserve Banks.

Currently, the Treasury sells bills at minimum amounts of $10,000. At one time it offered $1,000 bills, but commercial and savings banks argued that too many small customers were investing directly in bills and that deposits were falling because of disintermediation. What should be the denomination of Treasury issues?

## Debt Management Operations and Financial Markets

Treasury debt management operations are important to financial market participants for two reasons. First, newly issued government securities may be attractively priced relative to outstanding issues and thereby offer profitable investment opportunities. Second, actions to lengthen or shorten the debt may change the pattern of interest rates in the market for government and private securities. Any such changes have important implications for the earnings of financial institutions and for the allocation of savings among sectors of the economy. We can illustrate these effects of debt management policy by tracing changes in interest rates that might accompany a particular action by the Treasury.

Suppose that the Treasury pursues a countercyclical policy aimed at restraining aggregate borrowing during a period of inflation. To do this, the Treasury sells bonds and redeems Treasury bills. This debt-lengthening operation is intended to reduce the liquidity of the outstanding debt and/or to raise the average level of interest rates. As we will see, the success of such a program depends upon certain assumptions about the substitutability of Treasury bills for bonds and government securities for private claims.

Following the increase in Treasury bonds and the redemption of bills, we would expect bond yields to rise somewhat and bill yields to decline, *if* market participants view bills and bonds as *imperfect* substitutes. That is, bonds must be considered somewhat less liquid than bills or for other reasons certain groups of investors must prefer bonds to bills, or vice versa. The market will accept the new bonds but only at lower prices and higher yields. Because the amount of outstanding bills has been reduced, the bill price rises and the average bill yield declines. This development, of course, implies a segmented markets theory of the term structure of interest rates. Put differently, if Treasury bills and bonds are treated as one homogeneous financial asset, the yield spread will not change.

Assuming that bond yields rise while bill yields decline, we might expect investors to adjust their portfolios. The higher yield on Treasury bonds should induce some lenders to switch out of, say, corporate bonds, municipals, or mortgages and into the Treasury issues. If they do, the yields on private securities should rise until a new equilibrium is established in the capital markets. At this new position all long-term rates should be somewhat higher than they were before the sale of bonds by the Treasury. For similar reasons we would expect some downward pressure on the yields on private money market instruments, such as commercial paper and CDs. It is important to note that these portfolio changes occur only if government and private securities of the same maturity are considered fairly close substitutes for one another.

How will these changes in the structure of yields affect financial institutions? There will be differential effects on various intermediaries, depending upon their individual sources and uses of funds. As interest rates change, for example, some institutions may experience higher rates of return while others face a decline in operating income. Lenders specializing in long-term securities and loans should benefit; short-term lenders will find their interest return somewhat lower. These results depend, of course, on the nature of the demand for their loans by borrowers. It may be, for example, that even though a long-term lender realizes a higher yield on earning assets, the volume of loans is lower. But, if the demand for funds is fairly interest inelastic, long-term lenders should benefit relative to short-term lenders. Life insurance companies, pension funds, and thrift institutions should be able to improve their position while commercial banks lose ground.

But financial intermediaries also borrow funds in the market and each has somewhat different sources of funds. Those lenders who borrow short-term funds, such as commercial banks, should find their borrowing costs lower than before. And, with lower short-term interest rates, many institutions will be less apt to face disintermediation than when rates on market instruments were higher. A further consideration is that, when interest rates change, the market values of lenders' portfolios are altered. The rise or fall will, other things equal, be greater for long-term assets than for assets held by short-term lenders. The benefit of higher long-term rates on income may be offset by capital losses for long-term lenders who choose to sell market instruments prior to maturity.

As these changes in interest rates and in lending and borrowing occur, resources would be allocated somewhat differently among the various sectors of the economy. With higher long-term rates, we might expect less demand for housing and for other long-lived capital projects. Lower short-term rates, on the other hand, *may* stimulate business spending on inventories. These differential effects will be greater if borrowers have less flexibility in the maturity ranges in which they can obtain funds.

The scenario just outlined is hypothetical, not an empirically verified statement of fact. Little is known about the precise relationships among markets and interest rates. It is, for example, still a matter of debate whether debt management operations by the Treasury or Federal Reserve alter the structure of rates in the market. Further, when we suggest that long-term rates might, say, rise and short-term rates decline, the orders of magnitude are probably quite small. We can theorize that equilibrating forces would be set into motion that would tend to arrest the upward movement of long rates and the decline in short rates. Nonetheless, any policy prescriptions that call for changing the structure of rates imply the type of market behavior we described. For this reason, it is useful to understand the transmission mechanism.

## SUMMARY

Broadly, fiscal policy includes the workings of both automatic stabilizers and discretionary changes in taxes and expenditures by government. The personal income tax structure and the unemployment compensation program are the most important automatic stabilizers. They act to dampen swings in economic activity and require no conscious government actions to put them into operation. At times, discretionary changes in tax rates and in expenditures have also been used for stabilization purposes.

Many economists have used the "high-employment" budget, rather than the observed or actual budget, to determine the thrust of fiscal policy. The high-employment budget is useful to separate automatic from discretionary changes in taxes and expenditures. The larger the high-employment surplus, the more restrictive fiscal policy is believed to be during a given period. The larger the full-employment deficit, the more expansionary it is believed to be.

Government spending is financed mainly by taxation. When expenditures exceed tax receipts, the Treasury may draw down its cash balances or sell securities to raise needed funds. Securities may be sold to nonbank investors, commercial banks, or to the Federal Reserve. The most potentially inflationary means of financing a deficit is the sale of securities to the Federal Reserve. The Fed now cannot buy securities directly from the Treasury. But any purchases by the Federal Reserve add to the money supply and, more important, to bank reserves. Many observers believe that, unless the Fed provides additional reserves, deficit financing tends, at times, to "crowd out" some private spending. If the Fed *does* provide such reserves, the result may at times be excessive creation of money and high rates of inflation.

Debt management policy includes Treasury and Federal Reserve actions that affect the composition of the debt in the hands of the public. By shortening or lengthening the maturity of the marketable debt, policymakers seek to change the relative levels of interest rates in the term structure, or more broadly, the liquidity of the economy. Many economists believe that these changes may alter the overall level of economic activity, but that debt management is much less powerful than are monetary or fiscal policy actions. Some recent studies have supported the "segmented markets" theory of interest rates, in which it is assumed that securities with different maturities are *not* perfect substitutes in the view of investors, even if yields are the same. If so, changing the maturities of new debt issues could change yield curves.

Few believe that the goal of debt managers should be to minimize the cost of the debt. Nonetheless, financial analysts must take note of changes in Treasury budgets and monetary policy actions in evaluating the situation in the money and capital markets, in forecasting interest rates, and in determining appropriate actions in borrowing and in managing financial portfolios.

## Questions for Discussion

**1.** Distinguish "automatic" stabilizers from "discretionary" fiscal actions by government.

**2.** Why have government deficits been much more common than budget surpluses in recent years?

**3.** What kinds of taxes provide the bulk of federal government receipts? Which outlays are the largest? Do most of these expenditures return funds to those who pay the most taxes? What explanation can you give for this?

**4.** Why is the level of federal spending a better measure of the impact of government on the economy than the size of a budget deficit or surplus?

**5.** Under what conditions is a deficit financed by sales of securities to banks essentially the same as when securities are sold to nonbank investors?

**6.** Why are purchases of government securities by the Federal Reserve often described as the same as "printing money"?

**7.** If "crowding out" occurs, what does this imply about the effectiveness of fiscal policy in maintaining high employment?

**8.** If debt management operations are aimed at minimizing the interest cost on the federal debt, should the debt be shortened or lengthened during periods of inflation?

**9.** Why did the government increase the minimum denomination of Treasury bills from $1,000 to $10,000? What effect does this have?

**10.** If lengthening the maturity of the debt tends to raise the yields on private securities, for example, corporate bonds and mortgages, are government securities and private securities close substitutes or imperfect substitutes? What about Treasury bills and Treasury bonds?

## Selected References

A number of research studies on specific aspects of countercyclical fiscal policy are summarized in Albert Ando, E. Cary Brown, and Ann F. Friedlander, *Studies in Economic Stabilization* (Washington, D.C.: The Brookings Institution, 1968). Current studies on nearly all aspects of fiscal policy may be found in the periodical, *Brookings Papers on Economic Activity*.

A brief review that clarifies the deficit questions as much as possible in a short space is Rose McElhattan, "Understanding Federal Deficits," Federal Reserve Bank of San Francisco, *Weekly Letter*, October 29, 1982.

A longer analysis is readily available in "The Deficit Puzzle," Federal Reserve Bank of Atlanta, *Economic Review*, August 1982.

Some take the position that deficits cannot cause inflation *if* monetary policy is restrictive; for this view, see Scott E. Hein, "Deficits and Inflation," Federal Reserve Bank of St. Louis,

*Review*, March 1981, pp. 3–10. Many would argue that deficits, if large, cause heavy pressure on the Fed to "monetize" the debt, thus causing inflation.

For a very readable account of the controversy over the "crowding-out" effect of large deficits if they occur in future years, see Richard I. Kirkland, Jr., "The Reaganites' Civil War over Deficits," *Fortune*, October 17, 1983, pp. 74–80.

Also see Charles E. Dumas, "The Effects of Government Deficits: A Comparative Analysis of Crowding-Out," *Essays in International Finance*, No. 158, October 1985, Princeton University; and Michael Dotsey, "Controversy over the Federal Budget Deficit: A Theoretical Perspective," Federal Reserve Bank of Richmond, *Economic Review*, September–October 1985, pp. 3–16, and the many references cited in these publications.

A compendium of excellent papers on debt management was prepared for a conference at the Federal Reserve Bank of Boston; see *Issues in Federal Debt Management*, Conference Series No. 10, June 1973. A more recent article is V. Vance Roley, "Federal Debt Management Policy: A Re-examination of the Issues," Federal Reserve Bank of Kansas City, *Economic Review*, February 1978, pp. 14–23.

# INDEX